Waterfowl in Winter

Waterfowl in Winter

*Selected papers from Symposium and Workshop
held in Galveston, Texas, 7-10 January 1985*

EDITOR: MILTON W. WELLER

Professor, Caesar Kleberg Chair in Wildlife Ecology
Texas A&M University, College Station, Texas

Editorial Board:

BRUCE D.J. BATT
Scientific Director
Delta Waterfowl and Wetlands Research Station
Portage la Prairie, Manitoba, Canada

ROBERT H. CHABRECK
Professor, Forestry and Wildlife
Louisiana State University, Baton Rouge, Louisiana

LEIGH H. FREDRICKSON
Director, Gaylord Memorial Laboratory
University of Missouri, Puxico, Missouri

DENNIS G. RAVELING
Professor, Wildlife and Fisheries Biology
University of California, Davis, California

University of Minnesota Press, Minneapolis

The publication of this book was assisted by a bequest from Josiah H. Chase to honor his parents, Ellen Rankin Chase and Josiah Hook Chase, Minnesota territorial pioneers.

Financial Supporters of the Workshop and Publication:
Rob and Bessie Welder Wildlife Foundation, Sinton, Texas
Delta Waterfowl and Wetlands Research Station, Portage la Prairie,
    Manitoba, Canada
U.S. Fish and Wildlife Service, Division of Cooperative Research Units,
    Washington, D.C.
Wildlife Management Institute, Washington, D.C.
Caesar Kleberg Chair in Wildlife Ecology, Texas A&M University,
    College Station, Texas
Max McGraw Wildlife Foundation, Dundee, Illinois

Published by the University of Minnesota Press
2037 University Avenue Southeast, Minneapolis, MN 55414.
Published simultaneously in Canada
by Fitzhenry & Whiteside Limited, Markham.
Printed in the United States of America.

Library of Congress Cataloging-in-Publication Data

Waterfowl in winter.
    Includes bibliographies and index.
    1. Waterfowl — Wintering — Congresses. 2. Birds — Wintering — Congresses. I. Weller,
    Milton Webster.
QL696.A52W38 1987   598.4′1   86-30817
ISBN 0-8166-1570-5
ISBN 0-8166-1571-3 (pbk.)

Contents

Preface — Milton W. Weller ix

Acknowledgments — Milton W. Weller xi

Contributors xii

Reviewers xviii

I. ***Winter in Perspective***

1. Waterfowl in Winter: Past, Present, and Future 3
   Milton W. Weller and Bruce D. J. Batt

2. Some Considerations in Modeling the Mallard Life Cycle 9
   Douglas H. Johnson, James D. Nichols, Michael J. Conroy, and Lewis M. Cowardin

II. ***Reproductive and Social Behavior***

3. Pair Bond Duration and Timing of Its Formation in Barnacle Geese 23
   (Branta leucopsis)
   Myrfyn Owen, Jeffrey M. Black, and Halyna Liber

4. Variations in Pair Bond and Agonistic Behaviors in Barnacle Geese
   on the Wintering Grounds 39
   Jeffrey M. Black and Myrfyn Owen

5. Social Behavior and Pairing Chronology of Mottled Ducks during
   Autumn and Winter in Louisiana 59
   Stuart L. Paulus

6. Weak Family Associations in Cackling Geese during Winter: Effects
   of Body Size and Food Resources on Goose Social Organization 71
   James C. Johnson and Dennis G. Raveling

7. Formation of Feeding Flocks during Winter by Dusky and
   Taverner's Canada Geese in Oregon 91
   Loree H. Havel and Robert L. Jarvis

8.   Sex Specificity of Behavioral Dominance and Fasting Endurance
     in Wintering Canvasbacks: Experimental Results   103
     Matthew C. Perry, James D. Nichols, Michael J. Conroy, Holliday
     H. Obrecht III, and Byron K. Williams
9.   Workshop Summary: Courtship and Pairing in Winter   123
     Michael G. Anderson, Gary R. Hepp, Frank McKinney, and
     Myrfyn Owen

III.   *Activity Budgets*
10. Time-Activity Budgets of Nonbreeding Anatidae: A Review   135
     Stuart L. Paulus
11. Diurnal Behavior Patterns of Waterfowl Wintering on the Columbia
     River, Oregon and Washington   153
     Bruce C. Thompson, James E. Tabor, and Clarence L. Turner
12. The Need for Nocturnal Activity and Energy Budgets of Waterfowl 169
     Dennis G. Jorde and Ray B. Owen, Jr.
13. Workshop Summary: Techniques for Timing Activity of
     Wintering Waterfowl   181
     Guy A. Baldassarre, Stuart L. Paulus, Alain Tamisier, and
     Rodger D. Titman

IV.   *Community and Feeding Ecology*
14. Structure of the Winter Duck Community on the Lower Colorado
     River: Patterns and Processes   191
     Bertin W. Anderson and Robert D. Ohmart
15. Feeding Ecology of Canvasbacks Staging on Pool 7 of the Upper
     Mississippi River   237
     Carl E. Korschgen, Louis S. George, and William L. Green
16. Workshop Summary: Feeding Ecology   251
     Carl E. Korschgen, Frederic A. Reid, and Jerome R. Serie

V.   *Weights, Molts, and Condition*
17. Annual Body Weight Change in Ring-Necked Ducks   257
     (Aythya collaris)
     William L. Hohman, T. Scott Taylor, and Milton W. Weller
18. Spatial and Temporal Variation in Winter Weights of Mississippi
     Valley Canada Geese   271
     Dennis D. Thornburg, Thomas C. Tacha, Bridgett L. Estel, and
     James W. Spitzkeit
19. Examining Waterfowl Condition: Skewed Ideas on
     the Normal Procedure   277
     James K. Ringelman
20. Nutrient Reserve Dynamics of Female Mallards during Spring
     Migration through Central Iowa   287
     Theodore G. LaGrange and James J. Dinsmore

21. Workshop Summary: Nutrition, Condition, and Ecophysiology   299
     Kenneth J. Reinecke, C. Davison Ankney, Gary L. Krapu, Ray B.
     Owen, Jr., Harold H. Prince, and Dennis G. Raveling

VI. *Habitat Resources and Habitat Selection*
22. Waterfowl Use of Forested Wetlands of the Southern United
     States: An Overview   307
     Leigh H. Fredrickson and Mickey E. Heitmeyer
23. Potential Effects of Changing Water Conditions on Mallards
     Wintering in the Mississippi Alluvial Valley   325
     Kenneth J. Reinecke, Robert C. Barkley, and Charles K. Baxter
24. Duck Food Production in Openings in Forested Wetlands   339
     Andrew J. Harrison, Jr., and Robert H. Chabreck
25. Winter Body Condition of Northern Shovelers on Freshwater
     and Saline Habitats   353
     William D. Tietje and James G. Teer
26. Distribution and Numbers of American Black Ducks along the
     Maine Coast during the Severe Winter of 1980-1981   377
     Jerry R. Longcore and James P. Gibbs
27. Cover Type Relationships and Black Duck Winter Habitat   391
     James C. Lewis and Martin Nelson
28. Workshop Summary: Habitat Selection   399
     Richard M. Kaminski, Alan D. Afton, Bertin W. Anderson,
     Dennis G. Jorde, and Jerry R. Longcore

VII. *New Habitats and Habitat Management*
29. The Role of Parks in the Range Expansion of the Mallard in
     the Northeast   405
     H W Heusmann
30. Use of Catfish Ponds by Waterfowl Wintering in Mississippi   413
     Mark W. Christopher, Edward P. Hill, and David E. Steffen
31. Waterfowl Habitat Created by Floodwater-Retarding Structures
     in the Southern United States   419
     Gary Bates, Gary L. Valentine, and Frank H. Sprague
32. Experimental Plantings for Management of Crayfish and Waterfowl   427
     James R. Nassar, Robert H. Chabreck, and David C. Hayden
33. Production, Management, and Waterfowl Use of Sea Purslane, Gulf
     Coast Muskgrass, and Widgeongrass in Brackish Impoundments   441
     Peter K. Swiderek, A. Sydney Johnson, Philip E. Hale,
     and Robert L. Joyner
34. Workshop Summary: Habitat Management in Winter   459
     Roger L. Pederson, Robert H. Chabreck, Daniel P. Connelly,
     Leigh H. Fredrickson, and Henry R. Murkin

VIII. *Harvest, Distribution, and Population Status*

35. Recoveries of North American Waterfowl in the Neotropics   469
     Jorge E. Botero and Donald H. Rusch
36. Mobility and Site Fidelity of Green-Winged Teal Wintering on the
     Southern High Plains of Texas   483
     Guy A. Baldassarre, Eileen E. Quinlan, and Eric G. Bolen
37. History and Status of Midcontinent Snow Geese on Their
     Gulf Coast Winter Range   495
     Hugh A. Bateman, Ted Joanen, and Charles D. Stutzenbaker
38. Recent Changes in Wintering Populations of Canada Geese in
     Western Oregon and Southwestern Washington   517
     Robert L. Jarvis and John E. Cornely
39. Use of the Missouri River in South Dakota by Canada Geese in
     Fall and Winter, 1953-1984   529
     S. G. Simpson
40. Estimating Populations of Ducks Wintering in Southeast Alaska   541
     Bruce Conant, James G. King, John L. Trapp, and John I. Hodges
41. Dabbling Duck Harvest Dynamics in the Central Valley of
     California — Implications for Recruitment   553
     Michael R. Miller, John Beam, and Daniel P. Connelly
42. Workshop Summary: Species and Population Status and
     Distribution   571
     *James D. Nichols, Dirk V. Derksen, Robert L. Jarvis, and
     John T. Ratti*
43. Workshop Summary: Hunting Vulnerability and Mortality   575
     *Frank Montalbano III, Douglas H. Johnson, Michael R. Miller,
     and Donald H. Rusch*

IX. *Decimating Influences: Habitat Loss, Toxins, and Disease*

44. Wintering Waterfowl Habitat in Texas: Shrinking and
     Contaminated   583
     Brian W. Cain
45. Ingestion of Shotshell Pellets by Waterfowl Wintering in Texas   597
     *Daniel W. Moulton, Carl D. Frentress, Charles D. Stutzenbaker,
     David S. Lobpries, and William C. Brownlee*
46. Workshop Summary: Toxins, Disease, and Lead Poisoning   609
     Brian W. Cain and J. Scott Feierabend
47. Workshop Summary: Habitat Loss and Its Effect on Waterfowl   613
     *Robert E. Stewart, Jr., Gary L. Krapu, Bruce Conant,
     H. Franklin Percival, and David L. Hall*

Preface

In the spring of 1982, the staff of the Delta Waterfowl and Wetlands Research Station at Delta, Manitoba, called together a group of waterfowl biologists who had worked or who were working with ecological and behavioral aspects of waterfowl in winter and the postbreeding period. Their intent was to examine possibilities for future research programs. The meeting was held at the Gaylord Memorial Lab of the University of Missouri, where Leigh Fredrickson and his students have explored many aspects of nonbreeding waterfowl. At the close of that very impressive meeting, Bruce Batt of the station suggested that I host the next such meeting along the Gulf Coast, where so many of the North American waterfowl winter. I took this challenge seriously because of my own plans to reactivate research in this area and because of the impressive array of ongoing work that needed to be shared with other biologists. With the assistance of Bruce Batt, Leigh Fredrickson, and two other waterfowl biologists with years of experience with wintering waterfowl — Dennis Raveling of California and Robert Chabreck of Louisiana — we organized a symposium to document the state of our understanding and workshops to explore where we should be directing our research and management efforts in the best interests of science and the waterfowl resource.

This collection of papers on waterfowl in winter and other nonbreeding periods is the product of that symposium, which was held in Galveston, Texas, on January 7-10, 1985. More than 100 papers were presented orally or via posters, and 10 evening workshops allowed the 325 participants to discuss topics of concern or areas of interest in semistructured workshops related topically to the paper sessions. As with any symposium, coverage was influenced by contributing speakers, but the papers represented a reasonable balance of current research activities, state-of-the-art management strategies, and current issues. This volume retains some of the symposium format because that format was set by current research and management efforts, and the reports of workshop sessions follow clusters of related papers. Because many of the papers were given by workers whose research is still in progress and not ready for publication, or those presenting portions of more extensive data sets that will be published in entirety elsewhere, this group of papers represents a sample of what is going on in the study of migrant and wintering waterfowl today. All papers were subjected to reviews by experts in the subject area, a list of whom is presented on following pages.

Some of these reports concern issues and short-term field experiments; others represent long and detailed research investigations. But science is progressive, and the product often transient, so this work must be viewed as a statement of recent events. I hope that these papers, in conjunction with the workshop reports, also will help identify future research and management needs.

Acknowledgments

The symposium and this resulting volume could not have been produced without the stimulus, guidance, and assistance of many people. Individuals representing the five sponsoring agencies had both the foresight and the energy to arrange for funding, sometimes battling unexpected resistance: Bruce Batt and Peter Ward of the Delta Waterfowl and Wetlands Research Station, Jim Teer of the Rob and Bessie Welder Wildlife Foundation, Reid Goforth of the U.S. Fish and Wildlife Service, Larry Jahn of the Wildlife Management Institute, George Burger of the Max McGraw Wildlife Foundation, and Wallace Klussmann of Texas A&M University. In addition, thanks are due to the program committee that included Leigh Fredrickson of the University of Missouri, Robert Chabreck of Louisiana State University, and Dennis Raveling of the University of California at Davis, as well as Bruce Batt.

Helpers from Texas A&M University who facilitated operations before and during the symposium include Betsy Couch, Bridgett Estel, Craig Farquhar, Shannon Garner, Barry Grand, Nita Hazle, Mike Hoy, Mary Kae Hvizdos, Robert Richards, Will Roach, Cathrin Ryan, Ed Shanley, Bill Tietje, Dave Tilton, Jim Webb, Doris Weller, and Tommy Wright. Special thanks are due Nita Hazle for her tireless efforts in coordination of manuscript review and in copyediting.

Numerous persons ably chaired sessions and helped coordinate events: John "Frosty" Anderson, Dave Ankney, Bruce Batt, Frank Bellrose, Eric Bolen, Robert Chabreck, James Cooper, Leigh Fredrickson, Erwin Klaas, Gary Krapu, Frank McKinney, Ken Pollock, Dennis Raveling, Robert Stewart, Jr., and Roger Titman.

Finally, we acknowledge the many outstanding reveiwers who took their job seriously and put aside other chores to meet our unreasonable deadlines.

Contributors

Alan D. Afton, Minnesota Department of Natural Resources, 102 23rd St., Bemidji, MN 56601

Bertin W. Anderson, Center for Environmental Studies, Arizona State University, Tempe, AZ 85287

Michael G. Anderson, Delta Waterfowl and Wetlands Research Station, RR 1, Portage la Prairie, MB R1N 3A1, Canada

C. Davison Ankney, Department of Zoology, University of Western Ontario, London, Ontario, N6A 5B7, Canada

Guy A. Baldassarre, Department of Range and Wildlife Management, Texas Tech University, Lubbock, TX 79409. Present address: College of Environmental Science and Forestry, State University, Syracuse, NY 13210

Robert C. Barkley, U.S. Fish and Wildlife Service, 900 Clay Street, Vicksburg, MS 39180

Hugh A. Bateman, Louisiana Department of Wildlife and Fisheries, P.O. Box 15570, Baton Rouge, LA 70895

Gary Bates, U.S. Soil Conservation Service, 101 S. Main St., Temple, TX 76501. Present address: U.S. SCS, P.O. Box 665, Menard, TX 76859-0665

Bruce D. J. Batt, Delta Waterfowl and Wetlands Research Station, RR 1, Portage la Prairie, MB R1N 3A1, Canada

Charles K. Baxter, U.S. Fish and Wildlife Service, 900 Clay Street, Vicksburg, MS 39180

John Beam, California Department of Fish and Game, Los Banos Wildlife Area, 18110 W. Henry Miller Ave., Los Banos, CA 93635

Jeffrey M. Black, Wildfowl Trust, Slimbridge, Gloucester GL2 7BT, United Kingdom

Eric G. Bolen, Department of Range and Wildlife Management, Texas Tech University, Lubbock, TX 79409

Jorge E. Botero, Department of Wildlife Ecology, University of Wisconsin, 1630 Linden Drive, Madison, WI 53706

William C. Brownlee, Texas Parks and Wildlife Department, 4200 Smith School Rd., Austin, TX 78744

Brian W. Cain, U.S. Fish and Wildlife Service, Ecological Services, 17629 Camino Real, Houston, TX 77058

Robert H. Chabreck, School of Forestry, Wildlife, and Fisheries, Louisiana State University Agricultural Center, Baton Rouge, LA 70803

Mark W. Christopher, P.O. Drawer BX, Mississippi Cooperative Fish and Wildlife Research Unit, Mississippi State University, MS 39762-5603. Present address: Breedlove, Dennis, and Assoc., Inc., 2412 Forsyth Road, Orlando, FL 32807

Bruce Conant, U.S. Fish and Wildlife Service, Box 1287, Juneau, Ak 99802

Daniel P. Connelly, California Department of Fish and Game, 1416 Ninth St., Sacramento, CA 95814

Micheal J. Conroy, U.S. Fish and Wildlife Service, Migratory Bird and Habitat Laboratory, Laurel, MD 20708

John E. Cornely, U.S. Fish and Wildlife Service, Route 2, Box 208, Corvallis, OR 97333

Lewis M. Cowardin, U.S. Fish and Wildlife Service, Northern Prairie Wildlife Research Center, P.O. Box 1747, Jamestown, ND 58401

Dirk V. Derksen, U.S. Fish and Wildlife Service, 1011 East Tudor Road, Anchorage, AK 99504

James J. Dinsmore, Department of Animal Ecology, Iowa State University, Ames, IA 50011

Bridgett L. Estel, Illinois Department of Conservation, RR 2, Jonesboro, IL 62952. Present address: Cooperative Wildlife Research Unit, Cornell University, Ithaca, NY 14853

J. Scott Feierabend, National Wildlife Federation, Washington, D.C. 20036

Leigh H. Fredrickson, Gaylord Memorial Laboratory, University of Missouri, Puxico, MO 63960

Carl D. Frentress, Texas Parks and Wildlife Department, Rt. 3, Box 163-1A, Athens, TX 75751

Louis S. George, U.S. Fish and Wildlife Service, Northern Prairie Wildlife Research Center, P.O. Box 2226, La Crosse, WI 54601

James P. Gibbs, Wildlife Department, University of Maine, Orono, ME 04469

William L. Green, U.S. Fish and Wildlife Service, Northern Prairie Wildlife Research Center, P.O. Box 2226, La Crosse, WI 54601

Philip E. Hale, School of Forest Resources and Institute of Natural Resources, University of Georgia, Athens, GA 30602

David L. Hall, U.S. Fish and Wildlife Service, 1010 Gause Blvd., Building 936, Slidell, LA 70458

Andrew J. Harrison, Jr., RR 2, Box 3200, Plaquemine, LA 70764

Loree H. Havel, Department of Fisheries and Wildlife, Oregon State University, Corvallis, OR 97331-3803. Present address: P.O. Box 1073, Willamina, OR 97396

David C. Hayden, Indigo Island Research Station, RR 2, Box 3200, Plaquemine, LA 70764

Mickey E. Heitmeyer, Gaylord Memorial Laboratory, University of Missouri, Puxico, MO 63960. Present address: Department of Wildlife and Fisheries Biology, University of California, Davis, CA 95616

Gary R. Hepp, U.S. Fish and Wildlife Service, Patuxent Wildlife Research Center, Laurel, MD 20708. Present address: Savannah River Ecology Lab, Aiken, SC 29801

H W Heusmann, Division of Fisheries and Wildlife, Field Headquarters, Westboro, MA 01581

Edward P. Hill, Mississippi Cooperative Fish and Wildlife Research Unit, P.O. Drawer BX, Mississippi State University, Mississippi State, MS 39762-5603

John I. Hodges, U.S. Fish and Wildlife Service, Box 1287, Juneau, AK 99802

William L. Hohman, Department of Fisheries and Wildlife, University of Minnesota, St. Paul, MN 55108. Present address: U.S. Fish and Wildlife Service, Pacific Coast Field Station, University of California, Davis, CA 95616

Robert L. Jarvis, Department of Fisheries and Wildlife, Oregon State University, Corvallis, OR 97331-3803

Ted Joanen, Louisiana Department of Wildlife and Fisheries, Rt. 1, Box 20-B, Grand Chenier, LA 70643

A. Sydney Johnson, School of Forest Resources and Institute of Natural Resources, University of Georgia, Athens, GA 30602

Douglas H. Johnson, U.S. Fish and Wildlife Service, Northern Prairie Wildlife Research Center, Jamestown, ND 58401

James C. Johnson, Wildlife and Fisheries Biology, University of California, Davis, CA 95616

Dennis G. Jorde, Wildlife Department, University of Maine, Orono, ME 04469. Present address: U.S. Fish and Wildlife Service Patuxent Wildlife Research Center, Laurel, MD 20708

Robert L. Joyner, South Carolina Wildlife and Marine Resources Department, Tom Yawkey Wildlife Center, Georgetown, SC 29440

Richard M. Kaminski, Department of Wildlife and Fisheries, P.O. Drawer LW, Mississippi State University, Mississippi State, MS *James G. King,* U.S. Fish and Wildlife Service, Box 1287, Juneau, AK 99802

Carl E. Korschgen, U.S. Fish and Wildlife Service, Northern Prairie Wildlife Research Center, P.O. Box 2226, La Crosse, WI 54601

Gary L. Krapu, U.S. Fish and Wildlife Service, Northern Prairie Wildlife Research Center, Jamestown, ND 58401

Theodore G. LaGrange, Department of Animal Ecology, Iowa State University, Ames, IA 50011. Present address: Iowa Conservation Commission, 1203 North Shore Drive, Clear Lake, IA 50011

James C. Lewis, School of Forest Resources, University of Georgia, Athens, GA 30602. Present address: U.S. Fish and Wildlife Service, Albuquerque, NM 87103

Halyna Liber, Wildfowl Trust, Slimbridge, Gloucester GL2 7BT, United Kingdom

David S. Lobpries, Texas Parks and Wildlife Department, P.O. Box 248, Garwood, TX 77442

Jerry R. Longcore, U.S. Fish and Wildlife Service, Patuxent Wildlife Research Center, University of Maine, Orono, ME 04469

Frank McKinney, Department of Ecology and Behavioral Biology, University of Minnesota, Minneapolis, MN 55455

Michael R. Miller, U.S. Fish and Wildlife Service, Northern Prairie Wildlife Research Center, Dixon, CA 95620

Frank Montalbano III, Florida Game and Fresh Water Fish Commission, 3991 S.E. 27th Court, Okeechobee, FL 33472

Daniel W. Moulton, Texas Parks and Wildlife Department, Wildlife Division, 4200 Smith School Road, Austin, TX 78744

Henry R. Murkin, Delta Waterfowl and Wetlands Research Station, RR 1, Portage la Prairie, MB R1N 3A1, Canada

James R. Nassar, School of Forestry, Wildlife, and Fisheries, Louisiana State University Agricultural Center, Baton Rouge, LA 70803. Present address: Williams, Inc., Rt. 2, Box 3200, Plaquemine, LA 70764

Martin Nelson, Cooperative Wildlife Research Unit, School of Forest Resources, University of Georgia, Athens, GA 30602

James D. Nichols, U.S. Fish and Wildlife Service, Patuxent Wildlife Research Center, Laurel, MD 20708

Holliday, H. Obrecht, III, U.S. Fish and Wildlife Service, Patuxent Wildlife Research Center, Laurel, MD 20708

Robert D. Ohmart, Center for Environmental Studies, Arizona State University, Tempe, AZ 85287

Myrfyn Owen, Wildfowl Trust, Slimbridge, Gloucester GL2 7BT, United Kingdom

Ray B. Owen, Jr., Wildlife Department, University of Maine, Orono, ME 04469

Stuart L. Paulus, Department of Zoology/Entomology, Auburn University, Auburn, AL 36849; Louisiana Department of Wildlife and Fisheries, Grand Chenier, LA 70643. Present address: P.O. Box 731, Snoqualmie, WA 98065.

Roger L. Pederson, Delta Waterfowl and Wetlands Research Station, RR 1, Portage la Prairie, MB R1N 3A1, Canada

H. Franklin Percival, Cooperative Wildlife Research Unit, University of Florida, Gainesville, FL 32611

Matthew C. Perry, U.S. Fish and Wildlife Service, Patuxent Wildlife Research Center, Laurel, MD 20708

Harold H. Prince, Department of Wildlife, Michigan State University, East Lansing, MI 48823

Eileen E. Quinlan, Department of Range and Wildlife Management, Texas Tech University, Lubbock, TX 79409. Present address: College of Environmental Science and Forestry, State University, Syracuse, NY 13210

John T. Ratti, Department of Zoology, Washington State University, Pullman, WA 99164-4220. Present address: 2457 W. Twin Road, Moscow, ID 83843

Dennis G. Raveling, Wildlife and Fisheries Biology, University of California, Davis, CA 95616

Frederic A. Reid, School of Forestry, Fisheries, and Wildlife, University of Missouri, Columbia, MO 65211

Kenneth J. Reinecke, U.S. Fish and Wildlife Service, Patuxent Wildlife Research Center, 900 Clay Street, Vicksburg, MS 39180

James K. Ringelman, Colorado Division of Wildlife, Wildlife Research Center, Fort Collins, CO 80526

Donald H. Rusch, Wisconsin Cooperative Wildlife Research Unit, University of Wisconsin, Madison, WI 53706

Jerome R. Serie, U.S. Fish and Wildlife Service, Office of Migratory Bird Management, Laurel, MD 20708

S.G. Simpson, South Dakota Department of Game, Fish and Parks, 445 E. Capitol, Pierre, SD 57501

James W. Spitzkeit, Cooperative Wildlife Research Laboratory, Southern Illinois University, Carbondale, IL 62901

Frank H. Sprague, U.S. Soil Conservation Service, 101 South Main, Temple, TX 76501

David E. Steffen, Mississippi Department of Wildlife Conservation, P.O. Box 451, Jackson, MS 39205

Robert E. Stewart, Jr., U.S. Fish and Wildlife Service, National Wetlands Research Center, 1010 Gause Blvd., Slidell, LA 70458

Charles D. Stutzenbaker, Texas Parks and Wildlife Department, 10 Parks and Wildlife Dr., Port Arthur, TX 77640

Peter K. Swiderek, School of Forest Resources and Institute of Natural Resources, University of Georgia, Athens, GA 30602. Present address: College of Veterinary Medicine, University of Georgia, Athens, GA 30602

James E. Tabor, Washington Department of Game, 1668 David St., Moses Lake, WA 98837

Thomas C. Tacha, Cooperative Wildlife Research Laboratory, Southern Illinois *University, Carbondale, IL 62901*

Alain Tamisier, Centre d'ecologie de Camarque, Le Sambuc, 13200 Arles, France

T. Scott Taylor, Department of Fisheries and Wildlife, University of Minnesota, St. Paul, MN 55108. Present address: Gaylord Memorial Laboratory, University of Missouri, Puxico, MO 63960

James G. Teer, Welder Wildlife Foundation, P.O. Drawer 1400, Sinton, TX 78387

Bruce C. Thompson, Washington Department of Game, Olympia, WA 98504. Present address: Texas Parks and Wildlife Department, 4200 Smith School Road, Austin, TX 78744

Dennis D. Thornburg, Illinois Department of Conservation, RR 2, Jonesboro, IL 62952

William D. Tietje, Department of Wildlife and Fisheries Sciences, Texas A&M University, College Station, TX 77843. Present address: University of California Cooperative Extension, 2156 Sierra Way, San Luis Obisbo, CA 93401

Rodger D. Titman, Department of Renewable Resources, MacDonald College of McGill University, Ste. Anne de Bellevue, Quebec, Canada H9X 1C0

John L. Trapp, U.S. Fish and Wildlife Service, 1011 East Tudor Road, Anchorage, AK 99503

Clarence L. Turner, Washington Department of Game, 600 N. Capitol Way, Olympia, WA 98504. Present address: 1744 Vaughn Drive, Manhattan, KS 66502

Gary L. Valentine, U.S. Soil Conservation Service, 101 South Main, Temple, TX 76503

Milton W. Weller, Department of Fisheries and Wildlife, University of Minnesota, St. Paul, MN 55108. Present address: Department of Wildlife and Fisheries Sciences, Texas A&M University, College Station, TX 77843

Byron K. Williams, U.S. Fish and Wildlife Service, Patuxent Wildlife Research Center, Laurel, MD 20708

Reviewers

Alan D. Afton, Minnesota Department of Natural Resources, Bemidji
William C. Alexander, Brevard College, Brevard, N.C.
Charles E. Allen, Texas Parks and Wildlife Department, Austin
Bertin W. Anderson, Arizona State University, Tempe
Daniel W. Anderson, University of California, Davis
David R. Anderson, U.S. Fish and Wildlife Service, Fort Collins, Colo.
Michael G. Anderson, Delta Waterfowl and Wetlands Research Station, Portage la Prairie, Manitoba
C. Davison Ankney, University of Western Ontario, London
Michael Armbruster, U.S. Fish and Wildlife Service, Fort Collins, Colo.
David L. Baggett, St. Regis Paper, Groveton, Tex.
Robert O. Bailey, Canadian Wildlife Service, Ottawa, Ontario
Guy A. Baldassarre, State University, Syracuse, N.Y.
James C. Bartonek, U.S. Fish and Wildlife Service, Portland, Oreg.
Gary Bates, U.S. Soil Conservation Service, Menard, Tex.
Bruce D. J. Batt, Delta Waterfowl and Wetlands Research Station, Portage la Prairie, Manitoba
Frank C. Bellrose, Illinois Natural History Survey, Havana
Phillip Bettoli, Tennessee Tech University, Cookeville
Cynthia Bluhm, Max-Planck Institut, D-8138 Andechs, West Germany
Eric G. Bolen, Texas Tech University, Lubbock
Hugh Boyd, Canadian Wildlife Service, Ottawa, Ontario
Christopher J. Brand, U.S. Fish and Wildlife Service, Madison, Wis.
John Cary, University of Wisconsin, Madison
Robert H. Chabreck, Louisiana State University, Baton Rouge
Michael J. Conroy, U.S. Fish and Wildlife Service, Laurel, Md.
F. Graham Cooch, Canadian Wildlife Service, Ottawa, Ontario
Fred Cooke, Queen's University, Kingston, Ontario

James Cooper, University of Minnesota, St. Paul

Lewis M. Cowardin, U.S. Fish and Wildlife Service, Jamestown, N. Dak.

James T. Davis, Texas A&M University, College Station

Donald Delnicki, U.S. Fish and Wildlife Service, Vicksburg, Miss.

Ronald D. Drobney, Missouri Cooperative Wildlife Research Unit, Columbia

Alex Dzubin, Canadian Wildlife Service, Saskatoon, Saskatchewan

John R. Faaborg, University of Missouri, Columbia

Leigh H. Fredrickson, University of Missouri, Puxico

James B. Grand, Texas A&M University, College Station

William Grant, Texas A&M University, College Station

G. Michael Haramis, U.S. Fish and Wildlife Service, Laurel, Md.

Stephen P. Havera, Illinois Natural History Survey, Havana

Sue Hazeltine, U.S. Fish and Wildlife Service, Laurel, Md.

Mickey E. Heitmeyer, University of California, Davis

Gary R. Hepp, Savannah River Ecology Lab, Aiken, S.C.

H W Heusmann, Massachusetts Division of Fisheries and Wildlife, Westboro

Edward P. Hill, Mississippi Cooperative Fish and Wildlife Research Unit, Mississippi State

William C. Hobaugh, Wildlife Consultant, Columbus, Tex.

George Hochbaum, Canadian Wildlife Service, Winnepeg, Manitoba

William L. Hohman, U.S. Fish and Wildlife Service, National Wetlands Research Center, Baton Rouge, La.

Dale D. Humberg, Missouri Department of Conservation, Columbia

Roger Hunter, Fish and Wildlife Branch, Victoria, British Columbia

Robert L. Jarvis, Oregon State University, Corvallis

A. Sydney Johnson, University of Georgia, Athens

Michael A. Johnson, North Dakota Game and Fish Department, Bismarck

Dennis G. Jorde, U.S. Fish and Wildlife Service, Patuxent Wildlife Research Center, Laurel, Md.

Richard M. Kaminski, Mississippi State University, Mississippi State

Ronald E. Kirby, U.S. Fish and Wildlife Service, Fort Collins, Colo.

Carl E. Korschgen, U.S. Fish and Wildlife Service, La Crosse, Wis.

Gary L. Krapu, U.S. Fish and Wildlife Service, Jamestown, N. Dak.

James Kushlan, East Texas State University, Commerce

John Lazarus, Newcastle-on-Tyne University, United Kingdom

Jerry R. Longcore, U.S. Fish and Wildlife Service, Orono, Maine

Frank McKinney, University of Minnesota, Minneapolis

M. Robert McLandress, California Waterfowl Association, Suisan, Calif.

Harvey W. Miller, U.S. Fish and Wildlife Service, Golden, Colo.

Michael R. Miller, U.S. Fish and Wildlife Service, Dixon, Calif.

Daniel W. Moulton, Texas Parks and Wildlife Department, Austin

I.
Winter in Perspective

1

Waterfowl in Winter: Past, Present, and Future

Milton W. Weller and Bruce D. J. Batt

Abstract: Although waterfowl population and habitat management on migration and wintering areas have been studied more than publications reflect, basic biology of wintering waterfowl is poorly known. Much of the effort by waterfowl biologists working on wintering areas dealt with distribution, habitat, and other conservation issues. The lack of research effort on other basic problems can be explained by the prevalent idea that populations are controlled primarily by events on breeding areas. However, it has been obvious for some time that much of the pairing process of numerous species occurs on wintering areas, and recent observations on condition and fat deposition in relation to wintering and migration have demonstrated the need to understand cross-seasonal aspects of the life cycle of waterfowl. There are numerous gaps in our understanding of waterfowl on an annual basis, and the present focus on wintering and migrant birds is needed to allow a more holistic analysis of factors affecting reproduction, survival, and population dynamics of waterfowl.

Since the inception of modern research on the biology of waterfowl in the mid-1930s, the majority of effort has been on breeding birds (Fredrickson and Drobney 1979, Reinecke 1981). This emphasis has been sustained by the perception of waterfowl biologists that most of the critical events controlling annual recruitment and population size occur during the breeding period. Populations of waterfowl enter and leave this period at the lowest and highest population levels, respectively, in the annual cycle. Courtship, nest site selection, predation, laying, incubation, brood rearing, food habits, and bioenergetics have all been the subjects

Waterfowl in Winter. © 1988 University of Minnesota. Edited by Milton W. Weller and published by the University of Minnesota Press, Minneapolis.

of a great deal of study—more than for any other taxonomic group of wild birds. Attention also has been focused on the breeding grounds because of the dramatic losses of habitat there, a problem widely recognized as the ultimate control of wild populations.

This shortage of information on wintering waterfowl does not apply to management of wetlands to attract and sustain migrants and wintering waterfowl. However, published literature does not evenly reflect what has been learned, and what is routinely applied on public and private areas. For most marsh managers, the rewards of their toils come from establishing food plants through the timely application of water, drawing large numbers of birds to refuge or harvest areas, or the development of harvest strategies that maximize the kill while preventing excess disturbance. This information is passed on by word-of-mouth or field demonstrations; there is less necessity or reward for publishing information. There are notable exceptions (e.g., Lynch 1941; Glazener 1946; Chabreck 1959, 1979; Nelson 1954; Newsom 1968; Morgan et al. 1975; Connelly 1979; Fredrickson and Taylor 1982), and a great deal of information is contained in progress reports in various state and public agencies.

The greatest effort on migrant and wintering waterfowl by federal and state conservation agencies in North America has been on population management through harvest regulations and population monitoring (Hawkins et al. 1984). By legal authority, much of this work is associated with the federal governments of Canada, Mexico, and the United States. In the United States, the Fish and Wildlife Service (FWS), originally the Bureau of Biological Survey (BBS), is the responsible agency.

Many of the early naturalists who contributed much of our knowledge of the distribution of waterfowl in winter, both in the southern United States and Mexico, were employees of the BBS. For example, Wells W. Cooke set up a national team of observers to study bird migration and distribution. His report on waterfowl (Cooke 1906) was a landmark document in delineating breeding, migration, and winter areas and in setting the stage for understanding migratory routes of all birds in North America. Fredrick C. Lincoln later expanded on Cooke's work and, coupled with data from banded birds, elaborated the flyway concept. Although this study emphasized migratory movements and pathways, it related wintering areas and their problems to specific breeding populations (Lincoln 1935). In effect, it was one of the first ways biologists looked at birds in the context of the total annual cycle.

In 1936, Lincoln became the head of a team of "flyway biologists" who were to assess the waterfowl situation by flyways at each end of migratory movements north and south. Some of these biologists already had experience on both wintering and breeding areas, but this reorganization resulted in the first concerted effort by the federal conservation agency to learn about the waterfowl situation on an international scope (Hawkins et al. 1984). Harold S. Peters, working in the

Atlantic region, was among the first to use aircraft to survey waterfowl in winter. He also inventoried wintering birds in Cuba and other islands of the West Indies. Charles Gillham in the Mississippi Flyway spent some time in Mexico, but he devoted most of his time to the breeding ground surveys. George Saunders in the Central Flyway surveyed wintering waterfowl in southern Texas and northeastern Mexico in the same year and for several years thereafter. Complete aerial surveys were conducted in Mexico from 1947 through 1964 (Saunders and Saunders 1981). Pacific Flyway biologist Luther J. Goldman investigated the waterfowl situation on the west coast of Mexico (Saunders and Saunders 1981). Others of the BBS or FWS who visited wintering areas of the Gulf Coast and Mexico included Bureau Research Chief Logan Bennett, who had done the classic work on breeding blue-winged teal (*Anas discors*) and spent a little time in Mexico in 1936 (Bennett 1938), and Director Al Day, who explored commercial hunting in Mexico (Day 1949).

John J. Lynch has been called "the liveliest innovator waterfowl management has yet seen" (Boyd 1983). He was not one of the original four flyway biologists, but his work on wintering areas preceded the flyway crews. Among many achievements, he pioneered habitat management studies on Louisiana wintering areas (Lynch 1941), and he developed the winter measures of age ratio used in assessing the annual productivity of geese and swans (Lynch and Singleton 1964).

Several states or provinces also have had key biologists who influenced conservation and management programs for wintering waterfowl. In California, John Moffitt's pioneering studies included mortality estimates from banding data (Moffitt 1935) and California wintering issues such as oil pollution (Moffitt and Orr 1938). In the warmer areas of British Columbia, J. A. Munro (1939, 1943) devoted considerable effort to dealing with problems as well as biology of nonbreeding waterfowl. Another state-level biologist, Frank Bellrose of the Illinois Natural History Survey, has been one of the great pioneers in many areas of research on migrant and wintering waterfowl, and his influence is truly international (Bellrose and Chase 1950, Bellrose 1968, Bellrose et al. 1979).

Because most of Europe has few breeding birds, that continent is primarily important to waterfowl in winter. Population and habitat management have received much less effort than in North America, but there has been a sustained interest in population inventories and distributions of wintering birds (e.g., Evans et al. 1984, Tamisier 1985, Ruger et al. 1986). Much of this has been coordinated through the Wildfowl Trust of England and the International Waterfowl Research Bureau. The greatest effort is placed on the preservation and protection of the dwindling habitat base. However, some very important basic work on wintering waterfowl has been carried out by individuals in England (e.g., Owen et al. 1987), France (Tamisier 1974, Campredon 1981a, 1981b), Sweden (e.g., Nilson 1972, Pehrsson 1984), and the Netherlands (van Eerden 1984).

Thus, although there is a long history of interest in wintering waterfowl, relatively little work has concerned their basic biology. Some recent discoveries have challenged the philosophy of maintaining the sole research emphasis on breeding areas. We have long recognized that winter is the "pinch" period among resident wildlife because it is the time when food and cover are thought to be most limiting to the population. Our assumption has been that migratory birds avoid this pinch by seeking warmer areas where food and cover are better. But while being better than the "frozen north," conditions on the wintering grounds are not constant from year to year nor area to area. Moreover, we have assumed that waterfowl have special needs only during breeding and that they always return to the breeding areas in the same condition—ready to breed. These assumptions are unlikely. The influence of conditions during the winter on breeding ability has been known in resident wildlife (e.g., Watson and Moss 1972) and now is becoming better understood in waterfowl as well (Ankney and MacInnes 1978, Raveling 1979).

Waterfowl are most abundant in fall and early winter, are highly social, exert intense feeding pressure on reduced areas, and often have seasonally varying diets (Weller 1975). Much of courtship and pairing occur on wintering and migration areas, and perhaps plumage acquisition patterns in ducks should have made that obvious. Different species follow different strategies of energy accumulation and storage, and we are just beginning to appreciate that much of the energy used for reproduction arrives on the breeding areas with the bird—rather than being derived solely from local sources (Ankney and MacInnes 1978, Raveling 1979, Heitmeyer and Fredrickson 1981).

We have tended to assume that all controls on abundance are in the breeding component of the annual cycle. Rates of reproduction and factors influencing recovery are highly variable (Hochbaum 1946). Many researchers have over-emphasized this aspect of population regulation without appreciating that limiting influences may exist anywhere in the life cycle, including the wintering areas (Fretwell 1972). Although some studies have demonstrated patterns of potential competition and partitioning of breeding area resources (e.g., Poysa 1983a, 1983b; Nudds 1983), competition could be quite severe on wintering areas where the birds are often concentrated in great numbers. Indeed, recent studies have demonstrated patterns of resource partitioning in wintering assemblages of waterfowl (White and James 1970).

We need to examine the entire life cycle of waterfowl more objectively and to identify those possible components that could be limiting at any phase of the cycle. A focus on research and management needs for waterfowl in winter should be viewed as an important way to bring information on one segment of the life cycle into our understanding of the whole.

LITERATURE CITED

Ankney, C. D., and C. D. MacInnes. 1978. Nutrient reserves and reproductive performance of female lesser snow geese. Auk 95:459–471.

Bellrose, F. C. 1968. Waterfowl migration corridors east of the Rocky Mountains in the United States. Ill. Nat. Hist. Surv. Biol. Notes 61. 214pp.

———, and E. B. Chase. 1950. Population losses in the mallard, black duck and blue-winged teal. Ill. Nat. Hist. Surv. Biol. Notes 22. 27pp.

———, F. L. Paveglio, Jr., and D. W. Steffeck. 1979. Waterfowl populations of the changing environment of the Illinois River Valley. Ill. Nat. Hist. Surv. Bull. 32 (1):1–54.

Bennett, L. J. 1938. The blue-winged teal. Collegiate Press, Ames, Iowa. 144pp.

Boyd, H. 1983. Introduction. Pages 1-2 *in* H. Boyd, ed. First western hemisphere waterfowl and waterbird symposium. Int. Waterfowl Res. Bureau. 147pp.

Campredon, P. 1981a. Hivernage du canard siffleur *Anas penelope* L. en Camargue (France): stationnements et activites. Alauda 49:161–193.

———. 1981b. Hivernage du canard siffleur *Anas penelope* L. en Camargue: occupation de l'espace. Alauda 49:272–294.

Chabreck, R. H. 1959. Coastal marsh impoundments for ducks in Louisiana. Proc. Southeast. Assoc. Game Fish Comm. 14:24–29.

———. 1979. Winter habitat of dabbling ducks—physical chemical, and biological aspects. Pages 133–142 *in* T. Bookhout, ed. Waterfowl and wetlands—an integrated review. Proc. 1977 Symp., Northcent. Sect. Wildl. Soc., Madison, Wis. 152pp.

Connelly, D. P. 1979. Propagation of selected native marsh plants in the San Joaquin Valley. Calif. Dep. Fish Game Leaflet 15. 13pp. Bull. 26. 90pp.

Cooke, W. W. 1906. Distribution and migration of North American ducks, geese, and swans. U.S. Dep. Agric. Biol. Surv. Bull. 26. 90pp.

Day, A. 1949. North American waterfowl. Stackpole Books, Harrisburg, Pa. 363pp.

Evans, P. R., J. D. Goss-Custard, and W. G. Hale, eds. 1984. Coastal waders and wildfowl in winter. Cambridge Univ. Press, Cambridge. 331pp.

Fredrickson, L. H., and R. D. Drobney. 1979. Habitat utilization by postbreeding waterfowl. Pages 119 - 131 *in* T. Bookhout, ed. Waterfowl and wetlands—an integrated review. Proc. 1977 Symp., Northcent. Sect., Wildl. Soc., Madison, Wis. 152pp.

———, and T. S. Taylor. 1982. Management of seasonally flooded impoundments for wildlife. U.S. Dep. Interior Res. Publ. 148:29pp.

Fretwell, S. D. 1972. Populations in a seasonal environment. Princeton Univ. Monogr. Pop. Biol. 5. 217pp.

Glazener, W. C. 1946. Food habits of wild geese on the Gulf Coast of Texas. J. Wildl. Manage. 10:322–329.

Hawkins, A. S., R. C. Hanson, H. K. Nelson, and H. M. Reeves. 1984. Flyways. U.S. Fish Wildl. Serv., Washington, D.C. 517pp.

Heitmeyer, M. E., and L. H. Fredrickson. 1981. Do wetland conditions in the Mississippi Delta hardwoods influence mallard recruitment? Trans. N. Am. Wildl. Nat. Resour. Conf. 46:44–57.

Hochbaum, H. A. 1946. Recovery potentials in North American waterfowl. Trans. N. Am. Wildl. Conf. 11:403-418.

Lincoln, F. C. 1935. The waterfowl flyways of North America. U.S. Dep. Agric. Circ. 342. 12pp.

Lynch, J. J. 1941. The place of burning in management of Gulf Coast refuges. J. Wildl. Manage. 5:454-457.

———, and J. R. Singleton. 1964. Winter appraisals of annual productivity in geese and other water birds. Wildfowl Trust Annu. Rep. 15:114–126.

Moffitt, J. 1935. Waterfowl shooting losses indicated by band returns. Trans. N. Am. Game Conf. 21:305-308.

———, and R. T. Orr. 1938. Recent disastrous effects of oil pollution in the San Francisco Bay Region. Calif. Fish Game 24: 239-244.

Morgan, P. H., A. S. Johnson, W. P. Baldwin, and J. L. Landers. 1975. Characteristics and management of tidal impoundments for wildlife in a South Carolina estuary. Proc. Southeast. Fish Game Comm. 29:526-539.

Munro, J. A. 1939. Studies of waterfowl in British Columbia, Barrow's Golden-eye, American Golden-eye. Trans. Roy. Can. Inst. 22 (Pt. 2, No. 48):259-318.

———. 1943. Studies of waterfowl in British Columbia, mallard. Can. J. Res. 21:223-260.

Nelson, N. F. 1954. Factors in the development and restoration of waterfowl habitat at Ogden Bay Refuge, Weber County, Utah. Utah State Dep. Fish Game Publ. 6. 87pp.

Newsom, J. D., ed. 1968. Proceedings of the marsh and estuary management symposium. Louisiana State Univ., Baton Rouge. 252pp.

Nilson, L. 1972. Habitat selection, food choice, and feeding habits of diving ducks in coastal waters of south Sweden during the non-breeding season. Ornis Scand. 3:55-78.

Nudds, T. D. 1983. Niche dynamics and organization of waterfowl guilds in variable environments. Ecol. 64:319-330.

Owen, M., J. M. Black, and H. Liber. 1988. Pair bond duration and timing of its formation in barnacle geese (*Branta leucopsis*). Pages 23-38 *in* M. W. Weller, ed. Waterfowl in winter. Univ. Minnesota Press, Minneapolis.

Pehrsson, O. 1984. Diving duck populations in relation to their food supplies. Pages 101-116 *in* P. R. Evans, J. D. Goss-Custard, and W. G. Hale, eds. Coastal waders and wildfowl in winter. Cambridge Univ. Press, Cambridge. 331pp.

Poysa, H. 1983a. Morphology-mediated niche organization in a guild of dabbling ducks. Ornis Scand. 14:327-336.

———. 1983b. Resource utilization pattern and guild structure in a waterfowl community. Oikos 40:295-307.

Raveling, D. G. 1979. The annual cycle of body composition of Canada geese with special reference to control of reproduction. Auk 96:234-252.

Reinecke, K. J. 1981. Winter waterfowl research needs and efforts in the Mississippi Delta. Ducks Unlimited Int. Waterfowl Symp. 4:231-236.

Ruger, A., C. Prentice, and M. Owen. 1986. Results of the IWRB international waterfowl census 1967-1983. IWRB Spec. Publ. No. 6. Slimbridge, England. 118pp.

Saunders, G. B., and D. C. Saunders. 1981. Waterfowl and their wintering grounds in Mexico, 1937-64. U.S. Fish Wildlife Serv. Resour. Publ. 138. 151pp.

Tamisier, A. 1974. Etho-ecological studies of teal wintering in the Camarque (Rhone Delta, France). Wildfowl 25:107-117.

———. 1985. Hunting as a key environmental parameter for the Western Palearctic duck populations. Wildfowl 36:95-103.

van Eerden, M. R. 1984. Waterfowl movements in relation to food stocks. Pages 84-100 *in* P. R. Evans, J. D. Goss-Custard, and W. G. Hale, eds. Coastal waders and wildfowl in winter. Cambridge Univ. Press, Cambridge. 331pp.

Watson, A., and R. Moss. 1972. A current model of population dynamics in red grouse. Proc. Int. Ornith. Congr. 15:134-149.

Weller, M. W. 1975. Migratory waterfowl: a hemispheric perspective. Publicaciones Biologicas Instituto de Investigaciones Cientificas, U.A.N.L. 1(7):89-130.

White, D. H., and D. James. 1970. Differential use of fresh water environments by wintering waterfowl in coastal Texas. Wilson Bull. 90:99-111.

2

Some Considerations in Modeling the Mallard Life Cycle

Douglas H. Johnson, James D. Nichols, Michael J. Conroy, and Lewis M. Cowardin

Abstract: We outline a population model proposed to accommodate the full life cycle of the mallard (*Anas platyrhynchos*). Events during the breeding season are better understood than events at other times of the year, but recent findings suggest the importance of phenomena away from the breeding grounds. Several processes are discussed relative to mallard population dynamics. Compensatory mortality is a poorly understood concept, but one that can overwhelm many other components of a population model. Diseases and environmental contaminants can inflict indirect as well as direct mortality and can reduce reproduction. They interact with numerous other variables in complex and yet unknown ways. Recent evidence of a wintering-ground effect on subsequent recruitment provides one avenue for modeling phenomena occurring at different times of the year. Finally, the role of heterogeneity among individuals is widely acknowledged but not fully appreciated. We illustrate with an example the importance of heterogeneity to population processes, including compensatory mortality.

Waterfowl have been studied more closely than any other group of wild birds. Despite the attention given to these important and interesting birds, many key features of their biology are not understood. Among mallards (*Anas platyrhynchos*), for example, the mechanisms that regulate the North American population remain unknown. Numerous factors have been suggested, however, including hunting, predation, disease, and habitat.

Investigators have placed more emphasis on aspects of waterfowl biology during the breeding season than during other parts of the year. This disparate

Waterfowl in Winter.© 1988 University of Minnesota. Edited by Milton W. Weller and published by the University of Minnesota Press, Minneapolis.

attention is partly for convenience: waterfowl behavior, like that of most birds, is especially interesting then, and the sedentary nature of birds during that season facilitates their study. A more germane reason for focusing on breeding birds is the importance to population dynamics: all of the population increase from natality and a good portion of the natural mortality occur during a relatively short breeding season.

In contrast to the attention given breeding waterfowl, migrating and wintering birds have been studied with far less intensity. Some tantalizing observations and conjectures, however, recently have suggested that more must be learned about events away from the breeding grounds. One perception is that breeding habitat is no longer filled to capacity (Trauger and Stoudt 1978), an observation suggesting that factors elsewhere may be limiting. A second consideration is an increase in reported disease mortality (Friend 1981), much of which takes place in migrational or wintering areas. A third suggestion is that hunting mortality among mallards is largely compensatory to natural mortality (Anderson and Burnham 1976), an idea obviously important to harvest regulation. A fourth conjecture is that wetland conditions on wintering areas influence subsequent mallard reproduction, perhaps more so than conditions on breeding areas (Heitmeyer and Fredrickson 1981). These concepts are potentially important and must be acknowledged in the responsible management of waterfowl populations.

These ideas need to be put in proper context and related to other facts that we know about the birds. The phenomena should not be viewed in isolation, but as integral parts of a larger picture. One way to pull these diverse concepts together is with mathematical modeling. Modeling is no panacea for waterfowl management, but it often is a useful vehicle for consolidating what we know and for identifying what we do not know.

We are developing a model intended to encompass the entire annual cycle. Objectives of the model include identifying critical information gaps, investigating consistency of parameter values and assumed relationships, assessing the feasibility of selected hypotheses about mallard population dynamics, and investigating the anticipated effects of management actions.

The purpose of this paper is to describe the approach we are taking to develop this model. In this context, we discuss some recent results and hypotheses, particularly insofar as they relate to wintering, migrating, and breeding seasons. Although the paper is partly expository, we also offer it as a challenge to improve our understanding of waterfowl population dynamics and, more specifically, to identify and quantify the important relations among variables involved in the mallard life cycle.

R. M. Kaminski generously shared some unpublished findings with us. This report benefited from review by D. R. Anderson, K. P. Burnham, and T. L. Shaffer, who nonetheless should be held blameless for any errors or misinterpretations contained herein.

An Overview of the Model

Mallard numbers are controlled by two major processes (fig. 2.1): reproduction, including survival of young until fledging, and mortality, which we segregate into summer natural mortality, hunting kill (harvest and crippling loss), fall natural mortality, and winter-spring natural mortality. Each process is influenced by several variables. For simplicity, we focus on females; males seem not to be limiting to productivity.

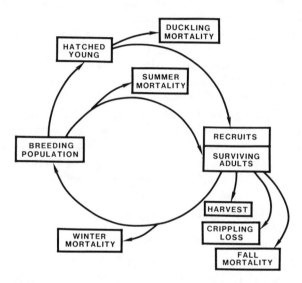

Fig. 2.1. Flow diagram of the mallard population during a year.

The reproductive component is understood better than the others. An existing model (Johnson et al. 1986) simulates mallard productivity in North Dakota and similar regions. Variables important to productivity include wetland conditions on breeding grounds, predator populations and composition, nesting habitat (influenced markedly by agricultural practices), weather phenomena, and condition of arriving hens in spring (related to feeding habitats on wintering and migrational areas). Density-dependence of reproduction is not incorporated in the existing productivity model, except that the number of breeding pairs in an area depends on the wetland habitat available there (Cowardin et al. 1983).

Mortality to adult hens during the summer or breeding season—which also is embodied in the existing productivity model—is largely affected by the numbers and composition of predators. It also is related to nesting effort and success: long periods of time spent on a nest expose the hen to greater risk of predation. Mortality forces also include diseases, which presumably relate to such variables as weather and which may be density-dependent in their effect.

Determinants of hunting kill are not as well known as might be expected from the prominence of sport harvest (but see Hochbaum and Walters 1984). We anticipate that the kill rate depends on the size of the fall flight and its age and sex composition (possibly including other duck species) and on hunting effort, which in turn relates to hunting regulations, number of birds in the fall flight, weather conditions, and the status of wetlands along the fall migration corridors.

Natural mortality during the fall probably is disguised by hunting mortality, but it may reasonably be assumed to relate to predator numbers and composition, disease, and possibly the size of the mallard population. Mortality during the winter and spring migration period is only beginning to be understood; however, it probably depends on wintering-ground wetland conditions, agricultural practices, weather, disease, and predator populations. Density-dependence cannot be eliminated as an influence on any of these mortality factors.

The North American mallard breeding population comprises several subpopulations that are likely to differ in reproductive and survival rates. Subpopulations may be defined on the basis of age as well as breeding and wintering areas, for it is known that both reproduction and survival vary by age and geography. Unfortunately, from the standpoint of population analysis, geographic subpopulations are not closed; mallards can and do move from one to another.

Some Important Processes

Compensatory Mortality

Anderson and Burnham (1976) suggested that natural mortality was largely compensatory to hunting mortality in mallards. Their conclusion was derived from an analysis of the extensive banding and recovery data for mallards, which showed that annual survival rates for this species did not vary in response to changes in hunting mortality rates. It contradicted previous conclusions that hunting mortality was additive, a finding that Anderson and Burnham indicated was based on flawed methodologies.

Rogers et al. (1979) reexamined the problem, using the same methodology as Anderson and Burnham (1976) but with data for five additional years, including some with relatively high harvest rates. They too found no relation between hunting mortality rates and overall annual mortality rates, a result consistent with compensation.

Nichols and Hines (1983) addressed the question with a different method, but one still based on analysis of banded mallards. They found that harvest rates and survival rates were inversely related among several groups of immature females, which is suggestive of additivity; but there was no evidence of a relationship among immature males or adults of either sex, which implies compensation. Burnham and Anderson (1984) returned to the question with improved analytic methods and an additional eight years of data. They again concluded that hunting mortalities among adults were largely compensated for by other forms of mortality. Burnham et al. (1984) also examined the hypothesis with the larger data set. They concluded that hunting mortality was largely compensatory among adult male mallards and evidently partly compensatory among adult female mallards.

Despite the fact that all five analyses reached much the same conclusion, we should not be completely comfortable with it, for three reasons. First, it condones an approach to management that is not conservative. A nearly optimal harvest strategy is to take as many birds as possible, up to some unknown and poorly understood threshold value. If complete compensation does not occur, or if the threshold is exceeded, this strategy could be detrimental to waterfowl populations.

The second concern is that all analyses have used much the same banding and recovery data (Burnham et al. 1984). The case for compensation will be strengthened considerably when studies using independent data sets and different methodologies reach the same conclusion. Moreover, inferences have been based on observational rather than the more desirable experimental studies that were recommended in the initial Anderson and Burnham (1976) report and that have been endorsed since (Burnham et al. 1984, Nichols et al. 1984).

The third problem with compensation is that there is no evidence of a specific mechanism that would account for it, other than general density-dependent mortality. If another mortality source compensates for hunting mortality, what is it, where and when does it operate, and how? Questions like these need to be addressed before we can rest comfortably with the conclusion about compensatory mortality.

Conversely, we can no longer proceed in the simple belief that hunting mortality is additive. Evidence for that hypothesis among mallards is weak, at best. Of the two extreme situations—full compensation and full additivity—evidence to date favors full compensation. More likely, compensation is probably partial and probably variable among subpopulations, years, and habitat conditions.

Despite the confusing situation, the concept of compensation is integral to modeling mallards on an annual basis. We could include hunting mortality as completely additive, completely compensatory, or somewhere in between these extremes. The conclusions reached about many processes by executing the model will be far different, however, depending on which assumption is made. We hope, at least, to be able to evaluate some hypotheses about compensation with a life cycle model, but we can reasonably conclude that the question will not be finally resolved until students of mallard biology identify and understand the mechanisms involved in compensation.

Diseases and Environmental Contaminants

Although diseases among wild waterfowl have long been recognized, they have received increased attention in recent years. There is a realization that waterfowl populations are no longer unlimited, and large losses have occurred from such diseases as avian cholera and duck virus enteritis, which were (or appeared) unimportant until recently (Friend 1981). The potential effects of lead poisoning have long been acknowledged as well (Bellrose 1959), but the issue still commands substantial attention. Other contaminants, including pesticides, polychlorinated biphenyls, mercury and other heavy metals, and petroleum, also can inhibit waterfowl survival or reproduction (White and Stickel 1975).

Diseases and contaminants directly kill many birds each year, although the total number is unknown. Estimates derived from counts of waterfowl found dead, such as those counts presented by Stout and Cornwell (1976), provide misleading estimates of the importance of disease (e.g., Hayes and Davidson 1978) because birds that concentrate in an area and succumb to disease in a major die-off are more likely to be found and reported than birds dying from other causes but dispersed over a wide geographic area.

The role of disease and contaminants is part of a complex web involving many other variables. In addition to causing direct mortality, diseases and contaminants may enhance the risk to waterfowl of other mortality factors, including hunting, predation, and weather stress. They can also diminish the reproductive performance of individual birds (White and Stickel 1975).

In turn, the function that disease and contaminants play is mitigated by numerous other variables, such as population size (e.g., Brand 1984), habitat quality, food availability, weather, and human activities and disturbances. It will be no easy task to account for the many ramifications of disease and contaminants in a population model.

Nonetheless, it is time to begin to understand the mechanisms by which these mortality factors operate and how they relate to external variables. One can model a disease or contaminant in any of several plausible ways, but each method will yield different results under analysis. Consider lead poisoning in mallards: we might model that mortality force as killing 300,000 mallards each winter. Alternatively, we could incorporate a 3% loss of the fall and winter population. Another approach might be to determine the lead mortality rate as a function of the number of lead shotgun shells sold during a particular year. A fourth method would be to base the lead mortality rate on a moving average of the number of lead shotgun shells discharged in key hunting areas (those most susceptible to lead poisoning).

Each of these approaches could yield "reasonable" values for output variables under current conditions; specifically, the number of mallards succumbing to lead poisoning might appear realistic. But they would give very different predictions about what to expect if certain changes occur. The first model, with a constant number of deaths, would show the lead mortality rate declining if the population increased; we would therefore conclude that the phenomenon was inversely density-dependent. The second model would not point to that conclusion, but it would miss completely the effect of a nationwide ban on lead shot for waterfowl hunting. The third model is more refined, but it still would not respond properly to a selective ban of lead shot in certain hunting areas. The final model would reflect that change but could be deceptive if feeding habits of susceptible mallards change, for example, from corn (which exacerbates lead mortality) to invertebrates (which do not).

Although each model might appear reasonable under present circumstances, its performance as a predictive or inferential tool would vary greatly. Improvements in the model come with an increase in the biological content: more knowledge permits better models.

Winter Habitat and Breeding Performance

An intriguing connection between wintering grounds and breeding grounds was suggested by Heitmeyer and Fredrickson (1981), who found a correlation between precipitation in the primary wintering area of the Mississippi Flyway and the subsequent age ratio of mallards harvested in the flyway. They concluded that precipitation improved wintering-ground wetlands, thereby enabling mallards to gain the nutrient reserves necessary for the first nesting attempt once they returned north.

The hypothesis is eminently reasonable. There are, nonetheless, some deficiencies in the analysis, several of which Heitmeyer and Fredrickson (1981) pointed out themselves. Primary among these is that age ratios of harvested birds may provide poor estimates of recruitment, especially for particular areas such as a flyway. Another consideration is that mallards can, and do, feed heavily and gain weight during spring migration, so that habitat conditions along the migration corridor also should be taken into consideration.

R. M. Kaminski (pers. commun.) examined the effect of wintering-ground conditions on productivity in two long-term studies, those of W. E. Leitch in south-central Saskatchewan grasslands and of J. H. Stoudt in southeastern Saskatchewan parklands. Kaminski looked for relations between brood/pair ratios and May and August pond counts and temperature and precipitation during the previous winter in the southern Mississippi Valley, the principal wintering area for these birds. Stoudt's data showed no significant effects, and in Leitch's data only the number of August ponds correlated significantly with the brood/pair ratio. The value of the brood/pair ratio as a measure of productivity in mallards is questionable, but the inconsistency between Kaminski's results and those of Heitmeyer and Fredrickson should nonetheless be explored.

The concept of the effect of wintering grounds on subsequent reproduction, as well as survival (J. D. Nichols, unpubl. data), of mallards is important as well as intriguing. Analyses such as that of Heitmeyer and Fredrickson should be replicated, preferably with productivity measures more accurate and area-specific than the age ratio in the harvest. The process of conditioning for reproduction will be better understood as studies on that subject are completed. The mechanism will be important in modeling the mallard's life cycle and integrating diverse geographic and temporal events. The current model of mallard productivity (Johnson et al. 1986) accounts for initial physical condition of hens by assigning each one a weight upon arrival on the breeding grounds. That weight is now generated randomly, but by firming the relationship between spring weight and habitat conditions on wintering and migrational areas, we will be able to incorporate those conditions in the model.

Heterogeneity

One consideration in population dynamics that has not received the attention it deserves is heterogeneity among individuals within a population. The fact that individuals and subpopulations may differ in life history parameters is well known. The consequences of this heterogeneity to population dynamics are not well known, but they can be investigated with population modeling.

Table 2.1. Percent composition, annual survival rates, and recruitment rates for a hypothetical population consisting of two subpopulations

Subpopulation	Composition (%)	Survival rate (%)	Recruitment rate
A	95	40	1.20
B	5	80	4.00
Average		42	1.34

Suppose a population of birds comprises two subpopulations (table 2.1). The majority one (95% of the total) survives the year at a 40% rate; at the end of the year, the survivors produce an average of 1.2 young each. A minority subpopulation (5% of the total) survives at a rate of 80% and each survivor produces 4 young, on the average. If we combine these population parameters (table 2.2), we find that for 1,000 birds at the beginning of a year, 950 will be in the first group of which 380 will survive to produce 456 young, for a total of 836. Of the 50 birds in the second group, 40 will survive and bear 160 young, for a total of 200. The survivors and young of both groups total 1,036, which represents a 3.6% increase; i.e., the population is growing.

Table 2.2. Calculated annual change in population based on subpopulations (upper)
and average rates (lower) of survival and recruitment

	Number of birds			
Basis of calculation	At start of year	Survive till end of year	Young	Total
Subpopulation				
A	950	380	456	836
B	50	40	160	200
Total	1,000	420	616	1,036
Average population	1,000	420	563	983

Suppose now that we do not or cannot recognize the two subpopulations and deal instead with a population of "average" individuals (table 2.1). The average survival rate is 0.95(0.40) + 0.05(0.80) = 0.42. The average reproductive rate is 0.95(1.20) + 0.05(4) = 1.34. Notice that these values are not very different from those of the majority subpopulation and likely would not be noticed in a typical analysis, even if differences were suspected. If we start with 1,000 of these "average" birds, 420 would survive and produce 563 young (table 2.2). The total is only 983, a 1.7% decline. Thus, the population, which actually is growing, appears to be decreasing. We draw erroneous conclusions from the analysis based on averages.

This phenomenon is an example of the statistical property that if X and Y are two random variables, say survival and reproduction, then the average of XY need not equal the average of X times the average of Y, if X and Y are not independent. Such heterogeneity has important consequences for population modeling, including the use of population models to assess the consistency of various parameter estimates.

Table 2.3. Percent composition and survival rates from hunting and natural mortality causes
during two years in hypothetical population

Subpopulation	Composition (%)	Year 1 survival rate (%)			Year 2 survival rate (%)		
		Hunting	Natural	Total	Hunting	Natural	Total
A	50	90	80	72	80	80	64
B	50	80	60	48	60	60	36
Total	100	85	70	60	70	70	50

Heterogeneity also can lend the appearance of compensation between hunting and natural mortality. Consider, for example, two subpopulations in equal numbers (table 2.3). In year 1, birds in group A survive natural mortality at a rate of 0.8 and hunting mortality at a rate of 0.9. Without compensation, annual survival is 0.72 (0.8 × 0.9). Birds in the second group have corresponding survival rates of 0.6 and 0.8, for an annual rate of 0.48. The annual survival rate for the combined population is 0.6. If rates of hunting survival and annual survival were known precisely, survival from natural mortality would be determined as annual survival rate divided by survival from hunting: 0.60/0.85 = 0.706. Suppose now that hunting mortality rates are doubled for each subpopulation (year 2); hunting survival rates then drop to 0.8 and 0.6, and annual survival rates to 0.64 and 0.36. The average annual survival rate is 0.5. Survival from natural mortality is now determined as 0.50/0.70 = 0.714. Thus, the natural mortality rate appears to decline from 0.294 (= 1 − 0.706) to 0.286 as the hunting mortality rate goes up. The two mortality forces appear partly compensatory, but only because of heterogeneity.

Several sources could contribute to heterogeneity. Age is one. Yearling mallards are known to survive at a lower rate than older ones, and they are also less effective reproductively (Krapu and Doty 1979). For these reasons, it is important to distinguish at least two age classes in a mallard population model. Condition is another feature to consider. Waterfowl in better physical condition are more successful than those in poorer condition with respect to both survival (Haramis et al. 1986; Hepp et al. 1986) and reproductive performance (Krapu 1979, 1981). An additional factor involves philopatry, especially the homing of successful breeders, which may cause local concentrations of highly productive birds. And not to be forgotten is the basis of evolution by natural selection: the genetic variation that exists in any population of animals. Genetic variability may underlie the other kinds of heterogeneity, as well as contribute other, unrecognized, variation.

Implications of such heterogeneity to population dynamics and models are indeed profound. At this time, we can offer little but suggestions. One is to continue recent efforts to investigate differences in life history parameters among individuals and subpopulations. The second recommendation is to recognize limitations in models imposed by unrecognized heterogeneity. We can also use models to investigate the consequences to population dynamics of such heterogeneity.

Conclusion

Five years ago, Weller (1982) summarized a workshop on the ecology of wintering waterfowl by noting that studies on that topic were individually excellent but that there was little coordination, relationship, or even communication among researchers. Results had not yet revealed the comprehensive patterns or processes needed for both science and management. From that workshop arose the recommendations that researchers (1) conduct long-term efforts, (2) collaborate in cross-disciplinary teams, (3) develop quantitative designs and analyses, (4) employ hypothesis-testing approaches, and (5) construct models for integrating data and guiding future research. These remain appropriate recommendations in which we concur.

LITERATURE CITED

Anderson, D. R., and K. P. Burnham. 1976. Population ecology of the mallard: VI. The effect of exploitation on survival. U.S. Fish Wildl. Serv. Resour. Publ. 128. 66pp.

Bellrose, F. C. 1959. Lead poisoning as a mortality factor in waterfowl populations. Ill. Nat. Hist. Surv. Bull. 27:235–288.

Brand, C. J. 1984. Avian cholera in the Central and Mississippi flyways during 1979-80. J. Wildl. Manage. 48:399–406.

Burnham, K. P., and D. R. Anderson. 1984. Tests of compensatory vs. additive hypotheses of mortality in mallards. Ecol. 65:105-112.

———, G. C. White, and D. R. Anders on. 1984. Estimating the effect of hunting on annual survival rates of adult mallards. J. Wildl. Manage. 48:350-361.

Cowardin, L. M., D. H. Johnson, A. M. Frank, and A. T. Klett. 1983. Simulating results of management actions on mallard production. Trans. N. Am. Wildl. Nat. Resour. Conf. 48:257-272.

Friend, M. 1981. Waterfowl management and waterfowl disease: independent or cause and effect relationships? Trans. N. Am. Wildl. Nat. Resour. Conf. 46:94–103.

Haramis. G. M., J. D. Nichols, K. H. Pollock, and J. E. Hines. 1986. The relationship between body mass and survival of wintering canvasbacks. Auk 103:506–574.

Hayes, F. A., and W. R. Davidson. 1978. Waterfowl diseases: status, contributing factors, and control. Int. Waterfowl Symp. 3:45–58.

Heitmeyer, M. E., and L. H. Fredrickson. 1981. Do wetland conditions in the Mississippi Delta hardwoods influence mallard recruitment? Trans. N. Am. Wildl. Nat. Resour. Conf. 46:44–57.

Hepp, G. R., R. J. Blohm, R. E. Reynolds, J. E. Hines, and J. D. Nichols. 1986. Physiological condition of autumn-banded mallards and its relationship to hunting vulnerability. J. Wildl. Manage. 50:177–183.

Hochbaum, G. S., and C. J. Walters. 1984. Components of hunting mortality in ducks. Can. Wildl. Serv. Occas. Pap. 52. 29pp.

Johnson, D. H., L. M. Cowardin, and D. W. Sparling. 1986. Evaluation of a mallard productivity model. Pages 23-29 in J. Verner, M. L. Morrison, and C. J. Ralph, eds. Modeling habitat relationships of terrestrial vertebrates. Univ. Wisconsin Press, Madison.

Krapu, G. L. 1979. Nutrition of female dabbling ducks during reproduction. Pages 59-70 in T. A. Bookhout, ed. Waterfowl and wetlands—an integrated review. Proc. 1977 Symp., Northcent. Sect., Wildl. Soc. Madison, Wis. 152pp.

———. 1981. The role of nutrient reserves in mallard reproduction. Auk 98:29–38.

———, and H. A. Doty. 1979. Age-related aspects of mallard reproduction. Wildfowl 30:35–39.

Nichols, J. D., M. J. Conroy, D. R. Anderson, and K. P. Burnham. 1984. Compensatory mortality in waterfowl populations: a review of the evidence and implications for research and management. Trans. N. Am. Wildl. Nat. Resour. Conf. 49:535-554.

———, and J. E. Hines. 1983. The relationship between harvest and survival rates of mallards: a straightforward approach with partitioned data sets. J. Wildl. Manage. 47:334–348.

Rogers, J. P., J. D. Nichols, F. W. Martin, C. F. Kimball, and R. S. Pospahala. 1979. An examination of harvest and survival rates of ducks in relation to hunting. Trans. N. Am. Wildl. Nat. Resour. Conf. 44:114–126.

Stout, I. J., and G. W. Cornwell. 1976. Non-hunting mortality of fledged North American waterfowl. J. Wildl. Manage. 40:681–698.

Trauger, D. L., and J. H. Stoudt. 1978. Trends in waterfowl populations and habitats on study areas in Canadian parklands. Trans. N. Am. Wildl. Nat. Resour. Conf. 43:187–205.

Weller, M. W. 1982. Summary. Pages 42-44 *in* Workshop on the ecology of wintering waterfowl. Delta Waterfowl Research Station. 51pp.

White, D. H., and L. F. Stickel. 1975. Impacts of chemicals on waterfowl reproduction and survival. Int. Waterfowl Symp. 1:132–142.

II.
Reproductive and Social Behavior

3

Pair Bond Duration and Timing of Its Formation in Barnacle Geese (*Branta leucopsis*)

Myrfyn Owen, Jeffrey M. Black, and Halyna Liber

Abstract: The duration and timing of the pair bond was studied in a population of barnacle geese *Branta leucopsis* wintering in northern Britain and breeding in Spitsbergen. Between 18 and 25% of the birds (ca. 2,000 geese) were individually marked, and the annual resighting rate was around 95%. Most pairs stayed together for life during this study, but 35 pairs separated while both partners remained alive ("divorce"). The annual divorce rate was 1.7%, but most separations probably were the result of birds that lost their partners on migration and rapidly re-paired. Birds involved in such separations had average breeding success with their old partners and reduced breeding success in the first year with their new mate. The penalty of re-pairing after separation or mate loss represented a loss of about 14% of the average lifetime production for a pair. This provides powerful adaptive reasons for lifelong monogamy in barnacle geese. It is argued that these results apply to all species of geese and swans. Pair formation occurred throughout the year, but young geese paired mostly in spring and summer. Although pairing did not occur until the second or third year of life, over 50% of young geese paired up with others molting in the same area in their second summer, against an expectation of only 20%. Thus, associations formed among yearlings were re-formed into pairs in later life. The strategy of pairing predominantly with birds from the same breeding segment had the advantage of concentrating genetic traits advantageous to exploiting the natal area.

It is widely assumed that geese pair for life, although there is very little information on pair stability from wild populations of migratory species. There is

Waterfowl in Winter.© 1988 University of Minnesota. Edited by Milton W. Weller and published by the University of Minnesota Press, Minneapolis.

ample evidence from captive or semicaptive situations to suggest that separation of partners while both are still alive (i.e., "divorce") is extremely rare in all species; lifelong monogamy is the accepted norm among geese and swans (Johnsgard 1965, Kear 1970). It is generally assumed that long-term monogamy confers selective advantages in breeding. The presence of an advantage has rarely been demonstrated, and the mechanism by which it might operate is unknown. Indeed, in lesser snow geese (*Anser caerulescens*), Cooke et al. (1981) found no difference in clutch size or the number of goslings leaving the nest between females that returned to the breeding area with the same or with different mates. There was no difference in the number of young surviving to fledging, though the sample available was small. Scott (in press) has shown that those tundra swans (*Cygnus columbianus bewickii*) that retained the same mate for a period of 10 years brought more young to the wintering grounds than those that had changed mates. A trend of lower output with an increasing number of mate changes was demonstrated for both sexes but was significant only for females (sample sizes were rather small).

Pair formation is here defined as the start of a long-term association of two partners of different sexes. In geese this generally is regarded as taking place on the wintering grounds, though there is little information from staging or breeding areas. Wintering ground pairing is the rule for Canada geese, according to Raveling (1969), but he quotes G. K. Brakhage who had evidence that yearling pairs seen in summer later separated but often re-paired again in the late winter and spring just before they were two years old. In snow geese, Cooke and Sulzbach (1978) argued that pairing took place outside the breeding area, and their data on return rates of the two sexes to a small breeding colony were generally consistent with that assumption. Pairing during the nonbreeding season likely would result in the intermixing of individuals from various breeding areas and prevent the genetic isolation of breeding subunits. However, the phenotypic distinction and isolated breeding distribution of the Tule race of the white-fronted goose (*Anser albifrons gambelli*) and many subunits or "races" of the Canada goose in North America suggest either that (1) the amount of pairing during the breeding season has been underestimated; or that (2) hitherto undescribed subtle differences in behavior effectively limit intermixing during winter when these units are sympatric with much larger numbers of conspecifics of diverse origins. This paper presents evidence on the timing of pair formation and the stability of the bond in the barnacle goose, a species restricted to Eurasia but very closely related to the Canada goose.

We are grateful to the many people who have helped in collecting the information and in ringing expeditions. The following have made major contributions: S. Berrow, R. Bridson, M. J. Brown, C. R. G. Campbell, S. Carter, C. Clunies-Ross, N. Davies, A. Dekker, R. H. Drent, B. Ebbinge, M. van Eerden, S. Ellis, R. Goater, M. J. Holloway, E. E. Jackson, J. Kirk, C. Miller, S. Montgomery, M. J.

Nugent, M. A. Ogilvie, M. Ounsted, A. Parkinson, C. Prentice, J. Prop, P. Reynolds, B. Sears, P. Vaux, P. Webb, R. L. Wells, R. White-Robinson, G. Williams, and B. Woijtowch. The Wildfowl Trust provided core support and the observation facilities at the Caerlaverock refuge on which most of the geese winter. The Trust's director, Sir Peter Scott, and director of research, Prof. G. V. T. Matthews, have been a constant source of advice and support. We would like to record our thanks to D. G. Raveling and M. R. McLandress for constructive criticisms on the manuscript.

Major financial contributions are acknowledged from Macmillan (London) Ltd., the North Atlantic Treaty Organization, The Natural Environment Research Council, the Royal Society, and Shell (UK) Ltd. Many other individuals and organizations have given assistance financially or in a practical way.

Study Area and Methods

Data have been collected between 1973 and 1983 from individually marked birds in a small population breeding in the Svalbard (Spitsbergen) archipelago and wintering in a small area (only 50-60 km in extent) of the Solway Firth in northern Britain. The population is discrete; there is a negligible amount of intermixing with the other two barnacle goose populations that winter in Europe. Geese from the three populations appear identical in plumage, and no significant differences have been demonstrated in body measurements despite the availability of large samples (Owen 1980 and unpubl. data). Total numbers in the study population during the 10-year period under consideration have ranged from 5,200 in 1973 to 9,050 in 1980.

Individual marking began in 1973 by fitting birds with engraved plastic leg bands (Ogilvie 1972); those fitted to barnacle geese are readable at 250 m in good conditions with the aid of a telescope. More than 3,000 geese have been ringed and, between 1977 and 1983, 18-25% of the population was individually marked at any one time. Geese were rounded up in two separate breeding areas as well as on the wintering grounds, when birds from the whole breeding range are potentially available. Resighting rate is high, averaging around 95% annually of birds alive and ringed. Plastic leg band loss is small, at least over the first five years, when the annual loss rate was calculated to be 0.14% per annum (Owen 1982).

Each marked bird is resighted between five and eight times each season. The number of resightings varies each year depending on the observational effort and accessibility of birds for viewing. More than 80,000 sightings of marked geese were recorded over the 10-year study period. The population is protected from hunting throughout the year and mortality is low, averaging 11.5% for adults and 16.8% for juveniles (Owen 1982). The high survival and sighting rate, together with the fact that all individuals are accessible for observation in winter, make this an ideal situation to study pair behavior of wild migratory geese.

Most of the observations have been made on the wintering area (late September to early May), but visits have also been made to spring staging areas in Helgeland, Norway, (mid May) each year since 1975; to the breeding grounds (late May-mid September) in four years; and to an autumn staging area on Bear Island (Svalbard) in late September/early October in three years. Thus, data on pairing are available from all times during the annual cycle.

At each sighting, observers attempted to ascertain the pair and family status of each goose. Birds usually were under observation for periods of one to five minutes. If no associations (birds remaining in close proximity, synchronizing behavior or performing pair-formation or maintenance displays [Black and Owen 1987]) were obvious during that time, no record of status was made or the bird was recorded as unpaired. Because of the large number of ringed birds available, observers rarely remembered the status of individual geese. Each observation can, therefore, be regarded as independent.

Ring sightings, including information on location, flock size, position in flock, mate and family members, and other associates (birds in same small flock or part of flock) are routinely entered on computer, sorted alphabetically, and merged so that each individual's records are consecutive. Because of the difficulty in many circumstances of gathering rigid data on pair and family associations, records were analyzed manually and a separate computer file of pair data was compiled. This contained information on each bird's mates, dates at which they were last unpaired, first and last observation with a mate, first seen unpaired if a mate was separated or lost, and status at the end of the 1982-83 season. Data from 1983-84 were used to establish the latest status if necessary. The number of days paired was computed for each pairing on the file.

The mean duration of pair bonds was calculated by adding the numbers of days all pairs had remained together and dividing by the number of known divorces, whether or not these involved the same or different individuals. This gave an expectation of stability expressed in years or as an annual divorce rate. The timing of pair formation was analyzed only for birds that were seen as unpaired and paired individuals within six months of each other. The pairing date was taken as the midpoint of the two dates. Records were amalgamated by half-months or longer periods.

Determination of breeding success in each year was based on family observations on the wintering grounds in autumn. The criterion of breeding success was, therefore, the production of surviving young at least to arrival on the Solway study area in late September/early October when juveniles average three months of age. Subsequent survival was high, about 85% reaching 15 months, 76% surviving 27 months or past the age at which they are physiologically capable of breeding. Nearly all breed at two years of age in captivity (Owen 1980 and unpubl. data).

Statistical comparisons were made using the chi-square test, unless otherwise stated.

Results and Discussion

Duration of the Pair Bond

Pair duration data for all ringed birds irrespective of ages and origins are given in table 3.1. Where pairs consisted of two marked individuals, data for both partners are analyzed and each bird treated as one-half of a pair. Pairings with unmarked birds are only used in a limited number of analyses where the status or fate of the pair is certain despite the mate being unmarked. For example, the re-pairing of a

Table 3.1. Status and fate of Barnacle goose pairs and analysis of pair bond duration.[a]

Status	No. of pairs (birds)	Pair years (bird years)	Years/pair (bird)
(a) Never paired while ringed (birds)	355		
(b) Mate unringed	1,056	1,992.0	1.89
(c) Alive and paired in 1982-83	454	1,238.9	2.73
(d) Both dead, last seen together	28	51.4	1.84
(e) Pair split by death	407	1,130.2	2.78
(f) Pair split by "divorce"	35	62.0	1.77
(g) Frequent mate changes (birds)	10	17.1	1.71
(h) Status uncertain (birds)	51	39.9	0.78
Total pairs (a+b+c+d+e+f)	1,980	4,474.5	2.26

Summary of stability data

Pair bond complete to present or death (c+d+e)		889 pairs	2,420.5 years
Pair bond split, both members survive (f)		35 pairs	62.0 years
Percentage of pairs split	3.79	[pairs (f)/pairs (c+d+e+f)]	
Years stable per split	60.72	[years (c+d+e+f)/pairs (f)]	
Annual divorce rate (%)	1.65	[pairs (f)/years (c+d+e+f+)∗100]	
Mean length of live bonds (years)[b]	2.73	[years (c)/pairs (c)]	
Mean length of bonds at death	1.90	[years (d+e)/pairs (d∗e)]	
Mean time to divorce	1.77	[years (f)/pairs (f)]	

[a] Where both pair members are ringed, each is counted as half a pair.

[b] The longest recorded pair bond lasted 3,455 days (9.46 years).

bird having originally an unringed partner with a new marked mate can be used in the analysis of mate changes, but whether the change is due to separation or to the death of the unringed bird is unknown since the fate of an unringed goose cannot be determined. A change from one unringed bird to another was included if the marked bird went through an unpaired period between mates. Mates that lost their rings were recognizable by the presence of a metal band on the other leg. Changes from ringed to metal-only were excluded unless the mate was known to be alive.

The majority of birds that were never paired while ringed died before they reached pairing age. The longest recorded bond was nearly nine and a half years, the whole of the study period; in fact, eight pairs were marked together in 1973 and survived as pairs until 1982-83. These birds were ringed as adults, so this is minimal pair bond duration.

The annual divorce rate is 1.7%—i.e., for every hundred pairs, 1.7 would be expected to split each year, although both partners remained alive.

Ten individuals were not consistent in their pair status: five alternated between two mates and the other five were seen periodically in association with a number of birds. Some of these may have involved sibling or parent-offspring associations, but this is unlikely since such associations of marked birds have not been recorded beyond the second year of offspring life in barnacle geese. Eight of the ten were females. There is a surplus of males in the population (Owen et al. 1978). and these probably are able to separate paired females from their mates temporarily, as recorded in studies of semi-captive barnacle geese (unpubl. data).

The Nature of Divorce

If both partners are ringed, the fate of both is known and a divorce is recorded only if both remain alive but separated (usually re-paired with other individuals). In view of the assumption of lifelong monogamy, a surprisingly large number of divorces was recorded during this study—nearly 4% of all pairs involved. The fact that the mean time from first observation to divorce was similar to that until death (table 3.1) indicates that such splits were not restricted to bonds that were of short duration. In fact, 16 of the splits were among pairs that had been together for at least two years, seven more than three years, and three more than four years. Divorce was not a characteristic of particular birds: the 35 splits involved 68 different individuals (only two were involved in two splits).

There was no significant difference in the divorce rate between geese caught at the two breeding areas or between that of either breeding area and the rate in birds caught on the wintering grounds.

The term *divorce* implies a separation while the birds are still in proximity. In migratory geese that make long journeys, however, it is possible that partners might be separated during these flights. Of the 32 splits for which good data existed around the time of the divorce, 23 were consistent with pairs separating on migration to the breeding grounds. Most of these were seen in spring with their original mate and returned in autumn with a new one. In one case, a bird was seen unpaired and then paired to a new mate in a spring staging area in the absence of its mate. In two further cases where both partners returned with new mates, one of the pair was seen molting apart from its original mate.

Two splits occurred either side of an autumn migration, and the remaining seven cases occurred during the winter season (October-April). Thus, about 80% of the divorces seem likely to have occurred through accidental separation on migration and rapid re-pairing of one or both partners. There is a possibility that some of the splits during winter were not deliberate since portions of the population spend some weeks in separate sites, especially late in the winter and in spring.

If divorce was a positive separation, one might expect pairs that were unsuccessful breeders to split more often than successful ones, as is the case, for example in kittiwake gulls (*Rissa tridactyla*) (Coulson and Thomas 1983). We examined the previous history of divorced birds with their original mates and found them to have brought young to the wintering grounds in 16 out of a possible 78 pair years (20.5%). The success rate of birds (all those in pairs) in the population at large was 21.33% (11,214 bird years), not significantly different from that of divorced birds. Indeed, 8 of 33 pairs (24%) for which good data on breeding success were available reared young in the season in which the divorce subsequently took place. These findings are consistent with the suggestion that most of the divorces documented during this study were accidental rather than deliberate separations.

The Consequence of Mate Change

If lifelong monogamy has an advantage in geese, birds should incur some penalty when they change their mates, for whatever reason. Geese involved in divorce were less successful in breeding in the year after they parted from their original mates ($P < 0.05$), though in the second year there was no significant difference

Table 3.2. Breeding success of "divorced" birds in previous years with old mates and in first and second years with new mates and success rate of those that changed mates and those that stayed together

Breeding success	Old mate	New mate	
		Year 1	Year 2
	Divorced birds		
Successful	32	5	8
Paired and failed	124	52	41
Unpaired	. . .	8	0
Successful (of those paired) (%)	20.5	7.7 (8.9)	16.3 (16.3)
	All changes		
Successful	2,392	30	87
Paired and failed	8,822	307	319
Unpaired	. . .	20	4
Successful (of those paired) (%)	21.3	8.4 (8.9)	21.2 (21.4)

(table 3.2). The frequency distribution of the last dates when birds involved in divorce that bred successfully were seen with their original mates is compared with the last-paired dates of all birds involved in change in figure 3.1. The distributions are significantly different, with (as might be expected) a much higher proportion of the successful split pairs being broken early in the season (60% in October and November). Birds involved in all mate changes had a much lower chance of breeding successfully then did those that retained the same mate (chi-square 30.5, df = 1, $P < 0.001$).

How important is the loss of breeding potential to a bird's breeding success? The average length of pair bonds in this study (total pair years/number of deaths and divorces) was 4.52 years. The potential lost (61% in year 1) by changing a mate thus represents 13.5% of the breeding potential of a pair—a powerful selection pressure against divorce in arctic geese.

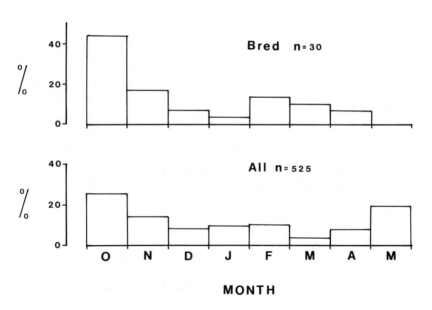

Fig. 3.1. Dates when birds that subsequently lost their mates were last seen with those mates. Upper histogram: birds that brought young to the wintering grounds the following year with their new mates; lower: all mate changes. Difference between distributions is significant (chi-square $P < 0.05$).

The Timing of Pair Bond Formation

The pattern of formation of the first and subsequent bonds was compared (fig. 3.2). Because up to six months elapsed between sightings, only an approximate estimate of pairing times was possible. About 60% of pairs are formed in winter and spring, but this may be an understatement. Because of the shortage of summer

PAIRING TIMES

First Mates   n = 225

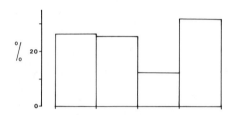

Subsequent Mates   n = 453

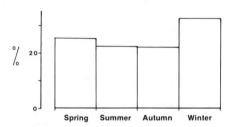

Spring Summer Autumn Winter

Fig. 3.2. Season at which barnacle geese form pair bonds. Upper histogram: first mates; lower: re-pairings.

sightings, some pairs formed in March and April may be excluded (see Black and Owen 1987). The two distributions are significantly different ($P < 0.05$), with very few initial bonds being formed in the autumn. Most mortality occurs in late summer and autumn, so it is not surprising that the peak of re-pairing occurs in winter and spring. A surprisingly high proportion (26%) of new pairs come together in the summer; sexual behavior and even copulation have been observed in molting flocks in Spitsbergen.

The Time Taken to Re-Pair

There was no difference in time to re-pair between males and females, so they are treated together here. The frequency distribution of re-pairing time (fig. 3.3) was estimated by two methods. The minimum estimate is given by the time from breakup to the last time the bird was seen without its new mate, and the maximum is the time between breakup and the first observation with its new mate. Periods over 18 months are omitted because most resulted from sparsity of data in the intervening period. A few birds may have taken longer to re-pair, but we believed it safter to omit these altogether to avoid a misleading impression.

TIME TO RE-PAIR

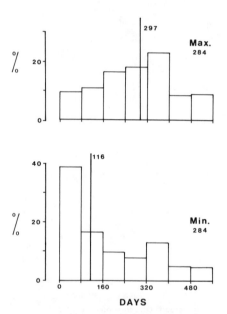

Fig. 3.3. Time taken for barnacle geese to re-pair after death of mate or "divorce." Maximum time is that between observations with the two mates; minimum is that between last observation with original mate and last time bird was later seen alone. Because of irregularity of records, times longer than 560 days (ca. 18 months) were excluded.

Re-pairing can be very rapid. Even when the maximum estimate was used, 13 geese (3%) had re-paired within 20 days, and rapid re-pairing was recorded in all seasons. Clearly there is great variation, and the median dates derived by the two methods differ widely. It seems likely that re-pairing takes place in most geese between three and nine months after the death of their partner or after separation. Information from other species is sparse; Abraham et al. (1981) describe a very rapid re-pairing of a single lesser snow goose. On the other hand, as in this study, some birds remain unpaired for more than 12 months following loss in the same species (Prevett and MacInnes 1980).

The Origins of Mates

Associations between groupings of Canada geese on the breeding and wintering grounds have been reported (Raveling 1969). We have been recording associations in units greater than families (flocks or parts of flocks) in our wintering population, and there is no obvious link between birds originating from the same breeding area and winter associations. On migration there is great loyalty of individuals to the particular part of the staging area, but the groupings found here bear no relation to breeding groups (Gullestad et al. 1984). Thus, outside the breeding area itself where the whole population is mixed, an individual has approximately equal chance of pairing or re-pairing with each other unpaired individual.

In 1977, 380 yearlings (hatched in 1976) were caught and marked on a 50 km stretch of breeding habitat that is separated from other breeding places by wide fjords (Owen et al. 1978). They represented 22% of the 1,720 yearlings estimated to be present in the population at the time (Owen 1984). The proportion of the population summering in the area was about 20% (nearly all were marked), so whether those yearlings paired with other yearlings or with older geese, they had about a 1 in 5 probability of doing so with birds from the same molting grounds. Since there is no molt migration in barnacle geese (Owen 1980), these geese probably originate from the same breeding segment.

The origins of the mates of those birds are given in table 3.3. Molting flocks are scattered along the coast, and the likelihood of pairing with birds from the same molting flock (maximum 350 geese), as opposed to the same area, also was examined. There was a significant association between eventual mates both

Table 3.3. Proportion of 1976 cohort ($N = 380$ ringed) that eventually paired with individuals from same and different breeding areas[a]

Population	Same segment	Different segment	Percentage the same	Expected percentage	P
			Origin of mate		
Males	60	65	48	22	<0.001
Females	88	63	58	22	<0.001
Catch 1: All	58	53	52	29	<0.001
Catch 2: All	33	32	51	36	<0.001

	Autumn 1977		Spring 1978		Autumn 1978		Later	
				Pairing date				
Origin of mate	No.	%	No.	%	No.	%	No.	%
Same segment	18	12.2	37	25.0	45	30.4	48	32.4
Different	4	3.1	16	12.5	38	29.7	70	54.7

[a]The chance of pairing within the same segment if pairing were random was 1 in 5 (see text).

within the general area and within the flock, even though most of the birds (73%) did not form pairs until a year later. The pairs of which both partners originated from the same breeding area were formed, on average, earlier ($P < 0.001$); 37% were formed before the spring migration compared with only 16% of pairs made up of geese of different origin. Thus, although most pairs are formed outside the breeding area, associations formed within it are clearly important in determining the origin of mates.

The Significance of Lifelong Monogamy

Although we have demonstrated a much higher rate of separation among geese than hitherto recorded, most of these divorces appear to arise incidentally, often involving separation on migration. We have produced several lines of evidence in support of this. In particular, the pairs that were involved had average breeding success with their original mates and their success was reduced after the split. Thus, although splits occur, they are disadvantageous.

Evidence from the wild is almost restricted to lesser snow geese. Prevett's (1973) detailed observations produced no evidence of divorce, although he knew for certain in very few cases that separation had been caused by death rather than divorce and movement to another wintering and breeding area. Cooke and Sulzbach (1978) assumed a very low divorce rate in snow geese, which enabled them to assess mortality by pair bond breakage. However, in both studies the rate was inevitably underestimated since the fate of only one partner was known. Cooke et al. (1981) did, however, note that five females at the La Perouse Bay colony had separated from their mates while both were still alive, but they did not indicate sample size. Studies on semicaptive barnacle geese have revealed no incidence of divorce in many hundreds of pair-years of observation (unpubl. data). Preliminary analyses from the wild involving 133 pairs for an average of 2.2 years (291 pair-years) yielded only a single divorce, an annual divorce rate of 0.34% (Owen 1980). There is little information from other species, but a single incidence of divorce in Canada geese has been well documented (Zicus 1984); separation in the same species had previously been reported with little comment (MacInnes et al. 1974). A rate as high as the 1.7% annually from this study would, however, have little impact on the survival estimates calculated for snow geese by Cooke and Sulzbach (1978).

How typical is the rate likely to be of geese in general? Assuming that accidental separation is responsible for most divorce, then the main factors affecting the rate of separation would be as follows: (a) size of the population, assuming that the larger the population, the more difficult it would be for partners to find each other after separation; (b) length and duration of migration, since longer journeys give greater opportunity for accidental separation; (c) size of the breeding and winter-ing range, since geese are more likely to relocate each other on small areas after losing touch on migration; and (d) amount of movement and disturbance in the nonbreeding season.

Except for (b) above, the barnacle goose population discussed here is exceptional. It is a tiny population with a very small breeding range, narrow migration corridors (Owen and Gullestad 1984), and circumscribed wintering area. It is also protected throughout its range and winters largely on effective refuges so that disruption of flocks by hunting and disturbance is minimal. It is not unique in its migration distance; of the 26 taxa considered by Owen (1980), 15 migrated longer and 10 shorter distances than the barnacle goose. Assuming that monogamy is the pattern in all geese, it seems likely that accidental separation leading to re-pairing would be lower in this species; therefore, the assumption of negligible divorce rate in other studies may be unwarranted in the absence of substantial positive evidence.

Although there is considerable evidence for both swans and geese that being in a pair or family confers feeding advantages (Boyd 1953, Raveling 1970, Scott 1980, Black and Owen 1984), only in swans has this been linked with an improvement in breeding success (Scott 1980). Indeed, the most extensive evidence for geese found no loss of reproductive potential after re-pairing (Cooke et al. 1981). In our study, we demonstrated a considerable loss of potential, accounting for up to one-sixth of a pair's lifetime output. This is true of both mates involved in divorce, as well as the surviving member of a pair separated by death.

We believe that there are two reasons for the failure of studies on snow geese (Cooke et al. 1981) to demonstrate an effect: most mortality in that species is in the early autumn during the shooting season; and it was only possible to measure success accurately up to the immediate posthatching period.

We have also demonstrated (fig. 3.1) that the successful breeders among re-paired birds predominantly lost their mates soon after the previous breeding season. The high proportion of early losses in snow geese would therefore reduce the penalty for mate loss. In the natural state, before large-scale hunting by man became the main source of mortality, most deaths probably were in late winter because of severe weather and competition for food. The penalty for mate loss at this time is high and produces a powerful selective pressure for retaining the same mate. Our criterion of success—bringing young to the wintering grounds—is obviously closer to "real" success in contributing to the next generation than those available to Cooke et al. (1981), and many losses intervene between hatching and this stage. Cooke et al. (1981) did demonstrate important behavioral differences between established pairs and remates that indicate that their performance as pairs and parents might well differ. In particular, they suggested that long-term mates were more efficient at nest defense. There is evidence from controlled studies in captivity that the body condition and survival of goslings is related to the aggressiveness of their parents as assessed by intensity of nest defense (Black and Owen, in press). This also is likely to extend to the defense of the brood from predation and feeding competition. Cooke et al. (1981) had little data on survival to fledging but could detect no difference there. However, the role of the pair in obtaining feeding opportunities and securing optimum growth rate of the young is vital (e.g., Raveling 1969, Prop et al. 1984). Poorly developed young may succumb at a much later stage, such as on autumn migration (Owen and Gullestad 1984), or overwinter survival may be adversely affected.

Thus, we believe that the loss of reproductive potential after re-pairing provides the selective advantage for lifelong monogamy in barnacle geese. We further believe that such a relationship exists in all goose species and will be demonstrated when more detailed data are available for other taxa.

The Significance of Timing of Pair Formation

Pair formation in barnacle geese is not limited to any one time of year. We have observed preassociations in several cases of two individuals that eventually became a pair up to one year later. Although pair formation behavior is most frequently seen in the spring when long days and favorable feeding conditions allow birds some leeway in their tight energy budget (Black and Owen 1987), the importance of spring pairing has been overemphasized, particularly in relation to the intermixing of populations or breeding segments. Despite the fact that most pairs may not be formed on the breeding area, young geese have a high probability of pairing with birds originating from the same breeding segment. It may be that associations initially formed on the molting grounds in the second summer are re-formed at some other stage in the annual cycle (see also Black and Owen 1987). No molt migration has been described in barnacle geese. In our population, yearlings molt in the same area as breeding birds and probably return to their natal area to molt. In species such as Canada geese, which molt in areas distant from the breeding grounds, associations at breeding areas before the molt migration may be important.

Bateson (1983) discusses the costs and benefits of outbreeding and inbreeding and concludes that the optimal inbreeding strategy is to choose a near relative but not a sibling as a mate. This strategy combines the advantages of outbreeding (i.e., maintaining genetic diversity) with the advantage of pairing with a similar individual adapted to the same environment. He produced evidence on mate selection in Japanese quail (*Coturnix coturnix*) (Bateson 1980). Controlled experiments showed that quail selected birds of intermediate relatedness (cousins) both over more closely related birds (siblings) and unrelated individuals.

Our evidence from the origins of mates of first-time pairing barnacle geese indicates that such a mechanism also may be at work. Bateson's (1983) statement that "sexual preferences are finely tuned by their early experience with members of the opposite sex" would certainly give rise to the pattern of pair formation and mate origins we have described in geese; this strategy allows geese to concentrate beneficial genetic traits, which are especially important in capitalizing on environmental change or occupying a newly available niche in the unpredictable arctic environment.

Management Implications

This barnacle goose population is protected throughout its range, and mortality is only about 12% annually (Owen 1982). The impact of the depressing effect of pair bond breakage on breeding success is small both because of low incidence of breakage and because in most years only a small proportion of pairs is able to breed successfully. In some heavily hunted populations, however, breakage through death may occur in as many as 30-40% of pairs annually. The disturbance caused by hunting also may cause a higher incidence of separation without death, if such disturbance disrupts movements and migrations. In species where a large proportion of the breeding potential is commonly realized, the effect of a high rate of pair bond breakage could be considerable.

We have demonstrated that pairs that split in autumn and early winter have a greater chance of breeding that those that do so later; re-pairings in spring rarely yielded successful breeders in our study. Initial pair formation in young birds predominantly occurs in spring, and any factor that disrupts this process will lower the population's production of young. For these reasons and because of the disturbing effect of hunting on the potential for accumulating body reserves even in unbroken pairs, moves to extend the shooting season into late winter and spring should be resisted.

LITERATURE CITED

Abraham, K. F., P. Mineau, and F. Cooke. 1981. Re-mating of a lesser snow goose. Wilson Bull. 93:557–559.

Bateson, P. P. G. 1980. Optimal outbreeding and the development of sexual preferences in Japanese quail. Z. Tierpsychol. 53:231–244.

———. 1983. Optimal outbreeding. Pages 257-277 in P. P. G. Bateson, ed. Mate choice. Cambridge Univ. Press, Cambridge.

Black, J. M., and M. Owen. 1984. The importance of the family unit to barnacle goose offspring—a progress report. Nor. Polarinst. Skr. 181:79–85.

———, and ———. 1988. Variations in pair bond and agonistic behaviors in barnacle geese on the wintering grounds. Pages 39-57 in M. Weller, ed. Waterfowl in winter. Univ. Minnesota Press, Minneapolis,

———, and ———. Determinants of social ranking in goose flocks: Acquisition of social rank in young geese. Behav. In press.

Boyd, H. 1953. On encounters between wild white-fronted geese in winter flocks. Behav. 5:85–129.

———, and D. S. Sulzbach. 1978. Mortality, emigration and separation in mated snow geese. J. Wildl. Manage. 42:271–280.

Cooke, F., M. A. Bousfield, and A. Sadura. 1981. Mate change and reproductive success in the lesser snow goose. Condor 83:322–327.

Coulson, J. C., and C. S. Thomas. 1983. Mate choice in the kittiwake gull. Pages 361-376 *in* P. P. G. Bateson, ed. Mate choice. Cambridge Univ. Press, Cambridge.

Gullestad, N., M. Owen, and M. J. Nugent. 1984. Numbers and distribution of barnacle geese *Branta leucopsis* on Norwegian staging islands and the importance of the staging area to the Svalbard population. Nor. Polarinst. Skr. 181:57-65.

Johnsgard, P. A. 1965. Handbook of waterfowl behaviour. Cornell Univ. Press, Ithaca, N.Y. 378pp.

Kear, J. 1970. Adaptive radiation of parental care in waterfowl. Pages 357-372 *in* J. H. Crook, ed. Social behaviour in birds and mammals. Academic Press, London.

MacInnes, C. D., R. A. Davis, R. N. Jones, B. C. Lieff, and A. J. Pakulak. 1974. Reproductive efficiency of McConnell River small Canada geese. J. Wildl. Manage. 38:686-707.

Ogilvie, M. A. 1972. Large numbered leg-bands for individual identification of swans. J. Wildl. Manage. 36:1261-1265.

Owen, M. 1980. Wild geese of the world. Batsford, London, 236pp.

———. 1982. Population dynamics of Svalbard barnacle geese 1970-1980. Aquila 89:229-247.

———. 1984. Dynamics and age structure of an increasing goose population—the Svalbard barnacle goose. Nor. Polarinst. Skr. 181:37-47.

———, R. H. Drent, M. A. Ogilvie, and T. M. van Spanje. 1978. Numbers, distribution and catching of barnacle geese *Branta leucopsis* on the Nordenskioldkysten, Svalbard in 1977. Nor. Polarinst. Arbok 1977:247-258.

———, and N. Gullestad. 1984. Migration routes of Svalbard barnacle geese with a preliminary report on the importance of the Bjornoya staging area. Nor. Polarinst. Skr. 181:67-77.

Prevett, J. P. 1973. Family behaviour and age dependent breeding biology of the blue goose *Anser caerulescens*. Ph.D. Thesis, Univ. Western Ontario, London. 192pp.

———, and C. D. MacInnes. 1980. Family and other social groups in snow geese. Wildl. Monogr. 71. 46pp.

Prop, J., M. van Eerden, and R. H. Drent. 1984. Reproductive success in the barnacle goose *Branta leucopsis* in relation to food exploitation on the breeding grounds, West Spitsbergen. Nor. Polarinst. Skr. 181:87-117.

Raveling, D. G. 1969. Social classes of Canada geese in winter. J. Wildl. Manage. 33:304-318.

———. 1970. Dominance relationships and agonistic behaviour of Canada geese in winter. Behav. 37:291-319.

Scott, D. K. 1980. Functional aspects of the pair bond in winter in Bewick's swans (*Cygnus columbianus bewickii*). Behav. Ecol. Sociobiol. 7:232-327.

———. Breeding success of Bewick's swans. *In* T. H. Clutton-Brock, ed. Reproductive success. Univ. Chicago Press, Chicago. In press.

Zicus, M. C. 1984. Pair separation in Canada geese. Wilson Bull. 96:127-130.

4

Variations in Pair Bond and Agonistic Behaviors in Barnacle Geese on the Wintering Grounds

Jeffrey M. Black and Myrfyn Owen

Abstract: Pair bond formation, pair bond maintenance, and agonistic behavior were monitored in barnacle goose flocks (*Branta leucopsis*) on wintering grounds in Scotland from October to May 1982-83 and 1983-84. Pair formation, Triumph Ceremonies, and agonistic behaviors peaked in March after a decrease in mid-winter from a less pronounced peak in October. The spring peak coincided with new growth of plants and subsequent accumulation of fat reserves as indicated by an abdominal profile field index. The pair formation process was identified and described in four chronological stages: Mate Searching, Herding, Mock Attacks (including wing displays), and Prolonged Triumph Ceremonies. Triumph Ceremonies and aggressive behaviors were most frequent in early morning and in midafternoon. Higher frequencies of Triumph Ceremonies and aggressive interactions were recorded in flocks that were dense than in scattered flocks. When temperatures were low, activities other than grazing reached a minimum. More pair bond and aggressive activities occurred in 1982-83 than in 1983-84 when there were greater numbers of parents and juveniles, which are more aggressive than nonbreeding geese, and more two year olds, which were pairing for the first time. The geese were also in better body condition through the winter in 1982-83, and thus had more time for activities other than feeding. Flock size and density decreased in March when pair bond behaviors and aggression increased. Triumph Ceremonies that involved both the male and female at high intensities were most frequent in February and March. As Triumph Ceremonies frequency increased, aggressive encounters became more intensive. We argue that Triumph Ceremonies and closely associated agonistic

Waterfowl in Winter. © 1988 University of Minnesota. Edited by Milton W. Weller and published by the University of Minnesota Press, Minneapolis.

behaviors aid paired birds in spring resource procurement prior to migration and breeding.

The pair bond is the principal mechanism by which individuals of monogamous species optimize resource procurement and maximize "reproductive" fitness (Wickler and Seibt 1983). In particular, geese and swans that are paired to the same mate for long periods produce more offspring than those that frequently change mates (Scott, in press; Owen et al. 1987). Pair bond formation, which occurs mainly during the nonbreeding season, includes displays and aggressive conflict when birds compete for mates (Collias and Jahn 1959, Johnsgard 1965). Most waterfowl biologists interpret the Triumph Ceremony display as instrumental in strengthening or maintaining the bond (Lorenz 1966) and aiding the pair in asserting themselves in aggressive encounters (Fischer 1965). In this study we attempted to identify the behaviors used by single or newly paired geese during the formation of new pair bonds and the behaviors used by established pairs to maintain their attachment. To detect the period of greatest importance for "strengthening" the pair bond, changes in social activities, including displays and agonistic behaviors, were recorded throughout the study period. An attempt was also made to identify a possible benefit of the pair bond prior to migration and breeding by linking changes in accumulation of fat reserves with changes in social displays.

We are grateful to several enthusiastic volunteer observers, including S. Berrow, J. Doherty, G. Nehls, K. Perry-Jones, B. Sears, and P. Webb. The Wildfowl Trust's staff gave their continual support and advice, especially G. V. T. Matthews and M. J. Nugent. We are particularly thankful to C. Clunies-Ross and H. Liber for their assistance in the field. J. B. Blossom kindly created the display drawings. M. R. McLandress, M. A. Ogilvie, and D. G. Raveling provided valuable comments on the manuscript. Financial support was granted by Overseas Research Awards; the University of Wales, Cardiff; and the Wildfowl Trust.

Study Area and Methods

Data were collected on the Svalbard (Spitzbergen) population of barnacle geese that wintered at the Caerlaverock Wildfowl Refuge on the Solway Firth, Scotland (55° N, 3.30° E). Observations were made during the entire period that the geese frequented the refuge from early October to early May 1982-83 and 1983-84. During this time, between 22% and 26% of the geese wore large plastic leg bands readable through a telescope up to 250 m (Ogilvie and Owen 1984). The population of 8,400-8,500 individuals spent about 50% of the study period on the refuge, which contains 95 ha of arable fields and 243 ha of marsh. The geese typically spend the whole day on the refuge before flying one or two kilometers on to mud flats to roost at night. We observed the geese from refuge towers and fiberglass blinds located along an elevated grass embankment that enabled inconspicuous approach.

Social behaviors were recorded using two methods of observation through a telescope: band reading and flock scans. Band reading is defined as the identification of coded plastic leg bands and the recording of information about the focal bird. Flock scans were comprised of one five-minute continuous watch on a representative sample of a flock and two counts, one before and after the continuous watch, of the number of birds that were involved in different activities. During the five-minute scan, the observer looked back and forth across the field of view recording social behaviors that were obvious breaks in predominant and nonconspicuous grazing postures. At least 10 such scans were made for each hour of the day within each month of the study period.

The information collected on each individually banded bird included a record of its pair or family status and a measure of its abdominal profile. Class status included single juvenile, single adult, paired adult, family juvenile, and family adult. Sex was recorded after cloacal examination during the ringing process. For unringed birds, sex was determined according to size and behavioral differences. Decisions on bird status were made according to proximity and behavior of the focal individual in relation to its neighbors; e.g., single birds did not maintain a close proximity to anyone and were frequently chased. A number between 0 and 4 was assigned to each bird according to the degree of convexity of the abdomen (Owen 1981). This profile was used as an index to spring fattening.

In 1982-83, four successive components of the pair formation process were identified. In 1983-84, we opportunistically recorded all pair formation events from October through April. The majority of pair formation events were observed while band reading, but also during flock scans. During the five-minute watches, all Triumph Ceremonies and agonistic encounters were recorded. Activities included grazing, vigilance types, resting, and comfort behavior. Using the percent activity data, we calculated an activity budget index (AI), which provides an indirect measure of the environmental constraints imposed on the geese feeding time (e.g., day length, temperature, and food availability). The index was calculated as follows: $AI = [10 - 0.5(\%\text{ resting and comfort behaviors})] - (\%$ vigilance $- 3)$. Three was subtracted because the level of vigilance never fell below 3%, the other 97% being devoted to feeding. Ten was subtracted to avoid negative values; the lower the index, the more time the geese devoted to activities other than those required for maintaining energy for daily existence. A flock density index was estimated on a relative scale, from 1 to 7, based on interneighbor distance. The number of birds in the flock also was estimated. Data on flocks of fewer than 400 birds were omitted to control for possible differences in activities; e.g., percent vigilance is greater in small flocks (Inglis and Lazarus 1981). Statistical tests included Mann-Whitney U tests on frequencies of events (frequency = events/1,000 birds/minute); Spearman's Rank Correlation between proximate factors within years, months, and days; and Kruskal-Wallis's one-way analysis of variance for variation between years. All tests were two tailed.

Results

Description of Pair Formation Activities

The pair formation process was split into four chronological phases for identification purposes. The first two phases involve the establishment of a bond, and the last two involve the strengthening of new pair bonds before the first breeding attempt.

Mate Searching was recorded when unpaired males walked conspicuously through a flock while adopting a variety of forward neck extensions, head pumps, and erect postures. Vocalizations, which accompanied the postures, were similar to the sounds used during Triumph Ceremonies. Mate Searching was easily identified because of these vocalizations and because of its duration of up to 30 minutes, with the bird walking as far as 100 m. By these criteria, distinction could be made between this behavior and the searching behavior described by Fischer (1965), which is concerned with reunion of separated partners. The Angled Neck display is thought to allow males to approach females in greylag geese (*Anser anser*) (Lorenz

Fig. 4.1. Herding behavior — the second stage in the pair formation process. Male attempts to position himself between female and nearest neighbors. Reproduced from M. Owen, Wild geese of the world. Batsford, London, 1980.

1959), and Mate Searching in barnacle geese may have a similar function. We regarded this behavior as the first event in the pair formation process. During more intense situations this behavior, which was performed on the ground, may lead to pursuit flights especially during the breeding season (Prevett 1972). However, such aerial chases were rare in wintering barnacle goose flocks; they will not be considered further.

The next category, *Herding* (after Raveling 1967; *Shepherding* of Owen 1980), was recorded when a male located a female and unceasingly made attempts to separate her from the rest of the flock (Fig. 4.1). This was achieved when the male successfully and often forcibly placed himself between the female and the nearest neighbors.

The third category, *Mock Attack*, was performed solely by the male. The gander typically ran up to 15 m away from the female while adopting aggressive threat postures to attack "imaginary aggressors." The run always ended several meters away from other geese and rarely elicited a submission; sometimes it was aimed away from the flock. At the end of the run, the bird turned, lifted its head momentarily, resumed a lower neck posture and ran back toward the female. Sometimes after a male made his mock run he spread his wings to the side (perpendicular to the ground) before returning to the female (Fig. 4.2). This more

Fig. 4.2. Mock Attack with wing display — third stage in pairing process of new partners. Male runs away from female to attack imaginary neighbors and returns to female, who joins in exaggerated Triumph Ceremony.

intensive wing display was observed eight times in March. When the male ran back to the female, she usually responded by joining in an exaggerated Triumph Ceremony with wing-flicking and biting. We believe this category signifies the initiation of a trial liaison potentially leading to a long-term bond.

The next phase was identified when pairs exercised their Triumph Ceremony and aggressive display among neighbors. These new pairs were found to be highly aggressive during the displays, which can be described as prolonged agonistic Triumph Ceremonies. The behavior occurred when a pair performed a Triumph Ceremony that preceded an attack on nearby conspecifics, followed by another Triumph Ceremony and attack, etc. In one case the behavior lasted up to 15 minutes, with only brief pauses for foraging and preening. In this phase, the female played a more overt role than earlier. She often initiated the direction and first surge of the attack before the male ran past her toward neighbors. This behavior was first described by Raveling (1967) as the *Prolonged Triumph Ceremonies*.

Table 4.1. Individual records of pair formation events for ringed birds with known histories

Birds, sex	Observ. date	Bird's age[a]	Type of observation	Pair status Before	During	After observation	Total sightings
HKK, F	10/82	7+	P.T.C.[b]	Unpaired	Liaison	Paired with different bird[c]	40
DFG, M	"	7+	"	Unpaired	"	Paired with different bird	63
--A, F	01/83	...	P.T.C.	...	Liaison	...	...
$XI, M	"	7+	"	Unpaired	"	Paired with different bird[c]	76
YFT, F	01/83	4	P.T.C.	Unpaired	New pair	Paired together 3+ years	76
%VC, M	"	1+	"	Unpaired	"	Paired together 3+ years	83
UNR, F	02/83	...	P.T.C.	...	New pair	...	...
XJC, M	"	2	"	Unpaired	"	Paired together 3+ years	32
XHS, F	02/83	2	P.T.C.	Unpaired	New pair	Paired together 3 + years	26
UNR, M	"	...	"	...	"	...	...
CTI, F	02/83	7+	P.T.C.	Unpaired	New pair	Paired together 3+ years	32
UNR, M	"	...	"	...	"	...	...
$NS, F	03/83	2+	P.T.C.	Unpaired	Liaison	Paired with different bird[c]	68
XFX, M	"	2	"	Unpaired	"	Paired together 3+ years	61
CSS, F	11/83	7+	Herding[d]	Unpaired	Liaison	Paired with different bird[c]	49
UNR, M	"	...	"	...	"	...	...
$JT, F	02/84	3	Herding[d]	Paired	Liaison	Remained paired with mate	33
X--, M	"	3	"	...	...	...	...

[a] Age is measured by the number of summers in a bird's lifetime; "+" indicates that the bird was ringed as an adult.

[b] Prolonged Triumph Ceremony.

[c] After trial liaisons with four to seven different birds.

[d] Associated fight between two males.

Individual Cases of Pair Formation

About 15,000 band sightings were made in each year during hundreds of observation hours. In both years, 96% of all ringed birds were seen and resighted an average of seven times a year. Table 4.1 documents pair formation observations on 10 potential pairs when at least one partner was ringed and whose pair status was known before and after the observation. In five cases, the participants formed long-term bonds. The other five groups of participants did not pair with each other; they either remained unpaired or later paired with a different bird. Females, in particular, participated in several trial liaisons before actually pairing for an extended period. Although most of the pair formation was observed in unpaired birds or new pairs, one observation of an old pair's vigorous Triumph Ceremonies and agonistic behaviors toward neighbors was very similar to a Prolonged Triumph Ceremony. It seems, therefore, that Prolonged Triumph Ceremonies may not be an exclusive pair formation event. In three additional observations of unringed birds involved in Herding where two males fought, the female ended up with the winner each time.

Seasonal Variation in Pair Formation Behavior

Only 5% of displays recorded during 1,533 continuous scans (about 128 scan hours) were classified as pair formation behaviors. Mate Searching and Mock Attacks were the only pair formation events recorded during the five-minute scans. The mean number of birds scanned was 132 (SE = 8.2) in a flock size of 1,860 (SE = 77). A total of 24 Mate Searchings and 21 Mock Attacks was seen during 430 scans from February to April. No pair formation events were observed during 469 scans before February; 71% of both Mate Searchings and Mock Attacks occurred in March. Their frequencies (events per 1,000 birds/minute) were much lower than other displays: 7.0×10^{-4} Mate Searchings and 6.2×10^{-4} Mock Attacks, levels that were not significantly different at any time.

During many hours of band reading sessions and flock scans, 114 opportunistic observations of pair formation events were recorded (Table 4.2). The proportion of different events differed significantly through the season (chi-square = 38.8, df = 4, $P < 0.001$). Whereas Mate Searching was not observed until the end of February, Herding was recorded at least once in every month in the study period. All displays (except associated fights) peaked in March. Mock Attacks occurred infrequently from October through January and increased in February and March. Prolonged Triumph Ceremonies appeared only twice before January and then increased until April. There were fewer observations of each type in April than in March. The monthly mean frequency of pair formation events correlated with seasonal frequencies of Triumph Ceremonies (Spearman Rank Correlation rs = 0.86, $P < 0.05$) (Fig. 4.3). The frequencies of initial pair-formation displays (Mate Searching and Herding) were not correlated; however, the relative number of each was not significantly different in any month.

Table 4.2. Relative frequency of initial pair formation and new pair activities in a season on the wintering grounds

Event	October	November	December	January	February	March	April	Total
Mate								
Searching	0	0	0	0	2	17	5	24
Herding	4	2	1	1	3	5	2	18
Fights	5	1	0	2	2	2	1	13
Mock Attacks	0	1	0	0	12	21[a]	5	39
Prolonged Triumph								
Ceremony	1	1	0	3	4	8	3	20
No. of Events	10	5	1	6	23	53	16	114
Frequency[b]	2.3	1.5	1.1	4.3	4.5	15.6	5.9	

[a]Includes eight records of the intensified wing-speading display (fig. 4.2).
[b]Based on an estimate of total hours of observations per goose, goose-hours.

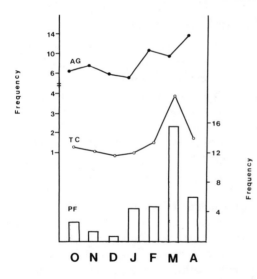

Fig. 4.3. Comparison in frequencies of pair formation (PF), Triumph Ceremonies (TC), and agonistic behaviors (AG) from October to April, showing average values for two years. Frequency equals number of events per 1,000 birds per minute.

Factors Influencing Triumph Ceremony Activities: Seasonal Variation

There were significantly more Triumph Ceremony activities in spring (March and April) than in autumn (October and November) ($P = 0.001$) and midwinter (December to February) ($P = 0.0004$). The frequency of Triumph Ceremonies in March was at least double that of other months (Table 4.3). Activity index and Triumph Ceremonies frequencies were significantly correlated in March and April ($P < 0.01$; $P < 0.05$). Table 4.4 lists the activity index, flock size, density index, number of scans for each month, and percent grazing for each month in the two

Table 4.3. Frequency (number of events per 1,000 birds/minute) and variation of intensity in Triumph Ceremonies in different months

	October	November	December	January	February	March	April
Frequency, 1982-83							
Mean	1.4	0.7	1.0	1.1	1.2	4.1	1.5
(SE)	(0.2)	(0.1)	(0.2)	(0.2)	(0.3)	(0.6)	(0.3)
Frequency, 1983-84							
Mean	1.2	1.5	0.8	1.0	1.8	3.6	1.9
(SE)	(0.2)	(0.2)	(0.1)	(0.2)	(0.2)	(0.4)	(0.2)
Intensity, 1983-84							
No. of ceremonies	95	118	60	73	116	255	202
Reduced (%)	49	12	32	34	51	44	38
Moderate (%)	24	18	13	14	3	2	15
Exaggerated (%)	27	70	55	52	50	51	47

years of study. Triumph Ceremony events and flock density were significantly correlated in October and April (both $P < 0.01$), when Triumph Ceremonies were more frequent. Within flocks, we found that a higher frequency of displays occurred at moderate or high densities than at extremely low densities ($0.04 > P > 0.008$). Flock size was not correlated with Triumph Ceremony frequency.

There was a correlation between time of day and Triumph Ceremony activity in four different months ($0.05 > P > 0.001$). More Triumph Ceremonies occurred in the early morning (0600-0900) than the remainder of the day ($P = 0.005$), and the

Table 4.4. Seasonal differences in mean activity index, flock size, density index, number of five-minute scans, and percent grazing

Variable	October	November	December	January	February	March	April
Activity index	3.1	4.9	8.2	9.3	8.4	7.9	10.4
Flock size	2,290	2,170	1,955	1,260	2,060	1,000	1,525
Density index	3.2	3.7	3.5	3.4	3.7	3.1	3.1
Number of scans	124	114	114	117	120	139	171
Percent grazing, 1982-83[a]	76	79	85	93	94	85	89
(SE)	2.0	2.2	1.7	0.6	0.6	2.9	0.7
Percent grazing, 1983-84	85	90	92	94	93	90	91
(SE)	0.6	0.4	0.8	0.4	0.4	0.4	0.5

[a]Sample sizes for percent grazing are more than twice that of five-minute scans on flocks of more than 100 birds.

frequency was lowest at the end of the day (1600-1800) before returning to roost (P = 0.005). Fig. 4.4 shows the month of March when both Triumph Ceremonies and agonistic behavior peaked in the morning, declined around midday, and showed a

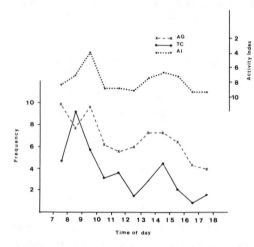

Fig. 4.4. Comparison in frequency of Triumph Ceremonies (TC) and agonistic behaviors (AG) in relation to activity index (AI) in average day in March (N = 139 scans). Frequency equals number of events per 1,000 birds per minute.

less pronounced peak in the afternoon. This relationship, however, may have been linked with the fact that time of day and density were correlated in four of seven months ($0.02 > P > 0.001$). However, density did not change much through the day until dusk in preroost flocks, when density was significantly greater than during the rest of the day ($P < 0.0001$) (see discussion).

Variation in Intensity of Triumph Ceremonies. The postures adopted by barnacle geese during Triumph Ceremonies were similar to those of their close relative the Canada goose (*Branta canadensis*) (Johnsgard 1965). As for other geese, the ceremony included several components determined by the angle of the head and neck relative to the ground and by vocalizations (Fischer 1965, Akesson and Raveling 1982). The distinctive postures consisted of brief upward and forward head and neck extensions (Rolling component) by the male toward the female's head. Otherwise the male maintained an upright posture while calling (Fig. 4.5). The female responded by retracting or turning her head away (Facing Away; Radesater 1974a) from the male's advances before or just after he made contact with his bill (Fig. 4.6). Similar head and neck postures were performed close to and parallel with the ground (Cackling component). Barnacle geese rarely displayed rotary head movements during the Rolling component and did not emit prolonged snoring vocalizations during the Cackling component. In this study, it was most instructive to classify the behaviors according to the degree of partner involvement to establish changes in affinity between pairs through the season. For ease of description, the following categories include the male and female, but many ceremonies involved parents and offspring (see below). Terminology approxi-

Fig. 4.5. Triumph Ceremony posture when both male and female hold upright stances while emitting cackling vocalizations.

mates that described or reviewed by McLandress and Raveling (1981) and Akesson and Raveling (1982). *Reduced Ceremony* involved the least amount of partner cooperation; the male Cackled at the female, who gave no response but continued with her current activity such as grazing or preening. *Moderate Ceremony* was identified when the female encouraged the male's behavior with vocalizations

Fig. 4.6. Triumph Ceremony posture when male extends his head and neck toward female's head. Female "Faces Away" before or after male makes contact with his bill.

similar to Yipping (Collias and Jahn 1959); both members were stationary and, if wing-flicking was observed, only the male performed it. *Exaggerated Ceremony* was recorded when both members performed vocalizations, wing-flicking, head and neck movements (extensions and Facing Away), and sometimes biting; the birds in this category usually were walking or running together.

Table 4.3 also shows that the intensity of Triumph Ceremony activities differed through the season (chi-square = 67.2, df = 12, $P < 0.0001$). Triumph Ceremony behaviors as a whole remained constant in autumn and winter but increased considerably in February and March and decreased in April. In October and February, the percentage of Reduced Ceremonies was highest; Exaggerated Ceremony predominated in all other months. Reduced and Exaggerated Ceremony frequencies were significantly different in autumn and spring ($P = 0.014$, $P = 0.0003$), and both Moderate and Exaggerated Ceremony frequencies were higher in spring than in winter ($P = 0.0002$, $P = 0.0006$).

Association between Triumph Ceremony and Agonistic Behavior

The close association between Triumph Ceremony and agonistic behavior has been well documented (Raveling 1970, Radesater 1974b). Partners normally perform Triumph Ceremonies either before or after agonistic situations or when they reunite after separations. McLandress and Raveling (1981) reported that 76% of displays were associated with aggressive conflict. Of 34 fights recorded in barnacle geese, 38% were associated with Herding behavior. About half of the remainder were observed in October, possibly because birds were reuniting after

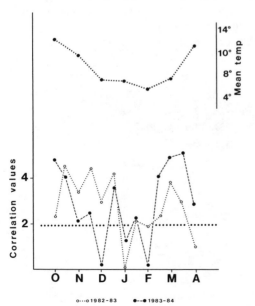

Fig. 4.7. Degree of significant correlation for both seasons between Triumph Ceremonies and aggression; significant points are above horizontal line. Chart also shows mean ambient temperatures per month.

o···o 1982-83   ●--● 1983-84

migration. Figure 4.7 shows the degree of significant correlation between Triumph Ceremony activities and aggressive behavior; 9 of the 14 months in the study period showed a significant correlation. The correlation was not significant in most midwinter months. Triumph Ceremony and agonistic behavior frequencies were correlated in each period of the day — early morning, late morning, afternoon, and evening $(0.05 > P > 0.001)$.

Factors Influencing Agonistic Activities: Seasonal Variation

Frequency of aggression differed significantly in various periods (table 4.5): between autumn and midwinter $(P < 0.0001)$, but not between the autumn and spring months. As with Triumph Ceremony events, the lowest frequency occurred in midwinter and the highest in spring. Nine of the 14 months in the study periods

Table 4.5. Frequency and variation of intensity in agonistic activities in different months

	October	November	December	January	February	March	April
Frequency, 1982-83							
Mean	8.7	7.1	6.4	7.1	15.8	13.0	14.0
(SE)	(0.8)	(1.2)	(1.1)	(1.0)	(2.1)	(1.2)	(1.1)
Frequency, 1983-84							
Mean	4.4	8.1	5.5	3.6	5.8	6.7	13.7
(SE)	(0.4)	(0.7)	(0.4)	(0.4)	(0.6)	(0.5)	(1.7)
Intensity, 1983-84							
Agonistic acts	678	646	386	248	416	541	1,435
Low-threat (%)	53	49	51	47	49	29	27
Mid-threat (%)	22	20	28	29	18	30	39
Contact (%)	15	7	15	17	26	19	19
Chase (%)	10	9	6	7	7	23	14

showed a significant $(0.05 > P > 0.001)$ or near correlation $(0.1 > P > 0.05)$ between aggressive activity and the activity index. January was the only month that did not show a correlation in either year. All months, except January, showed a significant correlation between threat frequency and density $(0.05 > P > 0.001)$. When density was extremely low, less aggression occurred than when it was intermediate or high $(P = 0.030, P = 0.027)$. Activity index and density showed a significant correlation only in April 1984 $(P < 0.01)$. Threat frequency and flock size were not correlated.

The highest frequency of agonistic behavior occurred in the morning after birds arrived in the fields. A significant difference in frequency was found between 0600-0900 and the remainder of the day $(P = 0.008;$ see fig. 4.4). The results from 1982-83 correlations showed that the frequency of agonistic events continued to increase from 0600 to 0900 and from 1200 to 1530 but decreased at the end of the day from 1530 to 1800 ($P < 0.05$, $P < 0.01$, $P < 0.02$). As with Triumph Ceremony activities, this relationship may be influenced by flock density. Time of day and the activity index correlated in two of seven months ($0.05 > P > 0.01$).

Variation in Intensity of Agonistic Encounters. Aggressive interactions were classified according to physical effort into five types. A *Low-threat* consisted of either Bent Neck or Forward postures (Blurton Jones 1960) given by a stationary goose. A *Mid-threat* included the same postures, plus a slight advancement of a couple of steps toward the opponent. A *Contact* was recorded when the aggressor bit or forcibly bumped the enemy, and *Chasing* occurred when the aggressor ran after a fleeing subordinate. *Fighting* males grasped one another with their bills and used their wings to hit their opponent. Agonistic behaviors that did not elicit some degree of submission by the opposition were not used in the analysis. We assume that the energy demand to execute these activities progressively increased from Low-threat to Fighting. As expected, with regard to efficiency in fighting strategies (Parker 1974), the frequency of threat types corresponded to the amount of energy demand required for their execution. The percentage of agonistic types decreased as the physical demand increased ($P < 0.01$).

The proportion of agonistic events of various intensities differed significantly through the season (chi-square = 330, df = 18, $P < 0.0001$). The frequency of all aggressive interaction types except Contacts decreased significantly from autumn to winter ($0.0002 > P > 0.0001$). There was an increase in all interactions that required more energy than Low-threat between winter and spring; frequencies were significantly greater in spring than autumn ($0.023 > P > 0.002$) and midwinter ($0.01 > P > 0.001$). Frequency of Low-threats, on the other hand, stayed the same in winter and spring, although it was significantly lower in spring than autumn ($P = 0.0001$). Chasing decreased slightly from 23% in March to 14% in April.

Variation in Body Condition: Abdominal Profile Index

Based on abdominal profiles recorded in the field, the period of hyperphagia in barnacle geese usually begins in February, proceeds through March and April on the wintering grounds, and peaks in May on the spring staging islands (Owen 1981 and unpubl. data). However, the exact timing and speed of buildup of body reserves vary each year depending on temperature, which controls the initiation of new plant growth. During the two study winters, a weighted median abdominal profile index was calculated for each 10-day period where samples exceeded 50 birds for each sex: weighted median (WM) = MP [NM + (NA − NB)]/NM, where MP = median profile, NM = number at median profile, NA = number above, and NB = number below median profile.

In 1982-83, the WM of females increased from 1.8 on arrival on the wintering grounds in early October to 2.5 in late November and stayed at that level until mid-February. It then increased to 3.0 at departure in the last week of April. In 1983-4, however, the birds arrived in better condition (WM of 2.1), but WM increased little in October-November (WM in late November = 2.2). In the cold weather of January, it fell to about 1.5 and increased in February to 1.9, a level that was maintained through March. Intensive hyperphagia therefore was delayed until April, when female profile index increased from 1.7 to 2.4. Samples of females weighed in January and April 1978 showed that a WM of 1.9 corresponded to a mean body weight of 1,640 g (January) and 3.0 to 1,965 g (April). Male abdominal profiles were very similar to female profiles except that they were consistently lower (see Owen 1981).

There were several differences in ecological situations between the two study years that influenced these differences in body condition. In 1982-83, there was ample grain left in the fields after the harvest in October-November. In autumn 1983, the geese were forced to feed on grass rather than grain because of a clean harvest. As a result, geese spent considerably less time feeding in the first three months of the 1982-83 season and continued to spend less time grazing in the remaining months as compared with 1983-84 (table 4.4). Mean January temperatures were higher (8.9C) in 1982-83 than in 1983-84 (5.4C), as were those in March (8.8C in 1982-83 compared with 7.4C).

Annual Variation in Triumph Ceremonies and Agonistic Activities

From the information that was collected during flock scans, it is not known what social class was responsible for the recorded activities. Several studies have found that family members were involved in more Triumph and agonistic behaviors per unit time than were nonfamily individuals (Dittami 1981; Akesson and Raveling 1982; J. M. Black, unpubl. data). In a separate study based on continuous observations of families, it was found that juveniles Cackled-at their parents twice as much as parents did at each other (J. M. Black, unpubl. data). We also know that many families break up through the winter and in spring (Owen 1980). The activities performed by family members should, therefore, decrease and activities by pairs and singles should increase as the season progresses. It follows that social activities in flocks vary with flock class structure. We found the same relationship on the population level between years. Table 4.6 shows that there were many more juveniles, parents, and two year olds in 1982-83 than in 1983-84. Monthly frequen-

Table 4.6. Population structure in 1982-83 and 1983-84

Year	Total	Juveniles	Parents	Two year olds
1982-83	8,500	13.5%	11.8%	19.0%
1983-84	8,400	8.0%	7.4%	2.5%

cy for both Triumph Ceremony and agonistic behavior varied slightly between years (each $P < 0.05$). The higher proportion of family members in 1982-83 may have resulted in the increased level of social behavior that year. Owen (1980) found that 58% of the two year olds are paired upon their departure from the spring staging areas for their second summer, and Dittami (1981) found that two year olds consistently performed more courting behaviors than other birds. The fact that there were eight times as many of these birds in 1982-83 than 1983-84 was probably responsible for the increase in displays in 1982-83. Another explanation for the different frequencies of Triumph Ceremonies and agonistic behaviors between years may be related to the fact that, the birds spent less time grazing in 1982-83 because they were consistently in better condition than in 1983-84. Because fat reserves were relatively large, they could devote more time to other activities.

Discussion

We agree with Akesson and Raveling (1982), who suggest that the female is largely responsible for the male's Triumph Ceremony and aggressive behaviors by her supportive responses (Facing Away and Yipping). Cooke and Davies (1983) suggest that the female is the choosier of the sexes with regards to plumage color in lesser snow geese (*Chen c. caerulescens*). From our observations on component stages of pairing, it seems that the female encourages a male to continue or cease his behavior. Mate Searching by males probably would not progress to Herding unless the female provided the correct postures and responses to the male's advances. It seems probable that a female chooses a mate based on his perform- ance in each of the different stages of displays. In functional terms, males compete in display quality and aggressive ability and females make decisions using these cues to choose a male with complementary phenotypes according to survival and fitness consequences (Wittenberger 1983, Partridge and Halliday 1984). The fact that some females form temporary liaisons with several males before actually pairing for an extended period suggests that the pair formation process is some- times repetitive. Triumph Ceremonies and conspecific aggression involving both participants in liaisons do not ensure long-term commitment and are evidently not exclusive to pairs with stable pair bonds. Wittenberger (1983) lists the alternatives for a female: she can "reject the male as unsuitable, accept the male as her mate, or defer a decision until further information about additional males has been ob- tained." The lack of any record of Mate Searching from October to February is puzzling since 44% of the Herding records were observed in this period. It is possible that yearlings and other nonbreeders could have located potential partners in molting flocks and migrated with them and continued the courting process upon arrival on the wintering grounds (see Owen et al. 1987).

When food is scarce, individuals in foraging flocks tend to decrease the amount of time allotted to resting and comfort activities and eventually to vigilance to increase feeding time (see also Pulliam and Caraco 1984). The activity index gave a single measure of major activities (other than social events) that were monitored during flock scans. The percentage of birds grazing increases during the coldest months when they are barely maintaining or losing weight. During these cold months, daylight feeding time is short and food availability is low. Because of these intense feeding periods, behaviors such as preening and sleeping are delayed until nighttime on the roost. This change in behavior is most evident in February through April, when display frequencies are significantly correlated to the index. Triumph Ceremonies and agonistic behaviors are most frequent early in the morning; they decrease through the afternoon and are very rare in the last hour before the birds fly to the mud flats. At dusk the birds pull together in large, compact flocks and move quickly across the fields to fill their esophagi with food to be digested on the roost (Owen 1972). This evidently cancels the positive effect of increased aggression and display with high densities. It seems that geese can best afford time to fight, form initial bonds, and reinforce old bonds during the long, warm spring days that coincide with spring plant growth.

Our results support the interpretation that Triumph Ceremonies promote and maintain pair bonds and thus aid geese in asserting themselves in aggressive encounters (e.g., Fischer 1965). The large number of Reduced Ceremonies in autumn indicates that the males were substantially more involved than the females at this time of the year. Females increasingly joined their partners in Moderate and Exaggerated displays through the winter and spring months. After the coldest midwinter months, Triumph Ceremonies and aggressive interactions were very closely related. We concluded from these findings, together with the recording of greater frequencies of Triumph Ceremonies and agonistic encounters in March, that the period of investment in strengthening old pair bonds is in the spring months, with its peak in March. Low-threats were no longer used as frequently in March, and the proportion of chases increased.

This population of barnacle geese undertakes two 1,500-km migratory flights over the sea before finally reaching the breeding grounds (Owen and Gullestad 1984). Their first flight (20 April to 10 May) is to the Helgeland Islands in Norway (65-66° N, 11° E), and the second (10-20 May) is to Spitsbergen (77-80° N, 15° E). It was previously shown that these geese have two phases of spring fattening; first in Scotland, then in Norway (Owen 1981). The peak frequencies and highest intensities of pair bond displays and threats occur during the first hyperphagic period (February to March), despite lower flock densities and sizes. Thereafter, agonistic encounter frequencies remain high. These peaks coincided with initial spring plant growth, and, subsequently, goose abdominal profiles became larger. We suggest that after pair bonds are strengthened, the benefits from stronger bonds (increased motivation in encounters is one example) are maintained through both periods of hyperphagia. Indeed, a well-accepted function of pair and family bonds is to aid in feeding competition (Raveling 1970, Scott 1980, Black and Owen 1984). Dittami

(1981) found in wintering feral bar-headed geese (*Anser indicus*) that successful breeders were more active in pair bond display and aggressive interactions than unsuccessful ones. In April, just prior to departure, Triumph Ceremony frequency in both years decreased. Agonistic behaviors increased while the most intensive threat, chasing, slightly decreased. It is possible that old pair bonds are sufficiently reinforced by April to enable increased motivation during conflict situations over food resources, thus the decline in Triumph Ceremony frequency and the continued overall increase in agonistic behaviors. Alternatively, the decline in Triumph Ceremony displays and chases may suggest that energy-draining activities, other than feeding, are ill adaptive so close to migration.

The April decline in pair formation displays illustrates this point further. It seems in April that young and unpaired birds devote more time to building up reserves for migration. A further reduction in social activities apparently occurs closer to nest initiation when the birds are in Norway. During the first two days after arrival on the islands, only 0.44% of the birds were involved in some form of social activity (all types lumped together). Two days later, the percentage dropped to 0.33%; then for the last four days prior to departure, the percentage remained at 0.22% (M. J. Nugent, pers. commun.). A similar relationship was found in giant Canada geese; despite an overall increase in Triumph Ceremony and agonistic behavior frequencies in April, the proportion of chases, fights, and exaggerated Triumph Ceremonies decreased (McLandress and Raveling 1981). The way in which the reinforcement of the pair bond and loyalty of partners affects individual survival and success is still poorly understood, although strong evidence for increased fecundity in long-term bonds is now established for barnacle geese (Owen et al. 1987). We hypothesize that pair bond strength, measured by the presence and exclusivity of partners and behavioral performances in the nonbreeding season such as feeding competition and vigilance synchrony in pairs, affects individual breeding performance.

LITERATURE CITED

Akesson, T. R., and R. G. Raveling. 1982. Behaviors associated with seasonal reproduction and long-term monogamy in Canada geese. Condor 84:188–196.

Black, J. M., and M. Owen. 1984. The importance of the family unit to barnacle goose offspring: a progress report. Nor. Polarinst. Skr. 181:79–85.

Blurton Jones, N. G. 1960. Experiments on the causation of threat postures of Canada geese. Wildfowl Trust Annu. Rep. 11:46–52.

Collias, N. E., and L. R. Jahn. 1959. Social behavior and breeding success in Canada geese (*Branta canadensis*) confined under semi-natural conditions. Auk 76:478–509.

Cooke, F., and J. C. Davies. 1983. Assortative mating, mate choice and reproductive fitness in snow geese. Pages 279–296 *in* P. Bateson, ed. Mate choice. Cambridge Univ. Press, Cambridge.

Dittami, J. P. 1981. Seasonal changes in the behavior and plasma titers of various hormones in bar-headed geese *Anser indicus*. Z. Tierpsychol. 55:289–324.

Fischer, H. 1965. Das triumphgeschrei der Graugans. Z. Tierpsychol. 22:247–304.

Inglis, I. R., and J. Lazarus. 1981. Vigilance and flock size: brent geese. The edge effect. Z. Tierpsychol. 57:193–200.

Johnsgard, P. A. 1965. Handbook of waterfowl behavior. Cornell Univ. Press, Ithaca, N.Y. 378pp.

Lorenz, K. 1959. The role of aggression in group formation. Pages 181-254 *in* B. Schaffner, ed. Group processes: transactions of the fourth conference. Josiah Macy, Jr., Foundation, New York.

————. 1966. On aggression. Harcourt Publ., New York.

McLandress, M. R., and D. G. Raveling. 1981. Hyperphagia and social behavior of Canada geese prior to spring migration. Wilson Bull. 93:310–324.

Ogilvie, M. A., and M. Owen. 1984. Some results from ringing of barnacle geese in Svalbard and Britain. Nor. Polarinst. Skr. 181:49–56.

Owen, M. 1972. Some factors affecting food intake and selection in white-fronted geese. J. Anim. Ecol. 41:411–428.

————. 1980. Wild geese of the world. Batsford, London. 236pp.

————. 1981. Abdominal profile—a condition index for wild geese in the field. J. Wildl. Manage. 39:227–230.

Owen, M., and N. Gullestad. 1984. Migration routes of Svalbard barnacle geese with a preliminary report on the importance of the Bjornoya staging area. Nor. Polarinst. Skr. 181:67–77.

————, J. M. Black, and H. Liber. 1988. Pair bond duration and timing of its formation in barnacle geese (*Branta leucopsis*). Pages 23-38 *in* M. Weller, ed. Waterfowl in winter. Univ. Minnesota Press, Minneapolis.

Parker, G. A. 1974. Assessment strategy and the evolution of fighting behaviour. J. Theor. Biol. 47:223–243.

Partridge, L. and T. R. Halliday. 1984. Mating patterns and mate choice. Pages 222–250 *in* J. R. Krebs and N. B. Davies, eds. Behavioural ecology: an evolutionary approach. 2nd ed. Blackwell Scientific Publications, Oxford.

Prevett, J. P. 1972. Family behavior and age-dependent breeding biology of the blue goose *Anser caerulescens*. Report to Canadian Wildlife Service, 192pp.

Pulliam, H. R., and T. Caraco. 1984. Living in groups: Is there an optimal group size? Pages 122-147 *in* J. R. Krebs and N. B. Davies, eds. Behavioural ecology: an evolutionary approach. 2nd ed. Blackwell Scientific Publications, Oxford.

Radesater, T. 1974a. On the ontogeny of orienting movements in the triumph ceremony in two species of geese (*Anser anser* L. and *Branta canadensis* L.). Behav. 50:1-15.

————. 1974b. Form and sequential associations between the triumph ceremony and other behavior patterns in the Canada goose *Branta canadensis* L. Ornis Scand. 5:87–101.

Raveling, D. G. 1967. Sociobiology and ecology of Canada geese in winter. Ph.D. Thesis, Southern Illinois Univ., Carbondale. 213pp.

————. 1970. Dominance relationships and agonistic behavior of Canada geese in winter. Behav. 37:291–319.

Scott, D. K. 1980. Functional aspects of prolonged parental care in Bewick's swans. Anim. Behav. 28:938–952.

————. Breeding success of Bewick's swans. *In* T. H. Clutton-Brock, ed. Reproductive Success. Univ. Chicago Press, Chicago. In press.

Wickler, W., and U. Seibt. 1983. Monogomy: an ambiguous concept. Pages 33-50 *in* P. Bateson, ed. Mate choice. Cambridge Univ. Press, Cambridge.

Wittenberger, J. F. 1983. Tactics of mate choice. Pages 435-447 *in* P. Bateson, ed. Mate choice. Cambridge Univ. Press, Cambridge.

5

Social Behavior and Pairing Chronology of Mottled Ducks during Autumn and Winter in Louisiana

Stuart L. Paulus

Abstract: Pairing chronology, agonistic and courtship behaviors, dominance relations, and spatial interactions of mottled ducks (*Anas fulvigula*) were studied in the coastal marshes of southwestern Louisiana during August through February 1980-82. Courting and agonistic activities comprised less than 1% of the time budget of mottled ducks, and time > spent in these activities was similar ($P > 0.05$) among paired and unpaired males and females. Courtship was initiated in late summer; by December, 90% of females were paired. Immature mottled ducks began forming pairs at five months of age. Mottled ducks and mallards (*Anas platyrhynchos*) were observed courting near each other in fall. However, only 0.4% of mottled ducks were observed paired with mallards or black ducks (*Anas rubripes*). Chasing, bill threats, and inciting were common agonistic activities, and most agonistic activity was observed in fall. Pairs were dominant to unpaired birds, as pairs won 94% ($P < 0.001$) of contests with unpaired birds. Mottled ducks usually were observed as solitary pairs or in small groups of fewer than 10 birds; 35% of all observations were of lone birds. Mottled ducks primarily associated with members of similar pair status. This study suggests that courtship displays may be more important in forming bonds between immature than adult mottled ducks. Early pair formation by mottled ducks may have minimized interspecific pairing between mottled ducks and mallards.

As part of a study on mottled duck (*Anas fulvigula*) behavior in Louisiana, special effort was directed toward a better understanding of the social activities of mottled ducks during autumn and winter. Investigation of these activities is

Waterfowl in Winter. © 1988 University of Minnesota. Edited by Milton W. Weller and published by the University of Minnesota Press, Minneapolis.

important for several reasons. First, although courtship displays and pairing chronology of captive mottled ducks were studied by Weeks (1969), little is known of these behaviors in wild mottled ducks. Second, Paulus (1983) suggested that pairing chronology might be related to foraging strategies in nonbreeding Anatinae, with those species feeding on poorer quality foods (such as leafy aquatic vegetation [Sugden 1973, Paulus 1982]) forming pairs earliest. However, mottled ducks pair early (Weeks 1969) but consume high-quality foods (such as plant seeds and invertebrates [Guidry 1977, Bellrose 1978]), suggesting that factors other than food choice influence pairing chronology. Third, mottled ducks associate with mallards (*Anas platyrhynchos*) during winter, yet cross-pairing is uncommon (Weeks 1969) despite similarities in courtship displays and overlap of time of pair formation. In some areas where mallards and black ducks (*Anas rubripes*) winter together, interspecific pairing is common (Brodsky and Weatherhead 1984). Fourth, little is known about the influence of sex and age on time of pairing in mottled ducks. Finally, the role of agonistic activities in influencing dominance relations and resource acquisition of mottled ducks is poorly understood.

The objectives of this study were to examine pairing chronology and displays, agonistic behaviors, dominance relations, and spatial interactions of mottled ducks. These data were used to examine the role of social behaviors and relationships in influencing mottled duck pair formation and distribution.

I wish to thank K. Paulus, T. Joanen, L. McNease, J. Kennamer, and M. K. Causey for their help during all phases of the project. I am grateful to D. Richard for his assistance in capturing and marking mottled ducks. I appreciate the help of G. Baldassarre, R. Mirarchi, G. Mullen, L. Wit, and M. Joanen for assistance in manuscript preparation and M. Weller, F. McKinney, G. Hepp, and C. Stutzenbaker for reviewing earlier drafts of the manuscript. Financial support was provided by the Louisiana Department of Wildlife and Fisheries.

Study Area and Methods

This study was conducted in coastal southwestern Louisiana, primarily on Rockefeller Wildlife Refuge and on privately owned lands within 35 km of the refuge. Mottled ducks were observed on brackish, intermediate, and freshwater natural marshes and impoundments. The study area has been described in detail (Paulus 1982, 1984b).

Data on social behavior and spatial relationships of mottled ducks were collected concurrently with activity budget observations during August through February, 1980-82. Observations were made with a 15-40× spotting scope, 7× binoculars, and 2× nightscope. Activities of a focal individual or pair were recorded at 20-second intervals during one-hour periods randomly selected during the day and at nonrandom periods at night. All courtship and intraspecific and interspecific aggressive behaviors involving focal individuals were recorded during observation periods. Most (93%) nocturnal observations occurred when the moon was between the first and last quarters. Nocturnal observations were limited to birds within 30 m of the observer.

Whenever possible, individually identifiable birds wearing nasal saddles labeled with number-letter combinations (Greenwood 1977) were observed. Individuals were marked to provide information on age of pair formation, movements, pair bond durability, and social interactions of mottled ducks. A total of 716 immature and adult mottled ducks was marked during the study.

Aggressive encounters involving mottled ducks were divided into five categories: (1) *Inciting*, performed by females, involving a rapid series of turns of the head over the shoulder with the beak usually pointed toward an intruder and accompanied by 'gagg' vocalizations (Johnsgard 1965); (2) *Biting*, one bird grabbing the other with its beak; (3) *Chasing*, one bird rushing another and forcing it to move away rapidly; (4) *Bill threats*, an open-bill display with the bill raised slightly upward from horizontal and toward another bird; and (5) *Fighting*, tugging and biting of an opposing bird's breast and side feathers as well as wing-slapping and chasing. Subtle avoidance (in which one bird moved out of the path of another bird as it approached) was observed but not included in the analysis because of the difficulty in detecting all occurrences of this behavior. Courtship displays of mottled ducks, which have been described by Johnsgard (1965) and Weeks (1969), included *Head shake, Introductory shake, Grunt-whistle, Head-up-tail-up, Nod-swimming, Preen-behind-the-wing, Down-up*, and *Jump-flights*. Copulatory and postcopulatory displays included *Head-pump, Bridling, Nod-swimming*, and *Turn-back-of-the-head*. The species, sex, pair status, and activity of birds involved in social interactions also were recorded.

Before each observation period, the number, sex, and pair status of all mottled ducks in the area were recorded. Because of similarity of plumages, sex was determined from bill coloration (Stutzenbaker 1984) and social behaviors. Birds were considered paired only if they mutually avoided or threatened other birds, synchronized their activities, and remained within 3 m of each other during most of the observation period (Paulus 1983).

During activity budget observations, the distance between focal birds and nearest bird was subjectively estimated at three-minute intervals and the species, sex, and pair status of the focal and nearest birds were recorded. From these data, intraspecific and interspecific associations and spatial relationships were determined. Frequencies of agonistic interactions and associations involving mottled ducks and sex ratios were evaluated via chi-square analysis of contingency tables (Snedecor and Cochran 1976, 250). When chi-square analyses indicated rejection of the hypothesis of independence, Goodman's (1964) simultaneous confidence-interval procedure was used to identify significant associations.

Results

Courting and Pair Formation

Courting activities comprised less than 1% (N = 1,188 hours) of the time budget of mottled ducks, with similar results for paired and unpaired males and females (P > 0.05). Courtship was initiated in August, and the greatest level of courting activity was observed during October through December. Most courting occurred in early morning and late afternoon, although 0.1% of time was spent courting at night.

The Introductory shake (26%, N = 566), Grunt-whistle (22%), Head-up-tail-up (15%), Head shake (13%), Nod-swimming (13%), and Preen-behind-the-wing (8%) were displays observed most often in males. The Down-up display (1%) and Jump-flights (1%) were rarely observed. Nod-swimming displays immediately followed other displays (23%), primarily the Head-up-tail-up (86%), as well as the Grunt-whistle (6%) and Down-up (6%) displays. Male displays, especially the Head-up-tail-up, often were highly synchronized among two to four males.

Courtship groups averaged 4.4 (range of 3-7) males and 2.2 (range of 1-7) females (N = 21). Courtship bouts involved only a few males and females at first, but they soon attracted other birds. Intensity of courting activity varied throughout the display period. Intervals of intense activity, with males courting or chasing away nearby birds and females, Nod-swimming or Inciting, would be followed by lulls in which birds fed or spent time in other activities. Individuals were observed leaving one courting group as courting activity waned and joining a nearby, more active courting group. During January and February, courting activities involved only two to three pairs and no unpaired birds (N = 3). Courting activities lasted less than 3 minutes, and no mate-switching was observed.

Mallards were observed courting near mottled duck courtship groups in fall. Although mallard and mottled duck displays and pairing chronology were similar, mallards and mottled ducks displayed to each other in only 2 of 21 courtship groups.

Of 63 mottled duck copulations observed, 2 took place in September (N = 231 hours), 23 in October (N = 195 hours), 11 in November (N = 150 hours), 9 in December (N = 206 hours), 13 in January (N = 252 hours), and 5 in February (N = 155 hours). Precopulatory and copulatory displays comprised 59.5% of courtship activities of mottled ducks. Postcopulatory displays by males consisted of Bridling followed by Nod-swimming around the female, Turn-back-of-the-head, and bathing. Females usually bathed while males performed postcopulatory displays. Pairs would copulate away from the main flock; on three occasions, copulatory activity ceased and no postcopulatory display was given when an intruder approached.

Females comprised 47% of the population during the nonbreeding season (table 5.1). The percentage of females observed in the population was lowest in

Table 5.1. Mottled duck sex ratios and percentage of females paired in Louisiana from August through February, 1980-82

Month	Males	Females	Percentage males	Percentage of females paired
August	53	47	53.0	21.3
September	203	153	57.0	70.6
October	259	204	55.9	82.8
November	176	156	53.0	84.0
December	150	142	51.4	93.0
January	222	216	50.7	95.8
February	150	141	51.5	100.0

September but was similar to that of males by December. The percentage of females paired was lowest during late summer (table 5.1), but it increased rapidly in the fall. First bonds may have been formed in late summer as males courted and associated with females while flightless in August and September. Over 90% of females were paired by December, and no unpaired females were observed in February. On no occasion were both members of a pair marked, and marked birds were not observed throughout the annual cycle to determine duration of the pair bond.

Only nine (0.4%) mottled ducks paired with a member of another species: four males paired with female mallards, four females paired with male mallards, and a male paired with a female black duck. The latter pair also copulated. Two mottled duck-mallard hybrids, showing plumage characteristic of both mallards and mottled ducks, were observed during the study.

Siblings that wore nasal saddles remained together until about 60-70 days of age ($N = 120$). During summer months, immature mottled ducks formed small groups, and 70% ($P < 0.001$, $N = 939$) of two-bird associations were with members of the same sex. More interaction among males and females was observed in late August, and first courtship activity by immature mottled ducks occurred in early September. Observations of five marked individuals showed that early bonds may be temporary, the male and female spending only part of a day to several days together. Immature males acted paired but later left the female to court other females. The earliest age that a nasal-saddled individual acted paired was at five months; both males and females were also observed copulating at this age. One unpaired immature female copulated with an unpaired male and then separated.

Agonistic Behavior

Agonistic activities were observed infrequently, and the percentage of time spent in these activities was similar among all mottled ducks ($P > 0.05$). Chasing was the predominant agonistic activity of pairs. Unpaired birds rarely chased other birds, giving mostly Bill threats (males) or Inciting (females) (table 5.2). Paired females Incited toward intruding males, other pairs, or their own mate, and these behaviors

Table 5.2. Relative frequency of agonistic activities of mottled ducks in Louisiana from September through February, 1980-82[a]

Type of display	Initiator of display		
	Pair ($N = 217$)	Unpaired male ($N = 34$)	Unpaired female ($N = 17$)
Inciting	26.3	0.0	58.8
Bite	6.0	17.7	11.8
Chase	34.6	8.8	5.9
Bill threat	28.1	67.7	23.5
Fight	5.0	5.9	0.0

[a]Values are percentages of activities observed for a given pairing class.

comprised 26% of agonistic activities by pairs. Fighting, which occurred infrequently, was initiated only by pairs and unpaired males toward other pairs or unpaired males. Agonistic activities lasted less than 30 seconds, although paired males were observed chasing other birds over 20 m. No differences were found in time spent in agonistic activities during day or night ($P > 0.05$).

Agonistic activities were observed most often in October and November, when threat behaviors comprised 0.5% ($N = 195$ hours) and 0.3% ($N = 150$ hours) of time spent by mottled ducks, respectively. During the remaining months, mottled ducks spent less than 0.2% ($N = 612$ hours) of their time in agonistic activities. Most conflicts (53.1%, $N = 273$) were between birds that were feeding prior to the dispute. Agonistic behavior involving courting birds occurred 8.8% of the time, even though courting comprised only 0.2% of the time budget of nonbreeding mottled ducks. Remaining conflicts involved birds that were resting (16.1%), locomoting (13.6%), preening (6.6%), or alert (1.8%) prior to the dispute. Most disputes involving resting birds appeared to be over use of loafing sites on land.

Pairs and unpaired males were more likely to threaten unpaired males than other birds ($P < 0.001$) (table 5.3). Unpaired females were never observed threatening paired mottled ducks. Most agonistic interactions involving other Anatinae were with blue-winged teals (*Anas discors*), green-winged teals (*A. crecca carolinensis*), gadwalls (*A. strepera*), or pintails (*A. acuta*).

Pairs were considered dominant to unpaired birds because pairs won 94% of contests with unpaired males ($N = 57$, $P < 0.001$) and 100% ($N = 14$, $P < 0.001$) of contests with unpaired females. Unpaired males and females rarely threatened each other and won similar numbers of contests ($P > 0.05$).

Table 5.3. Total number of agonistic interactions among paired and unpaired mottled ducks and other Anatinae in Louisiana from September through February, 1980-82

Loser of contest		Winner of contest			
	Pair	Unpaired male	Unpaired female	Mallard	Other Anatinae[a]
Pair	138	4	0	3	0
Unpaired male	53	20	8	0	0
Unpaired female	14	3	3	0	0
Mallard	6	0	0		
Other Anatinae	28	7	0		

[a] *Anas acuta, A. americana, A. clypeata, A. crecca carolinensis, A. discors, A. rubripes, A. strepera, Aythya affinis, A. americana, A. collaris, Lophodytes cucullatus.*

Associations

Mottled ducks usually were observed as solitary pairs or in small flocks of fewer than 10 birds. In 35% of observations, the nearest neighbor was more than 25 m from the individual or pair under observation. The largest flock observed on natural wetlands was about 100 birds, although concentrations of several thousand were observed in rice fields.

Mottled ducks primarily associated with members of similar pair status (table 5.4). Pairs also were more likely to be near unpaired females or alone than with unpaired males ($P < 0.05$). Unpaired males were observed more often with unpaired mottled ducks than with other species of Anatinae or alone ($P < 0.05$). Unpaired females associated with unpaired males in 86% of observations involving mottled ducks in which the unpaired female was the focal bird. Unpaired females also were more likely to associate with unpaired males than to be alone or with other Anatinae ($P < 0.05$).

Table 5.4. Total number of associations among paired and unpaired mottled ducks and other Anatinae in Louisiana from September through February, 1980-82

Individual observed		Nearest neighbor					
	Pair	Unpaired male	Unpaired female	Mallard	Blue- or green- winged teal	Other Anatinae[a]	None[b]
Pair	1,591	258	213	668	620	938	2,525
Unpaired male	94	118	75	32	137	54	172
Unpaired female	15	209	20	5	27	39	78

[a] *Anas acuta, A. americana, A. clypeata, A. rubripes, A. strepera, Aythya affinis, A. americana, A. collaris, Lophodytes cucullatus.*

[b] No bird within 25 m of focal bird.

Discussion

Courting and Pair Formation

Courtship, which allows ducks to assess the status and suitability of potential mates, is important in pair bond formation and reinforcement (Heinroth 1910, McKinney 1975, Cheng et al. 1978). However, mottled ducks, like mallards (Weidmann 1956) and gadwalls (Paulus 1984a), formed many pairs prior to peak courting activity. Courtship activities comprised only 0.1% of the time-activity budget of mottled ducks in September, yet 71% of females observed were paired. Presumably, early pairs arose through associations among individuals with few highly visible social displays or through re-formation of the previous year's bonds.

Adult male and female mottled ducks may remain paired until July or early August (Paulus 1984b). Males that had completed the wing molt were observed courting flightless females in August. Two males seemingly paired to flightless females left the hens each night to fly to other areas of the marsh.

Immature mottled ducks began forming pairs at about five months of age. Ducklings were first observed in late March and April, thus these birds may have begun forming pairs in September. These data suggest that adults formed early pairs and that the pairs formed after mid-September were comprised mostly of immature mottled ducks.

Higher levels of courtship activities involving mottled ducks began in October, five months after the peak of hatching. Lebret (1961) believed that the primary function of courting displays was to reduce hostile tendencies among individuals. Thus, an important function of courting displays may have been to reduce hostile tendencies among immature mottled ducks, allowing for subsequent formation of first-time bonds. Late-season courting displays involved only paired birds. These displays may have been important in reaffirming or testing bonds, or they may have reflected the male's interest in obtaining a new mate (see McKinney and Stolen 1982).

Mottled duck displays were similar to those of mallards (Johnsgard 1960, 1965). Head-up-tail-up and Down-up displays were performed by several male mottled ducks simultaneously, and often after females performed Nod-swim. Unlike mallards and black ducks (Johnsgard 1960), mottled ducks rarely performed Down-up displays. Down-up displays comprised 25-46% of displays (excluding Introductory shakes and Preening-behind-the-wing) by mallards and black ducks but only 1% of mottled duck displays. All Down-up displays by mottled ducks took place during the period of peak courting activity in late September and October. Johnsgard (1960) also noted that Down-up displays were most common during the period of peak courting activity in mallards and black ducks.

Down-up display frequency was correlated with the number of males in courting groups in mallards and black ducks (Johnsgard 1960). The low frequency of Down-up displays among mottled ducks may have resulted from the small size of courting groups and the few males. In penned mottled ducks, Weeks (1969) found that Down-up displays comprised 18% of courtship displays, presumably because close proximity induced sufficient stimuli to elicit that display.

Over 50% of mottled duck copulations during the study occurred in November and December. Copulatory activities may have been used by females to assess the male's suitability as a breeding partner (McKinney 1975), or may have served to strengthen pair bonds. Copulatory activity probably did not result in the insemination of females until late in the season, since mottled duck males are not reproductively fertile until late December or January (Allen 1980).

The time of pair formation in Anatinae has been related to resource use and food choice (Paulus 1983), energy costs and benefits of maintaining pair bonds (Daly 1978, Afton and Sayler 1982), time of nesting (Weller 1965), and time of acquisition of the alternate plumage (Sibley 1957, Weller 1965, Wishart 1983, Paulus 1984a). Birds consuming lower quality diets and spending much of their time feeding to meet nutrient needs may enhance their ability to acquire and defend preferred foods by forming pairs (Paulus 1983). However, food choice and competition appeared less significant as factors explaining early pairing in mottled ducks as compared with other *Anas* because mottled ducks (1) selected plant seeds and animal matter (Stutzenbaker 1984), foods of high nutrient content (Sugden 1973, Paulus 1982); (2) spent less than half their time feeding (Paulus 1984b); and (3) were widely scattered over available areas, rarely interacting aggressively with other individuals. The limited time spent in defense of pair bonds or food resources (Paulus 1984b) and the moderate temperatures during winter also suggest that energy costs of defending mates were minimal when compared with the potential benefits derived from early pairing (also see Afton and Sayler 1982).

Pairing chronology probably was influenced by time of nesting and plumage characteristics. Mottled ducks formed pairs but also began nesting in Louisiana about one to three months before mallards and pintails nested on northern breeding grounds. Except for bill coloration, mottled duck hens and drakes are nearly indistinguishable. Because courtship displays seem to play a limited role in forming bonds, early pair formation and long-term bonding may be favored to reduce chances for species recognition errors. Nearly equal sex ratios, early pairing, and limited aggressive interactions among mottled ducks add evidence supporting Brown's (1982) hypothesis that nearly equal sex ratios are favored in species that maintain the longest pair bonds and have reduced sexual dimorphism and intramale competition.

Early pair formation also appeared important in preventing cross-pairing between mottled ducks and mallards. Although mallards outnumbered mottled ducks by about a 10:1 ratio in late winter, the mallards do not arrive in large numbers until November or December (H. A. Bateman, unpubl. reps., La. Dep. Wildl. and Fish., 1980-82). By the time mallards were undergoing the period of rapid pair formation, most mottled ducks had already formed pairs. Pairs associated with mallards in numbers similar to that predicted by chi-square analysis, but it was uncommon for unpaired mottled ducks to be observed near mallards. Mottled ducks and mallards courted near each other, yet they rarely participated in courting groups of the other species. Because of similarity of display types among the two species, future studies should examine factors limiting interspecific courting activities among mallards arriving before November and mottled ducks in Louisiana.

Agonistic Behavior and Associations

Mottled ducks, like other Anatinae (Alexander and Hair 1979, Jorde 1981, Hepp 1982, Paulus 1984a), spent little time in agonistic activities. Agonistic behavior was common during mottled duck courtship activities. Males and females occurred in nearly equal numbers, and individuals of both sexes competed for mates. Many birds were already paired before the peak courting activities, probably intensifying competition among individuals for remaining potential mates.

Most wintering waterfowl form large congregations. However, White and James (1978) found that mottled ducks were the least social of waterfowl species observed in Texas; in this study, mottled ducks were observed alone in over one-third of observations. Several factors may have favored reduced sociality among mottled ducks. Their nonmigratory status may have allowed greater familiarity with local habitats (Southwick 1953) and lessened their need to rely on flocking as a means of gaining information about resource conditions (Ward and Zahavi 1973) or of detecting predators (Page and Whitacre 1975, Pulliam and Millikan 1982). Also, mottled duck displays associated with territorial defense were first observed in January. Lack of associations among pairs in winter may have reflected dispersal of pairs over the marsh in anticipation of breeding activities.

LITERATURE CITED

Afton, A. D., and R. D. Sayler. 1982. Social courtship and pairbonding of common goldeneyes, *Bucephala clangula*, wintering in Minnesota. Can. Field-Nat. 96:295–300.

Alexander, W. C., and J. D. Hair. 1979. Winter foraging behavior and aggression of diving ducks in South Carolina. Proc. Southeast. Assoc. Game Fish Comm. 31:226–232.

Allen, J. A. 1980. Nesting and productivity of mottled ducks in marshlands of southwest Louisiana. M.S. Thesis, Louisiana State Univ., Baton Rouge. 87pp.

Bellrose, F. C. 1978. Ducks, geese, and swans of North America. Stackpole Books, Harrisburg, Pa. 544pp.

Brodsky, L. M., and P. J. Weatherhead. 1984. Behavioral and ecological factors contributing to American black duck-mallard hybridization. J. Wildl. Manage. 48:846–852.

Brown, D. E. 1982. Sex ratios, sexual selection and sexual dimorphism in waterfowl. Am. Birds 36:258–260.

Cheng, K. M., R. N. Shoffner, R. E. Phillips, and F. B. Lee. 1978. Mate preference in wild and domesticated (game-farm) mallards (*Anas platyrhynchos*): I. Initial preference. Anim. Behav. 26:996–1003.

Daly, M. 1978. The cost of mating. Am. Nat. 112:771–774.

Goodman, L. A. 1964. Simultaneous confidence limits for crossproduct ratios in contingency tables. J. Roy. Sta. Soc. B. 26:86–102.

Greenwood, R. J. 1977. Evaluation of a nasal marker for ducks. J. Wildl. Manage. 41:582–585.

Guidry, K. P. 1977. An analysis of organochlorine pesticide residues and food habits study of the mottled duck in Southwest Louisiana. M.S. Thesis, Louisiana State Univ., Baton Rouge. 75pp.

Heinroth, O. 1910. Beitrage zur biologie, namentlich ethologie und psychologie der Anatiden. Verh. 5. int. ornith. Kongr. Berlin, 1910, 589–702.

Hepp, G. R. 1982. Behavioral ecology of waterfowl (Anatini) wintering in coastal North Carolina. Ph.D. Thesis, North Carolina State Univ., Raleigh. 155pp.

Johnsgard, P.A. 1960. A quantitative study of sexual behavior of mallards and black ducks. Wilson Bull. 72:133–155.

———. 1965. Handbook of waterfowl behavior. Cornell Univ. Press, Ithaca, N.Y. 378pp.

Jorde, D. G. 1981. Winter and spring staging ecology of mallards in south central Nebraska. M.S. Thesis, Univ. North Dakota, Grand Forks. 116pp.

Lebret, T. 1961. The pair formation in the annual cycle of the mallard, *Anas platyrhynchos* L. Ardea 49:97–158.

McKinney, F. 1975. The evolution of duck displays. Pages 331-357 *in* G. Baerends, C. Beer, and A. Manning, eds. Function and evolution of behavior. Clarendon Press, Oxford.

———, and P. Stolen. 1982. Extra-pair-bond courtship and forced copulation among captive green-winged teal (*Anas crecca carolinensis*). Anim. Behav. 30:461–474.

Page, G., and D. F. Whitacre. 1975. Raptor predation on wintering shorebirds. Condor 77:73–83.

Paulus, S. L. 1982. Feeding ecology of gadwalls in Louisiana in winter. J. Wildl. Manage. 46:71–79.

———. 1983. Dominance relations, resource use, and pairing chronology of gadwalls in winter. Auk 100:947–952.

———. 1984a. Activity budgets of nonbreeding gadwalls in Louisiana. J. Wildl. Manage. 48:371–380.

———. 1984b. Behavioral ecology of mottled ducks in Louisiana. Ph.D. Thesis, Auburn Univ., Auburn, Al. 152pp.

Pulliam, H. R., and G. C. Millikan. 1982. Social organization in the non-reproductive season. Pages 169-197 *in* D. S. Farner, J. R. King, and K. C. Parkes, eds. Avian biology Vol. 6. Academic Press, New York.

Sibley, C. G. 1957. The evolutionary and taxonomic significance of sexual dimorphism and hybridization in birds. Condor 59:166–191.

Snedecor, G. W., and W. G. Cochran. 1976. Statistical methods. Iowa State College Press, Ames. 593pp.

Southwick, C. 1953. A system of age classification for field studies of waterfowl broods. J. Wildl. Manage. 17:1-8.

Stutzenbaker, C. D. 1984. The mottled duck, its life history, ecology, and management. Draft. Fed. Aid Proj. W-96-R. Texas Parks Wildl. Dep. 279pp.

Sugden, L. G. 1973. Metabolizable energy of wild duck foods. Can. Wildl. Serv. Prog. Notes 35. 4pp.

Ward, P., and A. Zahavi. 1973. The importance of certain assemblages of birds as "information centres" for food finding. Ibis 115:517–534.

Weeks, J. L. 1969. Breeding behavior of mottled ducks in Louisiana. M.S. Thesis, Louisiana State Univ., Baton Rouge. 79pp.

Weidmann, U. 1956. Verhaltensstudien an der Stockente (*Anas platyrhynchos* L.). I. Das aktionssytem. Z. Tierpsychol. 13:208–271.

Weller, M. W. 1965. Chronology of pair formation in some nearctic *Aythya* (Anatidae). Auk 82:227–235.

White, D. H., and D. James. 1978. Differential use of fresh water environments by wintering watefowl of coastal Texas. Wilson Bull. 90:99–111.

Wishart, R. A. 1983. Pairing chronology and mate selection in the American wigeon (*Anas americana*). Can. J. Zool. 61:1733–1743.

6

Weak Family Associations in Cackling Geese during Winter: Effects of Body Size and Food Resources on Goose Social Organization

James C. Johnson and Dennis G. Raveling

Abstract: From August 1982 to May 1984, 1,629 cackling Canada geese (*Branta canadensis minima*) were individually marked with plastic neck collars and observed throughout their nonbreeding range in California and southern Oregon. Cackling geese, which are among the world's smallest geese, exhibited weaker pair and family associations during winter than reported for larger goose species and Canada goose subspecies. Only 5% of 820 marked adults seen in fall and winter were identified as paired or in families. Cohesiveness of the 21 pairs observed varied by location and season, increasing in late winter and early spring as cackling geese moved to locations where disturbance and flock size decreased. Only 5% of 312 marked juveniles that were resighted were in family groups. We concluded that most adults were paired but frequently were not closely associated. Cackling geese are primarily grazers during the nonbreeding season, and they can maximize availability of higher-quality food by repeatedly foraging on the same area in large, densely packed flocks, keeping grasses in a low growth stage. It appears that the advantages of feeding in large, dense flocks and the necessity of maintaining high food intake levels on low-calorie grasses offset advantages of maintaining close family associations in cackling geese. We suggest that other small, grazing geese may exhibit a similar social organization during winter and that winter food supplies have powerfully influenced diversification in feeding adaptations and social organization in geese.

Social organization of geese has long been a topic of widespread interest (e.g., see Phillips 1916). Mate fidelity, pair bond endurance, and close association of

Waterfowl in Winter.© 1988 University of Minnesota. Edited by Milton W. Weller and published by the University of Minnesota Press, Minneapolis.

offspring with parents (at least for the first winter of life) are legendary (see review in Owen 1980). However, relatively few studies of wild species have been conducted with individually identifiable animals. Until recently, most investigators tended to view social organization as a relatively fixed character of a species. Now, however, there is abundant evidence of variation in social organization within a species, especially in relation to effects of variation in resources abundance or quality and predation (see Lott 1984 for review).

Casual observation of autumn and winter flocks of cackling Canada geese (*Branta canadensis minima*), the smallest of the Canada goose subspecies, revealed no obvious family-based social organization such as that documented in large-bodied subspecies (*B. c. interior* and *B. c. maxima*; see, e.g., Raveling 1969a, 1970, 1979a, 1981). Cackling geese typically form large, densely packed flocks in fall and winter. This density, along with the absence of easily identified age-specific plumages under field conditions, makes observation of discrete families difficult.

The purpose of this paper is to report results of an investigation of cackling goose social organization during the nonbreeding season resulting from observations of individually identifiable animals marked with plastic neck collars. An attempt was made to determine the proportion of families and paired adults that remained together during winter and to quantify the extent to which pairs and families remained together during various time periods and in various locations throughout the nonbreeding season. Finally, we discuss the roles of body size, predation, food resources, and disturbances in determining the social organization of goose species during winter.

This study was a cooperative project funded partly by the California Department of Fish and Game (CDFG) and assisted by the U.S. Fish and Wildlife Service (USFWS). We gratefully acknowledged the support of J. R. LeDonne, D. P. Connelly, and J. A. Beam (CDFG), the Los Banos Wildlife Area (CDFG), as well as R. C. Fields, E. H. McCollum, E. J. Collins, and the staffs at the Klamath Basin and Sacramento Valley National Wildlife Refuges. Trapping and marking on the Yukon-Kuskokwim (Y-K) Delta, Alaska, were coordinated by D. V. Derksen, R. J. King, and M. R. Petersen (USFWS) and by staff of the Yukon Delta National Wildlife Refuge. M. R. Petersen provided observations of marked pairs of geese on the breeding grounds. W. C. Reinecker (CDFG) supervised trapping operations in California and greatly assisted with many other aspects of our fieldwork.

The cooperation of many private landowners who graciously granted us access to their property and of agency personnel and interested citizens who informed us of flock locations and read neck collars was vital to the study. We are grateful to M. R. McLandress for sharing with us his observations and thoughts on the social behavior of Ross's geese (*Anser rossi*), to L. H. Fredrickson for discussion about goose use of moist soil plants, to the Winema Hunting Lodge for providing lodging space, and to L. K. Hammersly for assistance in typing. M. W. Weller, J. Lazarus, F. McKinney, M. R. McLandress, A. Dzubin, and D. W. Anderson commented on an earlier draft of the manuscript.

Study Areas and Methods

We observed cackling geese from Mid-October to early May of 1982-83 and 1983-84 throughout their fall and winter range from the Willamette Valley, Oregon (44° 45'N, 123° 00'W), south to Merced County, California (37° 06'N, 120° 47'W). Observations were made primarily in four major geographic areas: the Klamath Basin of north-central California and southern Oregon (KB); Sacramento Valley, California (SAC); San Joaquin Valley, California (SJV); and intermountain valleys in the northeast corner of California (NE), (fig. 6.1). Northern portions of the Klamath Basin used by cackling geese in late winter-early spring but not during fall (Klamath Wildlife Area and Lost River Reservoir areas near Klamath Falls, Oregon) are included in the NE region for purposes of analysis. Thus, these geographic divisions also reflect seasonal distribution of cackling geese during the nonbreeding season (see below).

All our observations of geese in KB during autumn were made on Tule Lake and Lower Klamath National Wildlife Refuges. The majority of observations in other locations were made on or within 15 km of the Sacramento refuges in SAC and in the east grasslands area near Merced refuge in SJV, and over 75% of our observations in NE during late winter were made in Big Valley (fig. 6.1).

The objectives of our study required observation of individually identifiable geese of known sex and age class. To meet this requirement, cackling geese were captured and marked with yellow plastic neck collars (3.5 cm high, 3.5 cm inside diameter) that were engraved with black, three-digit alphanumeric codes. The distance at which codes could be read was maximized by arranging one digit in a horizontal position and two in a vertical position.

Flightless brood flocks were captured by water and land drives on breeding grounds of the Y-K Delta, Alaska, during late July and early August 1982 and 1983. Cackling geese also were captured by cannon-net trapping in October and early November 1982 and 1983 at the Tule Lake refuge and during mid-January and mid-December 1983 at the Sacramento refuge.

We attempted to identify and observe as many marked cackling geese as possible throughout their fall and winter range. Flocks were located by ground and aerial reconnaisance, aided by personal contacts with agency personnel and local residents who had observed marked birds.

In densely packed flocks, we rarely had confidence in identifying pairs and families comprised of one marked individual and one or more unmarked individuals. Therefore, we noted apparent pair and family associations only when at least two family members were marked. Agonism and triumph ceremonies were

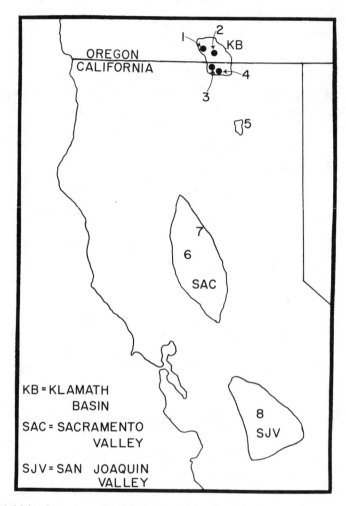

Fig. 6.1. Main winter range of cackling geese and locations of study areas: Klamath Wildlife Area (1), Lost River Reservoir (2), Lower Klamath National Wildlife Refuge (NWR) (3), Tule Lake NWR (4), Big Valley (5), Sacramento Valley NWRs (6), Chico (7), and Merced NWR (8).

conspicuously rarer in wintering flocks of cackling geese than in those of other geese (see below), so we relied almost entirely on consistent spatial associations for determining family relationships among marked geese. An adult male and adult female consistently observed near each other or moving together throughout an observation period were considered paired. Family groups were composed of at least two marked geese, including at least one juvenile, which we judged to be associated according to the same criteria.

Observations were categorized as "pair not together" when we saw pair members unaccompanied by mates known to be alive, or when we observed pair members spatially separated in the same flock. Multiple observations of a pair in the same status ("intact" or "not together") during any one day were considered one observation for purposes of analysis. When we observed pairs intact at least once and not together at least once during the same day, we categorized the data as one observation intact and one observation not together. Sightings of pair members later than the last date their mate was observed were not included in the analysis of pair cohesion.

Comparisons of the proportions of cackling goose pairs observed intact or apart between geographic areas and seasons were made using chi-square tests (Steel and Torrie 1960).

Results

A total of 1,629 cackling geese was color marked (table 6.1). By 2 May 1984, 71% of the marked individuals had been resighted a total of 6,490 times, an average of 5.6 sightings per individual. The percentages of marked adults and juveniles resighted were 73 and 68, respectively.

Table 6.1. Numbers, location, and time of neck-banding of cackling Canada geese

	Location and time of banding							
	Yukon Delta Refuge		Tule Lake Refuge		Sacramento Refuge		Totals		
Age class	Jul-Aug		Oct-Nov		Jan	Dec	Jul 1982-	Jul 1983-	
	1982	1983	1982 1983		1983	1983	Jan 1983	Dec 1983	All
Adult	74	39	435	293	173	142	682	474	1,156
Immature	150	71	81	108	17	44	248	223	471
Totals	224	110	516	401	190	186	930	697	1,627[a]

[a]Plus two of unspecified age, for a total of 1,629.

Paired Adults

Data on the numbers of marked cackling geese observed paired or in family groups during the study period are summarized in table 6.2. During two years of study, only 21 pairs of marked cackling geese were observed. Of these 21 pairs, one was first observed to be paired on the Y-K Delta breeding grounds the spring following marking. Three of these pairs consisted of a member marked during

Table 6.2. Numbers of marked cackling geese observed paired or in family groups during the fall and winter following marking, 1982-84

Mark date and location	Adults		Juveniles	
	Resighted first year	In pairs or families	Resighted first year	In families
1982, Alaska	43	8 (19%)	67	9 (13%)
1982, California	451	10 (2%)	86	0
1983, Alaska	26	4 (15%)	39	5 (13%)
1983, California	300	21 (7%)	120	1 (1%)
Total[a]	820	43 (5%)	312	15 (5%)

[a]Plus 21 adults and 6 juveniles resighted the second year following marking that were not seen the first year after marking, to yield a total of 841 adults and 318 juveniles used to calculate proportions resighted.

winter 1982-83 and a member marked during winter 1983-84. These 42 individuals represented 5% of all adults resighted and 7.8% of 538 adults resighted at least three times. Individuals of 19 of these 21 pairs (90%) were observed unaccompanied by their mate at least once during the study period.

Cackling geese arrived in mid-October in KB, where they fed in large flocks in harvested barley fields and emergent winter wheat. During this fall migration period, members of 18 pairs were observed 99 times (table 6.3). Cackling geese left KB for SAC and SJV throughout November and early December. The proportion of observations that were of intact pairs was greater in SAC than in KB ($P<0.001$) and greater in SJV than in KB ($P<0.001$) or in SAC ($P<0.05$). However, 14 of the 18 SJV sightings of intact pairs were of one particular pair. If these 14 observations are excluded from the analysis, the remaining six pairs were observed intact four times and not together twice, a proportion still greater than that in KB ($P<0.001$) but not significantly different than that in SAC.

Movement of cackling geese to the NE region (fig. 6.1) began in late January, and numbers peaked there in April. Pairs were observed intact during 80% of the sightings in NE, which was a higher proportion of intact observations than we observed in either KB ($P<0.001$) or SAC ($P<0.05$) but not significantly different from SJV. Strong pair behavior of unmarked geese (but not family association with offspring) was noted in Cook Inlet, Alaska, on 4-9 May 1982 immediately before their arrival on Y-K Delta nesting areas (D. G. Raveling and D. E. Timm, unpubl. data).

Pair cohesiveness varied with season as well as location, although seasonal distribution was highly dependent on geographic area. From mid-October to mid-January (hunting season), we observed 13 of 21 pairs (62%) intact at least once and 19 (90%) separated at least once. Of 125 observations of marked pairs during this time period, 24 (19%) were of intact pairs and 101 (81%) were of lone pair

Table 6.3. Variation in unity of 21 marked cackling goose pairs by location and season, October 1982 through May 1984

Location[a]	Time period	Pairs observed	Total observations	Observations of intact pairs	Observations of pair members not together
KB	Oct-Dec	18	99	13 (13%)	86 (87%)
SAC	Nov-Feb	14	28	14 (50%)	14 (50%)
SJV	Dec-Mar	7	22	18 (82%)[b]	4 (18%)[b]
NE	Mar-May	10	35	28 (80%)	7 (20%)

[a] KB = Klamath Basin, Oregon and California; SAC = Sacramento Valley, California; SJV = San Joaquin Valley, California; and NE = northeast corner of California.

[b] Fourteen of 18 observations of intact pairs and 2 of 4 observations of pairs not together were of one pair over a four-week period, which weights the sample. Excluding observations of this pair, 4 of 6 observations were of intact pairs.

members. After mid-January, 16 pairs were observed a total of 73 times. All 16 pairs were observed together at least once, and six (38%) were observed separated at least once. Ten observations (14%) were of lone pair members and 63 (86%) were of intact pairs. The difference in the frequency of pair cohesiveness between hunting and posthunting seasons was significant ($P < 0.001$).

During 1983-84, we observed five of the eight pairs we observed during 1982-83; four of these pairs were observed intact at least once, whereas one pair was never observed together during 1983-84. One of these pairs was also seen together on the Y-K Delta during the 1984 breeding season (M. R. Petersen, pers. commun.). A sixth pair observed in 1982-83 later was seen intact on the Alaska Peninsula during 13-18 October 1984 (J. S. Sedinger, pers. commun.).

Family Groups

During the entire study, we observed only eight family groups of marked cackling geese, containing 25 marked individuals (table 6.4). Only 5% of 312 marked juveniles observed during the fall and winter following marking were judged to be in families (table 6.2). These few marked families exhibited various degrees of cohesiveness during fall (table 6.5), but they were never observed together later than mid-December in either year.

One observation of group C illustrated the variable unity exhibited by cackling goose families. At 0744 on 8 November 1982, the adult male was observed landing at the edge of a flock feeding on winter wheat at the Tule Lake refuge. He began foraging immediately. One minute later, the three juvenile females of group C were observed foraging within 2 m of the adult. All four were observed together until 0803, when the entire flock took flight. They landed about a minute later in the same field from which they had just flown. At 0807, the

Table 6.4. Composition of marked cackling goose family groups observed during fall and winter, 1982-83 and 1983-84

| Group | Date and location marked | Number of marked geese | Age and sex of marked geese | | | |
			Adult male	Adult female	Juvenile male	Juvenile female
A	1982, Alaska	4	1		1	2
B	1982, Alaska	2		1		1
C	1982, Alaska	5	1		1	3
D	1982, Alaska	2		1	1	
E	1983, Alaska	3		1		2
F	1983, Alaska	3		1		2
G[a]	1983, Alaska	3	1	1		1
H[a]	1983, Klamath Basin	3	1	1		1

[a] Also included in observations of marked pairs of adults.

adult male was observed foraging alone, and 10 minutes later the three juveniles were observed together 25 m from the adult. At 0843, a golden eagle (*Aquila chrysaetos*) flushed the entire flock, which again landed in the same field. At 0846, all four family members were observed together, apparently having reunited during takeoff or while the flock was milling about over the field. We stopped observing the group at 0850. At 1120, when observation was resumed, the three juveniles were together at the flock edge, 40 m from the adult male.

In addition to the eight marked families, a family consisting of only one marked

Table 6.5. Observations of marked cackling goose family groups during the fall and winter following marking

Group[a]	All together	At least two together	Lone individuals
A	1	4	8
B	3	0	0
C	4[b]	3	0
D	2	0	4
E	1	0	7
F	1	0	9
G	1	0	10
H	3	1	8

[a] Group composition shown in Table 6.4.
[b] Juvenile male only observed once.

individual was observed extensively on 29 February and 1 March 1984 in SJV. The marked juvenile female was consistently accompanied by a leg-banded adult female, an unmarked adult male, and a goose of undetermined age and sex. Identity of age and sex of the unmarked pair was based on their size, behavior, and plumage. The marked juvenile female was never observed apart from the two adults during three hours of observation involving seven separate time periods. This was the only known instance of a marked juvenile cackling goose associated with adults later than mid-December.

During fall and winter 1983-84, we observed five yearling females that were members of family groups A and C in fall 1982 when they were juveniles. None of the five was ever observed near their marked siblings or parents during the 17 times they were seen in 1983-84.

Discussion

It is generally believed that all geese maintain family groups throughout the nonbreeding season. This evidence is largely based on observation of captives, but a few studies of marked, wild birds have confirmed this general conclusion. Sherwood (1967) demonstrated that marked giant Canada goose (*B. c. maxima*) families departing breeding grounds in autumn often returned intact the following spring. By using radiotelemetry, Raveling (1969a) quantified family cohesiveness in daily activities of *B. c. interior* throughout the winter where they were relatively less disturbed than at many other locations. He observed families intact 96% of the time, a remarkable degree of family unity. Pairs and families also were easily identified in a study of neck-banded giant Canada geese during autumn and winter, and 59% ($N = 140$) of yearlings rejoined parents and/or siblings (Raveling 1979a, 1981). Prevett and MacInnes (1980) observed families of lesser snow geese (*Anser caerulescens caerulescens*) intact 55% of the time on fall staging areas in the north-central United States and 95% of the time on their Gulf of Mexico coastal wintering grounds. Family groups of marked Pacific white-fronted geese (*Anser albifrons frontalis*) have also been observed intact throughout the nonbreeding season (C. R. Ely, unpubl. data).

The remarkably small number of marked cackling goose pairs and families observed in relation to the large sample marked indicates that most cackling goose pairs and families were not closely associated during fall and winter. What accounts for the low incidence of pairs and families observed and the frequent separation of the few cackling geese identified in such associations compared with other subspecies of Canada goose and other species? Weak family associations could have conceivably resulted from the study methods used, disturbances, or habitat alteration. However, they may be a long-term result of natural selection mediated by ecological factors such as food resources and predation.

Effects of Capture Methods, Disturbance, and Alteration of Roost Areas

Capture Methods. Capture methods may have separated pairs and families so that not all members of pairs and families were marked. However, banding drives on Y-K Delta breeding grounds were generally believed successful in capturing breeding adults with broods (and not nonbreeding, yearling geese) and few geese were believed to have escaped capture, although this was difficult to evaluate (M. R. Petersen, pers. commun.). Sex ratios of adults captured on the Y-K Delta were close to unity (1:0.97 in 1982, 1:0.86 in 1983). Only 15% of adults resighted were members of a marked pair.

Large cannon-net catches often do not capture all family members (Raveling 1966), but we believe that if pairs and families were intact during fall and early winter, we would have observed many more such associations than we did. Yearling geese, which were unlikely to be paired (see Hanson 1962; Raveling 1969a, 1981), were not identified in most captures. However, they would be unlikely to make up more than 10-15% of autumn captures (based on average age structure and survival rates; Raveling, unpubl. data). This relatively small number of yearlings marked as adults means that the proportion of true adult geese maintaining pair associations was slightly higher than the 5% indicated in table 6.2. In addition, some collar loss occurred during the study: responses to questionnaires sent to hunters who reported shooting banded cackling geese during the 1982-83 and 1983-84 hunting seasons indicated that up to 8% of the geese lost their collars within a few months after banding (Raveling et al. 1985). Neither of these biases would result in 95% of adults being paired to an unmarked mate.

We do not suggest that 95% of adults in autumn were not paired, but only that they rarely were close enough together to be captured at the same time. The frequent separation of even those pairs in which both members were marked, especially in the KB (table 6.3), supports this interpretation. We conclude that most adults probably were paired but that we were unable to identify these associations because only one member was marked; or, when both were marked, they were frequently not closely associated.

Disturbances. The effect of disturbances certainly contributed to the frequency of separation of pairs and families. Although associations of pairs were more frequent after the hunting season, we think that hunting per se was less important as a cause of disturbance resulting in weak pair and family associations than were other factors. About 70-75% of the cackling goose population congregated at one time at the Tule Lake refuge in autumn (Johnson and Raveling 1983, 1984). Several times per day, cackling geese took flight in milling, fast-moving flocks in response to disturbances by eagles (*Aquila chrysaetos* and *Haliaeetus leucocephalus*), coyotes (*Canis latrans*), airplanes, and other human activity. We were impressed with how difficult it must have been for individual geese to remain in immediate proximity to one another. Although related birds were rarely next to each other, they commonly would be in the same large flock, which tended to remain intact during daily activities.

Alteration of Roost Areas. Another factor that probably contributed to difficulty in cackling geese maintaining close pair and family unity in KB was the lack of natural lakeshore roost sites. Tule Lake was surrounded by diked levee roads or heavy emergent vegetation, and geese roosted mostly in large flocks on open water rather than close to and on shore during day as observed elsewhere (in the Central Valley of California and on bays in Alaska during migration). Traditional use of roost sites was a major mechanism of reunification of pair and family members of *B. c. interior* that were temporarily separated (Raveling 1969b).

Once cackling geese migrated south from KB, they spread out in smaller flocks (typically 200 to 2,500 birds each) in several locations in the Central Valley of California. Many roost sites were in natural, flooded depressions in grasslands, and disturbances, although still common, were less frequent than in KB. Here, pair cohesiveness was markedly greater than in the KB (table 6.3), even though the hunting season was often still in progress.

Thus, though we believe that most adults were paired during winter and that some pairs attempted to remain together, especially in late winter, the majority of cackling geese exhibited weak pair and family associations. The low frequency of marked pairs can be partly attributed to effects of capture methods, and weak pair and family associations were affected by disturbances and altered roost sites. However, we conclude that these factors are insufficient to explain our results and that weak family association in cackling geese during winter is a real phenomenon of ecological significance.

Effects of Body Size, Predation, and Food Resources

Differences in social organization of vertebrates have been attributed to differences in ecological factors, especially food resources and predation (Crook 1965, Wilson 1975). These factors may even result in variation in social systems within a species (Lott 1984). Proposed advantages to geese of maintaining family unity during the nonbreeding season include increased feeding time for juveniles and increased access to food and other resources because families are dominant over other groups (Jenkins 1944, Boyd 1953, Hanson 1953, Raveling 1970, Owen 1980). We suggest that differences in body size, gregariousness in relation to foraging behavior, food quality, and predation interact to negate these advantages, resulting in looser social organization in wintering cackling geese than in most other goose species and subspecies reported on to date.

Body Size and Predation. Cackling geese are much smaller than the North American geese that exhibit more cohesive pair and family relationships during winter (table 6.6). Smaller body size may make cackling geese susceptible to a larger variety of predators than other geese, thus increasing predator pressure on

Table 6.6. Average body weight in winter and culmen length of geese for which social organization has been determined in winter with individually identifiable animals

Species or subspecies	Data source	Adult male		Adult female	
		Body weight (kg)	Culmen (mm)	Body weight (kg)	Culmen (mm)
Branta canadensis minima	Raveling 1978	1.5	29	1.2	27
B. c. interior	Hanson 1965, Raveling 1968	4.2	56	3.6	50
B. c. maxima	Hanson 1965	5.7	61	5.0	57
Anser rossi	Trauger et al. 1971, McLandress 1983a	1.5	42[a]	1.3	39[a]
Anser caerulescens caerulescens	Flickinger and Bolen 1979, McLandress 1983a	2.1-2.3	58	2.0	56
Anser albifrons frontalis	Krogman 1979	2.2	50	2.0	48

[a]Feathers at base of bills are often obscured by caruncles.

them. Individual birds may reduce their risk of predation by joining flocks, thereby increasing the chances of early predator detection and of avoiding capture in the event of an attack (Hamilton 1971, Pulliam 1973, Lazarus 1978, Pulliam and Caraco 1984).

All geese form flocks during the nonbreeding season, but in our experience in North America only the Ross's goose tolerates the dense packing commonly observed in cackling geese (fig. 6.2). Notably, the Ross's goose is comparable in body size to the cackling goose (table 6.6). We suggest that higher predator pressure on cackling geese has favored formation of larger, denser flocks than are common in other geese. We do not suggest, however, that the antipredator functions served by dense flocking are the sole explanation or benefit derived, nor does this behavior by itself account for weak pair and family bonds.

Diet, Food Defensibility, and Foraging Time. Feeding behavior and quality of foods in relation to their defensibility also help explain variation in family unity in geese during winter. The cackling goose lies at or near the extreme of feeding specializations of geese, being nearly a pure grazer in winter. Cackling geese historically wintered in natural grasslands of California's Central Valley, where they used their short bills to feed rapidly and efficiently on very short, delicate grasses and forbs. They are still primarily grazers, although they do feed some on waste grains in KB and SAC.

Larger subspecies of Canada geese are believed to have used their long bills and necks for stripping grass and sedge seed heads (Hanson 1965), and they probably also made extensive use of moist soil seeds (e.g., smartweeds—*Polygonum* spp.)

Fig. 6.2. Dense packing of cackling geese grazing on winter wheat in California (A) compared with wider spacing of *Branta canadensis interior* grazing on winter wheat in Illinois (B).

and starchy plants and parts (e.g., *Sagittaria* spp.) before their wintering grounds were mostly converted to agricultural lands. They engage in high levels of aggressive behavior when feeding, but noticeably less so when grazing than when feeding on millet (*Echinochloa* spp.) seeds, a moist soil plant (Raveling 1970). Snow geese have heavy, strong bills well adapted for grubbing roots of the marsh plants upon which they feed where available, and white-fronted geese and medium-sized Canada geese have intermediate bills that were probably used for grubbing and seed-stripping as well as for grazing (Owen 1980).

Seeds and roots have a much higher calorie content per unit weight than grass and forb leaves (Cummins and Wuycheck 1971), and they occur in more concentrated patches. Geese feeding on concentrated food patches might well benefit from defending a patch against intruders, enabling them to meet their nutritional needs in a relatively short amount of time. On the other hand, grazing geese would benefit little from defending a patch of growing grass, since grass has low caloric content and is fairly uniformly and abundantly distributed throughout grassland areas. Grazing geese must forage longer and move almost constantly to harvest sufficient amounts of grass to meet their nutritional demands.

Raveling (1979b) calculated that cackling geese needed to forage 8-9 hours per day on grass or 5-5.5 hours per day on a mixture of grain and grass to meet their energy requirements during winter (based on gut contents of collected birds that had been feeding but would have also spent time in other activities). Cackling geese spent the following amounts of time in feed fields in the following habitats and locations (estimates are of time spent in feeding locations, not actual time spent feeding): KB—alternating between waste grain (barley) and winter wheat, 5 hours per day during October-November; SAC—alternating between harvested rice and pasture grasses, all day or 10-10.5 hours per day during November-January; SJV—in grasslands, all day or 10-12.5 hours per day during December-March. We do not have quantifiable data on nocturnal activity.

In comparison to cackling geese, *B. c. interior* in Illinois were in feeding areas (corn and soybean fields) 3.5-4 hours per day during winter (Raveling et al. 1972), whereas lesser snow geese fed 3.1 hours per day on corn during fall migration in Iowa (Frederick and Klaas 1982) and 7.2 hours per day on *Scirpus* roots during winter in British Columbia, Canada (Burton and Hudson 1978). Grazing European white-fronted geese (*A. a. albifrons*) and barnacle geese (*B. leucopsis*) foraged for 80-90% of available daylight hours in winter (Owen 1972, Ebbinge et al. 1975). Clearly, grazing requires a great deal more time for feeding by geese of all sizes than when they are using seeds.

If the costs of searching for partners and the alertness and aggression needed to maintain family cohesiveness exceed the benefits of that cohesion, then one would not expect strong family associations. Cackling goose pairs are pugnacious and highly aggressive toward conspecifics during the nesting season. However, they (and Ross's geese, according to McLandress 1983b) are the most sociable geese we have observed in winter (fig. 6.2). Occasional pecks at other geese occurred, but intense threatening postures, chases, and fights commonly observed in larger-bodied Canada geese (e.g., see Raveling 1970), snow geese, and white-fronted geese (see Jenkins 1944, Boyd 1953) were virtually nonexistent.

Costs of aggressive behavior include risk of injury, less time for feeding, and distraction from vigilance against predators. Cackling geese are more of an exploitative competitor (Morse 1980) than are larger geese, in which mates and offspring obtain food and space defended by the gander. There is little benefit to cackling goose family members to strive to constantly remain together. Rather, it is to their benefit to avoid aggression and maximize time spent foraging. Pairs will usually be in the same flock and able to reunify.

Flocking functions to lower the amount of time an individual goose spends alert and increases time available for feeding (e.g., see Lazarus 1978). Flocks of geese also may serve a function as an information center (Ward and Zahavi 1973), relating cues about food as well as predators (Drent and Swierstra 1977, Ydenberg et al. 1983). But, as with the antipredator functions noted above, these factors seem to operate to some degree in all goose species, regardless of food type, and do not by themselves explain the extreme density of cackling goose flocks with their attendant weak maintenance of pair and family associations.

Manipulation of Food Quality. We suggest that the extreme gregariousness of winter cackling goose flocks increases foraging efficiency by modifying vegetation structure to increase nutritive yield per bite. Several studies have demonstrated that animals that regularly graze in herds in the same area benefit from the increased nitrogen content and digestibility of graze maintained at a low growth status (see McNaughton 1984 for a recent review). Specifically, such selective repeated foraging in the same grazing areas functions to prolong the availability of higher-quality food for grazing brant (*Branta bernicla bernicla*) (Prins et al. 1980) and barnacle geese (Ydenberg and Prins 1981) during spring and for cackling geese (Sedinger and Raveling 1984) and lesser snow geese (Cargill and Jefferies 1984) in summer.

We conclude that the maintenance of extremely dense gregarious flocks of cackling geese during winter (fig. 6.2) is driven mainly by the need for these geese to exploit a widespread grass food supply by keeping it in its most nutritious, very low growth form. The time required for cackling geese to obtain needed nutrients from such delicate grasses, coupled with the small nutritional value per bite and relatively even distribution of grasses, makes it uneconomical to defend such a food supply compared with higher-energy-yielding, smaller patches of moist soil plants or tubers exploited by larger geese. Among geese, small body size may also be a prerequisite to depending solely on short graze during short winter days.

Implications for Other Geese

Our assessment of reasons why cackling geese exhibit weak pair and family relationships during winter suggests that other small-bodied, small-billed geese exhibiting extreme gregarious flocking behavior while primarily depending on grazing for their food supply may also exhibit a similar social organization in winter. Candidates would include the smallest of eastern North American Canada geese (those geese with 30- to 35-mm culmens, usually referred to as *B. c. hutchinsii*), brant, barnacle geese, the Ross's goose, possibly the lesser white-fronted goose (*Anser erythropus*, 1.8-2.0 kg and 31- to 34-mm culmen; Owen 1980), and especially the red-breasted goose (*Branta ruficollis*, 1.1-1.3 kg and 24- to 25-mm culmen; Owen 1980).

Two studies lend support to the idea that family breakup may occur more readily in small-bodied, grazing geese. Jones and Jones (1966) reported that black brant (*B. b. nigricans*) families (unmarked birds) broke up in October when the birds were highly concentrated in Izembek Bay, Alaska. This observation may have been affected by such an exceptional concentration of geese as noted by Maltby and Boyd (cited in Owen 1980, 87-88). Families of snow geese were less cohesive when at large concentration areas during autumn migration than when settled in smaller flocks on terminal wintering grounds (Prevett and MacInnes 1980), and similar observations were made during this study. On the other hand, the observations by Jones and Jones (1966) may have revealed a real and regular phenomenon of longer-lasting significance similar to the circumstances reported on here for cackling geese. Brant may be under severe pressure to optimize time spent feeding and minimize time in aggression and family maintenance when they are feeding on eelgrass (*Zostera marina*, a major food item) because of the effect of tidal rhythms in limiting feeding time.

The second study to indicate that pair and family cohesiveness in small geese is less than that of large geese is that of McLandress (1983b) on Ross's geese in California. Even though Ross's geese have a larger, more powerful bill than cackling geese (table 6.6), and they use seeds of moist soil plants and grains in autumn in migration both in Saskatchewan (Dzubin 1965) and at Tule Lake, they were thought to be primarily grazers in midwinter although they have recently adapted successfully to using rice (McLandress 1979). McLandress's observations suggest that pair and family relations are weak and very similar to that reported here for cackling geese (M. R. McLandress, pers. commun.).

Almost nothing is known of social behavior, and little information is available on food habits, of red-breasted geese and lesser white-fronts (Owen 1980) or *B. c. hutchinsii*. Individually marked (presumably colored leg-bands) barnacle goose pairs have stayed together for at least four years, and only one case of mate switching is known (Owen 1980). Barnacle geese are larger than cackling geese, and although extremely gregarious and adapted to grazing on short swards, they also feed extensively on stolens and roots of several plants and on the fleshy parts and seeds of glasswort (*Salicornia* spp.) (Owen 1980). Thus, the "threshold" in body size and the feeding specialization on grasses that may lead to weak family relations may lie below the size of these geese. However, apparently no information is published on levels of aggressive behavior or integrity of offspring with parents of barnacle geese.

Diversification in Feeding Niches and Social Behavior

A final implication of our study deals with the time period and habitat in which competition and major selective forces may have operated to produce niche specialization in geese. Owen (1976) considered that bill morphologies of geese in the British Isles were most adapted for foods outside the breeding grounds (for probing, seed stripping, and extracting roots and bulbils as well as for grazing, which nearly all geese seem to do in spring and summer). North American geese show the same pattern. This suggests that diversification of geese (even within a species such as the Canada goose) was strongly influenced by winter food supplies.

Larger geese dependent on swamps, coastal and riverine marshes, and openings in the forests probably were originally limited by winter food supplies. Concentrated patches of higher-calorie foods in these habitats would favor resource defense by the large geese. Because the dominance order of large geese is directly related to family size (Raveling 1970), family members benefit from remaining together, thereby increasing their access to defendable food and favored roosts. In contrast, small-billed grazing geese exploiting vast expanses of short winter grasses may have been limited by breeding habitat. Whether or not they were, an abundant, not easily defended winter food supply of short grasses would favor the exploitation, competition, and weak social dominance systems seen in cackling geese and expected in other small-bodied geese.

LITERATURE CITED

Boyd, H. 1953. On encounters between wild white-fronted geese in winter flocks. Behav. 5:85–129.

Burton, B. A., and R. J. Hudson. 1978. Activity budgets of lesser snow geese wintering on the Fraser River Estuary, British Columbia. Wildfowl 29:111–117.

Cargill, S. M. and R. L. Jefferies. 1984. The effects of grazing by lesser snow geese on the vegetation of a sub-arctic salt marsh. J. Appl. Ecol. 21:669–686.

Crook, J. H. 1965. The adaptive significance of avian social organizations. Symp. Zool. Soc. Lond. 14:181–218.

Cummins, K. W., and J. C. Wuycheck. 1971. Caloric equivalents for investigations in ecological energetics. Mitt. Int. Ver. Theor. Angew Limnol. 18. 158pp.

Drent, R., and P. Swierstra. 1977. Goose flocks and food finding: field experiments with barnacle geese in winter. Wildfowl 28:15–20.

Dzubin, A. 1965. A study of migrating Ross' geese in western Saskatchewan. Condor 67:511-534.

Ebbinge, B., K. Canters, and R. Drent. 1975. Foraging routines and estimated daily food intake in barnacle geese wintering in the northern Netherlands. Wildfowl 26:5-19.

Flickinger, E. L., and E. G. Bolen. 1979. Weights of lesser snow geese taken on their winter range. J. Wildl. Manage. 43:531-533.

Frederick, R. B., and E. E. Klaas. 1982. Resource use and behavior of migrating snow geese. J. Wildl. Manage. 46:601-614.

Hamilton, W. D. 1971. Geometry of the selfish herd. J. Theor. Bio. 31:295-311.

Hanson, H. C. 1953. Inter-family dominance in Canada geese. Auk 70:11-16.

──────. 1962. Characters of age, sex, and sexual maturity in Canada geese. Ill. Nat. Hist. Surv. Bio. Notes 49. 15pp.

──────. 1965. The giant Canada goose. Southern Illinois Univ. Press, Carbondale. 226pp.

Jenkins, D. W. 1944. Territory as a result of despotism and social organization in geese. Auk 61:30-47.

Johnson, J. C., and D. G. Raveling. 1983. Distribution and abundance of cackling Canada geese during winter 1982-83. Prog. Rep. to Calif. Dep. Fish Game and U.S. Fish Wildl. Serv. Univ. California, Davis. 14pp.

──────, and ──────. 1984. Distribution and abundance of cackling geese during winter 1983-84. Prog. Rep. to Calif. Dep. Fish Game and U.S. Fish Wildl. Serv. Univ. California, Davis. 18pp.

Jones, R. D., and D. M. Jones. 1966. The process of family disintegration in black brant. Wildfowl Trust Annu. Rep. 17:75-78.

Krogman, B. D. 1979. A systemic study of *Anser albifrons* in California. Pages 22-43 *in* R. L. Jarvis and J. C. Bartonek, eds. Management and biology of Pacific Flyway geese. Oregon State Univ. Book Stores, Corvallis.

Lazarus, J. 1978. Vigilance, flock size and domain of danger size in the white-fronted goose. Wildfowl 29:135-146.

Lott, D. F. 1984. Intraspecific variation in the social systems of wild vertebrates. Behav. 88:266-325.

McLandress, M. R. 1979. Status of Ross' geese in California. Pages 255-265 *in* R. L. Jarvis and J. C. Bartonek, eds. Management and biology of Pacific Flyway geese. Oregon State Univ. Book Stores, Corvallis.

──────. 1983a. Sex, age and species differences in disease mortality of Ross' and lesser snow geese in California: implications for avian cholera research. Calif. Fish Game 69:196-206.

──────. 1983b. Winning with warts? A threat posture suggests a function for caruncles in Ross' geese. Wildfowl 34:5-9.

McNaughton, S. J. 1984. Grazing lawns: animals in herds, plant form, and coevolution. Am. Nat. 124:863-886.

Morse, D. H. 1980. Behavioral mechanisms in ecology. Harvard Univ. Press, Cambridge, Mass. 383pp.

Owen, M. 1972. Some factors affecting food intake and selection in white-fronted geese. J. Anim. Ecol. 41:79-92.

──────. 1976. Factors affecting the distribution of geese in the British Isles. Wildfowl 27:143-147.

──────. 1980. Wild geese of the world. B. T. Batsford Ltd., London. 236pp.

Phillips, J. C. 1916. Two problems in the migration of waterfowl. I. Do American ducks reach the Marshall Islands? II. Behavior and makeup of the migrating flocks of Canada geese. Auk 33:22-27.

Prevett, J. P., and C. D. MacInnes. 1980. Family and other social groups in snow geese. Wildl. Monogr. 71. 46pp.

Prins, H. H. Th., R. C. Ydenberg, and R. H. Drent. 1980. The interaction of brent geese *Branta bernicla* and sea plaintain *Plantago maritima* during spring staging: field obervations and experiments. Acta Bot. Neerl. 29:585-596.

Pulliam, H. R. 1973. On the advantages of flocking. J. Theor. Bio. 38:419-422.

————, and T. Caraco. 1984. Living in groups: Is there an optimal group size? Pages 122-147 *in* J. R. Krebs and N. B. Davies, eds. Behavioural ecology: an evolutionary approach. 2nd ed. Sinauer Assoc., Sunderland, Mass.

Raveling, D. G. 1966. Factors affecting age ratios of samples of Canada geese caught with cannon-nets. J. Wildl. Manage. 30:682–691.

————. 1968. Weights of *Branta canadensis interior* during winter. J. Wildl. Manage. 32:412–414.

————. 1969a. Social classes of Canada geese in winter. J. Wildl. Manage. 33:304–318.

————. 1969b. Roost sites and flight patterns of Canada geese in winter. J. Wildl. Manage. 33:319–330.

————. 1970. Dominance relationships and agonistic behavior of Canada geese in winter. Behav. 37:291–319.

————. 1978. Morphology of the cackling Canada goose. J. Wildl. Manage. 42:897–900.

————. 1979a. Traditional use of migration and winter roost sites by Canada geese. J. Wildl. Manage. 43:229–235.

————. 1979b. The annual energy cycle of the cackling Canada goose. Pages 81-93 *in* R. J. Jarvis and J. C. Bartonek, eds. Management and biology of Pacific Flyway geese. Oregon State Univ. Book Stores, Corvallis.

————. 1981. Survival, experience, and age in relation to breeding success of Canada geese. J. Wildl. Manage. 45:817–829.

————, T. W. Aldrich, J. G. Silveira, and J. C. Johnson. 1985. Distribution and abundance of cackling Canada geese during winters 1982-83 through 1984-85 and their survival during 1982-83 and 1983-84. Prog. Rep. to U.S. Fish Wildl. Serv. and Calif. Dep. Fish Game. Univ. California, Davis. 40pp.

————, W. E. Crews, and W. D. Klimstra. 1972. Activity patterns of Canada geese in winter. Wilson Bull. 84:278–295.

Sedinger, J. S., and D. G. Raveling. 1984. Dietary selectivity in relation to availability and quality of food for goslings of cackling geese. Auk 101:295–306.

Sherwood, G. A. 1967. Behavior of family groups of Canada geese. Trans. N. Am. Wildl. Nat. Resour. Conf. 32:340–355.

Steel, R. G. D., and J. H. Torrie. 1960. Principles and procedures of statistics. McGraw-Hill, New York. 481pp.

Trauger, D. L., A. Dzubin, and J. P. Ryder. 1971. White geese intermediate between Ross' geese and lesser snow geese. Auk 88:856–875.

Ward, P., and A. Zahavi. 1973. The importance of certain assemblages of birds as "information-centres" for food-finding. Ibis 115:517–534.

Wilson, E. O. 1975. Sociobiology: the new synthesis. Belknap Press of Harvard Univ. Press, Cambridge, Mass. 697pp.

Ydenberg, R. C., and H. H. T. Prins. 1981. Spring grazing and the manipulation of food quality by barnacle geese. J. Appl. Ecol. 18:443–454.

————, ————, and J. Vandijk. 1983. The post-roost gatherings of wintering barnacle geese: information centres? Ardea 71:125–131.

7

Formation of Feeding Flocks during Winter by Dusky and Taverner's Canada Geese in Oregon

Loree H. Havel and Robert L. Jarvis

Abstract: Behavioral and environmental variables influencing the formation of flocks of dusky (*Branta canadensis occidentalis* [Baird]) and of Taverner's Canada geese (*B. c. taverneri* Delacour) were studied on Sauvie Island, Oregon, during winter (Oct-Apr) 1981-82. Geese occurred most frequently (80%) in skeins segregated according to subspecies affinity (at least 91% dusky or at least 90% Taverner's). In contrast, subspecies composition of flocks of feeding geese (feeding flocks) was frequently (73%) mixed (11-90% dusky/10-89% Taverner's). During the waterfowl hunting season, skeins composed of at least 90% Taverner's were larger, started approach and landing behaviors at higher elevations, circled more times before landing, and took a longer time to land than skeins composed of at least 91% dusky Canada geese ($P < 0.001$, all variables). On the average, skeins of Taverner's approached larger fields that contained more geese than did skeins of dusky Canada geese ($P < 0.001$, both variables). Taverner's frequented fields on privately owned land, located farther from a roost lake, whereas dusky Canada geese were more often associated with fields on a state wildlife management area, close to a roost lake. Taverner's Canada geese exhibited significant "seasonal" changes in patterns of behavior and use of fields from waterfowl hunting season to posthunting season. No significant changes were noted for dusky Canada geese between these seasons. We hypothesize that the observed differences between dusky and Taverner's Canada geese (within and between seasons) contributed to differential hunting vulnerability of these subspecies.

Dusky and Taverner's Canada geese are two of six subspecies of Canada geese known to winter in western Oregon (Bellrose 1976, 141-164). Dusky Canada geese comprised an estimated 95% of the Canada geese wintering in the Willamette Valley of Oregon in 1969-70 (C. F. Zeillemaker, unpubl. rep., Wm. L. Finley National Wildlife Refuge, Oregon, 1974). During winter 1975-76, nearly 45% of the 41,600 geese wintering along the lower Columbia River and in the Willamette Valley were Taverner's; by 1983-84, subspecies composition of the 69,000 wintering geese was approximately 15% dusky and 85% Taverner's Canada geese (Jarvis and Cornely 1987).

Hunting regulations, hunting techniques, and refuge management in western Oregon have been based primarily on information derived from research on dusky Canada geese (Timm et al. 1979). However, such management may be inadequate or inappropriate for the mixed flock of wintering geese (Simpson and Jarvis 1979, Timm et al. 1979), especially considering the declining population of dusky and increasing Taverner's Canada geese (Jarvis and Cornely 1987).

Our objectives were to determine similarities and differences in behavior and habitat use by dusky and Taverner's Canada geese where these subspecies winter in mixed aggregations. In particular, we examined flocking behavior to identify and explain factors that might account for the differential hunting vulnerability reported for dusky and Taverner's Canada geese (Simpson and Jarvis 1979).

We gratefully acknowledge the cooperation of R. L. Johnson, manager, Sauvie Island Wildlife Area, and private land owners on Sauvie Island, Oregon. Facilities, supplies, and equipment for this study were in part provided by the Oregon Department of Fish and Wildlife and by Oregon State University. Funds for computer-assisted data analysis were furnished by Milne Computer Center, Oregon State University. Many reviewers provided suggestions on the manuscript, including B. E. Coblentz, W. Hohenboken, and D. G. Raveling.

Study Area

Fieldwork was conducted from 15 October 1981 through 18 April 1982 on Sauvie Island at the confluence of the Willamette and Columbia Rivers, 40 km northwest of Portland (fig. 7.1). The area consists of about 5,500 ha of privately owned crop and pasture land and 4,900 ha managed as a wildlife area by the Oregon Department of Fish and Wildlife. A substantial portion of Sauvie Island is seasonally farmed and flooded to attract waterfowl. Public hunting on state-owned land occurred on alternate days from mid-October 1981 through mid-January 1982, whereas hunt schedules for privately owned land varied from daily (rare) to weekend-only hunts during this same time period. An unhunted, 1,300-ha lake (Sturgeon Lake; fig. 7.1) served as a sanctuary and roost for waterfowl. Total numbers of dusky Canada geese in the study area declined from January (8,200) through April (1,300), and total numbers of Taverner's increased (January, 8,300; April, 13,400).

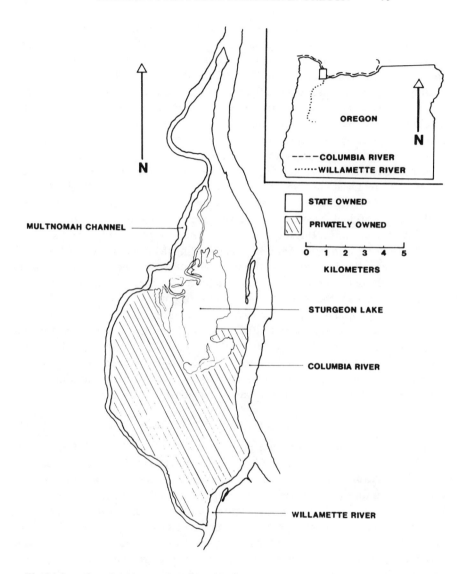

Fig. 7.1. Location of study area (inset) and distribution of land ownership on Sauvie Island.

Methods

Data Collection

We observed goose flocks from a vehicle or blind located in or near feeding fields (fields where geese fed). Observation periods generally spanned the time between sunrise and two hours after sunrise. Periodically, observations were conducted throughout daylight hours, and regular qualitative observations were made at night.

We collected data on numbers of geese, subspecies identity, and field approach and landing behaviors as feeding flocks formed in fields. Characteristics of the feeding fields that skeins (flocks of flying geese) approached or where geese already fed were measured or noted. Weather conditions and time of day were recorded for all observations. We made an estimate of approach elevation and started to time and count circles when at least one skein member terminated flapping flight, "set" its wings in a glide, and began to lose altitude.

Subspecies were identified on the basis of relative size and plumage differences as described by Delacour (1951; 1954, 167-172) and Johnson et al. (1979, 57). Data were not recorded when light level, heavy rain, fog, or distance from the birds prohibited confident classification of subspecies. On several occasions, a few cackling (*B. c. minima* Ridgway), lesser (*B. c. parvipes* [Cassin]), or Great Basin Canada geese (*B. c. moffitti* Aldrich) joined feeding flocks of dusky and Taverner's Canada geese. We assumed that the influence of these other subspecies on the formation of flocks of dusky and Taverner's Canada geese was insignificant and thus did not include them in our observations or counts.

The number and subspecies composition of geese feeding in a field were recorded as census scan samples (Altmann 1974, 259) at 15-minute intervals during an observation period. We measured field size, distance to Sturgeon Lake, and distance to the nearest potential "danger," which was defined as a feature in or near a feeding field that could provide cover for a predator (e.g., hunting blinds, fencerows, ditches, farm equipment, and roadsides).

Data Treatment and Analysis

Analyses were conducted on data partitioned by "season," where HUNT = 15 October 1981 through 17 January 1982 and NOHUNT = 18 January through 18 April 1982. Within each season, data were sorted into categories according to the subspecies composition of geese in feeding flocks and in skeins. We designated groups (feeding flocks or skeins) composed of 0-10% dusky Canada geese (i.e., 90-100% Taverner's) as groups of Taverner's and groups composed of 91-100% dusky (0-9% Taverner's) as groups of dusky Canada geese. Flock and skein subspecies compositions between these points were designated as groups of mixed Taverner's (11-50% dusky/50-89% Taverner's) or as groups of mixed dusky Canada geese (51-90%/10-49% Taverner's).

The nature of associations between subspecies compositions of feeding flocks and skeins and other study variables was determined through analyses of contingency tables. Chi-squared tests of independence or Kendall's Tau C statistics (Nie et al. 1975, 223–228) were used as measures of the strength and statistical significance of associations between and among variables. We compared the means for selected variables associated with behavior and use of field by dusky and Taverner's Canada geese with unpaired t-tests (Nie et al. 1975, 267–274).

Results

Subspecies Composition of Feeding Flocks and Skeins

While commuting from the roost lake to feeding fields, or from one field to another, subspecies occurred most frequently in segregated skeins. We classified about 80% of the skeins observed during both HUNT (N = 893) and NOHUNT (N = 483) as predominantly one subspecies or the other. In contrast to skeins, subspecies composition of feeding flocks was frequently mixed (72% during HUNT [N = 819] and 74% during NOHUNT [N = 423]).

Formation of Feeding Flocks and Characteristics of Feeding Fields

During HUNT, feeding flocks of Taverner's and mixed Taverner's Canada geese were associated with large feeding flocks (fig. 7.2), large fields (fig. 7.3), and fields

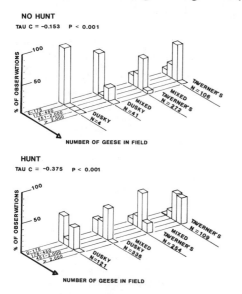

Fig. 7.2. Frequency distribution of feeding flocks of Canada geese according to subspecies composition during (HUNT) and after (NOHUNT) waterfowl hunting season on Sauvie Island, Oregon, 1981-82, for four size categories of number of geese in field. Dusky = flocks of 91-100% dusky, mixed dusky = 51-90% dusky, mixed Taverner's = 11-50% dusky, and Taverner's = 0-10% dusky.

located far from Sturgeon Lake (fig. 7.4) more frequently than expected ($P <$ 0.001, all variables). Conversely, feeding flocks of dusky and mixed dusky Canada geese were associated with small feeding flocks, small fields, and fields located close to Sturgeon Lake (figs. 7.2-7.4) more frequently than expected ($P < 0.001$, all variables). During NOHUNT, the negative relationship between subspecies composition (as percent dusky) and the number of geese in the field diminished (Tau C

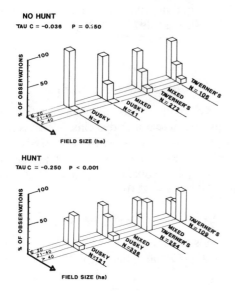

Fig. 7.3. Frequency distribution of
feeding flocks of Canada geese
according to subspecies composition
during (HUNT) and after (NOHUNT)
waterfowl hunting season on Sauvie
Island, Oregon, 1981-82, for three size
categories of fields. Dusky = flocks of
91-100% dusky, mixed dusky = 51-90%
dusky, mixed Taverner's = 11-50%
dusky, and Taverner's = 0-10% dusky.

for HUNT = −0.375, Tau C for NOHUNT = −0.153; fig. 7.2). After hunting ceased, all
feeding flocks were observed most frequently in small fields (63%, *N* = 423, ≤ 20
ha), close to Sturgeon Lake (87%, *N* = 377, ≤ 2,000 m; figs. 7.3 and 7.4). Distance to
danger was not strongly associated with subspecies composition of feeding flocks
during HUNT (Tau C for HUNT = −0.058). Following hunting, all feeding flocks

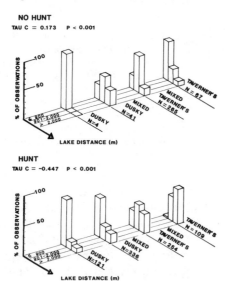

Fig. 7.4. Frequency distribution of
feeding flocks of Canada geese
according to subspecies composition
during (HUNT) and after (NOHUNT)
waterfowl hunting season on Sauvie
Island, Oregon, 1981-82, for three
categories of distance from Sturgeon
Lake. Dusky = flocks of 91-100%
dusky, mixed dusky = 51-90% dusky,
mixed Taverner's = 11-50% dusky, and
Taverner's = 0-10%.

except those composed of 91-100% dusky Canada geese (N = 4) frequented fields close to danger (70%, N = 419, $\leq$ 200 m; fig. 7.5).

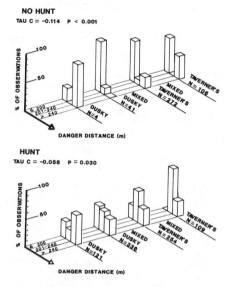

Fig. 7.5. Frequency distribution of feeding flocks of Canada geese according to subspecies composition during (HUNT) and after (NOHUNT) waterfowl hunting season on Sauvie Island, Oregon, 1981-82, for three categories of distance from danger. Dusky = flocks of 91-100% dusky, mixed dusky = 51-90% dusky, mixed Taverner's = 11-50% dusky, and Taverner's = 0-10% dusky.

During HUNT, about 2% (N = 109) of the feeding flocks of Taverner's and 80% (N = 121) of the flocks of dusky Canada geese were observed in fields on state-owned land. Following hunting, all feeding flocks of geese except those composed of 91-100% dusky Canada geese (N = 4) were observed most frequently (91%, N = 419) in fields on privately owned land.

On the average, skeins of Taverner's during HUNT were larger, started their feeding field approach from higher elevations, circled more times before landing, and took longer to land than skeins of dusky Canada geese ($P < 0.001$, all variables; table 7.1). Skeins of Taverner's approached feeding fields containing a larger mean number of geese, with a larger mean field size, than did skeins of dusky Canada geese ($P < 0.001$, both variables; table 7.1). Skeins of dusky Canada geese approached feeding flocks numerically dominated by their own subspecies (HUNT $\bar{x}$ = 72% dusky, N = 353), whereas skeins of Taverner's approached feeding flocks numerically dominated by Taverner's (Hunt $\bar{x}$ = 64% Taverner's, N = 303; $P \leq$ 0.001; table 7.1).

Following the hunting season, differences between subspecies were similar to those noted for the hunting season, but the magnitude of these differences was less (table 7.1). This reduction in the differences between subspecies from HUNT to NOHUNT resulted primarily from the reduction of mean values for the variables associated with skeins of Taverner's. The means for the number and subspecies composition of geese in a field, approach elevation, time interval from

Table 7.1. Means for selected variables associated with skeins of dusky (91-100% dusky) and Taverner's (90-100% Taverner's) Canada geese observed during (HUNT) and after (NOHUNT) waterfowl hunting season on Sauvie Island, Oregon, 1981-82

| Variable | Subspecies | HUNT | | | | NOHUNT | | | | |
		N	$\bar{x}$	SD	P^a	N	$\bar{x}$	SD	P^a	P^b
Geese in field	Taverner's	309	1,263	1,612	<0.001	279	681	591	0.146	<0.001
(no.)	Dusky	359	525	572		76	608	742		0.273
Approach elevation	Taverner's	324	121	83	<0.001	220	84	39	0.039	<0.001
(m)	Dusky	361	65	56		58	70	35		0.532
Geese	Taverner's	331	33	121	<0.001	319	20	45	0.002	0.061
in skein (no.)	Dusky	382	11	17		88	7	6		0.022
Circles	Taverner's	324	1.6	1.7	<0.001	220	1.5	1.3	0.001	0.610
(no.)	Dusky	361	0.8	1.0		58	1.0	0.8		0.241
Time interval to	Taverner's	324	84.5	64.4	<0.001	220	50.0	34.4	0.002	<0.001
first landing (sec)	Dusky	361	45.6	39.2		58	37.4	19.8		0.119
Time interval to	Taverner's	323	96.7	72.6	<0.001	220	63.6	46.9	<0.001	<0.001
last landing (sec)	Dusky	361	47.6	41.6		58	39.5	22.7		0.144
Field size	Taverner's	331	36.9	22.0	<0.001	319	21.9	18.3	0.032	<0.001
(ha)	Dusky	382	29.0	19.3		88	17.6	12.1		<0.001
Subspecies	Taverner's	303	35.5	27.6	<0.001	279	25.2	20.5	<0.001	<0.001
composition of	Dusky	353	72.5	24.3		76	35.8	18.0		<0.001
geese in field										
(% dusky)										

[a]Comparison between subspecies within each season.
[b]Comparison between seasons within each subspecies.

approach to landing, and field size associated with skeins of Taverner's were significantly smaller during NOHUNT than during HUNT ($P < 0.001$, all variables; table 7.1).

Differences between the seasons were not so notable for skeins of dusky Canada geese as they were for skeins of Taverner's. Skeins of dusky Canada geese observed during NOHUNT did approach smaller fields, containing a smaller proportion of their own subspecies in the feeding flock, than did skeins of dusky Canada geese observed during HUNT ($P < 0.001$, both variables); but the means for other variables associated with such skeins were similar during both seasons (table 7.1). The decline in total numbers of dusky Canada geese in the study area during winter 1981-82 probably accounts for the shift in subspecies composition of geese in fields approached by skeins of dusky Canada geese.

The observed univariate associations between subspecies composition of skeins and other study variables were influenced by interactions among study variables. For example, close to Sturgeon Lake ($\leq$ 900 m), approach elevation was not significantly associated (P = 0.391) with subspecies composition of skeins for HUNT data. Farther from the lake ($>$ 900 m), skeins of Taverner's and mixed Taverner's started their approach from high elevations more frequently than expected ($P < 0.001$), whereas dusky and mixed dusky Canada geese started their approach from low elevations more frequently than expected ($P < 0.001$). Overall, results from multifactor analyses were similar to the trends described for univariate analyses and did not change our interpretation of the data. Havel (1985) presented multifactor analyses in detail.

Weather and Time of Day

There were no significant associations between any of the weather variables and subspecies composition of either feeding flocks or of skeins during either season ($P > 0.050$, all variables, both seasons). Weather may affect behavior and use of fields by geese (Raveling et al. 1972, Frederick and Klaas 1982), but the two subspecies that we studied were not affected differently within the range of weather conditions recorded.

Time of day (diurnal) was not significantly related to subspecies composition of either feeding flocks or of skeins during either season ($P > 0.050$, for both flock types and both seasons). There was considerable nocturnal activity by geese, especially during NOHUNT, but we were unable to identify subspecies at night.

Discussion

Dusky and Taverner's Canada geese exhibit differences in certain aspects of their winter ecology, including their distribution (Simpson and Jarvis 1979), behaviors (e.g., approach and landing; current study), and use of feeding fields (e.g., field size and location; Simpson and Jarvis 1979 and current study). Regardless of the cause or causes for differences between subspecies, these differences probably affect the vulnerability of dusky and Taverner's Canada geese to hunting mortality in western Oregon (Simpson and Jarvis 1979).

Simpson and Jarvis (1979, 232) found dusky Canada geese to be approximately 2.7 times more likely to be shot during waterfowl hunting season (1976-78) than Taverner's. During waterfowl hunting season on Sauvie Island (1981-82), groups of Taverner's generally fed and flew in numerically larger groups and utilized larger fields than did groups of dusky Canada geese.

We did not directly examine the relationship between group size and hunting vulnerability of individual group members. Studies involving other species of birds indicate that foraging and flying in numerically "large" groups probably facilitate detection and avoidance of predators (Lazarus 1978, 1979; Greig-Smith 1981; and others). Owens (1977, 8) found that larger flocks of dark-bellied brent geese (*Branta bernicla bernicla*) took flight at greater distances from approaching humans than did smaller flocks. Because humans are probably the most important predators of adult geese (Bellrose 1976, 143-144), detection and avoidance of humans is obviously advantageous to individual geese. It is generally believed that large groups of waterfowl are more difficult to bring within shooting range of a "set" of decoys, and therefore more difficult to hunt successfully, than are small groups (Taylor 1974, 106; Simpson and Jarvis 1979, 237). Although skeins of Taverner's were in the air over a field for a relatively longer period of time than skeins of dusky Canada geese, Tavener's high approach elevation (66% of skeins of Taverner's and mixed Taverner's [N = 438] started approach at elevations > 60 m) kept them out of shooting range much of the time.

Use of large fields by Taverner's and use of small fields by dusky Canada geese may have affected their hunting vulnerability in more than one way. The midpoints of large fields on Sauvie Island were generally farther from potential danger than the midpoints of small fields (r = 0.578, N = 893, P = 0.001). Unless there was a blind located in a large field, or a flock of geese located near the field periphery (rare), a hunter could only find cover a considerable distance from geese landing in large fields. Large fields also were associated with privately owned land, whereas small fields were associated with state-owned land. In our opinion, state-owned land was more intensively hunted than privately owned land (alternate days and 1-3 days per week, respectively) on Sauvie Island.

Taverner's exhibited significant changes in behavior and use of fields from hunting to posthunting season, whereas dusky Canada geese exhibited essentially the same patterns throughout the study. The shift in Taverner's behavior and use of fields was from patterns that could make them less vulnerable to hunting (than dusky geese) during waterfowl hunting season to patterns similar to those of dusky Canada geese following the waterfowl hunting season. Although this shift in the patterns exhibited by Taverner's may be attributable to many factors, we believe that it is associated with hunting and its cessation. Although dusky Canada geese did change from feeding primarily in fields on state-owned land during hunting to fields on privately owned land following hunting, dusky Canada geese did not change their approach to fields and landing behaviors in response to hunting and its cessation.

Although generally allopatric during nesting, many of the subspecies of Canada geese are at least partially sympatric and occur in mixed flocks during the nonbreeding season. Our research demonstrates that differences in behavior and habitat use exist between two of these subspecies that winter in the same place at the same time. Management applied without regard for these differences can have differential consequences for subspecies (Raveling 1978). Recognition of ultimate similarities and differences between subspecies of Canada geese is necessary for the formulation of local management strategies that are appropriate for all subspecies involved.

LITERATURE CITED

Altmann, J. 1974. Observational study of behavior: sampling methods. Behav. 49:227–267.

Bellrose, F. C. 1976. Ducks, geese, and swans of North America. Stackpole Books, Harrisburg, Pa. 543pp.

Delacour, J. T. 1951. Preliminary note on the taxonomy of Canada geese, *Branta canadensis*. Am. Mus. Novitates 1537. 10pp.

————. 1954. The waterfowl of the world. Vol. 1. Country Life, London. 284pp.

Frederick, R. B., and E. E. Klaas. 1982. Resource use and behavior of migrating snow geese. J. Wildl. Manage. 46:601–614.

Greig-Smith, P. W. 1981. Responses to disturbance in relation to flock size in foraging groups of barred ground doves *Geopelia striata*. Ibis 123: 103–106.

Havel, L. H. 1985. Formation of feeding flocks during winter by dusky and Taverner's Canada geese in Oregon. M.S. Thesis, Oregon State Univ., Corvallis. 81pp.

Jarvis, R. L., and J. E. Cornely. 1988. Recent changes in wintering populations of Canada geese in western Oregon and southwestern Washington. Pages 517-28 *in* M. W. Weller, ed. Waterfowl in winter. Univ. Minnesota Press, Minneapolis.

Johnson, D. H., D. E. Timm, and P. F. Springer. 1979. Morphological characteristics of Canada geese in the Pacific Flyway. Pages 56-80 *in* R. L. Jarvis and J. C. Bartonek, eds. Management and biology of Pacific Flyway geese. Oregon State Univ. Bookstores, Corvallis. 346pp.

Lazarus, J. 1978. Vigilance, flock size, and domain of danger size in the white-fronted goose. Wildfowl 29:135-145.

————. 1979. The early warning function of flocking in birds: an experimental study with captive quelea. Anim. Behav. 27:855-865.

Nie, N., C. Hull, J. Jenkins, K. Steinbrenner, and D. Bent. 1975. Statistical package for the social sciences. 2nd ed. McGraw-Hill, New York. 675pp.

Owens, N. W. 1977. Response of wintering brent geese to human disturbance. Wildfowl 28:5-14.

Raveling, D. G. 1978. Dynamics of distribution of Canada geese in winter. Trans. N. Am. Wildl. Nat. Resour. Conf. 43:206-225.

————, W. E. Crews, and W. D. Klimstra. 1972. Activity patterns of Canada geese during winter. Wilson Bull. 84:278-295.

Simpson, S. G., and R. L. Jarvis. 1979. Comparative ecology of several subspecies of Canada geese during winter in western Oregon. Pages 223-240 *in* R. L. Jarvis and J. C. Bartonek, eds. Management and biology of Pacific Flyway geese. Oregon State Univ. Bookstores, Corvallis. 346pp.

Taylor, Z. 1974. Successful waterfowling. Crown Publishers, New York. 276pp.

Timm, D. E., R. G. Bromley, D. E. McKnight, and R. S. Rodgers. 1979. Management evolution of dusky Canada geese. Pages 322-330 *in* R. L. Jarvis and J. C. Bartonek, eds. Management and biology of Pacific Flyway geese. Oregon State Univ. Bookstores, Corvallis. 346pp.

8

Sex Specificity of Behavioral Dominance and Fasting Endurance in Wintering Canvasbacks: Experimental Results

Matthew C. Perry, James D. Nichols, Michael J. Conroy, Holliday H. Obrecht III, and Byron K. Williams

Abstract: Hand-reared canvasbacks (*Aythya valisineria*) of varying sex ratios were maintained in pens during winter 1980-81 (3M-3F, 6M-0F, 0M-6F) and winter 1981-82 (4M-2F, 2M-4F) and fed two diets (control and stress). They were observed during feeding trials to determine intrasexual and intersexual aggressive activity. There was little evidence that either diet or sex ratio affected the total number of aggressive encounters. Females fed both control and stress diets were more aggressive and spent more time in the small feeding areas than males in pens with 3M-3F, 4M-2F, and 2M-4F sex ratios. Stressed ducks tended to weigh less than controls throughout the study. Females in the 3M-3F and 4M-2F pens weighed less than those in the 0M-6F and 2M-4F pens, respectively. However, relative weight changes throughout the winter were similar for males and females. Thus, results of these experiments do not lead to conclusive rejection of either the behavioral dominance hypothesis or the fasting endurance hypothesis.

In a number of migratory bird species, females tend to winter farther south than males (Ketterson and Nolan 1976, Gauthreaux 1978, Nichols and Haramis 1980, Myers 1981, Sayler and Afton 1981). Early speculation (Allen 1931, Hochbaum 1944, Degraff et al. 1961) and recent evidence (Nichols and Haramis 1980, Alexander 1983, Haramis et al. 1985) suggest this tendency for canvasbacks (*Aythya valisineria*). Several hypotheses have been proposed to explain differential distribution of sexes during the nonbreeding period (Ketterson and Nolan 1976, Gauthreaux 1978, Nichols and Haramis 1980, Myers 1981, Sayler and Afton 1981, Hepp and Hair 1984). Nichols and Haramis (1980) suggested that two of

Waterfowl in Winter. © 1988 University of Minnesota. Edited by Milton W. Weller and published by the University of Minnesota Press, Minneapolis.

these hypotheses might apply to canvasbacks: the behavioral dominance hypothesis (BDH) and the fasting endurance hypothesis (FEH).

BDH suggests that sex-specific differences in winter distribution patterns evolved and are maintained as a result of behavioral interactions in which males control critical resources in periods of resource scarcity. FEH suggests the importance of sexual dimorphism in body size, which may render the smaller females especially susceptible to mortality during periods of inclement weather and food shortages. We report the results of two experiments designed to test predictions of these hypotheses using hand-reared canvasbacks held in pens.

We thank J. E. Hines for programming and statistical assistance and W. C. Alexander, M. G. Anderson, T. J. Dwyer, R. M. Erwin, G. M. Haramis, G. R. Hepp, H. F. Percival, and M. W. Weller for their comments on earlier drafts of this manuscript. M. E. Maj provided invaluable assistance with observations on both pen and wild canvasbacks. Assistance with word processing was provided by L. Hungerbuhler, R. Munro, and J. Wilcox, and L. Moyer assisted with graphs.

Methods

Procedures

Canvasbacks used in this study were adults hatched at Patuxent Wildlife Research Center from eggs collected in Manitoba in 1978. During winter 1980-81 (November-March), ducks were maintained in outdoor pens measuring 1.0×6.0 m that had water area of 1.0 m^2 (0.5 m deep) centered in each pen (A-pens). Twelve pens were used with six ducks in each pen, for a total of 72 ducks. During winter 1980-81, the sex ratio in each pen was either 3 males (M) and 3 females (F), 6M-0F, or 0M-6F. Ducks were randomly assigned to two replicates of each sex ratio from a captive flock of 85 canvasbacks. During the years before this experiment, canvasbacks had been maintained on ad libitum diets in the same group of pens with three males and three females per pen.

The 1980-81 experiment left several unresolved questions about the two-sex (3M-3F) pens, so a follow-up experiment was designed for the next winter. During winter 1981-82, canvasbacks were maintained in 12 pens measuring 1.8×6.0 m that had a water area of 1.8×4.6 m (0.3 m deep) (B-pens). The pen area was changed during the second year to provide more water area for ducks to better simulate natural conditions in regard to space. Overall space per duck increased almost twofold, from 1.0 m^2/duck in 1980-81 to 1.8 m^2/duck in 1981-82, and water space increased more than eightfold from 0.17 m^2/duck to 1.38 m^2/duck. Ducks were randomly selected into groups of six with sex ratios of 4M-2F and 2M-4F. The 4M-2F sex ratio was considered to simulate more natural sex ratios than the 3M-3F sex ratio used during winter 1980-81. Groups of ducks were randomly assigned to pens with three replications of each sex ratio.

Feed for all ducks was duck developer pellets (Beacon Feeds, Cayuga, N.Y.; use of trade names does not imply federal government endorsement of commercial products), which were fed in gravity-flow metal containers at the end of each of the A-pens and in flat, plastic trays in each of the B-pens. This ration, which contained 2,293 kcal of metabolizable energy per kilogram and 14% protein, was a complete diet fortified with vitamins and trace minerals. No natural food was available in the pens.

The ducks in six pens (designated *controls*) were given feed ad libitum, whereas ducks in the other six pens (designated *stress*) were given 75% of the control diet in November-December 1980 and 85% in January-March 1981 and during winter 1981-82. Stress diet was changed from 75% to 85% control when it was discovered that ducks fed the stress diet were losing too much weight. Control ducks were given feed in 1,300-g portions as necessary to assure constant availability of feed. At first, stress ducks were given 975-g portions (November-December); thereafter, 1,115-g portions were given whenever control ducks of the respective sex ratio received feed.

Energy intake was calculated based on records of grams of feed given to ducks (Perry 1985). The assignment of diet (control or stress) to each pen was by completely randomized design. Spilled feed from each pen was collected at the end of each month in 1980-81 to obtain an estimate of feed lost to spillage.

All ducks in the study were weighed at the end of each month to investigate weight changes as affected by each of the two diets and by different sex ratios. Behavioral observations were conducted between 0900 and 1100 once a week immediately preceding normal inspection of feed containers and feeding. Before observation, about 500 cc of corn was placed in the water to induce diving activity for food and aggressive behavior. Corn was placed in the center of the 1.0-m²-water area in the A-pens (1980-81) and in the center of a 1.0-m² feeding area delineated by four wooden stakes in each of the B-pens (1981-82). Previous studies (Perry 1985) indicated that there was little aggressive behavior at the feed tray and that corn was preferred to pellets during winter.

A one-minute adjustment period followed placement of corn. Then ducks were observed for five minutes and all aggressive encounters were recorded on a form. Aggressive encounters were defined as any overt attack by one duck on another, including pecking, chasing, pushing, bumping, and fighting. They did not include any of the more subtle threats that are sometimes observed, which apparently are ways of reinforcing social hierarchy. Colored nasal saddles on ducks enabled both initiators and recipients of each encounter to be recorded.

In both study years, ducks were recorded as being in or out of the 1.0-m² feeding area at the beginning of each minute during the five-minute period. During 1980-81, the feeding area was the total water area in each pen. These additional observations were recorded to help evaluate the control of the feeding area by ducks of each sex.

Unmarked wild canvasbacks were observed in several areas of Chesapeake Bay to obtain comparable data on aggressive behavior. Sex ratios of canvasback flocks were determined and all observed intrasexual and intersexual aggressive encounters within each flock were recorded while the flock was slowly scanned with a spotting scope. Observations of wild canvasbacks were made between 30 January and 5 March 1981 from 0800 to 1830 during periods of 0.5-3.5 hours. Ages of wild canvasbacks could not be determined.

Predictions

Our experiments and observations were designed to provide data that could be used to distinguish between BDH and FEH as potentially important selective factors affecting latitudinal segregation of sexes in wintering canvasbacks. We specify our a priori predictions under these two hypotheses.

FEH makes no predictions about the number of aggressive encounters occurring during the sampling period. If BDH is true, however, aggressive encounters (or possibly some other expression of behavioral dominance) should increase during periods of food shortage. Under BDH, therefore, we predicted more aggressive encounters for ducks fed the stress diet than for ducks fed the control diet for all sex ratios. If males tend to be behaviorally dominant over females, as suggested by BDH, then for the 1980-81 experiment, we might also expect more encounters in the 3M-3F pens than in the 6M-0F and 0M-6F pens because of the greater behavioral asymmetries.

BDH also leads to predictions about the initiators (virtually synonomous with "winners" in our experiments) and recipients of aggressive encounters. In two-sex pens, we would expect under BDH more M-F (initiator = M, recipient = F) and fewer F-M (initiator = F, recipient = M) encounters than expected under a null hypothesis of encounters occurring in proportion to the number of random encounters with individuals of both sexes. FEH again leads to no specific predictions about the relative frequencies of the four different sex-specific classes of encounters.

If BDH is true, then time spent in the feeding areas of the pens should be lower for females than for males in the two-sex pens, especially under the stress diet. This variable should also be higher for females in the 0M-6F and 2M-4F pens than in the 3M-3F and 4M-2F pens, respectively. FEH makes no specific prediction about sex-specific differences in this variable, although it is possible that time spent in the feeding area might even be greater for females than males, especially under the stress diet. However, FEH does predict similar time spent in the feeding areas for the different sex ratios.

BDH and FEH lead to different predictions about body-weight changes under the different treatments. Both hypotheses predict lower weights under the stress diets for all sex ratios. BDH predicts higher body weights of females on the 0M-6F sex ratio than on the 3M-3F sex ratio (1980-81 experiment) and on the 2M-4F sex ratio than on the 4M-2F sex ratio (1981-82 experiment), especially under the stress diets. In pens with no males or fewer males, there would be less aggressive behavior toward females, based on BDH, and thus females would have more access to feed.

Because the behavioral dominance of males is hypothesized to result in their excluding females and taking disproportionate shares of available resources, BDH predicts greater male weights in the 3M-3F and 2M-4F pens than in the 6M-0F and 4M-2F pens, respectively, at least under the stress diets. Under FEH, any disadvantages experienced by females are strictly a function of body size and physiological tolerance, and sex ratio should have no influence on body-weight changes.

Finally, we note that the deduction of specific predictions from very general hypotheses is not necessarily a simple or straightforward matter. The preceding represent the predictions that seemed most reasonable to us after considerable thought and discussion. They also correspond well to the mechanisms envisioned by Nichols and Haramis (1980) when they first suggested BDH and FEH as possible explanations for observed differences in winter distribution patterns of male and female canvasbacks. Nevertheless, we recognize that not everyone will agree with these predictions. In fact, we doubt that any two students of canvasbacks charged with the task of deducing detailed, a priori predictions of these hypotheses for our experiments would independently produce identical lists.

We believed that the results of our experiments would be very useful in providing us with information on the appropriateness of our predictions. For example, some of our predictions are based on the assumption that the initiation of an overt aggressive interaction is a reasonable indicator of the behavioral dominance of the initiator over the other bird. It was possible that this assumption was inappropriate (although our previous observations of captive canvasbacks suggested that this was unlikely) and that behavioral dominance would be exhibited only via more subtle behavioral interactions. Had this been the case, it would have become apparent during our observations. It would also have produced very different results for behavioral interactions and time spent in the 1.0-m² feeding area, and these data provided us with a check of the assumption.

The alternative to producing a set of specific predictions is to simply conduct the "experiment" and then build a story to "explain" the results afterwards. We prefer our approach of using a priori predictions, despite the fact that they provide ample opportunity for second-guessing. Also, we have tried to provide sufficiently detailed results to enable others to evaluate any alternative sets of predictions.

Statistical Analyses

Repeated-measures analysis of variance (ANOVA) procedures (Winer 1962) were used to examine the total number of aggressive encounters in each pen for each of the two study years without regard to which duck initiated the encounters. The repeated-measure approach was used because behavioral observations were made on the same individuals over time. Observations were classified by the sex ratio of the ducks in the pens (3M-3F, 6M-0F, 0M-6F in 1980-81, 4M-2F, 2M-4F in 1981-82), by diet (control and stress), and by month (November-March). For the two-sex pens (3M-3F, 4M-2F, and 2M-4F), a contingency chi-square analysis was used to test for differences in the sex-specific patterns of aggression from those expected under a null hypothesis of encounters occurring at random. For the chi-square analysis, interactions were aggregated across months.

Chi-square contingency table analysis was used to test for differences in time (number of one-minute segments of the five minutes observed) spent in the feeding area for males in the different-sex-ratio pens within each year and each diet, and similarly for females. Differences associated with diet and differences between males and females in the two-sex pens were also tested using chi-square contingency table analyses.

Hypotheses about differences and changes in body weight were investigated using repeated-measure ANOVA procedures (Winer 1962). The sex-ratio treatments required different numbers of ducks of a given sex in different pens. Thus, the very nature of the treatment yielded unbalanced data and necessitated the use of ANOVA procedures that were not as straightforward as might have been hoped. With respect to the 1980-81 data, the hypotheses of interest required comparisons of ducks from single-sex vs. two-sex pens and thus required separate analyses for males and females. Synthetic mean squares corresponding to hypotheses of interest were computed and used to obtain F statistics. All pens in 1981-82 contained both males and females, and the analysis of these data was approached differently. We first computed the mean weight of males and of females within each pen at each time period. We then conducted one analysis using the average of these two means and another using the difference between the sex-specific means. The inferences of interest are then based on the results of both analyses.

Energy intake was examined using a repeated-measure ANOVA for each winter. These analyses were based on the grams of feed supplied to each pen, as described under Procedures.

Results

Total Aggressive Encounters

Summary statistics on the number of aggressive encounters per bird-hour are presented in table 8.1. More encounters were observed in 1980-81, probably reflecting the difference in available water within the pens. There were significant month-to-month differences in total encounters during both 1980-81 ($F_{3,18}$ = 7.29, $P < 0.01$) and 1981-82 ($F_{4,32}$ = 7.97, $P < 0.01$). Diet appeared to affect the number of encounters in 1980-81, as more encounters were observed for the

Table 8.1. Rate of intrasexual and intersexual canvasback aggression (encounters per bird-hour) during the winters of 1980-81 and 1981-82

Diet	Sex ratio[a]	Nov	Dec	Jan	Feb	Mar	$\bar{x}$
			1980-81				
Control	3M-3F		4.2	13.8	7.8	9.5	8.8
	6M-0F		4.8	3.8	3.1	1.7	3.4
	0M-6F		1.8	7.2	3.8	3.0	4.0
	$\bar{x}$		3.6	8.2	4.9	4.7	5.4
Stress	3M-3F		11.0	12.9	8.3	7.7	10.0
	6M-0F		6.0	9.6	5.9	8.7	7.6
	0M-6F		17.5	19.0	7.8	4.0	12.1
	$\bar{x}$		11.5	13.8	7.3	6.8	9.9
			1981-82				
Control	4M-2F	4.6	5.2	1.5	2.6	4.2	3.6
	2M-4F	4.2	6.7	3.1	3.1	0.5	3.5
	$\bar{x}$	4.4	5.9	2.3	2.8	2.4	3.6
Stress	4M-2F	5.3	3.9	0.8	3.4	4.7	3.6
	2M-4F	4.7	3.7	2.8	2.9	5.9	4.0
	$\bar{x}$	5.0	3.8	1.8	3.2	5.3	3.8

[a] Two replications in 1980-81, three replications in 1981-82.

stress-diet birds, but this difference only approached significance ($F_{1,6}$ = 2.51, P = 0.16). There was no evidence of an effect of diet on total encounters in 1981-82 ($P >$ 0.20). The sex-ratio treatment did not affect the number of aggressive encounters in either 1980-81 or 1981-82 ($P >$ 0.20). None of the interactions was significant for either year.

Sex Specificity of Interactions

Observations of captive canvasbacks fed control and stress diets in 1980-81 revealed that females were more aggressive than males during feeding trials in pens with three males and three females (table 8.2). F-F and F-M aggressive encounters occurred with greater frequency than expected under a null hypothesis of encounters occurring at random for ducks fed the control diet. For ducks fed the stress diet, only F-M encounters occurred with greater frequency than expected. Males initiated fewer encounters than expected under the null hypothesis for both diets in 1980-81 (table 8.2).

It is clear that sex-specific aggressive encounters did not occur in proportion to the number of individuals available for encounters during the 1980-81 experiment.

Females initiated more encounters than males in all pens, and F-M encounters occurred with greater frequency than any other type of encounter in all pens but one, in which F-F encounters dominated.

Table 8.2. Chi-square values based on intrasexual and intersexual aggression for canvasbacks on different sex ratios, 1980-81 and 1981-82

Sex ratio	Interaction	Expected (H_o)[a]	Observed	χ^2
		Control diet		
3M-3F	M-M	48.6	33	5.0
	M-F	72.9	13	49.2
	F-M	72.9	124	35.8
	F-F	48.6	73	12.3
				102.3[b]
4M-2F	M-M	122.0	132	0.8
	M-F	81.3	41	20.0
	F-M	81.3	113	12.4
	F-F	20.3	19	0.1
				33.3[b]
2M-4F	M-M	16.7	18	0.1
	M-F	66.7	15	40.1
	F-M	66.7	142	85.0
	F-F	100.0	75	6.3
				131.5[b]
		Stress diet		
3M-3F	M-M	51.8	4	44.1
	M-F	77.7	9	60.7
	F-M	77.7	222	268.0
	F-F	51.8	24	14.9
				387.7[b]
4M-2F	M-M	122.4	123	0.0
	M-F	81.6	63	4.2
	F-M	81.6	117	15.4
	F-F	20.4	3	14.8
				34.4[b]
2M-4F	M-M	22.8	17	1.5
	M-F	91.2	22	52.5
	F-M	91.2	178	82.6
	F-F	136.8	125	1.0
				137.6[b]

[a] Null hypothesis expectations were based on a model assuming random encounters with individuals of both sexes.

[b] Totals for each sex ratio are distributed under H_o as χ^2 with 3 degrees of freedom. All are significant ($P < 0.01$).

In 1981-82, when sex ratios were changed, it was found that females were still more aggressive toward males than predicted by chance alone. With the 4M-2F and the 2M-4F sex ratios, F-M encounters occurred with greater frequency than expected under the null hypothesis for both diets (table 8.2).

Limited observations among unaged wild canvasbacks in Chesapeake Bay indicated that males were generally dominant over females in aggressive encounters (table 8.3). The number of M-M and F-F encounters observed was very close to that expected under a null hypothesis of random encounters. However, M-F encounters occurred much more frequently than expected and F-M encounters occurred much less frequently, leading to rejection of the overall null hypothesis (table 8.3; overall $\chi_3^2 = 42.27$, $P < 0.01$).

Table 8.3. Aggressive encounters between wild male and female canvasbacks in Chesapeake Bay, 30 January-5 March 1981

Flock composition			Intrasexual and intersexual aggression				
Males	Females	Sex ratio	MM	MF	FM	FF	Total
172	54	3.2:1	67	33	9	5	114
244	65	3.8:1	36	19	7	6	68
75	58	1.3:1	36	26	9	8	79
299	139	2.2:1	8	11	6	6	31
38	20	1.9:1	3	1	2	0	6
44	23	1.9:1	22	6	3	1	32
36	11	3.3:1	4	5	0	0	9
69	23	3.0:1	52	22	2	5	54
977	393	2.5:1	201	123	41	28	393
Expected encounters under null hypothesis:			200	81	81	32	

Time Spent in 1.0-m² Feeding Area

In the 1980-81 pens having a 3M-3F ratio, females consistently spent a larger proportion of their time in the feeding area than did males under both control and stress diets (table 8.4). In the single-sex pens, females also tended to spend more time in the feeding area than did males, under both diets. This tendency held true for the 1981-82 experiment. In only one case (4M-2F, stress diet) was there no significant difference between the sexes (table 8.4).

Weight Changes

In 1980-81, both male and female canvasbacks exhibited significant (male $F_{5,20} = 33.08$, $P < 0.01$; female $F_{5,20} = 12.76$, $P < 0.01$) temporal variation in body weight over the late fall and winter (fig. 8.1). The diet-time interaction was also significant for both sexes (male $F_{5,20} = 10.31$, $P < 0.01$; female $F_{5,20} = 10.82$, $P < 0.01$). Lowest

Table 8.4. Proportion of observed time canvasbacks spent inside the 1.0m^2 feeding area[a]

Diet	Sex ratio	Males	Females	M-F test[b] χ^2_1	P
			1980-81		
Control	3M-3F	0.85	0.93	13.12	<0.01
	6M-0F	0.76	. . .	28.01	<0.01
	0M-6F	. . .	0.87		
Stress	3M-3F	0.82	0.96	42.90	<0.01
	6M-0F	0.82	. . .	38.88	<0.01
	0M-6F	. . .	0.92		
			1981-82		
Control	4M-2F	0.72	0.78	8.77	<0.01
	2M-4F	0.74	0.84	24.77	<0.01
Stress	4M-2F	0.84	0.85	0.18	0.67
	2M-4F	0.72	0.89	73.21	<0.01

[a]Times were summed for all individuals over all replicates within a diet/sex-ratio treatment.
[b]A two-by-two χ^2 test with 1 df was used to test the hypothesis that the proportion of time spent in the feeding area was the same for males and females.

weights of males and females fed control diets occurred in February, whereas lowest weights for canvasbacks fed stress diets were recorded in December (fig. 8.1). This dramatic drop in weight in December 1980 is believed to have been caused by the very limiting diet (75% of ad libitum) fed to stressed ducks. Weights increased in January when ducks were fed 85% ad libitum stress diets, which was sufficient to stress ducks without causing excessive weight loss and possible mortality.

The overall diet effect in 1980-81 only approached significance ($F_{1,4} = 2.65$, $P = 0.18$) for males. Females did show significant overall weight differences associated with diet ($F_{1,4} = 6.20$, $P = 0.07$), with stress-diet ducks weighing less than control ducks.

There were no weight differences associated with sex-ratio treatment for males ($P < 0.20$). However, sex ratio did influence average weight for females ($F_{1,4} = 6.50$, $P = 0.06$). Females on the 0M-6F sex-ratio treatment tended to be heavier than those on the 3M-3F treatment. In addition, the interaction between diet and sex ratio approached significance for females ($F_{1,4} = 4.32$, $P = 0.11$). Females from the two sex-ratio treatments had very similar weights on the control diet, whereas on the stress diet, females from the 0M-6F treatment were heavier (fig. 8.1). This difference in weights of stressed females for the two sex ratios was especially pronounced toward the end of the experiment (fig. 8.1),

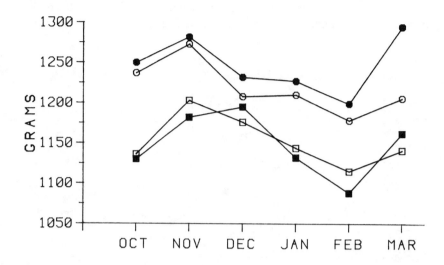

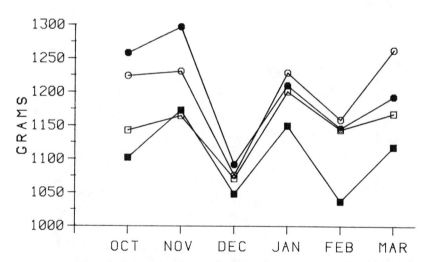

Fig. 8.1 Weights of male and female canvasbacks fed control (A) and stress (B) diets and maintained on three sex ratios from October 1980 to March 1981. Solid circle = male (3M-3F), solid square = female (3M-3F), open circle = male (6M-0F), and open square = female (0M-6F).

resulting in an interaction between sex ratio and time that approached significance ($F_{5,20}$ = 2.03, P = 0.12).

As indicated in Methods, we based our analyses of the 1981-82 data on the mean weights of males and females in each pen. The first analysis was based on the

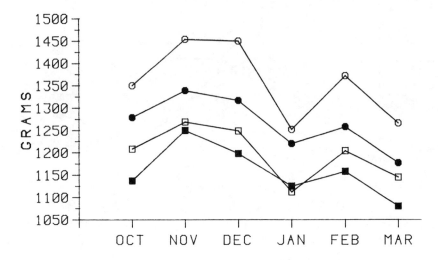

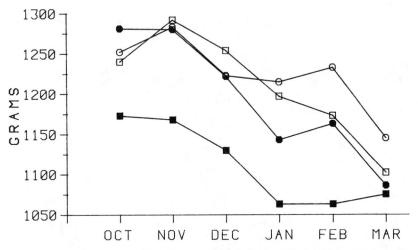

Fig. 8.2. Weights of male and female canvasbacks fed control (A) and stress (B) diets and maintained on two sex ratios from October 1981 to March 1982. Solid circle = male (4M-2F), solid square = female (4M-2F), open circle = male (2M-4F), and open square = female (2M-4F).

average of these means. This ANOVA showed significant diet ($F_{1,8}$ = 9.02, P =0.02), sex ratio ($F_{1,8}$ = 10.87, P = 0.01), time ($F_{5,40}$ = 26.84, $P < 0.01$), and diet-time interaction ($F_{5,40}$ = 2.69, P = 0.03) effects. Weights of both sexes varied from month to month, being lowest in January and March (fig. 8.2). Stress-diet ducks weighed less than control-diet ducks, especially during the period December-March. Canvasbacks in the 2M-4F sex-ratio pens weighed more than ducks in the 4M-2F pens (fig. 8.2).

The second analysis of the 1981-82 weight data, based on the difference between the mean male and female weights, was intended to provide insight into sex-specific differences in body-weight changes. This difference was affected significantly by diet ($F_{1,8}$ = 10.69, P = 0.01), as there was a tendency for male and female weights to be more similar on the stress diet (fig. 8.2). There was also a significant interaction between diet and sex ratio ($F_{1,8}$ = 5.64, P = 0.04), reflecting very similar weights of stressed males and females in the 2M-4F pens. These two significant effects (diet and interaction between diet and sex ratio) were largely a function of initial conditions, as our random assignment of ducks to pens resulted in similar weights of males and females in the 2M-4F, stress-diet pens. Biologically, the most interesting inference of this analysis involves the absence of significant month-to-month variation in the difference between male and female weights ($F_{5,40}$ = 0.71, P = 0.62). Males and females thus exhibited the same pattern of temporal variation in body weight (fig. 8.2).

Energy Intake

Energy intake was greater for control-diet than stress-diet ducks during both 1980-81 ($F_{1,6}$ = 169.82, $P < 0.01$) and 1981-82 ($F_{1,8}$ = 174.19, $P < 0.01$) as dictated by the diet treatment (table 8.5). Energy intake also exhibited temporal variation in both winters (1980-81 $F_{3,18}$ = 130.92, $P < 0.01$; 1981-82 $F_{4,32}$ = 78.68, $P < 0.01$). Ducks consumed the most feed during the beginning month of each experiment (December and November during 1980-81 and 1981-82, respectively), decreased consumption substantially during January and February, and increased consumption again in March (table 8.5). During 1980-81, the change in the stress diet from 75% to 85% of ad libitum led to much larger differences between diets during December and a resultant significant diet-month interaction ($F_{3,18}$ = 57.51, $P < 0.01$). The smallest difference in food consumption in 1980-81 was during January, the month of lowest food consumption. In 1981-82, there was also a significant diet-month interaction ($F_{4,32}$ = 2.46, P = 0.07), with very similar food intakes for two diets during the month of lowest consumption (February in 1981-82).

Energy intake differed for the different sex ratios in both years (1980-81 $F_{2,6}$ = 8.67, P = 0.02; 1981-82 $F_{1,8}$ = 6.40, P = 0.04). During 1980-81, food consumption was similar for the 3M-3F and 6M-0F pens, with ducks in the latter pens eating most (table 8.5). The 0M-6F pens consumed substantially less than the pens containing

Table 8.5. Energy intake (kcal/ bird-day) of canvasbacks fed two diets and on different sex ratios during the winters of 1980-81 and 1981-82

Diet	Sex ratio[a]	Nov	Dec	Jan	Feb	Mar	$\bar{x}$
			1980-81				
Control	3M-3F		256.4	171.0	208.2	222.2	214.5
	6M-0F		256.4	179.5	208.2	222.2	216.6
	0M-6F		247.9	162.4	189.3	213.7	203.3
Stress	3M-3F		191.5	174.2	176.8	188.8	182.8
	6M-0F		191.5	181.5	176.8	188.8	184.6
	0M-6F		185.1	167.0	168.8	181.5	175.6
	$\bar{x}$		221.5	172.6	188.0	202.9	196.2
			1981-82				
Control	4M-2F	270.9	222.2	199.5	164.0	216.6	214.6
	2M-4F	259.1	216.6	171.0	145.1	235.9	205.5
Stress	4M-2F	215.1	183.9	174.2	150.0	198.4	184.3
	2M-4F	235.1	188.8	154.9	144.7	193.6	183.4
	$\bar{x}$	245.0	202.9	174.9	151.0	211.1	197.0

[a]Two replications in 1980-81, three replications in 1981-82.

males. In 1981-82, the 4M-2F pens tended to exhibit higher energy intake than in 2M-4F pens (table 8.5). However, food consumption for the two sex ratios was more similar during some months than others, leading to a significant interaction between month and sex ratio ($F_{4,32}$ = 2.54, P = 0.06).

Waste feed collected at the end of each month for ducks fed the control diet did not differ between sex ratios. Waste feed for the winter was 3-4% of total feed for ducks on the control diet. Ducks fed stress diets had no waste feed.

Discussion

Total Aggressive Encounters

FEH does not lead to predictions about the number of aggressive encounters. Under BDH, however, behavioral interactions are important in obtaining resources, especially during periods of resource shortage. BDH thus leads to the prediction of more aggressive encounters for ducks on the stress diet. The ANOVA results indicated that diet effects were nonsignificant, although results were not clear-cut ($0.10 < P < 0.20$) for 1980-81. By far the largest difference in total interactions between the two diets occurred during December 1980 (table 8.2), following the most severe stress diet (75% of ad libitum) of the entire experiment.

It may be that relatively severe resource restrictions are needed to produce substantial increases in aggressive activity.

Under BDH, if one sex tends to be dominant over the other, then we would expect more interactions during 1980-81 in the 3M-3F pens than in the single-sex pens. Our results provided no evidence of different numbers of encounters for the different sex ratios in 1980-81. Similarly, there was no evidence of an effect of sex ratio on total encounters in 1981-82.

In conclusion, the data on total encounters provided little support for the predictions of BDH. There was little indication that total encounters were affected by diet, although more severe food restrictions might have yielded different results. There was no evidence that total encounters differed between the sex-ratio treatments.

Sex Specificity of Interactions

Under BDH, we expected males to be the initiators and females the recipients of aggressive encounters more frequently than would occur based on random encounters. The null-hypothesis expectations of sex-specific encounter frequencies were clearly rejected in our experiments. During both years and under all diet/sex-ratio treatments, F-M encounters occurred much more frequently than expected. The females definitely tended to be dominant over males in our experiments.

Because of published reports of behavioral interactions of wild canvasbacks (Alexander and Hair 1979) and indirect evidence of sex-specific spacing patterns within wintering canvasback flocks (Nichols and Haramis 1980), we were surprised at this result. In early 1981, when it had become clear that females tended to be dominant over males, we initiated observations on wild canvasbacks. These observations supported BDH, showing frequencies of M-M and F-F interactions extremely close to what was expected under a null model, but many more M-F (and fewer F-M) interactions than expected. These contrasting results led to our decision to continue the experiment in 1981-82 with a more realistic sex ratio (4M-2F) and pen situation (increased water area). As reported, however, F-M interactions again occurred much more frequently than expected during our second winter. We will return to this problem later.

Time Spent in 1.0-m² Feeding Area

Under BDH, we predicted that the behavioral dominance of males over females would result in females being excluded from the feeding area and thus spending a smaller proportion of their time there. We also predicted that females in single-sex pens would spend a larger proportion of their time in the feeding area than females in two-sex pens. Furthermore, we expected these differences (M vs. F in two-sex pens, F in two-sex pens vs. F in single-sex pens) to be greater under the stress diet. As was the case with sex-specific interactions, our results ran contrary to BDH expectations. In two-sex pens, females consistently spent more time in the feeding area than males. In 1980-81, females in the two-sex pens actually spent more time in the feeding area than females in the single-sex pens. These results were unexpected, but nevertheless consistent with the sex-specific interactions results.

It should be pointed out that the relationship between behavioral dominance and time spent in the feeding area is still not clear. Females did tend both to be dominant and to spend more time in the feeding area. However, in 1980-81, males in single-sex and two-sex pens spent similar amounts of time in the feeding area under the stress diet, and males in the single-sex pens actually spent less time there than those in two-sex pens under the control diet. Thus, results do not show the kind of "competitive release" that might be expected in the single-sex pens. We conclude that females tended to spend more time in the feeding area than males but that females were not necessarily excluding males from these areas.

Weight Changes

Both BDH and FEH lead to the prediction of generally lower body weights under the stress diet. This was true in 1981-82 and, at least during some months, in 1980-81. BDH predicts higher body weights of females in the 0M-6F pens than in the 3M-3F pens during 1980-81, with the difference being most pronounced on the stress diet. Our results matched this prediction closely. BDH also predicts higher female weights in the 2M-4F pens than in the 4M-2F pens during 1981-82. Females were heavier in the 2M-4F pens, and the difference was most pronounced on the stress diet. BDH also predicts higher male weights in the 3M-3F vs. 6M-0F pens and in the 2M-4F vs. 4M-2F pens. Sex ratio did not influence male weight in 1980-81; however, in 1981-82, males in the 2M-4F pens did weigh more than those in the 4M-2F pens. In the 1981-82 experiments, both BDH and FEH predict greater overwinter weight losses for females than males. However, our results indicated that relative weight changes through the winter were similar for both sexes. In summary, the body-weight differences associated with the sex-ratio treatments generally tended to support BDH. However, the similar patterns of temporal variation for males and females run counter to both BDH and FEH.

Energy Intake

The data on energy intake was collected to facilitate interpretation of other results and not to test specific predictions of FEH or BDH. Results indicated that energy intake was indeed less for stress-diet ducks than for control-diet ducks. Energy intake also differed among sex-ratio treatments in both years, reflecting greater absolute energy intake for males.

During both years there was significant month-to-month variation in energy intake, with lowest intake during January and February, the two coldest months. This pattern of temporal variation in food consumption is similar to that observed by Perry (1985). Low body weights of ducks during cold winter periods have often been interpreted as reflections of both increased energy expenditures for maintenance and decreased energy availability. Decreased food consumption appears to be an alternative, or at least a contributing, explanation for canvasbacks.

Evaluation of Results

Results of our studies do not consistently support either BDH or FEH. The similar relative weight losses of captive males and females on both diets are not consistent with the prediction of FEH that females experience greater relative weight losses, at least on the stress diet. The finding of substantial female aggressive behavior and behavioral dominance of females over males was not consistent with BDH.

This reversal of the sex specificity of behavioral dominance is the result that puzzles us most. Females were consistently more aggressive than males and able to obtain adequate feed supplies throughout the winter. Perry (1985) observed similar aggressiveness among females in his study of captive canvasbacks fed rations with varying nutrient levels. This behavioral dominance of penned females over males is the reverse of the situation we observed in wild canvasbacks. Similarly, Alexander and Hair (1979) studied diving ducks in South Carolina and found that male canvasbacks were dominant over females and excluded females from preferred foraging sites. Hepp and Hair (1984) studied wintering dabbling ducks in North Carolina and found that males were dominant over females when both were paired or both unpaired. Paired males and females, however, were dominant over both unpaired males and females. Paulus (1983) and Hepp and Hair (1984) reported that early pairing may be advantageous in controlling preferred food resources. We note that pairing occurred from mid-January through March in our ducks, whereas the aggressive behavior of females occurred throughout the study (i.e., not just after pairing).

Studies of dominance hierarchies with captive Northern shovelers (*Anas clypeata*) (March 1967) indicated that females were dominant to males from December to March. In late March and April, males became dominant, probably in response to increased secretions of male sex hormones. Observations by Hepp and Hair (1984), however, indicated that wild shovelers had the same dominance relationship as other dabbling ducks—i.e., males dominant to females throughout the winter.

We speculate that some aspects of our experimental situation may have been sufficiently different from conditions experienced in the wild to produce this reversal of behavioral dominance. The limited water space for the captive ducks could be an important factor controlling sexual aggression. Such space limitations are not normally encountered in the wild. The small number of ducks per treatment used in this study is seldom observed in the wild in major wintering areas. The preponderance of males in most large flocks may promote male aggressiveness in the wild.

Another possibility that should perhaps be considered is that our results are not anomalous and that our random groupings combined individuals that would not tend to be found together (and thus not observed interacting) in the wild. For example, it might be that aggressive females simply do not tend to frequent areas with large numbers of males and that observations on wild ducks view a very biased (with respect to aggression) subset of females. We have no evidence to support this idea and simply mention it as a possibility.

In summary, our results provided some evidence against the prediction of FEH that relative weight loss is greater for females than males, at least under stressful conditions. We did not stress ducks sufficiently to produce substantial mortality (one duck died in 1980-81), however, so perhaps our test was not sufficiently extreme. Our results definitely provided evidence against BDH, with the dominance of females over males. However, the sex specificity of behavioral dominance may somehow have been an artifact of our experimental situation. We initially set up our studies as a means of testing competing predictions of BDH and FEH. Despite what we thought was an experimental design consistent with this goal, our experiments did not yield results entirely consistent with either hypothesis. However, the substantial differences between our results and observations on wild ducks lead us to believe that some aspect of our experimental situation may have differed from the wild in some important respect. We believe that our results should not be used to reject either BDH or FEH, and we still view both hypotheses as viable possibilities.

LITERATURE CITED

Alexander, W. C. 1983. Differential sex distributions of wintering diving ducks (Aythyini) in North America. Am. Birds 37:26–29.

———, and J. D. Hair. 1979. Winter foraging behavior and aggression of diving ducks in South Carolina. Proc. Southeast. Assoc. Game Comm. 31:226–232.

Allen, A. A. 1931. The canvasback. Bird Lore 33:347–360.

DeGraff, L. W., D. C. Foley, and D. Benson. 1961. Distribution and mortality of canvasbacks banded in New York. N.Y. Fish Game J. 8:69–87.

Gauthreaux, S. A., Jr. 1978. The ecological significance of behavioral dominance. Pages 17-54 in P. P. G. Bateson and P. H. Klopfer, eds. Perspectives in ethology. Vol. 3. Plenum Press, New York.

Haramis, G. M., J. R. Goldsberry, D. G. McAuley, and E. L. Derleth. 1985. An aerial photographic census of Chesapeake Bay and North Carolina canvasbacks. J. Wildl. Manage. 49:449–454.

Hepp, G. R., and J. D. Hair. 1984. Dominance in wintering waterfowl (Anatini): effects on distribution of sexes. Condor 86:251–257.

Hochbaum, H. A. 1944. The canvasback on a prairie marsh. Am. Wildl. Inst., Washington, D.C. 201pp.

Ketterson, E. D., and V. Nolan, Jr. 1976. Geographic variation and its climatic correlates in the sex ratio of eastern-wintering dark-eyed juncos (*Junco hyemalis hyemalis*). Ecol. 57:679–693.

March, J. B. 1967. Dominance relations and territorial behavior of captive shovelers. *Anas clypeata*. M.S. Thesis, Univ. Minnesota, Minneapolis. 47pp.

Myers, J. P. 1981. A test of three hypotheses for latitudinal segregation of the sexes in wintering birds. Can. J. Zool. 59:1527–1534.

Nichols, J. D., and G. M. Haramis. 1980. Sex-specific differences in winter distribution patterns of canvasbacks. Condor 82:406–416.

Paulus, S. L. 1983. Dominance relations, resource use, and pairing chronology of gadwalls in winter. Auk 100:947–952.

Perry, M. D. 1985. Seasonal influence of nutrients on the physiology and behavior of captive canvasbacks (*Aythya valisineria*). Ph.D. Dis., Univ. Maryland, College Park. 157pp.

Sayler, R. D., and A. D. Afton. 1981. Ecological aspects of common goldeneyes *Bucephala clangula* wintering on the upper Mississippi River, USA. Ornis Scand. 12:99–108.

Winer, B. J. 1962. Statistical principles in experimental design. McGraw Hill, New York. 907pp.

9

Workshop Summary: Courtship and Pairing in Winter

Michael G. Anderson, Gary R. Hepp,
Frank McKinney, and Myrfyn Owen

This report offers recommendations for future research on courtship and pairing by waterfowl. We wish to acknowledge the helpful input of the 65 people who attended and contributed to our discussion in Galveston. In particular, D. G. Raveling stimulated several useful exchanges. Several of the topics we discussed also were identified by Raveling et al. (1982). We believe this reflects continuing interest in these subjects from both theoretical and practical points of view.

Interesting Problems for Future Research

Ecological Bases for the Distribution and Spacing of Birds

Most ethologists now believe that animal social behavior evolves as the product of selfish individuals competing in specific ecological settings (Wilson 1975, Brown 1975, Wittenberger 1981, Alcock 1983). Therefore, identifying factors that shape the basic social organization of a species is critical to our understanding of courtship and pair formation as these processes have evolved to meet the needs of individuals operating within specific social systems. Of key importance here is elucidating ecological and phylogenetic factors that shape the distribution and spacing patterns of birds, both geographically and on a micro scale. Knowledge of this habitat "template" is invaluable for identifying important selection pressures and for comparative studies of behavior. For instance, to understand why birds pair when they do, it is necessary to understand why birds flock or remain dispersed; how spacing and agonistic behavior are related to resource distribu-

Waterfowl in Winter.© 1988 University of Minnesota. Edited by Milton W. Weller and published by the University of Minnesota Press, Minneapolis.

tions, predator disturbance, etc.; and the effects of these factors on the costs and benefits of living in different social classes (e.g., paired vs. unpaired).

Studies of factors affecting flocking, philopatry, and distributions of nonbreeding birds also should help managers identify key factors affecting survival that might lead to more enlightened management.

Pairing in Winter

Nearly all northern hemisphere ducks form pairs away from their breeding grounds between midautumn and early spring (Cramp and Simmons 1977, Bellrose 1980). This pattern of winter pairing appears to be unique among migratory North American birds and thus of special interest to all ornithologists. Geese may pair year-round, but the timing and processes involved are not as well known (Ogilvie 1978, Akesson and Raveling 1982, Owen et al. 1987, Black and Owen 1987).

Few general hypotheses have been offered to explain why waterfowl pair in winter (Lack 1968, Wittenberger and Tilson 1980, Shields 1983), and none has been subjected to rigorous testing. Time of pairing also varies greatly among species (e.g., Bezzel 1959, Weller 1965, Paulus 1983, Hepp and Hair 1983), and only a few attempts have been made to assess what determines these temporal differences (Weller 1965, Paulus 1983).

Comparative and experimental studies and theoretical analyses are needed to determine why ducks pair away from the breeding grounds and what influences variation in the timing of pair formation among individuals and among different species. Further descriptive data are needed for many species, preferably from several locations, to enable rigorous comparative tests of current hypotheses.

Better data on pair bond durations for a variety of species also would be valuable. The question of why most swans and geese are perennially monogamous while most ducks form seasonal pair bonds has been addressed from several viewpoints (e.g., Kear 1970, Maynard-Smith 1977). The central question appears to be: What factors tip the scales in favor of prolonged male parental investment in some species, nonparental associations with brood-rearing mates in other species, and early mate desertion, often coupled with extra-pair copulations or rapid serial monogamy, in still others? Studies of such trade-offs in sedentary southern-hemisphere species (e.g., Siegfried 1974; McKinney 1985, 1986) or island forms, some of which switch mates (e.g., Moulton and Weller 1984), might offer especially valuable insights on this question.

Finally, studies of wild, marked birds might reveal details of liaison formations and switches throughout the period of courtship and pair formation that would be important for analyzing the process of social courtship and mate choice (see below).

Because many ducks pair in late autumn and early winter, numerous pair bonds undoubtedly are disrupted by hunting, which continues through January in the southern United States and even later elsewhere (as in portions of Central America and Europe). Goose families and pairs suffer similar disruption, and this may exact short-term reproductive costs (Owen et al. 1987). Shooting essentially prereproductive pairs seems risky at first glance because of probable costs associated with re-pairing. In some species of geese, late shooting may even prevent re-pairing before the breeding season. However, the costs of disruption are largely unquantified. We need imaginative research to determine the effects of mate loss on overwinter survival and subsequent reproductive performance of individuals, especially by geese and early-pairing female ducks.

Mate Choice

Because many waterfowl, particularly seasonally monogamous ducks, form pairs anew each year away from the breeding grounds, they are an especially attractive group for studies of mate choice. Such choices apparently must be made solely on the bases of phenotypic characteristics of potential mates uncomplicated by variation in breeding territory or habitat quality—a problem that generally complicates studies of mate choice in birds (for reviews, see Bateson 1983). We believe this is a field ripe for progress since little work on modern evolutionary questions of mate choice (e.g., Halliday 1983, Partridge and Halliday 1984) has been done with waterfowl (but see McKinney 1975, Cooke and Davies 1983, Williams 1983).

Studies are needed to test for the occurrence of nonrandom rate choice, the characteristics selected in various species, and the relationship of these criteria to reproductive success. The simple occurrence of nonrandom mate selection has been demonstrated convincingly in only a few species (e.g., wild *Anser caerulescens*, Cooke and Davies 1983; captive *Aythya valisineria*, Bluhm 1985; captive *Anas platyrhynchos*, Williams 1982, K. Holmberg, pers. commun.). This is not a trivial point. Parental investment theory (Trivers 1972) offers specific predictions concerning which sex should be "choosier" in different social systems, but this does not eliminate the possibility that both sexes exercise some degree of mate choice or that other factors might suppress its expression (Partridge and Halliday 1984). For instance, mate choice could be largely masked by strong intrasexual competition for mates, and separation of these two effects is fraught with practical problems. Also the "value" to an individual of any breeding partnership may differ between mates and over the course of a breeding cycle (Anderson 1984). Pair bonds are dynamic, complex relationships, and it is likely that mate assessment continues even after pair formation.

It would be interesting to know which phenotypic characteristics form the bases for mate choice, for both males and females and in a variety of species, and how selection for these characters might affect reproductive success. Following general suggestions of Trivers (1972), Halliday (1983), and others, we might identify a variety of characteristics (table 9.1) important in mate selection in waterfowl. This list certainly is not exhaustive, but it offers some examples of characteristics that might profitably be tested. Plumage, physical condition, dominance, age, and

Table 9.1 Phenotypic characteristics and selection criteria of possible importance in mate choice by waterfowl

Character selected	Possible selection criteria
Higher fecundity	Female age
Improved social status	Fighting skill, strength, stamina
	Body size
Parental abilities	Above plus vigilance, attentiveness
Complementarity	Degree of genetic relatedness
	Previous experience together
	Mutual experience with a breeding area
Strong reproductive effort	Physical condition (vigor, plumage)
Genetic "quality"	Any phenotypic trait with a genetic basis, additive variance, and high heritability

genetic strain all may be factors affecting mate choice in captive mallards (Klint 1975, 1978, 1980; Cheng et al. 1978, 1979; Goldsmith 1979; Bossema and Kruijt 1982; Williams 1982; K. Holmberg, pers. commun.), but more work is needed to sort out the interrelationships of these factors. Only preliminary studies have been carried out with wild ducks (*Anas americana*, Wishart 1983). Body size may affect mate choice in Canada geese (MacInnes 1966) and snow geese (Ankeny 1977, Cooke and Davies 1983). Large size may be advantageous in increasing clutch size in geese (Cooke and Davis 1983) or social rank in swans (Scott 1981). Links between the characteristic selected and reproductive success will be especially difficult to determine in wild birds but should be attempted in promising situations, such as with sedentary populations. Research combining field studies and captive experiments (e.g., Wishart 1983) seems especially promising.

Process and Functions of Social Courtship

Until about 10 years ago, the functions of courtship were viewed in a rather narrow way. Courtship was shown to synchronize the reproductive condition of mates, to increase the sexual motivation of partners, and to provide reproductive isolation among otherwise similar species (e.g., Tinbergen 1951, Bastock 1967). Questions concerning the strategies and tactics of individuals engaged in courtship only became an issue with the emergence of "selfish-individual" thinking. With a "good-of-the-species" perspective, getting the right species and sexes together and synchronized seemed sufficient. Now ethologists believe that courtship also may serve many complex functions (Trivers 1972, McKinney 1975, Erickson 1977, Dawkins and Krebs 1978, Alcock 1983, Wittenberger 1983, Krebs and Dawkins 1984). This revolution in approach is based on theoretical expectations and on observations that even simple displays from a complex repertoire may contain more than enough information to assure "correct" choice of mates (Nuechterlein 1981). Consequently, we have reason to suspect that much of social courtship in waterfowl may deal with salesmanship or the assessment of potential mates, generally resulting from the competing self-interests of the individual players involved.

We have a rich information base on waterfowl courtship (e.g., Heinroth 1911, Lorenz 1941, McKinney 1965, Johnsgard 1965) that has proved to be of great taxonomic importance and that still offers many clues for understanding waterfowl social systems. However, we have surprisingly little strong evidence on the function of complex social display (e.g., Laurie-Ahlberg and McKinney 1979). Observations and experiments on marked birds are badly needed to address the goals and tactics of individuals within their social system. We need a fresh look at waterfowl courtship, including an examination of hypotheses concerning mate assessment, conflicts of interest, and evolutionarily stable courtship strategies.

Issues of Perspective and Methodology

In addition to the research topics noted above, we believe that there are several issues of methodology and perspective that require comment or deserve further study.

(1) Studies of wild birds remain critical for gaining insights into selection pressures operating in nature, but expanded use of controlled experiments with captive birds to test many existing ideas will be very helpful and should be encouraged.

(2) As the questions we ask become more sophisticated and difficult to answer, it will be increasingly important to search for populations of birds that are amenable to particular studies. Situations that permit the use of individually marked birds will be invaluable, especially if the population can be followed year-round. At the same time, we sense a growing concern over possibly serious effects of various marking techniques on the behavior of study subjects, especially with regard to potentially subtle discrimination tasks such as mate choice (for finches and doves, see Goforth and Baskett 1965; Burley 1981; Burley et al. 1982; Immelmann et al. 1982). Critical

studies of marker biases should be carried out for a variety of effects on several species.

(3) More deliberate hypothesis-testing approaches would be helpful in this field and are overdue, considering the wealth of behavioral and ecological information available on waterfowl. These tests could occur via observational studies that take advantage of natural experiments, comparative studies, or controlled experiments. Others argue that inductive approaches are still essential to reveal the nature and range of variability in behavior, especially in different habitats. Certainly, basic descriptive data on wintering social behavior are still lacking for many species and are sorely needed for comparative purposes.

(4) Studies designed to examine intraspecific variations in social behavior in relation to geographical location, time, or local habitat conditions are badly needed. We suspect that considerable variability will be found both spatially and temporally, and it would be interesting to discover the causes of such variation. Spacing, agonistic behavior, and time of pairing may be especially interesting to examine in this way. We are hampered in attempts to generalize about social behavior because, for many species, data are available from only a single time and place.

(5) The union of bioenergetic and behavioral approaches has been very productive, and we agree with the conclusion of Raveling et al. (1982) that studies combining these disciplines remain especially promising.

(6) We stand to gain much insight and stimulation for our work by extending our horizons to consider the social systems of tropical and southern hemisphere waterfowl, and other birds in general, when developing research questions about northern hemisphere waterfowl.

(7) It is crucial for progress that we approach even very specific research questions from the broader perspective of the annual cycle of each species. Thus, questions of behavior during nonbreeding periods cannot be viewed in isolation, and important research questions on courtship and pairing in winter become an integral subset of broader questions concerning the evolution of waterfowl social behavior.

LITERATURE CITED

Akesson, T. R., and D. G. Raveling. 1982. Behaviour associated with seasonal reproduction and long-term monogamy in Canada geese. Condor 84:188–196.

Alcock, J. 1983. Animal behavior: an evolutionary approach. 3rd ed. Sinauer Associates, Sunderland, Mass. 722pp.

Anderson, M. G. 1984. Parental investment and pair-bond behavior among canvasback ducks (*Aythya valisineria* Anatidae). Behav. Ecol. Sociobiol. 15:81–90.

Ankney, C. D. 1977. Male size and mate selection in lesser snow geese. Evol. Theory 3:143–148.

Bastock, M. 1967. Courtship: an ethological study. Aldine Press, Chicago. 220pp.

Bateson, P. 1983. Mate choice. Cambridge Univ. Press, Cambridge, Mass. 462pp.

Bellrose, F. C. 1980. Ducks, geese and swans of North America. Stackpole Books, Harrisburg, Pa. 540pp.

Bezzel, E. 1959. Beitrage zur Biologie der Geschlechter bei Entenvogeln. Anz. Ornithol. Ges. Bayern 5:269–356.

Black, J. M., and M. Owen. 1988. Variations in pair bond and agonistic behaviors in barnacle gleese on the wintering grounds. Pages 39-57 *in* M. W. Weller, ed., Waterfowl in winter. Univ. Minnesota Press, Minneapolis.

Bluhm, C. K. 1985. Mate preferences and mating patterns of canvasback ducks (*Aythya valisineria*). Pages 45-56 *in* P. A. Gowaty and D. W. Mock, eds. Avian Monogamy. Ornithol. Monogr. 37.

Bossema, I., and J. P. Kruijt. 1982. Male activity and female mate acceptance in the mallard (*Anas platyrhynchos*). Behav. 79:313–324.

Brown, J. L. 1975. The evolution of behavior. W. W. Norton, New York. 761pp.

Burley, N. 1981. Sex ratio manipulation and selection for attractiveness. Science 211:721–722.

———, G. Krantzberg, and P. Radman. 1982. Influence of colour-banding on the conspecific preferences of zebra finches. Anim. Behav. 30:444–455.

Cheng, K. M., R. N. Shoffner, R. E. Phillips, and F. B. Lee. 1978. Mate preference in wild and domesticated (game-farm) mallards (*Anas platyrhynchos*): I. Initial preference. Anim. Behav. 26:996–1003.

———, ———, ———, and ———. 1979. Mate preference in wild and domesticated (game-farm) mallards: II. Pairing success. Anim. Behav. 27:417–425.

Cooke, F., and J. C. Davies. 1983. Assortative mating, mate choice and reproductive fitness in snow geese. Pages 279-295 *in* P. Bateson, ed. Mate choice. Cambridge Univ. Press, Cambridge, Mass. 462pp.

Cramp, S., and K. E. L. Simmons, eds. 1977. Handbook of the birds of Europe, the Middle East and North Africa. Vol. I. Oxford Univ. Press, Oxford. 722pp.

Dawkins, R., and J. R. Krebs. 1978. Animal signals: information or manipulation. Pages 380-402 *in* J. R. Krebs and N. B. Davies, eds. Behavioural ecology: an evolutionary approach. Blackwell Scientific Publ., Oxford.

Erickson, C. J. 1977. Sexual affiliation in animals: pair bonds and reproductive strategies. Pages 697-725 *in* J. B. Hutchinson, ed. Biological determinants of sexual behavior. John Wiley, New York.

Goforth, W. R., and T. S. Baskett. 1965. Effects of experimental color marking on pairing of captive mourning doves. J. Wildl. Manage. 29:543–553.

Goldsmith, A. R. 1979. Social behaviour, pair formation and the behavioural effects of testosterone in the mallard (*Anas platyrhynchos*). Ph.D. Thesis, Univ. Leicester, Leicester. 176pp.

Halliday, T. R. 1983. The study of mate choice. Pages 3-32 *in* P. Bateson, ed. Mate choice. Cambridge Univ. Press, Cambridge. 462pp.

Heinroth, O. 1911. Beitrage zur Biologie, namentlich Ethologie und Psychologie der Anatiden. Verh. Int. Ornithol. Kongr. 5:598–702.

Hepp, G. R., and J. D. Hair. 1983. Reproductive behavior and pairing chronology in wintering dabbling ducks. Wilson Bull. 95:675–682.

Immelmann, K., J. P. Hailman, and J. R. Baylis. 1982. Reputed band attractiveness and sex manipulation in zebra finches. Science 215:422.

Johnsgard, P. A. 1965. Handbook of waterfowl behavior. Cornell Univ. Press, Ithaca, N.Y. 378 pp.

Kear, J. 1970. The adaptive radiation of parental care in waterfowl. Pages 357-392 in J. H. Cook, ed. Social behaviour in birds and mammals. Academic Press, London.

Klint, T. 1975. Sexual imprinting in the context of species recognition in female mallards. Z. Tierpsychol. 38:385–392.

———. 1978. Significance of mother and sibling experience for mating preferences in the mallard (Anas platyrhynchos L.). Z. Tierpsychol. 47:50–60.

———. 1980. Influence of male nuptial plumage on mate selection in the female mallard (Anas platyrhynchos). Anim. Behav. 28:1230–1238.

Krebs, J. R., and R. Dawkins. 1984. Animal signals: mind-reading and manipulation. Pages 380-402 in J. R. Krebs and N. B. Davies, eds. Behavioural ecology—an evolutionary approach. 2nd ed. Blackwell Scientific Publ., Oxford.

Lack, D. 1968. Ecological adaptations for breeding in birds. Methuen and Co., London. 409 pp.

Laurie-Ahlberg, C. C., and F. McKinney. 1979. The nod-swim display of male green-winged teal (Anas crecca). Anim. Behav. 27:165–172.

Lorenz, K. 1941. Vergleichende Bewegungstudien an Anatinen. J. Ornithol. 89:194–294.

MacInnes, C. D. 1966. Population behavior of eastern arctic Canada geese. J. Wildl. Manage. 30:536–553.

Maynard-Smith, J. 1977. Parental investment: a prospective analysis. Anim. Behav. 25:1–9.

McKinney, F. 1965. The comfort movements of Anatidae. Behav. 25:120–220.

———. 1975. The evolution of duck displays. Pages 331-357 in G. Baerends. C. Beer, and A. Manning, eds. Function and evolution in behaviour. Clarendon Press, Oxford.

———. 1985. Primary and secondary male reproductive strategies of dabbling ducks. Pages 68-82 in P. A. Gowaty and D. W. Mock, eds. Avian monogamy. Ornithol. Mongr. 37.

———. 1986. Ecological factors in the evolution of social behavior of dabbling ducks. Pages 153-171 in D. I. Rubenstein and R. W. Wrangham, eds. Ecological aspects of social evolution. 551 pp.

Moulton, D. W., and M. W. Weller. 1984. Biology and conservation of the Laysan duck (Anas laysanensis). Condor 86:105–117.

Nuechterlein, G. L. 1981. Variations and multiple functions of the advertising display of western grebes. Behav. 76:289–317.

Ogilvie, M. A. 1978. Wild geese. Buteo Books, Vermillion, S.D. 350 pp.

Owen, M., J. M. Black, and H. Liber. 1988. Pair bond duration and timing of its formation in barnacle geese (Branta leucopsis). Pages 23-38 in M. W. Weller, ed. Waterfowl in winter. Univ. Minnesota Press, Minneapolis.

Partridge, L., and T. R. Halliday. 1984. Mating patterns and mate choice. Pages 222-250 in J. R. Krebs and N. B. Davies, eds. Behavioral ecology: an evolutionary approach. Sinauer Associates Sunderland, Mass.

Paulus, S. L. 1983. Dominance relations, resource use, and pairing chronology of gadwalls in winter. Auk 100:947–952.

Raveling, D. G., A. D. Afton, W. C. Alexander, M. G. Anderson, R. O. Bailey, D. F. McKinney, R. D. Sayler, R. D. Titman, and R. A. Wishart. 1982. Report of the social behavior discussion group. Pages 26-33 in M. G. Anderson and B. D. J. Batt, eds. Workshop on the ecology of wintering waterfowl. Delta Waterfowl Research Station, Portage la Prairie, Man.

Scott, D. K. 1981. Social behaviour of Cygnus columbianus bewickii. Pages 211-225 in Proc. 2nd Int. Swan Symposium, Int. Waterfowl Res. Bureau, Slimbridge, U.K.

Shields, W. M. 1983. Optimal inbreeding and the evolution of philopatry. Pages 132-159 in I. R. Swingland and P. J. Greenwood, eds. The ecology of animal movement. Clarendon Press, Oxford.

Siegried, W. R. 1974. Brood care, pair bonds and plumage in southern African Anatini. Wildfowl 25:33–40.

Tinbergen, N. 1951. The study of instinct. Clarendon Press, Oxford. 228pp.

Trivers, R. L. 1972. Parental investment and sexual selection. Pages 136-179 *in* B. Campbell, ed. Sexual selection and the descent of man, 1871-1971. Aldine Press, Chicago.

Weller, M. W. 1965. Chronology of pair formation in some nearctic Aythya (Anatidae). Auk 82:227-235.

Williams, D. M. 1982. Agonistic behaviour and mate selection in the mallard (*Anas platyrhynchos*). Ph.D. Thesis, Univ. Leicester, Leicester. 243pp.

————. 1983. Mate choice in the mallard. Pages 297-309 *in* P. Bateson, ed. Mate choice. Cambridge Univ. Press, Cambridge.

Wilson, E. O. 1975. Sociobiology, the new synthesis. Belknap Press, Cambridge, Mass. 697pp.

Wishart, R. A. 1983. Pairing chronology and mate selection in the American wigeon (*Anas americana*). Can. J. Zool. 61:1733-1743.

Wittenberger, J. F. 1981. Animal social behavior. Duxbury Press, Boston, Mass. 722pp.

————. 1983. Tactics of mate choice. Pages 435-447 *in* P. Bateson, ed. Mate choice. Cambridge Univ. Press, Cambridge, Mass.

————, and R. L. Tilson. 1980. The evolution of monogamy: hypotheses and evidence. Ann. Rev. Ecol. Syst. 11:197-232.

III.
Activity Budgets

10

Time-Activity Budgets of Nonbreeding Anatidae: A Review

Stuart L. Paulus

Abstract: Available literature on time-activity budgets of nonbreeding waterfowl demonstrates how environmental factors, social status, and physical condition of the individual influence the amount of time allocated to major activities. Non-breeding waterfowl spend most of their time feeding and loafing. Species that select foods of high nutrient content devote the least amount of time to feeding. For many Anatinae, time spent feeding is highest in fall (Aug-Nov), declines during winter (Dec-Jan), and increases in early spring (Feb-Apr). Time spent in locomotion, being alert, and preening remains nearly constant from fall to early spring. Waterfowl spend much of their time loafing diurnally and feeding at night. For birds using tidal areas, timing of daily activities is closely associated with the tidal cycle. Predation, hunting pressure, and physiological characters of the individual also influence timing of daily activities. Few differences exist in time budgets of males and females. Time spent foraging usually increases as ambient temperature declines. Cloud cover delays initiation of morning field-feeding flights, and high winds and rainfall lower feeding activity levels in many nonbreeding Anatidae. Time budgets can be used by managers to identify and protect habitats used by nonbreeding waterfowl, to monitor behavioral responses of waterfowl to habitat loss and changes in diet, and to determine optimum times for hunting, censusing, and viewing. Future studies should employ hypothesis testing, determine nocturnal activities and habitat use, and be used to construct energy budgets.

Time-activity budgets quantify how birds apportion time for various activities. Time budgets may be used to ascertain how individuals apportion energy between

Waterfowl in Winter. © 1988 University of Minnesota. Edited by Milton W. Weller and published by the University of Minnesota Press, Minneapolis.

productive and maintenance functions, assuming that each individual apportions its time in an optimal fashion for each environmental condition, that this time apportioned has adaptive value, and that estimates of time budgets closely approximate apportionment of time for a species studied. They may also be used to evaluate behavioral and physiological responses of waterfowl to environmental factors (Fredrickson and Drobney 1979), provide data on habitat use, assist in managing populations, or help identify further waterfowl research needs.

The purposes of this paper are to (1) review available literature on time budgets of nonbreeding waterfowl, with primary emphasis on how environmental factors, social status, and physical condition of the individual influence the amount of time allocated to major activities; (2) discuss potential uses of time-budget data in management of nonbreeding waterfowl; (3) and provide suggestions for future research.

I thank A. Afton, G. Baldassarre, M. Joanen, D. Jorde, M. Miller, A. Tamisier, R. Titman, and M. Weller for their assistance in manuscript preparation. Financial support was provided by the Louisiana Department of Wildlife and Fisheries.

General

Time spent in activities by anatids varies among and within species (tables 10.1 and 10.2). Species comparisons often are difficult because data are lacking on the nocturnal activities of many waterfowl. However, these data show that nonbreeding waterfowl spend most of their time loafing and feeding; time allocated to these activities varies greatly among species; time spent resting usually is inversely related to time spent feeding; and time allocated to other activities, including locomoting, preening, social display, and alert and agonistic activities, is similar

Table 10.1. Definition of terms used in text

Term	Definition
Feeding	Ingestion of food obtained by surface or subsurface feeding or grazing
Resting	Sleeping or loafing
Locomotion	Swimming, walking, and flying (flying activity is probably underestimated in most studies)
Alert	Attentive to nearby conspecifics or disturbances; bird usually assumes upright posture
Preening	Activities involved with body maintenance or bathing
Social display	Displays associated with pair formation and maintenance activities and copulations
Agonistic	Threat displays
Nonbreeding	Includes the period birds spend migrating to and from, and on, the wintering grounds

Table 10.2. Percentage of time spent by nonbreeding Anatidae in various activities

Species	Feed-ing	Rest-ing	Loco-motion	Alert	Preen-ing	Court-ing	Agon-istic	Other[a]	Diet[b]	References
Anserinae										
Chen c. caerulescens	30[c]	52	1	12	6				N	Burton and Hudson 1978
	13[c]	59	2		3		<1	24	Ag	Frederick and Klaas 1982
Anser anser	39[c]		42					19	N	Lebret 1970
Branta canadensis	13[d]							87	Ag	Raveling et al. 1972
Anser a. albifrons	39[d]							61	N	Howard 1940
	90[d]	3		3	2				N	Owen 1972
Branta leucopsis	83[d]	1		15	1		<1		N	Ebbinge et al. 1975
Dendrocygna viduata	<2[d]	43	10	23	20				N	Roux et al. 1978
Anatinae										
Anas penelope	56[c]	29	8		5			2	N	Campredon 1981
Anas strepera	64[c]	11	11	9	5	<1	<1		N	Paulus 1984a
Anas fulvigula	43[c]	36	6	7	7	<1	<1		N	Paulus 1984b
Anas platyrhynchos	35[c]	28	13	5	18	<1	<1		Ag	Jorde et al. 1984
Anas c. crecca	42[c]	33			14			11	N	Tamisier 1972
Aythya fuligula	21[c]	40	34		<1			3	N	Pedroli 1982
Anas querquedula	<2[d]	56	40	<1	4				N	Roux et al. 1978
Anas acuta	<2[d]	60	30	<1	10				N	Roux et al. 1978
	18[d]	48	13		13	4			Ag	Miller 1985
	5[d]	70	9		10			6	Ag	Tamisier 1976
	61[d]	29	5		3	1	<1	<1	N	Hepp 1982
Anas c. crecca	51[d]							49	Ag	Zwarts 1976
	5[d]	75	9		9				Ag	Tamisier 1976
Anas crecca carolinensis	56[d]	35	4		3	2	<1	<1	N	Hepp 1982
	14[d]	72	7		6			1	N	Quinlan and Baldassarre 1984
Anas rubripes	43[d]	40	9		7	1	<1	1	N	Hepp 1982
	34[d]	44	10		10			3	N	Hickey and Titman 1983
Anas strepera	75[d]	17	5		2	<1		<1	N	Hepp 1982
Anas americana	53[d]	32	9		4	<1	<1	<1	N	Hepp 1982
Anas clypeata	59[d]	29	8		4	<1	<1	<1	N	Hepp 1982

continued on next page

Table 10.2. Continued

Species	Feeding	Resting	Locomotion	Alert	Preening	Courting	Agonistic	Other[a]	Diet[b]	References
Tadorna tadorna 55[d]								45	N	Evans and Pienkowski 1982
45[d]								55	N	Thompson 1981
Anas undulata 34[d]	33	25		9					N	Skead 1977
Anas erythrorhyncha 26[d]	38	28		8					N	Skead 1977
Anas smithii 39[d]	34	18		8					N	Skead 1977
Anas capinsis 59[d]	26	9		7					N	Skead 1977
Aythya affinis, marila[e] 73[d]	8	15		4	<1				N	Noseworthy 1981
Aythya marila 9[d]								91	N	Nilsson 1970
Aythya fuligula 11[d]								89	N	Nilsson 1970
Aythya ferina 23[d]								77	N	Nilsson 1970
Bucephala clangula 86[d]								14	N	Nilsson 1970
Bucephala americana 84[d]	3	9		4	<1				N	Noseworthy 1981
Clangula hyemalis 79[d]								21	N	Nilsson 1970
Mergus serrator 50[d]								50	N	Nilsson 1970
Mergus merganser 19[d]								81	N	Nilsson 1970
Mergus albellus 46[d]								54	N	Nilsson 1970
Aythya collaris 35[d]	24	17	10	15	<1	<1			N	Hohman 1986

[a] Combined time spent in activities for which no values were given by author.

[b] Major food consumed, consisting either of natural marsh vegetation or animal matter (N) or agricultural seed grains (Ag).

[c] Observation of birds during day and night.

[d] Observation of birds only during the day.

[e] Time budgets combined for 2 species.

among species. Nonbreeding anatids average 20-70% of their time feeding; 10-50% resting; less than 20% preening, alert, or in locomotion; and less than 2% in social display and agonistic activities.

Diet

Diet choice and food availability apparently are important factors influencing the amount of time spent in various activities by nonbreeding waterfowl. Nonbreeding waterfowl consume diverse and large amounts of food to meet nutrient needs for molt and daily metabolic requirements and to acquire lipid reserves for winter storage, spring migration, and reproduction. Waterfowl differ greatly among and within species in their choice of foods during the nonbreeding season. In general, birds selecting foods of low water and high nutrient content, such as agricultural grains (Sugden 1973, Driver et al. 1974, Baldassarre et al. 1983), devote the least amount of time to feeding. For example, green-winged teal (*Anas crecca carolinensis*) in Texas, which fed mostly on corn (*Zea mays*), spent only about 15-20% of their time feeding during most of winter (Quinlan and Baldassarre 1984). In contrast, it is estimated that green-winged teal feeding upon rice in Louisiana, or common teal (*A. c. crecca*) feeding upon natural vegetation in the Camargue, France, spent 40-50% of their time feeding (Tamisier 1972, 1976). Consumption of agricultural seeds by nonbreeding waterfowl may benefit birds by reducing time needed to forage. These individuals spend much time resting and, even during periods of food shortage or increased food-intake requirements, should have sufficient time to meet nutritive needs. However, a diet of agricultural foods may be deficient in certain nutrients (Baldassarre et al. 1983).

Brodsky and Weatherhead (1985) found that black ducks (*Anas rubripes*) spent only 20% of daytime activity consuming corn. As birds selected lower-quality diets, time spent feeding usually increased. Individuals selecting highest-quality foods also initiated earlier and spent more time in social display than ducks selecting lower-quality foods.

Species consuming leafy aquatic vegetation, which usually is of high water and fiber content (Paulus 1982a), spent much of their time feeding. Gadwalls (*Anas strepera*) (Paulus 1984a) and European wigeon (*Anas penelope*) (Campredon 1981) spent over 50% of their time feeding. In areas with little disturbance, gadwalls spent 80% of their diurnal time feeding. In addition, time spent feeding by gadwalls increased as they selected aquatic plants of lower gross energy and higher fiber content (Paulus 1982a, 1984a). Intestines of these species are often elongated and enlarged, allowing birds to maximize consumption and nutritive extraction of foods (Paulus 1982b).

Inland diving ducks (*Aythya*) usually spend less than 30% whereas mergansers (*Mergus*) and goldeneyes (*Bucephala*) may spend over 50% of their diurnal time feeding on diets primarily containing animal matter (table 10.2). However, during the 24-hour period, tufted ducks (*Aythya fuligula*) (Pedroli 1982) spent only 21% of their time feeding. Because animal matter usually contains more gross caloric energy and a greater diversity of nutrients than vegetative foods (Driver et al. 1974), individuals selecting this diet are predicted to spend the least amount of time foraging. However, time spent feeding by *Aythya* foraging upon animal matter is similar to that of birds consuming seeds of aquatic vegetation and more than that of birds feeding upon agricultural grains. Time spent feeding by divers may be higher than expected if (1) birds must spend more time searching for, acquiring, and consuming animal than seed matter; (2) the high water content of animal foods results in the nutritional value per gram of wet weight being lower for animal matter than seeds, requiring greater intake of animal matter to meet nutrient needs; or (3) differences in the methods of data collection in time-activity budget studies elevate foraging levels of divers as compared with dabblers (A. Tamisier, pers. commun.). For example, feeding time of divers may include time spent diving, catching the food, rising to the surface, surfacing, and consuming the prey item. However, time recorded as feeding for dabblers usually consists only of time spent actually consuming foods.

Grazing geese also have enlarged guts that are useful in processing poorer-quality foods, but they still may spend most diurnal hours feeding. White-fronted geese (*Anser a. albifrons*) (Owen 1972) and barnacle geese (*Branta leucopsis*) (Ebbinge et al. 1975) may consume up to 25% of their body weight in grass each day and spend over 80% of daylight hours feeding to meet nutrient requirements. In contrast, geese consuming agricultural grains can meet daily nutritional needs in a few hours (Raveling et al. 1972, Frederick and Klaas 1982).

There are conflicting data regarding the effect of food availability on time spent feeding. Shelducks (*Tadorna tadorna*) spent more time feeding as food availability declined (Bryant and Leng 1975, Thompson 1981, Buxton 1981), whereas no such relationship existed with common teal (Tamisier 1972, 1974). Perhaps food densities were great enough in all study areas so that common teal could acquire and process foods at similar rates, or factors other than food density may have influenced feeding rates (see Buxton 1981). Frederick and Klaas (1982) noted that snow geese (*Chen c. caerulescens*) avoided areas heavily exploited by other foraging geese and flew longer distances to less exploited areas.

Temporal Factors

For many Anatinae, percentage of time spent feeding is highest in fall (Aug-Nov), declines in winter (Dec-Jan), and increases in early spring (Feb-Apr) (table 10.3). Seasonal trends in time budgets of nonbreeding waterfowl are closely related to food availability and quality and to energy requirements of individuals. In autumn, waterfowl spend much of their time feeding to meet energy requirements for accumulation of lipid reserves that serve as an energy source later in winter (Paulus 1980, 1983; Jorde 1981; Miller 1985). Molting waterfowl also may increase foraging rates in autumn to acquire specific nutrients required for feather formation (Quinlan and Baldassarre 1984). Because of shorter nights, diurnal feeding rates may be higher because birds need to spend part of the day feeding to meet nutrient needs (Nilsson 1970, Tamisier 1972). Time of peak social-display activity in fall and winter varies for each species, occurring during the period of pair formation (Afton and Sayler 1982, Paulus 1983, Hepp and Hair 1984).

In early winter, climatic conditions on many wintering areas generally are moderate. Most individuals have acquired large fat reserves and completed the prealternate molt, and consequently less energy intake is required than in autumn (Tamisier 1974, Campredon 1981). In many habitats, food availability and quality for waterfowl are greatest during early winter as natural marsh seeds (Paulus

Table 10.3. Percentage of time spend by nonbreeding Anatidae in various activities by time of year

Time Activity	Chen c. caerulescens[a] (Frederick and Klaas 1982)	Anas penelope (Campredon 1981)	Anas strepera (Paulus 1984a)	Anas c. crecca (Tamisier 1972)	Anas fulvigula (Paulus 1984b)	Anas acuta[b] (Miller 1985)	Aythya fulvigula[b] (Nilsson 1970)
Aug-Sept							
Feeding				48		33	
Resting				39		27	
Locomotion				1		11	
Alert							
Preening				12		21	
Courting						0	
Other						8	
Oct-Nov							
Feeding	13	55	47	33	33	13	2
Resting	58	28	12	36	42	55	
Locomotion	2	8	16	20	7	12	
Alert			13		7		
Preening	2	6	11	7	11	15	
Courting			1		<1	2	
Other	25	3	<1		<1	3	98
Dec-Jan							
Feeding	15	48	58	49	39	7	5
Resting	67	33	15	29	41	51	
Locomotion	2	11	13	20	6	13	
Alert			9		7		
Preening	3	5	4	2	8	12	
Courting			<1		<1	13	
Other	12	3	<1		<1	4	95
Feb-Mar							
Feeding		64	68	51	45[c]	20	19
Resting		25	7	32	33	50	
Locomotion		6	9	16	5	11	
Alert			10		9		
Preening	2	4	5	1	8	13	
Courting			<1		<1	3	
Other		1	<1		<1	3	81

[a] Diet consisted primarily of agricultural foods; all other species consumed diets primarily of aquatic vegetation.

[b] Observations conducted only during daylight.

[c] Includes data collected only in February.

1984b) and agricultural foods become increasingly available. Energy losses are minimized as birds select thermally favorable microhabitats and spend most of their time resting during the day (Tamisier 1974, Brodsky and Weatherhead 1984, Jorde et al. 1984, Paulus 1984b, Quinlan and Baldassarre 1984).

By late winter, time spent feeding increases due to a scarcity of food and premigratory hyperphagia (Tamisier 1972, 1974; Miller 1985). Energy intake and time spent feeding also may be elevated to meet nutrient needs for upcoming egg-laying and breeding activities (Paulus 1984b).

Gadwalls in Louisiana (Paulus 1984a) and ring-necked ducks (*Aythya collaris*) in Florida (Hohman 1986) differ in that feeding rates increased steadily from autumn to early spring. Gadwall diets consisted of 95% aquatic vegetation and algae, and food availability and quality were greatest in fall during the period of molt and lipid deposition. As winter progressed, gadwalls consumed diets of lower quality; by late winter, algae, a dilute source of nutrients (Paulus 1982a), was the predominant food in the diet. In addition, gadwalls, as do other species, increase foraging rates in late winter to obtain the greater energy reserves needed for spring migration.

Studies to date show that many Anatidae spend much of their time loafing diurnally and feeding and loafing at night (fig. 10.1), especially those individuals that forage upon seeds or sessile animal matter. Common goldeneyes (*Bucephala clangula*) and mergansers, which consume motile prey or sessile prey in flowing rivers, feed primarily during daylight hours while forming rafts on rivers and resting at night (Linsell 1969, Nilsson 1970, Sayler and Afton 1981, Afton and Sayler 1982). Individuals consuming low-energy, high-fiber diets spend much of the day and night foraging to meet nutrient requirements. Gadwalls (Paulus 1984a) spent 61% and 69% and European wigeon (Campredon 1981) 33% and 72% of their time feeding on leafy aquatic vegetation during the day and night, respectively. Rest periods were interspersed among feeding bouts during night and daytime hours for both species.

Timing of daily activity patterns is influenced by many factors. However, thermal conditions and diurnal avian predation pressure are cited most often as proximate factors influencing daily activity patterns (Tamisier 1972, 1974; Paulus 1984a, 1984b). Diurnal resting is favored because optimal thermal conditions during the day and reduced activity minimize energy costs. Nocturnal feeding would be favored if metabolic heat produced by feeding activity lowered thermoregulatory costs (Calder and King 1974).

Anatinae on the wintering grounds experience harassment by avian predators during the day and are observed flying to open water from feeding sites at the approach of an avian predator (Tamisier 1970, Paulus 1984b). Tamisier (1974) observed that common teal were disturbed up to 160 times per day by avian predators. Northern harriers (*Circus cyaneus*) will attempt to flush sick or crippled birds from flocks, and I have seen them trying to capture adult, healthy mottled

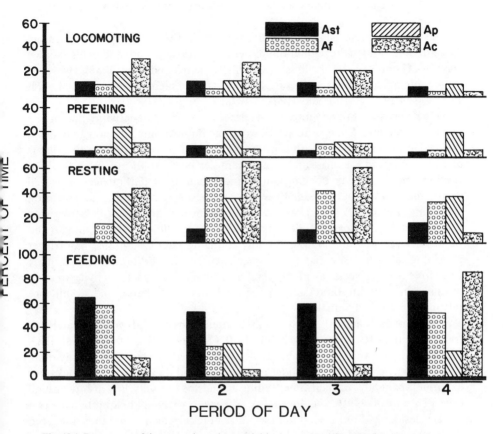

Fig. 10.1. Percentage of time spent in various activities by nonbreeding Anatidae (Ast = *Anas strepera*, Paulus 1984a; Af = *A. fulvigula*, Paulus 1984b; Ap = *A. platyrhynchos*, Jorde 1981; Ac = *A. c. crecca*, Tamisier 1972) in relation to period of day (1 = 0600-1000, 2 = 1000-1400, 3 = 1400-1800, and 4 = 1800-0600). Percentages less than 0.05 are not shown.

ducks (*Anas fulvigula*). Thus, during the day, Anatinae often select deeper water areas, which provide loafing habitat and areas for escape from predators but limited feeding habitat. At night, when threat of avian predation is less, birds may move into shallow-water foraging areas (Paulus 1984b).

Field-feeding Anatids, including mallards (*Anas platyrhynchos*) (Jorde et al. 1984) and green-winged teal (Quinlan and Baldassarre 1984), tend to forage during daylight or at dawn and dusk in winter. Common teal and green-winged teal (Tamisier 1976, Baldassarre and Bolen 1984), northern pintail (*Anas acuta*) (Tamisier 1976, Miller 1985), common goldeneyes (Breckenridge 1953, Sayler and Afton 1981), mottled ducks (Paulus 1984b), and other Anatinae (Thornburg 1973, Campbell 1978) make regular flights between habitats used mainly for loafing and those used for feeding.

Field-feeding geese using agricultural crops or pastures forage primarily during daylight hours and make regular flights between roosting ponds and fields at dawn and dusk (Lebret 1970, Raveling et al. 1972, Frederick and Klaas 1982). However, geese foraging in natural marshes feed during day and night (Howard 1940, Lebret 1970, Owen 1972, Burton and Hudson 1978).

Dawn and dusk provide important cues for the timing of activities and movement of waterfowl. Changes in activities of tufted ducks and common goldeneyes in Sweden were associated with sunrise and sunset (Nilsson 1970). Feeding flights often are observed at sunrise and sunset (Tamisier 1978-79). By moving in flocks at specific times of the day, flocking can aid individuals in predator detection as well as provide for information exchange regarding resource availability and location (Ward and Zahavi 1973, Kenward 1978). Social display and agonistic activity are common at dawn (Gorman 1970; Hepp 1982; Paulus 1984a, 1984b; Quinlan and Baldassarre 1984; Miller 1985). Rapidly changing light conditions may trigger physiological responses that favor social activity. In addition, because many waterfowl are less social at night (Paulus 1984a, 1984b), social activity in early morning may be an expression of reestablishment of spatial and dominance relations among individuals.

Timing of daily activities is closely associated with the tidal cycle for waterfowl using tidal areas (Gorman 1970, Lebret 1970, Campbell 1978, Albright et al. 1983, Hickey and Titman 1983, Ydenberg et al. 1984). Feeding activity is usually more common during ebb and flow tides and lowest at tidal extremes. Shelducks, for example, spent 80% of their time feeding at midtide but only 10% at low or high tides (Thompson 1981). Shelducks, like European wigeon, apparently need two tidal cycles per 24-hour period to meet nutrient requirements, and thus must feed during both day and night (Buxton 1981, Campredon 1981). Social activity of common eiders (*Somateria mollissima*) occurred more often during flood than ebb tides, although timing of social activities also was influenced by time of day (Gorman 1970).

Tides are an important factor influencing daily activities of greylag geese (*Anser anser*). In tidal areas, greylag geese fed during day and night; however, birds using pastures fed only diurnally (Lebret 1970). Absolute tidal height, and not tidal direction (ebb or flow), was most important in influencing lesser snow goose foraging on rhizomes, and at tidal extremes most birds rested (Burton and Hudson 1978). These researchers also observed that diurnal resting activity was lower for snow geese using tidal flats than for geese using marshes not influenced by tides.

Until recently, few studies examined the activities of individuals at night. Barnacle geese fed at night around the full moon, both day and night as the moon waxed, and during the day as the moon waned (Ebbinge et al. 1975, Ydenberg et al. 1984). Paulus (1984b) observed that mottled ducks began preening and resting at night as the moon dropped below the horizon, although some feeding was observed on moonless nights. Social activities also appear more important to Anatinae on moonlit than moonless nights (Jorde 1981; Paulus 1984a, 1984b).

Table 10.4. Percentage of time spent by nonbreeding Anatidae in various activities in relation to sex and pair status

Species Status	Feed-ing	Rest-ing	Loco-motion	Alert	Preen-ing	Other[a]	Reference
Anas strepera							Paulus 1984a
Paired male	64	11	10	10	5	1	
Paired female	64	11	10	8	6	0	
Unpaired male	65	1	16	11	6	1	
Unpaired female	66	6	11	10	7	0	
Anas fulvigula							Paulus 1984b
Paired male	39	38	6	8	9	0	
Paired female	39	38	6	7	9	0	
Unpaired male	40	21	17	11	11	1	
Unpaired female	39	24	12	15	11	0	
Anas platyrhynchos							Jorde 1981
Paired male	31	26	15	10	16	2	
Paired female	38	25	15	4	17	1	
Unpaired male	30	30	15	7	16	1	
Unpaired female	31	37	15	4	13	1	
Anas acuta[b]							Miller 1985
Male	15	46	15		13	11	
Female	15	56	10		13	6	
Anas crecca carolinensis[b]							Quinlan and Baldassarre 1984
Male	13	54	22	1	9	0	
Female	15	55	19	1	10	1	
Anas rubripes[b]							Hickey and Titman 1983
Male	32	43	10		11	4	
Female	38	42	10		8	2	
Bucephala americana[b]							Noseworthy 1981
Male	7	4	18		7	1	
Female	83	4	8		4	1	
Aythya marila, affinis[b,c]							Noseworthy 1981
Male	72	6	16		5	<1	
Female	68	12	18		4	<1	

[a]Combined time spent courting, in agonistic activities, or in activities listed for which no values were shown.

[b]Observations conducted only during diurnal hours.

[c]Time budgets combined for two species.

Sex, Age, and Social Status

Recently it has been shown that sex or social status of nonbreeding individuals influences time budgets. For many nonbreeding Anatinae, few differences are found in time spent feeding by males and females, whereas other studies have shown that females feed more than males (table 10.4). Age of the individual also influences how time is allocated. Frederick and Klaas (1982) found that juvenile lesser snow geese spent more time foraging than did adults, whereas adults spent more time alert than juveniles.

These data suggest that nutrient requirements of nonbreeding male and female waterfowl are similar or slightly greater for females. Males may sacrifice feeding opportunities to spend more time courting, locomoting, or protecting mates (Jorde 1981, Miller 1985). Feeding rates of females also may be higher than those of males because females are excluded from higher-quality feeding areas by dominant males (Hepp and Hair 1984). It has been suggested that females may migrate south to more favorable areas if they are unable to compete for and secure required nutrients (Tamisier 1972, Nichols and Haramis 1980, Sayler and Afton 1981, Hepp and Hair 1984).

Paired and unpaired gadwalls, mottled ducks, and mallards spent similar amounts of time feeding. However, unpaired gadwalls and mottled ducks spent more time locomoting and less time resting and unpaired mallards devoted more time to social displays than did pairs (Jorde et al. 1984; Paulus 1984a, 1984b).

Unpaired birds often are displaced to poorer habitats or to the periphery of the flock by dominant birds; they may spend more time in food search or agonistic activities and have larger activity centers (Hepp 1982, Jorde et al. 1984, Paulus 1984a). Paired females may benefit from improved foraging efficiency as mates defend against interactions with other birds (Ashcroft 1976). Since pairs often are dominant to unpaired birds (Paulus 1983, 1984a), energy costs may be greater and nutrient intake less for unpaired than paired birds. Thus, unpaired birds may be in poorer condition in winter and less likely to survive or breed than adults (Paulus 1980, 1983; Wishart 1983; see also Afton and Sayler 1982).

Weather

Foraging effort usually increases as the temperature declines (Nilsson 1970; Tamisier 1972, 1974; Jorde 1981; Paulus 1984a, 1984b) until the temperature reaches about 0C. Below this level, energetic costs of foraging may exceed gains (Frederick and Klaas 1982, Paulus 1984b); birds thus reduce activities that have excessive energy costs (Smith and Prince 1973; Hickey and Titman 1983; Brodsky and Weatherhead 1984, 1985) and spend more time resting. Raveling et al. (1972) noted that Canada geese (*Branta canadensis*) did not fly to nearby fields to feed when temperatures were less than –9C but that flights were common at temperatures greater than -7C. Common goldeneye morning flights were delayed on coldest days, but birds did feed and selected more favorable microclimates (Sayler and Afton 1981). Female common goldeneyes spent most of their time feeding (95%) during the day in cold weather (Nilsson 1970).

With lower temperatures, alert and agonistic activity levels often decline as birds spend more time foraging (Caraco 1979; Jorde et al. 1984; Paulus 1984a, 1984b). On coldest days (<-20C), black ducks selected sheltered roosts and spent most of their time resting (Albright et al. 1983, Brodsky and Weatherhead 1984). While resting, waterfowl often face into the sun, or, at high wind speeds, into the wind (Tamisier 1976, Mitgard 1978). Social displays were more common among black ducks and mallards in winter as temperatures increased (Reed 1971, Albright et al. 1983).

Cloud cover delays initiation of morning field-feeding flights in Canada geese (Raveling et al. 1972) and white-fronted geese (Owen 1972) and increases time spent by birds in fields. Raveling et al. (1972) suggested that a certain light level was required to trigger morning flights. Little or no relationship between cloud cover and flight time was noted for morning flights of common goldeneyes (Breckenridge 1953) or afternoon flights of Canada geese (Raveling et al. 1972).

High wind speeds and rainfall result in lower feeding activity levels in northern pintail, gadwalls, and mottled ducks (Paulus 1984a, 1984b; Miller 1985) as the ability of birds to find and obtain food probably is hampered. During high winds, when wave action makes it difficult for birds to feed, they often engage in preening and bathing or fly to more secluded marshes (Paulus 1984a, 1984b).

Hunting pressure and disturbance influence daily activities of waterfowl. Hunting pressure often discourages use of preferred wetlands by wintering waterfowl, and many species spend more time feeding at night in areas where they are hunted than in nonhunted habitats (Raveling et al. 1972, Thornburg 1973). Gadwalls, mottled ducks (Paulus 1984a, 1984b), and tufted ducks (Pedroli 1982) spent more time feeding, alert, and in locomotion and less time loafing, on hunted than on nonhunted areas. Energy costs of daily flights to and from hunted areas and increased levels of awareness by individuals using hunted areas may account for these behavior differences. However, Tamisier (1976), Roux et al. (1978), Burton and Hudson (1978), and Miller (1985) stated that hunting had little influence on daily time budgets of birds.

Management Implications

Time budgets are useful in identifying important habitats used by nonbreeding waterfowl (Fredrickson and Drobney 1979), assessing current and future habitat needs, determining the fundamental requirements of the species (Tamisier 1978-79), and predicting the behavior and bioenergetic response of waterfowl to projected habitat changes. Among variables measured in time budget studies, habitat choice often is most important in determining the amount of time spent by waterfowl in various activities (Paulus 1980, Frederick and Klaas 1982, Hohman 1986). By determining what activities are most important to a species and where they are performed, a wildlife manager can take steps to preserve or provide critical habitats. This intervention may be more important for less adaptable species or for those less able to modify their activity regimes (i.e., species consuming aquatic vegetation, using tidal areas, or wintering in more hostile climates).

Wildlife managers must not only be concerned with correctly interpreting time budget data when determining habitat needs, but also when assessing the ability of an area to provide for the fundamental requirements of waterfowl. The nutritive, spatial, and social requirements of waterfowl must be provided. Tamisier (1978-79) noted that many species loaf primarily during the day and feed at night. Because these activities often occur in geographically distinct areas, each area may require different strategies to meet management objectives. If the goal is to protect birds from harassment and hunting, it may be necessary to protect these distinct areas or provide loafing and feeding habitats in one area to meet the fundamental needs of the birds. Managers must also be cognizant of the importance of microhabitat choice (Jorde et al. 1984), seasonal variability in requirements of waterfowl, and the unique needs of individual species in influencing time budgets and habitat use.

In recent years, agricultural foods have comprised a greater portion of the diets of several species. Although agricultural foods are deficient in some nutrients important to waterfowl (Baldassarre et al. 1983), individuals can rapidly meet their energy requirements, as demonstrated by the time birds spend feeding on agricultural foods. If nutrient deficiencies can be met while foraging for short periods in natural marshes, overall foraging time may be greatly reduced.

Knowledge of the timing of daily activities may be useful in manipulating hunting or viewing hours. Closure of hunting in midafternoon in Illinois allowed Canada geese to leave refuges and feed unharassed during the evening feeding period (Raveling et al. 1972). Nature center tours in search of waterfowl can be arranged to coincide with periods when birds are feeding or courting and are most visible. Accuracy of winter population surveys can be enhanced by timing survey flights to coincide with periods of the day when most birds are engaged in activities that are conducted on open water or other easily observable areas. Finally, management practices should be concerned about the effects of harvest regulations on population social structure. Regulations favoring harvest of one sex over another may disrupt pair formation (Brown 1982). Since allocation of time by nonbreeding waterfowl is influenced by pair status, modifications in population social structure may adversely affect survivorship and reproductive potential of individuals.

Future Directions

Despite the recent explosion in knowledge concerning activities of nonbreeding waterfowl, much remains to be learned about their allocation of time to various activities. Most studies have concentrated on foraging activities, but little is known of the relative contribution of remaining activities toward an individual's well-being. Many environmental variables also have been examined in time budget studies, yet often less than 25% of the variance associated with time spent feeding and loafing, and much less for social activities, is explained by these variables (Burton and Hudson 1978, Paulus 1980). Future studies need to determine the factors that account for this variability so that we can better understand the role of environment, social status, age, and sex upon waterfowl fitness.

Nocturnal activities have often been ignored in time budget studies. Because waterfowl actively feed or engage in other activities at night, it is important that researchers examine the role of nocturnal activities and habitat choice to nonbreeding waterfowl. Where possible, these studies should also examine nocturnal activities during all moon phases (Paulus 1984b, Ydenberg et al. 1984).

Comparative studies of time budgets of species are also hindered by differences in methodology employed by researchers. Baldassarre et al. (1987) reviewed the merits of different techniques for evaluating time budgets of waterfowl. Care must be taken to evaluate activities in different habitats, in hunted and nonhunted areas, and of birds in different flock sizes (A. Tamisier, pers. commun.) to obtain an accurate portrayal of the time requirements of nonbreeding waterfowl.

Previous studies examining activities of the same species in different geographic regions have increased our understanding of the underlying factors influencing the allocation of time by waterfowl. These studies have shown that allocation of time for activities is modified by environmental factors characteristic of that region. Time budget data gathered in one area may not be applicable to birds in another region. Thus, determination of the time budgets of representative waterfowl species in an area may be a critical element in the proper management of local populations. More important, greater emphasis upon hypotheses testing may help explain much of the variability in time-activity budget studies. This would reduce the need for multiple time-budget studies on each species (A. Afton, pers. commun.). In addition more needs to be known about the activities of waterfowl during migration to or from the nonbreeding areas and concerning waterfowl wintering in the southern hemisphere.

Finally, time budgets of nonbreeding waterfowl can be used in conjunction with energy budgets to increase our understanding of nutrient requirements, energy storage and use, and energy cost of activity to basal metabolism and thermoregulation. These data would help explain behavioral strategies and habitat choice by nonbreeding waterfowl and thus be important in making sound management decisions.

LITERATURE CITED

Afton, A. D., and R. D. Sayler. 1982. Social courtship and pairbonding of common goldeneyes, (*Bucephala clangula*), wintering in Minnesota. Can. Field-Nat. 46:295-300.

Albright, J. J., R. B. Owen, Jr., and P. O. Corr. 1983. The effects of winter weather on the behavior and energy reserves of black ducks in Maine. Trans. Northeast Sect. Wildl. Soc. 40:118-128.

Ashcroft, R. E. 1976. A function of the pairbond in the common eider. Wildfowl 27:101-105.

Baldassarre, G. A., and E. G. Bolen. 1984. Field-feeding ecology of waterfowl wintering on the southern high plains of Texas. J. Wildl. Manage. 48:63-71.

———, S. L. Paulus, A. Tamisier, and R. D. Titman, 1988. Workshop summary: techniques for timing activity of wintering waterfowl. Pages 181-188 *in* M. W. Weller, ed. Waterfowl in winter. Univ. Minnesota Press, Minneapolis.

———, R. J. Whyte, E. E. Quinlan, and E. G. Bolen. 1983. Dynamics and quality of waste corn available to postbreeding waterfowl in Texas. Wildl. Soc. Bull. 11:25-31.

Breckenridge. W. J. 1953. Night rafting of American golden-eyes on the Mississippi River. Auk 70:201-204.

Brodsky, L. M., and P. J. Weatherhead. 1984. Behavioural thermoregulation in wintering black ducks: roosting and resting. Can. J. Zool. 62:1223-1226.

———, and ———. 1985. Time and energy constraints on courtship in wintering American black ducks. Condor 87:33-36.

Brown, D. E. 1982. Sex ratios, sexual selection and sexual dimorphism in waterfowl. Am. Birds 36:258-261.

Bryant, D. M., and J. Leng. 1975. Feeding distribution and behaviour of shelduck in relation to food supply. Wildfowl 26:20-30.

Burton, B. A., and R. J. Hudson. 1978. Activity budgets of lesser snow geese wintering on the Fraser River Estuary, British Columbia. Wildfowl 29:111-117.

Buxton, N. E. 1981. The importance of food in the determination of the winter flock sites of the shelduck. Wildfowl 32:79-87.

Calder, W. A., and J. R. King. 1974. Thermal and caloric relations of birds. Pages 259-413 *in* D. S. Farner, J. R. King, and K. C. Parkes, eds. Avian biology. Vol. 4. Academic Press, New York.

Campbell, L. H. 1978. Diurnal and tidal behavior patterns of goldeneyes wintering at Leith. Wildfowl 29:147-152.

Campredon, P. 1981. Hivernage du canard siffleur (*Anas penelope*) L. en Camargue (France), stationnements et activities. Alauda 49:161-193.

Caraco, T. 1979. Time budgeting and group size: a theory. Ecol. 60:611-617.

Driver, E. A., L. G. Sugden, and R. J. Kovach. 1974. Calorific, chemical and physical values of potential duck foods. Freshw. Biol. 4:281-292.

Ebbinge, B., K. Canters, and R. Drent. 1975. Foraging routines and estimated daily food intake in barnacle geese wintering in the nothern Netherlands. Wildfowl 26:5-19.

Evans, P. R., and M. W. Pienkowski. 1982. Behavior of shelducks (*Tadorna tadorna*) in a winter flock: Does regulation occur? J. Anim. Ecol. 51:241-262.

Frederick, R. B., and E. E. Klaas. 1982. Resource use and behavior of migrating snow geese. J. Wildl. Manage. 46:601-614.

Fredrickson, L. H., and R. D. Drobney. 1979. Habitat utilization by postbreeding waterfowl. Pages 119-131 *in* T. A. Bookhout, ed. Waterfowl and wetlands—an integrated review. Proc. 1977 Symp., Northcent. Sect., Wildl. Soc., Madison, Wis. 152pp.

Gorman, M. L. 1970. The daily pattern of display in a wild population of eider duck. Wildfowl 21:105-107.

Hepp, G. R. 1982. Behavioral ecology of waterfowl (Anatini) wintering in coastal North Carolina. Ph.D. Thesis, North Carolina State Univ., Raleigh. 155pp.

————, and J. D. Hair. 1984. Dominance in wintering waterfowl (Anatini): effects on distribution of sexes. Condor 86:261–257.

Hickey, T. E., and R. D. Titman. 1983. Diurnal activity budgets of black ducks during their annual cycle in Prince Edward Island. Can. J. Zool. 61:743–749.

Hohman, W. L. 1986. Diurnal time-activity budgets for ring-necked ducks wintering in central Florida. Proc. Southeast. Assoc. Game Fish Comm. 38:158–164.

Howard, W. J. 1940. Wintering of the greater snow goose. Auk 57:523–531.

Jorde, D. G. 1981. Winter and spring staging ecology of mallards in south central Nebraska. M.S. Thesis, Univ. North Dakota, Grand Forks. 116pp.

————, G. L. Krapu, R. D. Crawford, and M. A. Hay. 1984. Effects of weather on habitat selection and behavior of mallards wintering in Nebraska. Condor 86:258–265.

Kenward, R. E. 1978. Hawks and doves: factors affecting success and selection in goshawk attacks on wood-pigeons. J. Anim. Ecol. 47:449–460.

Lebret, T. 1970. Nachtelijk voedselzoeken en andere activiteiten van de grauwe gans (*Anser anser*) in het zoete getij-milieu in Nederland. Limosa 43:11–30.

Linsell, S. E. 1969. Pre-dusk and nocturnal behavior of goldeneye with notes on population composition. Wildfowl 20:75–77.

Miller, M. R. 1985. Time budgets of northern pintails wintering in the Sacramento Valley, California. Wildfowl 36:53–64.

Mitgard, V. 1978. Resting postures of the mallard (*Anas platyrhynchos*). Ornis Scand. 9:214–219.

Nichols, J. J., and G. M. Haramis. 1980. Sex-specific differences in winter distribution patterns of canvasbacks. Condor 82:406–416.

Nilsson. L. 1970. Food seeking activity of south Swedish diving ducks in the nonbreeding season. Oikos 21:145–154.

Noseworthy, S. M. 1981. Distribution, sex ratios, and behavior of diving ducks wintering on the Detroit River. M.S. Thesis, Univ. Michigan, Ann Arbor. 82pp.

Owen, M. 1972. Some factors affecting food intake and selection in white-fronted geese. J. Anim. Ecol. 41:79–92.

Paulus, S. L. 1980. The winter ecology of the gadwall in Louisiana. M.S. Thesis, Univ. North Dakota, Grand Forks. 357pp.

————. 1982a. Feeding ecology of gadwalls in Louisiana in winter. J. Wildl. Manage. 46:71–79.

————. 1982b. Gut morphology of gadwalls in Louisiana in winter. J. Wildl. Manage. 46:483–489.

————. 1983. Dominance relations, resource use, and pairing chronology of gadwalls in winter. Auk 100:947–952.

————. 1984a. Activity budgets of nonbreeding gadwalls in Louisiana. J. Wildl. Manage. 48:371–380.

————. 1984b. Behavioral ecology of mottled ducks in Louisiana. Ph.D. Thesis, Auburn Univ., Auburn, Ala. 152pp.

Pedroli, J. C. 1982. Activity and time budget of tufted ducks on Swiss lakes during winter. Wildfowl 33:105–112.

Quinlan, E. E., and G. A. Baldassarre. 1984. Activity budgets of nonbreeding green-winged teal on playa lakes in Texas. J. Wildl. Manage. 48:838–845.

Raveling, D. G., W. E. Crews, and W. D. Klimstra. 1972. Activity patterns of Canada geese during winter. Wilson Bull. 84:278–295.

Reed, L. W. 1971. An ecological evaluation of a thermal discharge. VI. Use of western Lake Erie by migratory and wintering waterfowl. Inst. Water Res. Tech. Rep. 18, Michigan State Univ., East Lansing. 71pp.

Roux, F., R. Maheo, and A. Tamisier. 1978. L'exploitation de la basse vallee du Senegal (quartier d'hiver tropical) par trois especes de canards palearctiques et Ethiopien. Terre Vie 32:387–416.

Sayler, R. D., and A. D. Afton. 1981. Ecological aspects of common goldeneyes (*Bucephala clangula*) wintering on the upper Mississippi River. Ornis Scand. 12:99–108.

Skead, D. M. 1977. Diurnal activity budgets of Anatini during winter. Ostrich Suppl. 12:65–74.

Smith, K. D., and H. H. Prince. 1973. The fasting metabolism of subadult mallards acclimatized to low ambient temperatures. Condor 75:330–335.

Sugden, L. G. 1973. Metabolizable energy of wild duck foods. Can. Wildl. Serv. Prog. Notes 35. Saskatoon, Sask. Can. Wildl. Serv.

Tamisier, A. 1970. Signification du gregarisme diurne et de l'alimentation nocturne des sarcelles d'hiver *Anas crecca crecca* L. Terre Vie 4:511–562.

———. 1972. Rhythmes nychtemeraux des sarcelles d'hiver pendant leur hivernage en Camargue. Alauda 40:107–135, 235–256.

———. 1974. Etho-ecological studies of teal wintering in the Camargue (Rhone Delta, France). Wildfowl 25:107–117.

———. 1976. Diurnal activities of green-winged teal and pintail wintering in Louisiana. Wildfowl 27:19–31.

———. 1978-79. The functional units of wintering ducks: a spatial integration of their comfort and feeding requirements. Verh. Ornithol. Ges. Bayern 23:229–238.

Thompson, D. B. A. 1981. Feeding behavior of wintering shelduck on the Clyde Estuary. Wildfowl 32:88–98.

Thornburg, D. D. 1973. Diving duck movements on Keokuk Pool, Mississippi River. J. Wildl. Manage. 37:382–389.

Ward, P., and A. Zahavi. 1973. The importance of certain assemblages of birds as information-centres for food finding. Ibis 115:517–534.

Wishart, R. A. 1983. Pairing chronology and mate selection in the American wigeon (*Anas americana*). Can. J. Zool. 61:1733–1743.

Ydenberg, R. C., H. H. Th. Prins, and J. Van Dijk. 1984. A lunar rhythm in the nocturnal foraging activities of wintering barnacle geese. Wildfowl 35:93–96.

Zwarts, L. 1976. Density-related processes in feeding dispersion and feeding activity of teal (*Anas crecca*). Ardea 64:192–209.

11

Diurnal Behavior Patterns of Waterfowl Wintering on the Columbia River, Oregon and Washington

Bruce C. Thompson, James E. Tabor, and Clarence L. Turner

Abstract: Daily activities of wintering Canada geese (*Branta canadensis*) and dabbling and diving ducks (Anatinae) were recorded during 320.5 hours of observation at nine major concentration areas along the Columbia River in Oregon and Washington from October 1977 through March 1978. Behavioral categories including feeding, preening, swimming, flight, agonistic, courtship, alert, walking, drinking, and inactive were recorded at 15-minute intervals during observations. For all species groups at all locations, inactivity was the most prevalent behavior. Behavioral repertoires were relatively stable among daily time periods. Loafing (preen, inactive) and swimming comprised 50-99% of the cumulative time budget among all sites for all species groups. Feeding by geese and dabbling ducks comprised less than 10% of the time budget for all sites. Feeding by diving ducks was more prevlant than for dabbling ducks or geese. Areas that contained shoals with bottom-rooted aquatic vegetation (*Potamogeton* spp., *Elodea* spp.) consistently supported feeding aggregations of diving ducks. Activity patterns did not differ on a daily basis within species groups but did differ among months and locations, indicating constant daily routines but flexible behavior during the wintering period among study sites. Water fluctuations associated with altered hydroelectric regimes are not expected to substantially alter diurnal waterfowl use of concentration areas. However, observed behavioral patterns should be considered with respect to future harvest management and redistribution of this wintering population.

Congressional action (House Document 413, 87th Congress, 2nd Session) during the early 1960s outlined a change in the Pacific Northwest's power supply

---

system from a hydroelectric to a thermal-based system, with peak power demands being met by hydroelectric projects primarily on the Columbia and Snake rivers. Implementation of this "power-peaking" regime was projected to occur gradually through 2020. During this time, structural modifications would be made to dams, altering water flows on the Columbia River to maximize power generation capabilities during peak demand periods. Under power peaking, substantial fluctuations are expected in forebay and tailwater areas near dams, and the water flow through reservoirs would differ from past schedules. The Columbia River system involves more than 1,400 km in Washington and Oregon; about 400 km remains free flowing, of which 230 km is a tidally influenced reach between Bonneville Dam and the Pacific Ocean.

Earlier reservoir projects had substantially reduced riparian habitats and associated wildlife (Lewke and Buss 1977), and the planned project alterations also had potential for impact on riparian or river-dependent wildlife. A Wildlife Work Group involving state and federal wildlife agencies and the U.S. Army Corps of Engineers (USACE) identified the need to investigate the effects of river regulation on wildlife and their habitat. Waterfowl were an important component of these studies because of the more than 450,000 ducks and geese wintering on the upper Columbia River and the nearly 900 pairs of Great Basin Canada geese (*Branta canadensis moffitti*) nesting and wintering there (Galbreath 1962, McCabe 1976, McKern 1976). Specific attention was directed at winter use patterns because of the magnitude of the waterfowl populations involved and the association of waterfowl concentrations with locations subject to tailwater and forebay fluctuations.

Our paper summarizes diurnal activity patterns of ducks and geese wintering on the Columbia River with respect to possible impacts from full implementation of power peaking. These activity patterns are discussed relative to future harvest and distribution of waterfowl wintering in the Columbia Basin. This research was accomplished under contract DACW68-76-C-0184 from the USACE to the Washington Department of Game. C. Detrick and B. Langstaff assisted with the collection and summary of field data, H. Horton identified invertebrate food items collected from ducks, and J. C. Howerton coordinated logistical support of field activities. Four anonymous reviewers provided important editorial suggestions on an earlier draft.

Study Area

The study area included the Columbia River from The Dalles Reservoir to Grand Coulee Dam in northeast Washington, except about 230 km from Priest Rapids Dam upstream to the mouth of the Okanogan River (fig. 11.1). The excluded area represented reservoirs under jurisdiction of local utility districts and outside the immediate area of interest to the USACE planning functions that established the scope of the study. The study area ranged from an ocean-influenced,

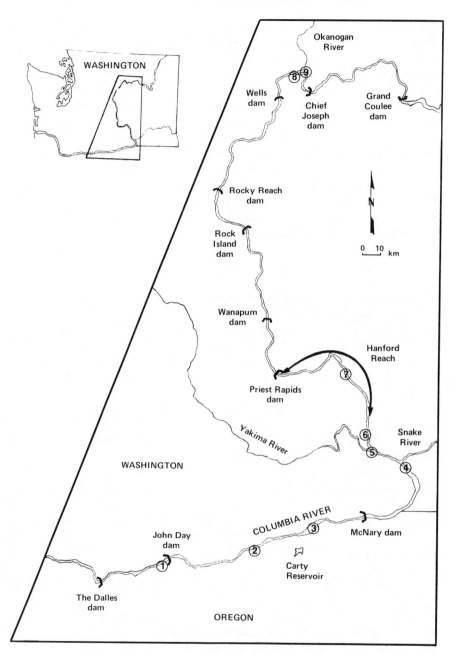

Fig. 11.1. Map of Columbia River study area depicting locations of dams, reservoirs, and waterfowl concentration areas. Circled numbers correspond to concentration area locations listed in text.

high-humidity belt dominated by coniferous forest to a relatively xeric shrub-steppe at approximately 290 m mean sea level at the upstream end. Detailed descriptions of physiography, climate, and vegetation in the study area were presented by Franklin and Dyrness (1973).

Observation sites were established at nine waterfowl concentration areas along The Dalles, John Day, McNary, and Wells reservoirs and the free-flowing Hanford Reach. These locations (numbers corresponding to those on fig. 11.1) and their distance in river miles (RM) from the mouth (established conventional reference) were: (1) unnamed gravel island (RM 214.3), (2) Threemile Island (RM 255.6), (3) Longwalk Slough (RM 275.0), (4) Foundation Island (RM 322.0), (5) Yakima River delta (RM 335.5), (6) Graduate Center (RM 342.2), (7) 100-F Slough (RM 366.0), (8) Cassimer Bar (RM 535.0), and (9) Washburn Island (RM 537.5). Sites were selected to provide reasonable accessibility for observers, but they also represented major concentration areas and several minor use areas.

Methods

Waterfowl were observed with 20-45× spotting scopes from distances of 200-1,000 m. Observations were made from a vehicle or portable seating, depending on the site; observers for each site were the same during all months. Two or three observation periods 4-10 hours long were made monthly at each site from October 1977 through March 1978. Observation periods within months were staggered temporally to ensure coverage from 0700 to 1645 PST (equivalent PDT in October). Earlier or later observations were not possible because of inadequate light. Observation days were chosen in advance as part of monthly work schedules, and observations were made as scheduled regardless of weather. All general weather conditions, including snowstorm, were represented in the data collection, but data were not sufficient to stratify analyses on these factors.

During each observation period, flocks of fewer than 1,000 birds at concentration areas were scanned and the behavior of the individual nearest the center of the 100 or 200 individual scope fields viewed throughout the area were recorded at 15-minute intervals (i.e., 0800, 0815, 0830, 0845). In large concentrations of 1,000-10,000 birds, flocks were visually subdivided into groups of 10-25 birds and the predominant behavior for each of at least 100 groups was recorded. Behavioral categories were feed, preen, swim, fly, agonistic, courtship, inactive, alert, and walk/drink. Walking and drinking were combined because of the close association resulting from birds walking to and from drinking locations. The same area was scanned each interval, but the same birds were not necessarily examined. Visual scans and associated behavioral classifications required 3-6 minutes per interval depending on abundance and distribution of birds at each site.

The observation procedures used, which were similar to those described by Siegfried (1974) and Burger (1976), represent a form of scan sampling having the limitation of greater margin of error for estimates of behavior duration (Lehner 1979, 122-123). This procedure requires the assumption that a behavior recorded during a count interval typically occurred in bouts of 15 minutes or greater duration. If the assumption did not hold, prevalent behaviors would be underestimated and less frequently occurring behaviors overestimated. Continuous observation of the flocks during collection of interval behavioral data indicated that the assumption generally held.

Interval observations, weather data (temperature, wind, cloud cover, precipitation), and an estimate of total number of birds present during each interval were recorded on prepared data sheets. Observers used manual event recorders initially to tally behavior classifications during interval counts to avoid looking away from the scope. Also, a written summary of arrivals, departures, disturbances, and grossly apparent flock activities provided background information helpful in interpreting interval counts. Before beginning their data collection, three observers were provided with explicit printed instructions describing observation and data-recording procedures. These observers were evaluated under field observation conditions to assess comparability. Observers were required to demonstrate ≤5% deviation in numerical estimates and behavioral classifications relative to the study coordinator before beginning data collection.

Percentage classifications in each behavioral category on an hourly basis were viewed as a series of multivariate response vectors representing location, month, and time of day. Data for each species or species group at each site each month were grouped by hour prior to performing analyses. On-the-hour through three-quarter-hour interval counts were grouped to calculate each hourly percentage (i.e., 0800 comprised 0800, 0815, 0830, and 0845 interval counts). Three to 12 interval counts were used to calculate hourly percentages, depending on the number of times each site had been observed during specific hours each month. Thus, hourly percentages were composite-weighted values, and arcsine transformations of percentages were used for analyses to "normalize" variances inherent to proportions (Snedecor and Cochran 1967, 327).

Location effects and daily and monthly patterns for the five most common behaviors were evaluated using factorial multivariate analyses of variance (MANOVA, Morrison 1976) available as standard analytical routines (Helwig and Council 1979). Only feed, preen, swim, inactive, and walk/drink were considered for final analyses because of primary interest in major time allocation and the need to eliminate matrix singularity for MANOVA. A probability level of $P = 0.05$ was used for all analytical decisions.

Associated food habits data for dabbling and diving ducks were obtained from hunter-killed ducks collected at hunting areas adjacent to the study sites during September through December in 1976 and 1977. Esophagi and proventriculi from 121 ducks that contained food items were removed in the field and preserved in 80% ethanol. Food items were later removed from esophagi, washed with tap water in a 100-mesh screen, and spread on newspaper to air dry for 48-72 hours. Air-dried samples were separated into plant and animal matter categories and identified taxonomically. Volume of the respective categories was estimated by water displacement in a graduated cylinder. Aggregate percent volume was calculated according to Swanson et al. (1974).

Results

Observations of Canada geese during 81.5 hours at five concentration areas indicated relatively consistent dedication of time to resting and maintenance activities (table 11.1). Inactivity was the prevalent behavior in nearly all instances. Loafing activities (preen, inactive) and swimming represented 50-97% of the time budget on a cumulative basis for each site (table 11.1, fig. 11.2). Feeding was prevalent during three monthly summary periods but generally represented less than 10% of the time budget (table 11.1). It was unlikely that geese obtained their principal dietary requirements from concentration areas. Routine morning and afternoon feeding flights to agricultural fields recorded during continuous observations exemplified the primary food sources used by geese.

Table 11.1. Estimated maximum number present and percentage of time spent by geese in six activity categories at five concentration areas along the Columbia River, October 1977 through February 1978

Location	Month	Maximum number present	Period observed	Interval counts (no.)	Feed[a]	Preen	Swim	Inactive	Walk/Drink	Other[b]
Island	Oct	1,200	1100-1645	44	0	30.6	13.4	46.6	5.5	3.9
(RM 214.3)	Nov	1,300	1000-1645	48	0	23.8	4.8	52.5	7.9	11.0
	Dec	2,000	1000-1545	22	8.6	10.8	6.1	67.5	6.0	1.0
Threemile	Oct	2,000	1000-1645	26	0.4	16.2	45.1	29.1	2.4	6.8
Island	Nov	450	1000-1445	20	0	13.6	19.8	51.0	7.6	8.0
	Dec	1,300	1000-1545	31	1.7	18.8	7.7	44.4	20.5	6.9
	Feb	200	1300-1645	15	7.1	10.3	0	71.3	1.6	9.7
Foundation	Oct	150	0900-1645	32	23.0	5.4	27.3	41.6	. . .	2.7
Island	Nov	240	0900-1245	16	2.1	15.7	19.3	62.2	. . .	0.7
Yakima Delta	Dec	70	0700-1145	37	28.4	10.6	23.6	37.3	. . .	0.1
Washburn Island	Nov	215	0800-1145	32	32.4	1.5	24.6	23.8	0.8	16.9

[a] Feeding activity may have included some time seeking grit.
[b] Includes agonistic, alert, and short flight activities.

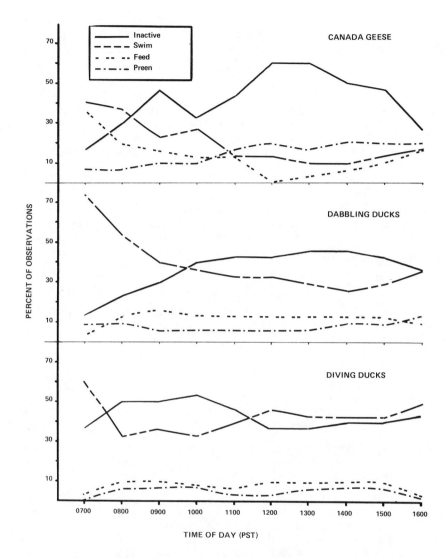

Fig. 11.2. Composite time budget for four prevalent behaviors of Canada geese, dabbling ducks, and diving ducks observed during 10 hourly periods at nine winter concentration areas on Columbia River, October 1977 through March 1978.

Generally, Canada geese appeared to spend most of the night on concentration areas and initiated feeding flights between 0700 and 0830 PST. They returned between 1030 and 1200 to loaf during late morning and afternoon hours. Feeding flights occurred again between 1600 and 1800, and geese returned during darkness.

This pattern was typical of the concentration areas used routinely by geese, such as RM 214.3 and Threemile Island. Deviations from this pattern occurred when late-winter "green-up" of grasses and forbs caused geese to feed and loaf during the day on sagebrush (*Artemisia-Chrysothamnus-Bromus-Agropyron* association)

Table 11.2. Estimated maximum number present and percentage of time spent by dabbling ducks in six activity categories at eight concentration areas along the Columbia River, October 1977 through March 1978

Location	Month	Maximum number present	Period observed	Interval counts (no.)	Feed[a]	Preen	Swim	Inactive	Walk/Drink	Other[b]
Threemile	Dec	7,000	1000-1645	35	0.1	4.6	30.1	59.9	5.1	0.2
Island	Jan	8,700	0700-1645	39	0.8	14.0	40.5	40.6	3.5	0.6
	Feb	1,500	1300-1645	16	0.2	8.0	28.4	60.3	2.9	0.2
Longwalk	Nov	10,000	0800-1645	64	0.3	15.2	35.8	42.9	3.4	2.4
	Dec	8,000	1000-1645	41	0.5	18.4	35.9	38.8	5.9	0.5
	Feb	2,000	1400-1645	12	2.3	14.6	26.7	47.1	8.2	1.1
Foundation	Oct	200	0900-1645	32	10.1	1.5	32.2	54.6	...	1.6
Island	Nov	530	0700-1645	60	6.1	11.0	34.9	47.0	...	1.0
	Dec	500	0900-1245	15	0.1	3.0	51.0	45.9	...	0
Yakima	Nov	1,090	0800-1645	50	13.8	11.3	25.6	42.3	...	7.0
Delta	Nov	275	0800-1645	50	39.9	11.5	40.3	5.2	...	3.1
	Dec	300	1100-1445	18	15.6	10.2	34.6	39.6	...	0
Graduate	Jan	500	0800-1545	49	0	4.8	32.3	62.9	...	0
Center	Feb	300	1000-1645	28	0.2	11.1	42.1	46.4	...	0.2
100-F	Oct	4,800	0900-1645	31	2.5	5.7	41.9	47.9	...	2.0
Slough	Nov	5,500	0800-1545	50	5.5	16.5	27.3	50.3	...	0.4
	Dec	6,000	0900-1545	28	1.3	7.3	23.0	67.5	...	0.9
Cassimer	Oct	200	0800-1345	31	24.4	6.3	65.5	2.4	...	1.4
Bar	Nov	500	0800-1545	43	29.8	3.3	51.2	11.6	...	4.1
	Dec	500	0800-1345	42	8.8	3.6	57.0	26.1	...	4.5
	Jan	300	0900-1545	48	36.2	4.5	23.9	32.7	2.0	0.7
	Feb	500	0800-1545	54	37.8	4.9	20.7	32.6	2.6	1.4
	Mar	500	0800-1545	62	11.5	7.5	34.8	43.9	1.5	0.8
Washburn Island	Nov	55	0800-1445	43	32.7	7.6	28.0	28.6	...	3.0

[a]Concentrations were composed of 80-95% mallards except for those at the Graduate Center, which were all mallards, and the first November entry under Yakima Delta, which was of green-winged teal (*Anas crecca*).

[b]Includes agonistic, alert, courtship, and short flight activities.

hillsides. Consequently, geese were observed on concentration areas during non-feeding periods, and the prevalence of loafing was expected.

Dabbling ducks, primarily mallard (*Anas platyrhynchos*), northern pintail (*Anas acuta*), and American wigeon (*Anas americana*), were observed for 239

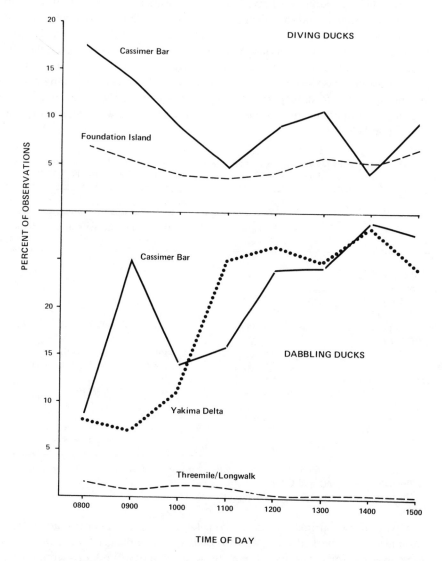

Fig. 11.3. Comparison of feeding prevalence by dabbling and diving ducks at five winter concentration areas on Columbia River, November 1977 through January 1978.

hours at eight concentration areas throughout the winter. Dabbling ducks occupied concentration areas during all daylight hours at most sites. Inactivity was most prevalent in 17 of 24 monthly comparisons (table 11.2). Loafing behaviors and swimming combined represented 57-99% of the time budget for all observations (fig. 11.2). Feeding was prevalent at the Cassimer Bar site, exceeding 25% in four of six months; Yakima Delta and Washburn Island also were important feeding areas (table 11.2, fig. 11.3). American wigeon commonly fed at Cassimer Bar in association with American coots (*Fulica americana*). However, dabbling ducks made feeding flights similar to those of geese, usually arriving and departing concentration areas during darkness or the low light of early morning and late afternoon. These feeding patterns were apparent from the grain and aquatic vegetation components in the diets of mallards and American wigeon in the study area (table 11.3).

Table 11.3. Frequency and aggregate percentage (volume) for 10 food item categories in the diet of four duck species wintering on Columbia River reservoirs, 1976-77

	Frequency (aggregate%)			
Food category	Mallard (N = 72)	American wigeon (N = 22)	Lesser scaup (N = 15)	Redhead (N = 12)
Plant materials				
Seeds				
Corn	59.7 (59.6)	0	0	0
Wheat	22.2 (19.4)	22.7 (22.7)	0	0
Aquatic[a]	8.3 (4.4)	4.5 (1.1)	26.7 (21.1)	16.7 (12.5)
Other parts				
Potamogeton	6.9 (6.6)	54.5 (54.1)	40.0 (27.0)	50.0 (50.0)
Elodea	2.8 (2.1)	22.7 (18.6)	53.3 (50.6)	41.7 (37.0)
Other aquatics	5.6 (4.0)	0	0	0
Unknown plant tissues	5.6 (3.7)	0	13.3 (tr)	0
Animal materials				
Insecta[b]	2.8 (tr)	9.1 (1.1)	0	0
Gastropoda[c]	0	4.5 (2.3)	20.0 (1.1)	8.3 (0.1)
Pelecypoda (*Corbicula*)	11.1 (0.1)	0	13.3 (0.2)	8.3 (0.4)

[a] Included *Carex*, *Chenopodium*, *Echinochloa*, *Panicum*, *Polygonum*, and *Potamogeton*.
[b] Included Coleoptera and Odonata.
[c] Included Lymnaceae, *Gyraulus*, *Heliosoma*, and *Physa*.

Diving ducks, primarily lesser scaup (*Aythya affinis*), canvasback (*Aythya valisineria*), ring-necked duck (*Aythya collaris*), and redhead (*Aythya americana*), were observed for 128 hours at three sites where inactivity and/or swimming were most prevalent during all observations (table 11.4). Feeding was a substantial percentage of activity at Washburn Island only in December; however, feeding percentages were consistently near 10% for all months at Cassimer Bar (table 11.4). The Cassimer Bar concentration area, which included shoal areas with submergent aquatic vegetation, was a routinely used feeding area (fig. 11.3). Aquatic seeds and plant parts were identified as primary food items for lesser scaup and redhead (table 11.3).

Table 11.4. Estimated maximum number present and percentage of time spent by diving ducks in five activity categories at three concentration areas along the Columbia River, October 1977 through February 1978

Location	Month	Maximum number present[a]	Period observed	Interval counts (no.)	Mean time spent (%)				
					Feed[a]	Preen	Swim	Inactive	Other[b]
Foundation Island	Nov	550	0800-1545	51	7.3	6.6	57.2	24.4	4.5
	Dec	500	0800-1545	42	1.5	4.7	36.5	57.3	0
	Jan	500	0700-1545	66	6.5	3.4	42.1	47.9	0.1
	Feb	250	0900-1645	32	6.6	7.2	53.6	32.5	0.1
Cassimer Bar	Nov	200	0800-1545	61	9.3	9.0	41.0	40.7	0
	Dec	300	0900-1345	19	11.4	6.7	40.9	40.2	0.8
	Jan	300	0900-1545	52	7.5	5.4	42.6	44.0	0.5
	Feb	300	0800-1545	54	11.8	5.5	47.0	35.3	0.4
	Mar	110	0800-1545	32	8.1	4.3	39.4	48.4	0
Washburn Island	Oct	500	0800-1545	39	1.8	4.7	25.4	64.6	3.5
	Dec	120	0800-1545	64	18.9	8.0	26.7	45.4	1.0

[a]Concentrations were comprised of scaup, canvasback, ring-necked duck, and redhead.
[b]Includes agonistic, alert, courtship, and short flight activities.

Diving ducks used most concentration areas that were used by dabblers, but generally fewer than 200 divers were observed. At Cassimer Bar and Foundation Island, however, 300-500 divers were observed consistently. Diving ducks fed at all concentration areas observed, but most time was spent loafing.

In tests using MANOVA for daily, monthly, and location effects, behavioral composition differed significantly among all locations within species groups and, with two exceptions, among months within species groups (table 11.5). Conversely, with the exception of Canada geese, there were no significant differences among hourly percentages for feeding or loafing when accounting for month and location effects. These analyses supported the consensus of observers that behavior levels were relatively constant during observations each day. However, at least subtle distinctions existed in how each species group used the different locations through the winter period as expected from month × location interactions (table 11.5). Examination of partial correlation matrices in MANOVA revealed significant negative correlations between feeding or swimming and inactivity (table 11.5),

Table 11.5. Temporal and spatial factor effects and interbehavioral correlations for ducks and geese observed at wintering areas on the Columbia River, October 1977 through March 1978

Species group	Location[a]	Month[b]	Time period	Wilks criterion probability for factor effects[c]					Partial correlation coefficient[c]					
				Location	Month	Time of day	Month × time	Month × location	Feed × Preen	Feed × Swim	Feed × Inactive	Preen × Swim	Preen × Inactive	Swim × Inactive
Canada geese	1,2	O,N,D	1100-1445	0.008	0.001	0.032	NS	0.007	NS	NS	NS	NS	-0.74	NS
	1,2,4	O	1100-1645	0.017	-	NS	-	-	NS	NS	-0.66	NS	NS	-0.79
Dabbling ducks	4,7,8	O,N,D	0900-1245	0.001	0.008	NS	NS	0.006	NS	-0.42	NS	NS	NS	-0.66
	2,6,8	J	0900-1545	0.001	-	NS	-	-	NS	NS	-0.76	0.55	NS	NS
	7,8	N,D	0900-1545	0.001	0.001	NS	NS	0.001	NS	-0.60	-0.65	NS	NS	NS
	6+7	O,N,D,J,F	1000-1545	-	0.001	NS	NS	-	NS	NS	NS	NS	-0.51	-0.89
	2+3	N,D,J	1000-1545	-	NS	NS	NS	-	0.56	0.56	-0.65	NS	-0.78	-0.90
	8	N,D,J,F,M	0900-1545	-	0.001	NS	NS	-	-0.44	-0.47	-0.86	NS	NS	NS
Diving ducks	4,8	N,D,J,F	0900-1645	0.002	NS	NS	NS	0.024	NS	0.43	-0.53	NS	NS	-0.94

[a] Location numbers are those given in the study area text and in figure 11.1. A plus sign indicates pooling of data from two sites.

[b] Letters represent the first letter of each month from October to March.

[c] NS = nonsignificant test criterion or correlation.

indicating that activity trade-offs among daily time intervals were primarily adjusted among these three behaviors, as is apparent from the composite time budgets (fig. 11.2).

Differences in time devoted to feeding were largely attributable to the prevalence of feeding by all species at the Cassimer Bar and Washburn Island sites (fig. 11.3). Variation in the relative proportions of the several "loafing" behavior categories contributed most extensively to the seasonal and geographic patterns of differences in site use. Grouping of swimming and loafing behaviors indicates relatively consistent, nonfeeding use of most concentration areas throughout the winter (tables 11.1, 11.2, and 11.4).

Discussion

Loafing behaviors predominated among geese and dabbling ducks concentrated along the Columbia River, as reported in other recent diurnal studies of wintering waterfowl (Jorde et al. 1984, Quinlan and Baldassarre 1984). Feeding comprised a relatively small percentage of daily and seasonal time budgets during diurnal use of these areas. Observations of nocturnal behavior might have uncovered an increased prevalence of feeding, as has been reported by Paulus (1984). Foods obtained at concentration areas by waterfowl species other than diving ducks probably were a minor component of the overall diet, given the multiple daily flights to upland agricultural sites to feed, a primary factor in dictating winter activity patterns (Raveling 1969). However submergent aquatic plants and macroinvertebrates may be an important dietary supplement to agricultural plants and grains (Jorde et al. 1983). The Columbia River offers most of the ice-free feeding and resting areas during periods of subfreezing temperatures and snow cover, especially north of the Yakima River confluence. Other behaviors should not be construed as unimportant, but they comprised little of the diurnal time budget.

Fluctuating water levels associated with power peaking, at least at operational levels expected throughout the 1980s, are not expected to have major, direct effects (either positive or negative) on diurnal feeding and resting patterns of migrant and wintering waterfowl populations because use is mainly for resting. However, some effect may be expected in areas with very shallow bottom topography, where slight variations in water level can inundate low islands, or conversely, expose large, open flats, as in the Longwalk Slough area. Close association of resting with the land-water interface would require movement by resting birds to compensate for fluctuating water. Such movements would involve additional energy expenditure.

The Cassimer Bar-Washburn Island area and similar sites also are of concern where altered water levels or scouring action related to peaking regimes could affect availability of aquatic plants and invertebrates at important feeding sites for diving ducks. This potential problem has been illustrated by a 92% reduction in diving ducks in Wells Reservoir in 1983, associated with water-level manipulations that reduced submerged aquatic vegetation, primarily *Potamogeton crispus* (Washington Dep. Game, unpubl. data). It is important in the future to anticipate and possibly mitigate these effects. Development of impoundments with water control capabilities adjacent to reservoirs is a promising approach to mitigate impacts on aquatic wildlife, although such "subimpoundments" are subject to freezing during extremely cold weather (Allen and Aggus 1983).

Although potential effects of altered water-level fluctuations on time-activity budgets of waterfowl may be considered minimal based on our investigations, these data bear heavily on the overall management of waterfowl in the Columbia Basin. The trend toward increasing goose and dabbling duck populations, as described by Galbreath (1962), has magnified in recent years with as much as a 300% increase in duck populations on the Columbia River, mostly in John Day and McNary reservoirs, from 1977 to 1984 (Wash. Dep. Game, unpubl. winter survey data). Relatively recent and rapid development of irrigation systems in the vicinity of John Day and McNary reservoirs (Barron and Butcher 1975) is associated closely with increased wintering waterfowl populations, particularly in southerly portions of the Columbia Basin where corn and alfalfa dominate the agricultural scene and provide a substantial food source for wintering ducks and geese.

Additionally, extensive areas closed to waterfowl hunting historically have existed along the Columbia River, and many continue to the present in large portions of The Dalles, John Day, Rock Island, Rocky Reach, and Chief Joseph reservoirs, plus 42 km of Hanford Reach (Oregon Dep. Fish Wildl. 1984, Washington Dep. Game 1984). Thus, large numbers of waterfowl in the Columbia River have a nearby agricultural food source and spend substantial time in relative seclusion, largely immune to exposure to hunters. This study demonstrated that ducks and geese spend extensive periods of time closely aggregated on the river. Many migrant geese and ducks move into the Columbia Basin in late summer and early fall; late-winter and early-spring migration through the area is substantial (Bellrose 1976). Therefore, crop depredation and potential for disease transmission exist during a lengthy period.

Potential disease exposure, harvest control, and crop depredation problems associated with seasonal overabundance of waterfowl on portions of the Columbia River have been identified for some time, and plans have been outlined to alter waterfowl population distribution (U.S. Fish Wildl. Serv. 1983). This plan specifies approaches to reduce population density along the lower Columbia River by authorizing hunting in limited portions of some previously closed areas, hazing of waterfowl aggregations at an off-river power plant reservoir (Carty Reservoir — fig. 11.1) that is closed to hunting, and providing hunting closures in the North Columbia Basin to lure waterfowl away from problem areas to the south. These approaches appear to be appropriate ones for balancing waterfowl use and distribution in much of the Columbia Basin, but the plan is largely limited to regulatory and procedural action related to hunting and provides for little monitoring of effects of the actions beyond changes in winter inventory counts. Our data concerning behavioral regimes at concentration areas can serve as a baseline for investigation of some effects of redistribution strategies on the winter waterfowl population.

LITERATURE CITED

Allen, H. H., and L. R. Aggus, eds. 1983. Effects of fluctuating reservoir water levels on fisheries, wildlife, and vegetation; summary of a workshop, 24-26 February 1981. Misc. Paper E-83-2, U.S. Army Engineer Waterways Experiment Station, Vicksburg, Miss.

Barron, J. C., and W. R. Butcher. 1975. Irrigation development in Washington: some public and private policy issues. Wash. State Univ. Coop. Ext. Serv. Em-3993. 10pp.

Bellrose, F. C. 1976. Ducks, geese, and swans of North America. Stackpole Books, Harrisburg, Pa. 544pp.

Burger, J. 1976. Daily and seasonal activity patterns in breeding laughing gulls. Auk 93:308-323.

Franklin, J. F., and C. T. Dyrness. 1973. Natural vegetation of Oregon and Washington, U.S. For. Serv. Gen. Tech. Rep. PNW-8. 417pp.

Galbreath, D. S. 1962. Waterfowl population increase in the Columbia Basin of central Washington. Wash. Game Bull. 14(3):6-7.

Helwig, J. T., and K. A. Council, eds. 1979. SAS user's guide, 1979 ed. SAS Inst. Inc., Raleigh, N.C. 494pp.

Jorde, D. G., G. L. Krapu, and R. D. Crawford. 1983. Feeding ecology of mallards wintering in Nebraska. J. Wildl. Manage. 47:1044-1053.

———, ———, ———, and M. A. Hay. 1984. Effects of weather on habitat selection and behavior of mallards wintering in Nebraska. Condor 86:258-265.

Lehner, P. N. 1979. Handbook of ethological methods. Garland STPM Press, New York. 403pp.

Lewke, R. E., and I. O. Buss. 1977. Impacts of impoundment to vertebrate animals and their habitats in the Snake River Canyon, Washington. Northwest Sci. 51:219-270.

McCabe, T. R. 1976. Productivity and nesting habitat of Great Basin Canada Geese; Umatilla National Wildlife Refuge. M.S. Thesis, Oregon State Univ., Corvallis. 72pp.

McKern, J. L. 1976. Inventory of riparian habitats and associated wildlife along the Columbia and Snake Rivers. Vol. 1. Summary. U.S. Army Engineers, Walla Walla, Wash. 100pp.

Morrison, D. F. 1976. Multivariate statistical methods. McGraw-Hill, New York. 415pp.

Oregon Department of Fish and Wildlife. 1984. Oregon game bird regulations, 1984. Portland, Oreg. 4pp.

Paulus, S. L. 1984. Activity budgets of nonbreeding gadwalls in Louisiana. J. Wildl. Manage. 48:371-380.

Quinlan, E. E., and G. A. Baldassarre. 1984. Activity budgets of nonbreeding green-winged teal on playa lakes in Texas. J. Wildl. Manage. 48:838-845.

Raveling, D. G. 1969. Roost sites and flight patterns of Canada geese in winter. J. Wildl. Manage. 33:319-330.

Siegfried, W. R. 1974. Time budget of behavior among lesser scaups on Delta Marsh. J. Wildl. Manage. 38:708-713.

Snedecor, G. W., and W. G. Cochran. 1967. Statistical methods. Iowa State Univ. Press, Ames. 593pp.

Swanson, G. A., G. L. Krapu, J. C. Bartonek, J. R. Serie, and D. H. Johnson. 1974. Advantages in mathematically weighting waterfowl food habits data. J. Wildl. Manage. 38:302-307.

U.S. Fish and Wildlife Service. 1983. Wintering waterfowl redistribution plan for the Columbia Basin of Oregon and Washington. 45pp.

Washington Department of Game. 1984. Upland game bird and migratory waterfowl seasons, 1984-85. Olympia, Wash. 16pp.

12

The Need for Nocturnal Activity and Energy Budgets of Waterfowl

Dennis G. Jorde and Ray B. Owen, Jr.

Abstract: Activity and energy budgets of waterfowl during the night have received little attention. Researchers often assume that the nocturnal period represents a time of inactivity or minimal activity for waterfowl. Recent studies during winter and breeding seasons indicated that waterfowl varied their activity at night and that this variation was often in response to changes in environmental and physiological conditions. In this paper we discuss methods to collect behavioral data at night, identify variables that influence the nocturnal behavior of waterfowl, and compare diurnal and nocturnal activity and energy budgets of several waterfowl species.

Photoperiod has a marked effect on diel activity patterns of animals. In general, photoperiod is divided into diurnal, crepuscular, and nocturnal periods, and animals are often classified according to the period in which they are most active. Unfortunately, waterfowl cannot be categorized this easily. For diurnal animals or animals for which no nocturnal data are available, researchers often assume that the nocturnal period represents a time of inactivity or minimal activity. Hence, the nocturnal period often has been given little importance and not included in experimental designs of field research. The literature contains many studies of waterfowl behavior conducted during daylight hours, but few studies of activities involving nocturnal observations (Paulus 1987).

Recent quantitative studies of the nocturnal behavior of waterfowl during winter (Tamisier 1974, 1976; Jorde 1981; Pedroli 1982; Paulus 1984a, 1984b), migration (Jorde 1981), and breeding (Talent et al. 1982, Moulton and Weller 1984)

Waterfowl in Winter. © 1988 University of Minnesota. Edited by Milton W. Weller and published by the University of Minnesota Press, Minneapolis.

indicated that different waterfowl species using a diversity of habitats are active at night and vary their activity under a variety of environmental and physiological stimuli. These studies suggested that the ecological importance of the nocturnal period may have been overlooked or misinterpreted if diurnal and nocturnal behavior patterns differ.

Several factors have contributed to the lack of information concerning water-fowl behavior at night: (1) equipment needed to collect detailed data on nocturnal behavior usually is expensive and not readily available; (2) information describing effective methods and techniques is limited; and (3) many biologists and other scientists are reluctant or unable to conduct field research at night.

Our objectives are to discuss methods to collect data on waterfowl behavior at night, identify ecological factors that influence nocturnal activity, compare diurnal and nocturnal activity of several waterfowl species, and illustrate temporal differences in energy budgets. This is Maine Agricultural Experiment Station publication 1064.

Collecting Nocturnal Behavior Data

There is little published information regarding techniques to collect waterfowl behavior data during the night. However, several methods used include auditory, visual observation, photography, remote-sensing systems, telemetry, penlights, and radar.

The auditory method involves listening for sound that indicates waterfowl activity. For example, vocalizations such as grunt-whistles and quacking may indicate courtship activity, whereas splashing suggests foraging, bathing, or agonistic behavior. This method provides a quick indication of waterfowl activity, effective for a wide range of cloud and light conditions. Major disadvantages are that specific behaviors may not be differentiated; time spent in various activities cannot be quantitated; lack of sound does not necessarily indicate inactivity; species and sex may not be ascertained; and effectiveness is influenced by weather conditions (e.g., wind). These disadvantages reduce the effectiveness of using auditory data to estimate time and energy budgets.

Visual observation can be a reliable method to record waterfowl at night under certain conditions. Generally, only silhouettes of birds are visible without special equipment, but some general behavior patterns often can be distinguished (court-ship, flight, swimming, diving, resting) (Hochbaum 1944). Low-power binoculars and spotting scopes can be efficient in moonlight and good weather conditions. An infared night-viewing device or starlight scope functions well under low light. Their effectiveness in image resolution and range increases as night-light conditions are improved by moonlight or snow. Using a night scope with a 300-mm lens, Jorde (1981) was able to determine the sex of mallards (*Anas platyrhynchos*) based on plumage patterns up to 100 m under these conditions. During high tide along the coast of Maine, general observations of black ducks (*Anas rubripes*) have been recorded at distances up to about 700 m using a 1,300-mm Questar catadioptric lens attached to a night-viewing scope. Because sea ducks are often at greater distances from shore, behavior observations are not possible or are limited to general categories (diving, swimming, inactivity).

Advantages of direct observation using binoculars, spotting scopes, and night-viewing devices are that activities of individuals and flocks can be studied in detail under suitable conditions and that the equipment is portable. Disadvantages are that distances observed and quality of data are dependent on good light conditions that may bias data for these conditions; ducks may be dispersed and difficult to locate, requiring many hours of nocturnal observation to obtain useful information; extreme cold may affect the electrical operation of night-viewing scopes and the efficiency of the observer; and purchase, maintenance, and repair costs of night scopes are high.

Photography is a technique originally used to study waterfowl during the day (e.g., Cowardin and Ashe 1965); more recently, it has been adapted to collect excellent data during the night (Moulton and Weller 1984). Camera systems range in technical complexity from simple, manually controlled cameras to integrated, automatic cameras controlled by timers, light beams, and other electronic devices. Time-lapse photographic techniques, which are most common, provide excellent results (Weller and Derksen 1972, Cooper and Afton 1981). However, electronic video systems with sound-recording capabilities offer a unique opportunity and challenge to collect detailed behavior/vocalization data.

Important advantages of photographic methods are increased sample size; a permanent record that can be reanalyzed to obtain supplemental data; the overcoming or standardizing of observer bias; relatively little or no disturbance to waterfowl; and adaptibility to many research objectives—determining numbers, species, sex, and age of individuals in a specific habitat or area, recording general activity patterns to specific behaviors, etc. Disadvantages are that the equipment may be expensive, bulky, and require auxiliary power supplies, custom-built controlling devices, camera mounts, etc.; the time required to develop and analyze film may be lengthy, and special equipment may be needed; the area covered by a camera is limited; variable light conditions may cause film to be overexposed or underexposed and limit detail; behaviors occurring in a duration less than the timing interval of the camera can be missed; an electronic flash and power source are needed for photography at night; and additional equipment is needed to protect photographic systems from adverse environmental conditions, (e.g., temperature extremes).

Remote-sensing systems employing thermisters, thermocouples, photoelectric cells, and mechanical switches connected to chart recorders have been used to record behavioral and physiological data of nesting waterfowl during the night (Low 1945, Caldwell and Cornwell 1975, Cooper 1979, Afton 1980, Cooper and

Afton 1981). Sensors can be positioned near or in the nest and on or in natural and artificial eggs. Recent advances in sensors, electronic data-logging devices, and microcomputers have increased efficiency of data collection and enhanced data analyses. A recorder or data-logger system operated concurrently with time-lapse photography offers a unique opportunity to collect detailed data during the night (Cooper and Afton 1981). Advantages of these remote-sensing systems are that more individuals, nests, and variables can be studied concurrently and continuously throughout the nesting season and that systems can be programmed or operated remotely, thereby reducing human disturbance and bias. Disadvantages are that equipment may be expensive, depending on the degree of complexity; sensors, wiring, and support equipment (e.g., power supplies, weather shelters) may be difficult to position near some nests without influencing the animal's behavior; and some disturbance may occur during periodic servicing of equipment.

Radiotelemetry can provide information about movements and general activity patterns of waterfowl and may be used to record the duration of some specific behaviors. For example, telemetry has been used to study waterfowl movement within and between habitats during winter (Jorde et al. 1983, 1984), nocturnal use of feeding sites (Tamisier and Tamisier 1981), nocturnal movements of duckling broods between wetlands (Talent et al. 1982), nest attentiveness of females (Ringelman et al. 1982), and activity of hens during the brood-rearing period (R. B. Owen, unpubl. data). Major advantages of radiotelemetry are that nocturnal activity data can be collected during adverse environmental conditions and when waterfowl occupy dense habitat; movements can be recorded easily and continuously throughout the nocturnal period; and telemetry signals can be put directly into a computer for rapid processing and analysis of data. Disadvantages are that specific behaviors may be difficult to differentiate; signal bounce may bias location and habitat use data; electronic errors may reduce the sensitivity of the telemetry system to detect subtle movements and activity; and the transmitters may alter normal behavior and may fail or come off (Gilmer et al. 1974, Wooley and Owen 1978).

An automated radiotelemetry system operated concurrently with direct observations on clear nights should provide the most comprehensive data on nocturnal behavior. This system would help verify both methods by aiding in the interpretation of telemetry signals and determining whether behavior observed on clear nights was representative of all light conditions.

Bellrose (1958) used penlights attached to the legs of waterfowl to study flight orientation at night. These lightweight devices can be attached with water-dissolving tape to allow release of the device soon after its useful life. Penlights can be seen up to 5 km with a spotting scope during optimal conditions (Bellrose 1963). Small lights powered by rechargeable batteries and solar cells could be used to study courtship and feeding behavior at night (M. W. Weller, pers. commun.). Major advantages of this technique are that the device is inexpensive, lightweight, and easily designed and that it can be easily attached. Disadvantages are that animals must be captured and handled; battery life is limited unless the unit is recharged by solar cells; and light may influence individual or group behavior.

Radar has been used primarily to study patterns of bird migration during various weather conditions (Hassler et al. 1963), during the nocturnal period (see Bellrose and Graber 1963), and more recently to estimate bird use of flight corridors (Korschgen et al. 1984). Advantages are that birds can be observed at long distances; data can be collected during most weather and all light conditions; large flocks of birds can be observed at the same time; and radar can scan all directions or focus on a specific airspace. Disadvantages are that equipment is expensive and not easily portable; special training and expertise usually are necessary to operate radar equipment and interpret images; sex, age, and species of individual birds cannot be determined by radar alone; and observations are restricted to general flight behaviors.

Variables Influencing Nocturnal Activity

Seasonal and daily activity budgets within and among waterfowl species vary widely (for review see Paulus 1987). Because there is little information about the nocturnal activity of waterfowl, comprehensive and unifying statements concerning nocturnal behavior and energy budgets of waterfowl cannot be made at this time. However, it is important to identify specific variables that influence the behavior of waterfowl at night, although these are often interactive (e.g., Pedroli 1982; Tamisier 1974, 1985) and it may be difficult to determine which variable governs an animal's periodicity. The variables include species, season, geographic location, weather, food resources, lunar and tidal cycles, physiological condition of the bird, and activity of potential predators, including humans.

Nocturnal activity patterns, especially feeding behavior, of waterfowl vary within and among taxonomic groups (Nilsson 1970; Paulus 1987). For example, wintering tufted ducks (*Aythya fuligula*), Canada geese (*Branta canadensis*), and common goldeneyes (*Bucephala clangula*) can be either day active or night active or both (Nilsson 1970, Raveling et al. 1972, Sayler and Afton 1981). Nocturnal activity of waterfowl has been reported for both nonmigratory species (Moulton and Weller 1984, Paulus 1984b) and migratory species (Jorde 1981; Paulus 1984a, 1987).

Seasonal differences in activity budgets are influenced by mainenance and reproductive strategies of birds and environmental variables. Photoperiods range from almost 24 hours of light at far northern breeding areas to less than 8 hours at some wintering sites. Therefore, differences in day length most likely influence nocturnal behavioral patterns and foraging strategies of waterfowl during winter as birds attempt to balance energy needs. Waterfowl may be active at night during the breeding season (Swanson and Sargeant 1972), winter (Nilsson 1970, Paulus 1980, Pedroli 1982), migration (D. Jorde, unpubl. data), and after breeding (Bailey

1982). Waterfowl can shift behavior patterns to be most active during the nocturnal period in winter and the diurnal period at other seasons (Nilsson 1970).

Waterfowl in different geographic areas exhibit variations in nocturnal activity during both the breeding and wintering seasons. For example, tufted ducks wintering in Sweden were night active on northern coastal sites but mostly day active on southern coastal areas (Nilsson 1970). Goldeneyes wintering on the Mississippi River formed rafts at roost sites during the night and flew to foraging sites during the day (Sayler and Afton 1981). In contrast, goldeneyes wintering along the coast of Maine often remained in small groups or pairs at night and continued to forage (D. Eggeman and D. Jorde, unpubl. data). Waterfowl that respond to human-induced habitat loss or modification (Buller 1975) most likely vary or adapt their activity patterns to conditions prevailing at new geographic locations.

Daily and seasonal climatic patterns influence waterfowl behavior. Cold temperatures may cause waterfowl to emigrate (Bennett and Bolen 1978) or partition behavior to conserve energy for thermoregulation. During severe weather, waterfowl may increase foraging intensity (Tamisier 1972) or adjust foraging activity to feed during the day and night (Nilsson 1970). Snow and ice cover may limit food resources and available roost sites and cause waterfowl to repartition daily activity patterns (Bourget and Chapdelaine 1975, Jorde et al. 1984). Microclimates warmed by the sun most likely influence waterfowl to spend more time loafing, resting, and in other energy-conserving behaviors during the day (Jorde et al. 1984) and to be more active during the night when heat energy generated by muscular activity and digestion offsets some of the costs of thermoregulation.

Abundance and availability of food resources also influence waterfowl behavior. Some waterfowl can be active both day and night when food resources are available during the entire 24-hour period (Nilsson 1970). The timing of feeding is influenced by food density and the proximity of foraging sites to roost areas (Bossenmaier and Marshall 1958). Because some aquatic invertebrates consumed by waterfowl are negatively phototactic (Newell 1970), foraging strategies and time budgets of waterfowl using some animal foods may differ from waterfowl relying on plant foods. Nilsson (1970) suggested that waterfowl feeding on sessile animal foods such as molluscs and chironomid larvae could forage night or day whereas those species feeding on mobile prey are predominately daytime feeders. We agree that these trends may occur; however, he specifically listed goldeneye in the latter category, and our observations of goldeneyes feeding at night in coastal Maine indicated that this division may vary. During the breeding season, adult and immature dabbling ducks forage intensively at night during periods of aquatic invertebrate emergence (Swanson and Sargeant 1972). Waterfowl feeding on agricultural foods by day may supplement their diet with aquatic invertebrates by foraging at night (Jorde et al. 1983).

Waterfowl adjust activity patterns to specific periods of the moon and tide. During nights when the moon was bright, geese often foraged in aquatic habitats (Lebret 1969, 1970) and in fields used during the day (Raveling et al. 1972, Ydenberg et al. 1984). However, lunar cycles may not affect the nocturnal feeding of other species (Tamisier 1972). Tidal cycles influence the availability of food resources and the timing of feeding. Waterfowl dependent on tidal cycles foraged during optimal tide heights both day and night (Lebret 1970, Burton and Hudson 1978, Campbell 1978, Campredon 1982). For example, black ducks wintering along the Maine coast fed during each low tide (Albright et al. 1983) unless severe weather conditions forced them to remain at roost sites (Albright 1981).

Waterfowl behavior at night is influenced by physiological condition and energy requirements. When energy demand is high, waterfowl may be forced to feed both during the day and night (Tamisier 1974). Activity often is modified to maintain body heat during periods of cold stress and to replenish fat and protein when stress conditions have lessened. Specific dynamic effect, the heat energy released when foods are digested, may influence noctural foraging activity during winter periods and molt when this source of energy would be most beneficial for thermoregulation (Jorde 1981, Bailey 1982, Quinlan and Baldassarre 1984). During prelaying, waterfowl may need to feed during both day and night to increase energy and nutrient input for egg production.

Predator activity and other disturbances influence the behavior of waterfowl (Campredon 1981). Avian predators tend to be most active during the day; therefore, it may be advantageous for waterfowl to be gregarious, more alert, and less active during the diurnal period (Tamisier 1974, 1976). Tamisier (1970, 1985) further suggested that nocturnal foraging observed in many species during the nonbreeding season may be a direct result of this response. He stated that the diurnal resting grounds provided such additional benefits as serving as an information center, favoring pair formation, and permitting extensive comfort activities related to sunbathing. Human disturbance and protection can cause waterfowl to change behavior and migration patterns (Hankla and Rudolph 1967). Hunting pressure often forces waterfowl to adjust daily patterns and feed at night (Girard 1941, Raveling et al. 1972).

Activity and Energy Budgets

Activity Budgets

Several studies that provide quantitative data on activity budgets of waterfowl throughout the entire diel period illustrate the differences among species and the significance of nocturnal activity (table 12.1). For many species, foraging is the dominant nighttime activity, consuming as much as 90% of the time for green-winged teal (*Anas crecca*) in France (Tamisier 1974). Tufted ducks wintering in

Sweden rested 85% of the day and not at all during the night (Pedroli 1982). In contrast, the same species wintering farther south was predominately day active (Nilsson 1970). Other waterfowl species formed rafts at night and did not seem to feed at roost sites (Linsell 1969, Sayler and Afton 1981).

Table 12.1. Diurnal and nocturnal activity budgets and estimated behavioral energy expenditures for six waterfowl species during winter

Species	Period	Feeding/ Diving	Loco- motion	Resting	Alert	Comfort	Court- ship	Agon- istic	Flight	Energy[a] (kj)
Green-winged teal	Day	5.0	33.0	60.0	. . .	2.0	--	--	--	130
(*Anas crecca*)[b]	Night	90.0	5.0	4.0	--	1.0	--	--	--	138
Mottled duck	Day	39.1	7.5	36.7	7.5	9.2	0.3	0.2	--	284
(*Anas fulvigula*)[c]	Night	50.8	2.5	34.2	5.8	7.5	0.1	0.2	--	283
Eurasian wigeon	Day	32.0	22.0	30.0	--	16.0	--	--	--	238
(*Anas penelope*)[d]	Night	74.0	4.0	19.0	--	2.0	--	--	--	235
Mallard	Day	29.9	12.5	29.9	6.3	13.4	0.4	0.6	5.8	423
(*Anas platyrhynchos*)[e]	Night	20.0	9.2	39.2	5.8	22.5	0.8	1.7	0.0	306
Gadwall	Day	60.8	12.5	8.3	10.8	6.7	0.3	0.5	--	255
(*Anas strepera*)[f]	Night	69.2	6.7	17.5	4.2	2.5	0.0	0.1	--	242
Tufted duck	Day	1.7	8.3	85.0	--	5.0	--	--	--	248
(*Aythya fuligula*)[g]	Night	40.0	56.7	--	--	3.3	--	--	--	356

[a] Energy estimates of basal metabolism rate and activity based on Wooley and Owen (1978).
[b] Tamisier (1974).
[c] Paulus (1984b).
[d] Campredon (1981).
[e] Jorde (1981).
[f] Paulus (1984a).
[g] Pedroli (1982).

Nocturnal observations and telemetry data indicated that black ducks along the coast of Maine foraged intensively during the night when the tidal cycle exposed ledges, mud flats, and mussel bars (Albright 1981; D. Jorde, unpubl. data). Activity budgets for this species are similar during the day and night in winter.

Further studies should help to discover whether certain ecological trends occur in activity patterns. For example, are there waterfowl that are exclusively day feeders and do they feed on mobile animal prey (Nilsson 1970)? Are seed and grass eaters active day and night? In winter, are species that consume natural foods predominantly night feeders whereas those waterfowl feeding on planted grains are mostly diurnal feeders, as A. Tamisier (pers. commun.) has suggested? These are important and interesting questions that await further exploration.

Energy Budgets

Energy expended for activity represents a major component of a species' total energy budget (Weathers et al. 1984); therefore, behavior needs to be recorded throughout the diel period. Behavioral energy budgets can illustrate temporal variation of energy requirements among different species of waterfowl. Some species (e.g., *Anas fulvigula*, *A. strepera*) exhibit similar behavior and energy expenditure throughout the entire diel period (table 12.1). Other species (e.g., *Anas crecca*, *A. penelope*) have very different activity patterns during the day and night, but energy expenditure for behavior is the same. In contrast, *Aythya fuligula* foraged almost exclusively at night (Pedroli 1982) and its energy cost for activity was 44% greater during that period. Few waterfowl studies have included estimates of flight, an energy-intensive behavior. In mallards, expenditure for flight increased the daytime energy estimate by 38%. Without flight, day and night energy expenditures for behavior were equal.

Although studies have described activity patterns at night, few have provided the quantifiable data needed to estimate daily energy budgets. Given the variability among species illustrated above, errors can be made when assuming activity patterns without supporting data. In addition, errors probably will occur in estimates of energy budgets if energy equivalents for different behaviors have not been determined in the laboratory and if thermal conditions around the bird are unknown at the time behavior data are collected (Weathers et al. 1984).

Conclusion

Waterfowl display unusual adaptability to changing environmental conditions. Thus, most species cannot be called strictly diurnal or nocturnal. As a group, waterfowl may be one of the most adaptable orders of birds with respect to this behavioral flexibility. Researchers have just begun to understand this aspect of waterfowl biology. Information gathered to date suggests that daily activity and energy budgets must accurately portray nocturnal behavior even though quantifying these data may be difficult and expensive. We strongly believe that this is a fertile area for research that will lead to a better understanding of waterfowl physiology and ecology.

LITERATURE CITED

Afton, A. D. 1980. Factors affecting incubation rhythms of northern shovelers. Condor 82:132–137.
Albright, J. J. 1981. Behavioral and physiological responses of coastal wintering black ducks (*Anas*

rubripes) to changing weather in Maine. M.S. Thesis, Univ. Maine, Orono. 72pp.

———, R. B. Owen, Jr., and P. O. Corr. 1983. Activity patterns and energy budgets of black ducks wintering on the Maine coast. Trans. Northeast Sect. Soc. Wildl.

Bailey, R. O. 1982. The postbreeding ecology of the redhead duck (*Aythya americana*) on Long Island Bay, Lake Winnipegosis, Manitoba. Ph.D. Diss., McGill Univ., Montreal, Que.

Bellrose, F. C. 1958. Celestial orientation by wild mallards. Birdbanding 29:75-90.

———. 1963. Orientation behavior of four species of waterfowl. Auk 80:257-289.

———, and R. R. Graber. 1963. A radar study of the flight directions of nocturnal migrants. Proc. Int. Ornithol. Congr. 13:362-389.

Bennett, J. W., and E. G. Bolen. 1978. Stress response in wintering green-winged teal. J. Wildl. Manage. 42:81-86.

Bossenmaier, E. F., and W. H. Marshall. 1958. Field-feeding by waterfowl in southwestern Manitoba. Wildl. Mongr. 1. 32pp.

Bourget, A., and G. Chapdelaine. 1975. Diving by wintering puddle ducks. Wildfowl 26:55-57.

Buller, R. J. 1975. Redistribution of waterfowl; influence of water, protection, and feeding. Int. Waterfowl Symp. 1:143-154.

Burton, B. A., and R. J. Hudson. 1978. Activity budgets of lesser snow geese wintering on the Fraser River estuary, British Columbia. Wildfowl 32:79-87.

Caldwell, P. J., and G. W. Cornwell. 1975. Incubation behavior and temperatures of the mallard duck. Auk 92:706-731.

Campbell, L. H. 1978. Diurnal and tidal behavior patterns of eiders wintering at Leigh. Wildfowl 29:147-152.

Campredon, P. 1981. Hivernage du canard siffieur *Anas penelope* L. en Camargue (France). Stationnements et activities. Alauda 49:161-193.

———. 1982. Conditions d'hivernage du canard siffleur *Anas penelope* en France, en zone littorale et continentals. Bull. Mens. Office Nat. Chasse 58:23-48.

Cooper, J. A. 1979. Trumpeter swan nesting behavior. Wildfowl 30:55-71.

———, and A. D. Afton. 1981. A multiple sensor system for monitoring avian nesting behavior. Wilson Bull. 93:325-333.

Cowardin, L. M., and J. E. Ashe. 1965. An automatic camera device for measuring waterfowl use. J. Wildl. Manage. 29:636-640.

Gilmer, D. S., I. J. Ball, L. M. Cowardin, and J. H. Riechmann. 1974. Effects of radio packages on wild ducks. J. Wildl. Manage. 38:243-252.

Girard, G. L. 1941. The mallard: its management in western Montana. J. Wildl. Manage. 5:233-259.

Hankla, D. J., and R. R. Rudolph. 1967. Changes in the migration and wintering habits of Canada geese in the lower portion of the Atlantic and Mississippi flyways—with special reference to national wildlife refuges. Proc. Southeast. Assoc. Game Fish Comm. 21:133-144.

Hassler, S. S., R. R. Graber, and F. C. Bellrose. 1963. Fall migration and weather, a radar study. Wilson Bull. 75:56-77.

Hochbaum, H. A. 1944. The canvasback on a prairie marsh. American Wildlife Institute, Washington, D.C. 201pp.

Jorde, D. G. 1981. Winter and spring staging ecology of mallards in south central Nebraska. M.S. Thesis, Univ. North Dakota, Grand Forks. 116pp.

———, G. L. Krapu, and R. D. Crawford. 1983. Feeding ecology of mallards wintering in Nebraska. J. Wildl. Manage. 47:1044-1053.

———, ———, ———, and M. A. Hay. 1984. Effects of weather on habitat selection and behavior of mallards wintering in Nebraska. Condor 86:258-265.

Korschgen, C. E., W. L. Green, W. L. Flock, and E. A. Hibbard. 1984. Use of radar with a stationary antenna to estimate birds in a low-level flight corridor. J. Field Ornithol. 55:369-375.

Lebret, T. 1969. Nocturnal observations on a roost of bean geese *A. fabalis* in the lake Neusiedl, Austria. Limosa 42:16–26.

———. 1970. Nocturnal feeding and other activities of the greylag goose in fresh water tidal habitat in the Netherlands. Limosa 43:11–30.

Linsell, S. E. 1969. Pre-dusk and nocturnal behavior of goldeneye, with notes on population composition. Wildfowl 20:75–77.

Low, J. B. 1945. Ecology and management of the redhead, *Nyroca americana*, in Iowa. Ecol. Monogr. 15:35–69.

Moulton, D. W., and M. Weller. 1984. Biology and conservation of the laysan duck (*Anas laysanensis*). Condor 86:105–117.

Newell, R. C. 1970. Biology of intertidal animals. Am. Elsevier Publ. Co., New York. 555pp.

Nilsson, L. 1970. Food seeking activity of south Swedish diving ducks in the nonbreeding season. Oikos 21:145–154.

Paulus, S. L. 1980. The winter ecology of the gadwall in Louisiana. M.S. Thesis, Univ. North Dakota, Grand Forks. 357pp.

———. 1984a. Activity budgets of nonbreeding gadwalls in Louisiana. J. Wildl. Manage. 48:371–380.

———. 1984b. Behavioral ecology of mottled ducks in Louisiana. Ph.D. Diss., Auburn Univ., Auburn, Ala. 152pp.

———, 1988. Time-activity budgets of nonbreeding Anatidae: a review. Pages 135–152 *in* M. Weller, ed. Waterfowl in winter. Univ. Minnesota Press, Minneapolis.

Pedroli, J. C. 1982. Activity and time budget of tufted ducks on Swiss lakes during winter. Wildfowl 33:105–112.

Quinlan, E. E., and G. A. Baldassarre. 1984. Activity budgets of non-breeding green-winged teal on playa lakes in Texas. J. Wildl. Manage. 48:838–845.

Raveling, D. G., W. E. Crews, and W. D. Klimstra. 1972. Activity patterns of Canada geese during winter. Wilson Bull. 84:278–295.

Ringelman, J. K., J. R. Longcore, and R. B. Owen, Jr. 1982. Habitat selection and home range of radio-marked black ducks in Maine. Can. J. Zool. 60:241–248.

Sayler, R. D., and A. D. Afton. 1981. Ecological aspects of common goldeneyes (*Bucephala clangula*) wintering on the upper Mississippi River. Ornis Scand. 12:99–108.

Swanson, G. A., and A. B. Sargeant. 1972. Observation of night-time feeding behavior of ducks. J. Wildl. Manage. 36:959–961.

Talent, L. G., G. L. Krapu, and R. L. Jarvis. 1982. Habitat use by mallard broods in south central North Dakota. J. Wildl. Manage. 46:629–635.

Tamisier, A. 1970. Signification du gregarisme divrne et de l'alimentation nocturne des sarcelles d'hiver *Anas crecca crecca* L. Terre Vie 4:511–562.

———. 1972. Rythmes nycthemeraux des sarcelles d'hiver pendant leur hivernage en Carmargue. Alauda 40:107–135, 235–256.

———. 1974. Etho-ecological studies of teal wintering in the Camargue (Rhone Delta, France). Wildfowl 25:122–133.

———. 1976. Diurnal activities of green-winged teal and pintail wintering in Louisiana. Wildfowl 27:19–32.

———. 1985. Some considerations on the social requirements of ducks in winter. Wildfowl 36:104–108.

———, and M. C. Tamisier. 1981. L'existence d'unités fonctionnelles démontrée chez les sarcelles d'hiver en Camargue par la bio-télémétrie. Rev. Ecol. (Terre Vie) 35:563–579.

Weathers, W. W., W. A. Buttemer, A. M. Hayworth, and K. A. Nagy. 1984. An evaluation of time budget estimates of daily energy expenditure in birds. Auk 101:459–472.

Weller, M. W., and D. V. Derksen. 1972. Use of time-lapse photography to study nesting activities of birds. Auk 89:196–200.

Wooley, J. B., Jr., and R. B. Owen, Jr. 1978. Energy costs of activity and daily energy expenditure in the black duck. J. Wildl. Manage. 42:739–745.

Ydenberg, R. C., H. H. Th. Prins, and J. Van Dijk. 1984. A lunar rhythm in the nocturnal foraging activities of wintering barnacle geese. Wildfowl 35:93–96.

13

Workshop Summary: Techniques for Timing Activity of Wintering Waterfowl

Guy A. Baldassarre, Stuart L. Paulus, Alain Tamisier, and Rodger D. Titman

The workshop on timing activity (TA) was unique among those at the Waterfowl in Winter Symposium because it focused on a research method currently used extensively for studying waterfowl ecology during the nonbreeding season. TA studies are important because natural selection should favor individuals optimally allocating time in space (Verner 1965); thus, time budgets relate importantly to many workshop topics (e.g., courtship and pairing, habitat selection, and feeding ecology). However, recent TA investigations of nonbreeding waterfowl (Tamisier 1976, Skead 1977, Roux et al. 1978, Burton and Hudson 1978, Campbell 1978, Frederick and Klaas 1982, Hepp 1982, Paulus 1984a, Quinlan and Baldassarre 1984, Jorde et al. 1984, Miller 1985, Hohman 1986) have diversified methodologies, which necessitates guidance in selecting and evaluating techniques.

Workshop participants agreed that (1) TA studies provide valuable data and insights into numerous aspects of avian ecology (see Wiens et al. 1970, Altmann 1974, Caraco 1979, Fredrickson and Drobney 1979, Reinecke 1981); (2) there are several TA techniques (e.g., focal vs. scan sampling), with no single one applicable to all research questions; and (3) TA is inexpensive, minimally requiring only a spotting scope or binoculars, timing device, and a tape recorder. With these favorable attributes as a foundation, we focused discussion on application and modification of existing methodologies relative to research of nonbreeding waterfowl. Workshop topics concerned focal-bird vs. scan sampling for collecting TA data, nocturnal studies, TA of diving ducks, concurrent measurement of environmental variables, statistical analysis, and interpretation and use of data.

Waterfowl in Winter. © 1988 University of Minnesota. Edited by Milton W. Weller and published by the University of Minnesota Press, Minneapolis.

Focal-Bird vs. Scan-Sampling Techniques

Because nearly all TA studies have used focal-bird or scan-sampling techniques, there was little discussion of other such techniques as ad libitum or one-zero sampling (Altmann 1974). The framework for using either focal or scan-sampling techniques is to divide each day into intervals and observe birds for set time periods within each interval.

Focal sampling involves observation of an individual bird for a specified time period. Activities are recorded continuously or instantaneously (e.g., every 10-15 seconds), with some variation of the latter most prevalent. Observations within a time period then are proportioned to determine the percentage of time spent in each behavioral activity.

Focal sampling is advantageous in recording infrequent behaviors such as social display and aggression, particularly if birds are observed continuously. Difficulties include observer fatigue; the random selection of individuals to observe, especially from large flocks; potential for losing the focal bird from view in dense flocks or heavily vegetated habitats; and maintaining accuracy in sampling of foraging diving ducks, unless ducks are in small groups.

Scan sampling records the activity of numerous individuals within a flock by instantaneously determining the behavior of each bird. Resultant data then are proportioned to determine the percentage of time the flock spends in each activity during a sampling period. Although observer fatigue is still a problem, large numbers of ducks can be sampled relatively quickly. However, because behavior of individuals must be assessed instantaneously, it is not possible to determine the social status of birds under observation (i.e., paired vs. unpaired).

Scan sampling may be the only alternative in dense vegetation where ducks may not be visible for long periods, which can limit opportunities for focal sampling. In dense cover, however, both focal and scan sampling can bias the observer toward birds in view. Scan sampling does eliminate choosing which individuals to observe, unless large numbers of birds are sampled. For example, sampling from large flocks may bias results because, by the time behaviors of the last birds are noted (perhaps several hours), activities may have changed significantly from those first sampled. Also, birds in the flock center may not be visible. These problems may be alleviated by shortening observation periods (i.e., subsampling).

Finally, scan sampling usually records behaviors of many individuals; thus, raw data often are tape-recorded and transcribed later at considerable time and expense to the investigator. Focal sampling also can necessitate data transcription. These costs can be overcome by using mechanical tabulators or portable microprocessors. Use of marked individuals and videotape equipment may eliminate or moderate many visibility problems associated with both focal-bird and scan-sampling techniques.

An investigator could increase flexibility in addressing research objectives during a given study by using both focal and scan-sampling techniques. For example, focal sampling is more suited for detailed analysis of behavioral patterns and for relating individual behaviors to energy budgets, whereas scan sampling is adapted more for broad analysis of large groups. The consensus of the workshop was that investigators should make TA flexible enough for the purposes at hand.

The concepts of behavioral events and states were discussed as being relevant to both techniques. An *event* is an instantaneous occurrence of a designated activity, whereas a *state* occurs in continuum. For example, green-winged teal feeding on a mud flat may walk, stop, filter feed for food, walk, etc., with the entire sequence occurring within several seconds. Event sampling would classify these behaviors separately, perhaps as locomoting, resting, and feeding. However, these activities represent the feeding state; thus, event sampling would underestimate the feeding bout by perhaps 75%. Social display may be particularly subject to this discrepancy, and this bias would explain why social display has comprised such a small percentage of wintering waterfowl time budgets (Quinlan and Baldassarre 1984, Paulus 1984a). State sampling may involve observer subjectivity, but data can be presented using both methods. Packard and Ribic (1982) have attempted to address this problem quantitatively in classifying behavior of sea otters (*Enhydra lutris*).

The group perceived a need for more detail when describing behavioral categories in publication to increase precision and facilitate comparison among studies. Subdivision of behavioral categories also may provide substantial new insights from TA studies. For example, valuable energetics data could be obtained by recording whether the general category of feeding behavior involved tipping-up, diving, surface feeding, above surface feeding, etc.

Nocturnal Studies

Waterfowl engage in important activities at night during winter, as indicated by both direct (e.g., nocturnal observation of feeding) and indirect evidence (e.g., diurnal observations showing lack of feeding). However, only a few TA studies of wintering waterfowl have included extensive nocturnal data (Tamisier 1972; Paulus 1984a, 1984b). This lack of data is significant because TA studies based only on diurnal data cannot reflect diel patterns. For example, it can be energetically advantageous for waterfowl to rest and sunbathe on cold winter days and to feed at night, but the daily inactivity might be misinterpreted unless nocturnal data were collected. However, nocturnal observation is difficult because investigators may be hampered by cold, fatigue, inadequate equipment, reduced visibility, insects, and poor mobility. Also, ducks must be approached more closely for observation at night. Indeed, these difficulties resulted in one workshop participant spending three to four hours to obtain each hour of nocturnal data.

Three means of obtaining nocturnal TA data include using moonlight, infrared night-vision scopes, and light-intensifying night-vision scopes. Binoculars aided by moonlight are sufficient for observation about 7-10 days per month if sky conditions are mostly clear. Infrared scopes have been replaced by more effective and versatile light-intensifying scopes, which are suitable in complete darkness if a supplemental light source invisible to ducks is provided (e.g., high-power light with an infrared filter). Best results are obtained when light sources shine on the subject from above or behind the observer.

The physical and technical constraints of obtaining nocturnal data dictate that observers be flexible in choosing sampling designs and schedules. Investigators should capitalize on situations when and where ducks are visible at night because an opportunity lost may not soon recur.

Timing Activity of Diving Ducks

Timing the activities of diving ducks poses unique and difficult problems for investigators because birds cannot be observed while underwater. There are few activity budget studies of wintering diving ducks (Klima 1966, Campbell 1978, Pedroli 1982, Hohman 1986), and the group agreed that additional TA work is needed in this area. There also are several problems with existing methodology.

Focal-bird sampling was deemed nearly impossible in large flocks unless marked individuals are available. Focal sampling of isolated individuals or small flocks is possible, but it could lead to biases because sampling may not reflect activity patterns occurring within larger groups. Scan sampling also is difficult because all birds diving are not tallied on each scan, which would underestimate diving (feeding) time. For example, assume 50 of 100 ducks in a flock begin feeding while the remaining 50 are resting. If 25 are below the surface during a scan sample, only 75 are tallied (50 resting, 25 feeding), and feeding effort by the group would be underestimated by 17%.

A possible solution would be first to count all the individuals in a flock when *not* diving. Then, recognizing that diving (feeding) consists of an emerging event (E) on the surface and a diving event (D) of time spent underwater, the feeding state (F) would equal E + D. Once diving activity begins, the observer can calculate the number of birds in F as all those seen in event E and assume all those not seen are in event D. These tallies then can be proportioned relative to the initial number of ducks known in the flock, and F again equals E + D. An index of feeding efficiency might be calculated as D ÷ E + D, the index varying by species and habitat (i.e., water depth). This technique may be difficult to apply in situations where an initial count of flock size is not possible (large flocks, densely vegetated habitats).

Measurement of Environmental Variables

TA studies of wintering waterfowl often concurrently record environmental variables (e.g., temperature, wind spend, cloud cover) to explain variation of time spent
in activities. Seldom have environmental factors accounted for more than 20% of
the variation in a given activity (Quinlan and Baldassarre 1984, Paulus 1984a), but
few studies have measured climatic variables from microhabitats actually used by
birds under observation (Jorde et al. 1984). Measurement of microhabitat climate
is highly desirable but could prove difficult and expensive because of the logistics
in positioning equipment in locations actually used by ducks. However, accurate
measurement of environmental variables should constitute an integral part of TA
studies because recent investigations demonstrate that waterfowl respond to severe
winter weather by seeking thermally favorable microhabitats (Jorde et al. 1984,
Brodsky and Weatherhead 1984).

Statistical Analysis

There was disagreement among investigators regarding statistical procedures for
analysis of TA data, perhaps because such a wide array of techniques is applicable.
We agreed that (1) large data sets commonly are obtained when undertaking TA
studies; (2) sound statistical and biological planning beforehand are paramount to
an efficient and effective TA study; (3) the research question should exert the most
influence on decisions made during the planning phase; and (4) TA data should be
subjected to a rigorous statistical analysis.

The minimum time a bird or flock should be observed was discussed because
differential opportunities result in observations for unequal periods of time. Thus,
some investigators discard data from birds observed less than a preset time (e.g., 15
or 30 minutes), although reasons for this are vague. Standardization within a study
would eliminate problems such as comparing an individual or group observed for
10 minutes with another observed for two hours. For example, a bird observed 10
minutes may not change behavior from an initial activity (i.e., it may rest 10
minutes), whereas a bird observed for a long period may change behavior several
times. The choice of a minimum time period will depend on study objectives;
however, if observation periods are greatly unequal, final analysis could weight
each by its time length.

The daily variability in activity patterns of wintering waterfowl is commonly
determined by dividing the day into sampling intervals and observing individuals
or flocks for given time periods within those intervals (Tamisier 1976, Skead 1977,
Burton and Hudson 1978, Hickey and Titman 1983, Paulus 1984a, Quinlan and
Baldassarre 1984, Miller 1985, and others). These data then are pooled to describe
overall diurnal, nocturnal, or diel activity patterns.

Bias occurs, however, when birds are sampled unequally throughout the day, regardless of sampling period length. For example, suppose that sampling is done by dividing a day into three equal intervals and that a given activity (e.g., feeding) dominates interval one. If most birds were sampled in interval one and calculation of the overall time budget based on the average of all birds observed, feeding time is overestimated. This bias can be eliminated by designating sampling intervals of equal length and observing equal numbers of birds per interval, or by calculating the mean of each sampling interval and averaging those means for each day. If sampling intervals are unequal, calculation of overall time budgets should weight averages based on sampling interval length and could also incorporate an additional weighting factor if individual birds are not observed for equal time periods. However, some caution should be exercised to avoid arbitrarily grouping sampling intervals, which could distort important behavior patterns. For example, grouping "day" and "night" will not depict patterns, if any, within those times. Statistical and biological justifications should dictate how observation intervals are grouped.

Few TA studies have addressed differential activity patterns among habitats (Paulus 1984a). Equal sampling among available habitats is difficult to accomplish, but studies should not be confined to easily observable, large flocks because resultant data could mask real habitat/behavior interactions. For example, if feeding dominates activity within a particular habitat and all birds are sampled from that habitat, interpretations of activity patterns would be misleading.

Finally, we discussed the choice of a replication unit within TA studies. For example, assume that 10 birds are observed for one hour each and, in another instance, 10 hours are spent observing a different bird every half hour. The sample size is 10 in the first situation, regardless of whether the replication is considered the individual bird observed or the time (one hour) each bird was under observation. However, sample size is 20 in the second instance, assuming that the birds observed are the replications. These differences have major ramifications in statistical testing and must be considered before subjecting TA data to analysis. Most workshop participants agreed that the individual bird or flock observed should be the replication unit.

Interpretation and Use of Data

Several concerns in interpretation and use of data were discussed. First, percentage of time spent in activities should not be construed as indicative of the importance of different activities. For example, time spent alert usually comprises less than 5% of a time budget but undoubtedly is an extremely important activity. Second, percentage values obtained from TA studies may vary from an individual's actual time budget depending on the technique used (e.g., focal vs. scan sampling). A study comparing TA techniques using long-term, continuous data of marked individuals would be very useful in this regard. Third, studies conducted in one area may not apply elsewhere. There is need for repetition within species from different geographical areas, but studies designed to test specific hypotheses could reduce the need for this duplication.

Finally, we recognized that investigators collecting TA data provide useful information to avian ecologists, but they also have a clientele among wildlife biologists seeking direction in management of wintering waterfowl. Most TA studies describe basic behavior patterns of a given species but have not addressed other questions. For example, TA techniques are useful in the investigation of the effects of hunting or predation on waterfowl behavior in winter, the effects of harvest regulations on behavior, and the impacts of habitat manipulation on activity patterns. Overall, workshop participants agreed that TA techniques will continue and expand as a major method used to investigate the ecology of wintering waterfowl.

LITERATURE CITED

Altmann, J. 1974. Observational study of behavior: sampling methods. Behav. 49:227–267.

Brodsky, L. M., and P. J. Weatherhead. 1984. Behavioral thermoregulation in wintering black ducks: roosting and resting. Can. J. Zool. 62:1223–1226.

Burton, B. A., and R. J. Hudson. 1978. Activity budgets of lesser snow geese wintering on the Fraser River Estuary, British Columbia. Wildfowl 29:111–117.

Campbell, L. H. 1978. Diurnal and tidal behavior patterns of goldeneyes wintering at Leith. Wildfowl 29:147–152.

Caraco, T. 1979. Time budgeting and group size: a theory. Ecol. 60:611–617.

Frederick, R. B., and E. E. Klaas. 1982. Resource use and behavior of migrating snow geese. J. Wildl. Manage. 46:601–614.

Fredrickson, L. H., and R. D. Drobney. 1979. Habitat utilization by postbreeding waterfowl. Pages 119-131 in T. A. Bookhout, ed. Waterfowl and wetlands—an integrated review. Proc. 1977 Symp., Northcent. Sect., Wildl. Soc., Madison, Wis. 152pp.

Hepp, G. R. 1982. Behavioral ecology of waterfowl (Anatini) wintering in coastal North Carolina. Ph.D. Diss., North Carolina State Univ., Raleigh. 155pp.

Hickey, T. E., and R. D. Titman. 1983. Diurnal activity budgets of black ducks during their annual cycle in Prince Edward Island. Can. J. Zool. 61:743–749.

Hohman, W. L. 1986. Diurnal time-activity budgets for ring-necked ducks wintering in central Florida. Proc. Southeast. Assoc. Game Fish Comm. 38:158–164.

Jorde, D. G., G. L. Krapu, R. D. Crawford, and M. A. Hay. 1984. Effects of weather on habitat selection and behavior of mallards wintering in Nebraska. Condor 86:258–265.

Klima, M. 1966. A study on diurnal activity rhythm in the European pochard, *Aythya ferina* (L.) Zool. Listy. 15:317–332.

Miller, M. R. 1985. Time budgets of northern pintails wintering in the Sacramento Valley, California. Wildfowl 36:53–64.

Packard, J. M., and C. A. Ribic. 1982. Classification of the behavior of sea otters (*Enhydra lutris*). Can. J. Zool. 60:1362–1373.

Paulus, S. L. 1984a. Activity budgets of nonbreeding gadwalls in Louisiana. J. Wildl. Manage. 48:371–380.

————. 1984b. Behavioral ecology of mottled ducks in Louisiana. Ph.D. Diss., Auburn Univ., Auburn, Ala. 139pp.

Pedroli, J.-C. 1982. Activity and time budget of tufted ducks on Swiss lakes during winter. Wildfowl 33:105–112.

Quinlan, E. E., and G. A. Baldassarre. 1984. Activity budgets of nonbreeding green-winged teal on playa lakes in Texas. J. Wildl. Manage. 48:838–845.

Reinecke, K. J. 1981. Winter waterfowl research needs and efforts in the Mississippi Delta. Int. Waterfowl Symp. 4:231–236.

Roux, F., R. Maheo, and A. Tamisier. 1978. L'exploitation de la basse vallée du Sénégal (quartier d'hiver tropical) par trois espéces de canards paléarctiques et éthiopien. Terre Vie 32:387–416.

Skead, D. M. 1977. Diurnal activity budgets of Anatini during winter. Ostrich Suppl. 12:65–74.

Tamisier, A. 1972. Rythmes nycthéméraux des sarcelles d'hiver pendant leur hivernage en Camargue. Alauda 40:107–135, 235–256.

————. 1976. Diurnal activities of green-winged teal and pintail wintering in Louisiana. Wildfowl 27:19–31.

Verner, J. 1965. Time budget of the male long-billed marsh wren during the breeding season. Condor 67:126–139.

Wiens, J. A., S. G. Martin, W. R. Holthaus, and F. A. Iwen. 1970. Metronome timing in behavioral ecology studies. Ecol. 51:350–352.

IV.
Community and Feeding Ecology

14

Structure of the Winter Duck Community on the Lower Colorado River: Patterns and Processes

Bertin W. Anderson and Robert D. Ohmart

Abstract: Food and habitat relationships of ducks were studied along the lower 400 km of the Colorado River during seven winters (1975-82). The objective was to examine habitat and dietary relationships of the 17 species commonly occurring in the area and to determine the extent, if any, to which congeneric species might be ecologically isolated. We also considered separation through time within each year. Dabbling ducks tended to be associated with areas of high-standing crop of submerged and emergent aquatic vegetation. Most diving ducks were associated with the areas immediately downstream from hydroelectric dams. This pattern was consistent across four years of censusing. Before dam construction in 1910, diving ducks of the genus *Bucephala* apparently were absent from the river or were rare. Their association with dams was related to large numbers of hydropsychid insects and the Asiatic clam (*Corbicula fluminea*), the major food of the bufflehead (*Bucephala albeola*) and common goldeneye (*B. clangula*). Pochards (*Aythya* spp.) also were associated with areas immediately downstream from hydroelectric dams but not as strongly as *Bucephala* spp.; they also overlapped in diet and habitat with dabbling ducks. Ecological separation between species was apparent for nearly all congeneric species pairs. That could reflect competition for food, but other processes, including a difference in habitat use patterns, probably are more important. The hypothesis that the size ratio of the largest-to-the-next-largest congener should be 1.25 was not supported, either statistically or biologically, for dabblers or pochards, but was supported statistically for goldeneye and bufflehead. Construction of major dams on the lower Colorado River has produced a more stable ecosystem with abundant food resources. Different hunter-avoidance

Waterfowl in Winter. © 1988 University of Minnesota. Edited by Milton W. Weller and published by the University of Minnesota Press, Minneapolis.

reactions further explain observed ecological differences in habitat use. The ability of dabbling ducks to shift from high-protein diets in summer to seed and plant diets in winter and opportunistically forage on locally superabundant food resources also contributed to the observed structure of the wintering duck community.

Measured in a straight line, the lower Colorado River (fig. 14.1) extends about 300 km from Davis Dam (Nevada-Arizona border) to the Mexican boundary; river meanderings increase the length to about 450 km. The total wintering

Fig. 14.1. Map of lower Colorado River region. Areas censused are designated as segments 1-14.

50 mi
80 km

population in this reach area varies from 10,000 to 25,000 ducks (present study; unpubl. data, Calif. Dep. Fish Game) originating from breeding areas located in several western states and Canadian provinces (Bellrose 1980). Constructed modifications on the river's lower reach include two hydroelectric and five irrigation-diversion dams. Thousands of visitors are attracted to the Colorado River annually (Greey and Jaten 1978), and there is pressure to develop the few remaining relatively undisturbed reaches.

The major objectives of this study were to quantify patterns of habitat use and dietary preferences throughout the winter and to search for processes that may account for these patterns. We strive to quantitatively describe processes that may be affecting the community structure of wintering ducks on the lower Colorado River. Grinnell (1914) and his party floated the Colorado River from Needles to Yuma between February and mid-May 1910. Duck numbers observed by them were compared with numbers we observed over the same route during the same time of year. General differences in the presence or absence of ducks were interpreted in terms of human impact on the river.

We wish to thank the several field biologists who helped with field work, particularly G. F. Drake, M. J. Kasprzyk, and R. J. Dummer. S. C. Cunningham, J. T. Fiedler, and M. A. Carr identified food items and computerized the data. Collectively, J. R. Durham, S. M. Cook, C. D. Zisner, and M. A. Carr kindly edited and typed the manuscript and prepared the illustrations. We thank D. W. Warner, M. W. Weller, J. K. Meents, R. W. Engel-Wilson, and D. E. Brown for critically reading the manuscript. J. Rice provided much useful insight on the use of statistics. Funds were provided by the U.S. Bureau of Reclamation through contrasts 1-07-34-X0176 and 2-01-30-13500 and also by the Center for Environmental Studies at Arizona State University.

Methods

Data Collection

All birds were counted by boat in 14 segments (table 14.1) of the river three times each month, August through April. In the Colorado River area, ducks are virtually absent during May, June, and July. Censusing was conducted from 1977 to 1981. Throughout this paper, *temporal* and *time* refer to distributions across this nine-month period unless otherwise stated.

To census as great a diversity in habitats as possible, and to consider effects of latitude, we divided the river from Davis Dam to Imperial Dam into three latitudinal reaches of approximately equal length. Within these areas we censused segments with reservoirs; those immediately downstream from hydroelectric dams; highly modified segments; and relatively undisturbed segments, except that no undistributed segment was available in the northern part of the study area, nor was a hydroelectric dam located in the southern part (fig. 14.1). Three additional segments, one undisturbed and two highly disturbed, were used in the middle of the study area.

Duck use of the various segments was determined by summing numbers of each species for all months within each year, which yielded a single number for each species for each river segment each year. The peak month of occurrence for each species was determined by summing the number present for a given month for all 14 segments for all four years, resulting in a single number for each species each month.

Table 14.1. Physical features of river segments studied on lower 443 km of Colorado River[a]

River segment	Length (km)	Area (ha)	Bank modification (%/km)	Use by humans ($\bar{x}$/km/month)	Latitude	Distance from discharge area of dam (km)
Channelized						
4	4.84	72	58	373	33° 34'	93.4
5	6,45	96	86	1,088	33° 21'	127.2
13	4.84	72	75	2,239	34° 05'	25.8
Pristine						
2	6.45	96	4	608	34° 06'	26.6
3	6.45	96	4	608	33° 58'	32.2
6	6.45	96	4	328	33° 17'	128.8
14	8.05	120	5	608	34° 02'	27.4
Below dams						
1	6.45	96	65	642	34° 59'	2.4
8	3.22	48	50	643	35° 06'	2.4
10	4.03	60	65	2,376	34° 17'	2.4
12	4.84	72	75	2,290	34° 08'	3.0
Through canyon						
7	29.03	432	35	579	33° 00'	148.1
Reservoirs						
9	8.06	388	100	1,521	35° 09'	64.4
11	12.90	500	100	1,521	34° 19'	93.4

[a]Latitude and distance from dam were determined at the center of each river segment.

Gizzards were saved from 702 ducks collected by shooting (by the authors and two other staff members) between October and January, 1976-82. All were collected between 0.5 hour before sunrise and sunset in segments 2, 3, 10, 12, 13, and 14, where peak or near-peak populations occurred for all species. The gizzard and esophagus were saved from each specimen. Since many esophagi were empty, but nearly all gizzard contained some identifiable material, our analysis was based largely on gizzard contents. Gizzards were preserved in a mixture of glacial acetic acid, ethyl alcohol, and formalin. Food items were separated into 10 categories: leaves and stems, algae, seeds, gastropods, other molluscs, crayfish, fish, mixed plant and animal parts, insects, and unidentified. Seeds were identified to species when possible. Plant parts were composed almost exclusively of fennelleaf pondweed (*Potamogeton pectinatus*). The proportion of unidentified material was small. All food items were weighed (wet weight) to the nearest 0.1 mg.

Data concerning use by recreationists in various river segments are from Greey and Jaten (1978). An index to standing crop of emergent vegetation was determined by measuring the area occupied by stands of cattail (*Typha* spp.) and bulrush (*Scirpus* spp.) on islands and along the river edge. An index to submerged vegetation was determined by estimating the area occupied by stands of submerged vegetation—primarily fennelleaf pondweed. Proportion of the channel and bank that had been channelized, dredged, riprapped, or in other ways disturbed was estimated from aerial photographs for each of the 14 river segments studied. Invertebrate biomass data are from Minckley (1979). Distance downstream from a hydroelectric dam was determined by measuring the distance from the dam to the middle of a river segment in the downstream direction. This measure was used as rough inverse indicator of water flow rate.

Analyses

Analyses employed nonparametric statistics. It is far from clear what type of distribution (normal, skewed, kurtotic) sets of species abundances should display, especially when abundances were determined on segments of the river specifically selected to reflect a range of habitat variations. Rather than relying on a set of transformations that might have produced a normal distribution, we chose a conservative treatment. All data were converted to relative abundances, with the segment with highest density of each species valued at 1.0. Segments were simply rank ordered for each species, and rank orders were compared between species or between species and environmental variables.

The 14 segments were considered representative of the available habitat. The extent to which a species was distributed over this habitat was determined by calculating habitat breadth (H') from $-\Sigma p_i \log_n p_i$, where p_i is the proportion of the total number of ducks in a given river segment. Differences in habitat breadths for two species were tested with a t-test (Zar 1974). Breadth of distribution through time and diet for each species was calculated in a like manner where p_i was the proportion of the total ducks present during each of the nine months studied each year or the proportion of a dietary category included in the gizzard, respectively.

Although two species may be found to have significantly different dietary habitat breadths (H_D), this information reveals nothing about the specific dietary or habitat preferences of each species—i.e., two species could have different habitat breadths and have either different or the same preferred areas or food items. Spearman rank correlation coefficients (Siegel 1956) were calculated to determine the extent of correlation (similarity) between the distribution of two species through time or through space (i.e., among the river segments) or in diet. If, for example, the correlation of their respective distributions through space was significant, the two species were considered to have shown similar relative use of various river segments. As similarity in use altered, the correlation weakened; thus, nonsignificant rank correlations were interpreted as indicating significant deviations from identical use of the 14 segments.

However, rank correlations cannot discriminate between cases where river segments (or month of presence or some dietary category) were being treated as equally different by two species and cases where there was a pronounced differentiation between segments but the relative order of use was similar. In such cases, the difference could be thought of as a difference in the shape of a distribution. The hypothesis of difference in shape was tested with the Kolmogorov-Smirnov (K-S) test (Sokal and Rohlf 1981). With this procedure, river segments (or dietary items or months) were ordered by relative abundance. The K-S test then determined whether the species being compared differed in the cumulative proportion of all segments below each relative rank from 0 to 100% of maximum abundance. For example, if there were substantially more segments where one species was absent or more rare than another species, the test was significant. Differences in shape of the distributions of two species in the habitat also were localized by the procedure, i.e., whether or not the disparity was due to differing numbers of segments where the species was rare, intermediate, or common.

Errors in the outcome of the K-S test can result when the relative abundance of one of the compared species is very low ($\leq$100 detections). In such cases, a censuser in a given area might miss an individual of a scarce species. Missed detections in one area would increase the estimated relative abundance in areas where the species was detected. A significant K-S test in such cases would not necessarily suggest a difference in the shape of the distributions; missed birds account for the apparent difference in shape. To address this problem, we randomly selected census data from river segments for the most abundant species until the total population of the sampled segments equaled the total population of the scarcer species. The K-S test was then redone. If the outcome was the same, the original outcome was considered valid; if not, the results of the second test were used.

Different combinations of significant results for the analyses above reflect particular adaptive patterns of the various species. For example, two species may have different habitat breadths and similar distributions among the 14 river segments (i.e., significant rank correlations) but significantly different cumulative proportions of detections occurring among the 14 segments (significant K-S test). Different possible combinations and ecological interpretations and schematic diagram are presented in figure 14.2. Each pairwise species comparison could show three differences (breadth, rank order, and shape of distribution) in temporal and spatial distribution and in diet. Thus, a pair of species could differ from each other in nine ways.

Relationships between each species and environmental variables were determined with Spearman rank coefficients. A significant correlation indicated close relationship between distribution of a species and some environmental variable. However, if a species was associated with two environmental variables, the rank correlation with each variable separately was often nonsignificant. This problem was overcome by first standardizing data for each environmental variable so that the mean was zero and the standard deviation was 1.0. Then any combination of variables to which the species was associated could be determined by adding any combination of variables together, ranking these values, and calculating another

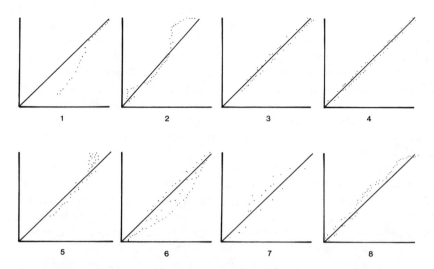

Fig. 14.2. Idealized graphs of distribution patterns (classes) of outcomes, with the X-axis representing segments of the river. Solid line represents distribution of species 1 and dots represent distribution of species 2. Graph 1: One species occupies greater proportion of available habitat relative to the other; both have same preferences, but cumulative differences in preferences at some point are greater in one species—i.e., habitat use shapes are different (HB, r_s, K-S all significant). Graph 2: Both species occupy about same proportion of habitat and have same general preferences, but habitat use shapes are different (HB nonsignificant, r_s and K-S significant). Graph 3: One species occupies greater proportion of available habitat; but among parts occupied, preferences are similar (HB and r_s significant, K-S nonsignificant). Graph 4: Both occupy about same proportion of habitat preferences and habitat use shapes are nearly identical (HB and K-S nonsignificant, r_s significant). Graph 5: One species occupies significantly greater proportion of habitat; preferences and thus habitat use shapes are different (HB and K-S significant, r_s nonsignificant). Graph 6: Both species occupy about same proportion of habitat, but preferences and thus habitat use shapes are different (HB and r_s nonsignificant, K-S significant). Graph 7: One species occupies greater proportion of habitat and preferences are different, but differences are small; thus, habitat use shapes are about the same (HB significant, r_s and K-S nonsignificant). Graph 8: Both species occupy about same proportion of habitat; even though preferences are different, cumulative differences are small. Thus, habitat use shapes are similar (HB, r_s, K-S all nonsignificant).

Spearman rank coefficient. There was no a priori reason to assume that multiplying or dividing or treatment in some other way would not yield significant results. We chose to add the variables because it was simple and yielded results that corresponded to observable field phenomena.

This procedure worked as long as the relationship of the species to each variable was either positive or negative. If the relationship was negative to one variable and positive to another, it was necessary to change the sign on the standardized scores of one of the variables before adding them together. Since there was no a priori way of knowing which combination of variables might be involved, it was necessary to calculate coefficients for all different combinations of variables for each species. This increased the type-2 error rate, but it did not mean that correlation with some combination of variables was inevitable. In reality, many of the combinations were redundant; for example, if variable 1 was added to variable 2 after reversing the signs, it would be the same as reversing the signs on variable 1 and adding it to variable 2. In all, only 26 combinations were different. In all cases we used the variable or combination of variables with which the correlation was greatest.

Friedman two-way analysis of variance (ANOVA; Siegel 1956) was used to determine whether distributions through time and space or in diets were similar across years. With this test, ranks were added across years. If the sum of ranks of population levels in the various river segments or dietary items did not vary from that expected by chance, the test was not significant. If the ranked river segments or dietary items were similar across years, the test was significant.

With the Friedman test, an apparently significant outcome might not be detected if, for example, several segments of river had no individuals of a given species. Such areas would all receive a tied rank and would tend to make the sum of ranks appear to result from a random distribution. Such a conclusion would be incorrect because absence of individuals of that species in some areas does not mean that all such areas are equally "bad" at all population densities. If densities had been larger, some areas without detections would probably have been selected before others. In the absence of insight into the precise rank of the least used areas, we omitted, for this test, all areas where no individuals of a given species were detected.

Correlation among Environmental Variables

Physical features associated with each river segment are presented in table 14.1. Rank correlations among environmental variables (table 14.2) revealed that standing crop was significantly negatively correlated with the extent of bank and stream modifications. The relationship was so near unity that we used only bank and stream modification in all subsequent analyses, with the understanding that this represented standing crop as well. Extent of bank and stream modification was also a measure of standing crop of submerged vegetation. Standing crop of emergent and submerged vegetation was also highly intercorrelated. Bank and stream modifications were greater at higher latitudes. Human activity tended to be greater in disturbed areas, near dams, and at higher latitudes.

Minckley (1979) collected invertebrate samples on six of the river segments in 1974-76. Invertebrates reached greatest densities either near dams or in areas of

Table 14.2. Spearman rank correlation coefficients among environmental variables

Environmental variable	Bank and stream modification	Distance downstream from dam	Human use	Latitude	Standing crop
Submergent vegetation	−0.785**[a]	−0.057	−0.420	−0.409	0.789**
Bank and stream modification		−0.108	−0.720**	0.530*	−0.996**
Distance downstream from dam			−0.600*	−0.701*	0.103
Human use				0.652*	−0.719**
Latitude					−0.505*

[a]*$0.05 \geq P \geq 0.01$; **$0.01 \geq P \geq 0.001$.

slower water flow with relatively large standing crops of emergent vegetation and low bank and stream modification (fig. 14.3).

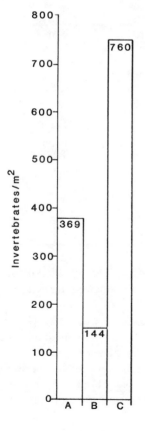

A ≤5 km from dam, bank and stream modification >50%

B ≥5 km from dam, bank and stream modification >50%

C >5 km from dam, bank and stream modification <5%

Fig. 14.3. Relationship of invertebrate abundance to bank and stream modification and to distance from discharge of dams.

Annual Variation in Duck Numbers, Distribution, and Diets

Numbers

Although substantial year-to-year differences existed in the number of detections for individual species (table 14.3), rank orders of abundances of the 17 species were similar between any pair of years (Spearman rank correlation ≥ 0.90, $P < 0.001$).

Table 14.3. Annual numbers of 17 species of ducks detected along lower Colorado River from August through following April

| Species | Detections | | | |
	1977-78	1978-79	1978-80	Total
Dabbling ducks				
American wigeon	3,314	4,916	3,420	11,650
Cinnamon teal	969	3,755	682	5,406
Gadwall	373	324	595	1,292
Green-winged teal	3,129	5,998	4,573	13,700
Mallard	1,302	1,239	3,193	5,734
Northern pintail	410	637	2,207	3,254
Northern shoveler	55	102	36	193
Pochards				
Greater scaup	17	160	3	180
Lesser scaup	691	854	796	2,341
Redhead	425	307	351	1,083
Ring-necked duck	339	377	226	942
Bucephala				
Barrow goldeneye	117	202	90	409
Bufflehead	1,807	2,297	1,247	5,351
Common goldeneye	6,886	10,253	13,819	30,958
Mergansers				
Common	1,522	2,294	4,487	8,303
Red-breasted	119	77	177	373
Ruddy duck	534	253	224	1,011
Total	22,009	34,045	36,126	92,180

Friedman ANOVA also was significant ($\chi^2 = 45.4$, 16 df, $P < 0.001$), suggesting that the most abundant or least abundant species in one year tended to remain in that status from year to year.

Common goldeneye were the most common species every year. Grinnell (1914) recorded neither common goldeneye nor bufflehead—the fourth most abundant species during our study. Green-winged teal (*Anas crecca*), the most numerous species in 1910, ranked second or third depending on year in our study. From Grinnell's account, we estimate that his party saw about 1,000 ducks of eight species between Needles and Yuma. We detected an average of about 17,800 ducks of 18 species each year in the same stretch of river at the same time of year. Even though count procedures were undoubtedly different, it seems clear that there were more individuals of a greater variety of species during our study than in 1910. Grinnell and his party did not record a single individual of common or Barrow goldeneyes (*Bucephala islandica*) or bufflehead. These species accounted for 40% of the detections in our study (table 14.3). One of Grinnell's objectives was to list all species that occurred in the area. The fact that he identified only 8 species, whereas we detected 18 species each year, attests to the current increase in the species richness relative to 1910.

Distribution

Among 21 rank correlations for distribution across 14 habitats during each of three years for seven species of dabbling ducks, 20 were significant (table 14.4). Northern shoveler (*Anas clypeata*) distribution in 1977-78 did not correlate with its distribution in the following year. Seventeen of 21 correlations were significant at $P \leq 0.01$. Gadwall (*Anas strepera*) and northern shoveler, the two species showing the weakest correlations in distribution among years, were the least abundant within the genus. To demonstrate the relationship of ducks to distribution by habitats and years simultaneously, a Friedman ANOVA was calculated for each species. The analyses were significant for all species but the shoveler, suggesting a tendency for all but northern shoveler to be most abundant in the same areas year after year.

All 12 correlations between years was significant among the four species of *Aythya* (table 14.4). Friedman tests revealed that each of the four species was distributed similarly among the three years. The three species of *Bucephala* and two species of *Mergus* all had significant rank distributions during any pair of years. Friedman tests were significant for these five species (table 14.4), all of which showed a remarkably consistent distribution pattern for the three years studied. Ruddy duck (*Oxyura jamaicensis*) distributions also were significantly correlated between years (table 14.4). Distribution of ducks on the segments of the river during the years of our study was remarkably similar from year to year.

Time of Occurrence

Temporal distribution of observations (August-April) for each species tended to be similar for all of the major species (table 14.5). Exceptions primarily involved species that were consistently scarce even during months of peak abundance (gadwall, northern shoveler, greater scaup [*Aythya marila*]). But even among these species, there was at least one significant correlation across time. Ruddy duck distribution through time did not deviate significantly from random.

Table 14.4. Mean Spearman rank correlation (r_s) between distributions of ducks in 14 habitats in each of three years on lower Colorado River[a]

Species	Number of significant correlations	Mean r_s	SD	Friedman χ^2
Dabbling ducks				
American wigeon	3	0.88	0.03	29.2**[b]
Cinnamon teal	3	0.69	0.03	27.9**
Gadwall	3	0.66	0.17	27.6*
Green-winged teal	3	0.87	0.03	30.5**
Mallard	3	0.91	0.05	30.3**
Northern pintail	3	0.79	0.15	26.1*
Northern shoveler	2	0.56	0.23	8.8 NS[c]
Pochards				
Greater scaup	3	0.77	0.12	35.3**
Lesser scaup	3	0.65	0.12	27.7***
Redhead	3	0.62	0.13	26.0*
Ring-necked duck	3	0.68	0.12	27.3*
Bucephala				
Barrow goldeneye	3	0.96	0.06	24.4*
Bufflehead	3	0.88	0.01	34.3**
Common goldeneye	3	0.90	0.03	36.2***
Other				
Common merganser	3	0.78	0.10	30.1**
Red-breasted merganser	3	0.84	0.01	33.1***
Ruddy duck	3	0.77	0.08	22.6**

[a] For the Friedman tests, a significant outcome indicates a similar distribution across years; there were 13 degrees of freedom, except for ruddy duck (df = 7), and an outcome of $P \leq 0.05$ was considered significant.

[b] $*0.05 > P > 0.01$; $**0.01 > P > 0.001$; $***P < 0.001$.

[c] NS = nonsignificant.

Diets

Overall, there were significant rank correlations in 89 (82%) of 109 comparisons of diet, in spite of frequent small sample sizes. Twelve of 15 species showed significant Friedman tests, indicating that intraspecific diets for most species of ducks wintering along the lower Colorado River were similar from year to year in the rank order of dietary items.

Variation in diet was greater from year to year than temporal or spatial distribution. Diet analyses were hampered, however, by lack of an adequate number of specimens in several comparisons among years (table 14.6). At least three comparisons between years, where sample sizes consisted of five or more individuals each year, could be made for seven species. American wigeon (*Anas*

Table 14.5. Mean Spearman rank correlations (r_s) of distributions of ducks across (August-April) in each of three years on lower Colorado River[a]

Species	Number of significant correlations	Mean r_s	SD	Friedmanχ^2
Dabbling ducks				
American wigeon	3	0.87	0.06	22.5**[b]
Cinnamon teal	2	0.69	0.17	18.6*
Gadwall	2	0.71	0.15	16.6*
Green-winged teal	3	0.86	0.04	21.0**
Mallard	3	0.91	0.05	19.9**
Northern pintail	2	0.80	0.20	19.7*
Northern shoveler	1	0.50	0.16	11.4 NS[c]
Pochards				
Greater scaup	1	0.55	0.25	4.8 NS
Lesser scaup	3	0.90	0.07	18.9*
Redhead	3	0.84	0.09	32.1**
Ring-necked duck	2	0.71	0.16	17.8*
Bucephala				
Barrow goldeneye	3	0.93	0.03	19.7*
Bufflehead	3	0.95	0.03	17.8*
Common goldeneye	3	0.93	0.04	22.5*
Other				
Common merganser	3	0.78	0.04	20.5**
Red-breasted merganser	3	0.76	0.13	25.0*
Ruddy duck	0	0.27	0.25	10.2 NS

[a]In all cases there were eight degrees of freedom (columns). An outcome of $P \leq 0.05$ was considered significant.

[b]$*0.05 > P > 0.01$; $**0.01 > P > 0.001$.

[c]NS = nonsignificant.

americana), green-winged teal, mallard (*A. platyrhynchos*), and northern pintail (*A. acuta*) had significant rank correlations in 27 of 31 comparisons, and all species were significant for the Friedman test (table 14.7). Not only was there a similarity in all pairwise comparisons for ranked dietary items, but those items most frequently eaten in one year tended to be those most frequently eaten in all years. For cinnamon teal (*A. cyanoptera*), gadwall, and northern shoveler, no comparisons involving samples of 5 or more were available; thus, we used whatever data were available. These results revealed significant correlations between compared years in 14 of 23 cases. Cinnamon teal and gadwall were significant for the Friedman test, indicating similarity in diet across all years. For cinnamon teal, 6 of 15 between-year comparisons were significant at $P = \leq 0.025$; all of them had a P of ≤ 0.1. All seven between-year comparisons were significant for gadwall; thus, even very small samples suggested similarities in diets across years. Among all species,

Table 14.6. Number of specimens (*N*) of 17 duck species collected from October through January, 1976-83, for food habits analyses

Species	Mean/year	SD	Range	*N*
Dabbling ducks				
American wigeon	15	11	7-37	89
Cinnamon teal	3	2	1-7	20
Gadwall	4	7	0-18	22
Green-winged teal	17	12	3-37	101
Mallard	4	2	0-8	25
Northern pintail	5	3	2-8	29
Northern shoveler	1	1	0-3	4
Pochards				
Greater scaup	<1	. . .	0-1	2
Lesser scaup	1	1	0-4	7
Redhead	4	1	2-5	21
Ring-necked duck	5	6	0-14	29
Bucephala				
Barrow goldeneye	0	. . .	0	0
Bufflehead	17	11	6-31	103
Common goldeneye	38	43	1-116	227
Mergansers				
Common merganser	2	3	0-8	14
Red-breasted merganser	2	2	0-5	9
Ruddy duck	0	0	0	0
Totals	118	64	59-205	702

Table 14.7. Mean Spearman rank correlations (r_s) for all possible between-year comparisons for dietary contents of gizzards for seven species of dabbling ducks collected along lower Colorado River

Species	Number of comparisons	Number of significant correlations at $P < 0.05$	Mean r_s	SD	Range	Friedman χ^2
American wigeon	15	15	0.87	0.10	0.69-1.00	26.5***[a]
Cinnamon teal	15	6	0.66	0.12	0.57-1.00	18.8**
Gadwall	7	7	0.85	0.14	0.73-1.00	64.5***
Green-winged teal	10	8	0.83	0.13	0.63-1.00	14.8*
Mallard	3	1	0.65	0.23	0.53-0.91	14.1*
Northern pintail	3	3	0.87	0.12	0.77-1.00	24.1**
Northern shoveler	1	1	0.77	. . .	--	7.0 NS[b]

[a]*$0.05 > P > 0.01$; **$0.01 > P > 0.001$; ***$P < 0.001$.
[b]NS = nonsignificant.

41 of 54 cases (76%) had significant within-species correlations between compared years, indicating that for any given dabbling duck species the rank order of dietary items was similar each year.

Among the four species of *Aythya*, 15 of 22 between-year comparisons of diet were significant ($P \leq 0.05$; table 14.8); all but greater scaup had significant Friedman tests. For two *Bucephala* species, all intraspecific, between-year comparisons in rank abundance of dietary items were significant ($P \leq 0.05$), as were the Friedman tests (table 14.8). Mergansers (*Mergus* spp.) ate nothing but fish each year and thus had significant ($P \leq 0.05$) between-year correlations and significant ($P \leq 0.05$) Friedman tests.

Table 14.8. Mean Spearman rank correlation (r_s) between years for dietary contents of four pochards and two species of *Bucephala* (last two species)

Species	Number of comparisons	Number of significant correlations at $P < 0.05$	Mean r_s	SD	Range	Friedman χ^2
Greater scaup	1	0	0.00	...	--	0.0 NS[a]
Lesser scaup	3	1	0.65	0.16	0.52-0.83	12.4*[b]
Redhead	15	13	0.78	0.16	0.53-1.00	15.9**
Ring-necked duck	3	1	0.49	0.36	0.20-0.89	45.6***
Bufflehead	15	15	0.81	0.10	0.69-0.98	28.9***
Common goldeneye	10	10	0.91	0.06	0.80-0.96	30.8***

[a]NS = nonsignificant.

[b]*$0.05 > P > 0.01$; **$0.01 > P > 0.001$; ***$P < 0.001$.

Associations with Environmental Variables

All seven dabbling duck species tended to be associated with segments high in the amount of submerged aquatic vegetation in the 14 segments of the river (table 14.9). This association was significant ($P \leq 0.05$) in 18 of 21 between-year cases. Nonsignificant correlations occurred for gadwall, northern pintail, and northern shoveler. Redhead (*Aythya americana*), lesser scaup (*A. affinis*), and ring-necked duck (*A. collaris*) distributions were associated positively with submerged aquatic vegetation and negatively with distance from a hydroelectric dam; i.e., these species tended to occur in areas ranked high for submerged aquatic vegetation or near hydroelectric dams (table 14.9). Primarily because of their occurrence on only two or three river segments each year, greater scaup never had significant correlations with environmental variables. However, 82% of all detections of this species occurred on three segments near discharge areas of dams.

Bufflehead and common goldeneye always were negatively associated with distance from dams. Barrow goldeneye was associated with areas of high human

Table 14.9. Correlation between duck distributions and various habitat variables over period of three years[a]

Species	Number of river segments with species present	Variable[b]	Number of years with significant r_s at $P \le 0.05$	Mean r_s	SD
American wigeon	12	SUBAQ	3	0.79	0.04
Cinnamon teal	11	SUBAQ	3	0.62	0.17
Gadwall	11	SUBAQ	2	0.53	0.14
Green-winged teal	13	SUBAQ	3	0.70	0.09
Mallard	8	SUBAQ	3	0.79	0.05
Northern pintail	9	SUBAQ	2	0.74	0.25
Northern shoveler	8	SUBAQ	2	0.36	0.37
Lesser scaup	12	DD(−), SUBAQ	3	0.64	0.08
Redhead	12	SUBAQ, DD(−)		0.67	0.17
Ring-necked duck	14	DD(−), SUBAQ	3	0.77	0.05
Barrow goldeneye	5	LAT	3	0.71	0.09
Bufflehead	9	DD	4	−0.69	0.04
Common goldeneye	14	DD	3	−0.79	0.07
Common merganser	14	LAT	1	−0.38	0.13
Red-breasted merganser	11	DD(−)			

[a]Species for which there were no significant correlations (greater scaup and ruddy duck) are not listed.

[b]SUBAQ = standing crop of submerged aquatic vegetation; DD = distance from hydroelectric dam; LAT = latitude.

use, namely hydroelectric dams and reservoirs, in the northern portion of the study area (table 14.9). These rank correlations did not reveal a correlation with hydroelectric dams because this species also occurs on reservoirs, which are the farthest points downstream from a dam. Dam areas and reservoirs are characterized by relatively high human use, and both dams were in the northern half of the study area (table 14.1). Red-breasted merganser (*Mergus serrator*), was most abundant below dams or in the northern portions of the study area. Nearly 65% of all common merganser (*M. merganser*) detections (after correction for size of area) were recorded in the two segments immediately downstream from the discharge area of dams. Correlations with this variable were not significant because segment 7, which was among those areas farthest from a dam, ranked first or second for common merganser detections; with segment 7 omitted, common mergansers were significantly associated with discharge areas of dams. Ruddy ducks were not significantly associated with any variable or combination of variables.

This analysis reveals several findings: (1) There was a definite pattern to the distribution of nearly all species: dabbling ducks were associated with those areas with the most submerged aquatic vegetation; pochards with submerged aquatic vegetation or with discharge areas of dams; and mergansers, goldeneyes, and buffle-head with discharge areas of dams. (2) This pattern was virtually identical during each of three years. (3) In 27 of 31 between-year comparisons for dabbling ducks and pochards, submerged aquatic vegetation was an important variable. Bank and stream modification was significantly but negatively associated with standing crop of submerged aquatic vegetation (table 14.2). Therefore, bank and stream modifi-cation such as channelization and riprapping apparently reduce habitat quality for many species.

Although distribution through time, space, and diets varied somewhat from species to species, there was a tendency for each species wintering along the lower Colorado River to occur at the same time and place and to take food items falling within the same dietary category year after year. One variable, distance from a dam, involves an artificial structure. Individuals of any species probably are not found near dams because they like dams but because some attribute such as food is available there.

Minckley (1979) reported the presence of certain invertebrate groups below major dams because conditions found there are not present elsewhere in the channel. Filter-feeding invertebrates, including the hydropsychid trichopterans, were abundant below dams, indicating an abundance of finely divided organic matter originating from the hypolimnion of upstream reservoirs (Colwell 1967, Minckley 1979). The Asiatic clam was also incredibly abundant below dams (up to hundreds per square meter; Minckley 1979) and tended to decrease in abundance downstream. On this basis, one might expect diets of duck species associated with dams to include these as major food categories.

In addition to a potentially unique food source, dams also add potential for a high degree of resource stability to the entire habitat in several ways. Water coming through the turbines is from the hypolimnion; therefore, water temperature and microhabitats below dams are relatively constant and unaffected by the vicissi-tudes of climate (Minckley 1979). Dams also add stability to the habitat through flood control. Grinnell (1914) pointed out that cattail and bulrush were scarce in 1910, probably the result of annual scouring action by floods. Temporary pools probably dried too quickly to allow development of emergent vegetation (Ohmart et al. 1977). Relative river and reservoir water-level stability that followed dam construction allowed cattail, bulrush, and other aquatic and semiaquatic vegeta-tion to develop and persist (Ohmart et al. 1977). Slowed water flows and reduction in turbidity (Ohmart et al. 1975, Minckley 1979) further stimulated growth of aquatic vegetation and its associated invertebrate fauna. High turbidity, which characterizes flood conditions, reduces light penetration and plant productivity, leading to a decrease in richness and density of the invertebrate fauna inhabiting such water. Thus, dams have created habitats with relatively high stability in annual resource availability. Greater instability and lower resource availability must be a substantial part of the explanation for the relatively low duck densities and diversities observed by Grinnell (1914). This interpretation is substantiated by the fact that, with the release of unusually large amounts of water in summer 1983, the 1983-84 Colorado River duck population was at its lowest point in the past decade. These high water flows also scoured out all major beds of fennelleaf pondweed and many of the major stands of cattail. The absence of dams in Grinnell's time seems to explain the near total historical absence of invertebrates and vertebrates now abundant near dams.

Of the 14 river segments, 11 were censused for four years. This additional information corroborates what was found over three years for all 14 segments (Anderson and Ohmart, unpubl. data). Since diets and distributions through time and space tended to be similar annually, subsequent interspecific analyses were carried out for the combined data for all three years for each of 14 segments. Year-by-year analysis of interspecific differences and similarities would greatly increase the volume of material presented but would add little, if anything, to our knowledge of interspecific differences in use of the river habitat. We have shown that major patterns of temporal and spatial distribution existed during the years of our study. We next make interspecific comparisons in search of ecological differences among species.

Table 14.10. Rank of abundance by month for 1977-79 along lower Colorado River

Species	H_T[a]	Aug	Sep	Oct	Nov	Dec	Jan	Feb	Mar	Apr
Dabbling ducks										
American wigeon	0.71	9	8	6	4	1	3	2	5	7
Cinnamon teal	0.77	8	5	3	4	9	6	1	2	7
Gadwall	0.72	9	8	6	5	3	2	1	4	7
Green-winged teal	0.74	9	8	6	4	3	2	1	5	7
Mallard	0.61	7	8	6	5	2	3	1	4	9
Northern pintail	0.57	8	7	3	5	4	2	1	6	9
Northern shoveler	0.67	9	8	4	3	5	1	6	2	7
Pochards										
Greater scaup	0.63	8	8	8	6	1	4	3	2	5
Lesser scaup	0.72	8.5	8.5	6	3	1	2	4	5	7
Redhead	0.42	8.5	8.5	6	7	5	2	1	3	4
Ring-necked duck	0.54	6.5	8.5	5	4	3	1	2	6.5	8.5
Bucephala										
Barrow goldeneye	0.51	7	7	7	7	3	1	2	4	7
Bufflehead	0.57	8	8	8	3	1	2	4	5	6
Common goldeneye	0.65	8.5	7	8.5	5	3	1	2	4	6
Other										
Common merganser	0.59	8	8	8	5	4	2	1	3	6
Red-breasted merganser	0.62	7.5	7.5	7.5	7.5	3	5	2	1	4
Ruddy duck	0.72	8	6	3	7	2	4	6	1	6

[a] H_T = breadth of distribution across nine months.

Ecological Separation among Dabbling Ducks

Temporal

Peak months of dabbling duck occurrence were January and February (table 14.10). Cinnamon teal had the broadest distribution through time, as judged by H_T (0.77), and northern pintail the narrowest (0.57). Interspecific differences in breadth of distribution through time, rank order, or shape of distribution (K-S

Table 14.11. Comparison of habitat breadth, rank correlations, and shape of distributions of seven species of dabbling ducks from August through April along the lower Colorado River[a]

Compared species	Probability of equal breadth (H'_T)	Rank correlation (r_s)	Probability that shape of distributions is equal	Class of difference[b]
American wigeon:				
Cinnamon teal	0.01	0.13	0.01	5
Gadwall	NS	0.93**[c]	0.01	2
Green-winged teal	NS	0.95**	0.01	2
Mallard	0.01	0.90**	0.01	3
Nothern pintail	0.01	0.77*	0.01	3
Northern shoveler	NS	0.56	NS	8
Cinnamon teal:				
Gadwall	NS	0.37	0.01	6
Green-winged teal	NS	0.34	0.01	6
Mallard	0.01	0.29	0.01	5
Northern pintail	0.01	0.46	0.01	5
Northern shoveler	NS	0.33	0.01	6
Gadwall:				
Green-winged teal	NS	0.98**	0.01	2
Mallard	0.01	0.92**	0.01	1
Northern pintail	0.01	0.84**	0.01	1
Northern shoveler	NS	0.65*	NS	4
Green-winged teal:				
Mallard	0.01	0.90**	0.01	1
Northern pintail	0.01	0.85**	0.01	1
Northern shoveler	NS	0.34	NS	8
Mallard:				
Northern pintail	NS	0.84**	0.01	2
Northern shoveler	NS	0.52	0.01	6
Northern pintail:				
Northern shoveler	NS	0.52	0.01	6

[a] Nonsignificant differences (NS) in habitat breadth and shape of distribution and significant rank correlations (r_s) were interpreted as indicating similarities in habitat use.

[b] As defined and illustrated in figure 14.2

[c] $*0.05 \geq P \geq 0.01$; $**0.01 \geq P \geq 0.001$.

test) were numerous. Five of 21 comparisons (table 14.11) were class 6 (classes interpreted in fig. 14.2); i.e., compared species had similar breadths of distribution across months (H_T), but rank orders and therefore distribution shapes through time were significantly different. Cinnamon teal relationships with American wigeon, mallard, and northern pintail illustrated situations where cinnamon teal were more evenly distributed across months and differed from the others in rank order of abundance and, therefore, in shape of their distributions across months. These species showed the greatest number of differences possible between two species. No differences were found between the gadwall and northern shoveler. In nine comparisons, there were two differences in the time dimension (classes 1 and 6); in six cases, there was a single difference (classes 2 and 8). Significant differences in shape of distribution through time were more common (18 of 21 cases) than for breadth of distribution (9 of 21 cases) or rank order of abundance (10 or 21 cases). There was at least one difference between compared species in 20 or 21 comparisons.

Mallard and northern pintail reached greatest densities on river segments 3 and 6 (fig. 14.4). Four additional species reached peak densities on segment 6, but segment 2 was second ranking for cinnamon teal and segments 10, 12, and 14 for gadwall, American wigeon, and northern shoveler, respectively. Segments 3 and 6

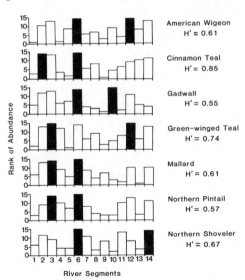

American Wigeon
H' = 0.61

Cinnamon Teal
H' = 0.85

Gadwall
H' = 0.55

Green-winged Teal
H' = 0.74

Mallard
H' = 0.61

Northern Pintail
H' = 0.57

Northern Shoveler
H' = 0.67

Fig. 14.4. Rank of abundance for seven species of dabbling ducks on 14 segments of lower Colorado River. Greatest abundance was assigned highest rank.

were areas with high-standing crops of emergent and submerged vegetation and low bank and stream modifications. Green-winged teal reached peak densities on segments 3 and 12. Cinnamon teal had the widest distribution through space (H_S' = 0.85) and gadwall the narrowest (H_S' = 0.55; fig. 14.4).

Eight of 21 interspecific comparisons of spatial distribution were class 2—i.e., both species in each comparison occupied about the same proportion of the habitat and rank orders of abundance were significantly correlated, but distribution shapes were different (table 14.12). Comparisons of cinnamon teal: gadwall, cinnamon teal: mallard, gadwall: green-winged teal, and gadwall: northern pintail revealed differences for all three tests (class 5). Cinnamon teal: northern

Table 14.12. Comparison of habitat breadth, rank correlations, and shape of distributions for seven species of dabbling ducks across 14 segments of lower Colorado River[a]

Compared species	Probability of equal breadth (H')	Rank correlation (r_s)	Probability that shape of distributions is equal	Class of difference[b]
American wigeon:				
Cinnamon teal	0.01	0.77**[c]	0.01	1
Gadwall	NS	0.54*	0.01	2
Green-winged teal	0.01	0.66**	0.01	1
Mallard	NS	0.71**	0.01	2
Northern pintail	NS	0.51*	0.01	2
Northern shoveler	NS	0.34	0.01	6
Cinnamon teal:				
Gadwall	0.01	0.13	0.01	5
Green-winged teal	NS	0.73**	0.01	2
Mallard	0.01	0.31	0.01	5
Northern pintail	0.01	0.57*	0.01	1
Northern shoveler	NS	0.56*	NS	4
Gadwall:				
Green-winged teal	0.01	0.36	0.01	5
Mallard	NS	0.52*	0.01	2
Northern pintail	0.01	0.32	0.01	5
Northern shoveler	NS	0.15	0.01	6
Green-winged teal:				
Mallard	0.01	0.66**	0.01	1
Northern pintail	0.01	0.81**	0.01	1
Northern shoveler	NS	0.43	0.05	6
Mallard:				
Northern pintail	NS	0.71**	0.01	2
Northern shoveler	NS	0.66**	0.05	2
Northern pintail:				
Northern shoveler	NS	0.56*	0.01	2

[a] Nonsignificant differences (NS) in habitat breadth and shape of distribution and significant rank correlations (r_s) were interpreted as indicating similarities in habitat use.

[b] As defined and illustrated in figure 14.2

[c] $*0.05 \geq P \geq 0.01$; $**0.01 \geq P \geq 0.001$.

shoveler comparisons revealed no significant differences in their respective distributions among the river segments (class 4). These species were relatively scarce and, as noted earlier, differed in two ways with respect to their distributions through time (table 14.12). Among 21 comparisons, 20 species pairs differed in their use of space in at least one way. Thus, as with distribution through time, there were many significant differences in spatial distribution of ducks on the lower Colorado River.

Dietary

Gadwall and American wigeon consumed more than 80% vegetation, and northern pintail and northern shoveler consumed more than 50% vegetation (table 14.13). Because we had only four specimens of northern shoveler, conclusions

Table 14.13. Number of ducks of seven species with various predominant food items

Food category	American wigeon (N = 89)	Cinnamon teal (N = 20)	Gadwall (N = 22)	Green-winged teal (N = 101)	Mallard (N = 25)	Northern pintail (N = 29)	Northern shoveler (N = 4)
Insects	3 (96)[a]	3 (93)	1 (87)	14 (87)	1 (75)		
Shelled invertebrates	1 (100)			3 (73)	5 (87)		
Seeds	3 (100)	7 (92)		39 (94)	7 (98)	7 (90)	
Vegetation	81 (99)	2 (94)	16 (82)	37 (93)	8 (92)	16 (95)	3 (99)
Shelled invertebrates— other		8 (65,44)				2 (42,58)	1 (60, 40)
Insect—other	1 (50,50)			4 (43,57)			
Vegetation— seeds				4 (48,49)	2 (61,34)	6 (53,46)	
H_D^b	0.33	0.72	0.058	0.69	0.76	0.55	0.43

[a] Mean percentage of the dietary category is given in parenthesis.
[b] H_D = diet-niche breadth.

about their diets are impossible. Green-winged teal and northern pintail consumed primarily seeds and vegetation; cinnamon teal ate seeds and insects. Mallard consumed significant amounts in all three categories, a fact reflected by their relatively large diet-niche breadth (0.76). Northern pintail and American wigeon had the narrowest diet-niche breadths $H_D' = 0.55$ and 0.33, respectively; table 14.13) among species for which there were 20 or more gizzards.

Ten of 21 interspecific comparisons were of class 1—i.e., one species of the two being compared had a significantly greater niche breadth and, even though the rank of abundance of items in various food categories was similar, the distribution shapes were significantly different (table 14.14). Cinnamon teal:green-winged teal had about the same diet-niche breadth, rank orders were similar, and the shape of

Table 14.14. Comparison of diet-niche breadths (H_D'), correlation of ranks of dietary items, and shape of distributions across dietary categories for seven species of dabbling ducks[a]

Compared species	Probability of equal breadth (H_D')	Rank correlation (r_s)	Probability that shape of distributions is equal	Class of difference[b]
American wigeon:				
Cinnamon teal	0.01	0.88**[c]	0.01	1
Gadwall	0.01	0.80*	NS	3
Green-winged teal	0.01	0.95**	0.01	1
Mallard	0.01	0.91**	0.01	1
Northern pintail	NS	0.88**	0.01	2
Northern shoveler	0.05	0.68*	0.01	1
Cinnamon teal:				
Gadwall	0.01	0.84**	0.01	1
Green-winged teal	NS	0.95**	NS	4
Mallard	NS	0.95**	0.01	2
Northern pintail	0.01	0.68*	0.01	1
Northern shoveler	0.05	0.76*	NS	3
Gadwall:				
Green-winged teal	0.01	0.75*	0.01	1
Mallard	0.01	0.79*	0.01	1
Northern pintail	NS	0.82*	0.01	2
Northern shoveler	0.01	0.90**	0.01	1
Green-winged teal:				
Mallard	NS	0.93**	0.01	2
Northern pintail	NS	0.85**	0.01	2
Northern shoveler	NS	0.66*	0.01	2
Mallard:				
Northern pintail	0.01	0.68*	NS	3
Northern shoveler	0.01	0.82*	0.05	1
Northern pintail:				
Northern shoveler	NS	0.56	NS	8

[a]Nonsignificant differences (NS) in niche breadth and shape of distribution and significant rank correlations (r_s) were interpreted as indicating similarities in diet.
[b]As defined and illustrated in figure 14.2
[c]*$0.05 \geq P \geq 0.01$; **$0.01 \geq P \geq 0.001$.

the diet niche (class 4) was about the same. Gadwall and American wigeon, those with the narrowest diet-niche breadths, differed significantly in only one aspect of diet (table 14.13). No species pair differed in diet in all three ways (class 5), but in 20 of 21 comparisons there was at least one significant difference in diet.

Although our data for diets are minimal, we believe they are reasonably valid as used because they were consistently similar across years (table 14.7) and because most species consumed a large proportion of vegetation parts; submerged aquatic vegetation was associated with the distribution of all dabbling species. Submerged aquatic vegetation was also significantly associated with standing crop of emergent vegetation (table 14.2).

Ecomorphological Relationships

Because of the more or less regular morphological spacing of sets of coexisting species, size ratios of adjacent pairs of species often have been cited as evidence supporting competition-based theory of community structure. Hutchinson (1959) drew attention to the fact that birds (and mammals) differed in measurements by ratios (larger to smaller) of 1.1 to 1.4, with a mean of 1.28. Nudds et al. (1981) and Nudds (1983), using data from Bellrose (1980), found that the mean ratio of differences in weights between seven species of dabbling ducks was 1.2. Following Wiens and Rotenberry (1979), we used specimens collected only in our study area.

Table 14.15. Ratios (largest to smallest) between adjacent pairs of species or sexes of dabbling ducks

Species	Sex	N	Weight (g)	Ratio	Culmen length (mm)	Ratio
Green-winged teal	Female	19	287		34.8	
				1.09		1.06
	Male	50	314		36.9	
				1.14		1.19
Cinnamon teal	Female	16	358		43.3	
				1.08		1.05
	Male	19	385		45.4	
				1.31		1.37
Northern shoveler	Female	6	506		62.3	
				1.15		1.06
	Male	5	582		66.1	
				1.10		1.31
American wigeon	Female	18	642		34.5	
				1.12		1.18
Gadwall	Female	12	720		40.8	
				1.01		1.14
American wigeon	Male	19	725		35.9	
				1.01		1.21
Northern pintail	Female	11	730		45.3	
				1.15		1.04
Gadwall	Male	10	837		43.5	
				1.04		1.19
Northern pintail	Male	16	871		51.8	
				1.10		1.02
Mallard	Female	4	962		52.7	
				1.09		1.03
	Male	10	1,045		54.2	

Correlations between Morphological Traits. Sample sizes and means for weight and culmen length, the morphological measures most frequently used in these analyses (Wiens and Rotenberry 1981), are presented by species and sex in table 14.15. In addition, we followed Nudds's (1980) suggestion that the number of lamellae per centimeter be considered. Because only minor differences were found between sexes in this measure data on sexes were combined.

The two most highly intercorrelated morphological traits were mean weight and upper mandible lamellae per centimeter (r_s = 0.72, $P < 0.05$). Culmen length: lamellae and culmen length:weight were not significantly correlated ($r_s \leq 0.3$, $P > 0.05$). Thus, it would seem that either weight and lamellae are important or that the culmen is, but not all three. This was further tested by calculating correlation

Table 14.16. Spearman rank correlations between morphological characteristics of dabbling ducks and proportion of dietary items found in gizzards[a]

	Vegetation	Insects	Seeds	Molluscs-gastropods
Number of lamellae	−0.19	0.09	0.28	−0.05
Culmen length	−0.14	−0.40	0.11	0.40
Weight	0.50	−0.62	−0.57	−0.01

[a]None obtained significance at $P \leq 0.05$.

coefficients between morphological characteristics and proportions of various food items identified in gizzards. The analysis (table 14.16) revealed that morphological characteristics were not significantly ($P \geq 0.05$) associated with the proportion of any of the major dietary categories; weights were only weakly correlated with proportion of both insects and seeds ($P \leq 0.1$) and with vegetation ($P < 0.25$). Among the variables considered, weights seem the most likely to reveal ecological insights into interpretation of ratios of adjacent pairs, but at best even this seems rather poor. We continue to explore these relationships because our dietary data may be inappropriate for one or more reasons (too coarse-grained, dietary items not measured) to reveal meaningful relationships that actually exist.

Morphological Ratios Observed. Since there were significant differences between sexes for most measurements and weights, the problem was that of deciding whether significant differences between sexes should be ignored, as done by Nudds et al. (1981) and Wiens and Rotenberry (1981). If ignored, the ratios between adjacent pairs of species for weights were 1.24, 1.46, 1.26, 1.14, 1.03, and 1.25, with a mean of 1.23. But what sex ratios should be used? When the sex of the adjacent pair was taken into account, the ratios between adjacent pairs (table 14.15) had a mean of 1.11, and only one reached the predicted ratio of 1.28. Ratios between sexes had a mean of 1.13. If the sexes are combined, it must be assumed that a ratio of 1.1 or more between sexes are unimportant ecologically but that such ratios between species bear ecological significance. A similar situation exists for culmen length, but the ratios were smaller. Lamellae per centimeter were, for mallard, 1.8; northern pintail, 2.3; gadwall, 2.8; American wigeon, 2.8; cinnamon teal, 3.0; green-winged teal, 3.0. The ratios are 1.28, 1.00, 1.22, 1.00, 1.07, and 1.00, respectively, with a mean of 1.1. We now have two questions to consider: Which among the three characters are most appropriate for explaining ecological questions relative to competition? Is it legitimate to ignore differences between sexes? We chose weights on the basis of precedence and the data above, which indicate a closer relationship between weights and diets than between any other trait and diets.

Our samples of gizzards were too small to yield much insight into the extent of dietary differences between the sexes. However, 21 (30%) of the green-winged teal males but only 5 (17%) of the females ate primarily seeds. In addition, 7 (10%) of the males but only 1 (3%) of females had mixtures of vegetation and insects. Four (36%) of the male northern pintail gizzards contained nearly all seeds, but only one (9%) gizzard from a female contained only seeds. These differences, in conjunction with morphological differences between the sexes, suggest to us that the sexes should not be lumped when considering size ratios.

Morphological Spacing in Dabbling Ducks. If the ratio of adjacent pairs of species for mean weight of the sexes combined was 1.25 in all cases and if the ratio between the sexes was about 1.15 for all species, the relationship of the seven species of dabbling ducks would be nonoverlapping (left part of fig. 14.5). But the observed ratio of weights between adjacent species was 1.1. If this ratio existed between all species, and if the ratio of female of the larger species to male of the smaller species remained 1.15 for all species, the seven species would occupy the same ecological space occupied by six species if true "Hutchinson ratios" existed (middle part of fig. 14.5). But the mean ratio between adjacent pairs was not consistent; hence, the seven species occupied only 78% of the area predicted by the theoretical relationship (right part of fig. 14.5). Perhaps more important, American wigeon, northern pintail, and gadwall should theoretically include 52 units on the graph, but in reality they include about 30 units, only 58% of the expected space. Under careful scrutiny, it is difficult to ascribe any validity to Hutchinsonian theory for explaining structure of the duck community in our area. The observed ratios seem to represent a stochastic relationship with respect to community structure.

Summary of Ecological Separation of Dabbling Ducks

Our analyses revealed that among the 21 between-species comparisons, 12 pairs differed in at least two of three ways in their distribution through space, thus indicating fundamentally different uses of the river habitat. Among the nine remaining comparisons in which member species were similarly distributed in space were five pairs in which member species differed fundamentally in temporal

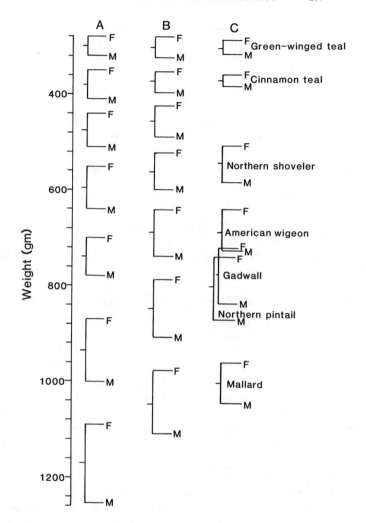

Fig. 14.5. Spacing between adjacent pairs of dabbling ducks if (A) ratio of 1.25 existed between mean weight for all adjacent pairs and mean ratio between largest sex of one species and smallest of the next was approximately 1.08; (B) ratios actually found to exist (1.11) were the same between adjacent pairs and ratio of largest sex of one species to smallest of the next was approximately 1.08; and (C) spacing between adjacent pairs as it actually occurred with mean ratio between adjacent pairs of 1.11. M = male, F = female.

distribution. Thus, 16 interspecific comparisons differed substantially in their use of space or in their distribution through time. Among the remaining four pairs (American wigeon:gadwall, mallard, northern pintail; mallard:northern pintail), members of one pair differed substantially in diet (American wigeon:mallard).

Members of the remaining three pairs differed significantly in at least one way in their distribution through time, space, and in diet. In the foregoing analysis we were looking for differences between species, and we have stressed these differences. We could have looked for and stressed similarities (i.e., nonsignificant differences), and similarities between species were nearly as common as differences (89 similarities, 100 differences).

The difference in morphological ratios between adjacent pairs of species was less than 1.2 for most adjacent pairs. There were minimal morphological differences between American wigeon, gadwall, and northern pintail, which also had similar distributions through space and time and had similar diets.

Processes Determining the Patterns of Separation among Dabbling Ducks

Hunting. Duck hunting season usually opens in early October before many ducks have reached the valley and continues into late January. Conceivably, hunting is a factor affecting the total number of ducks present and their distribution. As soon as the hunting season closed, dabbling duck numbers increased; January detections totaled (all years) 8,449; in February, detections increased to 15,699 (+86%). It seems that hunting keeps duck numbers relatively low, although some migrating influx may occur in February. Hunting also could affect dispersal, causing ducks to concentrate in areas where hunting was restricted (e.g., segments 10 and 12) and to avoid "preferred" areas (e.g., segments 3 and 6).

Reduction in total numbers because of hunting could reduce competitive interaction for food. One might predict that with population increases associated with a sudden decrease in hunting, a dramatic increase in competitive interactions would occur. This increase should correspond to a reduced overlap in space in February relative to that for the rest of the year, assuming that natural selection had operated long enough for mechanisms to have evolved that prevent or reduce competitive interactions (Diamond 1978). However, the mean number of differences in distribution through space decreased from a mean of 1.9 (SD = 0.7) per pair of species overall to 1.4 (SD = 0.9) in February. Thus, we not only failed to find a decrease in similarities in the use of space, but we actually observed a substantial (26%) increase. Mean rank correlations between the distribution of species increased significantly (t = 2.1, 40 df, $P < 0.05$) from r_s = 0.53 overall to 0.65 in February. There was thus an increasing tendency for any pair of species to occur in the same place at the same time as their populations increased, whether the increase resulted from absence of hunters or influx of migratory birds or both.

Diffuse Competition. It is possible that the overall effect of relatively weak competitive interaction per species summed over several species, i.e., diffuse competition, offers at least a partial explanation for the differences we have observed among dabbling ducks. With diffuse competition, as species richness increases the number of ecological differences between potential competitors should increase (MacArthur and Pianka 1966; MacArthur 1972; Pianka 1972, 1974). To test for diffuse competition, we summed the number of significant differences between species for diets and distribution across time and space for each pair of dabbling duck species. The average number of ecological differences between pairs should be positively correlated with species richness at the 14 segments. As predicted, the average number of differences could be forecast from species richness ($0.7 + 0.2$ species richness = mean number of differences between species; $r = 0.63$, $r^2 = 0.39$, $N = 34$, $P < 0.001$). This correlation explains 39% of the variance in the mean number of differences between species; thus, diffuse competition seems to contribute to community structure at a moderate level.

Past Competition. If explanation for observed ecological separation lies with the outcome of past competition, we should find, for example, similarity between species in diet to be correlated with differences in one or both of the other dimensions (space, distribution through time [Schoener 1974]). We found that correlation between the number of differences in diet and space was 0.10; diet:time, −0.3; diet:space + time, −0.02; and space:time, 0.27. Thus, the similarity or difference between species in one dimension was unrelated to the extent of difference or similarity between them in another. At the very least, we might expect to find more temporal and spatial differences for the three species that consumed mainly pondweed than for the other species. In fact, just the opposite was true: the mean number of differences in space and time for the three species that consumed mainly pondweed was 3.0, whereas for all other comparisons the mean was 4.3. Past interspecific competition does not seem to be the mechanism that accounts for the observed differences between species.

Wiens and Rotenberry (1979), in their study of grassland and shrubsteppe birds, suggested that in a variable environment—one in which resources are often superabundant—competition could not be responsible for existing species assemblages, niche breadths, or niche overlaps. Under conditions of superabundant resources, birds might be expected to forage opportunistically. Several species may take advantage of a temporarily superabundant food resource (Rosenberg et al. 1982). This superabundance often occurs under unstable climatic conditions (Wiens and Rotenberry 1979).

Two recent studies (Toft et al. 1982, Nudds 1983) have investigated interspecific competition on the breeding grounds for the same dabbling duck species discussed here. These studies agree with Rotenberry (1978) that, under unstable climatic conditions, species diversity varied as a function of evenness, whereas under more benign conditions, diversity varied as a function of species richness. It is under such benign and predictable conditions that competition is postulated to occur most frequently (Rotenberry 1978, Rotenberry et al. 1979). In unpredictable and harsh climatic regimes, competition develops only during times of ecological "crunches" (Wiens 1977). In such situations, year-to-year variation in species composition, niche breadths, and niche overlaps can be expected to be large.

Environmental Predictability and Colorado River Dabbling Ducks. Diversity ($-\Sigma\ p_i\log_n p_i$, where p_i is the proportion that species i contributes to the total population) is a function of the number of species present and the evenness in the distribution. The partial correlation of richness with diversity was significant ($P < 0.01$), but partial correlation of evenness with diversity was not. According to Rotenberry (1978), this indicates a stable environment typical of a competitive situation rather than unpredictable conditions associated with opportunism. The year-to-year similarities, as described above for diets and distribution, also comply with the situation theoretically associated with a competitive situation.

Perhaps there are situations of environmental stability in which at least some food resources are superabundant. In such situations, there could be opportunistic foraging. For example, in one of our study areas (segment 12), standing crop of emergent vegetation (and, therefore, presumably seed production of semiaquatic and aquatic emergent vegetation) was low, but standing crop of submerged aquatic vegetation and invertebrates was high. At another locality (segment 3), standing crop of emergent and submerged vegetation was high, but invertebrate numbers were only moderately high. American wigeon and green-winged teal were relatively abundant at both places, and reasonably large samples of these two species were collected at both sites. In both river segments, American wigeon consumed primarily parts of submerged vegetation; but in segment 3, where seeds were more abundant, seed consumption was highest, and at segment 12, where invertebrates were most abundant, American wigeon consumed a larger portion of insects and molluscs (table 14.17). For green-winged teal, where standing crop of emergent and submerged vegetation was highest (segment 3), seeds and vegetation made up 89% of the diet, compared with 53% in segment 12. In segment 12, where invertebrates were most abundant, molluscs and insects comprised 48% of the diet, compared

Table 14.17. Comparison of gizzard contents of American wigeon and green-winged teal in two segments of habitat where available food items varied[a]

River segment	Drift[b] (kg/ha × 10⁵)	Rank for standing-crop emergent vegetation	Standing-crop submerged aquatic vegetation (kg/ha × 10⁵)	Invertebrates (kg/ha × 10⁵)	American wigeon % of total diet[d]					Green-winged teal % of total diet				
					N	Mo	In	Vg	Se	N	Mo	In	Vg	Se
3	1.65	2	8.1	3.6	32	0	4	92	4	43	2	10	37	51
12	1.22	11	7.9	4.7	10	5	5	90	0	18	10	38	36	16

[a] Drift, standing crop, and invertebrate data from Minckley (1979).
[b] Including 70-75% fennelleaf pondweed.
[c] N = number of gizzards.
[d] Mo = molluscs, In = insects, Vg = vegetation, and Se = seeds.

with 10% in segment 3. This pattern seems to reflect opportunistic foraging under circumstances of superabundant food resources.

Possible Superabundance of Food

To know whether food is superabundant, we must know something about how much is required by the ducks present relative to supply. On cold winter days, mallards eat about 15% of their weight per day (Jordan 1953). Thus, in the lower Colorado River valley, where they weighed about 1,000 g (table 14.18), they probably ate 150 g daily. Since smaller birds must eat proportionately more and because the "average" dabbling duck weighs about 630 g, we make the liberal

Table 14.18. Weights and ratios of weights between adjacent pairs (largest to smallest) of species and sexes of pochards

Species	Sex	N	Weight (kg)	Ratio
Ring-necked duck	Female	12	0.68	
	Male	13	0.73	1.08
Lesser scaup	Female	4	0.76	1.04
	Male	5	0.82	1.08
Greater scaup	Female	2	0.98	1.20
Redhead	Female	6	0.99	1.01
Greater scaup	Male	4	1.05	1.06
Redhead	Male	12	1.10	1.05

assumption that dabblers consume 25% of their body weight per day (about 160 g). During the four months of peak abundance (mid-November through mid-March), there were 264 dabbling ducks present per day on segment 3, requiring about 42 kg of food per day or about 5,000 kg for the four-month period. On segment 3 (96 ha), there were roughly 13.4×10^5 kg of potential food (table 14.17). Of this total, only 0.05% would have to be available as dabbling duck food to supply the necessary 25% of their weight. The estimates for segment 12 are about the same, suggesting that food resources were not limiting; in fact, they were probably superabundant relative to the duck population present.

We have frequently observed American wigeon and green-winged teal picking drift from or near the surface of the water; the former fed predominantly in this fashion. If only 0.3% of the drift is available as duck food over the four months of peak duck abundance, it would be more than enough for their entire winter food supply. Observations during our study revealed that pondweed, rooted and drifting on or near the surface of the water, was still abundant by the end of March when most ducks have left the area. Beds of fennelleaf pondweed were so dense in large areas, especially in segments 3, 6, and 12, that boats with motors could not cut through them. The amount of drift in the channel was truly astounding.

Table 14.19. Comparison of habitat and diet-niche breadths, rank correlations, and shape of distributions of pochards for time, space, and diet[a]

Compared species	Probability of equal breadth (H′)	Rank correlation (r_s)	Probability that shape of distributions is equal	Class of difference[b]
		Time		
Greater scaup:				
Lesser scaup	NS	0.73*[c]	NS	4
Redhead	0.05	0.76*	0.05	1
Ring-necked duck	NS	0.73*	0.01	2
Lesser scaup:				
Redhead	0.05	0.58	0.01	5
Ring-necked duck	NS	0.85**	0.05	2
Redhead:				
Ring-necked duck	NS	0.55	NS	8
		Space		
Greater scaup:				
Lesser scaup	0.001	0.58*	<0.01	1
Redhead	0.001	0.34	0.01	5
Ring-necked duck	0.001	0.33	0.01	5
Lesser scaup:				
Redhead	0.001	0.81**	NS	3
Ring-necked duck	<0.05	0.70**	NS	3
Redhead:				
Ring-necked duck	<0.01	0.90**	NS	3
		Diet		
Greater scaup:				
Lesser scaup	NS	0.34	0.01	6
Redhead	NS	0.55	0.01	6
Ring-necked duck	NS	0.31	0.01	6
Lesser scaup:				
Redhead	NS	0.50	0.01	6
Ring-necked duck	0.01	0.47	0.01	5
Redhead:				
Ring-necked duck	0.001	0.84**	0.01	4

[a]Nonsignificant differences (NS) in breadth and significant correlations were interpreted as indicating similarities in habitat use.

[b]As defined and illustrated in figure 14.2

[c]$*0.05 \geq P \geq 0.01$; $**0.01 \geq P \geq 0.001$.

Ecological Separation among Pochards

Temporal

December, January, and February included the months of peak abundance for all four pochards (table 14.10). Greater and lesser scaup reached peak densities in December, ring-necked ducks in January, and redheads in February. Among the six possible interspecific combinations, the greater scaup:lesser scaup showed no significant differences (class 4) in their distribution through time (table 14.19). At the other extreme, lesser scaup:redhead differed in breadth of distribution, rank order of abundances, and in the shape of their distributions through time (class 5). Greater scaup:redhead differed significantly in two ways through time (class 1), whereas the scaup each differed in one way (class 2) from the ring-necked duck (table 14.19).

Spatial

All species reached peak densities in river segments 10 or 12 (fig. 14.6). Segment 1 was important for greater scaup and segment 3 for redhead. Redhead had the broadest distribution (13 segments) and greater scaup the narrowest, being confined to four segments. Three of the six possible comparisons between the four pochard species showed significantly different uses of space in one way (class 3;

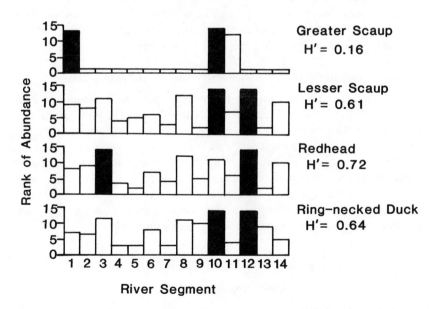

Fig. 14.6. Ranks of abundance for four species of pochards on 14 segments of lower Colorado River. Greatest abundance had highest rank.

table 14.19). Greater and lesser scaup did not differ significantly in any way in their distribution across the 14 river segments, but greater scaup differed in all three ways from the redhead and ring-necked duck (class 5).

Dietary

Redhead ate primarily plant parts; lesser scaup, clams; and greater scaup, snails (table 14.19). Ring-necked duck ate more algae and had the greatest diet-niche breadth. Redhead:ring-necked duck did not differ significantly in any of the three dietary comparisons (class 4), but lesser scaup:ring-necked duck differed in all three ways (class 5; table 14.19). The other species differed from each other in two ways (class 6).

Size Ratios and Ecological Interpretations

As with dabbling ducks, if the sex of adjacent pairs of pochards is considered, the weight ratios of adjacent pairs is not very close to the predicted ratio of 1.25 (table 14.18). Yet, differences between sexes in weights should be considered because we found differences between sexes in diet. Male ring-necked ducks had vegetation or vegetation-animal mixtures significantly (binomial $P < 0.01$) more frequently than females, and females had significantly ($P < 0.025$) more animal matter. Eleven of the gizzards from male redheads contained only vegetation; three (5%) of the gizzards from females contained only vegetation. Although sample sizes are small, the findings certainly do not justify combining the sexes, especially since size ratios between sexes are as great as ratios between some species.

Summary of Ecological Separation in Pochards

Greater scaup differed significantly in two or three ways in distribution through time and diet from the other species (table 14.19). Among the three species pairs differing in only their distribution through space, lesser scaup:redhead differed in two ways in distribution through time and in diet; lesser scaup:ring-necked duck differed in one way across time and in all three ways in diet. Redhead:ring-necked duck did not differ significantly either through time or in diet. Redhead was the habitat generalist among these species and ring-necked duck the dietary generalist. That there was past selection for morphological relationships between the suite of species that would reduce competitive interaction seems unlikely.

Ecological Separation among Bufflehead and Goldeneyes

Temporal, Spatial, and Dietary

Barrow and common goldeneyes reached peak densities in January and bufflehead in December (table 14.10). Common goldeneye was more broadly distributed

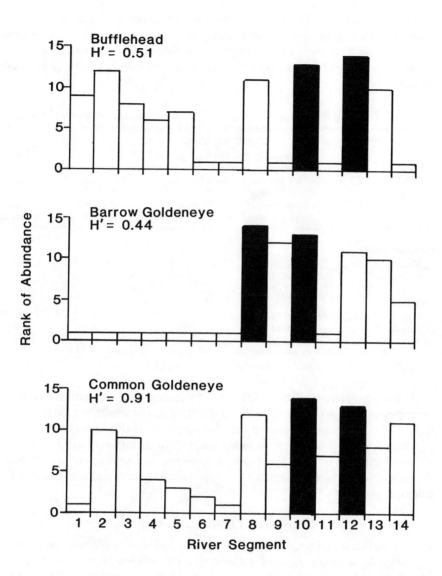

Fig. 14.7. Rank of abundance for three species of *Bucephala* on 14 segments of lower Colorado River. Greatest abundance had highest rank.

across months than either of the other species. Bufflehead and common goldeneye reached peak abundances on river segments 10 and 12, Barrow goldeneye on segments 8 and 10 (fig. 14.7). Barrow goldeneye was very narrowly distributed, having occurred on only six of the river segments studied. Common goldeneye occurred on all segments and bufflehead, on nine. Insects, mainly trichopteran larvae, and molluscs were the most common goldeneye dietary item (table 14.20). Common goldeneye had a somewhat broader diet-niche breadth (0.48) than bufflehead (0.39).

Table 14.20. Comparison of insect composition in the diet as determined from gizzard contents of common goldeneye and bufflehead collected along lower Colorado River

		Gizzard contents					
		60-100% Insects		20-59% Insects[a]		0-19% Insects[a]	
Species Sex	N	Proportion of total specimens	N	Proportion of total specimens	N	Proportion of total specimens	Total specimens
Common goldeneye							
Male	50	0.562	13	0.146	26	0.292	89
Female	104	0.753	14	0.101	20	0.145	138
Total	154	0.679	27	0.119	46	0.203	227
Bufflehead							
Male	49	0.740	10	0.145	10	0.145	69
Female	32	0.941	0	0.000	2	0.059	34
Total	81	0.786	10	0.145	12	0.117	103

[a] Mainly trichopteran larvae mixed mainly with Asiatic clams.

There was one significant difference in spatial distribution among three interspecific comparisons (table 14.21). Bufflehead and common goldeneye also differed in one way in distribution through time and one way in diet. No specimens of Barrow goldeneye were obtained for dietary analysis, but the two goldeneye species differed significantly in one way in distribution through time. There was less separation among these species than we found among dabbling ducks or pochards.

Size Ratios and Ecological Interpretations

Size Ratios and Diet. For common goldeneye and bufflehead, sexes were separated by a weight ratio of 1.4 and by a culmen length ratio of 1.1 (table 14.22). Male bufflehead were separated from female common goldeneye by a ratio of 1.5 for weight and 1.2 for culmen length.

We used the weight of each sex of each species each year and Pearson product-moment correlations to assess the relationship between size and proportion of insects and molluscs in the gizzards. Log_{10} of weight was negatively correlated with proportion of insects in gizzard contents ($r = -0.91, z = 3.2$, 11 df,

Table 14.21. Comparison of habitat and diet-niche breadths, rank correlations, and shape of distributions of goldeneyes and bufflehead for time, space, and diet[a]

Compared species	Probability of equal breadth (H')	Rank correlation (r_s)	Probability that shape of distributions is equal	Class of difference[b]
		Time		
Barrow goldeneye:				
Bufflehead	NS	0.75**[c]	NS	4
Common goldeneye	0.001	0.92**	NS	3
Bufflehead:				
Common goldeneye	0.001	0.87**	0.01	1
		Space		
Barrow goldeneye:				
Bufflehead	NS	0.57*	0.01	2
Common goldeneye	0.001	0.69**	NS	3
Bufflehead:				
Common goldeneye	0.001	0.69**	NS	3
		Diet		
Bufflehead:				
Common goldeneye	0.05	0.97***	NS	3

[a]Nonsignificant differences (NS) in habitat breadth and shape of distribution and significant (r_s) correlations were interpreted as indicating similarities in habitat use.
[b]As defined and illustrated in figure 14.2
[c]$*0.05 \geq P \geq 0.01$; $**0.01 \geq P \geq 0.001$; $***P < 0.001$.

$P < 0.01$. Culmen length was correlated at 0.85 ($z = 2.95$, 11 df, $P < 0.01$. These data quantify the impression (table 14.20) that, as size increases, the proportion of insects in the diet decreases and the proportion of molluscs increases. The result accords with Hutchinsonian theory of a relationship between body size or culmen

Table 14.22. Mean weight and culmen length (1 SD) of bufflehead and common goldeneye and ratio of largest to that of next smallest in series

Species	Sex	N	Weight (g)	Ratio	N	Culmen length (mm)	Ratio
Bufflehead	Female	31	314		23	25.4	
				1.40			1.10
	Male	89	440		34	28.0	
				1.52			120
Common goldeneye	Female	123	670		14	33.7	
				1.40			1.11
	Male	73	940		10	37.4	

length and diet. Our data differ in that they suggest that ratios between the sexes within species may also have ecological significance.

For both species, trichopteran larvae and molluscs were predominant foods. Differences were mainly small ones in the proportions of these items. Most individuals of both species (68% of common goldeneyes and 79% of buffleheads) had consumed primarily insects (table 14.20). These species were also more similar in their distribution through space and time than almost any other congeneric species pair wintering on the lower Colorado River. Perhaps there was a difference in size of items eaten by the two species, but this factor was not measured. If true, it would lend credence to the interpretation that differences in food size have a role in ecological isolation, if it could also be demonstrated that food was in short supply.

Food Supply. In the 60 ha encompassed by river segments 10 and 12, there were roughly 6×10^6 kg and 3.4×10^6 kg of invertebrates, respectively; clams were frequently found in densities of more than 100 individuals per cubic meter (Minckley 1979). Species of *Bucephala* reached peak densities in these areas: in 1978-79, when duck densities were highest, there were about 508 and 295 individuals of the three species of *Bucephala* per day on segments 10 and 12, respectively. If we assume a mean weight per duck in this group of 650 g and further assume that they consume 25% of their weight daily, the ducks in segment 10 would require 83 kg per day and 7,470 kg for the months of peak densities (December through February), which is just over 0.1% of the total food potentially available in segment 10. In segment 12, the requirement for the average number of 295 ducks per day would be 48 kg of 4,328 kg for the winter months—almost exactly the same proportion of food potentially available in segment 12. It seems that food was not limiting. The phenomenally high abundance of clams alone suggests a superabundant food supply.

Earlier we developed the argument that environmental conditions, and therefore food supplies, were relatively constant on the lower Colorado River. If true, and if food were a limiting factor, we would expect the greatest separation in diet between common goldeneye and bufflehead to have occurred in 1979-80 when populations of common goldeneyes were greatest. However, the extent of difference was no greater at that time than in any other year. Assuming a constant food supply, this fact would reduce the likelihood that there was competition for food in any other year.

Ecological Separation between Mergansers

Common mergansers reached peak densities in February (table 14.10) and redbreasted mergansers in March; both had about equal niche breadths (H') across the nine months studied. The rank correlation of their monthly densities was significant ($r_s = 0.83$, $P < 0.01$), but the shape of their distributions was different (K-S $P < 0.01$), thus exhibiting class 2 separation across months.

Both species reached peak abundance on river segments 8 and 10, but the common merganser had a significantly (t = 6.0, 411 df, $P < 0.01$) broader distribution through space (fig. 14.8). The shapes of the distributions for these two species over the 14 river segments did not differ significantly (K-S $P < 0.1$).

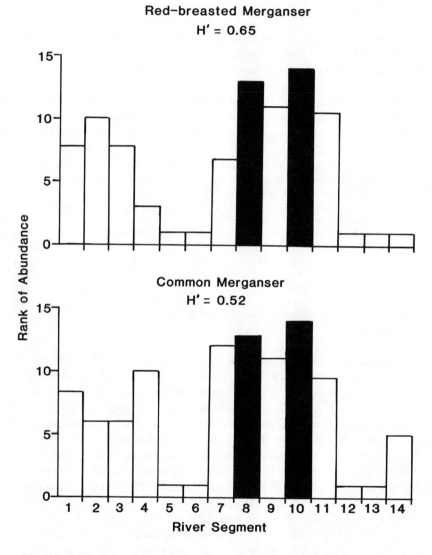

Fig. 14.8. Rank of abundances for two species of mergansers on 14 segments of lower Colorado River. Greatest abundance had highest rank.

Evaluation of Intergeneric and Intrageneric Separation

If a situation involving past competition among closely related species is responsible for present-day community structure, one would predict that statistically significant ($P \leq 0.5$) intrageneric correlations would be less frequent than expected by chance because selection would favor the isolation of competing species pairs. A second prediction is that competing pairs similar in one dimension—e.g., distribution through space—would tend to differ more in diet or in their occurrence through time. We have already shown that this prediction did not hold for dabbling ducks. Nonetheless, it seemed desirable to repeat the test for a pool of correlations involving all species.

Tests of the first prediction indicated that, for each dimension, intrageneric correlations were more common than predicted by chance and that this was significant for space and diet (table 14.23). In other words, species pairs that had

Table 14.23. Number of significant intergeneric and intrageneric correlations compared with number expected if significant correlations were randomly distributed

Variable	Number of significant correlations	Intrageneric		Intergeneric		χ^2	Probability
		Observed	Expected	Observed	Expected		
Space	29	21	6.6	8	22.4	40.7	<0.001
Time	64	18	14.6	46	49.4	1.0	NS[a]
Diet	31	22	9.1	9	21.9	25.9	<0.001
Total	124	61	30.3	63	93.7	42.4	<0.001

[a]NS = nonsignificant.

significantly similar distributions across the available habitat tended to be members of the same genus more often than expected by chance. Similarly, those species that tended to have similar diets also tended to be congeneric more often than expected by chance. Thus the first prediction fails. This suggests that the second prediction, that species using the environment in a similar way in one dimension would be more different in another, would occur frequently.

By chance alone, two species occupying the habitat in a similar way (i.e., significant rank correlations [29 of the 136 cases]) would also have similar diets (31 of 105 cases) in $(29/136)(31/105) = 6.3\%$ of the cases. The number of intrageneric combinations would be $(21/29)(22/31)(0.063) = 0.032$. Thus, among 105 combinations, there should have been 3.36 cases (105×0.032) among congeneric forms where distribution through space and diets were both similar. We actually observed 15 such cases. Significant correlations in all three dimensions where both species were congeneric would be $(0.213)(0.295)(0.471)(0.492)(105) = 1.5$. We actually found 10 such combinations. Conversely, more distantly related species, such as those in different genera, tended to be separated in at least two ways (space, time, or diet) more frequently than expected by chance. Does this reflect differentiation in these species as a result of past competitive interactions? We think not, but it could mean that intrageneric competition is still strong and needs further differentiation among congeners before community structure is significantly affected. One might argue that we would have found differentiation of congeneric species had our analysis been more fine grained (further subdivisions of habitat, division of diets by size of food items) and if feeding methods (tipping up, gleaning from surface of water, foraging on land, etc.) had been considered. But based on these data, we conclude that structure in the duck community on the lower Colorado River is not the outcome of past competitive interactions.

Processes Other Than Competition and Duck Community Structure

Given that differences (distributional, dietary, etc.) found between species are real, and we believe that they are, what processes led to them? Differences between species usually can be found when one looks for them (Wiens 1977), but interpretation is not necessarily easy. That observed differences serve as a means of ecological separation of congeneric species in the study area could be true, but superabundance of food resources, at least in some areas, and relative stability of lower Colorado River habitats since construction of hydroelectric dams would argue against a purely ecological interpretation of the data. What were the driving forces, if not exclusively competition?

Intraspecific variation in diet probably indicates that some dabbling duck species were opportunistic foragers (table 14.17). Some species ate a wide variety of items, among which the predominantly chosen foods were those most abundant and seemingly readily available within the river segment occupied. In avifaunal studies of North American grasslands (Wiens and Rotenberry 1979) and a shrub-steppe community (Rotenberry 1980), similar conclusions were drawn. Rice et al. (1983) found no need to invoke competition as an explanation for observed interspecific differences in avian use of riparian vegetation along the lower Colorado River. In a study of two similar but geographically separated habitat types, Paulus (1982) also found an opportunistic feeding pattern for wintering gadwalls in Louisiana. Landres and MacMahon (1983) interpreted evidence as suggesting that some competition occurred at one of their two sites but that opportunistic foraging predominated at the other.

White and James (1978) presented data for wintering waterfowl that suggested that species in Texas are separated by habitat in much the same way as species in our study were. They did not present data concerning the overall abundance of food resources, but only showing that certain species consistently fed in places where certain potential food items were consistently present.

Two species exposed to different selection regimes during their life histories, quite independent of any interspecific interactions (e.g., competition), can be expected to have evolved differences. Such evolved differences should not be interpreted in terms of their immediate ecological relationships.

The fact that two species belong to different genera infers considerable genetic difference between them. One would expect intergeneric similarities in the dimensions we considered (time, space, and diet) to be relatively few. Nonetheless, two species from different genera could overlap in one dimension from time to time by pure chance. We would expect overlap in more than one dimension from time to time by pure chance. We would expect overlap in more than one dimension to be scarce, exactly as observed (table 14.23 and associated discussion). Similarities are largely stochastic events; when multiple overlaps are considered, they become increasingly less likely. On the other hand, congeneric species have a broader set of similarities. Given that this is true, we would expect random overlaps to occur at a higher rate than between species of different genera. Overlaps in more than one dimension (time, space, and diet) would be rarer than for a given single dimension, but intrageneric occurrences should be more common than intergeneric occurrences. Expectations based on evolutionary history explain the data in table 14.23 better than competition. We conclude that at least part of the observed ecological differences is the result of chance in past evolutionary history.

Fretwell (1972) argued that winter is the time when competition for food is likely to be greatest and that adaptations for avoiding competition are likely to develop at that time, but such competition does not occur during summer when food may often be superabundant. Many duck species are insectivorous in summer but eat mainly vegetable material in winter. Because vegetable material is more abundant than invertebrates, it may be that this shift in diet often prevents competition among wintering dabbling ducks. This, of course, would not be true for goldeneyes, bufflehead, and mergansers, which eat primarily animal matter.

Recent studies presented some evidence for interspecific competition for food among breeding duck species (Patterson 1976, Toft et al. 1982, Nudds 1983). Given that this is true, at least some of the isolation of species observed in winter may actually mirror processes that prevent competition on the breeding grounds.

In their study of food-habitat relationships of sea ducks, Stott and Olson (1973) found little evidence for competition, but evidence indicated that hunting kept some populations from reaching levels at which competition would occur. In our study, we found that dabbling ducks tended to avoid areas where human activities were greatest (a form of predator avoidance). Predator avoidance accounted for at least some of the observed ecological differences among species in our study, and it extended beyond the hunting season.

Climate is another factor affecting the population structure of the duck community in our area. Harsher winter conditions farther north force more ducks into southern areas (e.g., Anderson and Timken 1972). In addition, climatic conditions that create favorable breeding conditions can lead to higher wintering populations, whereas low brood production leads to smaller wintering populations. Population levels are an integral part of community structure.

Migration permits ducks to leave an area any time there is an inadequate supply of food, when hunting pressure is too great, or in response to any other environmental feature they find unacceptable. We did not quantify this process in any way but intuitively believe that it had some effect.

Construction by humans, mainly of hydroelectric dams, is the main factor affecting the overall structure of the winter duck community along the lower Colorado River. At least 6 of the 17 species considered here were positively associated with dams. Beyond that, construction activities, such as channelizing the river and riprapping the banks, affected the structure of the dabbling duck community by altering the availability of food. Subaquatic vegetation was significantly negatively associated with these activities, but all seven dabbling species were associated with this variable.

Conclusions

Tilman (1982) pointed out that any one of a number of factors, including predation, disease, at least occasional resource superabundance, perfect substitutability of resources, immigration, and emigration, can result in indefinite competitive-free co-occurrence of a set of potential competing species. Most of these factors appear to have operated in structuring the Colorado River duck community. It is quite appropriate to conclude that observed "ecological" differences are probably not exclusively the result of competition because (1) a majority of the predictions expected in a competitive situation failed; (2) it is reasonable to expect differences between species in habitat choice, diets, and so forth to evolve more or less at random during the time species pairs were allopatric; (3) random selection rather than competition is a probable source of morphological variation (e.g., in bill size and weight) among species; (4) the ability to switch from insects to vegetation reduces the probability of competition; and (5) opportunism and the migratory habit permits the exploitation of superabundant food resources over a broad area. Intraspecific competition could have been one of the driving forces in (4) and (5).

We conclude that structure of the wintering duck community along the lower Colorado River can be explained realistically only by considering a number of processes. In order of importance they are: construction of dams, dredging the channel, and riprapping the bank; ability to shift from diets requiring high protein content (i.e., insects) in summer to seed and plant diets in winter for dabblers; opportunistic foraging on superabundant food resources; avoidance of human activities, especially hunting; the migratory habit; and the evolutionary history of the species.

Appendix 1. Use of Gizzards in Food Habits Analysis

Several food habits investigations have revealed biases resulting from different digestive rates of animal and plant material in the esophagus and proventriculus and in the gizzard (e.g., Dillon 1958, Perrett 1962, Bartonek and Hickey 1969, Swanson and Bartonek 1970). Hard seeds of plants remained longer in the gizzard than soft-bodied animals or plant parts. However, Stott and Olson (1973) found no differences between gizzards and esophagi of sea ducks. For 88 specimens in this study, the rank correlation of esophagus and gizzard contents was r_s = 1.0 (table 14.A-1). Data from the gizzard and esophagus analysis would lead to the same

Table 14.A-1. Contents of 88 specimens that contained food in both esophagi and gizzards[a]

Food category	Number of specimens containing category		Relative quantities of each food category	
	Gizzard	Esophagus	Gizzard	Esophagus
Vegetation	64	61	207	216
Insects	47	34	162	129
Seeds	30	18	137	61
Molluscs	23	12	58	29
Unknown	7	8	9	8
Tubers	2	1	5	5
Gastropods	1	0	4	0

[a] Included were 56 bufflehead, 9 gadwall, 12 common goldeneye, 6 green-winged teal, 3 mallard, and 1 each of northern shoveler and northern pintail. The relative abundance of a food item was determined by multiplying the number of times that item ranked first by 4, by 3 when second most numerous, etc., and then adding these values. No score was given if the item was absent.

conclusions—namely, that vegetation, insects, seeds and molluscs, in that order, were primary dietary categories. Bufflehead, gadwall, common goldeneye, and green-winged teal, examined separately, also revealed esophagus and gizzard contents that were identical with respect to rank orders. It is clear that in comparing relative amounts, however, seeds and molluscs were relatively more abundant in gizzards than in esophagi, exactly as indicated by the studies cited. Such biases would have little impact on our conclusions where relative proportions were not used for comparisons (rank tests) but could affect dietary-niche shapes (K-S tests).

Esophagi of American wigeon, northern shoveler, northern pintail, and gadwall contained primarily soft parts of plants; thus, little bias is likely to have occurred with these species. In addition, gizzard contents of cinnamon teal were separable from other species on the basis of the relatively large number of soft-bodied insects. If these results are biased in favor of soft foods, more insects would only make their diets more separable from diets of gadwall, American wigeon, northern shoveler, and northern pintail. Use of esophagus contents would probably do little to differentiate cinnamon teal from green-winged teal and mallard because all three consumed insects, the proportion of which would presumably be biased in the same direction as for cinnamon teal.

LITERATURE CITED

Anderson, B. W., and R. L. Timken. 1972. Weights and age and sex ratios of common mergansers. J. Wildl. Manage. 36:1127–1133.

Bartonek, J. C., and J. J. Hickey. 1969. Food habits of canvasbacks, redheads, and lesser scaup in Manitoba. Condor 91:280–290.

Bellrose, F. C. 1980. Ducks, geese, and swans of North America. Stackpole Books, Harrisburg, Pa. 540pp.

Colwell, B. C. 1967. The Copepoda and Cladocera of a Missouri River reservoir: a comparison of sampling the reservoir and the discharge. Limn. Ocean. 12:125–136.

Diamond, J. M. 1978. Niche shifts and the rediscovery of interspecific competition. Am. Sci. 66:322–331.

Dillon, O. W., Jr. 1958. Food habits of wild ducks in the rice-marsh transition area of Louisiana. Proc. Southeast. Assoc. Game Fish Comm. 11:114–119.

Fretwell, S. D. 1972. Populations in a seasonal environment. Monogr. Popul. Biol. 5. Princeton Univ. Press, Princeton, N.J.

Greey, G. W., and A. Jaten. 1978. Divisional outdoor recreational use and participation inventory of the lower Colorado River. USDI Bur. Reclam., Lower Colo. Reg., Boulder City, Nev.

Grinnell, J. 1914. An account of the mammals and birds of the lower Colorado River valley with especial reference to the distributional problems presented. Univ. Calif. Publ. Zool. 12:51–294.

Hutchinson, G. W. 1959. Homage to Santa Rosalia, or why are there so many different kinds of animals? Am. Nat. 93:145–149.

Jordan, J. S. 1953. Effects of starvation of wild mallards. J. Wildl. Manage. 17:304–311.

Landres, P. B., and J. A. MacMahon. 1983. Community organization of arboreal birds in some oak woodlands of western North America. Ecol. Monogr. 53:183–208.

MacArthur, R. H. 1972. Geographical ecology. Harper and Row, New York.

———, and E. R. Pianka. 1966. On optimal use of a patchy environment. Am. Nat. 100:603–609.

Minckley, W. L. 1979. Aquatic habitats and fishes of the lower Colorado River, southwestern United States. USDI Bur. Reclam., Lower Colo. Reg., Boulder City, Nev.

Nudds, T. D. 1980. Resource variability, competition, and the structure of waterfowl. Ph.D. Diss., Univ. Western Ontario, London.

———. 1983. Niche dynamics and organization of waterfowl guilds in variable environments. Ecol. 64:319–330.

———, K. F. Abraham, C. D. Ankney, and P. D. Tebbel. 1981. Are size gaps in dabbling and wading-bird arrays real? Am. Nat. 118:549–553.

Ohmart, R. D., W. O. Deason, and C. Burke. 1977. A riparian case history: the Colorado River. U.S. For. Serv. Gen. Tech. Rep. RM-43:35–47.

Patterson, J. H. 1976. The role of environmental heterogeneity in the regulation of duck populations. J. Wildl. Manage. 40:22–32.

Paulus, S. L. 1982. Feeding ecology of gadwalls in Louisiana in winter. J. Wildl. Manage. 46:71–79.

Perrett, N. G. 1962. The spring and summer foods of the common mallard (*Anas platyrhynchos platyrhynchos* L.) in southcentral Manitoba. M.S. Thesis, Univ. British Columbia, Vancouver.

Pianka, E. R. 1972. *r* and *K* selection or *b* and *d* selection? Am. Nat. 106:581–588.

———. 1974. Niche overlap and diffuse competition. Proc. Natl. Acad. Sci. USA 71:2141–2145.

Rice, J., R. D. Ohmart, and B. W. Anderson. 1983. Habitat selection attributes of an avian community: a discriminant analysis investigation. Ecol. Monogr. 53:263–290.

Rosenberg, K. V., R. D. Ohmart, and B. W. Anderson. 1982. Community organization of riparian breeding birds: response to an annual resource peak. Auk 99:260–274.

Rotenberry, J. T. 1978. Components of avian diversity along a multifactorial gradient. Ecol. 59:693–699.

———. 1980. Dietary relationships among shrubsteppe passerine birds: competition or opportunism in a variable environment? Ecol. Monogr. 50:93–110.

———, R. E. Fitzner, and W. H. Pockard. 1979. Seasonal variation in avian community structure: differences in mechanisms regulating diversity. Auk 96:499–505.

Schoener, T. W. 1974. Resource partitioning in ecological communities. Science 185:27–39.

Siegel, S. 1956. Nonparametric statistics for the behavioral sciences. McGraw-Hill, New York.

Sokal, R. R., and F. J. Rohlf. 1981. Biometry. 2nd ed. W. H. Freeman, San Francisco.

Stott, R. S., and D. P. Olson. 1973. Food-habitat relationship of sea ducks on the New Hampshire coastline. Ecol. 54:996–1007.

Swanson, G. A., and J. C. Bartonek. 1970. Bias associated with food analysis in gizzards of blue-winged teal. J. Wildl. Manage. 34:739–746.

Tillman, D. 1982. Resource competition and community structure. Monogr. Popul. Biol. 17. Princeton Univ. Press, Princeton, N.J.

Toft, G. A., D. L. Trauger, and H. W. Murdy. 1982. Tests for species interactions: breeding phenology and habitat use in subarctic ducks. Am. Nat. 120:586–613.

White, D. H., and D. James. 1978. Differential use of fresh water environments by wintering waterfowl in coastal Texas. Wilson Bull. 90:99–111.

Wiens, J. A. 1977. On competition and variable environments. Am. Sci. 69:590–597.

———, and J. T. Rotenberry. 1979. Diet niche relationships among North American grassland and shrubsteppe birds. Oecologia 42:253–292.

———, and ———. 1981. Morphological size ratios and competition in ecological communities. Am. Nat. 117:542–599.

Zar, J. H. 1974. Biostatistical analysis. Prentice-Hall, Englewood Cliffs, N.J.

15

Feeding Ecology of Canvasbacks Staging on Pool 7 of the Upper Mississippi River

Carl E. Korschgen, Louis S. George, and William L. Green

Abstract: Foods consumed by canvasback ducks (*Aythya valisineria*), food availability, and energetic relationships were studied on Navigation Pool 7 of the upper Mississippi River in 1978, 1979, and 1980. Canvasbacks fed primarily upon winter buds of American wildcelery (*Vallisneria americana*) and tubers of stiff arrowhead (*Sagittaria rigida*). In 1980, waterfowl consumed 40% of 380,160 kg of wildcelery winter buds on a portion of Pool 7 referred to as Lake Onalaska. Daily energy expenditure based on estimates from the literature suggests that individual canvasbacks require a minimum of 125 g (dry wt) of wildcelery winter buds each day. Extrapolation of use-days and the daily energy requirement suggests that 3,470 ha of wildcelery are required to support a canvasback population represented by 5 million use-days.

Migration in most species of birds is a costly activity that is anticipated by the deposition of fat as an energy reserve before and during migration (Kendeigh et al. 1977). Adequate food resources at strategic locations along the migration route provide energy for migration and prepare birds for arrival on breeding and wintering areas. Migration routes become traditional, to a large extent, in response to food availability as birds interrupt their flight to replenish energy reserves (Bellrose and Crompton 1970, King 1974). The increasing impact of humans on wetlands has increased the need to determine habitat and nutritional requirements during migration to develop a proper perspective for management (Fredrickson and Drobney 1979).

Waterfowl in Winter. © 1988 University of Minnesota. Edited by Milton W. Weller and published by the University of Minnesota Press, Minneapolis.

Shifts in the fall distribution of canvasbacks (Mills et al. 1966, Trauger and Serie 1974, Bellrose et al. 1979, Serie et al. 1983) in the Upper Midwest have prompted concerns regarding the availability and quality of migration habitat. Canvasbacks no longer use Minnesota, Wisconsin, and Illinois staging areas as extensively as they once did (Serie et al. 1983). A major proportion of the canvasback population migrating in the Atlantic and Mississippi flyways now stages on the upper Mississippi River (UMR). Navigation pools 7, 8, and 9 of the UMR attract migrating canvasbacks because of their strategic location between the principal prairie nesting grounds and the wintering areas along the Atlantic and Gulf coasts (Stewart et al. 1958, Serie et al. 1983). Numbers of canvasbacks staging on the UMR increased steadily from the mid-1960s through the 1970s (Serie et al. 1983).

Canvasback concentrations on UMR navigation pools probably developed because habitat quality of formerly important migration areas declined and natural successional development produced favorable habitat in these navigation pools (Trauger and Serie 1974). The primary objectives of this study were to determine the fall food habits of canvasbacks and to assess the production and use of foods by canvasbacks on Pool 7 of the UMR. A secondary objective was to determine the carrying capacity of this habitat and to make recommendations on the amount of habitat necessary to sustain a probable fall flight.

We acknowledge those who helped in the field and laboratory. Douglas H. Johnson provided statistical advice. Special thanks also to Harold H. Prince, Jerome R. Serie, and Gary L. Krapu for suggestions on the manuscript. Leigh H. Fredrickson arranged for analyses of plant parts.

Study Area

Pool 7, which is an impoundment that was constructed on the UMR to facilitate navigation, is approximately 17.8 km long and comprises 8,500 ha. The open-water portion, known as Lake Onalaska, is located at the pool's downstream end and covers about 3,036 ha. Water depth in Lake Onalaska ranges from 0.6 to 2.5 m, with a mean depth of about 1.3 m. Water level is relatively stable, except during major floods, because of the proximity of the lake to the lock and the dam and spillways. Water level is maintained for operation of the commercial navigation channel. Lake Onalaska is predominantly open water fringed with emergent plants. It is separated from the main navigation channel by a series of small, narrow, wooded islands. (See Jackson et al. [1981] for a further description.)

Methods

Food habits of canvasbacks were determined during the fall (October and November) migrations of 1978, 1979, and 1980. Birds were collected by shotgun from a mobile floating blind in shallow water in the southern half of Lake Onalaska (fig. 15.1). All birds were collected during early morning hours to avoid disturbances by recreational boaters. After collection, 70% ethanol was immediately squirted down the esophagus to prevent digestion of food items before dissection of the

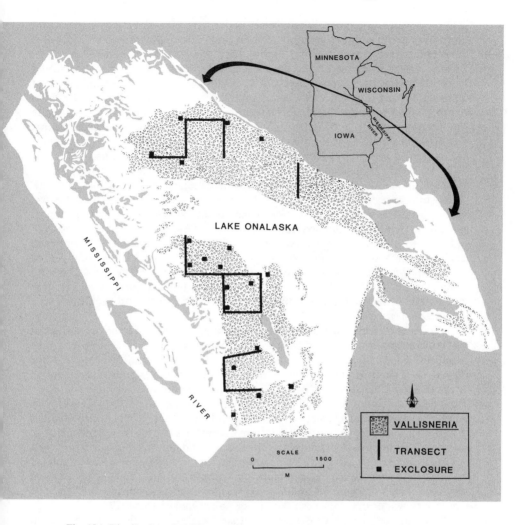

Fig. 15.1. Distribution of *Vallisneria* in Lake Onalaska, Navigation Pool 7, upper
Mississippi River, July 1980.

bird. Esophagus contents of actively feeding birds were analyzed following
methods described by Swanson and Bartonek (1970). Foods were preserved in
70% ethanol before analysis. Aggregate volume, aggregate percent, and percent
occurrence were calculated for each food item (Martin et al. 1946). All birds were
weighed to the nearest gram on a pan scale.

The standing crop of American wildcelery (*Vallisneria americana*) winter buds
was determined by sampling along transects with a heavy-duty core sampler.

Transects were located within wildcelery beds along a 0.8-km grid (fig. 15.1), and cores were taken at approximately 15-m intervals along the transects. Fifty cores were taken along every transect except one, along which 35 cores were taken because it was shorter than the others. The core sampler head was constructed from 10-cm-diameter copper pipe with an inside diameter of 9.9 cm and length of 39 cm. The area sampled was 75 cm², and all core samples were longer than the depth at which winter buds occur. The core sampler was pushed into the substrate and then raised with a davit. Sampling was done from the front deck of a large flat-bottomed boat. Core samples were taken in early October 1980 before canvasbacks arrived and in mid-November after most of the population had left.

In addition, 20 wire exclosures (5 × 5 × 1.2 m each) were randomly placed throughout the wildcelery beds. One exclosure damaged in a storm was removed. Exclosures were constructed with 5-cm hex-mesh wire and secured in place by steel fence posts. The wire extended to the substrate to exclude ducks as well as most large fish. Twine with attached fluorescent orange flagging was strung across each exlosure to discourage bird use. Fifteen core samples were removed from each exclosure in November. Five of 14 transects were again sampled in April to determine whether the standing crop of winter buds was further reduced during winter by any other herbivore. Mean winter bud biomass along transects was compared between sampling months and between transects and exclosures with unpaired t-tests.

Winter buds were washed from the substrate, frozen, and later oven-dried at 50 C to a constant weight and weighed to the nearest 0.01 g. The mean weight of winter buds per core was extrapolated to estimate total standing crop for Lake Onalaska. The gross energy content of 30 samples of winter buds taken from all areas of Lake Onalaska was determined with a Parr bomb calorimeter.

Wildcelery winter buds and tubers of stiff arrowhead (*Sagittaria rigida*) were analyzed for crude fat, crude protein, nitrogen-free extract (NFE), and crude fiber by the Agricultural Experiment Station Chemical Laboratories, University of Missouri, Columbia. Ash content of the foods was determined in our laboratory. Analyses were made using AOAC procedures (Horwitz 1980). NFE was calculated as the difference between the sum of the other components and 100%. The percent dry matter was determined by linear regression of 95 arrowhead tuber and 585 wildcelery winter bud samples taken from Lake Onalaska in 1979.

Total surface area and distribution of submerged vegetation were measured from vertical, 23-cm (9-in.) format color photography (scale 1:15,840) taken 23 July 1980. Wildcelery beds were delineated directly on photographs and the surface area was determined with a planimeter.

Estimates of waterfowl numbers and their distribution were determined at about seven-day intervals from 25 September to freeze-up by aerial surveys flown about 50 m above the water. Use-days were calculated by multiplication of census numbers by days between surveys for the fall migration period.

Results

Food Habits

Fifty-eight canvasbacks were collected during the period from 9 October 1978 to 15 November 1980. The sample was composed of 33 adult males (57%), 13 yearling males (22%), 9 adult females (16%), and 3 yearling females (5%). The high proportion of males was the result of limitations of the scientific collecting permit.

Fifty of the fall-staging canvasbacks contained adequate foods for analysis. The diet of the birds was made up almost exclusively of plant foods (table 15.1). Winter buds of wildcelery and tubers of stiff arrowhead were the principal foods con-

Table 15.1. Aggregate percent, percent aggregate volume, and percent occurrence of food items in the diet of 50 canvasbacks on the upper Mississippi River[a]

Food item	Aggregate percent	Percent aggregate volume	Percent occurrence
Plant			
Vallisneria americana winter bud	39.0	42.5	44.0
Sagittaria rigida tuber	49.6	56.0	46.0
Potamogeton crispus winter bud	4.8	0.2	6.0
Vallisneria americana leaf	3.1	0.9	8.0
Ceratophyllum demersum leaf	2.2	T[b]	2.0
Potamogeton pectinatus tuber	0.1	0.1	2.0
Scirpus fluviatilis seed	T	T	2.0
Potamogeton richardsonii seed	T	T	2.0
Potamogeton pectinatus seed	T	T	2.0
Other seeds and tubers	T	T	8.0
Total	98.8	99.7	
Animal			
Oligochaeta	0.7	0.2	2.0
Hexagenia spp.	0.5	0.1	2.0
Hyalella azteca	T	T	2.0
Other invertebrates	T	T	12.0
Total	1.2	0.3	

[a]Total food volume was 243.9 cm^3.
[b]T = trace.

sumed, accounting for nearly 99% of the aggregate percent of all foods. We believe that both of these foods are preferred by canvasbacks. However, the contribution of wildcelery to the diet of the population is much greater than is apparent from our food-habits study. Large numbers of canvasbacks began to arrive at the Mississippi River pools around 10 October. Before this time, the wildcelery winter buds have been produced and rosettes (leaves attached to an apical crown) become senescent; the entire plant, except for the winter bud, which is in the substrate, floats to the surface. This process permits canvasbacks to feed in areas of high densities of winter buds without diving through rank vegetation. Birds that arrived first fed in the location of the wildcelery beds.

In contrast, beds of stiff arrowhead are found in shallower water (approximately 1.0 m), and the plants do not senesce until after several frosts. Canvasbacks do not feed in such emergent vegetation until the plants wither and the areas appear as more open water. Arrowhead tubers were not found in any of the birds we collected before 25 October, when 300,000 use-days (56% of the total) had been met by birds feeding almost exclusively on wildcelery. The difficulty of collecting birds feeding in deeper water biased our data in favor of arrowhead tubers. Only 2 of 50 samples contained both foods, indicating that birds selected a habitat to feed in that provided a certain food.

Other species of diving ducks, such as the ring-necked duck (*Aythya collaris*), redhead (*A. americana*), ruddy duck (*Oxyura jamaicensis*), and bufflehead (*Bucephala albeola*), also consumed wildcelery winter buds (table 15.2). Of these, only

Table 15.2. Aggregate percent volume and percent occurrence of *Vallisneria americana* winter buds in esophagi of diving ducks collected in the fall (1978-80) on Pool 7 of the upper Mississippi River

Species (N)	Aggregate percent	Percent occurrence
Redhead (9)	65.3	66.7
Ring-necked duck (40)	52.1	62.5
Canvasback (50)	39.0	44.0
Ruddy duck (5)	20.0	20.0
Bufflehead (14)	7.1	7.1

ring-necked ducks used the area long enough and in sufficient numbers to account for significant use-days (63,745). On the basis of use-days, we estimated that canvasbacks accounted for over 90% of wildcelery cropping by waterfowl.

Use of Food Resources

Wildcelery occurred in 36% (1,056 ha) of Lake Onalaska in 1980 (fig. 15.1). From 685 core samples taken along the 14 transects in October (table 15.3), the mean dry weight of winter buds was calculated to be 35.8 ± 14.6 (SD) g/m². This extrapolated to 380,160 kg for the entire study area.

Analysis of transect and exclosure data on a gram-per-core basis showed a 40% decrease ($t = -3.21$, $P < .005$) in winter bud biomass between October and November transects, whereas there was no difference ($t = 0.67$, $P > 0.5$) between October transects and November exclosures. In addition, no difference was detected in the standing crop along selected transects from November to April ($t =$

Table 15.3. Proximate analyses of important plant food items in the diet of canvasbacks

| | Dry matter (%) | Percent dry matter | | | | | | | Gross calories (kcals/g dry wt) |
		Crude protein	Ash-free fiber	Ash-free NCF[a]	Ash	Crude fiber	Crude fat	NFE[b]	
Vallisneria									
Winter buds (Donnermeyer 1982)	24.8	9.9	13.0	82.2	4.7				3.9780
Winter buds (this study)	30.2	11.0			4.6	2.8	0.8	80.8	4.075
Sagittaria									
rigida tubers (this study)	41.1	11.6			5.2	2.0	0.6	80.6	
Latifolia tubers[c] (Reinecke 1977)		18.6			4.7	3.1	3.2	70.4	4.056

[a] Non-cell-wall fraction.
[b] Nitrogen-free extract.
[c] Provided as a comparison to *S. rigida* for the caloric content.

1.00, $P > 0.2$). These results suggest that waterfowl, primarily canvasbacks, were responsible for removing 40% (152,400 kg) of the standing crop of winter buds. Our aerial observations during waterfowl surveys indicated that waterfowl, primarily canvasbacks, exploited wildcelery beds throughout the study area.

We also estimated the standing crop of stiff arrowhead tubers (128.7 g [dry wt] per square meter) by core sampling in a single plot and extrapolating the results based upon the combined surface area of the beds determined by planimetering aerial photographs. The standing crop of tubers in October was estimated to be 12,950 kg (dry wt) in Lake Onalaska.

Proximate Analyses

Proximate analyses of wildcelery winter buds and arrowhead tubers (table 15.3) indicate that these foods have very similar compositions. The high NFE values, which yield the digestible portion of foods, are nearly the same as the non-cell-wall fraction determined by Donnermeyer (1982). The ash-free, non-cell-wall fraction contains soluble carbohydrates, proteins, starches, lipids, and other soluble materials that are highly digestible (Van Soest 1967). The neutral detergent-fiber procedure (Van Soest and Wine 1967), which Donnermeyer used to determine the ash-free, non-cell-wall fraction, provided a conservative estimate of digestibility for most nonruminant herbivores (Polisini and Boyd 1972). We estimated that at least 80% of the gross caloric content of winter buds and tubers should be metabolizable on a dry-weight basis based upon the 84.3% ash-free, non-cell-wall fractions. The gross caloric content of winter buds and arrowhead tubers (table

15.3) is about 4.0 kcal/g (dry wt) and therefore both would yield about 3.2 kcal/g (dry wt). Selection between winter buds or tubers probably is determined by their availability (water depth, residue cover, tuber depth, substrate type) and density.

Body Weights

Body weights obtained from the 58 collected birds averaged $1,422.2 \pm 137.6$ (SD) g. The mean body weight of adult males, which comprised 58% of the collected birds, increased from 1,234 g to 1,527 g ($F = 13.76$, $P = 0.0008$) when analyzed by 10-day periods from 1 October to 9 November. Mean body weights of 13 (22%) young males increased from 1,263 g to 1,463 g ($F = 5.907$, $P = 0.034$) from 11 October to 9 November. Sample sizes of females were not well distributed by 10-day periods and were small. Therefore, a mean body weight of 1,422.2 g was used in the following discussion even though there are temporal changes in body weight.

Discussion

Fat grain prior to or during migration increases a bird's theoretical maximum flight range (Odum et al. 1961, Wypkema and Ankney 1979). Fat deposition prior to migration is made possible partly by increasing efficiency in the assimilation of food, partly by reducing energy use in normal activities, but principally by increasing food intake, or hyperphagia (Kendeigh et al. 1977, 164).

Canvasbacks staging on Mississippi River pools in which there is an abundance of wildcelery winter buds and arrowhead tubers have an opportunity to increase fat reserves. These foods are high in carbohydrates, which are more efficiently converted to fat (Ricklefs 1974, 171) than are animal foods such as invertebrates, which would be high in protein content (Krapu and Swanson 1975, Drobney 1977, Reinecke 1977). Although winter buds and tubers do not have as high a gross caloric content as a variety of seeds (Kendeigh and West 1965, Reinecke 1977), they may contain as much or more metabolizable energy on a dry-weight basis as many domestic feed grains reported on by Sugden (1971). The relative softness of the winter buds would facilitate rapid processing through the digestive tract. Thus, birds may be able to increase fat reserves in a relatively short time.

Prince (1979) discussed the energetics of postbreeding dabbling ducks and described a technique to predict the amount of habitat required to support a population. The prediction compares metabolizable energy of food items, amount of food, and the energy requirement of each bird per day. This simplistic model is useful for making management recommendations, and it has been used for many species in a variety of habitats (e.g., Laughlin 1974, Lien 1978, Nilsson 1980, and Kirby and Obrecht 1980).

There are no direct methods of determining the exact amount of food eaten by free-living birds; therefore, the daily energy budget, a function of body weight, activity, and the environment, is calculated and translated into food consumed (Kendeigh et al. 1977). The best estimate is provided by calculation of the daily existence metabolism for nonpasserine birds at 0 C and a 10± hour photoperiod during winter or migration (Kendeigh et al. 1977, 5.31, p. 143). The temperature of 0 C approximates the average temperature regime of birds staging on Lake Onalaska in the October/November period. Canvasbacks with a mean weight of 1,422 g would have an existence metabolism of 201 kcal/day. Following the example of Nilsson (1980), the estimated daily caloric requirement is assumed to be about twice the existence metabolism because existence metabolism does not include energy for molting, migration, growth, or fat deposition (Kendeigh et al. 1977). Canvasbacks are estimated, therefore, to have a daily energy requirement of about 400 kcal/day. To meet this daily energy requirement, each canvasback would need to consume a total of 125 g (dry wt) of wildcelery winter buds and/or arrowhead tubers.

In 1980, canvasbacks accounted for 541,135 use-days on Lake Onalaska. If the average bird required 125 g of winter buds, the population would have consumed 67,640 kg, which represents 44% of the 152,400 kg that was estimated to have been removed based upon our transect and exclosure data. Several explanations for this discrepancy seem likely, foremost of which is that use-days are not adequately representing the number of birds using this staging area. In other words, the turnover rate of birds between our aerial surveys might be high. If the average bird was consuming about 125 g/day, the area provided food sufficient for 1,219,200 use-days. As indicated earlier, other species of ducks also consumed wildcelery, and their use-days could also have been underestimated, which would have reduced the amount that could potentially be consumed by canvasbacks. The tubers of arrowhead in the study area also provided a certain amount of food that was used later in the migration period. Therefore, this area has a potential carrying capacity much higher than the number of ducks observed on aerial surveys.

Canvasback food consumption has been studied by Longcore and Cornwell (1964) and by Anderson and Low (1976). However, these studies did not utilize an energetic approach based on the metabolic needs of the birds or energy content of the available foods. Longcore and Cornwell (1964) fed captive young canvasbacks a diet consisting of leaves, stems, and root stocks of wildcelery (63.7%) and Canadian waterweed (*Elodea canadensis*) (15.1%) and of invertebrates (13.3%). Winter buds and root stocks of wildcelery were highly preferred over other foods provided in the feeding trials (Longcore 1963). Wild birds do not eat appreciable quantities of leaves or stems of aquatic plants, preferring instead tubers, root stalks, and winter buds (Cottam 1939). The captive birds maintained weight (mean of 908 g) by consuming 31.8 g of natural foods per day in a 31-day period from 12 November to 12 December. The leaves and stems of the two plants in this diet have relatively low gross caloric content (Muztar et al. 1978) and low digestible fractions (Nelson and Palmer 1939). The contribution of the invertebrates to the daily energy requirement of the captive canvasbacks was not established. These captive canvasbacks may have had enough energy for maintenance, but the trials may have underestimated food consumption (i.e., daily energy requirement) of canvas-backs when applied to wild birds. Jordan (1953) and Sugden (1979) estimated that several species of captive waterfowl would require proportionately much greater intakes of a variety of feed grains each day, and these grains contain significantly more metabolizable energy than aquatic plant leaves and stems.

Anderson and Low (1976) estimated consumption rates of fennelleaf pondweed (*Potamogeton pectinatus*) by wild canvasbacks staging on Delta Marsh, Manito-ba. Based upon Longcore and Cornwell's study, they assumed that wild canvas-backs would consume 40 g (dry wt) of fennelleaf pondweed tubers per bird per day if 77% of the diet was provided by this source. This assumption may have led to an underestimation of the quantity of fennelleaf pondweed tubers necessary to sup-port a canvasback population represented by 340,000 use-days unless the re-mainder of the diet had a very high metabolizable energy.

Sincock (1962) calculated consumption of food by wintering waterfowl as 10% dry weight of the wet body weight. Our estimate that the birds have a daily food intake of 125g (dry wt) of wildcelery winter buds and arrowhead tubers is similar to Sincock's estimate of 123 g/day for canvasbacks wintering in the Back Bay-Currituck Sound area of Virginia and North Carolina. If the parameters necessary for the energetic approach to estimating the amount of food are unknown, then Sincock's estimate can be extrapolated to provide the minimum amount of food for a population as long as it is recognized that the habitat should provide on the order of two times as much food as could potentially be consumed.

Management Implications

Canvasbacks have been recognized as omnivorous, but plant foods appear to be preferred when and where available. Traditionally, canvasbacks have fed on two principal foods during the fall migration—fennelleaf pondweed and wildcelery (Cottam 1939, Perry 1982). At the present time, canvasbacks have few staging areas that provide an abundance of food resources. The primary northern staging areas (pools 7, 8, and 9 of the UMR; Lake St. Clair, Michigan; and Long Point, Ontario) (Serie et al. 1983) are large water areas where wildcelery is still abundant. Keokuk Pool (Navigation Pool 19 of the UMR) is a southern staging area (Serie et al. 1983) where birds feed on wildcelery (D. Steffeck and F. Paveglio, unpubl. data), which is increasing in abundance (Steffeck et al. 1985), and on benthic invertebrates (Thompson 1973). Management of food resources on canvasback staging areas must emphasize wildcelery and other plants that produce tubers, such as *Sagittaria* sp. and fennelleaf pondweed.

Management of canvasbacks on the UMR requires management of wildcelery. If we estimate the need for 125 g of wildcelery per day and an average of 36 g per square meter, wildcelery surface acreage on navigation Pools 7, 8, and 9 must equal about 1,735 ha to support 5 million canvasback use-days (1978 peak). Allowing for 50% consumption (we documented 40%), the total wildcelery area required would exceed 3,470 ha. Wildcelery beds in pools 7, 8, and 9 of the UMR totaled about 3,040 ha in 1980; some wildcelery beds are present in pools above and below pools

7, 8, and 9. If the birds do not crop more than 50% of the wildcelery because it is physically or energetically unavailable, then the arrowhead tubers are very important, even though distribution and abundance are limited.

We believe that consumption of wildcelery may indeed be greater in years when more birds are present; however, a threshold is eventually reached at which the density of food resources is too low for efficient feeding. At that point, the birds may fly to another area along the river or to the next staging area. The 40% reduction of the standing crop of winter buds that we documented in Lake Onalaska could represent a large proportion of the winter buds that are actually available to the feeding birds. The core sampler that we used was potentially more efficient than canvasbacks in harvesting winter buds since the corer could sample deeper and also in harder substrates. The surface acreage of American wildcelery has not decreased on Lake Onalaska as a result of feeding by canvasbacks.

The importance of wildcelery as a preferred food item is illustrated by our documentation of an abrupt decrease of 550 ha (80% of total) of wildcelery in Pool 8 with a corresponding 92% decrease (from 476,000 to 40,000) in canvasback use-days between 1978 and 1979 (C. E. Korschgen, unpubl. data). Because the UMR and its associated biotic communities will undoubtedly be stressed further in the future, management for canvasbacks should provide a variety of alternate migrational use areas that would contain a diversity of food resources for acquisition of required lipid reserves. Pools of the UMR probably will always be important in this regard, but other staging areas should be identified, restored, protected, monitored, and managed. We theorize that birds that cannot acquire sufficient energetic reserves for long-distance migration must remain in an area longer to build energy reserves or make comparatively short migration flights. We also suggest that because of reduced condition these individuals probably have lower survival potential.

More information is needed concerning the ecology of wildcelery and other preferred foods so that staging habitats can be developed or rehabilitated for canvasbacks and other waterfowl species.

LITERATURE CITED

Anderson, M. G., and J. B. Low. 1976. Use of sago pondweed on the Delta Marsh, Manitoba. J. Wildl. Manage. 40:233–242.

Bellrose, F. C., and R. D. Crompton. 1970. Migrational behavior of mallards and black ducks as determined from banding. Ill. Nat. Hist. Surv. Bull. 30:167–234.

———, F. L. Paveglio, Jr., and D. W. Steffeck. 1979. Waterfowl populations and the changing environment of the Illinois River valley. Ill. Nat. Hist. Surv. Bull. 32. 54pp.

Cottam, C. 1939. Food habits of North American diving ducks. U.S. Dep. Agric. Tech. Bull. 6743. 139pp.

Donnermeyer, G. N. 1982. The quantity and nutritive quality of *Vallisneria americana* biomass, in Navigation Pool 9 of the Upper Mississippi River. M.S. Thesis, Univ. Wisconsin, La Crosse. 93pp.

Drobney, R. D. 1977. The feeding ecology, nutrition, and reproductive bioenergetics of wood ducks. Ph.D. Thesis, Univ. Missouri, Columbia. 170pp.

Fredrickson, L. H., and R. D. Drobney. 1979. Habitat utilization by postbreeding waterfowl. Pages 119-131 *in* T. A. Bookhout, ed. Waterfowl and wetlands—an integrated review. Proc. 1977 Symp., Northcent. Sect., Wildlife Soc., Madison, Wis. 152pp.

Horwitz, W., ed. 1980. Official methods of analysis. 13th ed. Assoc. Off. Anal. Chem., Washington, D.C. 1,018pp.

Jackson, G. A., C. E. Korschgen, P. A. Thiel, J. M. Besser, D. W. Steffeck, and M. H. Bockenhauer. 1981. A long-term resource monitoring plan for the Upper Mississippi River System. Upper Mississippi River Basin Commission, Comprehensive Master Plan for the Management of the Upper Mississippi River System. Tech. Rep. F, vols. 1 and 2, Minneapolis, Minn.

Jordan, J. S. 1953. Consumption of cereal grains by migrating waterfowl. J. Wildl. Manage. 17:120-123.

Kendeigh, S. C., V. R. Dol'nik, and V. M. Gavrilov. 1977. Avian energetics. Pages 127-204 *in* J. Pinowski and S. C. Kendeigh, eds. Granivorous birds in ecosystems. Cambridge Univ. Press, Cambridge, Mass.

————, and G. C. West. 1965. Caloric value of plant seeds eaten by birds. Ecol. 46:553-555.

King, J. R. 1974. Seasonal allocation of time and energy resources in birds. Pages 4-85 *in* R. A. Paynter, Jr., ed. Avian energetics. Nuttall Ornithol. Club, Cambridge, Mass. 334pp.

Kirby, R. E., and H. H. Obrecht III. 1980. Atlantic brant—human commensalism on eelgrass beds in New Jersey. Wildfowl 31:158-160.

Krapu, G. L., and G. A. Swanson. 1975. Some nutritional aspects of reproduction in prairie nesting pintails. J. Wildl. Manage. 39:156-162.

Laughlin, K. F. 1974. Bioenergetics of tufted ducks (*Aythya fulvigula*) at Lock Levin, Kinross. Proc. Roy. Soc. Edinb. B. 74:383-389.

Lien, L. 1978. Energy consumption of ducks of Ovre Heimdalsvatn. Holarctic Ecol. 1:301-303.

Longcore, J. R. 1963. Consumption of natural foods and effects of starvation on canvasbacks and lesser scaup. M.S. Thesis, Univ. Michigan, Ann Arbor. 68pp.

————, and G. W. Cornwell. 1964. The consumption of natural foods by captive canvasbacks and lesser scaup. J. Wildl. Manage. 28:527-531.

Martin, A. C., R. H. Gensch, and C. P. Brown. 1946. Alternative methods in upland gamebird food analysis. J. Wildl. Manage. 10:8-12.

Mills, H. B., W. C. Starrett, and F. C. Bellrose. 1966. Man's effect on the fish and wildlife of the Illinois River. Ill. Nat. Hist. Surv. Biol. Notes 57. 24pp.

Muztar, A. J., S. J. Slinger, and J. H. Burton. 1978. Chemical composition of aquatic macrophytes. I. Investigation of organic constituents and nutritional potential. Can. J. Plant Sci. 58:829-841.

Nelson, J. W., and L. S. Palmer. 1939. Nutritive value and chemical composition of certain freshwater plants of Minnesota. Minn. Agric. Exp., Stn. Tech. Bull. 136. 34pp.

Nilsson, L. 1980. Wintering diving duck populations and available food resources in the Baltic. Wildfowl 31:131-143.

Odum, E. P., C. E. Connell, and H. L. Stoddard. 1961. Flight energy and estimated flight ranges of some migratory birds. Auk 78:515-527.

Perry, M. C. 1982. Distribution and food habits of canvasbacks in the northeast. Trans. Northeast Sect. Wildl. Soc. 39:56-67.

Polisini, J. M., and C. E. Boyd. 1972. Relationships between cell-wall fractions, nitrogen, and standing crop in aquatic macrophytes. Ecol. 53:484-488.

Prince, H. H. 1979. Bioenergetics of postbreeding dabbling ducks. Pages 103-117 *in* T. A. Bookhout, ed. Waterfowl and wetlands—an integrated review. Proc. 1977 Symp., Northcent. Sect., Wildl. Soc., Madison, Wis. 152pp.

Reinecke, K. J. 1977. The importance of freshwater invertebrates and female energy reserves for black ducks breeding in Maine. Ph.D. Thesis, Univ. Maine, Orono. 113pp.

Ricklefs, R. E. 1974. Energetics of reproduction in birds. Pages 152-292 in R. A. Paynter, Jr., ed. Avian energetics. Nuttall Ornithol. Club, Cambridge, Mass. 334pp.

Serie, J. R., D. L. Trauger, and D. E. Sharp. 1983. Migration and winter distributions of canvasbacks staging on the Upper Mississippi River. J. Wildl. Manage. 47:741-753.

Sincock, J. L. 1962. Estimating consumption of food by wintering waterfowl populations. Proc. Southeast. Assoc. Game Fish Comm. 16:217-221.

Steffeck, D. W., F. L. Paveglio, and C. E. Korschgen. 1985. Distribution of aquatic plants in Keokuk Pool (Navigation Pool 19) of the Upper Mississippi River. Proc. Iowa Acad. Sci. 92:111-114.

Stewart, R. E., A. D. Geis, and C. D. Evans. 1958. Distribution of populations and hunting kill of the canvasback. J. Wildl. Manage. 22:333-370.

Sugden, L. G. 1971. Metabolizable energy of small grains for mallards. J. Wildl. Manage. 35:781-785.

———. 1979. Grain consumption by mallards. Wildl. Soc. Bull. 7:35-39.

Swanson, G. A., and J. C. Bartonek. 1970. Bias associated with food analysis in gizzards of blue-winged teal. J. Wildl. Manage. 34:739-746.

Thompson, D. 1973. Feeding ecology of diving ducks on Keokuk Pool, Mississippi River. J. Wildl. Manage. 37:367-381.

Trauger, D. L., and J. R. Serie. 1974. Looking out for the canvasback. Part III. Ducks Unlimited 38:44-45, 60, 64, 71-72.

Van Soest, P. J. 1967. Development of a comprehensive system of food analyses and its application to forages. J. Anim. Sci. 26:119-128.

———, and R. H. Wine. 1967. Use of detergents in the analysis of fibrous feeds. IV. Determination of plant cell wall constituents. J. Assoc. Off. Anal. Chem. 50:50-55.

Wypkema, R. C. P., and C. D. Ankney. 1979. Nutrient reserve dynamics of lesser snow geese staging at James Bay, Ontario. Can. J. Zool. 57:213-219.

16

Workshop Summary: Feeding Ecology

Carl E. Korschgen, Frederic A. Reid,
and Jerome R. Serie

Feeding ecology of waterfowl is the study of interactions between the foods available in the environment and the physiological needs and behavior of the birds. Feeding ecology studies typically entail three basic elements: food habits of birds, food availability within the habitat, and the extent of utilization of the food resources. Many researchers use this information to investigate energetic and nutritional implications.

The quality and quantity of the food selected are influenced by the biological demands, feeding behavior, and morphological adaptations of the bird; the ecology of the prey; and the general nature of the aquatic ecosystem as determined by the hydrology and geology of the area (Swanson and Meyer 1973). Therefore, food and food-related studies are an area of research that can provide an understanding of habitat use and resource allocation in relation to the requirements of the organism (Fredrickson and Drobney 1979). At the present time, little is known about the relationship between food resources and population size, distribution, and condition. A systematic approach that incorporates feeding ecology studies as the third of four broad goals of habitat research and management will be required to fully determine the wintering requirements of waterfowl. These goals are as follows:

(1) Understand the structure and function of the diverse ecosystems utilized by wintering birds. Such studies necessarily involve long-term, interdisciplinary research to determine and understand nutrient and energy cycles, hydrology of wetlands (timing, duration, and depth of flooding

Waterfowl in Winter.© 1988 University of Minnesota. Edited by Milton W. Weller and published by the University of Minnesota Press, Minneapolis.

both in present and historical regimes), and autecology of plant and animal prey species.

(2) Determine time and energy budgets for all species of wintering waterfowl on a diel basis. Such budgets will provide insight into the physiological state of wintering birds. The technical challenges that exist in observing or collecting at night or in heavy cover need to be addressed. We recognize that it was not until researchers began to understand and separate the differing energy demands that occur during the breeding cycle that some aspects of the reproductive ecology of birds became apparent. We must strive to identify physiological states and nutritional needs of wintering birds and secure data based upon these states. Time and energy budgets will dictate where and when (physiological or real time) feeding ecology studies should be conducted.

(3) Conduct feeding ecology studies. Data should be analyzed to determine whether particular foods are being selected because of the physiological state of the birds. Even more effort should be given to documenting food preferences (i.e., selection vs. availability) by better sampling of food availability. Also, there is a need to describe in detail the habitat qualities of study areas so that valid comparisons may be made among geographic areas. Researchers must be aware of biases, especially when sampling birds in disturbed environments—which is why time/activity budget information is important. There also is a need to determine whether birds themselves are having an impact on the habitats or food resources. Data need to be collected over the course of a winter season and for a long time in the same habitats.

(4) Develop a broader perspective about management. Once the requirements of the birds have been determined, wetland complexes can be managed for species diversity and optimum productivity. We must know much more about the long-term consequences of our management practices, which seem presently to be very regimented on an annual basis, primarily because of recreational hunting. Researchers should communicate information to managers by being aware of their needs and keeping them informed during research projects.

Waterfowl have evolved a broad range of adaptations for efficient feeding in a variety of habitats. Only recently have we recognized that wintering areas are not only important in the context of maintenance or survival, but also in the annual condition of the birds (Heitmeyer and Fredrickson 1981). Additional research efforts are required to determine the value and functions of wetland communities and species, the ways in which wintering and migrating birds use them, and the overall carrying capacity. Manipulation of wetland communities can then be based upon sound management practices so that an optimum environment for waterfowl can be maintained.

LITERATURE CITED

Fredrickson, L. H., and R. D. Drobney. 1979. Habitat utilization by postbreeding waterfowl. Pages 119-131 *in* T. A. Bookhout, ed. Waterfowl and wetlands—an integrated review. Proc. 1977 Symp., Northcent. Sect., Wildl. Soc., Madison, Wis. 152pp.
Heitmeyer, M. E., and L. H. Fredrickson. 1981. Do wetland conditions in the Mississippi Delta influence mallard recruitment? Trans. N. Am. Wildl. Nat. Resour. Conf. 46:44–57.
Swanson, G. A., and M. I. Meyer. 1973. The role of invertebrates in the feeding ecology of Anatinae during the breeding season. Pages 143-185 *in* The Waterfowl Habitat Manage. Symp., Moncton, N.B. 306pp.

V.
Weights, Molts, and Condition

17

Annual Body Weight Change in Ring-Necked Ducks (*Aythya collaris*)

William L. Hohman, T. Scott Taylor, and Milton W. Weller

Abstract: Body weights were obtained (1978-84) from 2,376 ring-necked ducks (*Aythya collaris*) during breeding, postbreeding, and wintering stages of the annual cycle. Seasonal fluctuations in body weight were extensive especially during reproduction. Body weight declined through reproduction as birds expended stored nutrients. Seasonal minima were observed in breeding males after their mate initiated incubation and in hens attending class I ducklings. Birds regained body weight before the postbreeding wing molt. Maximum male body weight was observed in birds staging in southwestern Manitoba for fall migration. Male and female ring-necked ducks in southern Florida put on body fat and showed a constant weight gain over winter. The rate of increase, greater in yearlings than adults, varied annually. Yearlings in fall initially were lighter than adults, but body weights were equivalent by late winter. Based on body weights, ring-necked ducks use energy reserves accumulated on wintering and spring-staging areas to meet subsequent reproductive requirements. Body weight data highlight the importance of spring arrival condition to breeding ring-necked ducks and indicate a need for additional work on wintering birds and spring migrants.

There is increased interest in nonbreeding waterfowl and a heightened awareness of the interrelationship between the nonreproductive and reproductive periods of the annual cycle. Few studies to date, however, have addressed waterfowl on an annual basis. Body weights are a useful index for examining changes in nutrient reserve levels in waterfowl (Ankney and MacInnes 1978, Bailey 1979, Raveling 1979, Wishart 1979, Ankney 1982, Drobney 1982, Hohman 1986b). Together with

Waterfowl in Winter. © 1988 University of Minnesota. Edited by Milton W. Weller and published by the University of Minnesota Press, Minneapolis.

behavioral and ecological data, body weights may be used to elucidate strategies of survival and reproduction in waterfowl and evaluate patterns of habitat use.

Ring-necked ducks (*Aythya collaris*) are small-bodied diving ducks (Tribe Aythyini). They winter inland in the Gulf and southern Atlantic seaboard states and commonly nest in northern bog marshes, wetlands characterized by low primary production (Reader 1978) that are little used by other waterfowl species. This paper summarizes body weight data we collected on ring-necked ducks at various stages of the annual cycle and relates changes in body weight to the breeding biology of ring-necked ducks.

We are grateful to R. D. Drobney, C. E. Korschgen, and J. R. Serie for their helpful comments on the manuscript. This research was supported by the North American Wildlife Foundation through the Delta Waterfowl and Wetland Research Station; the University of Minnesota, Department of Fisheries and Wildlife, Computing Center, Agricultural Experiment Station and Graduate School; the U.S. Fish and Wildlife Service, Patuxent Wildlife Research Center (contract 14-16-009-79-019 awarded to M. W. Weller); the Minnesota Department of Natural Resources; the Florida Game and Fresh Water Fish Commission; and the Minnesota Waterfowl Association. We wish to thank the staff at Loxahatchee National Wildlife Refuge, especially T. Martin (refuge manager) and J. Takekawa (refuge biologist), for their generous assistance with our work in southern Florida.

Methods

Studies of breeding and postbreeding birds were conducted in northwestern Minnesota and southwestern Manitoba between 1977 and 1984. Ring-necked ducks wintering in southern and central Florida were studied from November to February, 1979-81. Fresh body weights were taken from birds collected by shooting, decoy trapping (Anderson et al. 1979), nest trapping (Weller 1957), drive trapping (Cowan and Hatter 1952), or night lighting (Lindmeier and Jessen 1961). We also obtained body weights from hunter-killed birds in southern Florida. All birds were weighed to the nearest 5 g using a Pesola spring scale.

We determined the age (yearling = first-year bird, before prebasic II molt; adult = after-first-year bird, after prebasic II molt) of wintering ring-necked ducks by inspection of the cloaca (Gower 1939) and rectrices (Pirnie 1935). Wing feathers (5th primary, 5th secondary, 12th and 13th greater secondary coverts) were removed from breeding birds, and age was assigned later on the basis of discriminant function analysis of feather measurements (Hohman 1986b).

Females and their mates were assigned to the following reproductive categories, based in part on Krapu (1974): *arrival*—females returning to the breeding grounds with ovary weight of less than 3 g; *follicle growth*—preovulating females; with ovary weight greater than 3 g; *laying*—ovulating females; *early incubation*—postovulating hens captured on nest, estimated days of incubation less than 10 as determined by field candling (Weller 1956) or inspection of embryos (Caldwell and Snart 1974); *mid-incubation*—eggs incubated 10-18 days; *late incubation*—eggs incubated longer than 18 days; *early brood*—hens attending age class I ducklings (Gollop and Marshall 1954); *late brood*—hens attending age class II ducklings; *postbreeding*—birds collected in July and August on molting areas before wing molt; *early molt*—flightless birds before rupture of remigial follicles; *late molt*— flightless birds after rupture of remigial follicles; and *postflightless*—birds staging for fall migration. Females initiated ovarian follicle growth after 6 May, as verified by back-dating on hens of known reproductive status. Consequently, all birds handled before 6 May were placed in the arrival category. Pairing status was assigned to marked males on the basis of behavioral observations made following capture. Paired individuals were birds showing active association, i.e., copulation, mutual display, female tolerance of male, or nonrandom spacing.

The extent of seasonal body weight fluctuation was calculated as a percentage of maximum mean body weight after Reinecke (1977). Statistical comparisons of body weight by reproductive status and 10-day Julian date intervals were made using one-way analysis of variance. Multivariate analysis of variance (factors = age, year, date, and reproductive status) was performed on body weight data using BMDP-4V Statistical Software (Dixon and Brown 1981). Regression procedures followed Weisberg (1981). The significance level was set at $P = 0.05$.

Results

We obtained body weights from 2,376 ring-necked ducks during breeding, post-breeding (molting and fall-staging), and wintering periods of the annual cycle (table 17.1). Although males (adult male body-weight range of 542-900 g, $N = 611$) are generally heavier and structurally larger than females (adult female body-weight range of 490-894 g, $N = 685$) (Hohman 1986b), considerable overlap between sexes occurs during the annual cycle (fig. 17.1). The extent of annual body weight fluctuation in our sample amounted to 19% (160 g) for adult males and 27% (208 g) for adult females.

Body weight changed substantially during reproduction, especially in females (fig. 17.2). Female body weight increased significantly from arrival to maximum seasonal levels at the initiation of ovulation, but it declined after laying as birds expended stored nutrients. Minimum female body weights were recorded in birds attending class I broods. Body weight recovered somewhat in hens with class II ducklings in late July.

Body weight of paired males also changed with female (mate) reproductive status (fig. 17.2). Males were heaviest during their mate's arrival and rapid ovarian follicle growth periods. A significant decrease in the body weight of males attending ovulating females occured in middle and late May. The seasonal minimum in mean weight of breeding males was recorded after females began incubation.

Table 17.1. Sample size, mean, and standard deviation (SD) for adult (after-first-year) male and female ring-necked duck body weights by 10-day Julian date intervals

Julian date	Month	Location[a]	Female			Male		
			N	Mean	SD	N	Mean	SD
001-009	January	FL	63	638.8	51.6	39	717.0	54.7
010-019	January	FL	97	662.2	52.3	65	733.3	51.3
020-029	January	FL	18	658.0	39.7	20	722.2	52.1
030-039	February	FL	5	691.0	71.2	3	792.3	9.6
040-049	February	FL	3	680.0	50.2	6	779.0	68.6
050-059	February	FL	7	738.7	50.2	2	820.5	7.8
100-109	April	MN	2	698.0	53.7	7	758.7	45.4
110-119	April	MN	13	722.3	50.8	47	742.8	58.8
120-129	May	MN	9	763.4	51.0	18	735.0	73.6
130-139	May	MN	11	741.2	74.8	22	756.3	57.7
140-149	May	MN	8	740.6	72.4	27	703.8	48.9
150-159	June	MN	2	771.0	114.6	16	673.3	35.2
160-169	June	MN	9	643.0	57.6	12	673.8	34.8
170-179	June	MN	9	620.8	67.8	2	672.0	11.3
180-189	July	MN	9	585.8	53.2	4	701.8	50.0
190-199	July	MN, MB	36	577.2	37.6	5	746.4	79.1
200-209	July	MN, MB	36	571.6	39.8	7	726.1	63.4
210-219	August	MN, MB	23	613.1	48.7	1	620.0	0.0
220-229	August	MB	6	629.5	27.6	25	713.0	70.6
230-239	August	MB	4	603.8	59.4	64	668.2	51.7
240-249	September	MB				3	795.0	57.7
260-269	September	MB				2	897.5	3.5
310-319	November	FL	8	642.9	29.0	1	648.0	0.0
320-329	November	FL	38	606.6	44.9	17	687.6	49.8
330-339	November	FL	86	631.4	46.7	54	712.7	45.2
340-349	December	FL	33	638.0	57.4	36	708.8	41.2
350-359	December	FL	84	640.5	45.0	73	710.8	50.7
360-365	December	FL	54	644.3	41.9	33	732.9	38.7

[a]Location in which body weights were obtained; FL = southern Florida, MN = northwestern Minnesota, and MB = southwestern Manitoba.

Patterns of body weight change for breeding male and female ring-necked ducks varied among years and by female age (Hohman 1986b). Differences among years were greatest early in the reproductive cycle. Arrival birds (adult and yearling) were significantly lighter in 1980 than birds in previous years (table 17.2).

Breeding adult and yearling males exhibited similar patterns of weight change, but body weights of adult and yearling females changed differently through reproduction (Hohman 1986b). Yearlings females returned to breeding areas lighter than adults and did not gain body weight before rapid ovarian follicle growth, as

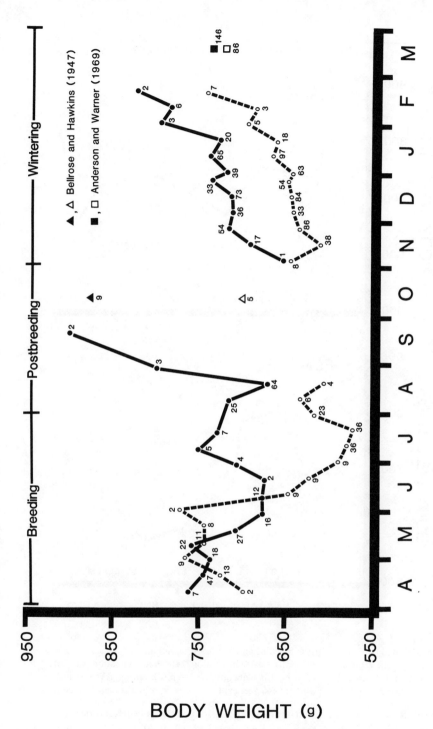

Fig. 17.1. Annual cycle of body weight changes in adult male (solid symbols) and female (open symbols) ring-necked ducks. Mean body weights, sample sizes, and standard deviations are given in table 17.1.

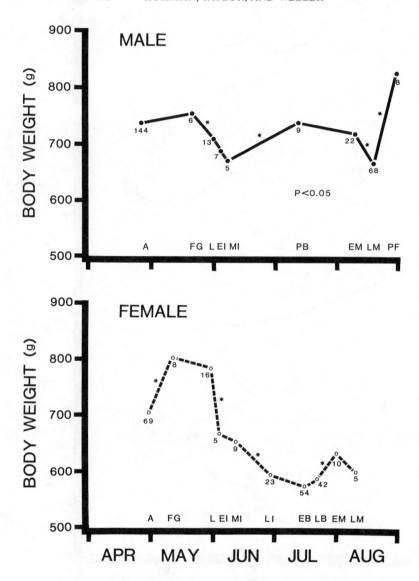

Fig. 17.2. Body weight changes in breeding and postbreeding ring-necked ducks. A = arrival, FG = follicle growth, L = laying, EI = early incubation, MI = mid-incubation, LI = late incubation, EB = early brood rearing, LB = late brood, PB = postbreeding, EM = early molt, LM = late molt, and PF = postflightless. See text for criteria used to distinguish categories.

did adult females. Consequently, adult females captured or collected before 6 May were significantly heavier than yearling birds in both 1979 and 1980 (table 17.2).

Table 17.2. Mean (±1 SE) arrival body weights (g) from breeding ring-necked ducks collected in northwestern Minnesota

Year	Female			Male		
	Yearling[a]	Adult[b]	All	Yearling	Adult	All
1978			700 ± 13			731 ± 8
n			(15)			(44)
1979	715 ± 20	777 ± 18	742 ± 16	772 ± 21	793 ± 15	787 ± 12
n	(9)	(7)	(16)	(6)	(16)	(22)
1980	632 ± 12	705 ± 9	670 ± 11	700 ± 12	726 ± 7	718 ± 6
n	(12)	(13)	(25)	(20)	(50)	(70)

[a] First-year.
[b] After-first-year.

Annual extremes in male body weight occurred during the postbreeding period, August to September. Males regained body weight after their departure from breeding areas before wing molt. Annual minima were recorded in males during late wing molt and maxima during fall staging. Body weight data for postbreeding female ring-necked ducks are limited, but females seem to gain weight before migrating to molting areas and to maintain their body weight through wing molt at levels above those observed during late incubation and early brood rearing.

Ring-necked ducks arrived in southern Florida in mid-November at low body weights. They put on body fat (T. S. Taylor, unpubl. data) and showed a constant weight gain through the wintering period (fig. 17.3). The rate of increase was significantly greater in yearlings than adults, but varied annually (fig. 17.4). Although yearlings were lighter in the fall than adults, body weights were equivalent by late winter.

Discussion

Endogenous nutrient reserves play a prominent role in ring-necked duck reproduction (Hohman 1986b), as well as that of many other waterfowl species (Korschgen 1977, Ankney and MacInnes 1978, Raveling 1979, Krapu 1981, Drobney 1982, Ankney 1984, Tome 1984). During egg production, females incur significant energetic costs, which are large for ducks and geese relative to those of other major groups of birds (King 1973, Ricklefs 1974). Ring-necked duck females deplete fat reserves during rapid ovarian follicle growth and ovulation, and after laying they are highly dependent on ambient food resources for their metabolic requirements (Hohman 1986b). As in other small-bodied waterfowl, ring-necked ducks draw the protein required for egg production almost exclusively from the diet during ovarian follicle growth (Hohman 1986b). To secure protein requirements for egg

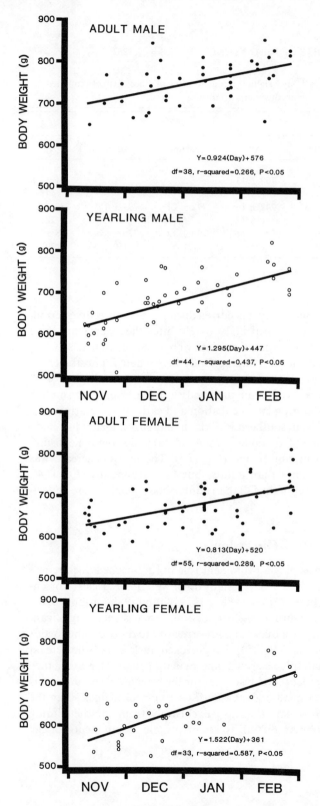

Fig. 17.3. Regression of body weights on date for ring-necked ducks collected in southern Florida, 1979-80.

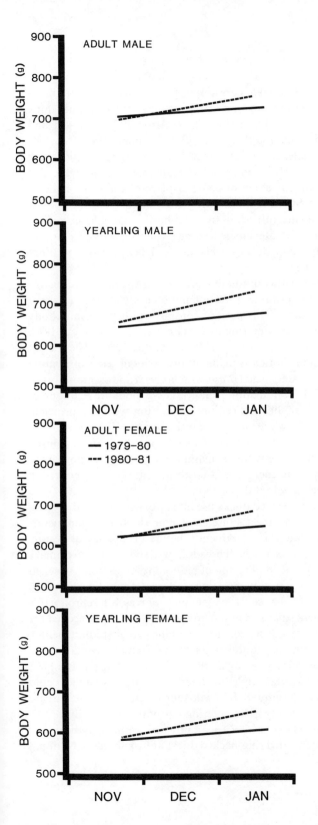

Fig. 17.4. Regression of body weights on date for hunter-killed ring-necked ducks taken at Loxahatchee National Wildlife Refuge, Florida, in 1979-80 (solid line) and 1980-81 (dashed line). All regressions significant at $P < 0.05$.

production, female ring-necked ducks, consuming predominantly invertebrate foods, feed intensively during prelaying and laying, as do females of other duck species (Dwyer 1975, Miller 1976, Derrickson 1978, Afton 1979, Steward and Titman 1980, Seymour and Titman 1981, Titman 1981, Hohman 1985).

Paired ring-necked duck males reduce feeding while attending prelaying/laying mates and expend lipid reserves (Hohman 1986b). Presumably, close attendance of the female minimizes the male's chances of being displaced by another male or having his mate inseminated by other males (McKinney et al. 1983). Moreover, male defense of the female against intrusions by other birds and vigilance against potential predators probably facilitate female feeding (Ashcroft 1976). This attention may be especially important during prelaying and laying when nutrient demands of females are greatest.

Activities of wintering waterfowl ultimately are tied to species reproductive strategies. Ring-necked ducks in southern Florida put on body fat and showed a constant weight gain over winter. This pattern contrasts with the erratic body weight changes observed in other wintering ducks (Folk et al. 1966, Ryan 1972, Owen and Cook 1977, Peterson and Ellarson 1979, Paulus 1980). The diet of ring-necked ducks wintering in Florida is made up primarily of seeds of floating pad plants, such as Schreber watershield (*Brasenia schreberi*) and fragrant water-lily (*Nymphaea odorata*) (T. S. Taylor, unpubl. data). These foods are rich sources of carbohydrate (Landers et al. 1977). Feeding and resting were the principal activities of ring-necked ducks wintering in central Florida (Hohman 1986a). Further, Florida birds exhibited low levels of alert, courtship, and agonistic behavior. Consumption of high-energy foods, maintenance of high feeding levels, and minimization of time spent in energetically costly activities such as courtship and aggression probably facilitated fat deposition.

Based on body weights, ring-necked ducks use fat stores accumulated on wintering and spring-staging areas to meet subsequent reproductive requirements. Acquisition of reserves adequate for reproduction before occupancy of nesting areas may be essential for this species, which breeds in wetlands with low primary production (Hohman 1986b). The implication of reduced reserves in ring-necked duck females entering reproduction, as in renesting mallards (*Anas platyrhynchos*) (Krapu 1981), is an increased reliance on exogenous sources for reproductive nutritional requirements. Deficiencies in initial lipid reserve (i.e., lipid needed for egg production and energy costs associated with obtaining protein requirements), which further increase exogenous requirements for reproduction, may cause breeding adjustments such as delayed laying or clutch size reduction (Krapu 1981, Drobney 1982). Inadequate reserves coupled with reduced food availability could result in deferred breeding (Hohman 1986b). Male reproductive strategies are no doubt affected by their reserve levels when entering reproduction as well.

The amount of weight gained over winter apparently varies annually; the rate of body weight increase in hunter-killed ring-necked ducks at Loxahatchee National

Wildlife Refuge in 1980-81 was greater than that observed in 1979-80. Water levels on the Loxahatchee refuge were lower in 1980-81 than in the previous year (J. Takekawa, pers. commun.), but our assessment of habitat conditions (e.g., food availability) and bird activities was inadequate to account for annual differences in rate of body weight change in ring-necked ducks.

The extent to which body weight gained on wintering areas influences the amount of fat reserve carried by returning breeding birds is unknown. The interval between wintering and breeding stages is clearly a critical period. Ring-necked ducks defer pairing until spring migration (Weller 1965); thus, they simultaneously incur in March and April the energetic costs of both migration and courtship. Reductions in the body weights of birds arriving on breeding areas from their winter maxima presumably reflect these costs. Our data do not indicate the fractions of body reserves provided by wintering and spring-staging areas; however, they do highlight the importance of spring arrival condition to breeding ring-necked ducks and indicate a need for additional detailed work on wintering birds and spring migrants.

LITERATURE CITED

Afton, A. D. 1979. Time budget of breeding northern shovelers. Wilson Bull. 91:42–49.

Anderson, B. W., and D. W. Warner. 1969. A morphological analysis of a large sample of lesser scaup and ring-necked ducks. J. Field Ornithol. 40:85–94.

Anderson, M. G., R. D. Sayler, and A. D. Afton. 1979. A decoy trap for diving ducks. J. Wildl. Manage. 44:217–219.

Ankney, C. D. 1982. The annual cycle of body weight change in lesser snow geese. Wildl. Soc. Bull. 10:60–64.

———. 1984. Nutrient reserve dynamics of breeding and molting brant. Auk 101:361–370.

———, and C. D. MacInnes. 1978. Nutrient reserves and reproductive performance of female lesser snow geese. Auk 95:459–471.

Ashcroft, R. E. 1976. A function of the pair bond in the common eider. Wildfowl 27:101–105.

Bailey, R. O. 1979. Methods of estimating total lipid content in the redhead duck (*Aythya americana*) and an evaluation of condition indices. Can. J. Zool. 57:1830–1833.

Bellrose, F. C., and A. S. Hawkins. 1947. Duck weights in Illinois. Auk 64:422–430.

Caldwell, P. J., and A. E. Snart. 1974. A photographic index for aging mallard embryos. J. Wildl. Manage. 38:298–301.

Cowan, I. McT., and J. Hatter. 1952. A trap and technique for the capture of diving waterfowl. J. Wildl. Manage. 16:438–449.

Derrickson, S. R. 1978. Mobility of breeding pintails. Auk 95:104–114.

Dixon, W. J., and M. B. Brown. 1981. Biomedical computer programs, P-Series. Univ. California Press, Berkeley. 880pp.

Drobney, R. D. 1982. Body weight and composition changes and adaptations in breeding wood ducks. Condor 84:300–305.

Dwyer, T. J. 1975. Time budget of breeding gadwalls. Wilson Bull. 87:335–343.

Folk, C., K. Hudec, and J. Taufar. 1966. The weight of the mallard, *Anas platyrhynchos* and its changes in the course of the year. Zool. Listy. 15:249–260.

Gollop, J. B., and W. H. Marshall. 1954. A guide for aging duck broods in the field. Mississippi Flyway Council Tech. Sect. Rep. 14pp.

Gower, W. C. 1939. The use of the bursa of Fabricius as an indication of age in game birds. Trans. N. Am. Wildl. Conf. 4:426–430.

Hohman, W. L. 1985. Feeding ecology of ring-necked ducks in northwestern Minnesota. J. Wildl. Manage. 49:546–557.

Hohman, W. L. 1986b. Changes in body weight and body composition of breeding ring-necked ducks (Aythya collaris). Auk 103:181–188.

———. 1986a. Diurnal time-activity budgets for ring-necked ducks wintering in central Florida. Proc. Southeast. Assoc. Game Fish Comm. 38:158–164.

King, J. R. 1973. Energetics of reproduction in birds. Pages 78-107 in D. S. Farner, ed. Breeding biology of birds. Natl. Acad. Sci., Washington, D.C.

Korschgen, C. E. 1977. Breeding stress of female eiders in Maine. J. Wildl. Manage. 41:360–373.

Krapu, G. L. 1974. Feeding ecology of pintail hens during reproduction. Auk 91:278–290.

———. 1981. The role of nutrient reserves in mallard reproduction. Auk 98:29–38.

Landers, J. L., T. D. Fendley, and A. S. Johnson. 1977. Feeding ecology of wood ducks in South Carolina. J. Wildl. Manage. 41:118–127.

Lindmeier, J. P., and R. L. Jessen. 1961. Results of capturing waterfowl in Minnesota by spotlighting. J. Wildl. Manage. 25:430–431.

McKinney, E., S. R. Derrickson, and P. Mineau. 1983. Forced copulation in waterfowl. Behav. 86:250–294.

Miller, K. J. 1976. Activity patterns, vocalizations, and site selection in nesting blue-winged teal. Wildfowl 27:33–43.

Owen, M., and W. A. Cook. 1977. Variations in body weight, wing length, and condition of mallard, Anas platyrhynchos platyrhynchos and their relationship to environmental changes. J. Zool. Lond. 183:377–395.

Paulus, S. L. 1980. The winter ecology of the gadwall in Louisiana. M.S. Thesis, Univ. North Dakota, Grand Forks. 357pp.

Peterson, S. R., and R. S. Ellarson. 1979. Changes in oldsquaw carcass weight. Wilson Bull. 91:288–300.

Pirnie, M. D. 1935. Michigan Waterfowl Management. Mich. Dep. Conserv., Lansing. 328pp.

Raveling, D. G. 1979. The annual cycle of body composition of Canada geese with special reference to control of reproduction. Auk 96:234–252.

Reader, R. J. 1978. Primary production in northern bog marshes. Pages 53-62 in R. E. Good, D. F. Whigham, and R. L. Simpson, eds. Freshwater wetlands: ecological processes and management potential. Academic Press, New York.

Reinecke, K. J. 1977. The importance of freshwater invertebrates and female energy reserves for black ducks breeding in Maine. Ph.D. Diss., Univ. Maine, Orono. 113pp.

Ricklefs, R. E. 1974. Energetics of reproduction in birds. Pages 152-292 in R. A. Paynter, Jr., ed. Avian energetics. Nuttall Ornithol. Club, Cambridge, Mass. 334pp.

Ryan, R. A. 1972. Body weight and weight changes of wintering diving ducks. J. Wildl. Manage. 36:759–764.

Seymour, N. R., and R. D. Titman. 1981. Changes in activity patterns, agonistic behavior and territoriality of black ducks (Anas rubripes) during the breeding season in a Nova Scotia tidal marsh. Can. J. Zool. 56:1773–1785.

Steward, G. R., and R. D. Titman. 1980. Territorial behaviour of prairie pothole blue-winged teal. Can. J. Zool. 58:639–649.

Titman, R. D. 1981. A time-activity budget for breeding mallards (Anas platyrhynchos) in Manitoba. Can. Field-Nat. 95:266–271.

Tome, M. W. 1984. Changes in nutrient reserves and organ size in female ruddy ducks breeding in Manitoba. Auk 101:830–837.

Weisberg, S. 1981. Applied linear regression. John Wiley, New York. 181pp.

Weller, M. W. 1956. A simple field candler for waterfowl eggs. J. Wildl. Manage. 20:111–113.

———. 1957. An automatic nest-trap for waterfowl. J. Wildl. Manage. 21:456–458.

———. 1965. Chronology of pair formation in some Nearctic *Aythya* (Anatidae). Auk 82:227–235.

Wishart, R. A. 1979. Indices of structural size and condition of American widgeon (*Anas americana*). Can. J. Zool. 57:2369–2374.

18

Spatial and Temporal Variation in Winter Weights of Mississippi Valley Canada Geese

Dennis D. Thornburg, Thomas C. Tacha,
Bridgett L. Estel, and James W. Spitzkeit

Abstract: Winter (Oct-Mar) weights of 5,281 Canada geese (*Branta canadensis*) varied ($P < 0.05$) among age and sex classes, years, periods within years, and locations in southern Illinois. Regression modeling of 3,412 weights from Union County Conservation Area (UCCA) explained 47% of variation and ranked age/sex classes, years, and periods within years in descending order of importance. Severe winter weather and reduced food production in 1983-84 were associated with lower weights ($P < 0.001$) than in 1982-83 in all age/sex classes at UCCA. Weights did not vary ($P < 0.10$) among locations until late winter in 1983-84 when weights of three age/sex classes were lower ($P < 0.05$) at Rend Lake than at UCCA, presumably because of higher energy expenditures and more dispersed food resources.

Canada geese (*Branta canadensis interior*) of the Mississippi Valley Population (MVP) winter in southern Illinois, western Kentucky, and northwestern Tennessee (Hanson and Smith 1950). Southern Illinois refuges, including Rend Lake, Crab Orchard National Wildlife Refuge (CONWR), Union County Conservation Area (UCCA), and Horseshoe Lake Conservation Areas, provide critical sanctuary and winter habitat for this flock. Raveling (1968) reported winter weight variability of Canada geese at CONWR, and Hanson (1962) studied weights of Canada geese at Horseshoe Lake Conservation Area and CONWR. Our objectives were to investigate factors affecting winter weight variability of MVP Canada geese and to develop hypotheses regarding the condition of geese wintering in southern Illinois.

Waterfowl in Winter.© 1988 University of Minnesota. Edited by Milton W. Weller and published by the University of Minnesota Press, Minneapolis.

W. D. Klimstra, Southern Illinois University, and W. L. Anderson, Illinois Department of Conservation, reviewed the manuscript. D. Jaques, Illinois Department of Conservation, provided technical assistance.

Methods

Weights were obtained from 5,281 Canada geese captured by rocket nets and swim-in bait traps and from geese harvested on public hunting areas at Rend Lake, UCCA, and CONWR in southern Illinois. Weights were obtained with a Chatillon spring scale. Data were collected from early October to late February in 1982-83 and 1983-84. Fall and winter seasons were divided into five periods to facilitate data analysis: early fall (Oct to early Nov), late fall (Nov to mid-Dec), early winter (mid-Dec to Jan), late winter (Jan to early Feb), and spring (Feb to early Mar).

Monthly summaries of National Weather Service data were furnished by A. Robertson, Southeast Missouri State University, Cape Girardeau, Missouri. Information about known yields of corn and grain sorghum on farms in the area surrounding UCCA and Rend Lake Refuge were obtained from the USDA Agriculture Service Centers in Union and Jefferson counties. Average corn and grain sorghum yields for 1982 and 1983 were calculated from 10 randomly selected farms near each of the areas. Average yields on UCCA, Rend Lake Refuge, and surrounding private land were used to estimate food availability for Canada geese.

Weights of Canada geese from all age/sex classes, periods, years, and locations were initially subjected to multiple regression analysis. However, empty cells and small sample sizes precluded use of location in the regression analyses. Subsequently, location was treated separately as a variable, and only Union County data were subjected to further regression analysis. All main effects (age/sex, periods, and years) of the Union County regression were significant ($P < 0.05$). However, only the age/sex by year and period by year interactions were significant ($P < 0.05$). Thus, comparisons between years were analyzed by age/sex class and comparisons among periods were analyzed by year. Statistical analyses were performed using the Statistical Analysis System (Helwig and Council 1979).

Results

Winter weights of MVP Canada geese in southern Illinois varied (one-way ANO-VAS, $P < 0.05$) among four age/sex classes, two years, five periods within years, and three locations. Regression modeling of 3,412 weights from UCCA explained 47% of the variation and ranked age/sex classes, years, and periods within years in descending order of importance. Male Canada geese were heavier ($P < 0.01$) than females and adults weighed more ($P < 0.01$) than juveniles, except that juvenile males were heavier ($P < 0.01$) than adult females.

All age/sex classes of geese at UCCA were lighter ($P < 0.05$) in all periods of 1983-84 than in 1982-83 (table 18.1). Geese of all age/sex classes at UCCA

Table 18.1. Variation between years in mean winter body weights (g) of Mississippi Valley Population Canada geese at Union County Conservation Area, Illinois, 1982-83 and 1983-84

Age/Sex[a]	1982-83			1983-84			Weight difference[b]
	N	$\bar{x}$	SE	N	$\bar{x}$	SE	
AM	253	4,269	27	674	3,996	14	273
JM	406	3,816	20	381	3,510	20	306
AF	315	3,730	22	707	3,421	13	309
JF	368	3,344	19	301	3,069	20	275

[a]A = adult, J = juvenile, M = male, and F = female.
[b]All between-year mean comparisons were significantly different (t-tests, $P < 0.001$).

increased weight throughout the fall and winter of 1982-83 (table 18.2). Peak weights occurred in late winter. In contrast, no significant weight gains were observed at UCCA in 1983-84. Weights of all age/sex classes declined ($P < 0.05$) during spring of 1983 and 1984. This decline occurred after the spring migration had begun and the geese were leaving southern Illinois.

Table 18.2. Variation among periods within years in mean body weights (g) of Mississippi Valley Population Canada geese at Union County Conservation Area, Illinois, 1982-83 and 1983-84

Period	1982-83				1983-84			
	N	$\bar{x}$	SE	DMRT[a]	N	$\bar{x}$	SE	DMRT
Early fall	187	3,613	35	A	347	3,599	24	A
Late fall	139	3,686	54	A	304	3,578	31	A
Early winter	118	3,741	42	A	381	3,569	26	A
Late winter	258	3,917	31	B	870	3,628	16	A
Spring	640	3,741	19	A	161	3,227	37	B

[a]Duncans multiple range test; difference letters denote significant differences ($P < 0.05$).

Weights of Canada geese did not vary ($P > 0.10$) among CONWR, Rend Lake, and UCCA until late winter 1983-84, when weights of three age/sex classes were lower ($P < 0.05$) at Rend Lake than at Union County (table 18.3). By late winter 1983-84, most geese had abandoned CONWR.

The fall and winter of 1982-83 in southern Illinois were unusually mild, with mean monthly temperatures staying above 0C throughout the entire five-month

Table 18.3. Variation in winter weights (g) of Mississippi Valley Population Canada geese between Rend Lake and Union County Conservation Area during late winter 1983-84

Age/Sex[a]	Union County			Rend Lake			Weight difference	P[b]
	N	$\bar{x}$	SE	N	$\bar{x}$	SE		
AM	284	4,021	21	92	3,763	41	258	0.001
JM	157	3,588	29	31	3,613	59	. . .	0.722
AF	316	3,456	19	129	3,203	33	253	0.001
JF	113	3,178	32	39	3,006	50	172	0.001

[a] A = adult, J = juvenile, M = male, and F = female.
[b] P for two-group t-tests between locations.

period. October and November of 1983 were mild, but mean monthly temperatures were well below 0C for both December and January 1983-84. Early winter (15-31 Dec) 1983 included 12 days with temperatures below −12C and five days below −18C. In contrast, the same period in 1982 had only four days below freezing and none below −12C. Late winter (1 Jan to 10 Feb) mean daily temperatures averaged 20% lower in 1984 than in 1983.

Corn yields in 1982 on farms in the vicinity of UCCA and Rend Lake averaged 11,482 and 10,777 liters per hectare, respectively. Grain sorghum yielded an average of 7,784 liters per hectare in the Union County vicinity and 6,903 liters per hectare on lands near Rend Lake. Heavy rains throughout southern Illinois in 1983 delayed spring planting. The summer months followed with one of the most severe droughts on record. As a result, both corn and grain sorghum yields in the Union County area declined 38% from the previous year. The effects of drought were even greater in the Rend Lake area, where average corn and grain sorghum yields declined 44% and 40%, respectively.

Discussion

Raveling (1968) suggested that interpretation of weight data could be biased by differential sampling of subspecies. Morphological measurements from a subsample of the trapped and harvested geese revealed that approximately 98% were *B. c. interior* (Spitzkeit 1985). Morphometric measurements and thus subspecific composition did not vary ($P > 0.05$) among years, locations, or periods within years in southern Illinois. However, morphometry did vary among age and sex classes. Thus, within age and sex classes, weight variations were not confounded with sampling of different subspecific groups.

Capture methods were a possible source of bias in interpretation of waterfowl weight data (Weatherhead and Ankney 1984). However, weights did not vary ($P > 0.10$) among the three different capture methods in this study.

Our weight data were comparable to findings of Hanson (1962) and Raveling (1968), although they separated yearlings from adult geese. Both Hanson and Raveling found that fall-winter weights varied by age and sex class in descending order among adult males, juvenile males, adult females, and juvenile females. Hanson and Raveling also noted seasonal or monthly variation of weights within years and age/sex classes. Raveling noted differences between locations by comparing his data from CONWR with Hanson's data from Horseshoe Lake, and Hanson noted annual variation in weights at Horseshoe Lake. Hanson further suggested that body weights of wintering geese were directly affected by availability of food supplies and that body weight was a valid indication of physiological condition. Following the severe winter of 1977-78, mean body weights of both adult and immature Canada geese in early February at Union County and Horseshoe Lake were nearly 30% less than February weights following the mild winter of 1982-83 (Estel 1983).

Weights of MVP Canada geese in southern Illinois were affected by weather and resource availability in this study. Canada geese began weight gains shortly after arrival on the wintering areas in the year of mild weather and abundant food resources, and weights continued to increase gradually throughout the winter. Lower weights were associated with a year of more severe weather and reduced food production. Weight variations between Union County and Rend Lake were observed only after severe weather in a year of reduced crop production, which may have resulted in lower food availability.

Our weight data support the hypothesis of Joyner et al. (1984) that spatial and temporal variation in condition of wintering geese is affected by resource availability and ambient weather conditions. Data from Joyner et al. and our study counter the hypothesis of Williams (1965) that mid- or late-winter weight declines are a result of intrinsic control mechanisms.

Canada goose weight declines occurred in early spring regardless of winter weather and food conditions. These declines could not be attributed to an influx of smaller subspecies in February and March, as suggested by Raveling (1968). Rather, spring weight declines may be the product of paired and parent geese that are older or in better physiological condition that are leaving southern Illinois wintering areas at the earliest opportunity.

Further research is needed to test these and other useful hypotheses. For example, information is needed to delineate how annual variation in weather and resource distribution and abundance affects both distribution and condition of geese. Improved management of wintering Canada geese is dependent upon understanding these basic bird/resource relationships.

LITERATURE CITED

Estel, B. L. 1983. Winter weights of Canada geese in southern Illinois. Ill. Dep. Conserv. Per. Rep. 38. 5pp.

Hanson, H. C. 1962. The dynamics of condition factors in Canada geese and their relation to seasonal stress. Arct. Inst. N. Am. Tech. Pap. 12. 68pp.

———, and R. H. Smith. 1950. Canada geese of the Mississippi Flyway with special reference to the Illinois flock. Ill. Nat. Hist. Surv. Bull. 25:67–210.

Helwig, J. T., and K. A. Council, eds. 1979. SAS user's guide. SAS Inst., Raleigh, N.C. 494pp.

Joyner, D. E., R. D. Arthur, and B. N. Jacobson. 1984. Winter weight dynamics, grain consumption, and reproductive potential in Canada geese. Condor 86:275–280.

Raveling, D. G. 1968. Weights of *Branta canadensis interior* during winter. J. Wild. Manage. 32:412–414.

Spitzkeit, J. W. 1985. Morphometric and taxonomic characteristics of Mississippi Valley Canada geese wintering in southern Illinois. M.A. Thesis, Southern Illinois Univ., Carbondale. 27pp.

Weatherhead, P. J., and C. D. Ankney. 1984. Comment: a critical assumption of band-recovery models may often be violated. Wildl. Soc. Bull. 12:198–199.

Williams, J. E. 1965. Energy requirements of the Canada goose in relation to migration and distribution. Ph.D. Thesis, Univ. Illinois, Urbana. 112pp.

19

Examining Waterfowl Condition: Skewed Ideas on the Normal Procedure

James K. Ringelman

Abstract: A condition index (CI) was calculated for mallards captured during winter in northeastern Colorado. As mean values of CI increased, standard deviations of CI decreased (rho = -0.462) and some distributions became negatively skewed. Data from wild and captive birds support the hypothesis that competition during periods of severe winter weather alters the habitat selection of subordinate individuals, particularly juvenile female mallards. Changes in habitat selection cause differential foraging success and lead to a high variability in CI. It is important to consider this variability when estimating the percentage of a population below a given level of CI.

Temporal changes in the relative magnitude of nutrient reserves, as indexed by physiological condition, can be used as indicators of energy balance. For this reason, condition indices are being used to investigate the cross-seasonal relationship between winter nutrition and spring reproductive performance (J. K. Ringelman, unpubl. data; G. R. Hepp, pers. commun.), as well as differential winter survival (Hepp et al. 1986) and habitat selection by waterfowl (Tietje and Teer 1987). Yet, despite the utility of condition indices, little is known about the variability in condition within waterfowl populations during winter or the biological basis for that variability.

Tests commonly used to compare sample means (*t*-test, analysis of variance) require that samples come from populations that are normally distributed with equal variances. However, after performing preliminary analyses on a condition index (CI) calculated for wintering mallards (*Anas platyrhynchos*), I noted that

Waterfowl in Winter.© 1988 University of Minnesota. Edited by Milton W. Weller and published by the University of Minnesota Press, Minneapolis.

sample distributions often were skewed and heteroscedastic. This finding prompted additional analyses on the distribution of condition index values. An outcome was the recognition that nonnormality and heteroscedasticity, rather than being viewed as inconveniences to be surmounted with data transformations or nonparametric procedures, have a biological basis that may enhance our understanding of winter waterfowl ecology. My purpose here is to discuss how sample standard deviations correlate with mean values of condition index, the implications of this association for investigations of winter waterfowl condition, and a possible biological basis for the relationship.

I thank M. R. Szymczak, J. F. Corey, and other personnel of the Colorado Division of Wildlife who helped in trapping and other phases of data collection. I am also grateful to D. C. Bowden for statistical advice and D. C. DeLong for coding and entering data and preparing figures. R. O. Bailey, C. E. Braun, T. E. Remington, M. R. Szymczak, and two anonymous referees offered helpful comments on drafts of this manuscript.

Methods

Mallards were captured in Salt Plains bait traps (Szymczak and Corey 1976) at waterfowl concentration areas in northeastern Colorado. Forty mallards of each age and sex class were measured at four locations during midwinter (12-21 January, 1983 and 1984). Age determinations were made using the techniques described by Carney (1964) and Krapu et al. (1979). At one of these areas (Bonny Reservoir, 225 km east of Denver), a similar number of mallards also was captured during early (2-9 December) and late (22 February-1 March) winter of both years. Birds were held until all esophageal corn was digested, then weight (nearest 10 g) and wing length (nearest 1 mm) measurements were recorded. Sex-specific equations were used to estimate total body fat of measured birds (Ringelman and Szymczak 1985), and a CI was calculated according to the equation: $CI = fat \div (weight - fat)$.

Summary statistics, including measures of skewness and kurtosis, were generated using the condescriptive procedure of SPSS (Nie et al. 1975). Because I was interested in the variability within a data set, irrespective of the magnitude of CI values, the coefficient of variation (CV) was used as the preferred measure of variability in CI. However, to avoid inducing correlation (D. C. Bowden, pers. commun.), I used the standard deviation as a measure of variability when performing Spearman Rank correlations. Differences between coefficients of variation were tested directly (Zar 1974, 104). Normal deviates were calculated to determine the proportion of a normal distribution lying below a given value of CI (Zar 1974, 74). Normal curves were fitted to CI data by computing the frequencies to be expected if the data were normal (Zar 1974, 81).

Results

When comparing all age and sex groups using January 1983 data, the sample standard deviations for CI increased with decreasing mean values of CI (rho = −0.462, 1-tailed test, $P = 0.04$; table 19.1). Standard deviations averaged 0.041 but

Table 19.1. Means and standard deviations of condition index calculated for mallards trapped at four northeastern Colorado locations during January 1983[a]

| Area | Condition index ± standard deviation | | | |
	Adult female	Juvenile female	Adult male	Juvenile male
1	0.152 ± 0.053	0.166 ± 0.047	0.173 ± 0.044	0.156 ± 0.035
2	0.174 ± 0.055	0.188 ± 0.052	0.168 ± 0.045	0.180 ± 0.037
3	0.187 ± 0.038	0.189 ± 0.048	0.195 ± 0.031	0.175 ± 0.038
4	0.211 ± 0.033	0.208 ± 0.041	0.188 ± 0.032	0.195 ± 0.035

[a]Each datum represents a sample of 40 birds.

ranged from 0.031 (CI = 0.195) to 0.055 (CI = 0.174). The frequency distributions of CI values for juvenile female mallards during early, middle, and late winter 1983-84 exemplify how CI and sample coefficients of variation change over time (fig. 19.1). During a period of moderately severe winter weather, CI averaged 0.141 and CV equaled 37.6%. As weather conditions became more severe during midwinter, mean CI (0.120) changed insignificantly ($P > 0.05$) but CV increased (49.8%, $P < 0.05$, variance ratio test). When severe weather abated in late winter, mean CI increased (0.171; $P < 0.05$) and variability in CI showed a marked decline (CV = 18.6%; $P < 0.001$).

Although asymmetries in the distributions of CI usually were not statistically significant, there was a tendency for distributions with high mean values of CI to be leptokurtic and negatively skewed. For juvenile female mallards (fig. 19.1), late winter birds were not only in better condition, but several individuals had CI values near and to the right of the mean (kurtosis = 0.224, skewness = −0.629). The distribution of CI values among midwinter females in poorer condition was platykurtic (−0.269) and slightly skewed (−0.205). Thus, mean values of CI may not provide a good measure of central tendency in some instances.

During early, middle, and late winter of 1982-83 and 1983-84, the CV in CI for adult male mallards was nearly constant (SD = 1.72), despite changes in weather and mean values of CI (table 19.2). In contrast, large changes in both the mean value and CV (SD = 10.44) in CI were apparent among juvenile females during the same period.

Although a continuum of body condition exists in any population of wintering waterfowl, it is reasonable to expect that suboptimal condition may impact

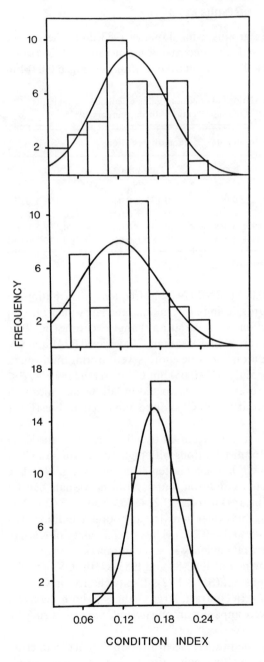

Fig. 19.1. Actual (histogram) and normalized (solid line) frequency distributions of condition index values for juvenile female mallards during early (top), middle (center), and late (bottom) winter 1983-84. Ducks were captured at Bonny Reservoir, Colorado. Sample sizes are 40 (early and late winter) and 39 ducks (midwinter).

Table 19.2. Means and coefficients of variation (CV) of condition index (CI) calculated for four age/sex classes of mallards captured at Bonny Reservoir, Colorado[a]

Age/sex class	Years	Mean CI	CV of CI (%)	Standard deviation of CV values
Adult female	1983-84	0.183	22.6	
		0.163	32.3	
		0.168	23.6	
	1982-83	0.210	25.6	
		0.152	35.1	
		0.170	23.4	5.28
Juvenile female	1983-84	0.141	37.6	
		0.120	49.8	
		0.171	18.6	
	1982-83	0.169	34.3	
		0.166	28.0	
		0.150	37.1	10.44
Adult male	1983-84	0.146	27.2	
		0.141	25.7	
		0.157	25.7	
	1982-83	0.168	30.1	
		0.173	25.6	
		0.156	26.8	1.72
Juvenile male	1983-84	0.129	32.6	
		0.139	32.2	
		0.154	23.5	
	1982-83	0.150	33.5	
		0.156	22.6	
		0.140	33.0	5.07

[a]Sample size equals about 40 birds per datum.

population parameters (i.e., survival, reproductive potential) only below a threshold level. If that is the case, investigators should carefully examine variability in CI. The variance as well as the mean of a distribution influence the estimate of the number of individuals below a given value of CI. Consider two sets of CI frequency distributions for juvenile female mallards. The first set (fig. 19.2, top) depicts the frequencies expected in a normal distribution where sample means and variances are taken to be the actual population mean and variance. The second set (fig. 19.2, bottom) illustrates samples with the same number of individuals (40) and mean values of CI, but with a hypothetical common variance equal to the average of the three real sample variances. If a hypothetical threshold of suboptimal condition is 0.09, then 16.8%, 30.7%, and 0.5% of the individuals in the population would have CI values <0.09 during early, middle, and late winter, respectively (shaded area, fig. 19.2, top). However, samples with the same means but a common variance would

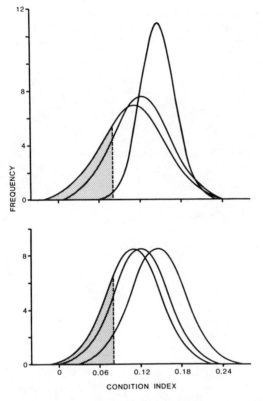

Fig. 19.2. Normalized frequency distributions of condition indices for juvenile female mallards during three winter periods (top) vs. frequency distributions with actual means and sample sizes ($N = 40$) but equal variances (bottom). Shaded areas denote those portions of curves below condition index of 0.09.

have 14.5%, 26.8%, and 4.7% of the individuals below of CI of 0.09, in the same order (shaded area, fig. 19.2, bottom). Thus, two populations might have equal mean values of CI but different percentages of birds below a threshold condition. Conversely, samples with different CI means could have the same percentage of individuals below a given CI.

A reduction in the CV of CI among female mallards during late winter could reflect a buildup of endogenous reserves preparatory to breeding. To test that hypothesis, I calculated CI values and associated CV for female mallards measured during early, middle, and late winter, 1982-83. No consistent decrease in CV during late winter was noted among either adult or juvenile female mallards at two locations, but CV did increase with decreasing CI as described earlier (table 19.1).

I also determined the early winter condition of 32 captive, female mallards (16 adult, 16 juvenile) held for three months on a nutritionally balanced, ad libitum diet. When compared with the coefficients of variation in CI among wild female mallards (table 19.1), which ranged from 35.1% ($\bar{x}$ CI = 0.152) to 15.6% ($\bar{x}$ CI = 0.211), data from captive mallards continued the trend of decreasing variability in CI (CV = 12.8%) with increasing condition ($\bar{x}$ CI = 0.258).

Discussion

Correlation between the mean value and the variability of CI suggests a biological causation. Condition reflects the energy balance of the individual, so it is necessary to consider both energy expenditure and acquisition when considering a plausible mechanism. The most energetically costly activities, such as flight and vigorous feeding, often occur synchronously during field-feeding bouts. During interludes between feeding, mallards in Colorado spend nearly all day and night concentrated in large flocks on lakes or rivers. Thus, thermoregulatory costs may differ among local populations but (except for differences attributable to body size) they should be similar within a flock. These similarities in behavior and thermoregulation suggest that only small differences in energy expenditure would be expected among mallards wintering in Colorado.

Several hypotheses can be advanced to explain the variability in body condition related to mean values of CI. Since an upper limit exists in the amount of fat reserves a bird can carry, I hypothesize that a reduction in the CV of CI at high levels of CI may be a simple function of the population approaching this maximum value. This relationship would also explain the tendency toward a negatively skewed distribution at high levels of CI. Theoretically, the CV of CI should also decrease at very low levels of CI because of death through starvation, although I did not observe evidence of this decrease among wild mallards even under the most severe winter conditions. However, the changes I observed in the CV of CI were evident in wild mallards with fat levels far less than maximum, as evidenced by the very high CI values I present for captive mallards and by the fat levels reported for wild mallards overwintering in other regions (Whyte and Bolen 1984) that far exceed fat reserves carried by mallards in Colorado. Thus, this hypothesis does not explain the changes in CV that I observed within a relatively narrow, moderate range of CI values.

Weather-induced changes in the behavior of field-feeding waterfowl were observed in early studies of waterfowl ecology during winter (Bellrose 1944, Hochbaum 1955, Bossenmaier and Marshall 1958) and continue to be addressed in recent studies (Baldassarre and Bolen 1984). The tendency of mallards to modify their traditional morning and evening field-feeding behavior during cold, blustery weather (Bellrose 1944) or during periods of snowfall (Baldassarre and Bolen 1984) is particularly noteworthy. My second hypothesis presumes that weather, the ultimate factor regulating condition of mallards in Colorado, causes differential foraging success among individuals. Differences in net energy acquisition are correlated with this variable foraging success and are the basis for the high variability in condition during severe winter periods.

During severe weather, small groups of mallards forage throughout the day, utilizing a wide variety of cornfields located near roosting areas (Bellrose 1944; J. K. Ringelman, unpubl. data). Because of the large differences in waste corn abundance among fields (Baldassarre and Bolen 1984), this increase in the number of different cornfields used results in variable foraging success. If my second hypothesis is correct, and the sex and age composition of small feeding flocks is representative of the local population, variability in CI within all age and sex groups should increase during severe weather. However, variations in the CV of CI were greatest among juvenile mallards, particularly females (table 19.2). Thus, this hypothesis does not provide a satisfactory explanation for these age- and sex-specific differences.

If field-feeding situations pressure birds to maximize energy intake over time, and if juvenile mallards are less efficient foragers than adults, variability in CV over the range of CI values should be higher among juveniles during times of food scarcity. Contrasts between adult males and juvenile females lend support to this third hypothesis (table 19.2), although the difference in the variability in CV between juvenile males and adult females is slight.

My final hypothesis is that competition causes differential foraging success by altering the habitat selection of subordinate individuals. Such intraspecific competition is thought to occur among wintering waterfowl (Nichols and Haramis 1980, Saylor and Afton 1981), particularly during periods of severe weather (Jorde et al. 1984). During periods of good weather and nonlimiting food supply, competition may be minimal and subordinate individuals are able to forage effectively. But when food becomes limiting, as occurs after a snowfall, competition increases and subordinate individuals may be excluded from preferred feeding sites.

Paired individuals and adult males are the dominant birds in the social structure of wintering mallard flocks (Jorde 1981). Adult female black ducks (*Anas rubripes*) pair earlier in the winter than juvenile females (Stotts and Davis 1960). If a similar behavior exists among wintering mallards, then juvenile females probably are subordinate individuals throughout much of the winter. Thus, during periods of intense competition, dominant birds should be in better condition and have lower CV in CI than do juvenile females. Data presented here (table 19.2) best fit this latter hypothesis, which implies that adult male mallards were not subject to the same variability in foraging success experienced by juvenile birds. Intraspecific competition, which resulted in juvenile females being displaced to suboptimal feeding areas, is one plausible explanation for these results.

LITERATURE CITED

Baldassarre, G. A., and E. G. Bolen. 1984. Field-feeding ecology of waterfowl wintering on the Southern High Plains of Texas. J. Wildl. Manage. 48:63–71.

Bellrose, F. C. 1944. Duck populations and kill. Ill. Nat. Hist. Surv. Bull. 23:327–372.

Bossenmaier, E. F., and W. H. Marshall. 1958. Field-feeding by waterfowl in southwestern Manitoba. Wildl. Monogr. 1. 32pp.

Carney, S. M. 1964. Preliminary keys to waterfowl age and sex identification by means of wing plumage. U.S. Fish Wildl. Serv. Spec. Sci. Rep. Wildl. 82. 47pp.

Hepp, G. R., R. J. Blohm, R. E. Reynolds, J. E. Hines, and J. D. Nichols. 1986. Physiological condition of autumn-banded mallards and its relationship to hunting vulnerability. J. Wildl. Manage. 50:177–183.

Hochbaum, H. A. 1955. Travels and traditions of waterfowl. Univ. Minnesota Press, Minneapolis. 301pp.

Jorde, D. G. 1981. Winter and spring staging ecology of mallards in south central Nebraska. M.S. Thesis, Univ. North Dakota, Grand Forks. 116pp.

———, G. L. Krapu, R. D. Crawford, and M. A. Hay. 1984. Effects of weather on habitat selection and behavior of mallards wintering in Nebraska. Condor 86:258–265.

Krapu, G. L., D. H. Johnson, and C. W. Dane. 1979. Age determination of mallards. J. Wildl. Manage. 43:384–393.

Nichols, J. D., and G. M. Haramis. 1980. Sex-specific differences in winter distribution patterns of canvasbacks. Condor 82:406–416.

Nie, N. H., C. H. Hull, J. G. Jenkins, K. Steinbrenner, and D. H. Bent. 1975. Statistical package for the social sciences. McGraw-Hill, New York. 675pp.

Ringelman, J. K., and M. R. Szymczak. 1985. A physiological condition index for wintering mallards. J. Wildl. Manage. 49:564–568.

Saylor, R. D., and A. D. Afton. 1981. Ecological aspects of common goldeneyes wintering in the upper Mississippi River. Ornis Scand. 12:99–108.

Stotts, V. D., and D. E. Davis. 1960. The black duck in the Chesapeake Bay of Maryland: breeding behavior and biology. Chesapeake Sci. 1:127–154.

Szymczak, M. R., and J. F. Corey. 1976. Construction and use of the Salt Plains duck trap in Colorado. Colo. Div. Wildl. Div. Rep. 6. 13pp.

Tietje, W. D., and J. G. Teer. 1988. winter body conditin of northern shovelers on fresh water and saline habitats. Pages 353–376 in M. Weller, ed. Waterfowl in winter. Univ. Minnesota Press, Minneapolis.

Whyte, R. J., and E. G. Bolen. 1984. Impact of winter stress on mallard body composition. Condor 86:477–482.

Zar, J. H. 1974. Biostatistical analysis. Prentice-Hall, Englewood Cliffs, N.J. 620pp.

20

Nutrient Reserve Dynamics of Female Mallards during Spring Migration through Central Iowa

Theodore G. LaGrange and James J. Dinsmore

Abstract: We collected 43 paired female mallards (*Anas platyrhynchos*) during the 1983 and 1984 spring migrations through Iowa to determine lipid and protein reserve status. The 1984 collections were grouped into early, peak, and late periods. Late-period mallards had greater body and lipid weights than mallards in the two earlier periods, or mallards collected during January and February on the wintering grounds, and equaled the body and lipid weights reported for mallards collected just before departure from the wintering grounds and for those on the breeding grounds. Female mallards maintained or acquired lipid reserves during the spring migration, especially late in the migration. We propose that these reserves are used for flight and thermoregulatory costs and that they allow a shift to invertebrate foods on the breeding grounds. Protein reserves changed little throughout the migration. Moist-soil areas and seasonally flooded agricultural lands that contain high-energy and nutritious seeds need to be provided throughout the spring migratory range of the mallard, especially close to the breeding grounds.

In response to the hypothesis that factors away from the breeding grounds may affect waterfowl production (Heitmeyer and Fredrickson 1981), there has been a proliferation of wintering-waterfowl studies. Krapu (1981) suggested that lipid reserves acquired by females before arrival on the breeding grounds influenced mallard reproduction, but it was not known when and where female mallards acquired these lipids.

Waterfowl in Winter. © 1988 University of Minnesota. Edited by Milton W. Weller and published by the University of Minnesota Press, Minneapolis.

Mallards often undergo weight loss on the wintering grounds (Whyte and Bolen 1984a, Heitmeyer 1985) because of a reduction in lipid reserves, possibly resulting from periods of negative energy balance (Jorde 1981, Heitmeyer 1985). Yet, upon arrival at the breeding grounds, near-maximum weight has been reached (Krapu 1981). This gain is most likely to occur on wintering grounds just before departure (Heitmeyer 1985) or during spring migration. Determining when and where female mallards acquire lipid reserves is important for delimiting potentially critical periods in the annual cycle and identifying important habitats, especially in light of continuing habitat losses (Tiner 1984).

The objectives of this paper are to document the nutrient reserves of spring migratory female mallards in central Iowa; evaluate the relationship between nutrient reserves and age, reproductive condition, and molt; and compare these findings with studies conducted on breeding and wintering areas.

We acknowledge the support and funding provided by Delta Waterfowl and Wetlands Research Station and Iowa State University. T. Eischeid, R. Johnson, J. White, E. Klaas, A. van der Valk, J. Coats, P. Pattee, and the Iowa Conservation Commission provided technical assistance, time, and equipment. M. Thompson and numerous private landowners allowed access to collection sites. This is journal paper J-11742 of Iowa Agriculture and Home Economics Experiment Station, Ames; Project 2466.

Methods

This study was conducted in central Iowa within a 50-km radius of Ames. Few mallards nest or winter here, and the number is miniscule compared with the numbers that migrate through the area. Numerous basins, planted primarily to corn and soybeans, fill with melt and rainwater in the spring and are extensively used by migratory waterfowl.

During the spring migrations of 1983 and 1984, respectively, 15 and 28 paired female mallards were shot while using seasonally flooded agricultural ponds. A male and female staying and moving together or exhibiting pair behavior (Johnsgard 1965) for a five-minute period were considered paired. In 1984, collections were divided into the premigratory peak (early), migratory peak (peak), and postmigratory peak (late) periods as determined from counts during a 97-km roadside survey conducted every three days (LaGrange 1985).

Collected birds were weighed to the nearest 10 g and the contents of the esophagus, proventriculus, and gizzard were removed and stored for analysis of food habits. These organs were replaced in the carcass, and the birds were double-bagged and frozen.

Total body weight (wet) of the birds was measured to the nearest 0.1 g after thawing. Prebasic molt was scored by estimating the percentage of incoming contour feathers on 20 body regions and estimating the percentage of new down over the entire body. The following were removed and weighed wet to the nearest 0.01 g: right breast muscle (pectoralis and supracoracoideus), right leg muscle (originating from or inserting to the femur, tibula, and fibula), gizzard, small and large intestines, heart, liver, ovary, and oviduct. Birds were aged by presence or absence of a bursa (Hochbaum 1942). The eviscerated carcass (carcass less the gastrointestinal and reproductive tracts, heart, liver, kidneys, feathers, and feet distal to the tibiotarsus) was weighed wet to the nearest 0.1 g, then homogenized. Two homogenate subsamples were freeze-dried for 120 hours to determine tissue moisture content. A 20-g aliquot was selected from each dried subsample and extracted for 22 hours by the Soxhlet process using petroleum ether (Horwitz 1975). Extracted aliquots were oven-dried at 55C for 24 hours and reweighed to the nearest 0.01 g. The extracted aliquot (fat-free dry weight) was used as an index of protein reserves.

Differences between paired means were tested by analysis of variance (ANOVA). Multiple comparisons were made using the least significant difference test (Ray 1982). All null hypotheses were tested at the $P \leq 0.05$ significance level.

Several factors make it difficult to interpret data about spring migratory waterfowl energetics, so comparisons must be made with caution. First, the past histories of collected individuals are unknown. Where a migrant spent the winter and where it will nest could significantly influence its nutrient reserve status. This problem is particularly severe with mallards because their breeding and wintering ranges span a vast latitudinal range (Bellrose 1980). Second, turnover time of mallards on the spring migratory grounds is unknown. The date a bird arrives at the collection location and how long the bird stays in the area will affect its nutrient reserves.

Results

Migration Chronology

In 1983 and 1984, mallards began arriving in central Iowa during the third week of February, several weeks earlier than average (Dinsmore et al. 1984). In 1983, collections were made between 8 March and 9 April. For 1984, collections were divided into the early (23 February to 4 March), peak (24-30 March), and late (9-17 April) periods. Mean roadside-survey mallard counts were 166 for the early period, 538 for the peak period, and 50 for the late period (LaGrange 1985).

Nutrient Reserve Dynamics

No annual differences in body and reserve weights were found ($P > 0.05$; table 20.1). Body and reserve weights did not differ between juveniles (birds hatched the previous year) and adults in 1983 ($P > 0.05$), but in 1984 adults had greater water ($P = 0.01$) and fat-free dry weights ($P = 0.04$) than juveniles (table 20.2). No

Table 20.1. Mean body and carcass constituent weights (g) for paired female mallards
in 1983 and 1984

| Basis of weight | 1983 | | | 1984 | |
	Mean ± SE	(N)	P	Mean ± SE	(N)
Field-measured body	1,167 ± 20.8	(15)	NS[a]	1,119 ± 26.3	(28)
Corrected body[b]	1,140.4 ± 23.6	(11)	NS	1,062.3 ± 24.5	(25)
Eviscerated carcass[c]	850.0 ± 19.1	(15)	NS	807.4 ± 19.3	(28)
Water	485.5 ± 6.3	(15)	NS	486.3 ± 7.5	(28)
Lipid	155.8 ± 14.5	(15)	NS	115.4 ± 14.3	(28)
Fat-free dry	208.7 ± 3.6	(15)	NS	205.7 ± 3.2	(28)

[a]Nonsignificant (ANOVA; $P \leq 0.05$).
[b]Gastrointestinal contents removed.
[c]See text for description.

Table 20.2. Mean body and carcass constituent weights (g) for juvenile and adult paired
female mallards in 1983 and 1984

| Basis of weight | 1983 | | | | | | 1984 | | | | | |
| | Juvenile | | | Adult | | | Juvenile | | | Adult | | |
	Mean ± SE	(N)	P	Mean ± SE	(N)		Mean ± SE	(N)	P	Mean ± SE	(N)
Field-measured body	1,143 ± 25.4	(7)	NS[a]	1,188 ± 31.7	(8)		1,105 ± 34.3	(14)	NS	1,134 ± 40.8	(14)
Corrected body[b]	1,119.4 ± 29.7	(5)	NS	1,157.9 ± 36.2	(6)		1,043.5 ± 30.3	(13)	NS	1,082.7 ± 39.6	(12)
Eviscerated carcass[c]	852.8 ± 23.8	(7)	NS	847.5 ± 30.7	(8)		787.9 ± 25.0	(14)	NS	827.0 ± 29.5	(14)
Water	483.7 ± 7.3	(7)	NS	487.1 ± 10.5	(8)		467.8 ± 10.4	(14)	0.010	504.8 ± 8.5	(14)
Lipid	158.2 ± 20.0	(7)	NS	153.8 ± 22.1	(8)		120.9 ± 16.7	(14)	NS	109.9 ± 23.8	(14)
Fat-free dry	210.9 ± 6.7	(7)	NS	206.7 ± 3.8	(8)		199.1 ± 5.0	(14)	0.039	212.3 ± 3.3	(14)

[a]Nonsignificant.
[b]Gastrointestinal contents removed.
[c]See text for description.

differences were detected in water and fat-free dry weights between the three 1984 migratory periods ($P > 0.05$; table 20.3) Field-measured and corrected body weights were greater during the late period than during the peak period ($P \leq 0.05$). Eviscerated carcass and lipid weights were greater during the late period than during either of the two earlier periods ($P \leq 0.05$).

Table 20.3. Mean body and carcass constituent weights (g) for paired female mallards for three migratory periods in 1984

	Early			Peak			Late		
Basis of weight	Mean ± SE	(N)		Mean ± SE	(N)		Mean ± SE	(N)	
Field-measured body	1,076 ± 32.0	(7)	AB[a]	1,051 ± 30.1	(9)	B	1,196 ± 46.8	(12)	A
Corrected body[b]	1,031.7 ± 23.3	(5)	AB	998.9 ± 26.7	(9)	B	1,128.1 ± 43.6	(11)	A
Eviscerated carcass[c]	784.2 ± 15.6	(7)	A	738.7 ± 20.1	(9)	A	872.5 ± 33.3	(12)	B
Water	506.7 ± 10.1	(7)	A	478.2 ± 13.6	(9)	A	480.5 ± 12.5	(12)	A
Lipid	69.4 ± 11.6	(7)	A	58.0 ± 8.7	(9)	A	185.4 ± 17.6	(12)	B
Fat-free dry	208.2 ± 5.2	(7)	A	202.5 ± 5.3	(9)	A	206.7 ± 5.9	(12)	A

[a] According to least significant difference tests, weights with shared letters are not significantly ($P \leq 0.05$) different.
[b] Gastrointestinal contents removed.
[c] See text for description.

Organ Weights and Molt Chronology

The only significant change for five body organs and two muscles between the three 1984 migratory periods was the increase of small intestine weights ($P \leq 0.05$; table 20.4). Ovary weights in adults were significantly greater than in

Table 20.4. Mean body organ and muscle weights (g) of paired female mallards for three migratory periods in 1984

	Early			Peak			Late		
Organ or muscle	Mean ± SE	(N)		Mean ± SE	(N)		Mean ± SE	(N)	
Gizzard	45.8 ± 2.6	(7)	A[a]	37.9 ± 2.8	(9)	A	40.4 ± 2.8	(11)	A
Small intestine	18.7 ± 0.7	(7)	A	19.8 ± 0.4	(9)	AB	21.4 ± 0.8	(12)	B
Large intestine	2.5 ± 0.2	(7)	A	2.3 ± 0.1	(9)	A	2.2 ± 0.1	(12)	A
Liver	25.6 ± 4.0	(7)	A	33.3 ± 3.8	(9)	A	31.2 ± 1.9	(12)	A
Heart	12.8 ± 0.4	(7)	A	12.3 ± 0.6	(9)	A	12.4 ± 0.4	(12)	A
Breast muscle	121.2 ± 2.4	(7)	A	118.6 ± 3.8	(9)	A	123.8 ± 4.0	(12)	A
Leg muscle	34.1 ± 1.7	(6)	A	31.8 ± 1.6	(9)	A	33.7 ± 1.2	(12)	A

[a] According to least significant difference tests, weights with shared letters are not significantly ($P \leq 0.05$) different.

juveniles in 1984 ($P = 0.01$) and approached significance in 1983 (table 20.5). Ovary weights were greater during the late period than during the early period ($P \leq 0.05$; table 20.6).

We detected no differences in percentage of incoming contour feathers be-

Table 20.5. Mean ovary weights (g) and extent of prebasic molt (%) for juvenile and adult paired female mallards in 1983 and 1984

| | 1983 | | | | 1984 | | | |
| | Juvenile | | | Adult | Juvenile | | | Adult |
Variable	Mean ± SE (N)	P	Mean ± SE (N)	Mean ± SE (N)	P	Mean ± SE (N)
Ovary weight	0.49 ± 0.11 (7)	NS[a]	0.72 ± 0.09 (8)	0.64 ± 0.06 (14)	0.010	1.10 ± 0.15 (14)
Incoming contour feathers	14 ± 3.2 (7)	NS	13 ± 2.1 (8)	9 ± 1.7 (14)	NS	10 ± 1.8 (14)
New (black) down	54 ± 0.1 (6)	NS	65 ± 13.2 (8)	42 ± 7.7 (14)	0.009	70 ± 6.4 (14)

[a] Nonsignificant.

tween age groups ($P > 0.05$; table 20.5). In 1984, adults had a greater percentage of new (black) down than did juveniles ($P = 0.009$); table 20.5). Percentage of new down did not differ between the three migratory periods ($P > 0.05$; table 20.6). The percentage of incoming contour feathers was less during the late period than during the peak period ($P \leq 0.05$; table 20.6).

Table 20.6. Mean ovary weights (g) and extent of prebasic molt (%) for paired female mallards for three migratory periods in 1984

| | Early | | | Peak | | | Late | | |
Variable	Mean ± SE	(N)		Mean ± SE	(N)		Mean ± SE	(N)	
Ovary weight	0.51 ± 0.04	(7)	A[a]	0.81 ± 0.12	(9)	AB	1.13 ± 0.16	(12)	B
Incoming contour feathers	12 ± 2.3	(7)	AB	13 ± 2.7	(9)	B	6 ± 0.9	(12)	A
New (black) down	44 ± 14.8	(7)	A	64 ± 6.4	(9)	A	56 ± 8.8	(12)	A

[a] According to least significant difference tests, weights with shared letters are not significantly ($P \leq 0.05$) different.

Discussion

Weight and Lipid Dynamics

A comparison between body and lipid weights of Iowa spring migratory mallards with mallards during other periods of the annual cycle helps identify periods of body and lipid weight change. These comparisons are most appropriate when made with areas where Iowa mallards winter, migrate, and breed (Munro and Kimball 1982). Spring migratory mallards weighed more than mallards in winter (January/February) in Arkansas (Wright 1960), Mississippi (Delnicki and Reinecke 1986), and Missouri (White 1982) and slightly less than mallards in midwinter alternate plumage and initiation of prebasic molt status categories in southeastern Missouri (Heitmeyer 1985).

Mallards collected late during the wintering period (March) or during the early stages of spring migration on the wintering grounds often regained weight lost during January and February (Jorde 1981, Heitmeyer 1985). Spring migratory mallards in Iowa weighed more than mallards in some areas late in the wintering period or during spring migration (Jorde 1981, White 1982) but less than mallards on wintering areas or departing on spring migration farther south (Whyte and Bolen 1984a, Heitmeyer 1985).

Average lipid weights of female mallards collected in Iowa during spring migration were less than average lipid weights of mallards collected on the wintering grounds or during spring migration (Jorde 1981, White 1982, Whyte and Bolen 1984a, Heitmeyer 1985). But, by the final migratory period, Iowa-collected birds were fatter than mallards collected by White (1982) and Jorde (1981) during winter and spring, fatter than mallards collected by Whyte and Bolen (1984a) during all winter periods except their midwinter period, and fatter than mallards collected by Heitmeyer (1985) except for late prebasic molt and predeparture status birds. Extraction methodologies, geographic locations, and years varied among studies, making comparisons and interpretation difficult.

Spring migratory mallards had lower body and lipid weights than birds collected on arrival at the North Dakota breeding grounds (Krapu 1981). When the Iowa collections were divided into migratory periods, it was evident that female mallards were not at breeding body or lipid weights in the two earliest migratory periods; but, by the late migratory period, they had weights equivalent to mallards arriving on the breeding grounds (Krapu 1981).

Possible Strategies for Weight and Lipid Gains

Maintenance or gain of body and lipid weight occurs during spring migration, a period of the annual cycle when paired female mallards incur a variety of energetic costs, including migratory flight (Prince 1979), thermoregulation (Prince 1979), gonadal growth (Ricklefs 1974), and prebasic molt (Jorde 1981, Heitmeyer 1985). It must be to a mallard's ultimate advantage not only to meet these energetic costs but also to maintain or gain body weight and lipid reserves.

There are several possible advantages to mallards of maintaining body and lipid weight gained just before departure from the wintering grounds or of acquiring body and lipid weight during spring migration. One would be that these reserves are used as an energy source to meet the flight costs of migration. Second, since a mallard's winter energy balance can be adversely affected by inclement weather (Jorde 1981, Heitmeyer 1985), it would be advantageous for migrants to add lipid reserves during periods of favorable weather and food supply (Whyte and Bolen 1984b) to be used when environmental conditions deteriorate either during migration or on the breeding grounds. A third possible advantage, proposed by Krapu (1981), would be for the female mallard to acquire lipid reserves before arrival on the breeding grounds and expend them there in search of the invertebrates (Swanson et al. 1985) that are used for the exogenous protein required to produce the first clutch. Most likely, the ultimate strategy is that lipid reserves are used to meet the costs of the migratory flight, are stored as a "hedge" against inclement weather, and, finally, provide an energy source that allows the female to switch to invertebrate foraging on the breeding grounds.

Determining when during spring migration lipid reserves are acquired helps identify when and where habitats are needed. Collections made in 1983 were not partitioned, but it appeared that reserves were accumulating by mid-March, which suggests a steady rate gain in reserves. Collections were partitioned into three periods during 1984. A buildup of reserves was not detected during peak migration (late March) but had occurred by the last migratory period (April). Several factors may have been responsible for the delay in lipid gains during 1984. Below-normal temperatures in March may have increased thermoregulatory costs enough to prevent a buildup of reserves. Conditions were more favorable in April, perhaps accounting for the weight and lipid gains in the late period. Another possibility is that maintaining low body weight early during migration reduces flight costs (Pennycuick 1969). This explanation is less likely because mallard weight gains often begin prior to migration departure (Jorde 1981, Heitmeyer 1985). Finally, mallards collected during the late period were closer to nest initiation, evidenced by greater ovary weights, and may have carried maximum reserves to meet the demands of reproduction. So, in most years, reserves are likely to be added at a steady rate throughout migration, peaking just before departure from the last staging area (Raveling 1979). This pattern suggests that migratory habitats located nearest breeding areas may be the most important to ensure that adequate reserves are acquired.

Several factors enable spring migration to be a time of favorable energy balance for paired female mallards moving through Iowa. Abundant precipitation, along with melting snow, creates many seasonally flooded habitats that contain high-energy foods (corn, moist-soil plant seeds, and tubers) heavily used by paired female mallards (LaGrange 1985). Also, the paired female has the advantage of spending more time feeding (LaGrange 1985) while the male defends the foraging site (Jorde 1981).

Age-Related Aspects

Reproductive output of mallards has been related to age and possibly to age-related differences in female mallard lipid reserves upon arrival at the breeding grounds (Krapu and Doty 1979). No significant differences were detected between body and lipid weights of juvenile and adult spring migratory mallards in Iowa. The results of other mallard studies have varied. Juvenile mallards weigh less than adults in fall (Bellrose and Hawkins 1947) and winter (Gordon 1981, Whyte and Bolen 1984a), but age-related differences in body weight were not found during winter and early spring in other studies (Jorde 1981, Heitmeyer 1985). Upon arrival at the breeding grounds, juvenile hens are lighter than adults (Krapu and Doty 1979). In certain years, geographic locations, and times of year, juveniles can equal or even exceed adult body weights. This was the case for both 1983 and 1984 in Iowa, partly because collected birds of both age classes were paired, and because juvenile mallards on the spring migration are healthy, experienced, and able to add reserves at a rate equal to that of their adult counterparts. More research is needed into these age-related factors, including why juveniles are lighter in weight and lower in lipid reserves in some years than adults upon arrival at the breeding grounds.

Protein Reserves

Weight changes of certain organs and muscles may indicate storage or catabolization of protein (Ankney and MacInnes 1978) or changes in food habits (Ankney 1977, Drobney 1984). The lack of significant changes in female mallard protein reserves during spring migration agrees with some winter studies (Jorde 1981, Whyte and Bolen 1984a), but protein reserves did vary significantly in wintering female mallards in Missouri (Heitmeyer 1985). On the breeding grounds, Krapu (1981) found that protein reserves varied little between arrival, laying, and incubation. Therefore, female mallards do not acquire large reserves of protein during the spring migration, unlike some waterfowl species (Milne 1976, Ankney and MacInnes 1978, Peterson and Ellarson 1979, Raveling 1979), and do not use substantial endogenous protein reserves to produce a clutch (Krapu 1981). The slight changes that do occur are more likely the result of changes in food habits and molt (Heitmeyer 1985) than storage of protein for reproduction.

Management Implications

The implications of failing to meet the energetic needs of spring migratory mallards are many. It is possible that female mallard mortality could increase either through starvation (Jordan 1953) or decreased physical condition and possible increased risks of predation or disease. We did not observe that these were major problems for spring migrants in central Iowa. Potentially more serious are the sublethal effects of not meeting the energetic requirements of spring migrants, since a positive relationship between lipid reserves and clutch size has been shown for mallards (Krapu 1981, Rohwer 1984). It is possible that failure to meet a female mallard's nutritional needs during spring migration, especially in years when habitat conditions on the wintering grounds are poor (Heitmeyer 1985), will result in reduced recruitment to the North American mallard population (see Heitmeyer and Fredrickson 1981).

To ensure that the needs of spring migrants are met, we need to provide adequate habitat in the appropriate geographic locations. The results of this and other studies (LaGrange 1985) suggest that habitats providing a diversity of high-energy and nutritious food resources are needed. Moist-soil areas (Fredrickson and Taylor 1982) and the vegetatively similar, seasonally flooded (sheetwater) agricultural ponds (LaGrange 1985) can provide such resources. It is important to provide these habitats throughout the spring migratory range of the mallard, especially where the habitats are near the breeding grounds.

LITERATURE CITED

Ankney, C. D. 1977. Feeding and digestive organ size in breeding lesser snow geese. Auk 94:275–282.
———, and C. D. MacInnes. 1978. Nutrient reserves and reproductive performance of female lesser snow geese. Auk 95:459–471.
Bellrose, F. C. 1980. Ducks, geese and swans of North America. Stackpole Books, Harrisburg, Pa. 540pp.
———, and A. S. Hawkins. 1947. Duck weights in Illinois. Auk 64:422–430.
Delnicki, D., and K. J. Reinecke. 1986. Mid-winter food use and body weights of mallard and wood ducks in Mississippi. J. Wildl. Manage. 50:43–51.
Dinsmore, J. J., T. H. Kent, D. Koenig, P. C. Petersen, and D. M. Roosa. 1984. Iowa birds. Iowa State Univ. Press, Ames. 356pp.
Drobney, R. D. 1984. Effect of diet on visceral morphology of breeding wood ducks. Auk 101:93–98.
Fredrickson, L. H., and T. S. Taylor. 1982. Management of seasonally flooded impoundments for wildlife. U.S. Fish Wildl. Serv. Resour. Publ. 148. 29pp.
Gordon, D. H. 1981. Condition, feeding ecology and behavior of mallards wintering in north central Oklahoma. M.S. Thesis, Oklahoma State Univ., Stillwater. 68pp.
Heitmeyer, M. E. 1985. Wintering strategies of female mallards related to dynamics of lowland hardwood wetlands in the upper Mississippi delta. Ph.D. Diss., Univ. Missouri, Columbia. 378pp.
———, and L. H. Fredrickson. 1981. Do wetland conditions in the Mississippi delta hardwoods influence mallard recruitment? Trans. N. Am. Wildl. Nat. Resour. Conf. 46:44–57.
Hochbaum, H. A. 1942. Sex and age determination of waterfowl by cloacal examination. Trans. N. Am. Wildl. Conf. 7:299–307.
Horwitz, W. 1975. Official methods of analysis. 12th ed. Assoc. Off. Anal. Chem. Washington, D.C. 36pp.
Johnsgard, P. A. 1965. Handbook of waterfowl behavior. Cornell Univ. Press, Ithaca, N.Y. 378pp.
Jordan, J. S. 1953. Effects of starvation on wild mallards. J. Wildl. Manage. 17:304–311.
Jorde, D. G. 1981. Winter and spring staging ecology of mallards in south-central Nebraska. M.S. Thesis, Univ. North Dakota, Grand Forks. 166pp.
Krapu, G. L. 1981. The role of nutrient reserves in mallard reproduction. Auk 98:29–38.
———, and H. A. Doty. 1979. Age-related aspects of mallard reproduction. Wildfowl 30:35–39.

LaGrange, T. G. 1985. Habitat use and nutrient reserves dynamics of spring migratory mallards in central Iowa. M.S. Thesis, Iowa State Univ., Ames. 81pp.

Milne, H. 1976. Body weights and carcass composition of the common eider. Wildfowl 27:115–122.

Munro, R. E., and C. F. Kimball, 1982. Population ecology of the mallard. VII. Distribution and derivation of the harvest. U.S. Fish Wildl. Serv. Resour. Publ. 147. 127pp.

Pennycuick, C. J. 1969. The mechanics of bird migration. Ibis 111:525–556.

Peterson, S. R., and R. S. Ellarson. 1979. Changes in oldsquaw carcass weight. Wilson Bull. 91:288–300.

Prince, H. H. 1979. Bioenergetics of postbreeding dabbling ducks. Pages 103–117 in T. A. Bookhout, ed. Waterfowl and wetlands—an integrated review. Proc. 1977 Symp., Northcent. Sect., Wildl. Soc., Madison, Wis. 152pp.

Raveling, D. G. 1979. The annual cycle of body composition of Canada geese with special reference to control of reproduction. Auk 96:234–252.

Ray, A. A., ed. 1982. SAS user's guide: statistics. SAS Inst. Inc., Cary, N.C. 584pp.

Ricklefs, R. E. 1974. Energetics of reproduction in birds. Pages 152–292 in R. A. Paynter, Jr., ed. Avian energetics. Publ. Nuttall Ornithol. Club 15. 334pp.

Rohwer, F. C. 1984. Patterns of egg laying in prairie ducks. Auk 101:603–605.

Swanson, G. A., M. I. Meyer, and V. A. Adomaitis. 1985. Foods consumed by breeding mallards on wetlands of south-central North Dakota. J. Wildl. Manage. 49:197–203.

Tiner, R. W., Jr. 1984. Wetlands of the United States: current status and recent trends. U.S. Fish Wildl. Serv., Natl. Wetlands Inventory. 59pp.

White, D.C. 1982. Leaf decomposition, macroinvertebrate production, and wintering ecology of mallards in Missouri lowland hardwood wetlands. M.S. Thesis, Univ. Missouri, Columbia. 293pp.

Whyte, R. J., and E. G. Bolen. 1984a. Variation in winter fat depots and condition indices of mallards. J. Wildl. Manage. 48:1370–1373.

———, and ———. 1984b. Impact of winter stress on mallard body composition. Condor 86:477–482.

Wright, T. W. 1960. Weights of mallards in Arkansas. Proc. Southeast. Assoc. Game Fish Comm. 14:14–17.

21

Workshop Summary: Nutrition, Condition, and Ecophysiology

Kenneth J. Reinecke, C. Davison Ankney,
Gary L. Krapu, Ray B. Owen, Jr., Harold H. Prince,
and Dennis G. Raveling

Attendance at the evening discussion session and papers appearing in this volume illustrate the high level of current interest in research on ecophysiology (also see Anderson and Batt 1983). Recent studies in this area have made substantial contributions both to the management (e.g., Krapu 1979) and basic biology (e.g., Raveling 1979) of waterfowl. In this limited review, we summarize selected background data, research opportunities, and problems to avoid.

Nutrition

Early efforts to solve waterfowl conservation problems via propagation stimulated research on nutrient requirements (e.g., Holm and Scott 1954). Interest subsequently declined during the 1960s, but it recovered in the 1970s when field studies (e.g., Krapu 1979) and experimental work (Krapu and Swanson 1975) focused on the role of invertebrates as a protein source for nesting females. However, the nutrition of waterfowl in winter has received little study to date.

Examples of areas where contributions are needed include the basic macronutrient requirements of nonbreeding waterfowl and the nutritional requirements for specific activities such as molt and pair formation. Existing data for domesticated birds often are of limited value for interpreting the nutritional requirements of wild waterfowl. For example, commercial diets generally are formulated with grains, whereas wild geese must cope with diets containing high concentrations of complex structural chemicals whose metabolizability is unknown (Sedinger and Raveling 1984). The response of geese to improved winter

Waterfowl in Winter. © 1988 University of Minnesota. Edited by Milton W. Weller and published by the University of Minnesota Press, Minneapolis.

forage quality (e.g., Owen 1975) should provide many opportunities for research and management.

Interpretation of the nutritional implications of molt in waterfowl is difficult given current data. King (1980) summarized early experiments, mostly on small passerines, and concluded that molt is limited more by the intake of energy than of sulfur amino acids, although the latter are more concentrated in feathers than in the diet. Recent experiments with white-crowned sparrows (*Zonotrichia leucophrys*) support this interpretation (Murphy and King 1984), but field studies of the mallard (*Anas platyrhynchos*) suggest interactions of protein intake and nutrient reserves during the prebasic molt of females (Heitmeyer 1985; but also see Young and Boag 1982; King and Murphy 1985). Nutritional relationships during molt are not necessarily the same in both species, because of differences in body size and duration of the molt.

Nutritional interpretations of winter feeding ecology data for nonmolting birds also are limited (e.g., Junca et al. 1962, McLandress and Raveling 1981), primarily because basic macronutrient requirements for the maintenance of waterfowl have not been studied. Experiments similar to those conducted with breeding mallards (Foster 1976) would provide some of the necessary data.

Condition

Research on nutrient reserves in waterfowl began with Hanson's (1962) study of Canada geese (*Branta canadensis*). However, most data currently available (e.g., Korschgen 1977, Ankney and MacInnes 1978, Raveling 1979, Krapu 1981, Drobney 1984, and others) were collected in the 1970s and 1980s. Waterfowl researchers have been more concerned than other ornithologists with both lipid and protein reserves and, consequently, with integrated measures of nutrient status—i.e., "condition."

Although the concept of condition provides a valuable means of comparing the status of nutrient reserves in individuals from different habitats or social contexts, it also presents some theoretical problems. It is not always clear whether fat, protein, body weight, structural size, or some function of these variables is the best measure of condition, or whether birds with the highest condition scores are necessarily the most fit.

There are two basic designs for studies involving condition: in the first, data on resource use, social status, or some other variable of interest are obtained before a bird is collected for carcass analysis. In the second, birds are captured for condition measurements and then released for subsequent observation. The first method, which has been more popular to date, has several advantages: more data are obtained for each bird, a detailed analysis of nutrient dynamics is possible, the condition data and other observations represent essentially the same point in time, and the data obtained facilitate studies using the second method. The primary disadvantage is that high costs may limit sample size. Advantages of the second method are that collecting is avoided and large samples can be obtained. It also has several disadvantages: the condition data and other observations are sampled at different times; and, the data analyses involve either general ratios of weight and size, which may have undesirable statistical properties (Blem 1984), or species-specific condition indices, which are derived from data obtained in studies using the first method (e.g., Johnson et al. 1985).

Ecophysiology

A thorough review of ecophysiology exceeded the scope of our discussion. Consequently, we limited our consideration to some opportunities for research on energy relationships. Probably the most common use of energy concepts in waterfowl studies today is in the conversion of time budgets to energy requirements. The validity of estimates obtained in this way depends on the accuracy of data derived from laboratory studies of behavioral and thermoregulatory energy costs and on the conceptual model used to combine the time budget and energetics data (see Weathers et al. 1984).

Two other methods have been developed in recent years for estimating the energy requirements of free-living birds. Heat-transfer and doubly-labeled water techniques both are improvements over traditional time-activity-energy methods and provide a means of evaluating estimates developed from time-budget data. Initial results from such studies indicate that time-activity-energy estimates are only general averages, subject at times to errors of 20-40% (Weathers et al. 1984).

The new methods are not without limitations, however. Sample size is restricted in the doubly-labeled water method by the cost and availability of technology for working with isotopes, and in heat-transfer analysis by the detailed data required to characterize behavioral energy costs in the laboratory and thermal environments in the field. Also, doubly-labeled water estimates are averages for intervals, during which a variety of different activities might occur, and the heat-transfer methods are most effective in static situations such as at nest or roost sites.

Standardization of Methods

Although members of the panel supported standardizing methods, recommendations are difficult to make. Even for basic concepts like metabolizable energy, terminology and experimental methods remain controversial (e.g., Pesti and Edwards 1983, Miller and Reinecke 1984). However, certain practices clearly should be avoided. For example, fecal samples from experiments investigating nitrogen or protein retention should be analyzed wet, freeze-dried, or dried in a convection oven at a low temperature. Vacuum ovens, and convection ovens operated at high temperatures, cause substantial losses of nitrogen as ammonia

(Shannon and Brown 1969). Although procedures for drying tissues in carcass analysis research apparently are less restrictive (Kerr et al. 1982), subsequent extraction of lipids should follow recommended methods (Horwitz 1980) and, in particular, avoid using methanol as a solvent (Dobush and Ankney, in press).

General Remarks

Participants in the evening discussion session debated the relative merits of observational and experimental methods in future waterfowl research. Some members of the group were interested in collecting new or more complete data, and others in designing experiments to test predictions developed from existing data or theories. As noted by Wiens (1980 and related comments), the two approaches are complementary when effective communication occurs. We expect that waterfowl researchers not only will continue to collect observational data in response to the needs of management and interests of basic research, but also will increase their use of experimental methods (e.g., Rohwer 1985). Although limited, our review indicates that opportunities exist for maintaining the current level of interest in ecophysiology.

LITERATURE CITED

Anderson, M. G., and B. D. J. Batt. 1983. Workshop on the ecology of wintering waterfowl. Wildl. Soc. Bull. 11:22–24.

Ankney, C. D., and C. D. MacInnes. 1978. Nutrient reserves and reproductive performance of female lesser snow geese. Auk 95:459-471.

Blem, C. R. 1984. Ratios in avian physiology. Auk 101:153–155.

Dobush, G. R., C. D. Ankney, and D. G. Krementz. 1985. The effects of apparatus, extraction time, and solvent type on lipid extractions of snow geese. Can. J. Zool. 63:1917–1920.

Drobney, R. D. 1984. Body weight and composition changes and adaptations for breeding in wood ducks. Condor 84:300–305.

Foster, J. A. 1976. Nutritional requirements of captive breeding mallards. Ph.D. Thesis, Univ. Guelph, Ontario. 93pp.

Hanson, H. C. 1962. The dynamics of condition factors in Canada geese and their relation to seasonal stresses. Arct. Inst. N. Am. Tech. Pap. 12. 68pp.

Heitmeyer, M. E. 1985. Wintering strategies of female mallards related to dynamics of lowland hardwood wetlands in the Upper Mississippi Delta. Ph.D. Thesis, Univ. Missouri, Columbia. 378pp.

Holm, E. R., and M. L. Scott. 1954. Studies on the nutrition of wild waterfowl. N.Y. Fish Game J. 1:171–187.

Horwitz, W., ed. 1980. Official methods of analysis. 13th ed. Assoc. Off. Anal. Chem., Washington, D.C. 1,018pp.

Johnson, D. H., G. L. Krapu, K. J. Reinecke, and D. G. Jorde. 1985. An evaluation of condition indices for birds. J. Wildl. Manage. 49:569–575.

Junca, H. A., E. A. Epps, and L. L. Glasgow. 1962. A quantitative study of the nutrient content of food removed from the crops of wild mallards in Louisiana. Trans. N. Am. Wildl. Nat. Resour. Conf. 27:114–121.

Kerr, D. C., C. D. Ankney, and J. S. Millar. 1982. The effect of drying temperature on extraction of petroleum ether soluble fats of small birds and mammals. Can. J. Zool. 60:470–472.

King, J. R. 1980. Energetics of avian moult. Proc. Int. Ornithol. Congr. 17:312–317.

———, and M. E. Murphy. 1985. Periods of nutritional stress in the annual cycles of endotherms: fact or fiction? Am. Zool. 25:955–964.

Korschgen, C. E. 1977. Breeding stress of female eiders in Maine. J. Wildl. Manage. 41:360–373.

Krapu, G. L. 1979. Nutrition of female dabbling ducks during reproduction. Pages 59-70 in T. A. Bookhout, ed. Waterfowl and wetlands—an integrated review. Proc. 1977 Symp., Northcent. Sect., Wildl. Soc., Madison, Wis. 152pp.

———. 1981. The role of nutrient reserves in mallard reproduction. Auk 98:29–38.

———, and G. A. Swanson. 1975. Some nutritional aspects of reproduction in prairie nesting pintails. J. Wildl. Manage. 39:156–162.

McLandress, M. R., and D. G. Raveling. 1981. Changes in diet and body composition of Canada geese before spring migration. Auk 98:65–79.

Miller, M. R., and K. J. Reinecke. 1984. Proper expression of metabolizable energy in avian energetics. Condor 86:396–400.

Murphy, M. E., and J. R. King. 1984. Sulfur amino acid nutrition during molt in the white-crowned sparrow. 1. Does dietary sulfur amino acid concentration affect the energetics of molt as assayed by metabolized energy? Condor 86:314–323.

Owen, M. 1975. Cutting and fertilizing grassland for winter goose management. J. Wildl. Manage. 39:163–167.

Pesti, G. M., and H. M. Edwards, Jr. 1983. Metabolizable energy nomenclature for poultry feedstuffs. Poultry Sci. 62:1275–1280.

Raveling, D. G. 1979. The annual cycle of body composition of Canada geese with special reference to control of reproduction. Auk 96:234–252.

Rohwer, F. C. 1985. The adaptive significance of clutch size in prairie ducks. Auk 102:354–361.

Sedinger, J. S., and D. G. Raveling. 1984. Dietary selectivity in relation to availability and quality of food for goslings of cackling geese. Auk 101:295–306.

Shannon, D. W. F., and W. O. Brown. 1969. Losses of energy and nitrogen on drying poultry excreta. Poultry Sci. 48:41–43.

Weathers, W. W., W. A. Buttemer, A. M. Hayworth, and K. A. Nagy. 1984. An evaluation of time-budget estimates of daily energy expenditure in birds. Auk 101:459–472.

Wiens, J. A. 1980. Theory and observation in modern ornithology: a forum. Auk 97:409.

Young, D. A., and D. A. Boag. 1982. Changes in physical condition of male mallards (*Anas platyrhynchos*) during moult. Can. J. Zool. 60:3220–3226.

VI.
Habitat Resources and Habitat Selection

22

Waterfowl Use of Forested Wetlands of the Southern United States: An Overview

Leigh H. Fredrickson and Mickey E. Heitmeyer

Abstract: Forested wetlands of the southern United States tend to occur along a flooding gradient rather than as distinct basins. The timing, duration, and depth of flooding determine the structure and composition of vegetation. A complex of habitat types provides a rich source of plant and animal foods for the eight species of waterfowl commonly using southern forested wetlands in winter. The species include a carnivore (hooded merganser, *Mergus cucullatus*), two grazing herbivores (Canada goose, *Branta canadensis*; gadwall *Anas strepera*), three seed-eating herbivores (northern pintail, *Anas acuta*; green-winged teal, *Anas crecca*; ring-necked duck, *Aythya collaris*), and two omnivores (mallard, *Anas platyrhynchos*; wood duck, *Aix sponsa*). Annual and long-term fluctuations in flooding create a resource base that provides for the constantly changing needs of birds with different age, sex, pair, and social status. Management to ensure the survival and reproduction of waterfowl requires careful decisions on size, location, and type of acquisitions that enhance or simulate historical hydrologic regimes, and that maintain rich plant communities. Additional research must elucidate the relationships among short- and long-term flooding and food production as well as the distribution of southern wetlands. Integration of these results with information on waterfowl energetics, behavior, and habitat use will provide a framework for new management directions.

Waterfowl communities of breeding areas, such as those of the glacial prairie marshes of southern Canada and the north-central United States, are well known (Bellrose 1979) compared with our understanding of waterfowl use of wetlands in

Waterfowl in Winter. © 1988 University of Minnesota. Edited by Milton W. Weller and published by the University of Minnesota Press, Minneapolis.

winter (Fredrickson and Drobney 1979). Variations in nesting chronology (Bell-rose 1980), body sizes (Bellrose 1980), foraging modes (Siegfried 1976), social systems (McKinney 1973), and resource requirements on breeding areas (Swanson et al. 1979) allow exploitation of the same habitats by high densities of several species. Wetland complexes composed of ephemeral, temporary, semipermanent, and permanent waters in juxtaposition to good upland nesting cover provide high productive sites for breeding waterfowl. Preliminary evidence from southern habitats suggests that wintering waterfowl form feeding guilds similar to associations on breeding areas, and that wintering waterfowl species are distributed among habitats by water depths and structural features (White and James 1978, Thomas 1982).

Our purpose here is to provide an overview of published and unpublished research concerning the waterfowl community of forested wetlands in the southern United States, and to offer a conceptual framework that describes relationships among habitats and waterfowl. These forested wetlands support a community of waterfowl that respond to the annual hydrologic cycle by exploiting the constantly changing resources within wetlands. We use wood ducks and mallards to provide more specific examples of how waterfowl exploit similar habitats and how nutritional requirements and behavior aid in formulating management plans. Our perspectives were shaped primarily by experiences and data collection in the Upper Mississippi Alluvial Valley (UMAV) in southeastern Missouri.

We acknowledge stimulating discussions with P. W. Brown, R. D. Drobney, D. G. Raveling, K. J. Reinecke, and J. P. Rogers. The long-term support of G. K. Brakhage and J. P. Rogers, Office of Migratory Bird Management, is greatly appreciated. Wetland managers in the MAV are recognized for their cooperation and keen insights—especially T. G. Bell, J. L. Boyles, G. L. Claw-son, J. C. Johnson, W. D. Rundle, D. A. Schafer, and S. J. Young. P. W. Brown, D. G. Raveling, and F. A. Reid kindly reviewed the manuscript. K. J. Reinecke provided many helpful suggestions. Research was supported by the U.S. Fish and Wildlife Service through project numbers USDI 14-16-0009-80-1029, USDI-14-16-0009-83-945, USDI-FWS-14-16-0009-78-974, USDI-FWS-14-16-0009-1509-4, and USDI-FWS-14-16-0008-1195. Contribution from Gaylord Memorial Laboratory (School of Forestry, Fisheries, and Wildlife, University of Missouri at Columbia and Missouri Department of Conservation cooperating), Missouri Agricultural Experiment Station project 170 and 183, journal series 9845.

Characteristics of Southern Forested Wetlands

Southern forested wetlands include several types of the palustrine system (Cowardin et al. 1979) occurring along flooding gradients in drainage basins, regardless of their size. In the southeastern United States, forested wetlands usually occur as interconnected wetland types along a flooding gradient, rather than as distinct basins. Vegetation with decreasing flood tolerance occurs along a continuum from the lowest to the highest elevations (fig. 22.1; also see Teskey and Hinckley 1977, Bedinger 1978, Fredrickson 1978). Although some authors distinguish

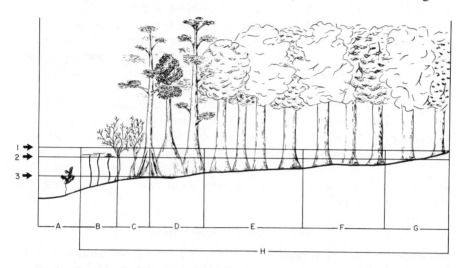

Fig. 22.1. Flooding gradient of southern forested wetland showing duration and depths of seasonal flooding. 1 = Maximum high water, 2 = annual mean high water, and 3 = annual mean low water. A-H are wetland habitats, with flood duration (months) shown in parentheses: A = openwater, submergent plant (11-12); B = robust emergent (10-12); C = shrub/scrub (8-12); D = forested, cypress-tupelo (6-8); E = forested, overcup oak-red maple (4-6); F = forested, pin oak/sweet gum (1-6); G = forested, cherrybark oak/willow oak (1-3); and H = moist-soil, occurring throughout depending on season (variable).

vegetation types along flooding gradients as *zones* or *bottoms*, the irregular land surface and the range of flood tolerance for each tree species usually create a mosaiclike patchwork of forest types rather than extensive areas or zones of a single tree species.

Types of Flooding

The hydrologic conditions of southern forested wetlands are driven by annual and long-term fluctuations in precipitation. Between 1961 and 1978, annual rainfall averaged 114 cm and varied from 64 to 191 cm in Mingo Swamp of southeastern Missouri (U.S. Dep. Commerce 1961-78). Although the heaviest rainfall normally occurs in April or May, any month may have 25 cm of precipitation in a few days. These annual variations in precipitation provide the proximate cues that determine when biological events occur, whereas long-term variations ultimately influence morphology and social systems of waterfowl. Observations in the Mingo Basin of southeastern Missouri suggest that three distinct types of flooding occur

(Fredrickson 1979, Heitmeyer 1985). Puddling, which is the most common, occurs when shallow depressions in the rather flat landscape gradually fill with surface water from on-site rainfall. Individual depressions may fill and dry several times during the annual cycle. With cooler temperatures in fall, senesced trees stop transpiring and evaporation decreases about the time precipitation increases. These processes initiate backwater flooding, which typically occurs during the dormant season. As surface water accumulates, puddles become small pools, small pools become large pools, and large pools become interconnected as entire drainage basins gradually fill with water. In northern portions of the MAV, backwater flooding of most drainage basins occurs at least once annually. The third type of flooding, known as flash flooding, is the least frequent (5- to 10-year periodicity). Flash floods follow brief periods of heavy rainfall when 15-30 cm of precipitation fall in a day. Characteristics of such rainfall include immediate flooding throughout entire drainage basins, large allochthonous inputs from the surrounding watershed, extensive scouring action, deposition of heavy sediment loads, and modification of drainage patterns.

Distribution of Vegetation

In the lowest elevations, permanent water may be present in old oxbows (fig. 22.1). Vegetation such as watermilfoil (*Myriophyllum* spp.), hornwort (*Ceratophyllum* spp.), naiad (*Najas* spp.), and Canadian waterweed (*Elodea canadensis*) are common submergents. Where water depths are 1 m or less, rooted emergents including American Lotus (*Nelumbo lutea*), white waterlily (*Nymphaea tuberosa*), spatterdock cowlily (*Nuphar advena*), and Schreber watershield (*Brasenia schreberi*) are often abundant. Shrub/scrub habitats with common buttonbush (*Cephalanthus occidentalis*), swamp privet (*Forestiera acuminata*), and waterelm (*Planera aquatica*) occur as distinct zones or intermixed with robust emergents. Depending on seasonal variation of flooding, annual plants such as smartweeds (*Polygonum* spp.) and millets (*Echinochloa* spp.) germinate on sites that are exposed before mid-June (Fredrickson and Taylor 1982). Exposure of mud flats in June or later results in germination of sprangletop (*Leptochloa* sp.), beggarticks (*Bidens* spp.), and flatsedges (*Cyperus* spp.).

The most flood-tolerant trees, common baldcypress (*Taxodium distichum*) and water tupelo (*Nyssa aquatica*), are abundant in sites where forests are flooded to the greatest depths for the longest periods (Fredrickson 1978; fig. 22.1). Somewhat higher in elevation, but where flooding usually extends at least one month into the growing season, overcup oak (*Quercus lyrata*), red maple (*Acer rubrum*), and waterlocust (*Gleditsia aquatica*) are abundant. As elevations increase, flooding duration and depth decrease, and water hickory (*Carya aquatica*), pin oak (*Quercus palustris*), American sweetgum (*Liquidambar styraciflua*), American elm (*Ulmus americana*), willow oak (*Quercus phellos*), and red ash (*Fraxinus pennsyl-*

vanica) are present (Fredrickson 1978). Where flooding is shallow and infrequent, southern red cherrybark oak (*Quercus falcata* var. *pagodaefolia*), sugar hackberry (*Celtis laevigata*), and hickories (*Carya* spp.) become abundant.

In general, baldcypress/tupelo are flooded for six to eight months, overcup oak/red for maple for four to six months, pin oak/Nuttall oak (*Quercus nuttallii*) for one to six cherrybark oak/willow oak for one to two months (fig. 22.1). Variation in flooding among these wetland types makes plant and animal resources available throughout the annual cycle for waterfowl and other wildlife (table 22.1). The exact timing of resource availability during a given cycle is dependent on the amounts and timing of precipitation. These different forest components represent sites within southern wetlands having differing hydrologic regimes (Bedinger 1978).

Table 22.1. Types of waterfowl foods produced in forested wetlands.

Wetland type	Plant	Animal
Aquatic bed		
Open water—submergent	Browse	Insects
		Snails
		Crustaceans
Floating—watershield	Seeds	Insects
Emergent wetland		
American lotus	None	None
Moist-soil	Seeds	Insects
	Tubers	Crayfish
	Browse	Snails
Scrub/shrub wetland	Seeds	Insects
		Crayfish
		Snails
Forested wetlands		
Baldcypress/water tupelo	Tupelo drupes	Crayfish
Overcup oak/red maple	Samaras	Small crustaceans
		Crayfish
		Spiders
Pin oak/Nuttall oak	Acorns	Small crustaceans
	Samaras	Crayfish
		Spiders
Willow oak/cherrybark oak	Acorns	Small crustaceans
	Samaras	Crayfish
		Spiders

Large, shallow depressions and single-tree openings within forested sites (moist-soil habitats) provide an abundance of seeds, tubers, browse, and some invertebrates (Fredrickson and Taylor 1982) in fall, but resources are often depleted or flooded too deeply in spring for efficient utilization by waterfowl (table 22.1). Although robust floating-leaf plants like waterlilies and watershield are seed producers, their growth form is not conducive to high invertebrate populations (Reid 1983). Seeds from emergents like American lotus are large and rarely used by waterfowl (Drobney and Fredrickson 1979, Heitmeyer 1985). Shrub/scrub habitats provide some seeds as well as browse and insects. The baldcypress/ tupelo wetlands provide good cover, but food production is primarily insects and tupelo drupes.

Overcup oak acorns are too large for waterfowl use. Nevertheless, crustaceans and dipteran larvae inhabiting litter, as well as samaras produced by red maples associated with this flooding regime, provide important foods. Samaras are valuable spring foods for wood ducks (Drobney and Fredrickson 1979) because of their protein and lipid content (Drobney 1977). Pin, Nuttall, cherrybark, and willow oaks provide acorns of high energy and ideal size for waterfowl consumption. Crayfish (*Procambarus* sp.) are abundant in these forest habitats, and isopods (*Asellus intermedius*), amphipods (*Crangonyx* sp.), and fingernail clams (*Pisidium fallux*) are present in flooded leaf litter. At higher elevations, small crustaceans, especially aquatic isopods, are abundant in leaf litter of pin oak sites (White 1985).

Although there are similarities in the composition of invertebrate resources between overcup oak and pin oak habitats, some differences are apparent in invertebrate numbers and the timing of responses to flooding (Batema et al. 1985). Overcup and pin oak sites support a relatively small number of invertebrate species including fingernail clams, oligochaetes, snails, freshwater shrimp (*Palaemonetes* sp.), isopods, amphipods, and insect larvae and nymphs. Pin oak habitats tend to have a greater population density of chironomids, fingernail clams, and amphipods in fall, whereas more of these individuals are present in overcup oak sites in spring (Batema et al. 1985). Isopod density is greater in both forest types in late winter and spring.

Greentree reservoir management is a common technique used in southern forests with acorn-producing trees. Levees are constructed around forests and the sites are flooded in fall by pumping or gravity flow. Managed flooding typically occurs more quickly, earlier in the season, and to greater depths than natural flooding in forests. Although acorns have long been the target foods in greentree reservoirs, samaras, as well as invertebrates and other fruits, berries, and seeds, are produced in abundance (Hubert and Krull 1973, White 1985). Managed flooding appears to influence forest composition (Fredrickson 1979, Newling 1981) and the abundance and composition of foods as well (Batema et al. 1985). Naturally flooded habitats have a greater abundance of invertebrates than greentree reservoirs (Batema et al. 1985). Abundance of invertebrates in forested wetlands is closely associated with the litter decomposition process (White 1985, Batema et al. 1985, Wylie 1985). Once litter accumulates on the forest floor and is flooded, it is colonized by bacteria and fungi. Pin oak leaves provide a relatively stable nutrient source: after one year, 52% of the biomass (dry weight) remains; after 21 months, 30% remains (Wylie 1985). Peak duck use of these habitats occurs during the first two to three months after flooding when rapid decomposition occurs (Wylie 1985, Heitmeyer 1985).

Annual Events of Waterfowl

Migratory Anatinae undergo at least three important biological processes within an annual cycle (Weller 1964, 1965, 1980; Palmer 1976; Heitmeyer 1985): reproduction (pairing, laying, incubation, brood-rearing), migration (fall and spring), and molt (at least one complete and one partial; Humphrey and Parkes 1959). Migrations may overlap with the molts and/ or pairing (Weller 1957). Migratory distance, location, and chronology vary within and among species. Migratory geese have only a single body molt/ cycle, and they generally pair for life; thus, Anserinae have fewer energetically expensive events in the annual cycle. Each of these biological processes requires different quantities and types of nutrients (Nat. Res. Council 1977) that influence social and behavioral constraints on individuals (Heitmeyer 1985).

Timing of these annual events and the geographic location where the event is undertaken vary both within and among species. For mallards, the sequence of events starting with postbreeding dispersal is premigratory staging, fall migration, fall-winter molt, pairing, winter-spring molt, spring migration, laying, incubation, brood-rearing, and summer molt (Heitmeyer 1985). Differences within a species are related to sex, age, physiological condition, social status, habitat, and weather variables. Most migratory waterfowl undergo portions of two or three of these major annual events during the five to eight months they spend on southern wetlands in winter.

We use the term *wintering* in a broad context to mean the time spent by an individual on southern wetlands following fall migration and preceding major movements northward in spring. Local and regional movements (often northward) occur in some waterfowl species and locations especially in late winter. These movements are usual phenomena within the "wintering strategies" of many species and appear commonly among those using dynamic forested habitats.

Use of Forested Wetlands by Waterfowl

Eight species of waterfowl regularly use forested wetlands in the southern United States for varying lengths of time in winter where they undergo different biological events. Categorized by their food consumption while using forested habitats, these include one carnivore—hooded merganser; five herbivores—gadwall, Canada goose, northern pintail, green-winged teal, ring-necked duck; and two omnivores—

mallard and wood duck. Historically, trumpeter swans (*Cygnus buccinator*) also were present during winter on forested wetlands, where they primarily grazed on aquatic vegetation and consumed *Sagittaria* and *Cyperus* tubers (Banko 1960). Although these eight species commonly use similar habitats within forested wetlands, they have different feeding niches and are temporally and spatially segregated.

Carnivores—Hooded Merganser

Hooded mergansers are present on forested wetlands in the MAV throughout the year, concentrating their use in deeper and more permanently flooded sloughs, backwaters, rivers, dead-tree, beaver pond, scrub/shrub, and overcup oak habitats. Use of different wetland types by hooded mergansers seems to coincide with crayfish abundance and availability. Shrub/scrub habitats are particularly important during prebreeding and breeding. Tree cavities used by hooded mergansers must be of proper size and located in trees that are within or immediately adjacent to water. Hooded mergansers utilize forested wetlands in the UMAV less in midwinter than in spring, summer, and fall, whereas Lower Mississippi Alluvial Valley (LMAV) wetlands are used throughout the year.

Grazing Herbivores—Canada Goose, Gadwall

Large Canada geese (*B. c. interior* and *B. c. maxima*) historically wintered in large numbers in forested wetlands in the MAV (Hanson and Smith 1950, 116-125; Hanson 1965, 94-97) and nested along the Mississippi and Missouri rivers and within cypress swamps in southeastern Missouri, western Tennessee, and northeastern Arkansas (Kliph 1881; Widmann 1907, 46; Howell 1911). At present, the numbers of these "forest-adapted" Canada geese are reduced in the MAV and are more common in more northerly habitats. Many of them probably concentrated along the Mississippi riverine wetlands where they consumed moist-soil seeds, browse, and tubers along river bars, oxbows, and larger open areas within forested habitats. Specific food items probably included smartweed seeds, tender new shoots of *Eleocharis* and *Cyperus*, and roots and tubers of *Sagittaria* and *Cyperus*. Some Canada geese were distributed as far south as the coastal marshes of the Louisiana Deltaic Plain (Hankla and Rudolph 1967). Seeds were probably more commonly consumed in fall and winter, and sedges and grasses were consumed in spring (Korschgen 1955).

The maintenance of pair and family bonds (Raveling 1969, 1970) and a partial molt, which are important activities of wintering Canada geese, probably are influenced by seasonal changes in food type, quantity, and quality (McLandress and Raveling 1981a, 1981b; Johnson and Raveling 1987).

Gadwalls have strong traditions of spending fall, early winter, and late spring in scrub/shrub, dead-tree, and slough habitats in the UMAV (Bellrose 1980). During midwinter, most gadwalls move farther south where they concentrate on scrub/

shrub, slough, and freshwater marsh habitats. Some gadwalls complete two molts and become paired while on forested wetlands (Paulus 1980). Gadwalls consume moist-soil seeds, vegetative parts of aquatic plants, and a large amount of algae (Palmer 1976, Paulus 1982). Invertebrates increase as a component of their diets during late winter and spring (M. E. Heitmeyer, unpubl. data). The relationship between the biological processes and the use of marsh and forested habitats by gadwalls is largely unknown.

Seed-Eating Herbivores—Northern Pintail, Green-Winged Teal, Ring-Necked Duck

Pintails use flooded, open-marsh areas and single-tree openings within forested wetlands during fall and spring, primarily during migrational stopovers (Heitmeyer 1985). Large concentrations of pintails (more than 50,000) often occur on large, shallowly flooded open-marsh habitats where moist-soil vegetation is abundant and visibility great within forested locations. Pintails are omnivores in most other parts of the North American range, but they primarily consume seeds and tubers from moist-soil plants during their stay in these large forest openings. Both sexes of pintails molt while using openings in forested wetlands in fall and spring (M. E. Heitmeyer, unpubl. data).

Green-winged teal use flooded open-marsh areas, riparian zones of sloughs and river backwaters, and dead-tree habitats in forested wetlands in the MAV throughout fall and spring (Heitmeyer 1985). Green-winged teal actively engage in the fall-winter molt while on forested wetlands, and some individuals delay the wing molt until arrival on southern habitats (Rogers 1967). Green-winged teal also molt in spring, and many females are actively engaged in courtship and pairing while using forested wetlands in late winter. Green-winged teal primarily consume small moist-soil seeds (e.g., *Amaranthus*, *Eleocharis*, *Panicum*) but also may consume many invertebrates in fall and spring.

Ring-necked ducks utilize deeper open-marsh areas and deep-water sloughs extensively in fall and spring, and smaller numbers spend the entire winter within forested wetlands. Some ring-necked ducks undergo the fall-winter molt, pairing, and initiation of the winter-spring molt while on forested wetlands. Ring-necked ducks regularly consume seeds or tubers of aquatic vegetation (T. Scott Taylor, pers. commun.).

Omnivores—Mallards, Wood Ducks

Mallards and wood ducks are the most abundant and best understood waterfowl using southern forested wetlands. Traditionally, more mallards winter in the UMAV than in any other location in the Nearctic (Bellrose 1980). The MAV is also the primary breeding and wintering range of wood ducks (Bellrose 1980). Mallards begin arriving in the UMAV in large numbers by early November and most depart by mid—March. During their stay on southern forested wetlands, mallards complete the fall-winter molt, become paired, initiate the winter-spring molt (some individuals complete this molt while in the MAV), and some females store nutrient reserves used in spring migration and as reserves for reproduction (Krapu 1981, Heitmeyer 1985).

Forested wetlands provide all resources required by wood ducks during their annual cycle (Drobney 1977, Armbruster 1982). Likewise, forested wetlands often provide all nutritional and habitat requirements of mallards throughout winter (Heitmeyer 1985), but the abundance and availability of resources vary within seasons, among years, and among geographic locations (Fredrickson 1979, Heitmeyer and Fredrickson 1981, Heitmeyer 1985). Although mallards and wood ducks seem to utilize a greater biomass of resources from forested wetlands and have more overlap in habitat and food use than other waterfowl using forested wetlands, their respective life history strategies allow the two species access to similar resources within the same habitat.

Strategies of Mallards and Wood Ducks

Habitat Use—Geographic

Major concentrations of mallards and wood ducks are separated spatially in winter. Wood ducks tend to use forested wetlands throughout the MAV during reproduction, brood-rearing (March-July), and staging in early fall, but areas north of the White River within the MAV are used little in winter and rarely during severe winters. By mid-November, most wood ducks move south to spend the winter in the LMAV below Memphis. In contrast, most mallards utilize forested wetlands no farther south than Arkansas throughout winter (November-March; Bellrose 1980). Numbers of mallards utilizing Louisiana wetlands in winter increase during periods of extremely harsh weather. Overall, the geographic centers of wintering are different for the two species: mallards in northeastern Arkansas and wood ducks in Louisiana. Mallards readily use agricultural habitats, but this use may be related to abundance, quality, and availability of forested wetlands (Heitmeyer and Vohs 1984, Heitmeyer 1985). Wood ducks also use croplands but to a much lesser extent than mallards, especially where extensive forested wetlands are present.

Timing of Annual Events and Habitat Use

Within the forested wetlands of the Mingo Basin in southeastern Missouri, mallards and wood ducks tend to use different wetland types at different times in the annual cycle according to the biological process of molt, pairing, breeding, or staging that is in progress (fig. 22.2). Wood ducks generally return to the Mingo Basin in abundance in late February and initially concentrate on slough, river,

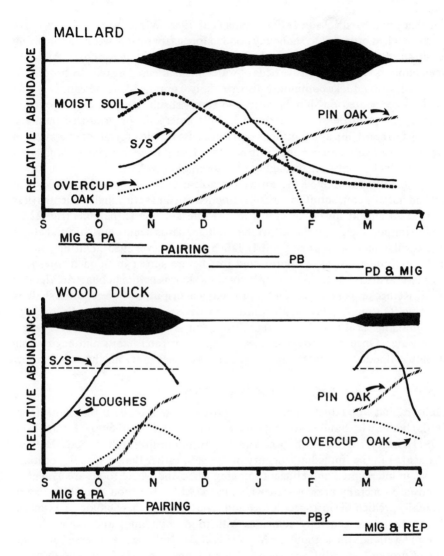

Fig. 22.2. Use of southern forested wetland complexes by wood ducks and mallards in relation to biological activities from September to April MIG & PA = migration and prealternate molt, PB = prebasic molt, PD & MIG = predeparture and migration, MIG & REP = migration and reproduction, and S/S = shrub/scrub. Data from Heitmeyer (1985).

shrub/scrub, and overcup oak habitats (fig. 22.2). Peak nest initiation in the Mingo Basin is middle to late March. During laying, wood ducks forage extensively in shallowly flooded forests where invertebrate foods occur in abundance

(Drobney and Fredrickson 1979, Batema et al. 1985, White 1985). Females move newly hatched broods into shallowly flooded forests for several weeks before using scrub/shrub and more permanently flooded wetlands with dense cover. At times, open habitats such as extensive beds of watershield are used heavily by broods. In early fall, wood ducks commonly disperse daily from the Mingo Basin. Daytime use is concentrated on slough, river, and scrub/shrub habitats. Night roosting usually occurs in dense scrub/shrub, robust emergent, or dead-tree habitats. During fall courtship and pairing, wood ducks use flooded forests of overcup and cypress-tupelo as well as scrub/shrub habitats. Use of these forested wetland types by wood ducks continues throughout winter in the LMAV.

Most mallards complete the fall-winter molt after arrival in the Mingo Basin in fall and initially concentrate on recently flooded openings with shallow depths (less than 15-25 cm) at lower elevations in live forest or marsh habitats (fig. 22.2). Following completion of the fall-winter molt, mallards begin courtship and about 90% of all females are paired by early January (Heitmeyer 1985). During pairing, mallards forage just after sunrise and just before sunset in flooded forests or agricultural areas. At times, mallards consume acorns before habitats are flooded (K. J. Reinecke, pers. commun.), but usually acorn utilization requires shallow flooding. During midday, small courting parties are present in sloughs, overcup oak sites, and scrub/shrub habitats. Throughout winter, mallards roost on larger open water. Once mallards pair, they change their food habits and begin using shallowly flooded forests throughout the day until they move northward in spring.

Feeding Niches

Mallards and wood ducks modify their consumption of foods as their nutritional needs change with biological events in the annual cycle (Drobney and Fredrickson 1979, Heitmeyer 1985). Both species are highly mobile in search of foods. Defense of the area in the immediate vicinity of the pair, rather than a specific location, allows uninterrupted and efficient foraging when and where foods are available. Foods are generally present somewhere in the MAV, but food availability is not generally predictable in a specific location. The timing of these biological events in the annual cycle generally coincides with food abundance and availability in forested wetlands throughout the MAV (fig. 22.3). Both species increase consumption of protein foods during molt and laying. Consumption of high-energy foods increases during periods of weight gain (initiation of pairing, molt, and spring migration) and during midwinter freezes. Within the Mingo Basin, mallards primarily consume moist-soil seeds and aquatic insects during the fall-winter molt, acorns and row crops during pairing and midwinter maintenance, and acorns and crustacean invertebrates during the winter-spring molt and predeparture phase of spring migration (Heitmeyer 1985). Wood ducks primarily consume aquatic

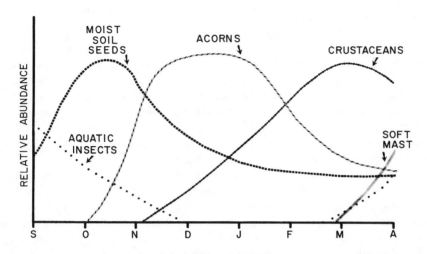

Fig. 22.3. Availability of food resources in southern forested wetlands from September to April. Data from Batema et al. (1985), Heitmeyer (1985), and White (1985).

insects, spiders, samaras, and crustaceans during reproduction; aquatic insects and seeds in summer; and acorns and tupelo drupes during courtship and pairing in midwinter (Drobney and Fredrickson 1979). Even though some of the same foods are consumed by mallards and wood ducks, timing of consumption of a specific food, geographic location, mode of feeding, and constantly changing water levels reduce potential competition. Mallards typically feed by subsurface dabbling on foods found intermixed with leaf litter on the bottom, whereas wood ducks typically feed by pecking at foods on or slightly below (1-3 cm) the surface (Drobney and Fredrickson 1979, Heitmeyer 1985).

Information on food and habitat use by mallards and wood ducks further implicates the importance of good wetland habitat conditions in winter for maintenance of continental populations. Because all members of a mallard or wood duck population are not engaged in the same biological process at the same time or location, a variety of nutritional and social requirements are met simultaneously by different wetland types at a location. These "good" wetland conditions include natural forested wetland complexes present throughout the MAV where flooding regimes resemble historical water fluctuations.

Both mallards and wood ducks utilize the entire complex of forested wetland types that are flooded during their stay in the Mingo Basin. No single habitat type provides all of their winter requirements; rather, all wetland types meet the constantly changing nutritional and behavioral needs of mallards and wood ducks over the annual cycle.

Implications for Management and Research

We believe that different morphological, behavioral, and physiological adaptations of waterfowl species have evolved with habitat structure and function. Because of complex interactions among waterfowl and their habitats, future research should be approached from a management perspective to integrate ideas from different disciplines relating to wetlands and avian ecology. Understanding the location, chronology, timing, benefits, and costs of the biological processes that waterfowl undergo while on southern wetlands will identify the type, value, location, and distribution of resources. Likewise, an understanding of food chains and hydrology will increase the potential to provide these resources.

We suggest some valuable research questions in relation to all southern wetlands and wintering waterfowl: (1) What are the distribution, size, and area of each wetland type within southern lowland forests? (2) What are the life histories of key plant species? (3) What are the dynamics of food, water, and cover in each wetland type? (4) What are the nutritional qualities of different foods? (5) What are the roles of aquatic detrital, nektonic, grazing, and terrestrial detrital food chains in different southern wetlands? (6) What, when, and where are the major biological processes undertaken by different species, sex, and age groups of waterfowl? (7) What is the cost in time and energy for these biological processes? (8) How do birds of each species, sex, age, and social status handle these biological processes and costs? Although this list of research needs is awesome, some progress has been made in improving the management of southern forests for waterfowl. The current state of our knowledge about forested wetlands and exploitation of their resources by wintering waterfowl has grown slowly. Nevertheless, these meager data suggest management scenarios useful in maintaining and preserving forested wetland systems and the waterfowl populations dependent upon them.

Remnant tracts of southern wetlands should be protected by acquisition, easements, favorable taxation, or regulations such as section 404 of the Clean Water Act. Efforts should be made to maintain a proportional area of each wetland type relative to the original composition. Whenever possible, the natural hydrology should be maintained or simulated. Deep and permanent flooding is undesirable and should be avoided. Availability of foods at optimum foraging depths should be enhanced. For example, optimum foraging depths for mallards are 15-25 cm, yet managed areas often exceed this depth. Water depth on moist-soil habitats, greentree reservoirs, and forests should be manipulated to optimize the area at depths used by foraging ducks. The timing of manipulations should be based on long-term and annual fluctuations in rainfall as well as historical flood cycles. Different habitats in juxtaposition (10 km or less) are important in providing a variety of resources in a locale. Size, distance between habitat types, and area with manageable water depths are important considerations in making decisions for acqusition, easements, permits, and management. Species richness should be maintained in wetland habitats. Acorns are valuable high-energy foods, but the red oak group has inconsistent acorn production. Red maple, elm, and ash produce samaras in abundance annually and should be maintained as important trees within lowland forests. Detritus (leaves from woody plants, entire structures from annuals) and timely flooding provide the nutrient base for macroinvertebrate production in forests. The recent losses and perturbations in southern wetlands require our immediate attention. Certain populations of waterfowl, as well as an array of other wildlife, are dependent upon imaginative and dedicated efforts by managers and researchers to maintain the vitality of these dynamic southern habitats.

LITERATURE CITED

Armbruster, J. S. 1982. Wood duck displays and pairing chronology. Auk 99:116–122.

Banko, W. E. 1960. The trumpeter swan: its history, habits, and population in the United States. N. Am. Fauna 63, Bur. Sport Fish Wildl. Washington, D.C. 214pp.

Batema, D. L., G. S. Henderson, and L. H. Fredrickson. 1985. Wetland invertebrates distribution in bottomland hardwoods as influenced by forest type and flooding regime. Pages 196-202 in J. O. Doson and K. A. Majerus, eds. Proc. 5th Central Hardwood Conference. Dep. Forestry, Univ. Illinois, Urbana/Champaign. 299pp.

Bedinger, M. S. 1978. Relation between forest species and flooding. Pages 427-435 in P. E. Greeson, J. R. Clark, and J. E. Clark, eds. Wetland functions and values: the state of our understanding. Am. Water Resour. Assoc., Minneapolis.

Bellrose, F. C. 1979. Species distribution, habitats, and characteristics of breeding dabbling ducks in North America. Pages 1-15 in T. A. Bookhout, ed. Waterfowl and wetlands—an integrated review. Northcent. Sect. Wildl. Soc., Madison, Wis. 152pp.

———. 1980. Ducks, geese and swans of North America. Stackpole Books, Harrisburg, Pa. 540pp.

Cowardin, L. M., V. Carter, F. C. Golet, and E. T. LaRoe. 1979. Classification of wetlands and deep-water habitats of the United States. U.S. Fish Wildl. Serv. FWS/OBS-79/31.

Drobney, R. D. 1977. The feeding ecology, nutrition, and reproductive bioenergetics of wood ducks. Ph.D. Diss., Univ. Missouri, Columbia. 170pp.

———, and L. H. Fredrickson. 1979. Food selection by wood ducks in relation to breeding status. J. Wildl. Manage. 43:109–120.

Fredrickson, L. H. 1978. Lowland hardwood wetlands: current status and habitat values for wildlife. Pages 296-306 in P. E. Greeson, J. R. Clark, and J. E. Clark, eds. Wetland functions and values: the state of our understanding. Am. Water Resour. Assoc., Minneapolis.

———. 1979. Floral and faunal changes in lowland hardwood forests in Missouri resulting from channelization, drainage, and impoundment. U.S. Fish Wildl. Serv. FWS/OBS-78191. 130pp.

———, and R. D. Drobney. 1979. Habitat utilization by postbreeding waterfowl. Pages 119-130 in T. A. Bookhout, ed. Waterfowl and wetlands—an integrated review. Northcent. Sect. Wildl. Soc. Madison, Wis. 152pp.

———, and T. S. Taylor. 1982. Management of seasonally flooded impoundments for wildlife. U.S. Fish Wildl. Serv. Resour. Publ. 148. 29pp.

Hankla, D. J., and R. R. Rudolph. 1967. Changes in the migration and wintering habitats of Canada geese in the lower portion of the Atlantic and Mississippi flyways—with special reference to national wildlife refuges. Proc. Southeast. Assoc. Game Fish Comm. 21:133–144.

Hanson, H. C. 1965. The giant Canada goose. Southern Illinois Univ. Press, Carbondale. 225pp.

————, and R. Smith. 1950. Canada geese of the Mississippi flyway with special references to an Illinois flock. Ill. Nat. Hist. Surv. Bull. 25:67–210.

Heitmeyer, M. E. 1985. Wintering strategies of female mallards related to dynamics of lowland hardwood wetlands in the upper Mississippi Delta. Ph.D. Diss., Univ. Missouri, Columbia. 448 pp.

————, and L. H. Fredrickson. 1981. Do wetland conditions in the Mississippi Delta hardwoods influence mallard recruitment? Trans. N. Am. Wildl. Nat. Resour. Conf. 46:44–57.

————, and P. A. Vohs, Jr. 1984. Distribution and habitat use of waterfowl wintering in Oklahoma. J. Wildl. Manage. 48:51–62.

Howell, A. H. 1911. Birds of Arkansas. U.S. Biol. Serv. Bull. 38:1–100.

Hubert, W. A., and J. N. Krull. 1973. Seasonal fluctuations of aquatic macroinvertebrates in Oakwoods Bottoms Greentree Reservoir. Am. Midl. Nat. 90:351–364.

Humphrey, P. S., and K. C. Parkes. 1959. An approach to the study of molts and plumages. Auk 76:1–31.

Johnson, J. C. and D. G. Raveling. 1988. Weak family association in cackling geese during winter; effects of body size and food resources on goose social organization. Pages 71-89 in M. W. Weller, ed. Waterfowl in winter. Univ. Minnesota Press, Minneapolis.

Kliph. 1881. The Franklin Club at Reelfoot. Forest Stream 16:244–245.

Korschgen, L. J. 1955. Fall foods of waterfowl in Missouri. Missouri Conserv. Comm. D. R. Prog. Rep. 14. 41 pp.

Krapu, G. L. 1981. The role of nutrient reserves in mallard reproduction. Auk 98:29–38.

McKinney, F. 1973. Ecoethological aspects of reproduction. Pages 6-21 in D. S. Farner, ed. Breeding biology of birds. Natl. Acad. Sci., Washington, D.C. 515 pp.

McLandress, M. R., and D. G. Raveling. 1981a. Changes in diet and body composition of Canada geese before spring migration. Auk 98:65–79.

————, and ————. 1981b. Hyperphagia and social behavior of Canada geese prior to spring migration. Wilson Bull. 93:310–324.

National Research Council. 1977. Nutrient requirements of domestic animals. 1. Nutrient requirements of poultry. Natl. Acad. Sci., Washington, D.C. 62 pp.

Newling, C. J. 1981. Ecological investigation of a greentree reservoir in the Delta National Forest, Mississippi. Environ. Lab., U.S. Army Engineer Waterways Exp. Sta. Misc. Pap. EL-81-5. Vicksburg, Miss. 59 pp.

Palmer, R. S. 1976. Handbook of North American birds. Vol. 2. Yale Univ. Press, New Haven, Conn. 521 pp.

Paulus, S. L. 1980. The winter ecology of the gadwall in Louisiana. M.S. Thesis, Univ. North Dakota, Grand Forks. 357 pp.

————. 1982. Feeding ecology of gadwalls in Louisiana in winter. J. Wildl. Manage. 46:71–79.

Raveling, D. G. 1969. Social classes of Canada geese in winter. J. Wildl. Manage. 33:304–318.

————. 1970. Dominance relationships and agonistic behavior of Canada geese in winter. Behav. 37:291–319.

Reid, F. A. 1983. Aquatic macroinvertebrate response to management of seasonally flooded wetlands. M.S. Thesis, Univ. Missouri, Columbia. 100 pp.

Rogers, J. P. 1967. Flightless green-winged teal in southeast Missouri. Wilson Bull. 79:339.

Siefried, W. R. 1976. Segregation in feeding behaviour for diving ducks in southern Manitoba. Can. J. Zool. 54:730–736.

Swanson, G. A., G. L. Krapu, and J. R. Serie. 1979. Foods of laying female dabbling ducks on the breeding grounds. Pages 47-57 in T. A. Bookhout, ed. Waterfowl and wetlands—an integrated review. Northcent. Sect. Wildl. Soc., Madison, Wis.

Teskey, R. O., and T. M. Hinckley. 1977. Impact of water level changes on woody riparian and wetland communities. Vol. 3. Central Forest Region. U.S. Fish Wildl. Serv. FWS/OBS-77160. 36 pp.

Thomas, C. 1982. Wintering ecology of dabbling ducks in central Florida. M.S. Thesis, Univ. Missouri, Columbia. 60pp.

U.S. Department of Commerce. 1961-78. Climatological data, Missouri. Vols. 65-82. Natl. Oceanic Atmos. Admin., Natl. Climatic Center, Asheville, N.C.

Weller, M. W. 1957. Growth, weights, and plumages of the redhead (*Aythya americana*). Wilson Bull. 69:5-38.

———. 1964. The reproductive cycle. Pages 35-79 *in* J. Delacour. The waterfowl of the world. Vol. 4. Country Life, London.

———. 1965. Chronology of pair formation in some Nearctic *Aythya* (Anatidae). Auk 82:227-235.

———. 1980. Molts and plumages of waterfowl. Pages 34-38 *in* F. C. Bellrose. Ducks, geese and swans of North America. 3rd ed. Stackpole Books, Harrisburg, Pa.

White, D. C. 1985. Lowland hardwood wetland invertebrate community and production in Missouri. Arch. Hydrobiol. 103:509-533.

White, D. H., and D. James. 1978. Differential use of fresh water environments by wintering waterfowl of coastal Texas. Wilson Bull. 90:99-111.

Widmann, O. 1907. A preliminary catalog of the birds of Missouri. Acad. Sci. St. Louis Trans. 17:1-288.

Wylie, G. D. 1985. Limnology of lowland hardwood wetlands in southeast Missouri. Ph.D. Diss., Univ. Missouri, Columbia. 146pp.

23

Potential Effects of Changing Water Conditions on Mallards Wintering in the Mississippi Alluvial Valley

Kenneth J. Reinecke, Robert C. Barkley, and Charles K. Baxter

Abstract: The history of federal flood control in the Mississippi Alluvial Valley (MAV) includes four periods: (1) regional settlement (1849-1927), with uncoordinated local drainage efforts; (2) flood protection (1928-43), with a national commitment to control major Mississippi River floods; (3) agricultural development (1944-72), with large-scale conversion of forested wetlands to croplands; and (4) agricultural intensification (1973 to the present), with emphasis on the improvement of existing agricultural lands. Superimposed on this trend toward increased drainage is substantial short-term variation in annual water conditions (C.V. = 0.37). Winter rainfall over an 86-year period at Yazoo City, Miss., was an independent, random, and noncyclic series with a trend ($P < 0.05$) toward slightly greater precipitation in recent years. Winter precipitation and January river stages are positively correlated ($P < 0.01$), and stage-area relationships on the Tallahatchie (Mississippi) and White (Arkansas) rivers indicate that potential habitat can increase fivefold to tenfold between dry (e.g., 1980-81) and wet winters (e.g., 1982-83). Mallards (*Anas platyrhynchos*) benefit from favorable winter water conditions in the MAV through changes in foraging opportunities, physical condition, distribution, habitat use, and, to some extent, survival and recruitment. Continued drainage will require more effort to preserve winter overflows, mitigate necessary losses, and improve management of existing habitat.

The Mississippi Alluvial Valley (MAV) or Delta is an area with substantial numbers of wintering waterfowl and drastic losses of forested wetlands, yet the research data that are essential for evaluating effects of habitat changes are limited.

Waterfowl in Winter. © 1988 University of Minnesota. Edited by Milton W. Weller and published by the University of Minnesota Press, Minneapolis.

The MAV is best known for its mallard concentrations; Bellrose (1976) described the Delta as the heart of the ancestral mallard wintering ground, with an average winter population of 1.5 million birds. Harvest statistics confirm the abundance of waterfowl in the MAV: Arkansas consistently leads the nation in total mallard bag (Carney et al. 1983).

Forested wetlands in the MAV have been drastically reduced (Forsythe and Gard 1980). By 1978, 79% of the original 9.8 million ha (24.2 million acres) of bottomland hardwoods in the Delta had been cleared, including 2.7 million ha (6.6 million acres) between 1937 and 1978. Attempts to mitigate wetland losses in the MAV have been only partially successful (Gard 1979). The U.S. Army Corps of Engineers (USACE) has either rejected the applicability or not enforced the provisions of Section 404 of the Clean Water Act regarding bottomland hardwoods (Office of Technology Assessment 1984). Also, agricultural trends that favor wetland conversion are expected to continue, especially in bottomland forests of the South (National Research Council 1982). On the brighter side, U.S. Fish and Wildlife Service (USFWS) waterfowl habitat acquisition objectives now recognize the importance of wintering areas, particularly the MAV (Ladd 1978; Tiner 1984, fig. 15).

Although hydrology is the driving force in alluvial environments (e.g., Larson et al. 1981), little attention has been given to the relationship between water conditions and the ecology of waterfowl during winter. In this paper, we review the history of federal flood control in the MAV, illustrate the variability associated with MAV wintering habitat, and summarize relationships between winter water conditions and mallard populations.

We acknowledge helpful comments on the manuscript from T. J. Dwyer, S. W. Forsythe, L. H. Fredrickson, M. E. Heitmeyer, J. A. Kushlan, and L. D. Vangilder. D. E. Delnicki and C. W. Shaiffer assisted with data management and preparation of the figures, respectively.

Study Area

The flora, fauna, and landforms of southern alluvial environments have been described by Larson et al. (1981) and Wharton et al. (1981) and (1982), respectively. Because the geologic-hydrologic development of the MAV has not been described in the waterfowl literature, we have included a brief overview here after Saucier (1974).

The MAV extends from southeastern Missouri to southern Louisiana (fig. 23.1); it is more than 800 km (500 miles) long, varying from 32 km (20 miles) to 128 km (80 miles) wide (Lower Mississippi Valley Division, USACE 1973). Although often referred to as the Delta, its soils and landforms are alluvial rather than deltaic. However, deltaic deposits of the Mississippi deltaic plain bound the MAV on the south, from Donaldsonville and Franklin, La., to the Gulf Coast.

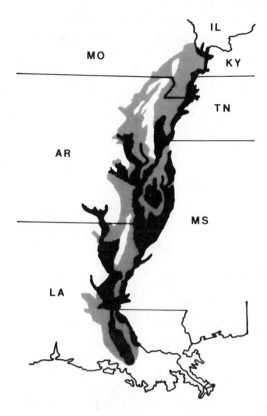

Fig. 23.1. Major features of Mississippi Alluvial Valley, illustrating areas subject to overflow before (shaded plus black) and after (black) construction of the principal Mississippi River levees. Data from Lower Mississippi Valley Division, USACE (1973, plate 12) and Saucier (1974).

The role of Pleistocene glaciation in the origin of prairie pothole wetlands is better known (e.g., Stewart and Kantrud 1973) than the less direct, but equally important, role of glaciation in the formation of waterfowl wintering areas in the lower Mississippi Valley. For example, the alignment of the contemporary Mississippi River and valley was established during the first continental glaciation. Subsequent glacial cycles have deepened and widened the valley with alternating periods of erosion, outwash, and alluviation, accompanied by changes in sea level (Saucier 1974).

Generally, first impressions are that the MAV is uniformly flat and monotonous. However, because recent glacial cycles did not completely erode alluvial deposits, and the Mississippi, Ohio, Arkansas, and other rivers have occupied various channels in postglacial times, there is considerable variation in local and regional landforms. Notable upland features include Macon Ridge, built by glacial outwash from the Arkansas River; the Grand Prairie, a Pleistocene terrace of Mississippi and Arkansas River alluvium; and Crowley's Ridge, a remnant of Tertiary marine deposits that escaped erosion during the Pleistocene. Three principal landforms dominate the floodplain: braided-stream terraces, meander belts, and backswamps. Braided-stream terraces are glacial outwash deposits of sand and gravel; they have a characteristic dendritic drainage pattern. Meander belts are areas of past or present channel migration that have numerous parallel, crescent-shaped ridges with intervening swales, the latter varying from open oxbow lakes to baldcyrpess (*Taxodium distichum*) sloughs (cf. Wharton et al. 1982, fig. 4). Backswamps are flat areas that remained peripheral to channel migration and slowly filled with even layers of fine sediment.

Methods

Our interpretation of the history of federal flood control in the MAV is based on a review of published and unpublished public documents. A summary of the benefits of favorable winter water conditions in the MAV to mallards is based on a review of recent and ongoing research.

We obtained monthly rainfall data from U.S. Department of Commerce, Climatological Data, Annual Summaries (Arkansas, Louisiana, Mississippi) for November through January 1897-98 to 1982-83 at Yazoo City, Miss. The same source was used for rainfall data for January through December, 1950 to 1984, at nine locations throughout the MAV (see Nichols et al. 1983, fig. 1). Stage-area curves for selected reaches of the White (Arkansas) and Tallahatchie (Mississippi) rivers were fitted by eye to unpublished data provided by the Little Rock and Vicksburg districts of the USACE. We planimetered the acreage of semipermanent wetlands (shrub and wooded swamps) in the same reach of the Tallahatchie River from National Wetland Inventory maps at 1:64,500. Statistical tests were conducted according to Sokal and Rohlf (1981) and included product-moment correlations, runs tests for randomness, linear regression, and goodness-of-fit tests.

Results

History of Federal Flood Control in the MAV

The Mississippi River drains 41% of the land area in the lower 48 states and is the third largest river in the world as measured by size of drainage basin and average annual flow (Lower Mississippi Valley Division, USACE 1973). The Mississippi River and Tributaries (MRT) Project, authorized by the Flood Control Act of 1928, had spent $5,384,179,271 (84.3% federal and 15.7% state and local funds) (USACE 1983) through fiscal year 1982 to control flooding in the MAV. It may be the largest such effort in the world in terms of expenditures and structural features implemented. For example, more than 16,000 km (10,000 miles) of Mississippi

Table 23.1. Selected structural flood control features of the Mississippi River and Tributaries Project as of 1974[a]

Structural features	Location	
	Main stem	Tributaries
Kilometers of levee	3,186	2,573
Kilometers of channel modification	1,535[b]	15,525[c]
Numbers (capacity) of pumping plants	. . .	27 (24,367 ft^3/sec)
Numbers (capacity) of flood storage reservoirs	. . .	5 (4,391,200 acre-ft)

[a]*Source:* Lower Mississippi Region Comprehensive Study Coordinating Committee (1974).

[b]Includes improvements for navigation on the Mississippi River from Cairo, Ill., downriver to the Head of Passes, below New Orleans, La.

[c]Includes channelization, channel realignment, snagging and clearing, and related activities.

River and tributary channels have already been modified (table 23.1). The history of federal flood control in the MAV can be divided into four time periods, each with certain fundamental differences in attitudes or objectives.

Regional Development. The first phase of flood control in the MAV was characterized by a single-purpose federal policy of wetland reclamation that began with the Swamp Lands Acts of 1849 and 1850 and continued for the next 75 years. The Swamp Lands legislation was simple in design and purpose; federal "swamp lands" were given to states with provisions whereby the states could sell the lands to individuals provided the revenues were used for reclamation. Subsequent state legislation enabled formation of local levee districts to sell bond issues and collect taxes. Widespread but generally uncoordinated projects resulted, and many drainage districts failed financially (Harrison 1961). Substantial settlement was stimulated in many areas (e.g., Korte and Fredrickson 1977), but long-term flood protection did not materialize.

The presence of the federal government in the MAV was generally confined to improvements for navigation on major waterways during the regional development phase. Prompted by major floods in 1912, 1913, and 1916, Congress passed the nation's first Flood Control Act in 1917 authorizing levee construction for flood prevention in the MAV. Thus, at the end of phase 1, the stage was set for federal and state governments to assume leadership roles in stimulating further regional development.

Flood Protection. Inspired by the great flood of 1927, Congress in 1928 passed comprehensive legislation directing flood control throughout the MAV. Thus, the second phase of flood control began with the federal government committed to a program that would protect existing settlements in the MAV from the greatest flood that might be expected to occur in 500 years. The Flood Control Act of 1928 simultaneously directed federal efforts on two fronts: one involving main-stem levees, floodways, and channel improvements for navigation and flood control and the other tributary basin improvements for flood control. Construction of the main-stem levee system is representative of phase 2 activities.

Agricultural Development. Phase 3 began with passage of the Flood Control Act of 1944, which is the acknowledged basis for federal flood control activity designed to achieve agricultural benefits. The era that followed was particularly destructive to fish and wildlife resources, because protection of existing development was secondary to the objective of draining forested wetlands for conversion to croplands. This philosophy was confirmed when Congress in 1954 directed a review of the comprehensive flood control and drainage program in the MAV. Completed in 1964 and commonly referred to as House Document No. 308, the review of the MRT project claimed economic benefits from project-induced conversion of 2,005,172 ha (4,954,712 acres) of bottomland hardwoods to croplands (U.S. House of Representatives 1964). Thus, the economic viability of federal flood control activities during phase 3 primarily depended on the benefits derived from land use conversions.

Agricultural expansion continued into the late 1960s and early 1970s, stimulated by favorable economic conditions. The Flood Control Act of 1965 renewed federal commitments and inspired confidence among developers that authorized MRT project features would be implemented. Farm commodity prices also had improved substantially by 1972, with particularly good export markets for grains and oilseeds (Office of Technology Assessment 1984). Conditions were especially favorable for increased soybean production. Soybeans were grown on most of the new acres brought into production in the MAV because they tolerate wet soils and can mature in the short growing seasons that follow spring floods (National Research Council 1982). At the same time, the contribution of agricultural exports to the national balance of payments increased during the energy crisis of the 1970s, with as much as 50% of the MAV soybean harvest entering foreign markets (Dideriksen et al. 1979). Farming cropland developed from forested wetlands was profitable during the latter part of phase 3 because of high prices for farm products and a period of 20 years without a major flood (Lower Mississippi Valley Division, USACE 1973).

Agricultural Intensification. Our choice of 1973 to mark the beginning of phase 4 was somewhat arbitrary. However, a flood in that year ended the temporary dry spell and changed the economics of farming wet soils without additional drainage. Thus, the agricultural intensification phase of flood control is a response to the need for flood protection on existing but marginal cropland developed during phase 3. Favorable cost-benefit ratios of phase 4 projects characteristically depend on controlling high-frequency flood events on cropland in areas previously dedicated for flood storage or designated as unprofitable for agriculture. This does not imply that conversion of bottomland hardwoods has ended, but rather that the present emphasis of federal flood control efforts is decreasing the wetness of cleared land. Actually, clearing has continued in recent years at a rate of 48,564 ha (120,000 acres) per year (Forsythe 1985).

Phase 4 flood control will include numerous local projects with cumulative effects and a few large operations. The Upper Yazoo Projects (UYP) in Mississippi are a major phase 4 activity. The UYP will reduce overflows from the average annual winter flood (i.e., the average flood during 1 December-28 February) by 14,772 ha (36,500 acres) (USACE, Vicksburg District, unpubl. data). Waterfowl use in this area is substantial; Leflore County in the center of the UYP area had the highest average annual harvest of mallards in the state during 1971-80 (Carney et al. 1983).

Annual Variation of Winter Water Conditions in the MAV

Winter precipitation (November + December + January) at Yazoo City, Miss. varied substantially (range = 13.2-82.0 cm, C.V. = 0.37) and averaged 38.2 cm (± 1.53 SE) over an 86-year period. A frequency distribution for the winter rainfall data (fig. 23.2) departed significantly from normality (Kolmogorov-Smirnov Test, $D = 0.1225$, $N = 86$, $P < 0.01$), with a skewness of 1.02 and kurtosis of 4.03. However, no departure from normality was detected after transformation of the data to natural logarithms ($D = 0.0598$, $P > 0.20$).

A runs test (Sokal and Rohlf 1981, 785-787) did not detect departures from randomness ($t = -1.387$, $0.10 < P < 0.20$) in the winter rainfall data series. Further analysis using serial correlation coefficients computed with time lags of 5-15 years also failed to detect evidence of cycles ($r = -0.13-0.14$, df = 69-79, $P > 0.10$). However, there was a linear trend toward increasing rainfall in recent winters ($F = 4.61$, df = 1,84, $P < 0.05$). The regression slope was significant ($t = 2.15$, df = 85, $P < 0.01$), but the model accounted for only 5.2% of the variation in the data.

The distribution of monthly rainfall at Jonesboro, Ark. in the White River basin, was similar to the mean for nine sites throughout the MAV (fig. 23.3). Rainfall was lowest during summer and fall, intermediate during winter, and highest in spring. Winter rainfall at Jonesboro was positively correlated with gauge readings on the White River at Clarendon, Ark. Correlations between mean January river stages at Clarendon (1951-81) and January, December + January, and November + December + January rainfall were 0.51, 0.68, and 0.71 (df = 29, $P < 0.01$).

Planimetry of National Wetland Inventory maps indicated that 2,585 ha (6,387 acres) of semipermanent wetlands (shrub and wooded swamps) were present in a selected reach of the Tallahatchie River in Mississippi at low river stages. A stage-area curve for the same reach (fig. 23.4) showed that water would cover about 2,000 ha (4,942 acres) during a dry winter (e.g., 1980-81) and 15,000-20,000 ha (37,064-49,419 acres) during a wet winter (e.g., 1982-83). Results were similar

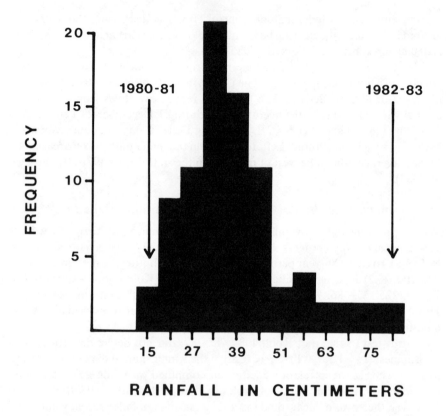

Fig. 23.2. Frequency distribution of winter rainfall (November + December + January) at Yazoo City, Miss. 1897-98 through 1982-83. (See Methods for source of data and Results for discussion of studies conducted during rainfall extremes in 1980-81 and 1982-83.)

for a reach of the White River in Arkansas. Overflows increased the area of potential habitat from 2,000-3,000 ha (4,942-7,413 acres) to 25,000-35,000 ha (61,774-86,484 acres).

Effects of Winter Water Conditions on Mallards

Published and ongoing research indicates that winter water conditions in the MAV can affect the welfare of mallards via changes in foraging opportuntities, physical condition, distribution, habitat use, survival, and reproduction (table 23.2). In Arkansas, Wright (1961) attributed greater use of acorns by mallards in some years to favorable water conditions. A similar relationship was observed in Mississippi with agricultural foods; mallards ate more rice than soybeans during winters with higher rainfall (Delnicki and Reinecke 1986). The physical condition

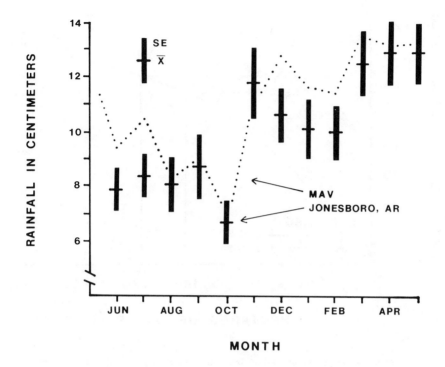

Fig. 23.3. Seasonality of precipitation in Missisisppi Alluvial Valley, 1950-84. (See Methods for source of data.)

of mallards also improved during wet years, presumably as a result of better food resources. For example, body weights decreased during the dry winter of 1980-81 and increased during the wet winter of 1982-83 (Delnicki and Reinecke 1986). In addition, Heitmeyer (1985) noted an earlier initiation of pair formation and prebasic molt in females during 1982-83.

Changes in water conditions also affect mallard distribution. Recent telemetry research in the MAV has shown that mallards often switch to newly flooded habitats within 24 hours after heavy rains (K. J. Reinecke, unpubl. data). On a larger scale, Nichols et al. (1983) have demonstrated that MAV winter habitats attract a greater proportion of midcontinent mallards, especially juveniles, during wet winters. Field studies also have detected the effects of winter water conditions on mallard survival; Reinecke (unpubl. data) found higher seasonal (i.e., winter) survival among females during the wet winter of 1982-83. Finally, Heitmeyer and Fredrickson (1981) reported a positive relationship between winter water conditions in the MAV and mallard recruitment during the subsequent breeding season.

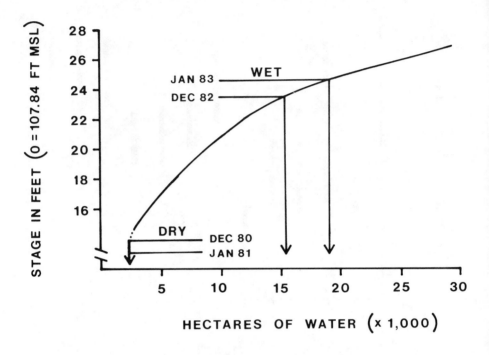

Fig. 23.4. Stage-area relationships on Tallahatchie River in upper Yazoo River basin, Mississippi (river miles 166-262). Data from Vicksburg District, USACE (unpubl. data).

Table 23.2. Benefits to mallards from favorable winter water (habitat) conditions in the Mississippi Alluvial Valley

Benefit	Reference
Improved foraging opportunities	
Natural foods (e.g., acorns)	Wright (1961)
Agricultural foods (e.g., rice)	Delnicki and Reinecke (1986)
Better physical condition	
Increased body weights in both sexes	Delnicki and Reinecke (1986)
Earlier prebasic molt in females	Heitmeyer (1985)
Changes in distribution and habitat use	
Rapid response to local floodwater	K. J. Reinecke (unpubl. data)
Regional increase in winter populations	Nichols et al. (1983)
Improved survival and recruitment	
Increased winter survival in females	K. J. Reinecke (unpubl. data)
Higher age ratio in subsequent fall population	Heitmeyer and Fredrickson (1981)

Discussion

The history of federal flood control in the MAV illustrates traditional floodplain management problems. Flood control designed during phase 2 to protect people and property stimulated extensive agricultural development during phase 3, which in turn required another cycle of flood control during phase 4. Most of the economic benefits justifying phase 4 flood control will result from drainage improvements on existing croplands, from which mallards wintering in the MAV now obtain much of their food (Wright 1961, Delnicki and Reinecke 1986). Unfortunately, single-purpose drainage structures could eliminate the benefits provided to waterfowl by the temporary flooding associated with heavy winter rains.

The outlook for mallard wintering areas in the MAV is not bright. The consensus among wildlife professionals is that future losses of wildlife habitat will be greatest for inland freshwater wetlands, particularly southern bottomland forests (National Research Council 1982, Office of Technology Assessment 1984, Tiner 1984). Thus, losses of natural habitat will continue concurrently with phase 4 drainage improvements on cropland. Habitat trends in the MAV are similar in many ways to those that have already occurred in California's Central Valley, where phase 4 drainage is more complete and serious waterfowl crowding has resulted (Gilmer et al. 1982).

In this report, we have used winter water conditions as a measure of waterfowl habitat and its variability. For example, stage-area relationships illustrated that potential habitat can increase fivefold to tenfold when rivers overflow after heavy winter rains. MAV wintering areas are therefore at least as dynamic as prairie nesting habitats (see also Heitmeyer and Fredrickson 1981), where the effects of variable water conditions are better understood and more conveniently measured as pond numbers (e.g., Pospahala et al. 1974, table 4; Krapu et al. 1983). At present, there are no annual estimates of either the number or acreage of waterfowl wintering areas in the Delta.

Although current mallard population analyses suggest that recruitment has the greatest influence on year-to-year changes in population size (Martin et al. 1979), the benefits of favorable winter habitat should not be overlooked. Intensive studies of mallard winter ecology have just begun, but preliminary results are providing evidence that winter habitat can have significant effects on mallard populations. The benefits of favorable winter water conditions in the MAV should be of particular concern in light of projected losses of natural and agricultural habitat.

The long-term decline in mallard winter habitat will continue, primarily because of flood control, drainage, and agricultural expansion. Short-term variation in winter water conditions obscures the long-term trend but provides a means of interpreting the effects of different levels of habitat availability on mallards. The resulting relationships between water conditions and the ecology of mallards wintering in the MAV should be of concern to waterfowl researchers and managers.

To be effective, researchers must often conduct studies that span the dynamics of natural systems (Wiens 1984). Since water conditions in the MAV are subject to substantial random variation, determining the functional role of mallard winter habitat will require research over a range of population levels and habitat conditions. Also, mallard population studies that are concerned with density effects should include a measure of winter habitat conditions in the MAV, because habitat availability is more variable than mallard numbers.

Managers should consider alternatives for counteracting future losses of winter habitat. Maintaining historical patterns of winter overflow must be emphasized. Where crop season drainage is a necessity, structures might be modified to provide floodwater storage and waterfowl benefits during winter. Wetland habitat managers must increase efforts and refine techniques for meeting the requirements of a diversity of species and the changing seasonal needs of individuals on a limited number of hectares.

LITERATURE CITED

Bellrose, F. C. 1976. Ducks, geese and swans of North America. Stackpole Books, Harrisburg, Pa. 543pp.

Carney, S. M., M. F. Sorensen, and E. M. Martin. 1983. Distribution of waterfowl species harvested in states and counties during 1971-80 hunting seasons. U.S. Fish Wildl. Serv., Spec. Sci. Rep. Wildl. 254. 114pp.

Delnicki, D., and K. J. Reinecke. 1986. Mid-winter food use and body weights of mallards and wood ducks in Mississippi. J. Wildl. Manage. 50:43-51.

Dideriksen, R. I., A. R. Hidlebaugh, and K. O. Schmude. 1979. Wet soils for crop production in the United States. Pages 632-641 in P. E. Greeson, J. R. Clark, and J. E. Clark, eds. Wetland functions and values: the state of our understanding. Am. Water Resour. Assoc., Minneapolis. 674pp.

Forsythe, S. W. 1985. The protection of bottomland hardwood wetlands of the Lower Mississippi Valley. Trans. N. Am. Wildl. Nat. Resour. Conf. 50:566-572.

———, and S. W. Gard. 1980. Status of bottomland hardwoods along the lower Mississippi River. Trans. N. Am. Wildl. Nat. Resour. Conf. 45:333-340.

Gard, S. W. 1979. Unmet mitigation in the Lower Mississippi River and tributaries. Pages 419-423 in G. A. Swanson, tech. coor. The mitigation symposium: a national workshop on mitigating losses of fish and wildlife habitats. U.S. For. Serv. Gen. Tech. Rep. RM-65. 684pp.

Gilmer, D. S., M. R. Miller, R. D. Bauer, and J. R. LeDonne. 1982. California's Central Valley wintering waterfowl: concerns and challenges. Trans. N. Am. Wildl. Nat. Resour. Conf. 47:441-452.

Harrison, R. W. 1961. Alluvial empire. Vol. 1. A study of state and local efforts toward land development in the Alluvial Valley of the Lower Mississippi River. Pioneer Press, Little Rock, Ark. 344pp.

Heitmeyer, M. E. 1985. Wintering strategies of female mallards related to dynamics of lowland hardwood wetlands in the Upper Mississippi Delta. Ph.D. Thesis, Univ. Missouri, Columbia. 378pp.

———, and L. H. Fredrickson. 1981. Do wetland conditions in the Mississippi Delta hardwoods influence mallard recruitment? Trans. N. Am. Wildl. Nat. Resour. Conf. 46:44-57.

Korte, P. A., and L. H. Fredrickson. 1977. Loss of Missouri's lowland hardwood ecosystem. Trans. N. Am. Wildl. Nat. Resour. Conf. 42:31–41.

Krapu, G. L., A. T. Klett, and D. G. Jorde. 1983. The effect of variable spring water conditions on mallard reproduction. Auk 100:689–698.

Ladd, W. N. 1978. The future U.S. Fish and Wildlife Service migratory waterfowl habitat acquisition program. Trans. N. Am. Wildl. Nat. Resour. Conf. 43:226–234.

Larson, J. S., M. S. Bedinger, C. F. Bryan, S. Brown, R. T. Huffman, E. L. Miller, D. G. Rhodes, and B. A. Touchet. 1981. Transition from wetlands to uplands in southeastern bottomland hardwood forests. Pages 225–273 *in* J. R. Clark and J. Benforado, eds. Wetlands of bottomland hardwood forests. Elsevier Sci. Publ., New York. 401pp.

Lower Mississippi Region Comprehensive Study Coordinating Committee. 1974. Lower Mississippi Region comprehensive study—Appendix E (Flood problems). U.S. Army Engineer, Vicksburg, Miss. 228pp.

Lower Mississippi Valley Division, USACE. 1973. Mississippi River and Tributaries post-flood report. U.S. Army Engineer, Waterways Exp. Stn., Vicksburg, Miss. 71pp.

Martin, F. W., R. S. Pospahala, and J. D. Nichols. 1979. Assessment and population management of North American migratory birds. Pages 187–239 *in* J. Cairns, G. P. Patil, and W. E. Waters, eds. Statistical ecology series. Vol. II. Int. Co-operative Publ. House, Fairland, Md. 438pp.

National Research Council. 1982. Impacts of emerging agricultural trends on fish and wildlife habitat. National Academy Press, Washington, D.C. 303pp.

Nichols, J. D., K. J. Reinecke, and J. E. Hines. 1983. Factors affecting the distribution of mallards wintering in the Mississippi Alluvial Valley. Auk 100:932–946.

Office of Technology Assessment. 1984. Wetlands: their use and regulation. U.S. Congress, Office of Technology Assessment, OTA-O-206, Washington, D.C. 208pp.

Pospahala, R. S., D. R. Anderson, and C. J. Henny. 1974. Population ecology of the mallard. II. Breeding habitat conditions, size of the breeding populations, and production indices. U.S. Fish Wildl. Serv. Resour. Publ. 115. 73pp.

Saucier, R. T. 1974. Quaternary geology of the Lower Mississippi Valley. Ark. Archeol. Surv. Res. Ser. 6. 26pp.

Sokal, R. R., and F. J. Rohlf. 1981. Biometry. 2nd ed. W. H. Freeman Co., New York. 859pp.

Stewart, R. E., and H. A. Kantrud. 1973. Ecological distribution of breeding waterfowl populations in North Dakota. J. Wildl. Manage. 37:39–50.

Tiner, R. W. 1984. Wetlands of the United States: current status and recent trends. U.S. Fish Wildl. Serv., National Wetlands Inventory, Washington, D.C. 59pp.

U.S. House of Representatives. 1964. Mississippi River and Tributaries Project. House Document No. 308, Vol. I. 88th Congress, 2d Session. 168pp.

USACE. 1983. Fiscal year 1982 annual report of the Chief of Engineers on civil works activities—extract reports of the Lower Mississippi Valley Division and Mississippi River Commission. U.S. Army Engineers, Vicksburg, Miss.

Wharton, C. H., W. M. Kitchens, E. C. Pendleton, and T. W. Sipe. 1982. The ecology of bottomland hardwood swamps of the Southeast: a community profile. U.S. Fish Wildl. Serv., Washington, D.C., FWS/OBS-81/37. 133pp.

————, V. W. Lambour, J. Newsom, P. V. Winger, L. L. Gaddy, and R. Mancke. 1981. The fauna of bottomland hardwoods in southeastern United States. Pages 87-160 *in* J. R. Clark and J. Benforado, eds. Wetlands of bottomland hardwood forests. Elsevier Sci. Publ. Co., New York. 401pp.

Wiens, J. A. 1984. Editorial. The place of long-term studies in ornithology. Auk 101:202–203.

Wright, T. W. 1961. Winter foods of mallards in Arkansas. Proc. Southeast. Assoc. Game Fish Comm. 13:291–296.

24

Duck Food Production in Openings in Forested Wetlands

Andrew J. Harrison, Jr., and Robert H. Chabreck

Abstract: The effect of forest openings on understory plant seed production was evaluated in natural forest openings within red maple (*Acer rubrum* var. *drummondii*), cypress-tupelo (*Taxodium-Nyssa*), and willow-buttonbush (*Salix-Cephalanthus*) zones of a southern Louisiana wetland. Understory vegetation stand size was positively related ($P < 0.01$) with forest opening size in all forest types, and seed production was positively related ($P < 0.01$) with forest opening size in the red maple site. Understory plant seed production was negatively correlated ($P < 0.01$) with canopy cover in all three forest types. Vegetation composition at artificially created forest openings (0.1 ha) was compared with that of adjacent control plots in cypress-tupelo and red maple sites to evaluate the potential of artificial openings to enhance production of understory plants commonly utilized for food by ducks in forested wetlands. Mean percentage of vegetative cover was greater ($P \leq 0.05$) in openings than controls for both types. Dense stands of water hyacinth (*Eichhornia crassipes*) grew where soil was flooded for prolonged periods and prevented growth of other plants.

Cypress-tupelo wetlands of the Atchafalaya-Lafourche and Blind River-Maurepas areas were excellent wintering habitat for waterfowl in Louisiana before the massive clearcuts of the 1800s and early 1900s (St. Amant 1959). Yancey (1970) noted that cypress-tupelo (*Taxodium-Nyssa*) brakes and sloughs sustained heavy utilization by wood ducks (*Aix sponsa*). Today, open water in this region has been reduced by encroachment of water hyacinth (*Eichhornia crassipes*), and production of moist-soil food plants has been reduced because of shading caused by

Waterfowl in Winter. © 1988 University of Minnesota. Edited by Milton W. Weller and published by the University of Minnesota Press, Minneapolis.

regeneration and second growth of clearcut forests (St. Amant 1959, Conner and Day 1976). Open water and an adequate food supply are important to wintering waterfowl, and use by waterfowl varies with habitat quality and preferences of individual species. Chabreck (1979) emphasized the importance of food for waterfowl and stated that removal of this essential element may cause an area to lose its attractiveness to dabbling ducks.

In recent years, large-scale conversion of bottomland hardwood habitat to row-crop farming (Yancey 1970, MacDonald et al. 1979) has placed additional pressures on remaining wintering habitat. Few studies have been directed at improving existing bottomland hardwood or cypress-tupelo wetlands for wintering waterfowl habitat. Efforts to improve winter habitat for waterfowl in forested wetlands should include maximizing production of seed-producing annuals by creating openings in forests. The occurrence and seed production of annual plants in the understory of bottomland hardwood forests are regulated largely by light penetration and water regimes (Fredrickson 1979a, 1979b; Wharton et al. 1982). Light is particularly important (Jones 1979), and many investigators (Crocker and Barton 1957, Miller 1965, Jones 1978, Helliwell 1980, and Williamson 1981) have related available light to inflorescence formation and subsequent seed production. While studying production of *Cyperus esculentus* at Catahoula Lake, Louisiana, Wills (1965) noted that production was higher in areas of open lake bed than in areas beneath a *Planera aquatica-Forestiera acuminata* canopy. He suggested that the "shading effect" of trees and shrubs was responsible for reduced production of *Cyperus esculentus*.

Other environmental factors also may affect germination, growth, and seed production of understory plants. Among these are water regime (Wiebe 1946, Crocker and Barton 1957, Fredrickson 1979a), soil pH (Helliwell 1980), and competition with other plants (Hammerton and Nuttall 1971). Evaluation of the combined effect of these factors is important to wildlife managers working to improve forested wetlands for waterfowl.

Objectives of this study were to determine the effects of size of forest opening on short-term plant succession and duck food production in cypress-tupelo, red maple (*Acer rubrum* var. *drummondii*), and willow-buttonbush (*Salix-Cephalanthus*) wetlands; and to correlate variation in duck food production with variation of selected environmental factors.

Funding was provided by William's Incorporated. We especially thank Frank B. Williams for his support. Special thanks are also extended to Carlos Garces and James P. Geaghan, Louisiana State University, for diligent efforts on the statistical portion of this paper.

Study Area

The study was conducted on the 931-ha Indigo Island Crayfish and Migratory Waterfowl Experiment Station located 40 km south of Baton Rouge near Pigeon, Iberville Parish, Louisiana. Predominant forest types on the study area include bottomland hardwoods, cypress-tupelo, and willow-buttonbush. The study was conducted at two sites in a zone transitional between bottomland hardwoods and cypress-tupelo habitats and in a cypress-tupelo wetland. A dense stand of red maple dominated the transitional zone. Other major tree species included green ash (*Fraxinus pennsylvanica*) and black willow (*Salix nigra*). The presence of decaying stumps indicates that the transitional zone once contained large bald-cypress (*Taxodium distichum*).

Understory vegetation in the cypress-tupelo site was characterized by floating aquatics and emergent plants. Dominant floating aquatics included water hyacinth (*Eichhornia crassipes*), common duckweed (*Lemna minor*), and mosquito fern (*Azolla carolinensis*), whereas predominant emergent plants were burmarigold (*Bidens laevis*) and smartweeds (*Polygonum* spp.). Dominant woody species included *Taxodium distichum*, tupelo gum (*Nyssa aquatica*), and buttonbush (*Cephalanthus occidentalis*). Estimates of basal area coverage averaged 30.6 m²/ha. The forest floor contained a soft, semifluid organic zone approximately 0.7 m deep.

Methods

Artificial Forest Openings

Six 0.1-ha plots were established in both the cypress-tupelo and red maple study sites to study plant succession in artificially created forest openings. In each study site, three of six plots that were in localities without openings were used as controls, and three were treated by creating artificial openings. All woody plants in treated plots in the cypress-tupelo site were felled; treated plots in the red maple site were cleared with a bulldozer. All treatments were completed by October 1981.

Twelve vegetation sampling units, each 1 m², were established at random within each plot in both study areas. Vegetation was sampled bimonthly between 28 September 1981 and 30 September 1982 by recording stem density, number of inflorescences of each species, and area (percentage) covered by plants.

Light intensity was measured at each sampling unit with a photographic exposure meter that was mounted facing downward on a frame 20 cm above a 400-cm² (20 cm each side) board painted alunimum. Reflected light was measured at each sampling unit and immediately thereafter in full light. Light measurements were measured as a fraction:

$$\frac{\text{Reading at sampling unit}}{\text{Reading in full light}} = \begin{array}{l}\text{Percentage of light admitted by cover} \\ \text{(understory light intensity).}\end{array}$$

Light measurements were taken biweekly between 1000 and 1400 hr on relatively cloudless days from March to September 1982. Water depth on all plots was recorded monthly during the same period.

Natural Forest Openings

Sixty plots, each 1 m², were established at equidistant points (50 m apart) from random starting points along five transect lines (50 m apart) to evaluate natural forest openings. Sixty additional plots, each 1 m², were selected in stands of *Polygonum* spp. to focus attention on the most commonly occurring waterfowl food plants in the area.

Environmental variables measured at these 120 plots included forest type, forest opening size (square meters), understory vegetation stand size (square meters), height of surrounding trees (meters), soil pH, and canopy cover (percentage). The width of forest openings and sites occupied by understory vegetation was measured at several points to allow computation of their areas. Soil pH was measured using a soil pH and humidity tester. Canopy cover (forest overstory density) was determined utilizing a spherical densiometer (Cowlin 1959). Vegetation was sampled by recording stem density and collecting 10 seed heads of each plant species in each plot during October 1982. Each seed sample was oven-dried at 100 C for 24 hours, and weight (grams) was determined using a Mettler balance. Seed weight (grams per square meter) was determined by multiplying the number of plants of the appropriate species in a sampling unit by the sampled weight and dividing by 10. During this study, special emphasis was placed on six common plant species that produce seeds commonly utilized by ducks (Martin et al. 1951): *Cyperus iria*, *Cyperus odoratus*, *Polygonum hydropiperoides*, *Polygonum punctatum*, *Polygonum setaceum*, and *Rhynchospora corniculata*. Reference to total seed production indicates the sum of seed production of these six species.

Statistical Analyses

The effect of treatment on percentage of vegetative cover and production of *Polygonum* spp. was analyzed using *t*-tests (Steel and Torrie 1980). The *t*-tests were conducted with consideration for equality of variances (SAS Institute 1982). In the seed production study, significant differences ($P \leq 0.01$) in stem density and seed production among forest types were found using analysis of covariance; therefore, the data were analyzed by forest type. Simple regressions were conducted to evaluate correlations between independent variables, forest opening size and canopy cover, and dependent variable seed weight for each forest type. The following model was linearized with logarithms and used to test for curvilinear relations: $Y = aX^b$.

Random and selected plot data were analyzed as one data set to increase sample size. Simple regressions were conducted to determine the relationship between forest opening size and vegetation stand size. Multiple regressions were conducted on data from all three forest types for stem density and seed weight of *Polygonum hydropiperoides* and *Polygonum punctatum* with independent variables canopy cover and soil pH.

Results

Artificial Forest Openings

Red Maple Study Site. Nine plant species producing foods commonly utilized by wintering waterfowl were recorded during vegetative sampling of control plots. Dominant species and frequencies were *Saururus cernuus* (33.3%), *Polygonum punctatum* (8.3%), and *Cephalanthus occidentalis* (5.6%) (table 24.1). Eleven waterfowl food plants were recorded in treated plots; dominant species and frequencies were *Rhynchospora corniculata* (47.2%), *Cyperus odoratus* (41.7%), and *Polygonum punctatum* (33.3%) (table 24.1).

Mean water depths were highest in treated (19.3 cm) and control plots (8.7 cm) during March; all plots were dry in June. Greater water depths in treated plots in most months probably were a result of soil compaction and creation of ruts by bulldozer. Mean understory light intensity in control plots ranged from 17.3% in March to 6.2% in August, whereas light intensity in treated plots was always less than 40%. Lower light intensity in red maple sites was the result of high tree density (2,700 stems per hectare).

Percentage of vegetative cover was greater (t = −4.15, df = 11.2, $P < 0.05$) in treated than in control plots. Plant cover of 10% or less was recorded in 72.2% of the sampling units in control and 33.3% of those in treated plots. Vegetation in treated plots was partially inundated during much of the growing season. Stem density of *Polygonum punctatum* was greater (t = −2.23, df = 11.2, $P \le 0.05$) in treated plots ($\bar{x}$ = 16.2/m²) than in control plots ($\bar{x}$ = 2.0/m²). Mean number of inflorescences was 102.0/m² in treated plots; none was recorded in controls.

Cypress-tupelo Study Site. Eichhornia crassipes was the dominant species in all sample plots and, in many instances, completely covered plots. Five plant species producing foods commonly utilized by wintering waterfowl were recorded during vegetative sampling of control plots. Dominant species and frequencies were *Bidens laevis* (72.2%), *Polygonum hydropiperoides* (30.6%), and *Lemna minor* (25.0%) (table 24.1). Nine waterfowl food plant species were recorded in treated plots. Dominant species and frequencies were *Bidens laevis* (72.2%), *Polygonum hydropiperoides* (66.7%), and *Lemna minor* (13.9%) (table 24.1).

Water depths did not vary greatly, and at no time during the study were any plots dry. Mean water levels were highest in treated and control plots (23.3 cm and

Table 24.1. Frequency (%) of plants commonly utilized by wintering waterfowl sampled in treated plots (n = 36) and control plots (n = 36) in forested wetlands during September 1982 near Bayou Pigeon, Louisiana

Species	Red maple		Cypress-tupelo	
	Treated plots	Control plots	Treated plots	Control plots
Rhynchospora corniculata	47.2	0.0	0.0	0.0
Cyperus odoratus	41.7	0.0	0.0	0.0
Polygonum punctatum	33.3	8.3	0.0	0.0
Cyperus iria	22.2	0.0	0.0	0.0
Saururus cernuus	16.7	33.3	0.0	2.8
Cephalanthus occidentalis	5.6	5.6	11.1	5.6
Polygonum hydropiperoides	5.6	0.6	66.7	30.6
Echinochloa colonum	2.8	0.0	0.0	0.0
Fraxinus pennsylvanica	2.8	2.8	0.0	0.0
Ilex decidua	2.8	2.8	0.0	0.0
Quercus nuttallii	2.8	2.8	0.0	0.0
Cyperus sp.	0.0	5.6	2.8	0.0
Lemna minor	0.0	2.8	13.9	25.0
Ulmus americana	0.0	2.8	0.0	0.0
Bidens laevis	0.0	0.0	72.2	72.2
Nyssa aquatica	0.0	0.0	11.1	0.0
Carex sp.	0.0	0.0	2.8	0.0
Planera aquatica	0.0	0.0	2.8	0.0
Taxodium distichum	0.0	0.0	2.8	0.0

16.0 cm, respectively) during May and lowest (15.7 cm and 8.3 cm respectively) in September. Continuous flooding of study plots probably facilitated the growth of *Eichhornia crassipes*. Monthly variations in light intensities were greatest in control plots; mean light intensities ranged from 53.3% in April and 46.7% in September to 17.0% in June. Mean understory light intensity in treated plots ranged from 89.6% in March to 97.6% during September.

Mean vegetative cover was greater (t = −5.62, df = 179, $P \leq 0.01$) in treated ($\bar{x}$ = 87.2%) than in control plots ($\bar{x}$ = 70.4%). Sample units with cover of 50% or more included 91.7% of those in controls and 100% of those in treated plots. *Polygonum hydropiperoides* was the only plant species in which density was significantly different between treated and control plots. Stem density was greater (t = −4.17, df = 24.3, $P \leq 0.01$) in treated plots ($\bar{x}$ = 42.4 stems/ per square meter) than in controls ($\bar{x}$ = 5.5 stems per square meter). Number of *Polygonum hydropiperoides* inflorescenes per square meter also was greater (t = −2.84, df = 33.0, $P \leq 0.01$) in treated ($\bar{x}$ = 138.6/ m²) than in control plots ($\bar{x}$ = 2.3/ m²).

Natural Forest Openings

Dominant understory waterfowl food plants occurring in the 120 plots and frequencies were *Rhynchospora corniculata* (33.8%), *Polygonum punctatum* (26.2%), and *Pontederia cordata* (18.8%) in red maple sites; *Rhynchospora corniculata* (90.0%), *Taxodium distichum* (40.9%), and *Polygonum punctatum* (36.4%) in cypress-tupelo sites; and *Polygonum punctatum* (50.0%), *Polygonum hydropiperoides* (50.0%), and *Rhynchospora corniculata* (33.3%) in willow-buttonbush sites (table 24.2).

Table 24.2. Frequency (%) of waterfowl food plants sampled in natural openings in forested wetlands, October 1982[a]

Species	Red maple (*n* = 80)	Cypress-tupelo (*n* = 22)	Willow-buttonbush (*n* = 18)
Rhynchospora corniculata	33.8	90.0	33.3
Polygonum punctatum	26.2	36.4	50.0
Pontederia cordata	18.8	22.7	16.7
Polygonum hydropiperoides	17.5	22.7	50.0
Saururus cernuus	8.8	0.0	5.6
Cyperus odoratus	2.5	18.2	5.6
Cyperus sp.	2.5	4.5	0.0
Taxodium distichum	2.5	40.9	0.0
Cyperus iria	1.2	4.5	0.0
Fraxinus pennsylvanica	1.2	0.0	0.0
Quercus nuttallii	1.2	0.0	0.0
Vitis rotundifolia	1.2	0.0	0.0

[a]Includes openings selected where stands of *Polygonum* spp. were present.

In red maple sites, 87.4% of the forest openings measured were less than 10 m², 95.8% were less than 30 m², and all were less than 60 m² (table 24.3). Openings less than 30 m² constituted 50%, openings 61-70 m² constituted 16.7%, and openings greater than 100 m² constituted 33.3% of the forest openings in cypress-tupelo sites. A positive relationship ($P \leq 0.01$) existed between total seed weight and forest opening size for the range of observed values in red maple sites (table 24.4). Relationships were not significant ($P > 0.05$) between total seed weight and forest opening size in cypress-tupelo or willow-buttonbush sites. Analysis revealed a negative relationship ($P \leq 0.01$) between total seed weight and canopy cover in all three forest types (table 24.4). Ranges of soil pH were 4.6-6.7, 5.2-6.2, and 5.2-6.5 in red maple, cypress-tupelo, and willow-buttonbush sites, respectively. No relationship was found between soil pH and total seed weight in any forest type.

Tree height varied from 3.5 to 31.0 m and averaged 12.8, 14.5, and 6.7 m in red

Table 24.3. Frequency (%) of forest opening sizes randomly sampled in forested wetlands near Bayou Pigeon, Louisiana, 1982

Opening sizes (m^2)	Swamp type	
	Red maple ($n = 48$)	Cypress-tupelo ($n = 12$)
<10	87.4	0.0
11-20	4.2	33.3
21-30	4.2	16.7
31-40	0.0	0.0
41-50	0.0	0.0
51-60	4.2	0.0
61-70	0.0	16.7
71-80	0.0	0.0
81-90	0.0	0.0
91-100	0.0	0.0
>100	0.0	33.3

maple, cypress-tupelo, and willow-buttonbush sites, respectively. Total seed weight was not related to tree height in any forest type. Understory vegetation stand size ranged from 0.0 to 1,024.0 m^2 ($\bar{x}$ = 107.0 m^2) in red maple sites and 10.4 to 160.9 m^2 ($\bar{x}$ = 65.2 m^2) in cypress-tupelo sites. Analysis showed a positive relationship ($P \leq 0.01$) between forest opening size and vegetation stand size in these forest types. No analysis was conducted on data for willow-buttonbush sites because of a lack of variation in forest opening sizes.

Stem density of *Polygonum hydropiperoides* ranged from 1.0 to 108.0/m^2 ($\bar{x}$ = 46.4/m^2) in the three forest types combined. Multiple regression analysis showed no significant relationships between stem density or seed weight and combinations of independent variables. Stem density of *Polygonum punctatum* ranged from 14.0 to 100.0/m^2 ($\bar{x}$ = 45.4/m^2) and seed weight ranged from 0.00 to 436.20 g/m^2 ($\bar{x}$ = 63.0 g/m^2) in the three forest types combined. Stem density decreased ($P \leq 0.05$) as canopy cover and soil pH increased. The same relationship was not found for seed weight.

Discussion

Because openings in the forest allow light to reach the understory, they are important to the production of waterfowl foods. Openings created in this study in forested wetlands increased light levels at the forest floor and resulted in increased growth of annual and perennial plants. Data from natural forest openings

Table 24.4. Summary of regression analyses of seed production in natural openings in forested wetlands near Bayou Pigeon, Louisiana, 1982[a]

Regression	Swamp type[b]	N	OSL[c]	R^2
Log total seed weight (g/ m²)				
vs. log forest opening size (m²)	I	80	0.01	0.550
	II	22	NS	
	III	18	NS	
Log total seed weight (g/ m²)				
vs. canopy cover (%)	I	80	0.01	0.448
	II	22	0.01	0.244
	III	18	0.01	0.529
Log total seed weight (g/ m²) vs.				
height of surrounding trees (m)	I	80	NS	
	II	22	NS	
	III	18	NS	
Log total seed weight (g/ m²) vs.				
soil pH	I	80	NS	
	II	22	NS	
	III	18	NS	
Stem density of *Polygonum hydropiperoides*				
vs. canopy cover (%) and soil pH	All	28	NS	
Seed weight (g/ m²) for *Polygonum*				
hydropiperoides vs. canopy cover (%) and soil pH	All	28	NS	
Stem density of *Polygonum punctatum*				
vs. canopy cover (%) and soil pH	All	38	0.05	0.274
Seed weight (g/ m²) for *Polygonum punctatum*				
vs. canopy cover (%) and soil pH	All	38	NS	

[a] Includes openings selected where stands of *Polygonum* spp. were present.
[b] I = red maple, II = cypress-tupelo, and III = willow-buttonbush.
[c] Observed significance level, NS (nonsignificant) = $P > 0.05$.

indicated that increased seed production of annual plants coincides with increasing forest opening size in red maple sites. Analysis of data for willow-buttonbush sites was difficult because of lack of variation in forest opening sizes. Although the data used to evaluate the relationships between seed production and forest opening size were analyzed by the significant linear models presented, there is obviously some point where the density of seed production would no longer increase as forest opening size increased. A probable assumption would be that the positive relationship remains rather continuous to a theoretical point where maximum seed production is attained; after this optimal level is reached, further increases in forest opening size have little or no additional beneficial effect on seed production on a density basis.

Generally, as forest opening size increases, canopy cover decreases; however, canopy cover is an important measure because it may vary in small forest openings as a result of the shading properties of overstory species and the varying abilities of these species to expand their canopies. Seed production was negatively related to canopy cover in all three forest types. Increases in seed production probably result from the marked difference in understory light as affected by canopy cover. Jenkins (1983) reported that percentage of crown cover accounted for 79% of the variation in understory light; McLaughlin (1978) found that percentage of crown closure accounted for 73.6% of the variation in light beneath *Pinus ponderosa*. Vezina and Pech (1964) also reported a relationship between understory light and crown closure in coniferous forests.

Stem density and number of inflorescences of *Polygonum hydropiperoides* were greater in forest openings (treated plots) than in forest sites without openings. However, stem density and seed production of *Polygonum hydropiperoides* were not significantly related to canopy cover or soil pH. The lack of significance may have resulted from small sample size. Stem density of *Polygonum punctatum* decreased as canopy cover and soil pH increased. Garner (1969) reported that production of *Polygonum hydropiperoides* was more than three times greater in thinned areas than in controls.

Effects of independent variables on stem density for both *Polygonum hydropiperoides* and *Polygonum punctatum* were similar to results obtained for total selected species, with one exception. When soil pH was tested in conjunction with canopy cover, higher soil pH levels had a negative effect on *Polygonum punctatum* and no effect on *Polygonum hydropiperoides*.

Water regimes were not evaluated during our study since they are not related to forest openings; nevertheless, water depth and the frequency and timing of inundation also affect germination, growth, and seed production of annual moist-soil plants (Fredrickson and Taylor 1982; Olinde et al., in press). Fredrickson and Taylor (1982) found that, in seasonally flooded impoundments in Missouri, time of drawdown and number of years since last disturbance were important factors in determining species composition. Their research indicated that *Polygonum* spp. were more likely to germinate after an early drawdown within three years of a soil disturbance, such as disking or long-term flooding. Although a soil disturbance was provided during our study, surface water remained in treated plots until June and accumulated again in August after above-average summer rains. Moist sites are generally favorable to growth and seed production in *Polygonum* spp. (Davis 1961, Bellrose et al. 1979, Staniforth and Cavers 1979); however, surface water prevents germination of most species (Davis 1961). Even if surface water disappears in the summer, shade, dense leaf litter, and quick-drying of surface soils are factors that reduce germination and growth (Fredrickson 1979a). Some *Polygonum* species are capable of continued growth if entirely submerged, but they usually are sterile under such conditions (Sculthorpe 1971).

Management Implications

Openings in forested wetland sites that become dry during the growing season allow light to reach the understory and stimulate growth of the seed-producing annuals that are important for producing food for waterfowl. However, it may not be beneficial to create openings where soils are frequently flooded and *Eichhornia crassipes* is the dominant plant. Where this species occurs, it may dominate the floral structure of the community and prevent growth of seed-producing annuals. Care should also be taken in wet areas when using heavy machinery since it may take years for bulldozer ruts to fill naturally.

Well-managed forest openings can provide a good food source for waterfowl, and habitat manipulation for production of waterfowl foods is important in areas where some natural phenomenon or human disturbances has altered production of natural waterfowl foods. Natural openings in mature forests are often created when individual or small groups of trees are killed by lightning, windthrow, or other causes. The openings usually provide excellent annual plant growth and a good food source for waterfowl. However, if natural or artificially created openings are to remain productive, annual mowing or disking will be necessary to prevent encroachment by trees and shrubs.

In forested wetlands where *Eichhornia crassipes* is not a problem and where natural openings are lacking, growth of seed-producing annuals can be increased by constructing artificial openings. Maximum seed productio on a density basis may be achieved in openings as small as 100 m². However, minimum effective opening size varies with the height of surrounding trees, and crown closure may reduce light penetration and seed production where large trees surround small openings. Therefore, artificial openings of at least 0.1 ha are recommended for greatest effectiveness. Even larger openings may be necessary to increase their attractiveness to waterfowl. This factor was not evaluated during the study but would be a worthy topic for further research. However, forested wetlands are rapidly being depleted, and artificial openings should not be constructed in a manner that would contribute significantly to that loss.

LITERATURE CITED

Bellrose, F. C., F. L. Paveglio, and D. W. Steffeck. 1979. Waterfowl populations and the changing environment of the Illinois river valley. Ill. Nat. Hist. Surv. Bull. 32:1–54.

Chabreck, R. H. 1979. Winter habitat of dabbling ducks—physical, chemical, and biological aspects. Pages 133-142 *in* T. A. Bookhout, ed. Waterfowl and wetlands—an integrated review. Proc. 1977 Symp., Northcent. Sect., Wildl. Soc., Madison, Wis. 152pp.

Conner, W. H., and J. W. Day, Jr. 1976. Productivity and composition of a bald cypress-water tupelo site and a bottomland hardwood site in a Louisiana swamp. Am. J. Bot. 63:1354–1364.

Cowlin, R. W. 1959. Use of the densiometer to estimate density of forest canopy cover on permanent sample plots. U.S. Dep. Agric. Pacific Northwest For. Range Exp. Stn. Res. Note 180. 5pp.

Crocker, W., and L. V. Barton. 1957. Physiology of seeds. An introduction to the experimental study of seed and germination problems. Chronica Botanica, Waltham, Mass. 267pp.

Davis, J. P. 1961. Foods available to waterfowl in fallow rice fields of Southwest Louisiana, 1960-1961. M.S. Thesis, Louisiana State Univ., Baton Rouge. 58pp.

Fredrickson, L. H. 1979a. Floral and faunal changes in lowland hardwood forests in Missouri resulting from channelization, drainage, and impoundment. U.S. Fish Wildl. Serv. OBS-78/91. 130pp.

——. 1979b. Lowland hardwood wetlands: current status and habitat values for wildlife. Pages 296-306 in P. C. Greeson, J. R. Clark, and J. E. Clark, eds. Wetland functions and values: the state of our understanding. Am. Water Resour. Assoc. Tech. Publ. 79-2, Minneapolis.

——, and T. S. Taylor. 1982. Management of seasonally flooded impoundments for wildlife. U.S. Fish Wildl. Serv. Resour. Publ. 148. 29pp.

Garner, G. W. 1969. Short-term succession of vegetation following habitat manipulation of bottomland hardwoods for swamp rabbits in Louisiana. M.S. Thesis, Louisiana State Univ., Baton Rouge. 181pp.

Hammerton, J. L., and M. Nuttall. 1971. Studies on weed species of the genus *Polygonum*. VII. Effect of nutrition and other factors on seed characteristics and germination behavior of *P. lapathifolium*. Weed Res. 11:94–98.

Helliwell, D. R. 1980. Germination and growth of *Primula vulgaris*. Watsonia 13:41–47.

Jenkins, M. W. 1983. Understory light intensity in bottomland hardwood stands as related to several stand characteristics and thinning intensities. M.S. Thesis, Louisiana State Univ., Baton Rouge. 57pp.

Jones, A. G. 1978. Asters. Am. Midl. Nat. 99:184–197.

Jones, G. 1979. Vegetation productivity. Longman Inc., New York. 100pp.

MacDonald, P. O., W. E. Frayer, and J. K. Clauser. 1979. Documentation, chronology, and future projections of bottomland hardwood habitat losses in the lower Mississippi alluvial plain. Vol. I. U.S. Fish Wildl. Serv., Washington, D.C.

Martin, A. C., H. S. Zim, and A. L. Nelson, 1951. American wildlife and plants. A guide to wildlife food habits. Dover Publications, New York. 500pp.

McLaughlin, S. P. 1978. Overstory attributes, light, throughfall, and the interpretation of overstory-understory relationships. For. Sci. 24:550–553.

Miller, H. A. 1965. Why wildlife openings in forest habitat. Proc. Southeast. Assoc. Game Fish. Comm. 19:171–173.

Olinde, M. W., L. S. Perrin, F. M. Montalbano III, L. A. Rowse, and M. J. Allen. Smartweed seed production and availability in south central Florida wetlands. Proc. Annu. Conf. Southeast. Assoc. Fish Wildl. Agencies. In press.

St. Amant, L. S. 1959. Louisiana wildlife inventory and management plan. Louisiana Wildl. Fish. Comm., New Orleans. 329pp.

SAS Institute. 1982. SAS user's guide: statistics. SAS Institute Inc., Cary, N.C. 584pp.

Sculthorpe, C. D. 1971. The biology of aquatic vascular plants. William Clowes, London. 610pp.

Staniforth, R. J., and P. B. Cavers. 1979. Field and laboratory germination responses of achenes of *Polygonum lapathifolium*, *P. pensylvanicum*, and *P. persicaria*. Can. J. Bot. 57:877–885.

Steel, R. D., and J. H. Torrie. 1980. Principles and procedures of statistics. A biometrical approach. 2nd ed. McGraw-Hill, New York. 481pp.

Vezina, P. E., and G. Pech. 1964. Solar radiation beneath conifer canopies in relation to crown closure. For. Sci. 7:257–264.

Wharton, C. H., W. M. Kitchens, E. C. Pendleton, and T. W. Sipe. 1982. The ecology of bottomland hardwood swamps of the southeast: a community profile. U.S. Fish Wildl. Serv. FWS/OBS-81/37. 133pp.

Wiebe, A. H. 1946. Improving conditions for migratory waterfowl on TVA impoundments. J. Wildl. Manage. 10:4–8.

Williamson, C. J. 1981. Variability in seedling progenies and the effect of light regimes during seed production on interspecific hybrids of *Poa*. New Phytol. 87:785–798.

Wills, D. W. 1965. An investigation of some factors affecting waterfowl and waterfowl habitat on Catahoula Lake, Louisiana. M.S. Thesis, Louisiana State Univ., Baton Rouge. 97pp.

Yancey, R. K. 1970. Our vanishing delta hardwoods. La. Conserv. 22 (3 and 4): 26–31.

25

Winter Body Condition of Northern Shovelers on Freshwater and Saline Habitats

William D. Tietje and James G. Teer

Abstract: Habitat factors and physiological body condition of northern shovelers (*Anas clypeata*) were studied on saline wetlands of the Texas Gulf Coast and on several freshwater lakes 18 km inland. The hypothesis considered was that freshwater and saltwater habitats do not provide equal resources for wintering shovelers and that this difference would be reflected in body condition. Aquatic vegetation persisted through the winters of 1982-84 in freshwater wetlands but died out of most saltwater ponds by late December in both years. Plankton biomass averaged 4× greater in freshwater than saltwater habitat during winter 1982-83, but little difference occurred the next year. Macroinvertebrate and seed biomass averaged 1.6× and 4.2× greater, respectively, in freshwater habitat during 1982-84. Birds that inhabited freshwater ate proportionately more vegetation and seeds than their saltwater counterparts, which presumably substituted a low-quality diet of Foraminifera. Average body, omental-fat, and sternal-muscle weights of shovelers of all age and sex classes were larger at freshwater than saltwater sites in 37 of 59 between-habitat comparisons. A notable exception to the trend of better habitat and body condition of shovelers in freshwater occurred during the record cold weather of 1983-84. Average body, omental-fat, and sternal-muscle weights were larger at saltwater sites, apparently because of ingestion of small, cold-stunned fish. In contrast, during the unusually cold weather, condition declined in freshwater habitat, presumably because of the unavailability of fish and reduced availability of plankton and macroinvertebrates. These data indicate that condition was influenced by food availability. During this study, saltwater habitat was generally inferior to freshwater habitat for wintering shovelers.

Waterfowl in Winter.© 1988 University of Minnesota. Edited by Milton W. Weller and published by the University of Minnesota Press, Minneapolis.

Winter habitat quality, especially food availability, influences the well-being of waterfowl. It affects pairing chronology of wintering gadwalls (*Anas strepera*) (Paulus 1983) and mallards (*Anas platyrhynchos*) (Brodsky and Weatherhead 1985) and is probably an important determinant of physiological condition. Condition has been implicated as a proximate factor affecting winter survival of green-winged teal (*Anas crecca carolinensis*) (Bennett and Bolen 1978) and black ducks (*Anas rubripes*) (Reinecke and Stone 1982) and productivity in common eiders (*Somateria mollissima dresseri*) (Korschgen 1977) and lesser snow geese (*Chen caerulescens caerulescens*) (Ankney and MacInnes 1978). Moreover, productivity of mallards has been related to winter habitat conditions (Heitmeyer and Fredrickson 1981). Therefore, data are needed on the relative value to wintering waterfowl of habitats of differing quality.

About half the waterfowl of the Central Flyway winter on about 917,000 ha of wetlands in Texas (Buller 1964). This diverse waterfowl habitat includes saline and brackish coastal marshes, freshwater lakes and ponds, playa lakes, reservoirs, stock ponds, and seasonally flooded agricultural lands. Not all of these habitats are of equal quality in terms of food availability and protective cover for wintering waterfowl. Populations of northern shovelers winter on both freshwater and saline wetlands in south Texas, providing an opportunity to compare food availability, body condition of shovelers by age and sex class in each habitat type, and relationships between environmental factors and body condition.

We are grateful to N. Silvy, F. Smeins and M. Weller for their help in discussion of the ideas or reviewing the manuscript. L. Wood, of Lambert Trusts, kindly permitted access to his land. We appreciate the assistance of M. Hvizdos, S. Garner, and L. Robinson with laboratory work. C. Gunn and S. Hatch helped with seed identification, as did J. Campbell and W. Clark with invertebrates. L. Folse and J. Roese provided statistical advice, and C. Cichra gave generously of his time to write computer programs to analyze the data. The Geochemical Services Laboratory, Department of Oceanography, Texas A&M University, conducted stable carbon isotope analyses on shoveler tissue samples. Research and support moneys were provided by the Welder Wildlife Foundation, Sinton, Tex.; this is Welder contribution 289.

Study Area

Study sites were established in freshwater and saltwater habitats within the Coastal Bend region of Texas. Murray (1961) described the physiography, climate, vegetation, and soils of the region. The freshwater study site was located on the Welder Wildlife Foundation Refuge (Welder site) in San Patricio County about 11 km north of Sinton, Tex. The saltwater study site comprised estuarine ponds and salt flats of the Mission-Copano Bay complex (Mission site) on the Texas coast in Refugio County about 18 km northeast of the Welder site.

Freshwater at the Welder Refuge includes stock ponds, swales, and several oxbow lakes formed by the Aransas River. Most data were collected from two oxbow lakes, Big Lake (56 ha) and Pollita Lake (29 ha), on the grounds of the refuge. Hog Lake (37 ha), located just north of the refuge boundary, also was sampled. These lakes contain water except during extreme drought. During the two study years, they averaged 1.5 m deep. Pondweed (*Potamogeton* spp.), water stargrass (*Heteranthera liebmannii*), southern naiad (*Najas guadalupensis*), and common hornwort (*Ceratophyllum demersum*) occurred in all but the deepest parts of the wetlands. American lotus (*Nelumbo lutea*) and waterlily (*Nymphaea* spp.) were the dominant floating-leaved plants. Emergents included smartweed (*Polygonum* spp.), arrowhead (*Sagittaria* spp.), and patches of cattail (*Typha* spp.) and tule or bullwhip bulrush (*Scirpus californicus*). Spikerush (*Eleocharis* spp.), burhead (*Echinodorus* spp.), and semiaquatic grasses (*Paspalum* spp. and *Panicum* spp.) occupied lake perimeters.

All census data and most shovelers and environmental samples from saltwater habitat were collected within 389 ha of estuarine ponds and bays of the Mission-Copano Bay complex. Water levels on the Mission study site vary considerably. The most notable fluctuations are referred to as wind tides (Collier and Hedgpeth 1950). Wind tides occurred frequently during early winter of the present study, and a sustained norther occasionally lowered the water level on the study site for several days.

Meuth-Alldredge (1984), using criteria from Cowardin et al. (1979), quantified habitat types on the Mission site. Of the few aquatic halophytes present, common widgeongrass (*Ruppia maritima*), frequently associated with filamentous algae (*Cladophora* and *Polysiphonia* spp.), predominated. Seashore saltgrass (*Distichlis spicata*), salt-flat grass (*Monanthochloë littoralis*), and salt-marsh bulrush (*Scirpus maritimus*) dominated areas surrounding the ponds and bays. These were interspersed with cattail, cordgrass (*Spartina alterniflora* and *S. spartinae*), bushy sea-oxeye (*Borrichia frutescens*), sea lavender (*Limonium nashii*), Carolina wolfberry (*Lycium carclinianum*), saltwort (*Batis maritima*), and glasswort (*Salicornia bigelovii* and *S. virginica*). Bigleaf sumpweed (*Iva frutescens*) was the only shrub species.

Methods

A total of 396 shovelers (175 adult males, 49 adult females, 109 juvenile males, and 63 juvenile females) was shot on the study sites during October-May of 1982-84. Of these, 182 were collected in freshwater and 214 in saltwater habitats. Nearly all were shot while feeding. Immediately after collection, the contents of the esophagus and proventriculus (upper digestive tract) were removed and preserved in 10% formaldehyde. Birds then were weighed (nearest 1 g) and frozen.

Habitat Sampling and Diet

Specific conductance (micromhos per square centimeter), water depth (centimeters), and biological factors were measured within a 6-m-diameter circle where shovelers were collected (shoveler feeding site). The percentage of cover of each plant species was determined with a square frame divided with a wire grid into 100 2.5×2.5-cm squares. At nine randomly selected locations within the circle, we recorded the number of squares in which each plant species occurred.

We sampled plankton by pouring 20 liters of water through a plankton net. In addition to those taken at feeding sites, in 1983-84 we took additional plankton samples ($n = 68$) about every two weeks at permanent sites, two in freshwater habitat and two in saltwater. Macroinvertebrate organisms were sampled with a 10 $\times$ 29-cm sweep net. A 1-m-long sweep was taken at six locations for an effective volume measurement of 0.17 m³. Seeds were measured from 10 5-cm-deep samples of benthos material taken with a 5-cm-diameter polyvinyl chloride core sampler. Benthos samples were washed in the field with a bucket fitted with a #30 screen.

Plankton, macroinvertebrates, and seeds from the habitat samples were sorted, identified, oven-dried, and weighed to 0.1 mg. We assigned 0.1 mg to any animal or seed material that occurred in a trace amount. Data were summarized by aggregate percent dry weight (Swanson et al. 1974). Dietary foods were treated as above except that plant parts were included in the analysis and diet samples that totaled less than 1 mg dry weight were excluded.

Body Condition

Shovelers collected at feeding sites also were used for body-condition analyses. Ducks were sexed and aged according to plumage characteristics (Palmer 1976) and by cloacal examination (Hochbaum 1942). Shovelers younger than one year were classed as juvenile and those older than one year as adult. We measured (nearest 1 mm) body length from the tip of the bill to the tip of the middle rectrix, with the bird firmly flattened on its back, and lengths of the flattened left and right wings from the anterior edge of the wrist joint to the tip of the longest primary. Birds then were dissected to obtain wet weights of the left sternal muscles (pectoralis, supracoracoideus, and coracobranchialis) (nearest 0.5 g) and the omental-fat depot (nearest 0.1 mg) excluding intestinal-mesenteric fat.

Wishart (1979) concluded that body length + wing length is a good predictor of structural size in wigeon (*Anas americana*), explaining 71% of the variation in skeletal weight. Therefore, to correct for structural size variation among shovelers collected in this study, we used those measurements to derive a structural index (SI) patterned after the one used by DuBowy (1980). Mean body length and wing length were calculated for each shoveler age/sex class. Individual birds within each class then were standardized by comparing the individual's body and wing length to the mean for its particular age/sex class by the formula:

$$SI_{ind} = BOD_{pop} \times WNG_{pop} / BOD_{ind} \times WNG_{ind}.$$

Here SI_{ind} = structural index of the individual shoveler, BOD_{pop} and WNG_{pop} = body and wing length, respectively, for the particular age/sex class, and BOD_{ind} and WNG_{ind} = the body and wing length for an individual within that class. For each duck, condition indexes were multiplied by the SI for that individual. All calculations and statistical tests were done only after the condition indexes were corrected by the SI. Analysis was limited to organs undamaged by shot; hence, sample sizes are variable.

Census

To determine shoveler use of freshwater and saltwater habitats during winter, ground counts on the Welder site and ground and boat counts on the Mission site were made each two weeks during October-May of 1982-84. Counts were conducted between 0700 and 1400 hr on days of good visibility, little or no precipitation, and light or no wind. On both study sites, the same census route was followed each count. This route resulted in minimal disturbance to the birds but afforded the observer a good view of all water areas. A spotting scope (15-60×) was used to identify and count waterfowl of all observed species. Water depth was taken in centimeters at a selected station on each study site during counts.

Cold Index and Assessment of Habitat Fidelity

To assess the effect of cold weather on shoveler body condition, we derived a cold index. The 141-day period between 19 November 1983 and 7 April 1984 was divided into 128 14-day periods by successively adding one day to the start and end of the preceding period (e.g., if a 14-day period started 5 January and ended 18 January, the next period would start 6 January and end 19 January, and so on). For each 14-day period, the number of days on which the mean of the minimum and maximum temperatures was 10C or less was plotted along with average omental-fat weights, by 10-day intervals, of adult male shovelers collected on the Welder site during 15 November-15 April 1983-84.

Habitat fidelity of wintering shovelers was assessed by two methods: First, stable carbon isotope analyses ($\delta^{13}C$) of shoveler tissues were conducted using techniques reviewed by Fry and Sherr (1984). The $\delta^{13}C$ values of plants is determined by the pathway followed by carbon during photosynthesis. Saltwater hydrophytes typically have $\delta^{13}C$ values more positive (-14 to $-20°/°°$) than plants of freshwater systems (-21 to $-27°/°°$) (K. Winters, pers. commun.). Consumers (including shovelers) acquire from their diet the isotopic value that is characteristic of the system. The time required for different animal tissues to attain a $\delta^{13}C$ value (about 28 days for duck sternal muscle tissue) (L. Tieszen, pers. commun.) varies depending on rates of body growth and metabolism. In the present study, sternal-muscle tissue samples were taken for $\delta^{13}C$ analyses from shovelers (19 adult males,

5 adult females, 1 juvenile male, and 4 juvenile females) collected during autumn (23 October-27 November) 1982 and winter (24 January-22 February) 1983 on the Mission and Welder study sites. The $\delta^{13}C$ analyses were conducted by the Department of Oceanography, Texas A&M University, College Station. These values are relative to the Peedee Belemnite (PDB) standard.

Second, we took the wet weight (nearest 0.1 mg) of the right supraorbital salt gland of adult male shovelers. Investigators have shown experimentally (Ellis et al. 1963, Benson and Phillips 1964, Schmidt-Nielsen and Kim 1964, and others), and with free-ranging waterfowl populations (Anderson and Warner 1969, Cornelius 1982), that the salt gland enlarges and atrophies in response to the salt content of ingested water. Hence, it seemed this relationship could be used to supplement the $\delta^{13}C$ values to indicate habitat fidelity.

Season Designations and Data Analysis

The period 6 October-6 May (winter) of 1982-84 was divided into the following seasons, designated largely on the basis of temperature, aquatic plant phenology, and shoveler migration chronology: (1) 6 October-11 November, (2) 12 November-16 December, (3) 17 December-19 January, (4) 20 January-22 February, (5) 23 February-27 March, and (6) 28 March-6 May. To increase sample sizes for some between-habitat comparisons, these six seasons were combined by twos into the following periods: (1) early winter (6 October-16 December), (2) midwinter (17 December-22 February), and (3) late winter (23 February-6 May).

Statistical analyses were conducted using the Statistical Analysis System (SAS) developed by Barr et al. (1976). One-way ANOVA was conducted using the GLM procedure for unequal sample sizes to test the significance of between-year (i.e., 1982-83 vs. 1983-84) differences, by habitat and season, in the biomass of macroinvertebrates and seeds that occurred in habitat samples. Student's t-tests were used to test the significance of between-habitat differences, by season or period, in the biomass of shoveler foods (plankton, selected macroinvertebrates, and seeds) in habitat samples; shoveler body, omental-fat, and sternal-muscle weights; the proportions of foods eaten by shovelers; shoveler density; $\delta^{13}C$ values; and shoveler salt-gland weights.

For body-condition data, between-habitat comparisons of seasonal means were made when three or more samples per habitat were available from each season within a period. If not, data from adjacent seasons were combined and, if $n \geq 3$ for each habitat, comparisons were made using the pooled data. These criteria resulted in 8 between-habitat comparisons within seasons and 12 within periods for each of the body and omental-fat weights data, and 8 and 11, respectively, for sternal-muscle weights. Furthermore, the total number of seasonal or period means that were larger for shovelers collected at freshwater or saltwater sites was compared by chi-square with the number expected, assuming habitat did not make a difference. The significantly different means (*t*-test) were weighted by a factor of 2. For example, if average omental fat was heavier at freshwater than saltwater sites in 16 of 20 comparisons, and if 3 of the 16 differences were significant, the observed chi-square value for data from freshwater habitat equaled 19 (3 significantly larger means × 2, plus 13 nonsignificantly larger means = 19). Finally, results of statistical tests were considered significant at $1 - \alpha \leq 0.05$.

Habitat Differences

Weather and Chemical and Physical Characteristics

December 1983 was the coldest December on record for coastal Texas (National Weather Service, Corpus Christi, Tex.), with the lowest temperatures during 17-31 December. The mean temperature of the coldest day (25 December) was −5C, 19.4C below normal. Temperatures were near normal during winter 1982-83.

Rainfall also differed between study years. Because winter water levels on the Welder site were determined by winter (October-May) rainfall and by rainfall the preceding summer and autumn, totals from those seasons were included in the following description. During the 12 months beginning with June 1982, only 51 cm of rain fell on the Welder Refuge (L. Drawe, unpubl. Welder Refuge data), but 126 cm fell during the following 12 months. Consequently, water levels averaged 1.4 m higher during 1983-84 than 1982-83 (fig. 25.1). In contrast, water levels on the Mission study site did not vary appreciably between years but did within years (fig. 25.1), primarily because of the influence of wind tides. During midwinter (17 December-22 February) of both study years, we estimated that up to half of the potential water area was periodically unavailable to shovelers because of drying of the ponds. Hence, there was considerable within-year variability in the availability of saltwater habitat for wintering shovelers during this study.

Specific conductance averaged 751 μmhos/cm² ± 54 (SE; *n* = 22 samples) in winter 1982-83 and 429 ± 45 (*n* = 18) in 1983-84 on the Welder site, and it averaged 26,821 ± 2,836 (*n* = 19) and 16,359 ± 2,679 (*n* = 22) for the two winters on the Mission site. Lower salt contents during 1983-84 were the result of dilution from rainfall. Highest salt contents (up to 48,000 μmhos/cm²) were recorded in very shallow ponds on the Mission site (<6 cm deep), which were partly dried as a result of evaporation and wind tides. On the Welder site, water depth at feeding sites averaged 25 cm ± 2 (SE; *n* = 25) in 1982-83 and 50 ± 8 (*n* = 18) in 1983-84. Deeper water at freshwater feeding sites in 1983-84 reflected higher water levels. Average water depth was comparatively shallow at shoveler feeding sites on the Mission site: 14 ± 2 (*n* = 22) in 1982-83 and 15 ± 2 (*n* = 22) in 1983-84.

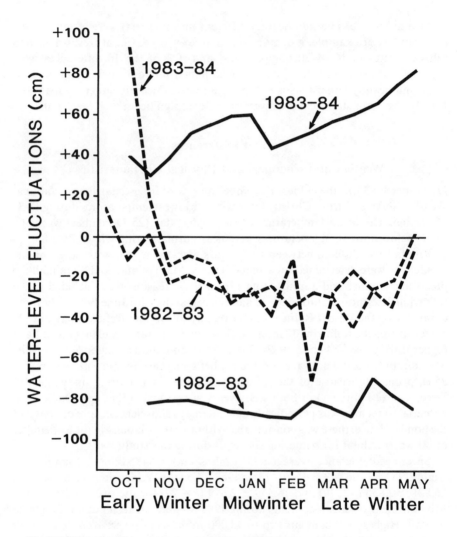

Fig. 25.1. Water-level fluctuations on the freshwater (solid lines) and saltwater (dashed lines) study sites during winters (6 October-6 May) of 1982-83 and 1983-84. The horizontal line is an arbitrary zero point.

Vegetative Cover

Widgeongrass flourished at most saltwater feeding sites during 6 October-16 December both study years: 45% occurrence in 1982-83 (*n* = 9 samples) and 78% in 1983-84 (*n* = 7). However, by late December, it had died out of nearly all ponds, presumably due to fluctuating water levels and cold weather. Hence, during middle and late winter, ponds on the Mission site were open: 11% occurrence of widgeongrass in 1982-83 (n = 7 samples) and 7% in 1983-84 (n = 6) during 17 December-22 February; 1% in 1982-83 (n = 8) and 3% in 1983-84 (n = 9) during 23 February-6 May. Widgeongrass did not regrow until mid-April. When widgeongrass was present on the Mission site, shovelers foraged in it for plankton and macroinvertebrates, but they foraged in many ponds even after all vegetation was gone. Unlike the saltwater ponds, Welder freshwater wetlands contained a variety of hydrophytes, and some of them, especially common hornwort in 1982-83 and semiaquatic grasses in 1983-84, were present at shoveler feeding sites all winter: 51% occurrence of common hornwort (n = 12 samples) during 6 October-16 December, 37% (n = 10) during 17 December-22 February, and 26% (n = 4) during 23 February-6 May 1982-83; 44% occurrence of semiaquatic grasses (n = 5), 85% (n = 5), and 82% (n = 6) during the three periods, respectively, in 1983-84.

Availability of Animal Foods and Seeds

Average plankton biomass in 1982-83 was significantly greater in freshwater than saltwater habitat during early winter (27 mg $\pm$ 6 [SE], n = 11, and 7 $\pm$ 3, n = 8, $P <$ 0.01); midwinter (57 $\pm$ 14, n = 10, and 6 $\pm$ 4, n = 6, $P <$ 0.006); and late winter (49 $\pm$ 16, n = 4, and 18 $\pm$ 6, n = 8, $P <$ 0.05) (fig. 25.2). In contrast, no difference in plankton availability was evident between the two study sites during any of the three periods in 1983-84 (7 $\pm$ 2, 5 $\pm$ 2, and 7 $\pm$ 4, n = 15, 17, and 30, respectively, in freshwater; 20 $\pm$ 15, 3 $\pm$ 2, and 6 $\pm$ 3, n = 19, 12, and 15, respectively, in saltwater; 0.41 $<$ P values $<$ 0.86). The comparatively large value for plankton biomass in saltwater during early winter (20 mg per sample) was due to one exceptional sample that contained 10× more plankton than any other in saltwater that period and 2× more than any sample collected during this study. During both years, copepods and cladocerans predominated in plankton samples from the Welder site, whereas copepods and ostracods did in saltwater samples.

Macroinvertebrate availability was indexed by the biomass of amphipods, chironomids, corixids, odonates, ephemeropterans, and gastropods that occurred in sweep samples. Other macroinvertebrates were excluded from this analysis because they constituted a small portion of the shoveler diet. Only those kinds of seeds from core samples that also occurred in diet samples were used to assess seed availability. The ANOVA test for between-year differnces in the biomass of macroinvertebrates and seeds indicated rejections in only 1 of 11 seasonal comparisons within each food group, showing little evidence of between-year differences. Therefore, years were combined in subsequent analyses.

The average macroinvertebrate samples from freshwater were 1.7, 1.6, and 1.6× as heavy as those from saltwater during the three winter periods, respectively (fig. 25.3). These differences, however, were not significant (0.15 $<$ P values $<$ 0.28). The greater macroinvertebrate biomass on the Welder site was largely the result of

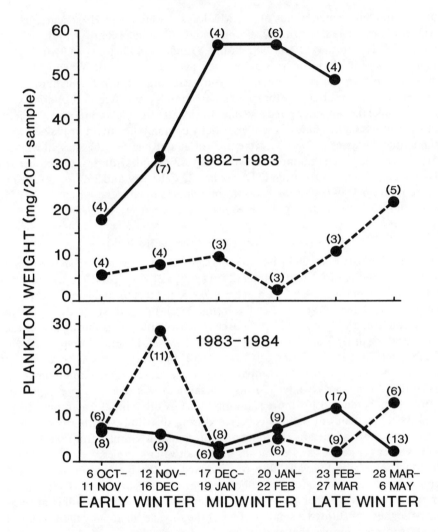

Fig. 25.2. Average seasonal availability of plankton on Welder (freshwater; solid lines) and Mission (saltwater; dashed lines) study sites during winters (6 October-6 May) of 1982-83 and 1983-84. Sample sizes are given in parentheses.

the abundance of gastropods during early (78% of the total) and midwinter (47%) and the abundance of corixids (72%) in late winter. In saltwater habitat, gastropods were the major macroinvertebrate food available to shovelers (40%) in early winter, but corixids were most abundant in middle (81%) and late (77%) winter. In both habitat types, average macroinvertebrate biomass was greater during early and late winter than during midwinter (fig. 25.3). The declines from early to

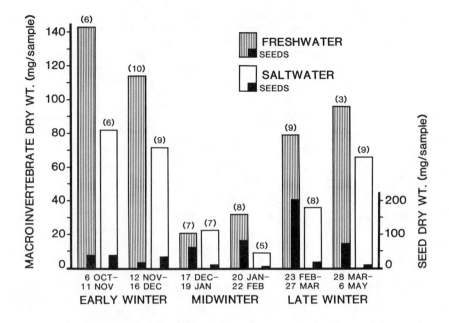

Fig. 25.3. Average seasonal availability of macroinvertebrates (amphipods, chironomids, corixids, odonates, ephemeropterans, and gastropods) on Welder (freshwater) and Mission (saltwater) study sites during winters (6 October-6 May) of 1982-84. Sample sizes are given in parentheses.

midwinter were significant: 126 mg $\pm$ 30 (SE; n = 16) to 27 $\pm$ 5 (n = 15), $P <$ 0.005, in freshwater; 76 $\pm$ 15 (n = 15) to 17 $\pm$ 8 (n = 12), $P <$ 0.003, in saltwater.

The average availability of seeds was not appreciably different during early winter in freshwater and saltwater: (25 mg $\pm$ 6 (SE; n = 16) and 37 $\pm$ 10 (n = 15), $P =$ 0.29 (fig. 25.3); but it was significantly greater in freshwater during middle (75 $\pm$ 24, n = 15, and 7 $\pm$ 2, n = 12, $P <$ 0.01) and late winter (172 $\pm$ 63, n = 12, and 14 $\pm$ 5, n = 17, $P <$ 0.03). In saltwater, seeds were most available during early winter and least during midwinter (37 and 7 mg/sample). In contrast, at freshwater sampling sites, seed biomass increased from the early- to late-winter periods (25, 75, and 172 mg/sample). Widgeongrass seeds constituted most of the saltwater seed biomass (91%), whereas several kinds of seeds were abundant in freshwater.

Shoveler Body Condition by Habitat

Body Weight

During the winters of 1982-84, in 20 between-habitat comparisons, average body weights of collected shovelers were heavier at freshwater than saltwater sites 16

Table 25.1. Summary and chi-square tests of total number of condition-data seasonal and period means that were larger for shovelers collected in freshwater or saltwater during winters (6 October-6 May) of 1982-84[a]

Body-condition index	Period[b]	Fresh $\bar{x}$ > salt $\bar{x}$[c]	Fresh $\bar{x}$ ~ salt $\bar{x}$[d] Fresh $\bar{x}$ larger	χ^2	Salt $\bar{x}$ larger	Salt $\bar{x}$ > fresh $\bar{x}$[c]
Body weight	1	1	5		0	0
	2	1	4		2	1
	3	1	4		1	0
Total		3	13	***e	3	1
Omental-fat weight	1	0	2		4	0
	2	2	3		3	0
	3	1	5		0	0
Total		3	10	*	7	0
Sternal-muscle weight	1	0	2		4	0
	2	0	2		4	1
	3	0	4		2	0
Total		0	8	NS	10	1

Between-habitat comparison of means

[a] For the chi-square tests, means found significantly different ($P \leq 0.05$) by t-test were weighted by a factor of 2.

[b] 1 = 6 Oct-16 Dec, 2 = 17 Dec-22 Feb, and 3 = 23 Feb-6 May.

[c] $P \leq 0.05$ that the means are different.

[d] $P > 0.05$ that the means are different.

[e] * indicates $P = 0.06$, ** indicates $P \leq 0.005$, NS = not significant ($P > 0.05$).

times, of which 3 were significant ($\chi^2 = 8.17$, $P < 0.005$) (table 25.1). During 17 December-19 January 1982-83, adult males at freshwater sites averaged 1.1× ($P < 0.006$) the weight of their saltwater counterparts (fig. 25.4), as did juvenile males ($P < 0.03$) at freshwater sites during 6 October-16 December 1982 and juvenile females ($P < 0.008$) during 23 February-6 May 1984 (table 25.2). Of the four exceptions to the trend of heavier birds in freshwater, three occurred in 1983-84 during the 17 December-22 February period (which included the 17-31 December record cold spell). One of the three was significant: during 17 December-19 January, adult males were heavier ($P \leq 0.05$) on the Mission than the Welder site. Their average body weight increased 14% from the previous season (12 November-16 December, $P < 0.05$), whereas that of adult males from freshwater sites declined 5% ($P > 0.05$) (fig. 25.5).

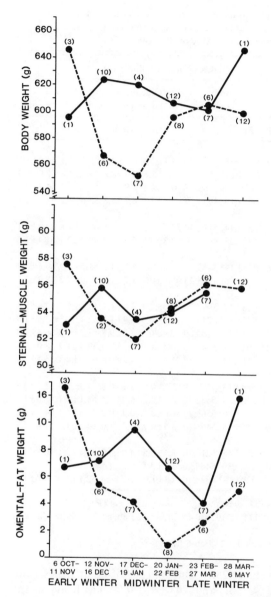

Fig. 25.4. Average seasonal body, sternal-muscle, and omental-fat weights of adult male shovelers collected on Welder (freshwater; solid lines) and Mission (saltwater; dashed lines) study sites during winter (6 October-6 May) of 1982-83. Sample sizes are given in parentheses.

Omental-Fat Weight

Patterns in average omental-fat weights in the winters of 1982-84 paralleled those of body weights (figs. 25.4 and 25.5). Among shovelers collected on the Welder site, the mean in 20 omental-fat comparisons was larger 13 times, of which 3 were

Table 25.2. Mean values of body, omental-fat, and sternal-muscle weights of shovelers collected in freshwater habitat on Welder study site and in saltwater wetlands on Mission study site during October-May of 1982-84[a]

				Index of body condition (g)							
				Sample size		Body weight		Omental-fat weight		Sternal-muscle weight	
Year	Cohort	Season[b]	Period[c]	Fresh	Salt	Fresh	Salt	Fresh	Salt	Fresh	Salt
1982-83	Adult male		1	11	5-9	622±13	593±20	7.1±1.6	9.1±2.5	55.7±1.1	56.0±1.3
		3		4	7	620±13*	552±13	9.6±1.8*	4.2±0.8	53.5±1.8	52.0±0.7
		4		12	8	607±18	596± 8	6.7±1.4*	0.9±0.2	54.0±1.6	54.4±0.8
			3	7-8	18	607±15	602± 9	5.5±1.6	4.3±0.8	55.6±1.2	56.0±1.1
	Adult female		1	8-9	5	531±14	511±30	3.7±0.5	4.5±1.6	49.4±1.8	49.0±1.1
			2	7	7	543±23	499±20	7.3±2.6	3.3±1.8	49.7±2.1	51.4±1.6
	Juvenile male		1	6	5-6	596±19*	546± 8	3.9±1.0	3.3±1.3	51.5±1.9	49.6±3.4
			2	3	3	556±28	492±23	4.2±1.6	1.2±1.0	51.0±2.3	48.3±2.7
1983-84	Adult male		1	7	9	618±17	598±26	7.1±2.1	4.4±1.1	53.4±1.5	53.8±2.1
		3		11-12	10-12	576±11*	624±15	4.6±0.9	6.9±1.5	52.4±1.5*	57.5±1.7
		4		9-12	10-11	581±12	578± 9	3.4±0.8	2.3±0.7	53.2±1.5	56.4±1.3
		5		9-10	9-11	604±11	594± 9	4.5±0.9	3.6±0.9	59.4±1.2	58.0±0.9
		6		3-4	7-10	616±33	574±17	10.7±4.6	4.2±0.8	61.3±4.4	56.1±2.1
	Juvenile male		1	6-7	14-15	584±13	578± 8	2.7±0.9	3.9±0.8	55.3±2.3	55.5±0.8
			2	14-15	9-10	560± 9	582±16	2.7±0.5	5.0±1.4	54.1±1.1	55.6±1.5
		5		9-10	8-10	546± 9	556±13	1.6±0.7	0.9±0.2	52.6±1.1	54.9±2.0
		6		8-9	7-9	565±13	546±10	3.5±0.9	2.8±1.0	54.5±1.5	51.6±1.7
	Juvenile female		1	4	11-14	529±15	521±10	3.6±0.8	4.9±0.9	48.4±3.1	50.8±1.1
			2	3	10	522±39	546±20	3.9±3.1	5.0±1.5		
			3	5	8-9	529± 8*	482±10	3.3±1.0*	1.2±0.4	52.1±1.4	49.4±1.2

[a]An asterisk between means indicates that they are significantly different ($P \leq 0.05$).

[b]1 = 6 Oct-11 Nov, 2 = 12 Nov-16 Dec, 3= 17 Dec-19 Jan, 4 = 20 Jan-22 Feb, 5 = 23 Feb-28 Mar, and 6 = 29 Mar-6 May.

[c]1 = 6 Oct-16 Dec, 2 = 17 Dec-22 Feb, and 3 = 23 Feb-6 May.

significant ($\chi^2 = 3.52$, $P = 0.06$) (table 25.1). Omental fat of adult males from freshwater sites averaged 2.3× ($P < 0.01$) and 7.4× ($P < 0.002$) as heavy as the omental fat of their saltwater counterparts during 17 December-19 January and 20 January-22 February, respectively, 1982-83. At freshwater sites, mean omental fat was heavier ($P < 0.04$) among juvenile females during 23 February-6 May 1984 (table 25.2). In the seven cases where average omental fat was heavier among

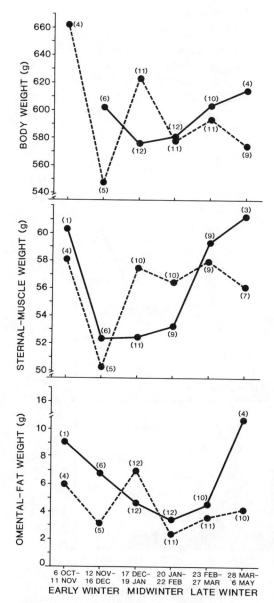

Fig. 25.5. Average seasonal body, sternal-muscle, and omental-fat weights of adult male shovelers collected on Welder (freshwater; solid lines) and Mission (saltwater; dashed lines) study sites during winter (6 October-6 May) of 1983-84. Samples are given in parentheses.

saltwater shovelers, three occurred during 17 December-22 February 1983-84, presumably because the 17-31 December cold spell which resulted in greatly increased ingestion of small fish in saline habitat.

Sternal-Muscle Weight

During the winters of 1982-84, sternal muscles were heavier about equal numbers of times among shovelers collected in each habitat (8 and 11 times, $x^2 = 0.80$, $P = 0.37$) (table 25.1), and only one difference was significant. During 17 December-19 January 1983-84, adult male sternals were heavier ($P<0.04$) on the Mission than the Welder site, increasing 15% from the 12 November-16 December season ($P<0.05$)

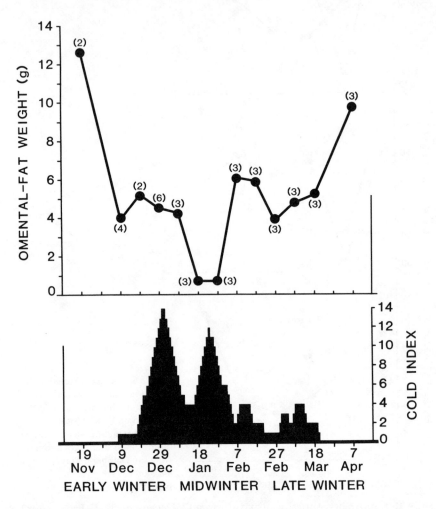

Fig. 25.6. Relationship between average weights of omental fat of adult male shovelers (top) collected on Welder site and temperature (bottom) during November-April 1983-84. Numbers of shovelers sampled per 10-day interval are shown in parentheses. See text for explanation of derivation of cold index.

(fig. 25.5), whereas sternals of freshwater shovelers changed little (0.3% increase, $P > 0.05$).

Relationship of Temperature to Condition

The record 17-31 December 1983 cold spell provided a unique opportunity to assess the effect of cold weather on shoveler body condition. Omental fat began to decline precipitously a few days after the peak of the cold spell (25 December) and reached a low point about three weeks later (fig. 25.6). The cold temperatures had ameliorated by then, and apparently because of this, shoveler condition improved. A similar pattern, but of lesser magnitude, occurred four weeks later. Declining omental-fat weights concurrent with the cold weather could have resulted from selective emigration of those shovelers in the best condition, but we have no evidence of that. During a few days of the 17-31 December 1983 cold spell, much of the water area on the Welder site froze, but small areas remained open where shovelers and other dabbling ducks congregated. Although some shovelers likely left the Welder site during this time, census data indicate that they returned within three to four days when the wetlands became free of ice.

Shoveler Diet and Numbers by Habitat

Diet

Esophageal-proventricular contents from shovelers collected on the Welder and Mission study sites were divided into five food groups: plankton, macroinvertebrates, fish, Foraminifera, and vegetation and seeds (fig. 25.7). In 10 of 12 seasons, shovelers ate proportionately more plankton in saltwater than freshwater habitat. During 2 of the 10 seasons, the between-habitat differences were significant ($P = 0.0002$ and 0.04). In contrast, vegetation and seeds constituted larger proportions of the diet of shovelers using freshwater habitat during most seasons (11 of 12). The between-habitat differences were significant ($0.0001 < P < 0.04$) seven seasons. No between-habitat pattern was detected in the proportions of macroinvertebrates eaten. During 7 of 12 seasons, the mean proportions were larger among shovelers using freshwater than saltwater habitat. The macroinvertebrate diet component was significantly larger among birds collected in freshwater one season and in saltwater habitat two seasons.

Foraminifera (a saltwater protozan, order Foraminifera) occurred in the freshwater diet of shovelers during only 23 February-27 March 1984, and fish occurred only during 20 January-22 February, in each case making up less than 5% of the diet. However, on the Mission site, Foraminifera occurred in the shoveler diet in 11 of 12 seasons and made up 5-40% of the diet in nine. As in the freshwater diet, fish usually were a small component of the saltwater diet (0% in eight seasons and between a trace and 7% in three others), but their importance increased dramati-

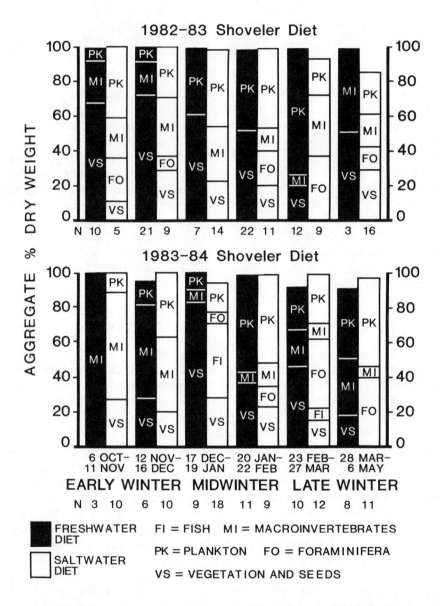

Fig. 25.7. Proportions of five food groups constituting diet of 122 shovelers collected on Welder (freshwater) and 134 on Mission (saltwater) study sites during winters (6 October-6 May) of 1982-83 and 1983-84. Seasonal proportions of foods that constituted less than 5% are not shown.

cally during the 17-31 December cold spell (fig. 25.7), when nearly all of the birds collected in saltwater were gorged with small fish (predominantly *Cyprinodon variegatus*). The upper digestive tract of one juvenile female contained 4.09 g by dry weight (19.3 ml by volume) of fish. Largely because they were eaten during the cold spell, fish made up 43% of the diet of shovelers on the Mission site during the 17 December-19 January 1983-84 season.

Numbers

Fewer shovelers were counted on the Mission site. The mean density there during October-May 1982-83 was 10 shovelers $\pm$ 2 (SE; n = 16 counts) compared with 183 $\pm$ 55 (n = 16) on the Welder site ($P < 0.006$). Densities were similarly different in 1983-84: 32 ± 8 (n = 15) and 143 ± 53 (n = 15) (P = 0.06). During both study years, the density of shovelers in saltwater was highest during migration, i.e., during early and late winter (years combined) (32 ± 11, n = 11 counts in early winter and 17 ± 5, n = 11, in late winter vs. 12 ± 4, n = 9, in midwinter), whereas most shovelers occurred on the Welder site in midwinter (409 ± 77, n = 9 counts in midwinter vs. 61 $\pm$ 17, n = 11, in early winter and 66 ± 30, n = 11, in late winter).

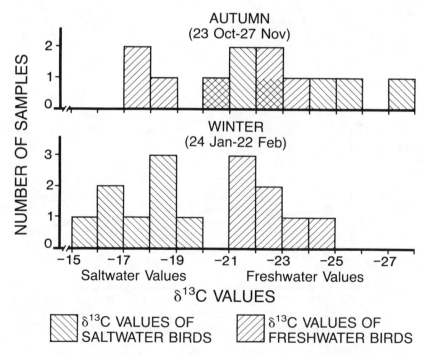

Fig. 25.8. Distribution of δ^{13}C values (-14 to $-20°/oo$) of sternal-muscle tissue from 29 shovelers collected during autumn (23 October-27 November 1982) or winter (24 January-22 February 1983) on Welder (freshwater) and Mission (saltwater) study sites.

Evidence for Habitat Fidelity

Stable Carbon Isotope Analysis

During autumn (23 October–27 November), $\delta^{13}C$ values of sternal-muscle tissues of seven shovelers collected in freshwater overlapped those of seven others from saltwater habitat (fig. 25.8). In fact, the average ($\pm$SE) $\delta^{13}C$ value of shoveler tissues sampled from the Welder site showed more of a saltwater affinity (i.e., they were more positive) than tissues from shovelers from the Mission site (-20.4 ± 0.9 and $-23.4 \pm 1.0°/oo$, respectively) ($P < 0.05$). However, average winter (24 January–22 February) $\delta^{13}C$ values of tissues of seven shovelers from freshwater

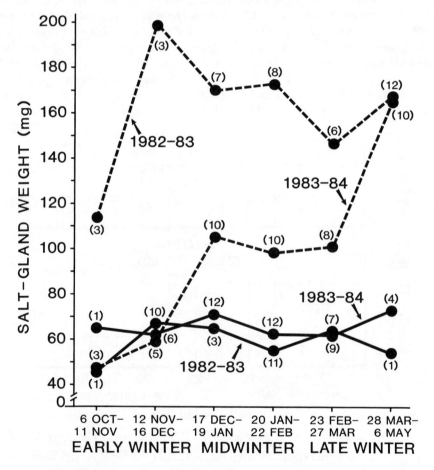

Fig. 25.9. Average seasonal salt-gland weights of adult male shovelers collected on the freshwater (solid lines) and saltwater (dashed lines) study sites during winters (6 October–6 May) of 1982-83 and 1983-84. Sample sizes are given in parentheses.

and eight from saltwater were disjunct and typical of the habitat where collected (−22.5 ± 0.05 and −17.6 ± 0.5°/∘∘, respectively) ($P < 0.0001$).

Salt-Gland Weight

Salt glands of adult male shovelers collected in saltwater habitat were significantly larger than those from freshwater sites during eight of nine seasons when sample size permitted between-habitat comparisons (i.e., $n ≥ 3$; $0.0001 < P$ values < 0.01 in 1982-83 and $0.0002 < P$ values < 0.01 in 1983-84) (fig. 25.9). In five of the eight seasonal comparisons, there was no overlap in gland weights. The mean gland weight in saltwater during the one exceptional season (12 November-16 December 1983) was apparently due to several heavy autumn rainstorms, which diluted the salt contents. Specific conductance at four of five feeding sites during that season was ≤9,000 μmhos compared with an average of 16,359 (n = 22) for winter 1983-84.

Discussion

We believe that stable carbon isotope ratios ($\delta^{13}C$) and salt-gland data collectively constitute strong evidence that shovelers did not move between habitats during the midwinter periods (17 December-22 February) of this study. In the only other study that applied the $\delta^{13}C$ technique to waterfowl (K. Winters, unpubl. data), redhead ducks (*Aythya americana*) exhibited dramatic isotopic changes between October and January upon switching from a freshwater diet during breeding and migration to one of primarily shoalgrass (*Halodule beaudettei*) (Cornelius 1975) on the Laguna Madre. The value of stable carbon isotopes to detect diet switches also has been demonstrated in field and laboratory experiments on brown shrimp (*Penaeus aztecus*) (Fry 1981, Fry and Arnold 1982) and in laboratory experiments on gerbils (*Meriones unguienlatus*) (Tieszen et al. 1983).

Anderson and Warner (1969) concluded that salt-gland data are of practical value to assess whether migrating lesser scaup (*Aythya affinis*) wintered in freshwater or saltwater habitat. However, Cornelius (1982) was skeptical of the technique because changes in gland size depend on salt concentration and occur rapidly upon exposure to contrasting hydrologic regimes. We used data from Holmes and Stewart (1968, 512) to compare salt-gland weights of mallards maintained on freshwater (353 mg, n = 12) and ducks exposed to saltwater for 1 day (625 mg, n = 3) and 14 days (773 mg, n = 9); after 1 day of exposure to saltwater, 65% of ultimate salt-gland weight (i.e., the 14-day weight) was reached. However, confidence in salt-gland data from the present study is gained from the complete lack of between-habitat overlap in weights of glands in most between-habitat comparisons. Such consistency seems improbable if movement between habitats was not infrequent.

Greater food availability in the freshwater wetland of the Welder Refuge, especially plankton and vegetation and seeds, is the most apparent factor that determined the better condition of shovelers there. Because the shoveler bill is highly modified for straining small foods, it is tempting to attribute better shoveler condition on the Welder Refuge in 1982-83 primarily to the high availability of plankton. But the data do not fully support this supposition; shovelers ate proportionately more plankton in saltwater concurrent with being in poorer condition. We did not, however, measure feeding efficiency, and we suspect that shovelers ate absolutely more plankton on the Welder site than did their counterparts in saltwater habitat. The relationship between plankton availability and shoveler body condition merits further study. The greater availability and ingestion of vegetation and seeds in freshwater than saltwater likely also contributed to the better condition of Welder site birds. Their contribution, however, is probably less than that of plankton because protein and fat contents of vegetable materials are generally less than those of animal foods (Sugden 1973).

Apparently because of the low biomass of animal and plant foods on the Mission site, resident shovelers ate large amounts of Foraminifera. Foraminifera are composed largely of calcareous shell and have little apparent food value. It is unknown whether shovelers foraged selectively for Foraminifera or whether their ingestion was incidental to that of more nutritious foods. It is also unknown whether the two study winters were unusual in that vegetation died out of the estuarine ponds and food availability was low, but we conclude they were not. Similar to our observations, saline wetlands in North Dakota contain less diversity of plant and invertebreate foods than nearby freshwater ponds (Serie and Swanson 1976). Notably, in the present study, when small fish became available on the Mission site, shovelers specialized on them and shoveler body condition improved appreciably. This corroborates our data implicating less food in saltwater as the reason for generally poorer shoveler condition there. It also points out the foraging plasticity of the shoveler, a species adapted morphologically to eat microorganisms.

In conclusion, if winter survival of waterfowl is affected by the availability of winter resources, or if productivity is influenced by winter habitat conditions, or if both of these phenomena are operative in shoveler populations, then the long-term effects of habitat changes in coastal Texas may negatively affect shoveler numbers and perhaps those of other waterfowl species. The present study raises several questions that warrant further study: If saltwater habitat is inferior to freshwater for wintering shovelers, why do populations occur in saltwater habitat? Are shoveler populations winter limited? Do other species of waterfowl that winter in freshwater and saline habitats do better in freshwater? Answers to these questions would assist in the development of appropriate winter-habitat management strategies and help in the understanding of the relationships between winter-habitat quality and the well-being of waterfowl.

LITERATURE CITED

Anderson, B. W., and D. W. Warner. 1969. Evidence from salt gland analysis for convergence of migratory routes and possible geographic variation in lesser scaup. Bird Band. 40:198–207.

Ankney, C. D., and C. D. MacInnes. 1978. Nutrient reserves and reproductive performance of female lesser snow geese. Auk 95:459–471.

Barr, A. J., J. H. Goodnight, J. P. Sall, and J. T. Helwig. 1976. A user's guide to SAS 76. Sparks Press, Raleigh, N.C. 329pp.

Bennett, J. W., and E. G. Bolen. 1978. Stress response in wintering green-winged teal. J. Wildl. Manage. 42:81–86.

Benson, G. K., and J. G. Phillips. 1964. Observations on the histological structure of the supraorbital (nasal) glands from saline-fed and freshwater-fed domestic ducks (Anas platyrhynchus). J. Anat. 98:571–578.

Brodsky, L. M., and P. L. Weatherhead. 1985. Time and energy constraints on courtship in wintering American black ducks. Condor 87:33–36.

Buller, R. J. 1964. Central flyway. Pages 209-232 in J. P. Linduska, ed. Waterfowl tomorrow. U.S. Gov. Print. Off., Washington, D.C.

Collier, A., and J. W. Hedgpeth. 1950. An introduction to the hydrography of tidal waters of Texas. Publ. Inst. Mar. Sci. Univ. Tex. 1:121–194.

Cornelius, S. E. 1975. Food choice of wintering redhead ducks (Aythya americana) and utilization of available resources in lower Laguna Madre, Texas. M.S. Thesis, Texas A&M Univ., College Station. 120pp.

———. 1982. Wetland salinity and salt gland size in the redhead Aythya americana. Auk 99:774–778.

Cowardin, L. M., V. Carter, F. C. Golet, and E. T. LaRoe. 1979. Classification of wetlands and deepwater habitats of the United States. U.S. Gov. Print. Off., Washington, D.C. 103pp.

DuBowy, P. J. 1980. Optimal foraging and adaptive strategies of post-breeding male blue-winged teal and northern shovelers. M.S. Thesis, Univ. North Dakota, Grand Forks. 122pp.

Ellis, R. A., C. C. Goertemiller, Jr., R. A. DeLellis, and Y. H. Kablotsky. 1963. The effect of a saltwater regimen on the development of the salt glands of domestic ducklings. Dev. Biol. 8:286–308.

Fry, B. 1981. Natural stable carbon isotope tag traces Texas shrimp migrations. Fish. Bull., U.S. 79:337–345.

———, and C. Arnold. 1982. Rapid $^{13}C/^{12}C$ turnover during growth of brown shrimp (Penaeus aztecus). Oecologia 54:200–204.

———, and E. B. Sherr. 1984. $\delta^{13}C$ measurements as indicators of carbon flow in marine and freshwater ecosystems. Contrib. Mar. Sci. 27:13–47.

Heitmeyer, M. E., and L. H. Fredrickson. 1981. Do wetland conditions in the Mississippi delta hardwoods influence mallard recruitment? Trans. N. Am. Wildl. Nat. Resour. Conf. 46:44–57.

Hochbaum, H. A. 1942. Sex and age determination of waterfowl by cloacal examination. Trans. N. Am. Wildl. Nat. Resour. Conf. 7:299–307.

Holmes, W. N., and D. J. Stewart. 1968. Changes in the nucleic acid and protein composition of the nasal glands from the duck (Anas platyrhynchos) during the period of adaptation to hypertonic saline. J. Exp. Biol. 48:509–519.

Korschgen, C. E. 1977. Breeding stress of female eiders in Maine. J. Wildl. Manage. 41:360–373.

Meuth-Alldredge, J. 1984. Habitat classification and wintering duck use of Mission Bay, Texas. M.S. Thesis, Texas A&M Univ., College Station. 125pp.

Murray, G. E. 1961. Geology of the Atlantic and Gulf Coastal Province of North America. Harper and Brothers, New York 692pp.

Palmer, R. S., ed. 1976. Handbook of North American birds. Vol. 2. Yale Univ. Press, New Haven, Conn. 521pp.

Paulus, S. L. 1983. Dominance relations, resource use, and pairing chronology of gadwalls in winter. Auk 100:947–952.

Reinecke, K. J., and T. L. Stone. 1982. Seasonal carcass composition and energy balance of female black ducks in Maine. Condor 84:420–426.

Schmidt-Nielsen, K., and Y. T. Kim. 1964. The effect of salt intake on the size and function of the salt gland in ducks. Auk 81:160–172.

Serie, J. R., and G. A. Swanson. 1976. Feeding ecology of breeding gadwalls on saline wetlands. J. Wildl. Manage. 40:69–81.

Sugden, L. G. 1973. Feeding ecology of pintail, gadwall, American widgeon and lesser scaup ducklings in Southern Alberta. Can. Wildl. Serv. Rep. Ser. 34. 43pp.

Swanson, G. A., G. L. Krapu, J. C. Bartonek, J. R. Serie, and D. H. Johnson. 1974. Advantages in mathematically weighting waterfowl food habits data. J. Wildl. Manage. 38:302–307.

Tieszen, L. L., T. W. Boutton, K. G. Tesdahl, and N. A. Slade. 1983. Fractionation and turnover of stable carbon isotopes in animal tissues: implications for $\delta^{13}C$ analysis of diet. Oecologia 57:32–37.

Wishart, R. A. 1979. Indices of structural size and condition of American wigeon (*Anas americana*). Can. J. Zool. 57:2369–2374.

26

Distribution and Numbers of American Black Ducks along the Maine Coast during the Severe Winter of 1980-1981

Jerry R. Longcore and James P. Gibbs

Abstract: Distribution and numbers of American black ducks (*Anas rubripes*) were determined by aerial survey along the eastern third of the Maine coast during the winter of 1980-81. Biweekly aerial surveys (five) were flown from 12 January through 5 March 1981. Survey units and subunits were those used for the Midwinter Waterfowl Inventory by the Maine Department of Inland Fisheries and Wildlife. The survey extended from Trenton to Eastport on the Canadian border. The numbers of black ducks, adjusted for estimation bias, averaged 5,695 (5,015-6,148) for the five surveys. Black duck numbers were associated with the index of shoreline irregularity of the units and with the number of clam flats. Although population size remained constant, the number of flocks declined from 71 to 57 from 12 to 21 January and then increased to 243 by 5 March. Mean flock size was larger ($P < 0.01$) during colder weather. Flocks observed at ambient temperatures below 0 C rested in the lee of landforms ($P < 0.01$); those observed at temperatures above 0 C did not ($P > 0.05$). These findings suggest adaptive behavior related to black duck distribution, flock size, and thermoregulation.

Prolonged low temperatures and reduced food availability during winter have caused periodic severe waterfowl losses in North America (Gromme 1936, Trautman et al. 1939, Hagar 1950, Hunt and Cowan 1963, Kirby and Ferrigno 1980) and in Europe (Boyd 1964, Nilsson 1984). Selective pressures on waterfowl in winter should favor adaptations for conserving energy and for obtaining food efficiently. The physiological and morphological mechanisms used for coping with cold stress are documented, but behavioral mechanisms have not been well studied (Walsberg

Waterfowl in Winter.© 1988 University of Minnesota. Edited by Milton W. Weller and published by the University of Minnesota Press, Minneapolis.

1983, 136). Behavioral adjustments in winter encompass habitat selection and changes in behavior within habitats (Walsberg 1983, 136). These changes in social organization during the nonreproductive season have costs and benefits to Darwinian fitness (Pulliam and Millikan 1982). Fitness during winter is approximated by the relative probability of survival, because anything that a bird does beyond surviving will have little influence on its reproductive success in spring (Pulliam and Millikan 1982, 170). Among wintering American black ducks (*Anas rubripes*), the two components of fitness are survival and, perhaps, accumulation of endogenous lipids (Krapu 1981). A favorable energy balance in winter, enhanced by low thermoregulatory costs, may increase survival probabilities and lipid reserves, thereby increasing fitness and perhaps reproductive success (Hepp 1984).

The study was part of the U.S. Fish and Wildlife Service's ongoing attempt to identify winter habitat of black ducks that may require protection by acquisition (U.S. Fish and Wildlife Service 1979). Our objectives were to determine the distribution and numbers of black ducks along a portion of the Maine coast during the winter of 1981 and to evaluate how environmental conditions affected distribution. The winter of 1980-81 was the coldest in the last 100 years, providing the opportunity to observe black ducks in habitats most critical to them during a severe winter.

We thank S. Fefer, J. Ringelman, and H. Spencer for assistance during the surveys. A. LaRochelle aided with data summary. S. Fefer and personnel of the U.S. Fish and Wildlife Service, Region 5, Boston, suggested the study and provided partial funding. M. Haramis, R. Kirby, L. McEwen, R. Owen, Jr., K. Reinecke, J. Ringelman, and two anonymous referees provided helpful manuscript reviews.

Study Area

Our study area included the coastal habitat between Trenton (44° 24'N; 68° 23'W) and Eastport (44° 55'N; 67° 00'W), Maine, a distance of 130 km (fig. 26.1). This estuarine system and intertidal subsystem (Cowardin et al. 1979) included the habitat classes of rock bottom, unconsolidated bottom, aquatic bed, reef, rocky shore, unconsolidated shore, and emergent wetland. Ecological characterization of these marine systems is provided by Bigelow Laboratories for Ocean Studies (1980) and by Larsen et al. (1980). The mean tidal range is 2.7 m at Portland and 5.5 m at Eastport. Between 1950 and 1978, the daily mean temperature in January recorded near Trenton at Bar Harbor ranged from -9.1C to -0.8C, with a 93-year mean of -4.9C (Baron et al. 1980). In comparison, at Bar Harbor, during our surveys in January 1981, the daily mean temperature was -9.4C, the coldest January in the last 100 years. In this 100-year period at Portland, Maine, only the January 1971 daily mean temperature was colder (-11.0C) (U.S. Dept. of Commerce 1981).

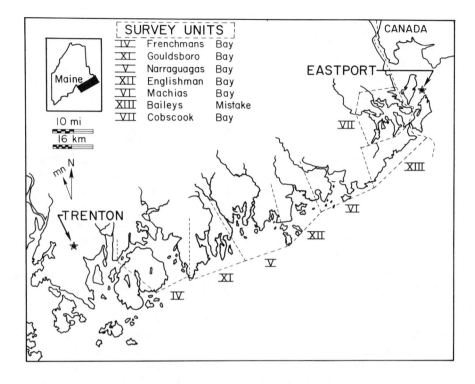

Fig. 26.1. Study area of Maine coast illustrating Mid-winter Waterfowl Inventory survey units between Trenton and Eastport.

Methods

Aerial surveys were flown on 12 and 21 January, 4 and 18 February, and 5 March 1981 to plot the location of black duck flocks and to estimate flock size. One or more ducks constituted a "flock." Surveys were conducted in a Skymaster-337, in-line, twin-engine aircraft piloted by Andrew Stinson, a 20-year veteran of the Mid-winter Waterfowl Inventory (MWI). The study area was surveyed at an altitude of 150 m at airspeeds between 104 and 113 knots. Flocks were plotted during the survey on county maps (scale: 2.5 cm = 6.4 km) that were modified to depict the MWI survey units (fig. 26.1) and subunits of the Maine Department of Inland Fisheries and Wildlife (MDIFW). Because the senior author was a novice aerial observer, he was accompanied by an experienced observer (H. E. Spencer, MDIFW) for the survey on 12 January, and each made independent estimates of black duck numbers to determine any necessary correction factors. During the next four surveys, 35-mm color transparencies of a sample of black duck flocks

(N = 11, 13, 7, 11) were taken to verify estimated flock sizes. A correction factor of +0.26% was applied to all flocks having 150 or more ducks for the surveys on 12 and 21 January.

Elapsed time of surveys for each unit was recorded to determine tidal stage. Surveys were completed between 0900 and 1630 hours on clear days. Flight direction alternated between east to west and west to east. Extent of ice was determined on 21 January by photographing (35-mm color transparencies) the study area from an altitude of 914 m for reference and then sketching ice cover on county maps. Ice cover was sketched on maps during the 18 February survey by a second observer. Area of ice then was determined using a Numonics electronic digitizer (use of trade names does not constitute endorsement by the federal government). Percentage of ice cover was calculated for each subunit, for the habitat within a zone extending 1 km from the shoreline of each subunit, and also around islands used by black duck flocks of more than 50 birds. Percentage data were normalized by arcsine transformations when necessary, and mean differences were tested by paired t-tests (Zar 1974).

The number of clam and mussel flats occurring in each subunit was obtained from Maine Coastal Inventory (Fish and Wildlife 1 and 2) maps (scale: 2.5 cm = 1,219 m) prepared in 1976 by the Maine State Planning Office. An index of shoreline irregularity (ISI) (Nilsson and Nilsson 1978) was calculated for each unit and subunit as follows: unit perimeter (meters) divided by 2 × square root of product of unit area (square meters) × pi. One unit that was of an atypical, linear shape that unduly influenced the ISI was deleted from the Spearman Rank Correlation analyses (Zar 1974). Distances to ice-free clam flats were measured from the center of flocks to the edge of clam flats for flocks of more than 100 ducks. Mean flock sizes (adjusted for estimation bias) were calculated for each survey unit and subunit.

Distribution of black duck flocks within 45-degree segments radiating from a point of the nearest landform was tested by chi-square analyses for flock sizes of fewer than 50, 50-99, and 100 or more birds. We considered four null hypotheses: (1) the distribution of flocks within the eight segments was uniform; (2) flock distribution was not related to the direction of the prevailing wind; (3) flock distribution was independent of ambient air temperature; and (4) flock size was independent of ambient air temperature. For flocks of fewer than 50 birds, 70 flocks were selected randomly from the 684 flocks to obtain a comparable sample; all data from the large flocks were used in analyses. Flock distribution also was determined for 100 flocks randomly chosen from those observed when air temperatures were below 0C (12 and 21 January, 4 February) and when air temperatures were above 0C (18 February, 5 March). Zero degrees was used as the dividing criterion because ice cover steadily increases below 0C, thereby reducing feeding areas (Albright 1981, 49). Records of the direction and duration of prevailing wind at Rockland, Maine, were obtained for January, February, and March 1981 (U.S. Dept. of Commerce 1983) to evaluate flock distribution.

Results

An unadjusted average of 5,289 (4,273–5,990) black ducks was estimated for the five surveys. After adjustment of survey data for underestimation in the 12 and 21 January surveys, a mean of 5,695 (5,015–6,148) black ducks was calculated (table 26.1). Three survey units—Cobscook Bay (1,717), Narraguagus Bay (1,497), and Frenchman Bay (934)—averaged the most ducks for the surveys (table 26.2), containing two to eight times as many ducks as the other units. All but Squirt Point and Pigeon Hill Bay of the 10 subunits with the greatest mean number of ducks were located in the three units used most by black ducks (table 26.3).

Table 26.1. Mean number of black ducks per flock by date for data unadjusted and adjusted for observer bias during aerial surveys of coastal habitats between Trenton and Eastport, Maine, in winter 1981

Date of survey	Number of flocks	Unadjusted		Adjusted[a]	
		Total number ducks	Mean flock size	Total number ducks	Mean flock size
12 Jan	71	4,858	68 a[b]	6,148	87 a
21 Jan	57	4,273	75 a	5,015	88 a
4 Feb	88	5,720	65 a	5,720	65 a
18 Feb	225	5,606	25 b	5,606	25 b
5 Mar	243	5,990	25 b	5,990	25 b
Mean		5,289		5,695	

[a] All flocks >150 adjusted by +0.26% for 12 and 21 Jan surveys.
[b] Means with the same letter are not different ($P > 0.01$).

For the survey units, ice cover was associated with ISI ($r = +0.94$, $P < 0.01$, $N = 6$). Mean number and mean density (number per square kilometer) of ducks of the unit were not significantly correlated with ISI ($r = +0.77$, $P = 0.07$, $N = 6$). Ice cover and ISI were correlated for subunits ($r = +0.33$, $P < 0.05$, $N = 38$; table 26.3). Mean number of ducks per subunit and ISI ($r = +0.35$, $P = 0.05$, $N = 38$) and mean density of ducks of the subunit and ISI were not significantly correlated ($r = +0.30$, $P = 0.06$, $N = 38$).

The adjusted mean flock sizes of 87, 88, and 65 for the 12 and 21 January and 4 February surveys were larger than the mean flock sizes of 25 and 25 for the 18 February and 5 March surveys ($F = 18.22$, df = 697, $P < 0.01$; table 26.1). The percentage of black ducks in flock sizes of fewer than 50, 50–299, and more than

Table 26.2. Survey unit area, index of shoreline irregulatiry, number of clam flats, and mean numbers of black ducks for all aerial surveys between Trenton and Eastport, Maine, in winter 1981

Unit name and number	Area (km^2) 1 km from shore	ISI[a]	Number of clam flats	Mean number and range of black ducks	
Cobscook Bay, VII	97.9	8.0	45	1,717	(1,210-2,356)
Narraguagus Bay, V	116.1	4.7	49	1,497	(1,359-1,650)
Frenchman Bay, IV	135.0	5.0	60	934	(494-1,695)
Englishman Bay, XII	59.8	4.1	41	485	(301-608)
Machias Bay, VI	84.4	4.5	29	444	(248-651)
Gouldsboro Bay, XI	90.4	4.4	32	416	(212-698)
Baileys Mistake, XIII	41.6	4.8	5	202	(43-435)

[a]Index of shoreline irregulatiry (ISI) equals unit perimeter (m) divided by 2 × square root of product of unit area (m^2) × pi.

Table 26.3. Index of shoreline irregularity, mean number of black ducks for 10 most-used subunits, percentage open water (based on area 1 km from shore), and number of ice-free clam flats for 21 January and 18 February between Trenton and Eastport, Maine, in winter 1981

		Unadjusted		Adjusted[a]			
				Percentage open water (A) and number ice-free clam flats (B)			
	Subunit		Mean	21 Jan		18 Feb	
Unit name	name and number	ISI[a]	number of black ducks	A	B	A	B
Cobscook Bay	Falls Bay, 5	3.5	723	65	1	85	2
Narraguagus Bay	Turner Pt., 1	2.6	563	82	13	100	28
Narraguagus Bay	N. River., 2	3.5	404	0	0	87	2
Frenchman Bay	Skillings R., 4	4.7	339	21	0	71	4
Englishman Bay	Squirt Pt., 3	3.0	279	65	8	92	8
Cobscook Bay	Johnson Bay, 1	1.9	267	95	4	98	5
Gouldsboro Bay	Pigeon Hill, 4	2.0	185	82	2	98	4
Cobscook Bay	Dennys Bay, 7	3.6	184	61	2	97	4
Narraguagus Bay	Back Bay, 3	2.1	182	0	0	100	2
Cobscook Bay	Middle Bay, 4	3.2	180	82	6	94	10

[a]Index of shoreline irregularity (ISI) equals unit perimeter (m) divided by 2 × square root of product of unit area (m^2) × pi.

300 birds shifted by flight date. In January and early February, most ducks (80-93%) were in flocks larger than 50, but only 52-61% were in this flock size by mid-February.

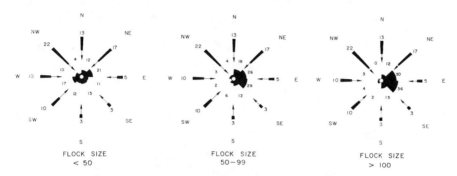

Fig. 26.2. Percentages (inner circle) of black duck flocks ($<$50, $P>$ 0.05, N = 70; 50-99, $P<$ 0.01, N = 69; $\geqslant$100, $P<$ 0.01, N =69) distributed among 45-degree segments around nearest landform as related to mean duration of wind (%) from various directions (outer circle).

For the three flock sizes designated ($<$50, 50-99, and $\geqslant$100), black ducks in the two larger categories selected the lee of landforms to rest with respect to the prevailing winds (50-99: χ^2 = 45.44, df = 7, $P<$ 0.01; $\geqslant$100: χ^2 = 59.69, df = 7, $P<$ 0.01) (fig. 26.2). We also compared the resting locations of a random sample of 100

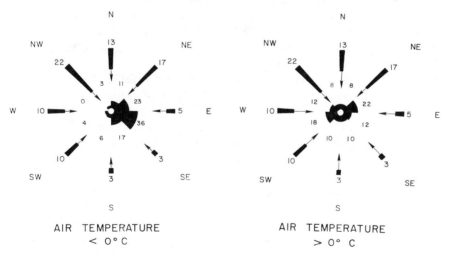

Fig. 26.3. Percentages (inner circle) of black duck flocks distributed among 45-degree segments around nearest landform as related to mean duration of wind (%) from various directions (outer circle) for random sample of 100 flocks when air temperature was below 0 C ($P<$ 0.01) and above 0C ($P>$ 0.05).

flocks recorded when air temperatures were below 0 C and another sample of 100 flocks when temperatures were above 0C. Black duck flocks rested in the lee of landforms when temperatures were below 0C (χ^2 = 83.67, df = 7, $P < 0.01$) but did not (χ^2 = 13.92, df = 7, $P > 0.05$) when temperatures were above 0C (fig. 26.3). Flock size (1-49 vs. 50 or more) was not associated strongly with tide height (χ^2 = 0.118, df = 1, $P > 0.05$).

There was less open water during the 21 January survey than during the 18 February survey, based on either total unit area (t = −8.5, df = 6, $P < 0.01$) (82% vs. 98%) or area 1 km from shoreline (t = −8.1, df = 6, $P < 0.01$) (71% vs. 96%) of units. Percentage of open water calculated on area 1 km from the shoreline (71%) on 21 January was smaller (t = 4.1, df = 6, $P < 0.05$) than that (82%) based on total area of units. By 5 March, only patches of ice remained in a few small coves.

Discussion

Black Duck Distribution among Survey Units

The number of black ducks wintering in our study area, excluding the Englishman Bay, Gouldsboro Bay, and Baileys Mistake units (fig. 26.1) (which were not part of the MDIFW survey until 1980), averaged 8,760 (4,300-12,400) from 1975 to 1984 (Steiner 1984). Our 1981 adjusted mean of 5,695 (table 26.1) is substantially lower, reflecting both the long-term decline of wintering black ducks in Maine and the southward migration prompted by below-normal temperatures in November (−17.2 to −15.5C) and December 1980 (−16.1 to −14.4C) (Albright 1981). Even after the wintering population has stabilized, black ducks may emigrate. Extreme low temperatures and extensive ice formation caused black ducks to move from New Jersey to North Carolina in 1984 (M. Conroy, pers. commun.), and similar southward shifts have been noted for scaup (*Aythya* spp.) and canvasback (*Aythya valisineria*) (Nelson 1978). Because our duck numbers varied slightly among surveys, we believe that birds did not leave after they chose wintering sites in 1981. Returns from banding stations in Maine indicate fidelity to specific wintering sites along the Maine coast (Albright 1981). In Massachusetts, after flocks formed in winter, black ducks remained in the locality regardless of weather changes (Grandy 1972).

The greater numbers of black duck in Cobscook, Narraguagus, and Frenchman Bay (table 26.2), when compared with the other, smaller survey units, would be expected to reflect unit size; but neither unit area (r = +0.08, P = 0.8, N = 6) nor subunit area (r = +0.25, P = 0.10, N = 6) was correlated with mean number of ducks. Correlation of mean number of ducks in survey units with ISI was only biologically significant (r = +0.77, P = 0.07, N = 6), but the mean number of ducks per subunit and ISI were correlated (r = 0.35, $P < 0.05$, N = 38). It seems that the beneficial effect of the irregular shoreline may be negated by the stronger relationship between ice cover and ISI for the units (r = +0.94, $P < 0.01$, N = 6) and the subunits (r = +0.33, $P < 0.05$, N = 38). Thus, when units are ice-free, the availability and benefit of the smaller coves and bays that contribute to the ISI are discernible. Nilsson and Nilsson (1978) reported that the number of summer waterbird species was correlated with shoreline development (=irregularity) in Swedish lakes. The Squirt Point (No. 3) subunit in Englishman Bay and Pigeon Hill Bay (No. 4) subunit in Gouldsboro Bay both averaged more than 250 ducks for the five surveys (table 26.3). Although these subunits were the only ones not included among those used most by black ducks, both always contained at least 65% open water, relatively large ISIs, and several ice-free clam flats, even during the coldest January temperatures.

Flock Distribution around Landforms

Selection of a favorable thermal environment is an important aspect of thermo-regulation in free-living birds (Calder and King 1974). The most conspicuous form of seasonal thermoregulatory behavior is that of shelter seeking. Our data (fig. 26.2) show that black ducks in flocks of either 50-99 or 100 or more birds selected the lee of landforms to rest ($P < 0.01$). Flocks observed at low temperatures ($< 0 C$) were located in the lee of landforms ($P < 0.01$) and those flocks observed when temperatures were above $0 C$ were not ($P > 0.05$; fig. 26.3). Flocks in this latter group still sought shelter, probably because the air temperatures of $5 C$ (5 March) and $13.8 C$ (18 February) were near or just below the lower critical temperature range of 8-14C for black ducks (Wooley and Owen 1977, 1978). Albright et al. (1983) also noted that, during periods of low temperatures ($-20 C$) in Frenchman Bay, black ducks crowded on the south side of dark-colored ledges. Lake Ontario dabbling ducks, including black ducks, concentrated inside and in the lee of intake groins of a power plant to avoid exposure to wind (Haymes and Sheehan 1982).

The distribution around landforms by flocks evidently was to avoid wind (figs. 26.2 and 26.3). A boundary layer of air surrounds and partly insulates the body; wind disrupts this layer, lowering insulative value and conducting more heat away at a greater rate when air temperatures are low (Gates 1968). Hickey (1980) calculated that the energy cost for thermoregulation for black ducks increased 186% as a result of change in wind-chill-equivalent temperatures of -5 to $-20 C$ on Prince Edward Island, Canada.

Changes in Flock Size

The change in flock size from early to late winter may reflect both a behavioral adjustment to cold temperature and a change in social organization related to the onset of breeding (table 26.1). During the first three surveys, when maximum air temperature was -4.4 to $-12.2 C$, mean flock sizes were larger, ranging from 65 to 88 ducks ($P < 0.01$), than for the last two surveys, when the average flock size was

25 ducks and air temperatures were 5 and 13.8C (table 26.1). Gathering in dense flocks is adaptive behavior permitting a more effective use of heat (Shilov 1968). Experiments have documented that the air temperature between roosting hens rises (up to 7C) as the number of birds sitting side by side increases and the distance between birds decreases (Bogolyubskii 1958; cited by Shilov 1968).

The dark body of the black duck is thermally advantageous because black absorbs thermal radiation well (Calder and King 1974). Dark plumages reflect only about 15% of the solar radiation (Birkebak 1966), whereas light plumages reflect more than 50% (Porter and Gates 1969). However, the advantage of dark plumage is lost at high wind speeds because disturbance of the boundary layer of air around black plumage lowers its radiative heat load below that of light plumage (Walsberg et al. 1978). Even plumage color becomes less important when a bird increases the angle of incidence to direct solar radiation through postural changes (Lustick et al. 1980). The combination of changes in a bird's direction to sun and in resting posture (Brodsky and Weatherhead 1984a), and, as we have observed, selection of sheltered sites for resting, and an increase in flock size when temperatures are below 0C seems to lower thermoregulatory costs of wintering black ducks.

The smaller flocks in late February and March may have been related to segregation of breeding pairs and dispersal of ducks to inland bays as ice disappeared from the units. Medium flock size increased and then declined (25, 30, 30, 12, 7) over the survey dates. Albright (1981) did not observe paired black ducks until late February on the Maine coast, but Brodsky and Weatherhead (1984b) reported a substantial increase in the number of paired black ducks during mid-February where ducks were fed in Ontario.

Distance between Resting Flocks and Feeding Sites

Mean distances (kilometers) to ice-free clam flats, by flight date, were relatively uniform for flocks of 100 or more birds ($N = 73$), averaging 0.56 km (0.26-0.87). The mean distance (0.52 km, $N = 48$) between flocks (>100) and ice-free clam flats when air temperatures were below 0C was not different $t = -0.089$, df = 72, $P > 0.05$) from that (0.54 km, $N = 25$) when air temperatures were above 0C. Clam flats are extremely important to wintering black ducks, especially those small flats near the low-tide area where strong currents prevent icing (Hartman 1963). Buxton (1981) reported that wintering shelducks (*Tadorna tadorna*) in the Ythan Estuary of Scotland generally stayed near areas in which food was abundant. Although distance from roosts to feeding sites may vary, Albright (1981) reported that the time in flight for black ducks remained relatively constant during winter.

Further, because the quantity and quality of foods obtained (energy intake) can differ greatly for black ducks (Grandy and Hagar 1971) even when feeding sites are clustered, the importance of behavioral adaptations to lower the costs of thermoregulation by individuals within flocks is evident. Jorde et al. (1984) suggest that mallards may feed on corn and forgo a nutritionally balanced diet to conserve energy for thermoregulation, especially during prolonged cold weather. Reinecke et al. (1982) have suggested that, for female black ducks, a decrease in energy reserves during winter may be internally programmed to reflect a shift in the relative advantages of maintaining energy reserves and disadvantages of carrying extra weight.

Black ducks on the Maine coast respond behaviorally to extreme and prolonged low temperatures by seeking shelter in the lee of landforms, forming denser flocks, and resting near foraging areas. In some year, conditions on wintering areas may affect normal breeding activities of black ducks because body condition of adult and juvenile female black ducks may be poor in late spring (Albright et al. 1983). Intensive, integrated studies encompassing all seasons are required to understand the effect of winter habitat conditions on black duck survival and subsequent breeding performance.

LITERATURE CITED

Albright, J. J. 1981. Behavioral and physiological responses of coastal-wintering black ducks (*Anas rubripes*) to changing weather in Maine. M.S. Thesis, Univ. Maine, Orono. 72pp.

———, R. B. Owen, Jr., and P. O. Corr. 1983. The effects of winter weather on the behavior and energy reserves of black ducks in Maine. Trans. Northeast Sect. Wildl. Soc. 40:118–128.

Baron, W. R., D. C. Smith, H. W. Borns, Jr., J. Fastook, and A. E. Bridges. 1980. Long-time series temperature and precipitation records for Maine, 1808-1978. Univ. Maine, Life Sci. Agric. Exp. Stn. Bull. 771. 235pp.

Bigelow Laboratories for Ocean Studies. 1980. The marine system. Pages 1-110 *in* S. I. Fefer and P. A. Schettig, eds. An ecological characterization of coastal Maine. U.S. Fish Wildl. Serv., Biol. Serv. Program FWS/OBS-80/29.

Birkebak, R. C. 1966. Heat transfer in biological systems. Int. Rev. Gen. Exp. Zool. 2:269–344.

Bogolyubskii, S. I. 1958. Osobennosti nochnogo otdykha (Pecularities of night rest in chicks). Zap. Leningr. S-Kh. t. 74, No. 15.

Boyd, H. 1964. Wildfowl and other waterfowl found dead in England and Wales in January-March 1963. Wildfowl Trust Annu. Rep. 15:20–23.

Brodsky, L. M., and P. J. Weatherhead. 1984a. Behavioral thermoregulation in wintering black ducks: roosting and resting. Can. J. Zool. 62:1223–1226.

———, and ———. 1984b. Behavioral and ecological factors contributing to American black duck-mallard hybridization. J. Wildl. Manage. 48:846–852.

Buxton, N. E. 1981. The importance of food in the determination of the winter flock sites of the shelduck. Wildfowl 32:79–87.

Calder, W. A., and J. R. King. 1974. Thermal and caloric relations of birds. Pages 259-413 *in* D. S. Farner, J. R. King, and K. C. Parks, eds. Avian biology. Vol. 4. Academic Press, New York.

Cowardin, L. M., V. Carter, F. C. Golet, and E. T. LaRoe. 1979. Classification of wetlands and deepwater habitats of the United States. U.S. Fish Wildl. Serv., Biol. Serv. Program FWS/OBS-79/31. 103pp.

Gates, D. M. 1968. Energy exchange and ecology. Biosci. 18:90–95.

Grandy, J. W., IV. 1972. Winter ecology of maritime black ducks *Anas rubripes* in Massachusetts: with special reference to Nauset Marsh, Orleans and Eastham. Ph.D. Thesis, Univ. Massachusetts, Amherst. 111pp.

———, and J. A. Hagar. 1971. Analyzing food habits of Maritime black ducks. Trans. Northeast Sect. Wildl. Soc. 28:207–212.

Gromme, O. J. 1936. Effect of extreme cold on ducks in Milwaukee Bay. Auk 53:324–325.

Hagar, J. A. 1950. Black duck mortality in the Parker River region, winter of 1949-50. Mass. Div. Fish. Game. 14pp.

Hartman, F. E. 1963. Estuarine wintering habitat for black ducks. J. Wildl. Manage. 27:339–347.

Haymes, G. T., and R. W. Sheehan. 1982. Winter waterfowl around Pickering Nuclear Generating Station. Can. Field-Nat. 96:172–175.

Hepp, G. R. 1984. Dominance in wintering Anatinae: potential effects on clutch size and time of nesting. Wildfowl 35:132–134.

Hickey, T. E., Jr. 1980. Activity budgets and movements of black ducks *Anas rubripes* in Prince Edward Island. M.S. Thesis, McGill Univ., Montreal. 94pp.

Hunt, G. S., and A. B. Cowan. 1963. Causes of deaths of waterfowl on the Lower Detroit River—winter 1960. Trans. N. Am. Wildl. Nat. Resour. Conf. 28:150–163.

Jorde, D. G., G. L. Krapu, R. D. Crawford, and M. A. Hay. 1984. Effects of weather on habitat selection and behavior of mallards wintering in Nebraska. Condor 86:258–265.

Kirby, R. E., and F. Ferrigno. 1980. Winter, waterfowl, and the saltmarsh. New Jersey Outdoors 7:10–13.

Krapu, G. L. 1981. The role of nutrient reserves in mallard reproduction. Auk 98:29–38.

Larsen, P., L. Doggett, C. Garside, J. Topinka, T. Mague, T. Garfield, R. Gerber, S. Fefer, P. Shettig, and L. Thornton. 1980. The estuarine system. Pages 1-148 *in* S. I. Fefer and P. A. Schetting, eds. An ecological characterization of coastal Maine. U.S. Fish Wildl. Serv., Biol. Serv. Program FWS/OBS-80/29.

Lustick, S., M. Adam, and A. Hinko. 1980. Interaction between posture, color, and the radiative heat load in birds. Science 208:1052–1053.

Nelson, H. K. 1978. Effects of the severe winter of 1976-1977 on waterfowl. Int. Waterfowl Symp. 3:39–44.

Nilsson, L. 1984. The impact of hard winters on waterfowl populations of south Sweden. Wildfowl 35:71–80.

Nilsson, S. G., and I. N. Nilsson. 1978. Breeding bird community densities and species richness in lakes. Oikos 31:214–221.

Porter, W. P., and D. M. Gates. 1969. Thermodynamic equilibria of animals with environment. Ecol. Mongr. 39:227–244.

Pulliam, H. R., and G. C. Millikan. 1982. Social organization in the nonreproductive season. Pages 169-197 *in* D. S. Farner, J. R. King, and K. C. Parkes, eds. Avian biology. Vol. 6. Academic Press, New York.

Reinecke, K. J., T. L. Stone, and R. B. Owen, Jr. 1982. Seasonal carcass composition and energy balance of female black ducks in Maine. Condor 84:420–426.

Shilov, I. A. 1968. Heat regulation in birds. Moscow Univ. Press. Translated from Russian by V. S. Kothekar, 1973. Amerind Publ. Co. New Delhi. 279pp.

Steiner, A. J. 1984. Mid-winter waterfowl inventory, Atlantic Flyway 1954-1984 trend analysis. U.S. Fish Wildl. Serv. Newton Corner, Mass. 284pp.

Trautman, M. B., W. E. Bills, and E. L. Wickliff. 1939. Winter losses from starvation and exposure of waterfowl and upland birds in Ohio and other northern states. Wilson Bull. 51:86–104.

U.S. Department of Commerce (NOAA). 1981. Climatological Data (New England). January 1981, vol. 93 (1): 1–37. The National Climatic Center, Asheville, N.C.

————. 1983. U.S. Coast Pilot. 1. Atlantic Coast: Eastport to Cape Cod. 19th ed. Climatological Tables, T-1.

U.S. Fish and Wildlife Service. 1979. Concept plan for black duck coastal wintering habitat— Atlantic coastal states, North Carolina to Maine. Newton Corner, Mass. 124pp.

Walsberg, G. E. 1983. Ecological energetics: What are the questions? Pages 135-158 *in* A. H. Brush and G. A. Clark, Jr., eds. Perspectives in ornithology. Cambridge Univ. Press, Cambridge.

————, G. S. Campbell, and J. R. King. 1978. Animal coat color and radiative heat gain: a re-evaluation. J. Comp. Physiol. 126:211–222.

Wooley, J. B., Jr. and R. B. Owen, Jr. 1977. Metabolic rates and heart rate-metabolism relationships in the black duck *Anas rubripes*. Com. Biochem. Physiol. 57 (A): 363–367.

————, and ————. 1978. Energy costs of activity and daily energy expenditure in the black duck. J. Wildl. Manage. 42:739–745.

Zar, J. H. 1974. Biostatistical analysis. Prentice-Hall Inc., Englewood Cliffs, N.Y. 620pp.

27

Cover Type Relationships and Black Duck Winter Habitat

James C. Lewis and Martin Nelson

Abstract: Habitat suitability indices, derived from area ratios of aquatic habitats used by American black ducks (*Anas rubripes*), were compared with winter waterfowl survey estimates of duck use along the Atlantic coast. Among the habitat variables tested, the percentage of shallow water (≤1 m deep) showed the highest correlation ($r = 0.37$, $P < 0.08$) with average duck use. We used an iterative process to compare the fit of duck use with more than 40 model variations. In this manner we derived nine equations that gave r values of 0.47 to 0.54 ($P < 0.01$ to 0.02), potentially explaining up to 29% of the variation in distribution of black ducks. The theorized requirements for open water shallows, and for tidal creeks and ponds within emergent and forested estuarine wetlands, appeared to explain much of the site use by ducks. Seven of the best models included a minimum area requirement for 25.9 km² of emergent marsh. Tidal flats did not appear to be an essential component influencing use of our study sites. Biological variables that we were unable to measure should be added to these best models of physical habitat characteristics, and the resultant new models should be tested to see how much they improve the ability to interpret habitat quality.

Black duck populations have been declining for several decades (Feierabend 1984). There is a need to understand black duck habitat requirements so that we can better interpret how habitat changes may be influencing duck numbers. No one knows whether existing habitat is fully utilized. High-quality habitat may not be utilized in proportion to its suitability because there may be a surplus of such habitat.

Waterfowl in Winter. © 1988 University of Minnesota. Edited by Milton W. Weller and published by the University of Minnesota Press, Minneapolis.

Based on the food habits and habitat use information for the Atlantic coast within the winter range of black ducks, Lewis and Garrison (1984) theorized that key physical habitat components include shallow (≤1 m) open water, tidal flats, emergent or forested wetlands, and tidal or permanent ponds and streams within the vegetated wetlands. Major habitats involved are estuarine emergent and forested wetlands and estuarine and marine open water (Cowardin et al. 1979). Key biological components include floating and submergent aquatic plants within shallow waters, snail populations within emergent wetlands, and clam populations on tidal flats, streambeds, bars, and banks (Lewis and Garrison 1984). These researchers further theorized that certain ratios of physical components provide optimum habitat.

Habitat quality for individual variables was numerically depicted as a suitability index of 0 (unsuitable) to 1 (ideal). For example, the black duck's requirement for shallow-water (≤ 1 m) feeding habitat was considered fully met if it made up a certain percentage of the subtidal open water (Lewis and Garrison 1984). The open water components (tidal flats and subtidal waters) and vegetated wetland were weighted by the proportion that they occupy of the total study area. Without such weighting, model output for a study area could be excessively low if one of the major subcomponents (open water or vegetated wetland) were scarce or absent. Good duck populations presumably can be supported where only one of the major subcomponents is present in a significant amount, but the optimum situation would exist where both subcomponents are present in reasonable amounts. The resulting suitability indices for individual habitat requirements were than combined in a model to derive an overall habitat suitability (U.S. Fish and Wildlife Service 1981).

The purpose of this investigation was to evaluate relationships between key habitat variables used in the habitat model and estimates of black duck use of wintering areas along the Atlantic coast. Because of limited funds, our investigations were restricted to those physical habitat features such as area and cover type identity that can be readily obtained from remote sensing.

This study was funded by the U.S. Fish and Wildlife Service National Coastal Ecosystem Team. Joe Clark selected the study sites and began analysis of National Wetland Inventory maps. Peter Dress, University of Georgia, gave statistical guidance. State and federal waterfowl biologists provided information about specific study sites; their assistance is appreciated. Joe Ware and George Haas, U.S. Fish and Wildlife Service (FWS), provided the original Winter Waterfowl Survey (WWS) data. John Montanari, project leader, national Wetlands Inventory (NWI), FWS, provided the National Wetland maps.

Study Area and Methods

The U.S. Fish and Wildlife Service has censused wintering waterfowl since the 1930s. These aerial counts in January are an inventory of all species and a measure of relative distribution of waterfowl in wintering habitats. The Concept Plan for Preservation of Black Duck Wintering Habitat (U.S. Fish and Wildlife Service 1979) listed 196 key Atlantic coast waterfowl wintering areas for which WWS data were available. From these potential sites we randomly selected 30 study areas. Seven study sites were omitted later because census data were incomplete, habitat maps were not yet available for these sites, duck use was influenced by artificial feeding, or duck use was measured by ground counts rather than aerial inventory. The remaining 23 areas, located from Maine to Virginia, appear representative of a wide geographic range of habitats and include areas with low, intermediate, and high black duck densities in winter. The areas are highly variable in terms of habitat, land ownership, and management.

Boundaries of the 23 study sites were determined for each WWS flight line on National Wetland Inventory maps. Areas where black ducks were censused during the WWS were largely open water sites where ducks could easily be seen and counted. Forested and emergent estuarine wetlands also are important for wintering black ducks and must be included in the habitat analysis. Therefore, we developed a systematic means of including within study area boundaries those forested and emergent estuarine wetlands that bordered an inventory site. A line was drawn on NWI maps along the maximum axis of each WWS inventory area. A plastic, transparent grid sheet, with squares 1.6 km on a side, was placed over the NWI map. The center point of the grid sheet was positioned over the midpoint of the maximum axis and the grid sheet aligned north-south. All the waterfowl habitat within an individual grid was included in the habitat analysis if any part of the grid was included in the black duck census area.

Physical habitat features at study sites were measured and calculated as follows: Water depths of 1 m or less were estimated from contour lines on U.S. Geological Survey topographic quadrangles (scale 1:24,000). Estuarine, and marine open water were identified on NWI maps and measured. The proportion of open water ≤ 1 m deep) at low tide, variable 1 (V1), was then calculated (table 27.1). Tidal flats (V3) are usually labeled on NWI maps, and the areas of these types were measured. Maps areas were determined with a digital polar compensating planimeter. Other physical habitat variables listed in table 27.1 were measured in a similar manner and their suitability indices calculated.

We compared long-term WWS data (1973-84) with model output (an index value between 0.0 and 1.0), assuming that the physical habitat variables are slow to change and that maps depict habitat that existed throughout 1973-84. A correlation test was performed to measure the closeness of linear relationship between the number of black ducks and model output for the study areas. By an iterative

Table 27.1. Physical habitat variables evaluated as components of models in this study

Variable	Description (hectares of)
V1	Subtidal open water ≤ 1 m deep
V2	Subtidal open water
V3	Tidal flats
V4	Tidal flats and open water
V5	Emergent and forested wetlands, ponds, creeks, and impoundments
V6	Inland wetlands (all waterfowl habitat exclusive of tidal flats and subtidal open water)
V7	Tidal creeks and ponds
V8	Nontidal ponds and impoundments
V9	Inland wetlands plus marine and estuarine open water habitat

process we compared individual habitat variables and more than 40 combinations of spatial variables to WWS estimates.

Results

The 23 study sites contained 166,577 ha of black duck habitat ranging from 1,554 to 17,353 ha ($\bar{x}$ = 7,242 ha). Average numbers of black ducks per study site ranged from 542 to 4,977 for 1973-84 (table 27.2). The habitat variable that showed the strongest association with black duck numbers was V1, the percentage of shallow marine and estuarine open water 1 m deep or less (r = 0.36, $P < 0.08$). When each was tested separately, the habitat variables of emergent and forested wetlands, tidal flats, tidal creeks and ponds, and nontidal ponds and impoundments did not appear to influence black duck numbers.

Nine models (table 27.3) had significant ($P < 0.02$) r values. The best model (8: r = 0.54, $P < 0.01$) indicated that the presence of physical variables could explain up to 29% of the variation in distribution of black ducks. Five spatial relationships are considered in model 8. Their relative contribution to habitat use is adjusted by the relationship between their area and total wetland habitat. In this model, the open water subcomponent was optimum habitat where it was 50% shallows and tidal flats. The vegetated wetland component was considered optimum habitat when 10% was tidal or permanent ponds, streams, and impoundments. Model 8 is also modified by the relationship between total area of emergent and forested wetland as the dividend and 2,590 ha (about 25.9 km²) as the divisor.

The same area component is present in seven of the nine models with the best r values. Our logic for including a hypothetical relationship between vegetated wetland and the divisor of 2,590 ha is that such an area was required to attract populations in excess of 500 black ducks and to provide them with food through the winter. This minimum area theoretically would provide the required diversity of plant and animal foods. Study sites with less vegetated wetland had a propor-

Table 27.2. Average black duck winter populations on 23 coastal study sites, 1973-84

Study site[a]	Location	Measured habitat (ha)	Average duck populations (1973-84)
ME-2	Lincoln Co., ME	5,771	680
ME-5	Washington Co., ME	15,799	3,532
MA-1	Essex Co., MA	12,015	3,309
MA-4	Suffolk Co., MA	6,162	648
MA-7	Barnstable Co., MA	8,208	1,868
MA-10	Barnstable Co., MA	14,763	3,842
MA-15	Dukes Co., MA	3,626	1,182
CT-2	Fairfield Co., CT	3,885	895
NY-26	Suffolk Co., NY	17,353	1,889
NJ-15	Atlantic Co., NJ	5,957	3,100
NJ-16	Atlantic Co., NJ	3,108	1,475
NJ-18	Atlantic Co., NJ	6,734	3,925
NJ-24	Cumberland Co., NJ	3,108	542
NJ-28	Cumberland Co., NJ	10,878	896
NJ-32	Auburn Co., NJ	5,180	877
DE-2	New Castle Co., DE	2,849	646
MD-7	Kent Co., MD	3,367	3,325
MD-11	Queen Anne Co., MD	3,108	717
MD-15	Talbot Co., MD	1,554	1,908
MD-21	Dorchester Co., MD	4,403	792
MD-27	Wicomico Co., MD	4,403	800
VA-14	Princess Anne Co., VA	13,986	2,096
VA-16	Accomack Co., VA	10,360	4,977

[a]Study site designations are those used in the concept plan for black duck wintering habitat (U.S. Fish and Wildlife Service 1979). Population figures are for survey areas smaller than the measured habitat area.

tionally lower value as a part of the equation. Since most of our best models hypothesized this area requirement for optimum habitat, we conclude that there is a minimum requirement for emergent marsh that is near 2,590 ha.

The high r value of model 9 indicates that the theorized requirements for open water shallows, and for tidal creeks and ponds within vegetated wetlands (Lewis and Garrison 1984), explain almost as much of the site use by ducks as do models that include several other physical variables. As the literature suggests, these two habitat components seem to be the most important. The presence of tidal flats did not appear crucial in influencing black duck use on our widespread study sites. Tidal flats are mainly used in the Maine to New Jersey coastal habitats and our evaluation suggests they are not important throughout the Atlantic coast winter range of black ducks.

Table 27.3. Linear correlation between spatial models and winter waterfowl survey average black duck populations on 23 study sites, 1973-84

Model[a]	r	$P<$
1. $\left(SI \dfrac{V5}{2,590} \times SI \dfrac{V7 + V8}{V6} \right)^{1/2}$	0.53	0.01
2. $\left(SI \dfrac{V5}{2,590} + SI \dfrac{V7 + V8}{V6} \right) \Big/ 2$	0.53	0.01
3. $\left[SI \dfrac{V1 + V3}{V4} \times \left(SI \dfrac{V5}{2,590} \times SI \dfrac{V7 + V8}{V6} \right)^{1/2} \right]^{1/2}$	0.52	0.01
4. $\left(SI \dfrac{V1 + V3}{V4} \right)^{\frac{V4}{V9}} \times \left[\left(SI \dfrac{V5}{2,590} \times SI \dfrac{V7 + V8}{V6} \right)^{1/2} \right]^{\frac{V5}{V9}}$	0.47	0.02
5. $\left(SI \dfrac{V1 + V3}{V4} \right)^{\frac{V4}{V9}} + \left[\left(SI \dfrac{V5}{V6} \times SI \dfrac{V7 + V8}{V6} \right)^{1/2} \right]^{\frac{V5}{V9}}$	0.50	0.02
6. $SI \dfrac{V1 + V3}{V4} \times \left(SI \dfrac{V5}{2,590} \times SI \dfrac{V7 + V8}{V6} \right)^{1/2}$	0.53	0.01
7. $\left[SI \dfrac{V1 + V3}{V4} + \left(SI \dfrac{V5}{2,590} + SI \dfrac{V7 + V8}{V6} \right) \Big/ 2 \right] \Big/ 2$	0.53	0.01
8. $\dfrac{V4}{V9} \left(SI \dfrac{V1 + V3}{V4} \right) + \dfrac{V5}{V9} \left[\left(SI \dfrac{V5}{2,590} + SI \dfrac{V7 + V8}{V6} \right) \Big/ 2 \right]$	0.54	0.01
9. $\left(SI \, V1 \times SI \dfrac{V7 + V8}{V6} \right)^{1/2}$	0.48	0.02

[a]SI = suitability index. Variables are listed in Table 1.

Discussion

Testing of habitat models for birds and mammals is in the formative stage and standardized techniques have not been developed for such a test. A basic assumption of most habitat models, including the Habitat Suitability Index models of the U.S. Fish and Wildlife Service, is that a direct linear relationship exists between habitat quality values and long-term carrying capacity (U.S. Fish and Wildlife Service 1981). In our tests, we treat black duck site-use data as being representative of carrying capacity and, thus, of habitat quality. But we are unable to interpret how frequently the existent populations accurately reflect habitat quality.

An important consideration in interpreting duck densities on winter habitat is the relationship between populations on winter areas and breeding areas. Mortality factors and habitat conditions that influence a population on wintering areas also affect it on breeding grounds, and vice versa (Feierabend 1984). Van Horne (1983) discussed factors that increase the probability that population density (of any species) will not be positively correlated with habitat quality. One of the factors listed was "seasonal habitat," referring to situations characteristic of migratory ducks; different habitats are preferred at various seasons. Black duck populations on wintering sites may reflect habitat and other circumstances on breeding grounds more than they reflect habitat quality on the wintering grounds.

Another potential difficulty in interpreting duck populations on winter habitat is our assumption that black duck numbers reflect the quality of feeding habitat. Factors other than feeding habitat quality could have a strong influence on where ducks winter. For example, ducks might concentrate on an area of moderate-quality feeding habitat if hunting was prohibited there or if it was a favored loafing site.

Finally, winter waterfowl surveys are assumed to be able to detect changes in relative population size over several years. However, according to Conroy (1981), there are problems with the survey technique—changes in aircraft, personnel, counting techniques, and survey areas—that make valid comparisons over time and between geographic areas questionable. Habitats surveyed often are those that are considered choice waterfowl habitat because of the high densities of birds wintering there (Conroy 1981). The presence of waterfowl in these habitats on a long-term basis indicates that they are important, but not necessarily essential. Conversely, the absence of waterfowl from a habitat may or may not reflect habitat quality.

Unfortunately, there are no other census data for black ducks nor any other census technique adequate for winter inventory of coastal sites. For our measure of black duck use, we had no choice other than the winter surveys. We hoped that data gathered over a series of years on several study areas would provide suitable estimates of habitat use that could be compared with our model indices of habitat quality.

Despite the difficulties described above, we know of no other technique that is suitable for testing these models. Van Horne (1983) suggested intensive field studies that included acquiring mortality and reproductive data for each study site population. Such studies would be more intensive, accurate, long-term, and expensive than our approach. We hope that our use of a number of years of survey data and a relatively large sample of study sites has eliminated the potential problems described above.

High r values between two variables can be coincidental. If a good ecological basis exists for a cause-effect relationship, then there is greater likelihood that the relationship is real. We believe that the relationships tested here have a strong ecological basis for a cause-effect relationship. Simple habitat suitability models that assume direct linear relationships probably cannot be expected to explain a high percentage of the variation in numbers of a species dependent on that habitat only seasonally. This conclusion is true particularly if relationships are not linear and when one is dealing with many complex factors (e.g., predation on nesting grounds, disease, hunting pressure, vagaries of weather, habitat quality at nesting and migration sites) that influence winter duck populations.

When one considers the factors that could mask any relationship between winter duck populations and local physical habitat variables, it is noteworthy that our relatively simplistic models detected r values as high as those found. With a relatively limited amount of effort and funds, we are able to evaluate some relationships between gross habitat features easily obtained from aerial photos and habitat maps and estimates of site use. The relationships evaluated here should be incorporated into new models with the biological variables (snail, clam, and aquatic plant populations) assumed to be important in explaining food requirements for wintering black ducks. These new models should be tested to evaluate further our ability to measure habitat quality.

LITERATURE CITED

Conroy, M. J. 1981. Appraisal of the winter waterfowl survey. U.S. Fish Wildl. Serv. Unpubl. rep. 15pp.

Cowardin, L. M., V. Carter, F. C. Golet, and E. T. LaRoe. 1979. Classification of wetlands and deepwater habitats of the United States. U.S. Fish Wildl. Serv. FWS/OBS-79/31. 103pp.

Feierabend, J. S. 1984. The black duck: an international resource on trial in the United States. Wildl. Soc. Bull. 12:128–134.

Lewis, J. C., and R. L. Garrison. 1984. Habitat Suitability Index models: American black duck (coastal wintering). U.S. Fish Wildl. Serv. FWS/OBS-82/10.68. 16pp.

U.S. Fish and Wildlife Service. 1979. Regions 4 and 5 concept plan, black duck wintering habitat. Region 5 U.S. Fish Wildl. Serv. 124pp.

———. 1981. Standards for the development of habitat suitability index models, 103 ESM. U.S. Fish Wildl. Serv.

Van Horne, B. 1983. Density as a misleading indicator of habitat quality. J. Wildl. Manage. 47:893-901.

28

Workshop Summary: Habitat Selection

Richard M. Kaminski, Alan D. Afton,
Bertin W. Anderson, Dennis G. Jorde,
and Jerry R. Longcore

The objectives of the Habitat Selection Workshop were to discuss habitat selection by waterfowl during the nonbreeding period and to summarize needs for future research. The authors served as discussion panelists or participated in preparation of this summary of the discussion of 42 workshop participants representing federal, state, provincial, and private institutions.

Habitat and Habitat Selection

Habitat is the place where an animal or plant normally lives (Ricklefs 1979, 871). Southwood (1977) entitled a paper "Habitat, the templet for ecological strategies." Implicit in this phrase is the notion that habitat imposes selective regimes upon organisms, causing them to survive and reproduce differentially. In response to these selective pressures, animals evolve or learn strategies of habitat use that may increase individual survival and ultimately fitness. Habitat selection may reflect an organism's exercising a choice among available habitats, or its differential occurrence among habitats in response to ecological consequences such as availability of resources, predation, competition, or disease. Here we define habitat selection as differential use of habitats relative to their availability.

Future Research

To establish a framework for discussion of needs for future research pertinent to waterfowl habitat selection, we reviewed the following general factors influencing

Waterfowl in Winter.© 1988 University of Minnesota. Edited by Milton W. Weller and published by the University of Minnesota Press, Minneapolis.

waterfowl habitat selection as documented by Nichols et al. (1983a): (1) food resources, (2) shelter, (3) behavioral interactions, (4) water, and (5) philopatry. Many of the issues documented by Nichols et al. (1983a) resurfaced during our forum. Prevailing interest in many of these issues, especially those listed below, indicates their perceived importance by waterfowl professionals participating in our forum and reflects the paucity of information on these issues for many species of North American waterfowl. The following list of needs for future research is not presented in any order of priority:

(1) Determine how human disturbances (e.g., hunting) influence habitat selection.

(2) Determine use of habitats and resources relative to their availabilities to discern preferences by waterfowl for each.

(3) Determine relationships between habitat selection and climate.

(4) Determine whether and how habitat selection during the nonbreeding period influences survival and subsequent reproductive performance.

(5) Determine relationships between habitat selection and sex, age, physio-logical-social status, body condition, survival, and reproduction.

(6) Determine how waterfowl assess habitat suitability. Do the birds sample habitats and resources within them to assess their relative suitability, and what are the important proximate cues and the resources being sought?

(7) Determine whether food resources become limited during the nonbreeding period, and quantify the effect of limitation on habitat selection, survival, and reproduction.

(8) Determine waterfowl use of constructed and human-modified habitats.

(9) Determine whether habitat selection and habitat suitability are density related (*in sensu* Fretwell 1972, Nichols et al. 1983b).

(10) Determine whether and how habitat selection varies among waterfowl subpopulations.

(11) Determine whether and how toxicants influence habitat selection.

(12) Determine short- and long-term effects of common wetland habitat management practices on plant, invertebrate, and waterfowl responses.

Ancillary Issues

A number of important ancillary issues emerged during our forum. We group related issues but do not imply any order of priority with sequence of presentation.

(1) Waterfowl scientists and those of other disciplines should increase communication and cooperation. Weller (1983) also pleaded for abandonment of the "lone wolf" syndrome among researchers, in favor of coordinated endeavors that expedite the understanding of natural phenomena as a prerequisite to implementing effective management programs.

(2) Researchers should feel obligated to promulgate results and management implications to public and private agencies engaged in waterfowl management.

(3) Communication should increase among the four flyway councils and technical sections. Such dialogue may reveal common problems that could be solved through coordinated research that might produce effective, large-scale management programs.

(4) University researchers should communicate with administrators of public and private natural resource agencies to uncover agency problems and then endeavor cooperatively to find solutions to problems. Moreover, natural resource agencies should solicit the cooperation of university scientists with appropriate training and interest.

(5) Researchers and administrators should co-develop research objectives to ensure agreement in program direction and fulfillment of goals.

(6) Basic research, designed tests of ecological theory, and efforts to integrate field and laboratory research should continue.

(7) Scientists should seek and use existing sets of data to test hypotheses and, thereby, increase cost-effectiveness.

(8) Researchers should prepare review papers that consolidate results on specific topics (e.g., habitat selection by wintering dabbling ducks) and emphasize ecological patterns within and among species.

(9) Researchers should replicate projects temporally and spatially (e.g., an experiment on habitat selection conducted simultaneously in two different flyways on the same species). Discovery of patterns across time and space could lead to formulation and refinement of broadly applicable habitat management practices.

Conclusions

Many of the issues discussed during the Habitat Selection Workshop had been addressed earlier in the report on the 1982 Workshop on the Ecology of Wintering Waterfowl (Anderson and Batt 1983). Reemergence of these issues suggests that now is the time to answer some of these persisting questions about the ecology and management of nonbreeding waterfowl. Researchers have answered many questions about breeding waterfowl over the past 50 years, but they cannot afford to invest another 50 years studying nonbreeding waterfowl, in view of the declining waterfowl populations and their habitats throughout the ranges of the species. Research should proceed swiftly, yet carefully and with cost-effectiveness, to fill voids in our understanding of the ecology and management of waterfowl during the nonbreeding period. Although waterfowl research in the immediate future may focus on studies of the nonbreeding period, we must remain cognizant of the biological interplay among phases of the annual cycle of waterfowl and should avoid conducting research on one phase to the exclusion of others.

LITERATURE CITED

Anderson, M. G., and B. D. J. Batt. 1983. Workshop on the ecology of wintering waterfowl. Wildl. Soc. Bull. 11:22–24.

Fretwell, S. D. 1972. Populations in a seasonal environment. Monogr. Popul. Biol. 1. Princeton Univ. Press, Princeton, N.J. 217pp.

Nichols, J. D., et al. 1983a. Report of the habitat selection discussion group. Pages 6-17 *in* Workshop on the ecology of wintering waterfowl. Delta Waterfowl Research Station Publ., Portage la Prairie, Manit., Canada.

———, K. J. Reinecke, and J. E. Hines. 1983b. Factors affecting the distribution of mallards wintering in the Mississippi Alluvial Valley. Auk 100:932–946.

Ricklefs, R. E. 1979. Ecology. Chiron Press, New York. 966pp.

Southwood, T. R. E. 1977. Habitat, the templet for ecological strategies? J. Anim. Ecol. 46:337–365.

Weller, M. W. 1983. Summary. Pages 42-44 *in* Workshop on the ecology of wintering waterfowl. Delta Waterfowl Research Station Publ., Portage la Prairie, Manit., Canada.

VII.
New Habitats and Habitat Management

29

The Role of Parks in the Range Expansion of the Mallard in the Northeast

H W Heusmann

Abstract: Wintering mallards (*Anas platyrhynchos*) in the Northeast have increased during the past 30 years according to midwinter inventories, but these inventories record only a portion of the wintering mallard population. Many mallards use park-type habitats where artificial feeding allows greater numbers of birds to overwinter than the sites could otherwise support. These park habitats enable mallards to exist year-round in areas formerly considered exclusive American black duck (*A. rubripes*) range.

The mallard has become an important game bird in the northeastern states, surpassing the black duck in some inland areas. Unlike the black duck, which winters along the coast, wintering mallards are largely restricted to freshwater or brackish sites, often in urbanized areas. The purpose of this paper is to examine the role artificial feeding plays in the maintenance of wintering mallard populations in the Northeast.

Special thanks are extended to F. Ferrigno and S. S. Sanford for comments on urban waterfowl and to C. L. Allin, G. Chasko, P. O. Corr, F. E. Hartman, L. J. Hindman, H. C. Lacaillade, J. Moser, and T. R. Myers for responses to my questionnaire. L. W. Hinds supplied banding data for the Parker River National Wildlife Refuge. G. Haas supplied computer graphics for mallard and black duck midwinter inventory trends. This study was a contribution of Massachusetts Federal Aid in Wildlife Restoration W-42-R.

Waterfowl in Winter. © 1988 University of Minnesota. Edited by Milton W. Weller and published by the University of Minnesota Press, Minneapolis.

Background

The mallard is a new bird to the Northeast. The early chroniclers recorded it as an uncommon migrant found in slightly greater numbers in the western reaches of the Northeast than in New England (Giraud 1844, Samuels 1870, Howe and Allen 1901, Knight 1908, Allen 1909, Chapman 1924). Their observations are supported by the study skin collection of the Harvard Museum of Comparative Zoology, where few mallards were collected in the Northeast before 1930. The number of specimens collected after 1930 increased, corresponding to releases by private and public sources in the early 1900s (Job 1915, Commissioners on Fisheries and Game 1919, Forbush 1929, Browne 1971). Hand-reared mallards also were re- leased by hunters after the use of live decoys was outlawed in 1935 (Heusmann and Burrell 1984).

Between 1934 and 1978, New York (Browne 1971), Pennsylvania (Pratt 1971, Hartman 1982), and Connecticut (G. Chasko, pers. commun.) released nearly a quarter-million hand-reared mallards. The effects of these releases on the mal- lard population in the Northeast are unclear because the mallard seemed to be naturally spreading eastward during this period (Johnsgard 1959, Johnsgard and DeSilvestro 1976). Britt (1971) believed that Pennsylvania's stocking program contributed to an increasing wild population; Hartman (1982), however, believed that the creation of numerous ponds and impoundments, combined with natural range expansion, was more important in light of the low survival rates of stocked mallards.

Wintering Mallards in the Northeast

Estimates of Winter Mallard Populations

The increasing mallard population in the Northeast is apparent from midwinter waterfowl inventories (fig. 29.1). An average of 56,160 mallards was observed during the 1982-84 winter inventories (Steiner 1984) for the six New England states, Long Island, mainland New York, Pennsylvania, and New Jersey. The inventories are normally conducted the first week of January and are based primarily on aerial observations. Surveys concentrate on coastal areas, major rivers and large lakes; inland areas are frequently not covered (Mid-Winter Waterfowl Workshop, Torrington, Conn., 28 February 1984; unpubl. data).

A second estimate of wintering mallard populations was provided by Audu- bon Christmas Bird Counts (table 29.1). An average of 98,600 mallards was recorded for the counts of 1981-83 (Heilbrun et al. 1982, 1983; Rubega et al. 1984). The Audubon counts generally are conducted the last half of December, imme- diately before the midwinter inventory (but falling into an earlier calendar year). Observers travel by car, boat, and on foot. Count areas, which reflect interest in birding by private citizens, consist of 24-km-diameter circles. Coverage varies

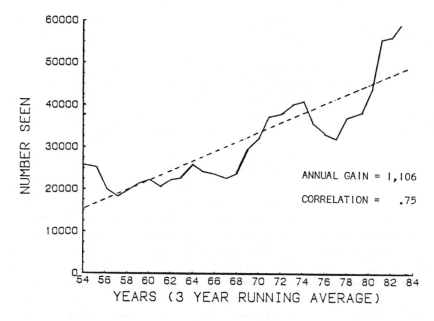

Fig. 29.1. Trends in midwinter inventory of mallards in New England states plus New York, Pennsylvania, and New Jersey in 1984-83 (adopted from Steiner 1984).

Table 29.1. Estimates of wintering mallard population in the northeastern states

Area	1981-82 through 1983-84		1984
	Average midwinter inventory[a]	Average Christmas count[b]	Biologists' park[c] mallard estimates
Maine	100	460	30
New Hampshire	70	1,180	1,400
Vermont	130	620	0
Massachusetts	1,130	8,950	13,000
Connecticut	1,970	11,270	No estimate
Rhode Island	370	1,350	800
Long Island	3,100	11,630	6,000
Mainland New York	17,060	17,150	16,000[d]
Pennsylvania	10,630	29,550	16,500
New Jersey	21,600	16,440	16,100
Total	56,160	98,600	69,830+

[a]U.S. Fish and Wildlife Service.

[b]National Audubon Society.

[c]Questionnaire responses.

[d]Incomplete estimate.

within assigned areas and among areas. Coverage of coastal marshes may be less extensive than on midwinter inventories, but coverage of small inland ponds usually is better.

Each of the above population estimates is incomplete. Each duplicates portions of the other, and each includes populations not surveyed by the other. The actual wintering population of mallards in the Northeast can be assumed to be greater than either estimate. I believe that a figure of 120,000 wintering mallards in the Northeast is an arbitrary but reasonably conservative estimate.

Parks as Winter Habitat

In Massachusetts, only about 1,000 mallards are counted on the coastal midwinter inventory; another 12,000 are missed. These birds winter in inland "parks" (Heusmann and Burrell 1984). Heusmann (1972) defined a park duck as a bird spending at least part of the day during part of the year in close company of humans and having access to artificial feed. Park ducks in Massachusetts use urban, suburban, and rural settings in freshwater, saltwater, and brackish environments. They use municipal parks and other public property, as well as privately owned areas. The main attraction of the parks is food. The ducks may be fed regularly either by public employees or private citizens, or they may rely on irregular handouts. Feeding enables ducks to utilize habitat that otherwise would not support them (Brodsky and Weatherhead 1984) and allows densities that otherwise could not be maintained (Heusmann and Burrell 1984).

The other requirement for park flocks is open water, which may be maintained by currents, tidal action, spring seepages, artificial aeration, or warm-water discharge. The physical movements of a large number of birds and the organic wastes associated with such flocks aid in keeping water open. When park areas do freeze, ducks move to nearby open areas and return when conditions moderate (Heusmann and Burrell 1984).

Northeast Park Mallard Populations

Because park mallards are not restricted to Massachusetts (Heusmann and Burrell 1984), I sent questionnaires to biologists in other northeastern states asking for information on wintering park mallard populations. Biologists varied in their knowledge of park waterfowl flocks in their jurisdiction. In some instances, estimates were expressed as a range. Responses to the questionnaire indicated that only about 45% of the known park mallard populations are counted on the midwinter inventory. I reviewed questionnaire responses and other comments and estimated a minimum park mallard population for the Northeast of 69,830 (table 29.1). Audubon Christmas Bird Counts, with greater inland coverage, probably give a better estimate of park mallard populations. For example, New York biologists could provide no estimate of the mallard population in the New York

City area or the region immediately north of the city. Christmas Bird Counts, however, indicate that more than 6,000 mallards winter in that highly urbanized area. These birds are not included in either the midwinter inventory (J. Hermes, pers. commun.) or the biologists' estimates of park mallard populations (table 29.1).

After reviewing all the data available, I estimate that 70-80% (84,000-96,000 birds) of the mallards wintering in the Northeast do so in areas where artificial feeding occurs.

Mallard Movements

The increasing population of mallards in the Northeast involves both an expansion of mallard range and growing numbers of local, feral birds, the progeny of human-released ancestors. Large-scale releases of mallards have ended in the northeastern states, but Maryland currently releases several thousand birds each year. Although the ducks are released in suitable natural habitat, many soon move to areas where they receive handouts in sanctuaries such as parks and marinas (L. J. Hindman, pers. commun.). Birds released in the Northeast probably behave similarly. I've captured mallards in parks that were released by Connecticut wildlife personnel as well as mallards released by Massachusetts sporting clubs.

Responses to the questionnaire indicated that most biologists believe 60-90% of the mallards wintering in parks to be state residents. Similar estimates were based on band recoveries for Massachusetts park mallards (Heusmann 1981). However, some mallards move longer distances: several Massachusetts winter-banded park mallards were recovered in the Midwest (Heusmann 1981). Figley and VanDruff (1982) also reported westward recoveries of New Jersey wintering suburban mallards. The origin of these birds is unknown.

Brodsky and Weatherhead (1984) reported that northern-wintering populations are predominantly male, perhaps because their larger body size enables them to conserve energy better. Some midwestern mallard drakes may migrate due east to winter, where they decoy into park flocks. However, during the period 1974-83, four adults and 11 immature mallards, preseason banded in Massachusetts, were reported as indirect recoveries in the midcontinent area. During this same period, Massachusetts hunters reported three indirect recoveries of preseason-banded, midcontinent adults and two direct recoveries of immatures from that region. All the birds except one were males. Movements of some mallards from the Midwest to the Northeast may involve the return of birds that were reared in the Northeast. For example, a male banded as an immature in Massachusetts in August 1979 was retrapped on a Minnesota refuge in September 1981 and subsequently shot in Massachusetts in December 1983. Had the duck not been previously banded, it would have been banded in Minnesota and considered a Midwest mallard when shot in Massachusetts.

Unlike the black duck, few mallards winter in salt marsh or tidal flat habitat in the Northeast, even though they use it during the summer. Banding records from the Parker River National Wildlife Refuge support this observation (table 29.2).

Table 29.2. Average number of ducks banded at Parker River National Wildlife Refuge, Newburyport, Mass.

	Summer		Winter	
Period	Mallard	Black duck	Mallard	Black duck
1968-71	111	538	17	613
1980-83	233	170	3	372

Mallards leave the coastal marshes, some migrating south; but others move into inland parks. I've recaptured mallards banded in summer on the refuge that wintered in nine different Massachusetts parks (Heusmann 1981). Conversely, a number of park mallards banded in winter were retrapped by refuge personnel during summer months.

Mallards vs. Black Ducks

Although mallard populations are increasing in the Northeast, North American black duck populations are declining. The factors most responsible for the decline are not fully known. Industrial development, urbanization, and changes in agricultural practices in the Northeast have created conditions unfavorable to black ducks but to which mallards have adapted (Rogers and Patterson 1984).

Between 1953 and 1972, the northeastern states lost over 35,200 ha (21%) of tidal marsh to filling and diking (F. Ferrigno, pers. commun.). Much of this terrain represents a loss in black duck wintering habitat. Loss of coastal wetlands is related to urbanization (Tiner 1984). The human population in the urban areas of the Northeast increased 26% from 1950 to 1970 (U.S. Department of Commerce 1983). Urbanization may be increasing mallard wintering habitat through the creation of artificial feeding sites.

Rogers and Patterson (1984) indicated that hybridization and competition between mallards and black ducks are a major problem in Ontario and Quebec. Heusmann (1974) reported that the maritime proclivities of the black duck limit its contact with mallards during the winter when pair-bond formation occurs, reducing chances of hybridization. During the winters of 1971-74, 8.1% of the ducks banded on the Massachusetts coast were hybrids, whereas the rate in parks was 12.9%. As the number of mallards has increased in Massachusetts, so has the number of hybrids. Park waterfowl banding ceased in 1976, but by 1979-82 the coastal hybrid rate had increased to 15.9% (Heusmann 1985). Brodsky and Weatherhead (1984) observed that mallards began pair formation earlier than black ducks and that surplus drake mallards were able to compete successfully for black duck females. Limited open water in northern regions and artificial feeding serve to bring the two species together, where disparate sex ratios favoring males increase the chances of hybridization.

Conclusions

In contrast to black ducks, mallards show little tendency to winter in salt marsh or tidal flats in the Northeast, and inland waters frequently freeze over. Small areas of open water where artificial feeding occurs provide the major source of winter habitat for mallards in this region, enabling mallards to exist in a part of the country that was originally black duck range. Black duck populations have been declining for 30 years (Steiner 1984), and hybridization with mallards is probably involved in this situation. Park waterfowl flocks also have the potential to become focal points for disease outbreaks that may then spread into natural areas (M. Friend, pers. commun.).

Currently, complaints about nuisance urban waterfowl center largely on Canada geese (Blandin and Heusmann 1974), but several Massachusetts communities have passed ordinances prohibiting the feeding of all waterfowl. Although it is unlikely that such restrictions will become widespread, the cessation of feeding would result in a major change in northeastern mallard habitat, possibly reversing the trend of a growing population.

LITERATURE CITED

Allen, G. M. 1909. Fauna of New England; List of Aves. Occas. Pap., Boston Soc. Nat. Hist. 230pp.

Blandin, W. W., and H. W. Heusmann. 1974. Establishment of Canada goose populations through urban gosling transplants. Trans. Northeast. Sect. Wildl. Soc. 31:83–100.

Britt, R. 1971. Views from production states: Pennsylvania. Pages 125-126 in Role of hand-reared ducks in waterfowl management—a symposium. Bur. Sport Fish. Wildl. and Max McGraw Wildl. Foundation, Dundee, Ill. 174pp.

Brodsky, L. M., and P. J. Weatherhead. 1984. Behavior and ecological factors contributing to American black duck-mallard hybridization. J. Wildl. Manage. 48:846–852.

Browne, S. 1971. The New York hand-reared duck program. Pages 9-19 in Role of hand-reared ducks in waterfowl management—a symposium. Bur. Sport Fish. Wildl. and Max McGraw Wildl. Foundation, Dundee, Ill. 174pp.

Chapman, F. M. 1924. Handbook of birds of eastern North America. D. Appleton and Co., New York. 530pp.

Commissioners on Fisheries and Game. 1919. Annual report. Pub. Doc. 25. Wright and Potter Printing Co., Boston. 296pp.

Figley, W. K., and L. VanDruff. 1982. The ecology of urban mallards. Wildl. Monogr. 81:1–39.

Forbush, E. H. 1929. Birds of Massachusetts and other New England states. Part 1: Waterbirds, marshbirds, and shorebirds. Mass. Dep. Agric., Boston. 481pp.

Giraud, J. P., Jr. 1844. Birds of Long Island. Wiley and Putnam, New York. 397pp.

Hartman, F. E. 1982. Evaluation of game farm duck stockings. Pennsylvania Game Comm., Harrisburg. Unpaged.

Heilbrun, L. H., and Christmas Bird Count Regional Editors. 1982. The eighty second Audubon Christmas Bird Count. Am. Birds 36:369–778.

———, and ———. 1983. The eighty third Audubon Christmas Bird Count. Am. Birds 37:369–792.

Heusmann, H. W. 1972. Mallards in the park. Massachusetts Wildl. 22:5–7.

———. 1974. Mallard-black duck relationships in the Northeast. Wildl. Soc. Bull. 2:171–177.

———. 1981. Movements and survival rates of park mallards. J. Field Ornithol. 52:214–221.

———. 1985. Plight of the black duck. Cape Naturalist 13:59–61.

———, and R. Burrell. 1984. Park waterfowl population in Massachusetts. J. Field Ornithol. 55:89–96.

Howe, R. H., Jr., and G. M. Allen. 1901. The birds of Massachusetts. Cambridge. Mass. 154pp.

Job, H. K. 1915. Propagation of wild birds. Doubleday, Page and Co., Garden City, N.Y. 276pp.

Johnsgard, P. A. 1959. Evolutionary relationships among the North American mallards. Ph.D. Thesis, Cornell Univ., Ithaca, N.Y. 159pp.

———, and R. DiSilvestro. 1976. Seventy-five years of change in mallard-black duck ratios in eastern North America. Am. Birds 30:904–908.

Knight, O. W. 1908. The birds of Maine. Charles H. Gloss Co., Bangor, Maine. 693pp.

Pratt, H. R. 1971. The mallard stocking program in Pennsylvania. Pages 21-42 in Role of hand-reared ducks in waterfowl management—a symposium. Bur. Sport Fish. Wildl. and Max McGraw Wildl. Foundation, Dundee, Ill. 174pp.

Rogers, J. P., and J. H. Patterson. 1984. The black duck population and its management. Trans. N. Am. Wildl. Nat. Resour. Conf. 49:527–534.

Rubega, M. A., and Christmas Bird Count Regional Editors. 1984. The eighty fourth Audubon Christmas Bird Count. Am. Birds 38:396–828.

Samuels, E. A. 1870. The birds of New England. Noyes, Holmes and Co., Boston. 591pp.

Steiner, A. J. 1984. Midwinter waterfowl inventory, Atlantic flyway, 1954-1984 trend analysis. U.S. Fish Wildl. Serv. Reg. 5. Newton Corners, Mass. 284pp.

Tiner, R. W., Jr. 1984. Wetlands of the United States: current status and recent trends. U.S. Fish Wildl. Serv. Washington, D.C. 59pp.

U.S. Department of Commerce. 1983. 1980 census of population. Vol. I, chap. A, part 1:1–49.

30

Use of Catfish Ponds by Waterfowl Wintering in Mississippi

Mark W. Christopher, Edward P. Hill, and David E. Steffen

Abstract: Aerial census of waterfowl on randomly selected clusters of channel catfish (*Ictalurus punctatus*) impoundments were conducted from November 1983 through March 1984 in a seven-county area of Mississippi River bottomland. Estimates of the total waterfowl population on catfish ponds were made from census counts using the ratio-to-size estimator. The average weekly estimate was 51,853 birds (range 19,628-92,857), including northern shoveler (*Anas clypeata*), 34%; ruddy duck (*Oxyura jamaicensis*), 24%; American coot (*Fulica americana*), 12%; lesser scaup (*Aythya affinis*), 12%; ring-necked duck (*Aythya collaris*), 6%; mallard (*Anas platyrhynchos*), 5%; gadwall (*Anas strepera*), 3%; canvasback (*Aythya valisineria*), 1%; and others making up the remainder.

Bottomland hardwood forests historically provided some of the essential habitat for wintering waterfowl, particularly mallards, in the lower Mississippi alluvial plain. There were 4.8 million hectares of bottomland hardwood forests in 1937. Conversion of bottomland hardwood area into croplands was accelerated as soybean and grain crops became more profitable than hardwood products (MacDonald et al. 1979). By 1978, the bottomland hardwood forests in this region had been reduced to 2.1 million hectares (MacDonald et al. 1979). In contrast to the decline of bottomland hardwood wetlands in the Delta region of Mississippi, impoundments for catfish, bait, and crawfish (*Procambarus clarki*) production were being constructed at a rate of 4,858 ha/year, or from 6,943 ha in 1977 to 27,477 ha in 1983 (Wellborn et al. 1983).

Notes from U.S. Fish and Wildlife Service (USFWS) midwinter waterfowl surveys indicated that catfish ponds contained increasing numbers of waterfowl. However, actual population estimates and seasonal trends of waterfowl use of catfish ponds have not been documented. This paper reports weekly population estimates for waterfowl and discusses some roles of catfish ponds in wintering waterfowl populations in the Mississippi Delta.

The authors wish to thank C. Mills for typing the manuscript; G. Hurst, R. Muncy, R. Kaminski, D. McDonald, P. Opler, K. Manci, E. Hackett, and anonymous reviewers for editorial review; and Triple C Aviation for providing flying services. This is a contribution of the Mississippi Cooperative Fish and Wildlife Research Unit: U.S. Fish and Wildlife Service, Mississippi Department of Wildlife Conservation, Mississippi State University, Department of Wildlife and Fisheries, and the Wildlife Management Institute cooperating.

Study Area

The study area consisted of parts of Humphreys, Holmes, Sharkey, Sunflower, Washington, Bolivar, and Leflore counties in the alluvial valley region of the Mississippi River, known locally as the Mississippi Delta. This area contains 80% (approximately 21,132 ha) of the catfish, bait, and crawfish ponds in that physiographic region of the state. This area also represents 75% of all aquacultural production in Mississippi and 65% of all catfish production in the Southeast. Bait and crawfish ponds make up 2% and 1%, respectively, of the aquaculture production in the study area.

Methods

Complexes of fish ponds delineated from Landsat imagery were organized into clusters according to arbitrary boundaries for single-stage cluster sampling (Cochran 1977, Shaeffer et al. 1979). All clusters ($N = 261$) then were numbered and about one-third ($N = 92$) were randomly selected for sampling. Total surface area for all clusters was calculated from the Landsat in hectares. The catfish pond clusters to be censused were organized into an aerial survey route encompassing all or portions of seven counties (fig. 30.1).

Aerial waterfowl censuses of the 92 sample clusters commenced on 5 November 1983 and continued at about weekly intervals until 10 March 1984. Estimated counts were made of the total waterfowl on each pond within each cluster. Waterfowl population estimates and standard errors for all ponds within the entire study area were estimated for each of the 19 aerial censuses using the ratio-to-size estimator (Shaeffer et al. 1979). This estimator is compatible with single-stage cluster sampling and uses a finite population correction factor. Confidence intervals were calculated at the 90% level.

Fig. 30.1. Aerial view of catfish pond complexes in Delta region of Mississippi.

Results

The mean number of total waterfowl estimated to be using catfish ponds in the study area was 51,853. Weekly estimates for all species were highest during mid-November, decreased gradually through mid-December, and showed significant declines in late December (fig. 30.2). Estimates indicated a population increase during the first census in January, followed by below-average levels throughout January and February before increasing during March (fig. 30.2). Confidence intervals for successive censuses overlapped until 16-26 December, when the weekly population projections differed significantly. During a freeze (19 December to 22 January 1983), weekly low temperatures averaged −5.5C, whereas normal weekly lows rarely fall below 0C (Hull et al. 1982). Marked declines in total waterfowl, ruddy duck, American coot, ring-necked duck, and canvasback population estimates occurred during the first week of freezing weather.

The mean population estimate of northern shoveler (17,778) was 34% of the mean total waterfowl population. The mean ruddy duck population estimate (12,347) averaged 24% of the total. The mean American coot estimate (6,324) was 12% of the total, as was the lesser scaup estimate (6,010). The mean ring-necked duck estimate (3,265) was 6% of the total. The means for mallard (2,653) and

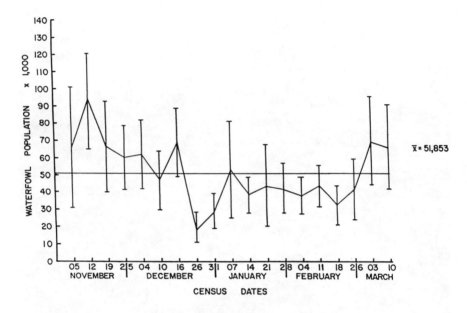

Fig. 30.2. Total weekly populations of waterfowl using catfish ponds in Mississippi River alluvial bottomland region of Mississippi, 1983-84. Populations calculated using ratio-to-size estimator with confidence intervals at $P < .10$.

gadwall (1,255) were 5% and 3% of the total, respectively. Lastly, the mean canvasback estimate (531) was 1% of the total. Miscellaneous species in which population estimates averaged 200 birds or fewer included hooded merganser (*Mergus cacullatus*), bufflehead (*Bucephala albeola*), redhead (*Aythya americana*), northern pintail (*Anas acuta*), American wigeon (*Anas americana*), green-winged teal (*Anas crecca*), and Canada goose (*Branta canadensis*).

Discussion

Catfish ponds in Mississippi represent a substantial area of permanent, artificial wetlands available to waterfowl in a region that has otherwise undergone major declines in natural permanent and seasonal wetlands. Aerial surveys conducted during the fall and winter of 1983-84 demonstrate that these ponds are used by wintering waterfowl. Because catfish ponds constitute most of the permanent open-water, lacustrine habitat in the Delta region, they may provide the major source of habitat available to shovelers, scaup, ruddy ducks, ring-necked ducks, coots, and canvasbacks.

Midwinter waterfowl survey data for the southern portion of the Delta show the yearly (1972-83) average total waterfowl population to be 178,200 birds (table 30.1). The estimated average waterfowl population on catfish ponds during 1983-84

Table 30.1. Average midwinter waterfowl survey counts for the southern portion of the Delta (1972-83)[a]

Species	Average count
Mallard	126,610
Northern pintail	10,621
Ring-necked duck	7,913
American wigeon	7,269
Ruddy duck	5,900
Gadwall	5,723
American coot	4,688
Scaup	4,144
Northern shoveler	4,069
Green-winged teal	3,596
Canvasback	1,156
Snow goose	1,108
Total waterfowl	178,200

[a]Averages computed from data supplied courtesy of B. R. Tramel.

represented 29% of the average total waterfowl observed in this seven-county area during midwinter surveys. USFWS waterfowl biologists noted that, during dry winters since the late 1970s, about half of the waterfowl observed on midwinter surveys in the Delta region were on catfish ponds (B. R. Tramel and S. Woodson, pers. commun.). Wells (1984) also suggested that catfish ponds are especially important during winters with low precipitation. Catfish ponds probably make their most vital contribution to waterfowl during the driest periods of the non-breeding season, such as late fall and late winter.

The majority of mallards, pintails, American wigeon, gadwalls, green-winged teal, and snow geese (*Chen caerulescens*) do not use the catfish pond habitat, whereas a small proportion of American wigeon and gadwalls use catfish ponds consistently. The estimated maximum population of mallards during the freeze (18,000) represents only 10% of the 1983-84 midwinter waterfowl survey (conducted at about the same time) estimate for the entire Delta region of Mississippi. Comparing the average populations calculated for northern shovelers, scaup, ruddy ducks, and American coots using catfish ponds and their average midwinter counts, we see that the majority of these species inhabit catfish ponds throughout the winter. Similar comparisons with canvasbacks and ring-necked ducks show that these species apparently use other wetlands in addition to catfish ponds. Northern shovelers, American coots, and ring-necked ducks were observed using flooded rice and soybean fields in addition to catfish ponds.

Midwinter survey data show general downward trends in diving duck use on large reservoirs outside the study area and on oxbow lakes adjacent to the

Mississippi River. Wells (1984) believed that a decrease in diving ducks observed on Mississippi reservoirs was probably the result of the catfish ponds. Diving ducks may be shifting from one habitat to another. The importance of catfish ponds to waterfowl may increase with time and as the surface area of this unique new habitat increases.

LITERATURE CITED

Cochran, W. G. 1977. Sampling techniques. 3rd ed. John Wiley, New York.

Hull, D. D., M. A. Brown, G. Rench, J. S. Hursh, and C. D. Ranney. 1982. Stoneville, Miss. Weather Normals, 1960-79. Agric. Res. Serv., Agric. Reviews and Manuals, South Series 24. 29pp.

MacDonald, P. O., W. E. Frayer, and J. K. Clauser. 1979. Documentation, chronology, and future projections of bottomland hardwood habitat loss in the lower Mississippi alluvial plain. U.S. Fish Wildl. Serv., Basic Rep., Vol. I, 133pp.

Shaeffer, R. L., W. Mendenhall, and L. Ott. 1979. Elementary survey sampling. 2nd ed. Duxbury Press, North Scituate, Mass. 278pp.

Wellborn, T. L., Jr., T. E. Schuedler, and J. R. MacMillian. 1983. For Fish Farming, Newsletter. 12 January 1983. Coop. Ext. Serv., Mississippi State

Wells, R. K. 1984. Periodic waterfowl inventories 1978-1982. Mississippi Dep. Wildl. Conserv. Jackson, Miss. 23pp.

31

Waterfowl Habitat Created by Floodwater-Retarding Structures in the Southern United States

Gary Bates, Gary L. Valentine, and Frank H. Sprague

Abstract: Floodwater-retarding structures provide valuable habitat to migrant and wintering waterfowl in the South. Although flood reduction is their primary purpose, waterfowl use is an incidental benefit that becomes more valuable as natural wetlands diminish. This paper reports the number of impoundments and total area of permanent water impounded by floodwater-retarding structures constructed with the assistance of the U.S. Soil Conservation Service in Alabama, Arkansas, Florida, Georgia, Kentucky, Louisiana, Mississippi, North Carolina, Oklahoma, South Carolina, Tennessee, and Texas. Numbers of structures planned or under construction as of 1983 and sizes of areas to be impounded also are provided. Findings of scientific and management studies on use of these structures by waterfowl are included. Features reported to enhance these structures for waterfowl are listed.

The construction of floodwater-retarding structures (FWRS) in the South since the early 1950s has created 133,261 ha (329,155 acres) of surface water, which provides waterfowl habitat of varying quality, primarily in the Mississippi and Central flyways. The U.S. Soil Conservation Service (SCS) assists in the construction of FWRS under the authority of the 1944 Flood Control Act, the 1954 Watershed Protection and Flood Prevention Act, and the Food and Agriculture Act of 1962 (Nord 1963, Lea and Mattson 1974).

FWRS are impoundments designed with flood control as a primary purpose. These impoundments have many names, including flood-detention structures, flood-prevention lakes, PL-566 impoundments, small watershed lakes, and pilot

Waterfowl in Winter. © 1988 University of Minnesota. Edited by Milton W. Weller and published by the University of Minnesota Press, Minneapolis.

watershed structures. All such impoundments will be referred to here as FWRS. In addition to FWRS, this survey includes impoundments built for grade stabilization, erosion control, and other limited uses. They are typically 2.0 ha (5.0 acres) and contain some or all of the features associated with FWRS.

The objectives of this paper are to describe the extent, location, and characteristics of existing and planned FWRS; to review current information about waterfowl use of these structures; and to discuss those features of structures that affect construction and management from a waterfowl perspective.

Description of Floodwater-Retarding Structures

FWRS have dams designed with a principal spillway consisting of a vertical concrete inlet and a conduit through the dam. Water flows through this spillway when levels exceed the elevation of the inlet. An emergency spillway is provided, but it seldom functions because of the large storage capacity. The structures impound excessive runoff from upstream sources and release the water slowly to prevent downstream flooding. Impoundments created by these structures also are designed to trap sediment and prevent its movement downstream.

FWRS differ from major reservoirs and farm ponds in many respects. Large reservoirs built on major streams and rivers generally are much larger and deeper than FWRS, which are impoundment-type structures that usually contain a greater proportion of shallow water in relation to the total water area than does the typical farm pond. Surface areas of FWRS typically range from 11.0 to 18.0 ha (27 to 44 acres); surface areas of farm ponds are typically less than 0.4 ha (1 acre). FWRS are subject to greater fluctuations in volume, water level, and surface area than are farm ponds. Water-exchange rates also are greater in FWRS than in ponds as a result of greater ratios of drainage area to surface area. Drain valves are routinely installed on FWRS to allow manipulation of water levels.

Farm ponds may be constructed by erecting a dam to create an impoundment-type pond or by excavating soil material to create a pit-type pond. Excavated ponds are typically less than 0.2 ha (0.5 acre) and contain a very limited littoral zone because slopes are steep.

Existing and Planned FWRS

SCS has provided assistance in the construction of 22,600 FWRS in the United States, which impound approximately 232,700 ha (574,800 acres) of surface water (U.S. Soil Conservation Service 1984a). Forty-five percent (10,091) have been constructed in the southern United States and impound 133,261 ha (329,155 acres) of surface water. Table 31.1 shows the number of structures and surface areas of water impounded in each of the 12 southern states. Forty-eight percent (4,852) of the FWRS built in the South are in the Central Flyway (table 31.1). The SCS has

Table 31.1. Number and surface areas of floodwater-retarding structures constructed in the southern states[a]

Flyway	State	Number	Hectares	Acreage
Central	Oklahoma	2,403	25,198	62,238
	Texas	2,449	32,620	80,572
	Subtotal	4,852	57,818	142,810
Mississippi	Arkansas	372	5,075	12,536
	Louisiana	120	1,841	4,548
	Mississippi	1,584	24,305	60,039
	Kentucky	319	4,249	10,495
	Tennessee	178	2,371	5,850
	Alabama	569	8,938	22,077
	Subtotal	3,142	46,779	115,545
Atlantic	North Carolina	294	5,261	12,994
	South Carolina	324	5,798	14,321
	Georgia	1,349	16,057	39,662
	Florida	130	1,548	3,822
	Subtotal	2,097	28,664	70,800
	Total	10,091	133,261	329,155

[a]Data compiled from watershed progress reports from U.S. Soil Conservation Service in Alabama (1984c), Arkansas (1983a), Georgia (1984b), Kentucky (1983b), Louisiana (1983c), Mississippi (1982), North Carolina (1983e), Oklahoma (1983d), Tennessee (1984d), and Texas (1984e) and from personal communications from SCS biologists J. Vance (Florida) and W. Melven (South Carolina).

assisted in the construction of 3,142 FWRS in the Mississippi Flyway and 2,097 FWRS in the Atlantic Flyway (table 31.1).

An additional 1,574 FWRS are planned for the South. These structures have the potential of impounding 21,315 ha (52,650 acres) of surface water (table 31.2).

Waterfowl Use Investigations

FWRS have been studied more extensively in Oklahoma than in any other southern state. Copelin (1961) flew five aerial surveys of FWRS in western Oklahoma from November 1960 to March 1961. The average number of ducks counted on utilized impoundments ranged from 54 to 88. Slimak (1975) counted 118,120 waterfowl of 23 species on 100 impoundments in north-central Oklahoma between September 1971 and August 1972. Most of the structures larger than 0.4 ha (1 acre) were FWRS. Sixty-two percent of the birds observed were puddle ducks. Heitmeyer and Vohs (1984) studied use of Oklahoma's constructed wetlands, including FWRS, by migrating and wintering waterfowl. He speculated that 50% of the state's puddle ducks may use natural wetlands, which constitute 10-15% of Oklahoma's wetland basins.

Table 31.2. Number and surface areas of floodwater-retarding structures planned in the southern states[a]

Flyway	State	Number	Hectares	Acreage
Central	Oklahoma	429	4,498	11,111
	Texas	393	5,234	12,929
	Subtotal	822	9,732	24,040
Mississippi	Arkansas	90	1,228	3,033
	Louisiana	12	184	455
	Mississippi	150	2,302	5,685
	Kentucky	50	666	1,645
	Tennessee	206	2,744	6,777
	Alabama	46	722	1,785
	Subtotal	554	7,846	19,380
Atlantic	North Carolina	25	447	1,105
	South Carolina	15	1,409	3,480
	Georgia	158	1,881	4,645
	Florida	0	0	0
	Subtotal	198	3,737	9,230
	Total	1,574	21,315	52,650

[a]Data compiled from watershed progress reports from U.S. Soil Conservation Service in Alabama (1984c), Arkansas (1983a), Georgia (1984b), Kentucky (1983b), Louisiana (1983c), Mississippi (1982), North Carolina (1983e), Oklahoma (1983d), Tennessee (1984d), and Texas (1984e) and from personal communications from SCS biologists J. Vance (Florida) and W. Melven (South Carolina).

Hobaugh and Teer (1981) studied waterfowl use of 55 FWRS in north-central Texas. They observed 41,855 waterfowl of 14 species between August 1976 and April 1977. Ducks accounted for 84% of the total and puddle ducks for 77% of all ducks.

Grizzell (1975) reported that 17,000 waterfowl used five Arkansas FWRS from October 1974 to March 1975; mallards were the most frequently observed species. In 1960, Grizzell reported that 53 species of waterbirds, including marsh and shorebirds, used water areas created by watershed projects in north Georgia.

Factors Affecting Waterfowl Use

Size

Several investigators suggested that larger impoundments were more heavily used than small ones. Most ducks used lakes larger than 10.0 ha (25 acres) in western Oklahoma (Copelin 1961), possibly because these larger western Oklahoma impoundments provide adequate food and security from human disturbance (Logan 1975). In north-central Oklahoma, fall migrants used larger, isolated impoundments, possibly to avoid hunting pressure (Slimak 1975). Hobaugh and Teer (1981) reported that seven of the most-used impoundments in Texas were larger than 16 ha (40 acres).

Aquatic Vegetation

Impoundments with abundant aquatic vegetation were used more than those with little or no aquatic vegetation (Copelin 1961, Hobaugh and Teer 1981). Spring migrants returned north at a leisurely pace, feeding on aquatic vegetation and macroinvertebrate populations (Slimak 1975). Aquatic plant species most frequently reported as important waterfowl foods in FWRS were southern naiad (busy pondweed), *Najas guadalupensis*; longleaf pondweed, *Potamogeton nodosus*; fennelleaf (sago) pondweed, *P. pectinatus*; muskgrass, *Chara* spp; marshpurslane (water primrose), *Ludwigia peploides*; longspike spikerush, *Eleocharis macrostachya*; and smartweeds, *Polygonum* spp. Dense stands of cattail, *Typha* spp, apparently discourage puddle duck use (Logan 1975).

Severe Winter Weather

Three authors suggest that waterfowl use is affected by severe winter weather. Fall migrants were observed on large impoundments near dams with east-west orientation, possibly attempting to avoid cold north winds (Slimak 1975). Large numbers of ducks were observed on 19 January 1977, using unfrozen flood-prevention pools when most smaller water bodies in north-central Texas were frozen (Hobaugh and Teer 1981). Large reservoirs, FWRS, and farm ponds in north-central Texas winter substantial numbers of waterfowl, particularly following severe weather in the Midwest (Gough 1984).

Proximity to Large Reservoirs and Refuges

Hatcher (1973) suggested that FWRS near refuges and flyways attract many waterfowl. Wintering mallards rested on large impoundments and fed in small impoundments (Slimak 1975). Daily feeding flights from large impoundments to small ones within a radius of 1.6 km (1.0 mile) were observed.

Value to Waterfowl

Some wildlife professionals have questioned the value of artificial impoundments as waterfowl habitat. Heitmeyer and Vohs (1984) suggested that protection of natural wetlands is more beneficial to wintering puddle ducks in Oklahoma than enhancing areas associated with large reservoirs and farm ponds. They stated that ponds built with steep sides to maximize water storage lack littoral zones that maintain the biological productivity of wetlands. Many FWRS, however, have extensive littoral zones, and as they store soil sediments during their functional life, a higher percentage of littoral zone is created.

Heitmeyer and Vohs (1984) stated that when natural wetlands are abundant in Oklahoma, mallards winter on fewer artificial reservoirs. However, constructed impoundments, including FWRS, provide migrating and wintering habitat for mallards in drought years when natural wetlands are scarce.

Other reports support the value of FWRS as wintering waterfowl habitat. Siegler (1945) suggested that more and larger lakes in eastern Texas would increase wintering waterfowl numbers. Thirty-six years later, Hobaugh and Teer (1981) reported significant waterfowl use of FWRS in north-central Texas. Barclay's (1976) analysis of Oklahoma's annual waterfowl inventories revealed a substantial increase in wintering ducks and geese between 1963 and 1972. He attributed this increase to construction of large impoundments, such as reservoirs built by the Corps of Engineers. A large number of FWRS were built in Oklahoma during the 1960s and early 1970s, which may also have contributed to the observed increase.

Enhancement of Waterfowl Value

Although waterfowl use of FWRS is an incidental benefit, the addition of specific features could enhance waterfowl values:

(1) Install a drawdown slot in principal spillways to facilitate exposure of shallow water areas for food plantings (Grizzell 1960, Copelin 1961, Gough 1984).

(2) Plant corn, grain sorghum, or other foods near impoundments (Hatcher 1973, Slimak 1975).

(3) Use FWRS a source of water to flood downstream food plantings or bottomland hardwoods (Dillon 1958, Copelin 1961, Dillon and Marriage 1973).

(4) Fence sections of shoreline to exclude livestock and encourage waterfowl food plants (Logan 1975, Hobaugh and Teer 1981).

(5) Seed areas disturbed during construction with annual grasses for turbidity control and waterfowl food (Copelin 1961, Hobaugh and Teer 1981).

(6) Design impoundments with 25-50% of surface area less than 0.9 m (3 ft) deep (Logan 1975, Slimak 1975).

(7) Manipulate water levels to encourage natural food plants (Copelin 1961, Gough 1984).

(8) Plant submergent, floating-leaved, and emergent aquatic plants for food and cover (Copelin 1961).

(9) Retain trees and brush in planned permanent water area during construction (Copelin 1961).

(10) Install wood duck nesting boxes (H. R. Huffstatler, SCS, Mississippi, pers. commun.).

Conclusions

The most extensive wetland losses in the United States have been in Arkansas, Florida, Louisiana, Mississippi, Nebraska, North Carolina, North Dakota, South Dakota, and Texas (Tiner 1984). FWRS constructed in the southern states do not replace losses of natural wetlands, but wintering waterfowl regularly use these impoundments. In Oklahoma and Texas, where most waterfowl use studies have been conducted, winter waterfowl habitat has been created in areas with few natural wetlands. The value of these FWRS will improve as they collect sediment and the littoral zone vegetation increases. During extended droughts, migrant and wintering waterfowl will have access to dependable water bodies.

In the remaining southern states, FWRS are potentially more valuable to wintering waterfowl because of the loss of natural wetlands along the Atlantic and Gulf coasts and the lower Mississippi Valley. Waterfowl use should be assessed on FWRS in these states to determine their present value to wintering birds.

Individuals who own existing impoundments should be encouraged to enhance the waterfowl value of their FWRS. The Oklahoma and Texas studies have identified important factors affecting waterfowl use. These factors should be used to identify those FWRS, both existing and planned, where enhancement measures will be most productive.

LITERATURE CITED

Barclay, J. S. 1976. Waterfowl use of Oklahoma reservoirs. Proc. Okla. Acad. Sci. Suppl. 5, pp. 141–151.

Copelin, F. F. 1961. Waterfowl inventory on small flood prevention reservoirs in western Oklahoma. Proc. Okla. Acad. Sci. 42:260–263.

Dillon, O. W., Jr. 1958. Biology notes on floodwater retarding structures. U.S. Soil Conserv. Serv., Rosenberg, Tex. Biol. Note 1. 3pp.

———, and L. D. Marriage. 1973. Fish and wildlife habitat improvement in watershed projects. Proc. Soil Conserv. Soc. Am. 28:166–171.

Gough, B. 1984. Trouble in the promised land, part 2. Tex. Parks Wildl. 42:28–31.

Grizzell, R. A., Jr. 1960. Fish and wildlife management on watershed projects. Trans. N. Am. Wildl. Nat. Resour. Conf. 25:186–192.

———. 1975. Waterfowl use of floodwater retarding structures in Arkansas 1974-1975. U.S. Soil Conserv. Serv., Little Rock. Biol. Tech Note AK-13. 2pp.

Hatcher, R. M. 1973. Floodwater retarding structures as fish and wildlife habitat. Proc. Soil Conserv. Soc. Am. 28:158–160.

Heitmeyer, M. E., and P. A. Vohs, Jr. 1984. Distribution and habitat use of waterfowl wintering in Oklahoma. J. Wildl. Manage. 48:51–62.

Hobaugh, W. C., and J. G. Teer. 1981. Waterfowl use characteristics of flood prevention lakes in north-central Texas. J. Wildl. Manage. 45:16–26.

Lea, D. M., and C. D. Mattson. 1974. Evolution of the small watershed program: changes in Public Law 566 watershed protection and flood prevention program, 1954-72. Econ. Res. Serv. Agric. Econ. Rep. 262. 58pp.

Logan, F. H. 1975. Characteristics of small impoundments in western Oklahoma; their value as waterfowl habitat and potential for management. M.S. Thesis, Oklahoma State Univ., Stillwater. 77pp.

Nord, W. H. 1963. Wildlife in the small watershed program. Trans. N. Am. Wildl. Nat. Resour. Conf. 28:118–124.

Siegler, R. H. 1945. Waterfowl and their management in inland Texas. Trans. N. Am. Wildl. Nat. Resour. Conf. 10:274–280.

Slimak, M. W. 1975. Waterfowl (Anatidae) utilization of impoundments in a north-central Oklahoma watershed. M.S. Thesis, Oklahoma State Univ., Stillwater. 189pp.

Tiner, R. W., Jr. 1984. Wetlands of the United States: current status and recent trends. U.S. Fish Wildl. Serv., Washington, D.C. 59pp.

U.S. Soil Conservation Service. 1982. Watershed progress report—Mississippi. Jackson. 58pp.

———. 1983c. Arkansas annual progress report. Little Rock. 28pp.

———. 1983b. Kentucky annual progress summaries FY 1983. Lexington. 23pp.

———. 1983c. Louisiana watershed progress report. Alexandria. 39pp.

———. 1983d. Oklahoma watershed summary. Stillwater. 65pp.

———. 1983e. Watershed progress—North Carolina. Raleigh. 32pp.

———. 1984a. Dams inventory base data. Washington, D.C. 2pp.

———. 1984b. Watershed development in Georgia—status report. Athens. 45pp.

———. 1984c. Watershed progress report—Alabama. Auburn. 48pp.

———. 1984d. Watershed progress report—Tennessee. Nashville. 30pp.

———. 1984e. Watershed progress report—Texas. Temple. 118pp.

32

Experimental Plantings for Management of Crayfish and Waterfowl

James R. Nassar, Robert H. Chabreck, and David C. Hayden

Abstract: Volunteer plants, rice (*Oryza sativa*), Japanese millet (*Echinochloa crusgalli* var. *frumentacea*), and browntop millet (*Panicum ramosum*) were evaluated as crayfish (*Procambarus* spp.) forage and for their ability to provide enough food to attract wintering waterfowl (both ducks and American coots—*Fulica americana*) to large impoundments. Crayfish abundance did not differ in impoundments with the four vegetation types, although rice produced the greatest total vegetation biomass. Crayfish production in all vegetation types was reduced by poor water quality in the fall and spring. Dabbling ducks, diving ducks, and American coots were most abundant in browntop millet habitat, even though it produced the least seed of the three domestic grains tested. Although rice produced the greatest amount of seed, waterfowl used these impoundments primarily at night and could neither be identified nor enumerated.

Impoundments for the commercial production of red swamp (*Procambarus clarkii*) and white river crayfish (*P. acutus acutus*), in Louisiana increased from 24 ha in 1949 (Lovell 1968) to 43,000 ha in 1984 (R. P. Romaire, pers. commun.). Annual crayfish harvest varies between 22 million and 32 million kg, with a wholesale value of $25-40 million (Louisiana Cooperative Extension Service 1983). Impoundment construction for crayfish is projected to increase as management techniques improve and farmers accept crayfish as a viable alternative to traditional crops.

Current crayfish management practices prescribe planting domestic rice (*Oryza sativa*) or small grains such as Japanese millet (*Echinochloa crusgalli* var.

Waterfowl in Winter. © 1988 University of Minnesota. Edited by Milton W. Weller and published by the University of Minnesota Press, Minneapolis.

frumentacea) or browntop millet (*Panicum ramosum*) as forage for crayfish (Huner and Barr 1984). These three species of commercial grains (rice, browntop millet, and Japanese millet) also are planted to attract waterfowl. Researchers (Martin et al. 1951, 462; Horn and Glasgow 1964: Givens et al. 1964) have emphasized the importance of rice in the management of wintering waterfowl in the southeastern United States. Neely and Davison (1966), Neely (1967), and Wright (1959) recommended planting millets on intensively managed, upland waterfowl areas.

Perry et al. (1970) reported that multiple-use management of impoundments for crayfish and waterfowl is a reasonable goal in southwest Louisiana. Optimal production of crayfish in Louisiana occurs in waters less than 47 cm deep (Huner and Barr 1984). These shallow waters also attract wintering dabbling ducks.

Chabreck (1979) stressed the importance of suitable wintering habitat to continental waterfowl populations. Fredrickson and Drobney (1979) emphasized the importance of the wintering grounds to postbreeding migratory waterfowl. They claimed that conditions on the wintering grounds play an important role in determining the breeding condition of waterfowl in the spring. If domestic small grains or cultural techniques favoring seed-producing annual plant species can be utilized to provide both crayfish forage and waterfowl food, then both groups should benefit from the improved habitat conditions.

The purpose of this study was to investigate the multiple-use potential of commercial impoundments for waterfowl and crayfish. Specific objectives were to determine vegetative biomass and domestic seed production of rice, browntop millet, Japanese millet, and native plant species in impoundments managed for crayfish and waterfowl; to ascertain waterfowl use in the impoundments; and to estimate relative crayfish abundance in the impoundments.

We thank Williams, Inc., New Orleans, La., for access to their properties, financial assistance, and use of equipment and personnel. We especially acknowledge R. P. Romaire and P. J. Zwank for assistance with data analyses and for manuscript review. Data presented herein were collected and analyzed under Louisiana Agricultural Experiment Station projects 1885 and 2063.

Study Area

The study was conducted in nine impoundments (2.8-10.1 ha) at the Indigo Island Crayfish and Waterfowl Research Station located about 40 km south of Baton Rouge, La. Soils on the site are predominantly Sharkey and Fausse associations. Soils are nearly level, drainage is poor, and air and water move slowly through them (Spicer et al. 1977, 16). The impoundments have been either planted with domestic vegetation (rice or millets) or allowed to revegetate in native species. The composition of species of natural vegetation in ponds not planted with rice or millets was often manipulated with selective use of herbicides, disking, or mowing. These cultural practices reduced rank vegetative species such as cockle-bur (*Xanthium pensylvanicum*) and hemp sesbania (*Sesbania exaltata*) and pro-moted abundant growth of seed-producing annual plants such as *Echinochloa* spp., *Fimbristylis* spp., *Polygonum* spp., *Leptochloa* spp., *Panicum* spp., and *Cyperus* spp. Many crayfish habitats (natural and managed) support numerous plant species that produce food for wintering waterfowl (Martin et al. 1951).

Methods

Impoundment Characteristics

Three impoundments (2.8, 3.6, and 4.5 ha) were planted in rice (var. Saturn) in 1978, one (6.5 ha) in browntop millet, one (8.1 ha) in Japanese millet, and four (104.5 ha) were allowed to revegetate in natural plant species. Waterfowl surveys were conducted in all four natural plant impoundments, but vegetative biomass and crayfish abundance were determined in only two (7.7 and 10.1 ha). Differential planting dates were used to achieve crop maturity at about the same time (late October): rice on 11 July 1978 at a rate of 151 kg/ha, Japanese millet on 4 August 1978 and browntop millet on 21 August 1978, both at a rate of 40 kg/ha.

Extant vegetation was mowed, stubble burned, and disked before the planting of all domestic crops. No fertilizer, pesticide, or herbicide was used, but the impoundments planted in rice were shallowly flooded to control undesirable plants. The four natural impoundments were disked to destroy rank plants that germinated after draining and then allowed to revegetate. All impoundments were flooded to a depth of approximately 0.5 m in late October-early November 1978 by pumping water from an adjacent river. Water was continuously pumped through impoundments in an effort to minimize poor water quality in fall and spring.

Vegetation Sampling

Vegetation was sampled using the clipped quadrat (approximately 0.09 m²) meth-od (Kirby and Gosselink 1976). Six equidistant, longitudinal transect lines were established in a stratified random manner within each impoundment. Five ran-dom vegetation samples were collected along each line before flooding. All aboveground vegetation was clipped in the 30 sampling plots in each impound-ment between 10 October and 4 November 1978.

Vegetation from each quadrat was dried in an oven for 24 hours at 38C and weighed to the nearest 0.5 g. Seeds were removed from domestic vegetation as the plants dried. Seeds of natural vegetation were not removed because they had matured and dispersed earlier. Number of stems, weight of all aboveground vegetation except seeds, and dry weight of seeds of planted vegetation were recorded for each sample. The first two parameters were also recorded for natural vegetation.

Avian Use

Waterfowl (both ducks and American coots, *Fulica americana*) use was estimated by total counts of birds at about three-week intervals. Censuses were made in the morning from one-half hour before sunrise to three hours after sunrise. Eleven inventories were made from 22 October 1978 until 27 May 1979.

Several factors may have influenced waterfowl use of the impoundments during the study. Impoundments planted with millets were more centrally located, possibly reducing disturbances that may have occurred. Disturbances consisted of construction, maintenance, and crayfish harvesting activities. These factors were minimized, but they affected waterfowl use, especially in impoundments immediately adjacent to them. Ducks were disturbed by moving objects, especially vehicles, at all times of the day and night, and they often abandoned the impoundments in response to their presence. Owen (1972) also noted that moving objects seriously disturbed white-fronted geese (*Anser albifrons*), which responded at first by night-feeding and eventually by deserting the area.

Additional factors, such as fluctuating impoundment water levels resulting from exhaust pump failure and heavy winter rains, probably influenced waterfowl numbers. Another potential source of error was flocks of about 6,000 dabbling ducks that commonly occurred in rice impoundments (totaling 10.9 ha) shortly after sunset during November and December but departed before daylight each morning. These were excluded from the samples since they could not be accurately identified or enumerated. This concentration of waterfowl obviously consumed a substantial portion of the available food resource in the rice impoundments but could not be considered in the data analysis.

Crayfish Abundance

Relative crayfish density was estimated in all impoundments on 9 April, 1 May, and 15 May 1979. Impoundments were divided into 0.2-ha blocks, and one crayfish trap was placed at a permanent trap point in the center of each block. Crayfish traps were constructed of 1.9-cm-mesh galvanized wire and had two entrance funnels. Traps were baited with 0.1-0.2 kg of fish and emptied 24 hours later. The number of crayfish in each trap and the total weight caught in each impoundment were recorded.

Statistical Analysis

Waterfowl habitat preference was determined using the procedure of D. Johnson (1980). Mean difference between ranks of use and availability (TBAR) determined the magnitude of relative preference. Vegetative biomass and crayfish abundance data were analyzed with the analysis of variance in a completely randomized design (Steel and Torrie 1960). The Duncan-Waller test was used to determine significant mean differences between impoundments.

Results

Waterfowl Utilization

A total of 10,826 ducks representing six species and 8,734 American coots were counted on 11 surveys of nine impoundments. Duck (dabbler and diver) use peaked during November-December 1978.

Shallow-water ducks (tribes Anatini and Cairinini) accounted for 98.8% of all ducks observed on the area, and their densities peaked during November-December 1978. Wood ducks (*Aix sponsa*), mallards (*Anas platyrhynchos*), blue-winged teal (*Anas discors*), and northern shovelers (*Anas clypeata*) were the most abundant species (table 32.1).

Diving ducks (tribe Aythyini) were not abundant on the area, making up less than 0.1% of the total duck population. Lesser scaup (*Aythya affinis*) and ring-

Table 32.1. Mean number (birds per hectare) of waterfowl by month in all impoundments, October 1978 through May 1979[a]

Species	October	November	December	January	February	March	April	May	Total	Group composition (%)
Dabbling ducks[b]										
Wood duck	2.45	52.61	62.37	0.07	0.00	0.00	0.15	0.00	117.65	52.3
Mallard	0.05	45.09	42.58	6.13	0.07	0.00	0.00	0.00	93.92	41.8
Blue-winged teal	0.05	0.04	0.81	0.00	0.00	1.41	3.94	0.41	6.66	3.0
Northern shoveler	0.05	3.28	1.13	0.45	0.30	0.00	0.30	0.00	5.51	2.5
Subtotal	2.60	101.02	106.89	6.65	0.37	1.41	4.39	0.41	223.74	
Diving ducks										
Lesser scaup	0.00	0.00	1.01	0.00	0.00	0.00	0.00	0.00	1.01	0.0
Ring-necked duck	0.00	0.00	0.00	0.08	0.01	0.00	0.01	0.00	0.10	0.0
Subtotal	0.00	0.00	1.01	0.08	0.01	0.00	0.01	0.00	1.11	
Total ducks	2.60	101.02	107.90	6.73	0.38	1.41	4.40	0.41	224.85	76.6
American coot	0.15	3.45	13.07	15.47	11.85	16.15	7.93	0.64	68.71	23.4
Total ducks and coots	2.75	104.47	120.97	22.20	12.23	17.56	12.33	1.05	293.56	. . .

[a]Dabbling ducks calculated on water area <45.7 cm and diving ducks calculated on water area >45.7 cm.

[b]For purposes of this report, wood ducks are grouped with dabbling ducks.

necked ducks (*Aythya collaris*) were the most common species, and their densities peaked during December-January 1979 (table 32.1).

Ducks preferred browntop millet areas over natural vegetation and rice areas and Japanese millet areas over natural vegetation (table 32.2, $P < 0.05$). Positive TBAR values indicate that availability of all vegetation types exceeded their use.

Table 32.2. Mean differences in ranks of use and availability (TBAR), ranks of preference (RANK), and multiple comparisons for all duck species in four vegetation types in 1978-79

Vegetation type	TBAR	RANK	Multiple comparisons[a]
Browntop millet	1.0	1	A
Japanese millet	2.0	2	AC
Rice	4.0	3	BC
Natural vegetation	5.0	4	B

[a]Differences between vegetation types followed by different capital letters are significant ($P < 0.05$).

All ducks preferred millet areas to natural vegetation. Browntop and Japanese millet areas did not differ, but browntop millet areas were preferred over rice areas (table 32.3, $P < 0.05$). Mean duck use of planted vegetation was 21.37 birds per hectare per survey day, as contrasted with 0.31 birds in natural vegetation. Ducks were 55.3% of all waterfowl observed.

Mean American coot utilization of planted vegetation was 6.60 birds per hec-

Table 32.3. Waterfowl preference for four vegetation types in 1978-79

Rank of pref- erence[a]	Wood duck		Mallard		Blue- winged teal		Northern shoveler		Lesser scaup		Ring- necked duck		American coot	
1	BTM[b]	A	BTM	A	BTM	A	BTM	A	BTM	A	BTM	A	BTM	A
		A		A		A		A		A		A		A
2	JM	AB	JM	AB	JM	AB	JM	AB	JM	A	JM	A	JM	AB
		B		B		B		B						AB
3	RICE	BC	RICE	C	RICE	BC	RICE	BC	RICE	B	RICE	B	RICE	AB
		C		C		C		C		B		B		B
4	NV	C	NV	C	NV	C	NV	C	NV	B	NV	B	NV	B

[a]Relative preferences for vegetation types followed by the same letter were not significantly different ($P > 0.05$) according to Waller-Duncan multiple comparison tests.

[b]Vegetation types: BTM = browntop millet, JM = Japanese millet, RICE = rice (var. Saturn), and NV = natural vegetation.

tare per survey day, as contrasted with 1.96 birds in natural vegetation (table 32.4). American coots were 44.7% of the total waterfowl usage of the area and were most abundant in March. They also preferred browntop millet over natural vegetation

Table 32.4. Mean number (birds per hectare) of waterfowl in each vegetation type, October-December 1978 and January-May 1979

Species	Rice	Browntop millet	Japanese millet	Natural vegetation
Dabbling ducks				
Mallard	2.73 (21.7)[a]	37.48 (93.5)	1.76 (17.1)	0.15 (55.6)
Wood duck	9.72 (77.3)	1.93 (4.8)	8.22 (79.7)	0.08 (29.6)
Blue-winged teal	0.07 (0.6)	0.69 (1.7)	0.04 (0.4)	0.03 (11.1)
Northern shoveler	0.06 (0.4)	0.00 (0.0)	0.30 (2.8)	0.01 (3.7)
Subtotal	12.58 (99.9)	40.10 (97.4)	10.32 (99.6)	0.27 (87.1)
Diving ducks				
Lesser scaup	0.00 (0.0)	1.06 (100.0)	0.04 (100.0)	0.03 (75.0)
Ring-necked duck	0.01 (100.0)	0.00 (0.0)	0.00 (0.0)	0.01 (25.0)
Subtotal	0.01 (0.1)	1.06 (2.6)	0.04 (0.4)	0.04 (12.9
Total ducks	12.59 (77.0)	41.16 (87.3)	10.36 (50.8)	0.31 (13.7)
American coot	3.76 (23.0)	6.00 (12.7)	10.04 (49.2)	1.96 (86.3)
Total ducks and coots	16.35 (19.0)	47.16 (54.7)	20.40 (23.7)	2.27 (2.6)
Duck utilization (%)[b]	19.5	63.9	16.1	0.5
Coot utilization (%)[b]	17.3	27.6	46.1	9.0

[a]Numbers in parentheses are percentages of relative abundance.
[b]By vegetation type.

but did not exhibit a preference between the three species of planted grains (table 32.5). Positive TBAR values indicate that availability of all habitat types exceeded their use.

Large flocks (5,000 ± 2,000) of wood ducks, accompanied by 1,000 ± 500 other ducks (primarily mallards), used rice fields (total area of 10.9 ha) after dark in early November. Browntop millet, Japanese millet, and natural vegetation (total area of

Table 32.5. Mean differences in ranks of use and availability (TBAR), ranks of preference (RANK), and multiple comparisons for all American coots in four vegetation types in 1978-79

Vegetation type	TBAR	RANK	Multiple comparisons[a]
Browntop millet	1.0	1	A
Japanese millet	2.0	2	AB
Rice	4.0	3	AB
Natural vegetation	5.0	4	B

[a]Differences between vegetation types followed by different capital letters are significant ($P < 0.05$).

119.1 ha) were simultaneously used at night by 1,000 ± 500 wood ducks and mallards. These crude estimates of nocturnal waterfowl use and flock species composition were obtained by stationing four observers around the impoundment system. Waterfowl utilized rice fields heavily at night until the abundant food supply in them was depleted in mid-December.

Crayfish Abundance

The average crayfish catch (kilograms per trap per day) did not differ ($P > 0.05$) among the four vegetation types. Average relative abundance ranged from 0.27 kg/trap per day (rice) to 0.50 kg/trap per day (Japanese millet) (table 32.6).

Table 32.6. Mean relative abundance of crayfish (kilograms per trap) in four vegetation types in 1979[a]

Date	BTM[b]	JM	RICE	NV
19 April	0.39[c]	0.40	0.30	0.49
1 May	0.48	0.75	0.41	0.56
15 May	0.52	0.35	0.10	0.24
Average	0.46 (0.05)[d]	0.50 (0.18)	0.27 (0.13)	0.43 (0.14)

[a] Differences among vegetation types were not statistically significant ($P > 0.05$).
[b] Vegetation types: BTM = browntop millet, JM = Japanese millet, RICE = rice (var. Saturn), and NV = natural vegetation.
[c] Average kilograms per trap.
[d] Standard deviations in parentheses.

Vegetation Biomass

Japanese millet produced significantly more stems (735/m²) than rice, natural vegetation, or browntop millet ($P < 0.01$). Rice produced more stems per square meter (330) than natural vegetation, and the difference in number of stems produced between rice and browntop millet approached significance ($0.05 < P < 0.10$) (table 32.7).

Rice produced a greater biomass of stems (0.59 kg/m²) than all other vegetation types ($P < 0.05$). Stem weights of natural vegetation (0.27 kg/m²) and Japanese millet (0.19 kg/m²) were not different ($P > 0.05$), but natural vegetation produced a greater weight of stems than browntop millet (0.02 kg/m²) (table 32.7). Differences in stem weight per square meter between Japanese millet and browntop millet approached significance ($0.05 < P < 0.10$) (table 32.7).

Rice produced a greater weight of seeds (0.40 kg/m²) than either Japanese millet (0.07 kg/m²) or browntop millet (0.01 kg/m²) ($P < 0.01$) (table 32.7). Seed weights in Japanese and browntop millet plots were not different ($P > 0.05$).

Table 32.7. Mean biomass and stem density estimates for planted and natural vegetation in 1978

Vegetation type	Production variables					
	Number of stems (per m²)	Weight of stems (kg/m²)	Seed produced (kg/m²)	No. of stems of natural vegetation (per m²)	Wt. of natural vegetation (kg/m²)	Total biomass (kg/m²)
Natural vegetation (n = 2)	. . .	. . .	. . .	165 (120) A[a]	0.27 (0.24) A	0.27 (0.24) A
Browntop millet (n = 1)	131 (184) AB	0.02 (0.04) B	0.01 (0.01) A	184 (125) A	0.41 (0.24) A	0.44 (0.22) A
Japanese millet (n = 1)	735 (500) C	0.19 (0.10) AB	0.07 (0.04) A	116 (161) AB	0.03 (0.04) B	0.29 (0.13) A
Rice (n = 3)	330 (134) B	0.59 (0.16) C	0.40 (0.14) B	53 (160) B	0.01 (0.03) B	1.00 (0.28) B

[a]Treatment means (vertical) within each production variable followed by the same letter were not significantly different ($P > 0.05$) according to Duncans New Multiple Range Test. Standard deviations are shown in parentheses.

Natural vegetation grew in all impoundments, including those planted with domestic small grains, making up from 1 to 92% of the total plant biomass in the planted areas (table 32.7). Impoundments planted with browntop millet contained a greater weight of natural vegetation (0.41 kg/m²) than those planted with either Japanese millet (0.03 kg/m²) or rice (0.01 kg/m²) ($P < 0.01$).

Rice impoundments produced the greatest total plant biomass (1.00 kg/m²) of the four vegetation types ($P < 0.01$) (table 32.7). No differences were noted in total plant biomass among impoundments planted with browntop millet, Japanese millet, and natural vegetation.

Discussion

Waterfowl Utilization

Browntop millet and Japanese millet were preferred over natural vegetation by all waterfowl. Their preference may have been influenced by location, water depth, and disturbance factors. The impoundments planted with millets were centrally located and disturbance was reduced. Kuyken (1969) reported that white-fronted geese utilized the central portion of protected areas to a greater extent than the margins and concluded that disturbance was the most important influence on this pattern. The preference for browntop millet may have been influenced by the large amount of seed-bearing, natural vegetation present in the impoundment. Fredrickson and Taylor (1982) estimated production of annual plant seeds with food value to wildlife at 0.14 kg/m² in seasonally flooded impoundments in southeast Missouri.

Crayfish and Vegetation

Crayfish are omnivorous, with the bulk of their diet composed of plant detritus and its associated colonies of unicellular decomposers and epiphytic organisms (Huner and Barr 1984). Japanese millet produced more stems and, consequently, should have provided more substrate for the production of epiphytic organisms than any of the four vegetation types tested. Increased stem production may have been responsible for impoundments planted with Japanese millet having the highest abundance of crayfish, although differences among vegetative types were not statistically significant. Rice produced the greatest total plant biomass of the four vegetation types tested and should have provided the most food to crayfish. Rice impoundments were expected to produce the greatest crayfish yield based on previous studies (Chien 1978, Miltner 1980), but they did not.

Our results differ from those of previous researchers who found rice to be a superior forage for crayfish production. However, previous research comparing crayfish production in ponds planted with different vegetation has been conducted in relatively small ponds (<0.40 ha), which did not experience the extremely low oxygen levels that were common in the large impoundments used for this study.

Decreased crayfish production in our study may have resulted from consistently low levels of dissolved oxygen (<2 mg/liter, November-December 1978) and high levels of hydrogen sulfide in all impoundments. All ponds in our study exhibited two common symptoms of oxygen-deficient water—water color was black, and a strong hydrogen sulfide odor commonly associated with anaerobic detrital decay in aquatic ecosystems was present.

The primary water quality factor limiting crayfish production in commercial ponds is dissolved oxygen. Dissolved oxygen levels in ponds should consistently exceed 2.5 mg/liter to ensure adequate survival. Substantial periods of dissolved oxygen levels below 2.5 mg/liter are deleterious to crayfish (Huner and Barr 1984).

Rice impoundments in this study produced a mean total plant biomass (1.00 kg/m²) within the ranges reported by previous researchers (Chien 1978, W. Johnson 1980, Miltner 1980). Miltner (1980) also evaluated Japanese millet as forage for crayfish in small ponds and reported that rice produced a greater total plant biomass (1.03 kg/m²) than Japanese millet (0.70 kg/m²). Rice also produced a greater total plant biomass than either Japanese millet or browntop millet in this study.

Browntop millet areas produced 13 times more natural vegetation (by weight) than Japanese millet did. Seed production in Japanese millet was eight times higher than in browntop millet, and the difference between them approached significance. Although vegetation growth varies with environmental conditions (rainfall, days of sunlight, temperature, etc.), it appears that browntop millet is not able to compete effectively with natural vegetation species on the wet Sharkey Clay soils indigenous to the site.

Site wetness and soil type did not seem to have the adverse effects on Japanese millet that they had on browntop millet. Japanese millet tended to reseed itself the following year after the impoundments were drained in early summer. We observed this characteristic of Japanese millet for three years on this site, but never witnessed reseeding by browntop millet.

Rice seed production compared favorably with the 1978 Louisiana statewide production of 0.432 kg/m² (U.S. Department of Agriculture 1980). Rice is well adapted to the heavy, organic soils of the site because it is a semiaquatic plant that benefits from flooded soil conditions during part or all of the growing season. Rice competed exceptionally well because water could be used to suppress natural vegetation growth.

Management Implications

High plant biomass in commercial-sized impoundments may increase oxygen demand and increase mortality of juvenile crayfish. Ponds dominated by annual terrestrial vegetation or millets may be largely depleted of suitable crayfish food in the spring. Although impoundments planted in rice initially produce more vegetative biomass, it may be depeleted by early to midspring. We believe that more research should be conducted on vegetation mixtures that decompose differentially and become available to crayfish as a food source at various times. Intensive management of vegetative composition and quantity in impoundments used for both crayfish production and waterfowl habitat should be accompanied by adequate intake-pump capacity to avoid water quality problems.

Waterfowl can benefit greatly from crayfish production impoundments if vegetation is managed to produced a food source. Although rice did not increase crayfish production or waterfowl utilization of impoundments in this study, it appears to be an excellent choice for multiple-use management applications (based on field observations during this study and on existing literature). Previous research indicates that rice will increase crayfish production, but we believe that poor water quality masked this effect in our study. Estimation of rice use by ducks was considerably biased by nocturnal feeding, which prevented their accurate identification and enumeration.

We believe that multiple-use impoundments offer a positive, small-scale option to the widespread destruction of waterfowl habitat that is continuing on the wintering grounds.

LITERATURE CITED

Chabreck, R. H. 1979. Winter habitat of dabbling ducks—physical, chemical and biological aspects. Pages 133-142 *in* T. A. Bookhout, ed. Waterfowl and wetlands—an integrated review. Proc. 1977 Symp., Northcent. Sect., Wildl. Soc., Madison, Wis. 152pp.

Chien, Y. H. 1978. Double cropping rice *Oryza sativa* and crawfish *Procambarus clarkii* (Girard). M.S. Thesis, Louisiana State Univ., Baton Rouge. 84pp.

Fredrickson, L. H., and R. D. Drobney. 1979. Habitat utilization by postbreeding waterfowl. Pages 119-131 *in* T. A. Bookhout, ed. Waterfowl and wetlands—an integrated review. Proc. 1977 Symp., Northcent. Sect., Wildl. Soc., Madison, Wis. 152pp.

———, and L. S. Taylor. 1982. Management of seasonally flooded impoundments for wildlife. U.S. Fish Wildl. Serv. Resour. Publ. 148. 29pp.

Givens, L. S., M. C. Nelson, and V. Ekedahl. 1964. Farming for waterfowl. Pages 599-610 *in* J. P. Linduska, ed. Waterfowl tomorrow. U.S. Fish Wildl. Serv., Washington, D.C. 770pp.

Horn, E. E., and L. L. Glasgow. 1964. Rice and waterfowl. Pages 435-443 *in* J. P. Linduska, ed. Waterfowl tomorrow. U.S. Fish Wildl. Serv. Washington, D.C. 770pp.

Huner, J. V., and J. E. Barr. 1984. Red swamp crawfish: biology and exploitation. Center for Wetland Resources Pub. LSU-T-80-001. Rev. ed. Louisiana State Univ., Baton Rouge. 135pp.

Johnson, D. H. 1980. The comparison of usage and availability measurements for evaluating resource preference. Ecol. 61:65–71.

Johnson, W. B., Jr. 1980. Evaluation of poultry wastes, rice (*Oryza sativa*), and delta duckpotato (*Sagittaria platyphylla*) as crayfish (*Procambarus* spp.) forages. M.S. Thesis, Louisiana State Univ., Baton Rouge. 94pp.

Kirby, C. J., and J. G. Gosselink. 1976. Primary production in a Louisiana Gulf Coast *Spartina alterniflora* marsh. Ecol. 57:1052–1059.

Kuyken, E. 1969. Grazing of wild geese on grasslands at Dame, Belgium. Wildfowl 20:47–54.

Louisiana Cooperative Extension Service. 1983. Agriculture and natural resources 1982. Louisiana State Univ. Agric. Center, Baton Rouge. 186pp.

Lovell, R. T. 1968. Development of a crawfish processing industry in Louisiana. Louisiana State Univ., Dep. Food Sci. Tech., Baton Rouge. 151pp.

Martin, A. C., H. S. Zim, and A. L. Nelson. 1951. American wildlife and plants: a guide to wildlife food habits. U.S. Fish Wildl. Serv., Washington, D.C. 500pp.

Miltner, M. R. 1980. Evaluation of domestic rice, *Oryza sativa*, and Japanese millet, *Echinochloa frumentacea*, as fodder for red swamp crawfish, *Procambarus clarkii*. M.S. Thesis, Louisiana State Univ., Baton Rouge. 106pp.

Neely, W. W. 1967. Planting, disking, mowing, and grazing. Pages 212-222 *in* J. D. Newsom, ed. Proceedings of the marsh and estuary management symposium. Louisiana State Univ., Baton Rouge. 250pp.

———, and V. E. Davison. 1966. Wild ducks on farmland in the south. U.S. Dep. Agric. Farmers' Bull. 2218. 13pp.

Owen, M. 1972. Movements and feeding ecology of white-fronted geese at the New Grounds, Slimbridge, J. App. Ecol. 9:385–397.

Perry, W. G., Jr., T. Joanen, and L. McNease. 1970. Crawfish-waterfowl, a multiple use concept for impounded marshes. Proc. Southeast. Assoc. Game Fish Comm. 24:506–519.

Spicer, B. S., S. D. Matthews, R. E. Dance, K. R. Milton, and W. H. Boyd. 1977. Soil survey of Iberville Parish, Louisiana. U.S. Soil Conserv. Serv., Washington, D.C. 68pp.

Steel, R. K., and J. H. Torrie. 1960. Principles and procedures of statistics. McGraw-Hill, New York. 481pp.

U.S. Department of Agriculture. 1980. Annual crop summary—Louisiana. Washington, D.C. 45pp.

Wright, T. W. 1959. Winter foods of mallards in Arkansas. Proc. Southeast. Assoc. Game Fish. Comm. 13:291–296.

33

Production, Management, and Waterfowl Use of Sea Purslane, Gulf Coast Muskgrass, and Widgeongrass in Brackish Impoundments

Peter K. Swiderek, A. Sydney Johnson, Philip E. Hale, and Robert L. Joyner

Abstract: Potential production, management, and waterfowl use of two little-known waterfowl food plants, Gulf Coast muskgrass (*Chara hornemannii*) and sea purslane (*Sesuvium maritimum*), were compared with use of common widgeongrass (*Ruppia maritima*) in brackish impoundments in South Carolina. Muskgrass, like widgeongrass, was grown under sustained flooding with brackish water. Vegetation production and chemical composition were similar to those of widgeongrass, and near total use by waterfowl occurred. Muskgrass tubercles, which were 95% nitrogen-free extract, were selected intensively by northern pintail (*Anas acuta*) and ruddy ducks (*Oxyura jamaicensis*). Muskgrass offers an attractive alternative to widgeongrass, but its growth is limited by soil and water characteristics not yet adequately understood. Sea purslane, which was grown in brackish impoundments drained to bed level during the growing season, produced significantly more seed biomass than widgeongrass. The seeds were higher in percentage of crude fat and crude protein than those of widgeongrass and were a preferred food of blue-winged teal (*Anas discors*), green-winged teal (*Anas crecca*), and northern pintail. Sea purslane grew best on organic soils. Under suitable conditions, it may be grown on a rotating schedule with widgeongrass, or both may be double-cropped in the same year by delaying flooding for widgeongrass until late summer.

Brackish impoundments are important habitat for wintering waterfowl in coastal areas of the southeastern United States, but there are few plant species having waterfowl food value that are suitable for culture in such impoundments,

Waterfowl in Winter.© 1988 University of Minnesota. Edited by Milton W. Weller and published by the University of Minnesota Press, Minneapolis.

especially where salinities exceed 10 ppt. Most such impoundments are managed by flooding during the growing season to produce widgeongrass, which has long been known as an important food plant for ducks (McAtee 1939, 16; Martin and Uhler 1939, 9). Though ecological requirements and management strategies for widgeongrass are well documented (McAtee 1939, Joanen and Glasgow 1965, Mayer and Low 1970, Richardson 1980), management can be difficult because of the plant's sensitivity to such environmental factors as heat, algae competition, and wave action (Joanen and Glasgow 1965, Prevost et al. 1978). Because of this and the desirability of greater diversity of management options, identification of other potential waterfowl foods that can be grown in brackish impoundments is needed. Previous observations at the Tom Yawkey Wildlife Center in South Carolina indicated that Gulf Coast muskgrass and sea purslane were readily eaten by waterfowl and might be suitable for management in certain situations. This paper reports on the management of these species at the Yawkey Center and research conducted there in 1979 and 1980 to compare their potential productivity, seasonal availability, and waterfowl food value with widgeongrass. Methods and results are reported in more detail by Swiderek (1982).

This study was a cooperative project of the South Carolina Wildlife and Marine Resources Department and the University of Georgia, with financial support provided by the Yawkey Foundation. Special thanks are due W. P. Baldwin, M. B. Prevost, and P. M. Wilkinson for assistance in designing the study, providing information and ideas throughout, and reviewing the manuscript. Personnel of the Yawkey Center provided much assistance during the field work.

Background

Gulf Coast muskgrass was identified in impoundments managed for widgeongrass at the Yawkey Center in 1960 but may already have been present for several years (W. P. Baldwin, pers. commun.). Muskgrasses (*Chara* spp.) of various species are eaten by many waterfowl, particularly diving ducks (Cottam 1939, 53; Martin and Uhler 1939, 20; Munro 1939; Bartonek and Hickey 1969). Gulf Coast muskgrass, one of a few members of the genus that grows well in brackish water, occurs from the central United States southward (Wood and Imahori 1965, 321-325). It is an important duck food on some coastal waterfowl areas in Florida (W. O. Stieglitz, unpubl. rep., U.S. Fish Wildl. Serv., 1966), but it is not a well-known plant and its management has not been described.

Sea purslane became well established in an impoundment at the Yawkey Center in 1976. The impoundment had been drained to bed level during the growing season to encourage growth of emergent vegetation to break up the large expanse of open water. An extensive growth of sea purslane developed on the moist bed, and the impoundment was used intensively by ducks in the fall when flooded by rainfall. The impoundment was manipulated in this way again in 1977 and 1978 with similar results. In 1978, P. M. Wilkinson (pers. commun.) noted that sea purslane invaded another impoundment near the Yawkey Center in which flooding for widgeongrass was delayed until midsummer, and several ducks taken from this impoundment had fed on the seeds.

Sea purslane is a small, fleshy, annual herb that produces numerous tiny seeds (≤ 1 mm in diameter). Although distributed along the coast from New York to Texas, it has not been recognized as a significant waterfowl food, probably because it occurs naturally only in irregularly flooded salt marsh and usually is not accessible to ducks. However, Chabreck (1964) reported that extensive stands of *Sesuvium portulacastrum* (later identified as *S. maritimum*) in Louisiana were used intensively by ducks. These stands developed when severe drought resulted in absence of standing water (in impoundments previously flooded with brackish water). Chabreck's observations and those at the Yawkey Center indicated that the sea purslane response to drainage of brackish impoundments might be replicated; if so, summer drawdown could be a feasible management strategy for brackish impoundments.

Study Area

The Tom Yawkey Wildlife Center, located on the Atlantic Coast 16 km from Georgetown, S.C. includes three islands (Cat Island, North Island, and South Island) and surrounding tidal marshlands. Wintering habitat for migratory waterfowl is provided on 1,214 ha of impoundments where growth of desirable food plants is encouraged by water manipulations made possible by a system of ditches, canals, and tide-operated water control structures. The area is a sanctuary, and waterfowl are not hunted. Other forms of disturbance are minimal.

Six closely associated salt marsh impoundments on South Island were selected for intensive study (fig. 33.1). Historically, water measurements in all of these impoundments have been generally in the following ranges: salinity, 10-30 ppt; pH, 7-9; and depth, 30-60 cm. Water temperature in summer has exceeded 30C. For more than 20 years before the study, all the impoundments had been managed for submerged food plants, except Lower Reserve, which was managed for sea purslane after 1976. During the study, four of the study impoundments were managed, as in previous years, with sustained flooding for growth of widgeongrass (Gibson and Rest ponds) and muskgrass (Wheeler and Sand Creek basins). The other two (Lower Reserve and Twin Sisters' Pond) were drained to bed level from April to August to encourage growth of sea purslane. When field work began, Lower Reserve was in its fourth year of drawdown management and Twin Sisters' Pond was in its first. In addition to the six intensively studied impoundments, Upper Pine Ridge Pond also was observed closely because extensive growth of sea purslane developed after the pond was drained to repair a water control structure. The impoundment was reflooded in late summer, and a good crop of widgeongrass developed.

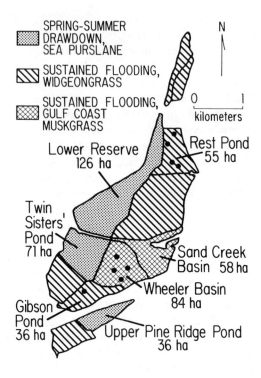

Fig. 33.1. South Island impoundments with study impoundments (those named) and management strategies identified, Tom Yawkey Wildlife Center, South Carolina, 1979. Position of each set of five vegetation exclosures is indicated by solid circle.

Methods

Vegetation Sampling

Widgeongrass and muskgrass vegetation (aboveground parts) were sampled in 1979 to estimate relative potential production and seasonal availability and to measure waterfowl use. For this purpose, we constructed 45 exclosures of 1-m² steel-rod frames covered with netting. These exclosures were designed to prevent waterfowl and other wildlife from eating or disturbing the enclosed vegetation, yet not interfere with environmental influences such as sunlight and water movement. We sampled muskgrass in Wheeler Basin only, because Sand Creek Basin (the only other muskgrass impoundment) was drained from April to July to correct a serious algae problem. We intended to sample widgeongrass in Gibson Pond, which historically had been the most productive impoundment for this species. But by late June, when the exclosures were to be emplaced, the crop of widgeongrass in Gibson Pond had declined by about 50% and we chose instead to sample in Rest Pond, which at that time had the best crop of widgeongrass in the complex. Twenty exclosures (four sets of five) were placed in Wheeler Basin and 20 in Rest Pond. In late August, the condition of the widgeongrass in Gibson Pond had improved considerably, and we put the remaining five exclosures (one set) there.

Exclosures within a set were arranged linearly and spaced 20 m apart; thus, a set of exclosures and associated outside samples required an area of about 10 m by 100 m. As shown in figure 33.1, the locations of the sets in Rest Pond and Wheeler Basin were not clustered together but were well dispersed over the impoundments. Because of characteristics of bottom configuration, soils, and water circulation, most impoundments have areas that do not produce good stands of aquatic vegetation. The portion consisting of such areas varies from one impoundment to another. We avoided sampling in those areas where the species of interest was absent or sparse; therefore, our results cannot be expanded to the entire impoundments. Our concern was not for a good comparison of average production in specific impoundments but for the more useful comparison of the potential productivity of muskgrass and widgeongrass under good growing conditions.

Each month, August through December, one sample from inside an exclosure was taken from each set and four samples were taken from outside the same exclosure, spaced uniformly 6 m from each corner. A box-shaped aluminum frame (0.5 m² in cross section), with its sides covered with hardware cloth, was used for sampling. One open end of the device was placed against the marsh bottom and all aboveground vegetation was removed, washed to remove sediment, drip-dried, and weighed to the nearest 0.1 g. Wet/dry weight conversion factors were obtained from subsamples. A series of t tests was performed to compare weights of vegetation inside and outside exclosures within sampling periods. Differences were assumed to reflect consumption by waterfowl.

Frequency of occurrence of sea purslane and associated plant species in Lower Reserve was measured in late August 1979 and 1980 and in Twin Sisters' Pond in August 1979. Lines were established 25 m apart throughout the two impoundments, and plots (10 cm × 10 cm) were located at 10-m intervals along each line. All species rooted inside a plot were identified and recorded.

Sea purslane biomass and seed production were estimated from a separate series of plots in Lower Reserve. Because sea purslane flowers and produces seeds over an extended period, samples were taken biweekly from 24 July through 21 August 1979. During each of these three sampling periods, 12 0.5-m² plots were established in the dense stands of sea purslane that covered virtually the whole impoundment. Entire plants in each of the 36 plots were picked and counted, then weighed both fresh and oven-dried. From nine randomly selected plots (three from each sampling period), seeds later were extracted from the dried plants and weighed to the nearest 10 mg.

Bottom Sampling

Estimates of production and waterfowl use of widgeongrass and sea purslane seeds and muskgrass tubercles were obtained from bottom exclosures. Some seeds and tubercles in bottom samples may have been produced in previous years. In midsummer 1979, bottom exclosures were placed adjacent to vegetation exclo-sures in Wheeler Basin (N = 20), Rest Pond (N = 20), and Gibson Pond (N = 5). Bottom exclosures were uniformly placed along transect lines spaced equidistantly throughout Twin Sisters' Pond (N =15) and Lower Reserve (N = 15). In late January 1980, bottom samples were taken from within the exclosures and 1 m outside. Each sample consisted of the top 10 cm of a substrate core 15 cm in diameter.

Seeds in bottom samples were extracted by washing the samples through a sieve, air-drying, and then separating seeds and debris. Seeds were then sorted by species and weighed. Before the bottom samples were dried, muskgrass tubercles were removed and weighed. Paired t tests were performed to detect differences in weights of seeds and tubercles of various food species between samples from inside and outside exclosures in each study impoundment.

Censusing

All 12 impoundments on the South Island complex of the Yawkey Center were censused semiweekly from 12 September through 23 December 1979 to determine relative use of individual impoundments by different waterfowl species. Censusing began about one hour after sunrise, and predetermined stops were made around each impoundment.

Dietary Contribution and Nutritional Value of Study Plants

To determine the extent to which waterfowl species fed upon sea purslane and muskgrass, the plant parts consumed, and relative use of the three foods under study, we collected a sample of waterfowl present during the middle of each month, September through December. Ducks were observed feeding and then shot on the water. Viscera were removed and frozen immediately after collection. The com-bined contents of the esophagus, proventriculus, and gizzard were sorted, mea-sured volumetrically, and recorded by taxa. Chemical composition of vegetation, seeds, and tubercles of the three study plants was determined by proximate chemical analysis (Georgia State Chemist Laboratory).

Results and Discussion

Growth, Production, and Availability

During this study, the largest standing crop of widgeongrass was measured on 3 August. It occurred in the southern portion of Rest Pond, where 10 plots taken inside and outside exclosures averaged 113.6 g/ m² oven-dry (SE = 6.3). This figure is about 80% of the greatest previously reported value (197.0 g/ m² air-dry; Single-ton 1951). On the same date, plots in the northern half of the pond averaged 62.1 g/ m² oven-dry (SE = 2.51). During August, widgeongrass in Rest Pond plots

Table 33.1. Vegetation (grams per square meter, oven-dry) inside and outside exclosures, Tom Yawkey Wildlife Center, South Carolina, 1979[a]

Species	Impoundment	N[b]	Jul 31- Aug 3	Aug 28- Aug 31	Sept 24- Sept 27	Oct 25- Oct 30	Nov 27- Nov 30	Dec 19- Dec 20
					Sampling period			
Chara hornemannii	Wheeler Basin							
	Inside	4	122.2	115.7	63.5	97.4	92.1*	42.3*
	Outside	16	127.4	107.9	50.8	84.3	35.0	8.7
Ruppia maritima	Gibson Pond							
	Inside	1			62.0	61.0	66.6	44.3
	Outside	4			71.4	36.2	8.9	4.8
	Rest Pond							
	Inside	4	93.7	61.1	21.0	5.0	1.8	3.2
	Outside	16	86.3	56.5	30.3	12.6	3.4	2.1

[a]Inside values followed by an asterisk differ ($P < 0.05$) from corresponding outside values. Gibson Pond values were not tested because of inadequate sample size.

[b]Sample sizes are as reported with the following exceptions: Wheeler Basin, 31 July and 28 August, outside N = 15.

decreased by about one-third, and by October little remained in the plots (table 33.1) or elsewhere in this impoundment. The loss of widgeongrass was similar inside and outside exclosures ($P > 0.05$) and there was no waterfowl use of the impoundment during this period, indicating that the reduction resulted mainly from unfavorable environmental conditions. (See Swiderek 1982, 77-98, for detailed data on environmental conditions of individual impoundments throughout summer and fall.) Vigorous growth of widgeongrass in Gibson Pond was evident in May and June, but the crop had declined noticeably by early July. By late August, there was renewed growth, standing crop was similar to that in Rest Pond, and natural deterioration was not evident until December (table 33.1). Although vegetation was more abundant initially in Rest Pond than in Gibson Pond, less seed was produced, probably because plants died before maturity. Widgeongrass seed production, estimated from bottom sampling inside exclosures, averaged 3.2 g/m² air-dry (SE = 0.5) for Rest Pond plots and 6.6 g/m² (SE = 1.1) in Gibson Pond. Prevost et al. (1978) reported widgeongrass seed at 1.2 g/m² from similar bottom sampling in widgeongrass stands within two other South Carolina coastal impoundments. In a dense but shallowly flooded (5-10 cm) stand of widgeongrass in Louisiana, Jemison and Chabreck (1962) estimated seed at 0.5 g/m² based on bottom sampling before arrival of most waterfowl. These values include an unknown amount of residual seed from previous years.

On 1 August 1979, maximum standing crop of muskgrass was measured in Wheeler Basin plots taken inside and outside exclosures ($\bar{x}$ = 126.3 g/m² oven-dry, SE = 17.4). These values are comparable to those of widgeongrass measured in this study and approach the maximum previously reported for widgeongrass. Muskgrass in the plots was reduced by half between August and September sampling dates, probably the result of Hurricane David buffeting the area on 5 September. By late October the muskgrass vegetation had increased to near prehurricane levels (table 33.1). Standing crops inside exclosures were comparable for October and November ($P > 0.05$) but were lower ($P < 0.05$) by late December, indicating that natural deterioration began in December. Muskgrass tubercles in bottom samples taken inside exclosures averaged 15.4 g/m² air-dry (SE = 1.7).

Fig. 33.2. Almost pure stand of sea purslane, representative of about 90% of 126-ha Lower Reserve impoundment, Tom Yawkey Wildlife Center, South Carolina, August 1979.

In 1979, sea purslane dominated Lower Reserve (fig. 33.2) and occurred in 70% of the frequency plots (N = 2,057). Other common plants were dwarf spikerush (*Eleocharis parvula*) (23%), smooth cordgrass (*Spartina alterniflora*) (10%), sprangletop (*Leptochloa filiformis*) (10%), glassworts (*Salicornia* spp.) (9%), and saltgrass (*Distichlis spicata*) (8%). From 1979 to 1980 (fourth to fifth year of drawdown management), occurrence of sea purslane and dwarf spikerush decreased considerably (to 57% and 11%, respectively: N = 2,429 plots in 1980), while saltgrass occurrence increased more than that of any other plant (to 16%). As measured in 12 0.5-m² plots in August 1979, mean density of sea purslane was 590 stems per square meter (SE = 114.4) and oven-dry weight was 217 g/m² (SE = 6.9). Sea purslane required about three months to mature. Although some capsule dehiscence and plant death were noticed in late June, standing crop of seeds attached to sea purslane plants in the plots increased from late July through late August, with the number of mature seeds roughly doubling each two weeks. In late August (115 days after drawdown), seeds on the plants averaged 35.2 g/m² air-dry (SE= 0.4). The plots were located in densely stocked stands that covered most of Lower Reserve (fig. 33.2). Bottom sampling in January within exclosures produced a somewhat lower estimate of sea purslane seed production (26.0 g/m² air-dry, SE = 5.6). These exclosures were uniformly placed along transects spaced equidistantly throughout Lower Reserve.

Sea purslane did not successfully invade Twin Sisters' Pond. Although some plants grew on portions of the bed exposed during normal flooding (10% of 209 frequency plots), the low bed remained bare. The few sea purslane plants that did germinate on the low bed (0.5% of 853 plots) soon died. The inability of plants of all species to become established may have resulted from stress caused by adverse soil conditions such as low pH (Swiderek 1982).

Waterfowl Use

During fall 1979, the most abundant waterfowl species on South Island impoundments in decreasing order were American coot (*Fulica americana*), green-winged teal, American wigeon (*Anas americana*), northern pintail, blue-winged teal, ruddy duck, gadwall (*Anas strepera*), and northern shoveler (*Anas clypeata*). These eight species made up 90% of all waterfowl censused. Ninety-one percent of all waterfowl were on Lower Reserve, Wheeler Basin, Sand Creek Basin, and Upper Pine Ridge Pond. The largest total count was 23,094 on 11 December.

Lower Reserve, managed for sea purslane, attracted most of the waterfowl arriving on South Island in early fall (fig. 33.3). During September, blue-winged teal were predominant and 99% of them were observed on Lower Reserve. In October, northern pintails predominated and concentrated on this impoundment during most of the month. During November, 96% of all green-winged teal used Lower Reserve, and intensive use continued in December. Twin Sisters' Pond received very little duck use during the study ($\bar{x}$ = 0.3 waterfowl per hectare per census).

Widgeongrass impoundments had little duck use until late in October (fig. 33.3). During November, Upper Pine Ridge Pond, which had good stands of widgeongrass, was used intensively ($\bar{x}$ = 43.8 waterfowl per hectare per census), especially by American wigeon. Rest Pond, with sparse widgeongrass, was used little, and Gibson Pond, with an intermediate amount of widgeongrass, had

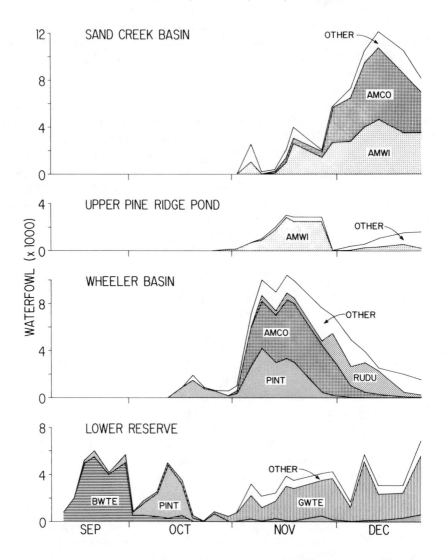

Fig. 33.3. Waterfowl use of selected South Island impoundments, Tom Yawkey Wildlife Center, South Carolina, 1979. These four impoundments received 91% of all waterfowl use. See figure 33.1 and text for description of major foods in these impoundments. AMCO = American coot, AMWI = American wigeon, PINT = pintail, RUDU = ruddy duck, BWTE = blue-winged teal, GWTE = green-winged teal, and OTHER = all other waterfowl species.

moderate usage ($\bar{x}$ = 1.9 and 8.9 waterfowl per hectare per census, respectively, during November-December).

Table 33.2. Foods of collected waterfowl, Wheeler and Sand Creek basins, Tom Yawkey Wildlife Center, South Carolina, fall 1979[a]

Food[b]	PINT (17)[d] Aggregate percentage	Percentage occurrence	AMWI (23) Aggregate percentage	Percentage occurrence	GADW (5) Aggregate percentage	Percentage occurrence	RUDU (8) Aggregate percentage	Percentage occurrence	NOSH (9) Aggregate percentage	Percentage occurrence	AMCO (9) Aggregate percentage	Percentage occurrence
Chara hornemannii												
Tubercles	42	100					30	100	25	55	89	100
Vegetation	13	59	87	100	77	100	2	12	tr	67	tr	33
Ruppia maritima	11	100	tr	35	tr	40	41	100	4	44	10	55
Vegetation	1	18	13	78	18	80			31	67		
Scirpus robustus	22	100	tr	4			5	87				
Echinochloa walteri	4	6										
Distichlis spicata	1	6										
Myrica cerifera	tr	88					6	100	tr	11	tr	11
Polygonum persicaria					4	20						
Seed fragments and debris	6	100					16	100	4	67		
Unidentified vegetation									4	11		
Animal matter	tr	41	tr	4					32	55		
Total	100		100		99		100		100		99	

[a]These contributed ≥0.5% each to the food volume (aggregate percentage; Martin et al. 1946) of one or more species.

[b]Seeds unless otherwise stated.

[c]PINT = pintail, AMWI = American wigeon, GADW = gadwall, RUDU = ruddy duck, NOSH = northern shoveler, and AMCO = American coot.

[d]Sample sizes are shown in parentheses.

Table 33.3. Foods of collected waterfowl, Lower Reserve, Tom Yawkey Wildlife Center, South Carolina, fall 1979[a]

	Waterfowl species[c]									
	PINT (12)[d]		BWTE (16)		GWTE (22)		GADW (10)		AMCO (5)	
Food[b]	Aggregate percentage	Percentage occurrence	Aggregate percentage	Percentage occurrence	Aggregate percentage	Percentage occurrence	Aggregate percentage	Percentage occurrence	Aggregate percentage	Percentage occurrence
Sesuvium maritimum	62	100	74	100	64	100	tr	80	tr	20
Ruppia maritima	tr	100	16	75	tr	82	tr	80	36	80
Vegetation			tr	6			100	100		
Scirpus robustus	3	83	4	62	tr	41				
Distichlis spicata	1	58	tr	19	tr	82				
Eleocharis parvula	tr	100	tr	81	3	82	tr	30	tr	40
Salicornia spp.	tr	8	tr	6	1	54			tr	20
Scirpus validus	tr	8	tr	6	4	18				
Leptochloa filiformis	tr	42	tr	12	5	73			tr	80
Vegetation					3	27			54	80
Polygonum persicaria					2	14				
Scirpus sp.										
Seed fragments and debris	34	100	7	100	18	100	tr	10		
Unidentified vegetation	tr		tr	6	tr				10	40
Animal matter	1	25	tr	6	tr	32				
Total	101		101		100		100		100	

[a] These contributed ≥0.5% each to the food volume (aggregate percentage; Martin et al. 1946) of one or more species.
[b] Seeds unless otherwise stated.
[c] PINT = pintail, BWTE = blue-winged teal, GWTE = green-winged teal, GADW = gadwall, and AMCO = American coot.
[d] Sample sizes are shown in parentheses.

The first major waterfowl use of a muskgrass impoundment was observed on 14 October when 500 northern pintails were seen feeding in Wheeler Basin. Northern pintails favored Wheeler Basin during November until they left South Island late in the month. American coots were 31% of all waterfowl on the island during November, and 74% of them were on this impoundment. American wigeon and American coots used Sand Creek Basin, which had extensive muskgrass, in late November and concentrated there during most of December. Ruddy ducks and northern shovelers were the predominant ducks on Wheeler Basin in December.

Of 149 waterfowl collected from Lower Reserve, Wheeler Basin, and Sand Creek Basin, 136 of eight species contained sufficient food for analysis. Plant foods composed 98% of the total aggregate volume; the three study plants accounted for 77%.

Muskgrass and widgeongrass were the primary foods of ducks collected from Wheeler and Sand Creek basins (table 33.2). The intensive use of muskgrass tubercles by northern pintails and ruddy ducks was unexpected. Tubercles are small, spherical growths (1-4 mm in diameter) that occur in the mud and are attached to the rhizoids. They store carbohydrates and are capable of vegetative propagation (Fritsch 1935, 465). They composed 42% of the food volume for northern pintails and 30% for ruddy ducks from Wheeler Basin (table 33.2). One northern pintail contained 1,800 tubercles.

Sea purslane seeds composed 74%, 64%, and 62% of the food volume from blue-winged teal, green-winged teal, and northern pintails, respectively, from Lower Reserve (table 33.3). One blue-winged teal ingested about 71,000 sea purslane seeds. Gadwalls and American coots from Lower Reserve contained much widgeongrass vegetation, produced after the early September flooding of the impoundment.

Samples from inside and outside exclosures (table 33.1) confirmed trends in use revealed by census and analysis of gullet contents. Widgeongrass use in Gibson Pond was first evident from vegetation sampling on 30 October; by 20 December, 89% of available widgeongrass had been consumed. Waterfowl use of Rest Pond was low, and this was reflected in comparable weights of vegetation inside and outside exclosures. In Wheeler Basin, differences in standing crop of muskgrass inside and outside exclosures in November and December ($P < 0.05$) reflected intensive waterfowl use.

Weights of seeds obtained from bottom samples were greater ($P < 0.05$) inside than outside bottom exclosures for widgeongrass in Gibson Pond only, and for sea purslane and dwarf spikerush seeds in Lower Reserve (table 33.4). Weights of muskgrass tubercles from Wheeler Basin also were greater inside exclosures ($P < 0.01$). These differences between samples from inside and outside exclosures were assumed to result from waterfowl use and supported census and food habits data showing intensive use of muskgrass tubercles and sea purslane seeds.

Table 33.4. Weight (grams per square meter, air-dry) of selected seeds and muskgrass tubercles based on marsh bottom sampling, Tom Yawkey Wildlife Center, South Carolina, January 1980

Impoundment	N[a]	Food	Inside exclosures	Outside exclosures	Duck use (%)[b]
Lower Reserve	15	*Sesuvium maritimum*	26.0	6.7	74
		Ruppia maritima	2.5	2.0	
		Eleocharis parvula	0.4	0.2	55
		Salicornia spp.	0.4	0.1	
		Leptochloa filiformis	0.2	0.1	
		Distichlis spicata	0.1	0.1	
Wheeler Basin	20	*Chara hornemannii*	15.4	4.4	71
		Ruppia maritima	2.1	2.2	
Gibson Pond	5	*Ruppia maritima*	6.6	2.6	60
Rest Pond	20	*Ruppia maritima*	3.2	2.9	

[a] Number of pairs of samples (inside and outside exclosures).
[b] Only reported where corresponding inside and outside exclosure values differed ($P < 0.05$).

Chemical Composition

Nutritionally, muskgrass vegetation was similar in composition to widgeongrass vegetation (table 33.5), although there were differences in elemental composition. Muskgrass had a higher calcium content than widgeongrass and a lower phosphorus content. Tubercles contained 95.8% nitrogen-free extract (NFE). This unusually high value is important because NFE is high in digestible energy. Sea purslane seeds were high in protein and fat compared with widgeongrass seeds (table 33.5) and most other seed foods (Spinner and Bishop 1950, Bardwell et al. 1962).

Table 33.5. Chemical composition (percentage dry matter) of selected waterfowl foods, Tom Yawkey Wildlife Center, South Carolina, 1979

Food	Crude protein	Crude fat	Crude fiber	Nitrogen-free extract	Ash	Ca	P
Ruppia maritima							
Vegetation	21.9	1.5	16.5	35.1	25.2	0.28	0.27
Seeds	7.8	2.9	35.2	51.0	3.1	0.58	0.19
Chara hornemannii							
Vegetation	17.8	1.3	17.7	30.8	32.6	0.68	0.18
Tubercles	2.1	0.7	1.0	95.8	0.4	0.09	0.03
Sesuvium maritimum							
Seeds	17.9	8.2	31.9	38.2	4.0	0.05	0.31

Management Implications

Both muskgrass and sea purslane yielded substantial amounts of waterfowl food. Under good growing conditions resulting in well-stocked stands, production of muskgrass vegetation and tubercles was at least equal to production of widgeongrass vegetation and seeds, and production of seeds of sea purslane was several times that of widgeongrass. Both muskgrass and sea purslane were readily eaten by waterfowl. These species offer managers viable alternatives to widgeongrass and an opportunity to increase diversity of food and waterfowl species. However, several limitations were evident.

On South Island, Gulf Coast muskgrass has been found in dense stands only in Wheeler Basin and Sand Creek Basin since its presence there was discovered more than 20 years ago (W. P. Baldwin, pers. commun.). It was transplanted into other impoundments on the Yawkey Center in late summer 1980, but no growth was observed in these impoundments during the following two years. This species may require rather specific environmental conditions. Unlike widgeongrass, which occurred on a wider range of soil types, muskgrass was restricted to soft, mucky substrates as found in Wheeler and Sand Creek basins. However, muskgrass tolerated turbidity and wave action better (see Swiderek 1982 for water quality data) and tolerated salinity near 35 ppt for about one week in 1979. But in summer 1981 (after completion of this study), when severe drought resulted in very high water salinity (38-40 ppt) and temperature (>32C) for about one month, there was a complete loss of muskgrass in both impoundments. The loss was temporary, and excellent muskgrass crops were produced in 1982 in both Wheeler and Sand Creek basins.

Requirements for sea purslane growth and management are still not fully understood. Lower Reserve seemed to provide almost ideal conditions. The attempt to grow sea purslane in Twin Sisters' Pond was unsuccessful after two years of drawdown; however, sea purslane has become established in several other impoundments on the South Carolina coast (M. B. Prevost, pers. commun.), and Chabreck (1981) has reported that it is managed in Louisiana. In South Carolina, the most obvious difference between areas where sea purslane occurred and where it did not was in soil type. Lower Reserve, the southern portion of Upper Pine Ridge Pond, and higher portions of Twin Sisters' Pond had organic or peaty soils, whereas the northern portion of Upper Pine Ridge Pond and the low bed of Twin Sisters' Pond were firm clay and supported no sea purslane. Prevost (pers. commun.) has noted a similar association of sea purslane with organic soils elsewhere on the South Carolina coast.

Insect damage to sea purslane occurred in all dewatered impoundments and sometimes was severe. The small beetles responsible were identified by E. G. Riley, University of Missouri, as *Erynephala maritima* (Le Conte), family Chrysomelidae.

Several major problems must be confronted when dewatering salt marsh impoundments for growth of sea purslane. Cat clay may develop, resulting in high acidity that inhibits or prevents plant growth (Neely 1958). Cat clay formation in Twin Sisters' Pond could have been responsible for the failure of sea purslane and other plants to become established. This condition, however, was not irreversible. The impoundment was reflooded after the second year of attempted sea purslane management and produced good growth of dwarf spikerush and some widgeongrass the first growing season and excellent widgeongrass the second year. A second major problem in the drawdown type of management is mosquito production. When an impoundment is drained, the surface may dry and crack, providing breeding areas for mosquitoes (primarily *Aedes solicitans* and *A. taeniorhynchos*). This may be an important public health consideration in some locations.

On suitable soils, such as in Lower Reserve, sea purslane may be encouraged by draining the impoundment to about 20-30 cm below bed level by 1 April, allowing it to remain dewatered during the growing season, and flooding 20-25 cm deep by 1 September. If this management is continued for several years, eventual encroachment by undesirable emergent vegetation will occur. A possible solution is to revert to widgeongrass management (flooding during the growing season) for one or two years, then to reinstitute sea purslane management after undesirable plants are under control. The effectiveness of this procedure was demonstrated in Lower Reserve after completion of this study.

Two South Island impoundments (Lower Reserve and Upper Pine Ridge Pond) and a privately owned impoundment within the boundaries of the Tom Yawkey Wildlife Center (P. M. Wilkinson, pers. commun.) demonstrated the possibility of growing crops of both sea purslane and widgeongrass in the same impoundment during the same year. When dewatered impoundments containing stands of mature sea purslane plants were flooded late in the summer, late crops of widgeongrass were produced. Some advantages of intentionally managing widgeongrass impoundments in this way include reduced problems of algae competition, summer die-out, and damage by wave action.

LITERATURE CITED

Bardwell, J. L., L. L. Glasgow, and E. A. Epps, Jr. 1962. Nutritional analyses of foods eaten by pintail and teal in South Louisiana. Proc. Southeast. Assoc. Game Fish Comm. 16:209–217.

Bartonek, J. C., and J. J. Hickey. 1969. Selective feeding by juvenile diving ducks in summer. Auk 86:443–457.

Chabreck, R. H. 1964. Refuge Division research. Pages 189-198 *in* Tenth biennial report, 1962-1963. Louisiana Wildl. Fish. Comm., New Orleans.

———. 1981. Effects of impoundments in marshes on wildlife and fisheries. Pages 21-29 *in* R. C. Carey, P. S. Markovits, and J. B. Kirkwood, eds. Proceedings of U.S. Fish Wildl. Serv. workshop on coastal ecosystems of the southeastern United States. FWS/OBS-80/59. U.S. Fish Wildl. Serv., Washington, D.C.

Cottam, C. 1939. Food habits of North American diving ducks. U.S. Dep. Agric. Tech. Bull. 643. 140pp.

Fritsch, F. E. 1935. The structure and reproduction of the algae. Vol. 1. Cambridge Univ. Press, London. 791pp.

Jemison, E. S., and R. H. Chabreck. 1962. The availability of waterfowl foods in coastal marsh impoundments in Louisiana. Trans. N. Am. Wildl. Nat. Resour. Conf. 27:288-301.

Joanen, T., and L. L. Glasgow. 1965. Factors influencing the establishment of widgeongrass stands in Louisiana. Proc. Southeast. Assoc. Game Fish Comm. 19:78-92.

Martin, A. C., R. H. Gensch, and C. P. Brown. 1946. Alternative methods in upland gamebird food analysis. J. Wildl. Manage. 10:8-12.

———, and F. M. Uhler. 1939. Food of game ducks in the United States and Canada. U.S. Dep. Agric. Tech. Bull. 634. 308pp.

Mayer, F. L., Jr., and J. B. Low. 1970. The effect of salinity on widgeongrass. J. Wildl. Manage. 34:658-661.

McAtee, W. L. 1939. Wildfowl food plants: their value, propagation, and management. Collegiate Press, Ames, Iowa. 141pp.

Munro, J. A. 1939. Foods of ducks and coots at Swan Lake, British Columbia. Can. J. Res. Sect. D Zool. Sci. 17:178-186.

Neely, W. W. 1958. Irreversible drainage—a new factor in waterfowl management. Trans. N. Am. Wildl. Conf. 23:342-348.

Prevost, M. B., A. S. Johnson, and J. L. Landers. 1978. Production and utilization of waterfowl foods in brackish impoundments in South Carolina. Proc. Southeast. Assoc. Fish Wildl. Agencies 32:60-70.

Richardson, F. D. 1980. Ecology of *Ruppia maritima* L. in New Hampshire (U.S.A.) tidal marshes. Rhodora 82:403-439.

Singleton, J. R. 1951. Production and utilization of waterfowl food plants on the east Texas Gulf Coast. J. Wildl. Manage. 15:46-56.

Spinner, G. P., and J. S. Bishop. 1950. Chemical analysis of some wildlife foods in Connecticut. J. Wildl. Manage. 14:175-180.

Swiderek, P. K. 1982. Production, management, and waterfowl use of sea purslane, Gulf Coast muskgrass, and widgeongrass in brackish impoundments. M.S. Thesis, Univ. Georgia, Athens. 105pp.

Wood, R. D., and K. Imahori. 1965. A review of the Characeae. Vol. 1, Monograph of the Characeae. Verlag Von J. Cramer, Weinheim, West Germany. 904pp.

34

Workshop Summary: Habitat Management in Winter

Roger L. Pederson, Robert H. Chabreck, Daniel P. Connelly, Leigh H. Fredrickson, and Henry R. Murkin

This report summarizes the current status of, and future needs for, research and management of habitat used by waterfowl during their nonnesting period. We are grateful for the interest and contributions of all participants who attended our discussion session. In addition, we would like to thank John Kadlec, Richard Kaminski, Loren Smith, and the editorial board for providing helpful comments and suggestions for improving this manuscript.

Habitat Management

Objectives

Waterfowl habitat management during the nonnesting period should provide food, cover, space, and water requirements of waterfowl. Our understanding of where and when to manage habitat will be predicated on our knowledge of factors affecting waterfowl distribution during the nonnesting phase of their life cycle (e.g., Bellrose et al. 1979, Raveling 1979, Howard and Kantrud 1983, Nichols et al. 1983, Heitmeyer and Vohs 1984, Lewis and Garrison 1984). Similarly, our understanding of how to manage habitat will depend on our comprehension of habitat processes and how resources required by waterfowl are produced and become available within different habitat types (e.g., Josselyn 1982, Wharton et al. 1982, Odum et al. 1984, Gosselink 1984). This information is essential for waterfowl habitat programs relating to acquisition, protection, and management.

Status

(1) Much of the habitat that waterfowl occupy during the nonnesting season is in the private sector or has limited management capability (Chabreck 1979, Sanderson 1980, Gilmer et al. 1982, Tiner 1984).

(2) Of the habitat that is actively managed for waterfowl, management usually is directed toward providing refuge areas or attracting birds for hunting. Generally, there are few provisions made to manage habitat for waterfowl requirements in the posthunting, premigration period (Sincock 1968, Fredrickson and Drobney 1979, Suring and Knighton 1985). Because requirements of waterfowl during the nonnesting period are only partially understood, state-of-the-art waterfowl habitat management has endeavored to use "natural management," i.e., the use of environmental forces (disturbance, water level changes, fire) to develop mosaics of native plant communities (Weller 1978). Mosaics of native plant communities are less costly to manage, more permanent, and provide more resources for waterfowl than do standard agronomic practices (Fredrickson and Taylor 1982). However, the successful development of a habitat complex requires a conceptual grasp of habitat change (e.g., vegetation dynamics), an understanding of the biological and physical factors that produce change, and a knowledge of the life-history attributes of species that occur in or utilize management areas.

(3) Habitat management is still considered more an art than a science, with local practitioners learning trial-and-error methods by apprenticeship. The advancement of waterfowl habitat management as a science is hindered by the different reward systems of academia and resource agencies; the fragmentation, abstraction, and complexity of scientific inquiry; the difficulty of applying scientific expertise in the resource management arena; and the limited capability of agencies and private individuals to use biological information (Bella and Williamson 1976, McCreary 1982, Weller 1982).

(4) There is a need to distinguish between the in-depth methodology and data required by researchers and the monitoring data required by managers. Managers need simple data-gathering techniques and criteria to tell them when to use or not use specific management procedures. They often cannot get the appropriate data that they need by research, nor are research techniques usually directly applicable to the gathering of monitoring data for use in devising management schedules. Consequently, managers and researchers have problems understanding or appreciating each other's methods of operation.

Habitat Management Research

Status

Present habitat-management research reflects individually excellent studies that, unfortunately, also represent a disjunct array with little coordination, relationship, or even communication among researchers (Weller 1982). The resulting research conclusions reflect this diverse approach, failing to reveal the comprehensive patterns of processes that are essential to both science and management (Weller 1982). Many waterfowl investigations recognize habitat values, but the most detailed wetland studies are those of botanists and wetland ecologists. In tracing the information evolution on the nesting grounds, we see that recent conceptual frameworks for management were obtained when waterfowl studies were integrated with wetland investigations (Weller and Spatcher 1965, Weller and Fredrickson 1974, van der Valk and Davis 1978, Kaminski and Prince 1981, Danell and Sjoberg 1982). The need to integrate waterfowl/habitat research on migration and wintering areas is just as important.

Because of the dynamic changes in waterfowl habitat, long-term, interdisciplinary research approaches are desirable for defining the causal factors that determine waterfowl use. Phenomena that seem to be detrimental to waterfowl in the short term (drought, flooding) may be critical for the long-term productivity of the habitat. Currently, there are several wetland research programs involving long-term, interdisciplinary efforts: e.g., National Science Foundation's long-term ecological research (Halfpenny and Ingraham 1984), Delta Waterfowl and Wetlands Research Station and Ducks Unlimited Canada's Marsh Ecology Research Program (Murkin et al. 1984), and Sea Grant Consortium's Coastal Wetland Impoundment Ecological Characterization Research Program (DeVoe 1984). Each sponsoring organization supplies progress reports and information that will aid administrators or prospective researchers.

Research Needs

We clearly need to develop waterfowl habitat models that identify functional levels of organization: system, community or life-form, and species. For example, Simpson et al. (1981) designed a diagrammatic representation of major pathways and compartments through which nutrients and heavy metals move in freshwater tidal wetlands. Major system components—producers, consumers, detritus, sediment, and nutrients—are coupled by biological and physical processes (for reviews, see Greeson et al. 1978, Good et al. 1978, Brinson et al. 1981) that transfer materials and energy (Simpson et al. 1983). Although wetland functions are ultimately controlled by climate, hydrologic parameters, such as duration and frequency of flooding (hydroperiod) and the velocity and source of water, determine the physical and chemical properties of wetland substrates (Gosselink and Turner 1978). In turn, substrate characteristics influence primary production, species diversity, decomposition, and uptake and release of nutrients (Simpson et al. 1983). System level information provides concepts for understanding the long-term cycling of nutrients and food resource availability in habitats and management areas used by waterfowl (Hussong et al. 1979, Smith and Odum 1981, Danell and Sjoberg 1982, Smith and Kadlec 1985). Unfortunately, data bases for applying a system level of organization to habitat management are rudimentary, and traditional concepts describing wetland phenomena may not be appropriate (Nixon 1980, van der Valk 1982, Nelson and Kadlec 1984, Verry 1985).

Systems level of organization can be further separated into life-form or functional group levels of organization. Wiggins et al. (1980) recognzied four groups of temporary pool invertebrates (system "consumers") on the basis of their strategy of toleration or avoidance of drought and their period of recruitment to the community. Knowledge of general requirements for invertebrate species in a particular functional grouping enabled White (in press) to elucidate invertebrate abundance in relation to flooding regimes in greentree reservoirs and bottomland hardwood forests in southeast Missouri. An example of life-form classification for vegetation is given in van der Valk and Davis' (1978) model of vegetation dynamics of prairie glacial marshes. They recognized three major groups of aquatic macrophytes (system "producers") on the basis of germination and establishment characteristics. Each group exhibited changes in abundance in response to such changes in environmental states as drought or prolonged flooding (van der Valk and Davis 1978). A life-form approach to vegetation management also was developed by Knighton (1985) to devise water-level prescriptions for impoundments in the Great Lakes states.

The level of information most useful for predicting and interpreting management effects in wetlands is found at the population or life-history level of individual species (Howard and Kantrud 1983, Allen and Hoffman 1984, Lewis and Garrison 1984, Pederson and van der Valk 1985). Life-history information is particularly important for controlling problem plant and animal species (Fontaine 1983, Spencer and Bowes 1985). Hall et al. (1946) provide a classic example of how seed germination, seed dispersal, and water tolerance data of wetland species were used to devise management regimes to control vegetation in Tennessee reservoirs. Harris and Marshall (1963) and Connelly (1979) detail how drawdown and irrigation schedules can be designed to the life-history of characteristics of certain wetland plant species. The life-history approach has also been used by van der Valk (1981, 1982) to develop a model for predicting vegetation change in marshes. When plant life-history information is combined with an understanding of the biological and physical factors that cause vegetation change (Kadlec and Wentz 1974, Hutchinson 1975, Davis and Brinson 1980, Olson 1981, Smith and Kadlec 1985), more reliable predictions about vegetation dynamics in management units can be made.

Recommendations

To improve the status of waterfowl habitat management and research, management agencies should endeavor to (1) hire personnel with strong backgrounds in wetland ecology (e.g., water chemistry, aquatic plant ecology and physiology, limnology, invertebrate zoology), (2) devise continuing education programs to train field staff, (3) establish an "ecological engineer" position with responsibilities for assembling and interpreting research findings into management formats, (4) invite scientists to participate as technical advisors and reviewers in research and management planning processes, and (5) provide funding for cooperative research programs.

The scientific community should (1) recognize the need for researchers to consult with their counterparts in resource agencies as a legitimate professional activity and provide rewards for this role, (2) cooperate with resource agencies in developing an applied research agenda, (3) develop programs of study to enhance educational opportunities for students interested in resource agency employment, and (4) become more involved with extension activities for the private landowner.

LITERATURE CITED

Allen, A. W., and R. D. Hoffman. 1984. Habitat suitability index models: muskrat. FWS/OBS-82/10.46, U.S. Fish Wildl. Serv., Off. Biol. Serv., Washington, D.C.

Bella, D., and K. Williamson. 1976. Conflicts of interdisciplinary research. J. Environ. Syst. 6:107.

Bellrose, F. C., F. L. Paveglio, Jr., and D. W. Steffeck. 1979. Waterfowl populations and the changing environment of the Illinois River Valley. Ill. Nat. Hist. Surv. Bull. 32:11–54.

Brinson, M. M., A. E. Lugo, and S. Brown. 1981. Primary productivity, decomposition and consumer activity in freshwater wetlands. Annu. Rev. Ecol. 12:123–161.

Chabreck, R. H. 1979. Winter habitat of dabbling ducks—physical, chemical, and biological aspects. Pages 133-142 in T. A. Bookhout, ed. Waterfowl and wetlands—an integrated review. Proc. 1977 Symp., Northcent. Sect., Wildl. Soc., Madison, Wis. 152pp.

Connelly, D. P. 1979. Propagation of selected native marsh plants in the San Joaquin valley. Calif. Dep. Fish Game Wildl. Manage. Leafl. 15.

Danell, K., and K. Sjoberg. 1982. Successional patterns of plants, invertebrates, and ducks in a man-made lake. J. Appl. Ecol. 19:395–409.

Davis, G. J., and M. M. Brinson. 1980. Responses of submerged vascular plant communities to environmental change. FWS/OBS-79/33, U.S. Fish Wildl. Serv., Off. Biol. Serv., Washington, D.C. 70pp.

DeVoe, M. R. 1984. Coastal wetland impoundments: ecological characterization and development of management strategies for productive uses. South Carolina Sea Grant Consortium mimeo. 29pp.

Fontaine, R. E. 1983. Mosquito control research—annual report. Extension Entomology, Univ. California, Davis. 132pp.

Fredrickson, L. H., and R. D. Drobney. 1979. Habitat utilization by postbreeding waterfowl. Pages 119-131 in T. A. Bookhout, ed. Waterfowl and wetlands—an integrated review. Proc. 1977 Symp., Northcent. Sect., Wildl. Soc., Madison, Wis. 152pp.

———, and T. S. Taylor. 1982. Management of seasonally flooded impoundments for wildlife. U.S. Fish Wildl. Serv. Resour. Publ. 148. 29pp.

Gilmer, D. S., M. R. Miller, R. D. Bauer, and J. R. Le Donne. 1982. California's Central Valley wintering waterfowl: concerns and challenges. Trans. N. Am. Wildl. Nat. Resour. Conf. 47:441–452.

Good, R. E., D. F. Whigham, and R. L. Simpson, eds. 1978. Freshwater wetlands: ecological processes and management potential. Academic Press, New York. 377pp.

Gosselink, J. G. 1984. The ecology of delta marshes of coastal Louisiana: a community profile. FWS/OBS-84/09, U.S. Fish Wildl. Serv., Off. Biol. Serv., Washington, D.C. 134pp.

———, and R. E. Turner. 1978. The role of hydrology in freshwater wetland ecosystems. Pages 63–78 in R. E. Good, D. F. Whigham, and R. L. Simpson, eds. Freshwater wetlands: ecological processes and management potential. Academic Press, New York. 377pp.

Greeson, P. E., J. R. Clark, and J. E. Clark, eds. 1978. Wetland functions and values: the state of our understanding. American Water Resources Assoc., Minneapolis. 674pp.

Halfpenny, J. C., and K. P. Ingraham. 1984. Long-term ecological research in the United States: a net of research sites. National Science Foundation, Washington, D.C. 28pp.

Hall, T. F., W. T. Penfound, and A. D. Hess. 1946. Water level relationships of plants in the Tennessee Valley with particular reference to malaria control. J. Tenn. Acad. Sci. 21:18–59.

Harris, S. W., and W. R. Marshall. 1963. Ecology of water-level manipulations on a northern marsh. Ecol. 44:331–343.

Heitmeyer, M. E., and P. A. Vohs, Jr. 1984. Distribution and habitat use of waterfowl wintering in Oklahoma. J. Wildl. Manage. 48:51–62.

Howard, R. J., and H. A. Kantrud. 1983. Habitat suitability index models: redhead (wintering). FWS/OBS-82/10.53, U.S. Fish Wildl. Serv., Off. Biol. Serv., Washington, D.C.

Hussong, D., J. M. Damare, R. J. Limpert, W. J. L. Sladen, R. M. Weiner, and R. R. Colwell. 1979. Microbial impact of Canada geese (*Branta canadensis*) and whistling swans (*Cygnus columbianus columbianus*) an aquatic ecosystems. Appl. Environ. Microbiol. 37:14–20.

Hutchinson, G. E. 1975. A treatise on limnology. Vol. 3. Limnological botany. John Wiley, New York. 660pp.

Josselyn, M., ed. 1982. Wetland restoration and enhancement in California. Workshop Proc., California State Univ., Hayward, February. Calif. Sea Grant Publ. La Jolla. 110pp.

Kadlec, J. A., and W. A. Wentz. 1974. Evaluation of marsh plant establishment techniques: induced and natural. Vol. 1. Tech. Pap. U.S. Army Engineer Res. Cent. Waterways Exp. Stn., Vicksburg, Miss. 266pp.

Kaminski, R. M., and H. H. Prince. 1981. Dabbling duck and aquatic macroinvertebrate responses to manipulated wetland habitat. J. Wildl. Manage. 45:1–15.

Knighton, M. D. 1985. Vegetation management in water impoundments: water-level control. Pages 39-50 in M. D. Knighton, ed. Water impoundments for wildlife: a habitat management workshop. U.S. For. Serv. Gen. Tech. Rep. NC-100, St. Paul, Minn. 136pp.

Lewis, J. C., and R. L. Garrison. 1984. Habitat suitability index models: American black duck (wintering). FWS/OBS-82/10.68, U.S. Fish Wildl. Serv., Off. Biol. Serv., Washington, D.C.

McCreary, S. 1982. Legal and institutional constraints and opportunities in wetlands enhancement. Pages 39-52 in M. Josselyn, ed., Wetland restoration and enhancement in California. Workshop Proc., California State Univ., Hayward, February. Calif. Sea Grant Publ., La Jolla. 110pp.

Murkin, H. R., B. D. J. Batt, P. J. Caldwell, C. B. Davis, J. A. Kadlec, and A. G. van der Valk. 1984. Perspectives on the Delta Waterfowl Research Station-Ducks Unlimited Canada Marsh Ecology Research Program. Trans. N. Am. Wildl. Nat. Resour. Conf. 49:253–261.

Nelson, J. W., and J. A. Kadlec. 1984. A conceptual approach to relating habitat structure and macroinvertebrate production in freshwater wetlands. Trans. N. Am. Wildl. Nat. Resour. Conf. 49:262–270.

Nichols, J. D., K. J. Reinecke, and J. E. Hines. 1983. Factors affecting the distribution of mallards wintering in the Mississippi Alluvial Valley. Auk 100:932–946.

Nixon, S. 1980. Between coastal marshes and coastal waters—a review of 20 years of speculation and research on the role of salt marshes. Pages 437-525 *in* P. Hamilton and K. Macdonald, eds. Estuarine and wetland processes. Plenum Press, New York.

Odum, W. E., T. J. Smith III, J. K. Hoover, and C. C. McIvor. 1984. The ecology of tidal freshwater marshes of the United States east coast: a community profile. FWS/OBS-83/17, U.S. Fish Wildl. Serv., Off. Biol. Serv., Washington, D.C. 177pp.

Olson, R. A. 1981. Wetland vegetation, environmental factors, and their interaction in strip mine ponds, stockdams, and natural wetlands. U.S. For. Serv. Gen. Tech. Rep. RM-85, Fort Collins, Colo. 19pp.

Pederson, R. L., and A. G. van der Valk. 1985. Vegetation change and seed banks in marshes: ecological and management implications. Trans. N. Am. Wildl. Nat. Resour. Conf. 49:271–280.

Raveling, D. G. 1979. The annual cycle of body composition of Canada geese with special reference to control of reproduction. Auk 96:234–252.

Sanderson, G. C. 1980. Conservation of waterfowl. Pages 43-58 *in* F. C. Bellrose. Ducks, geese, and swans of North America. Stackpole Books, Harrisburg, Pa. 540pp.

Simpson, R. L., R. E. Good, M. A. Leck, and D. F. Whigham. 1983. The ecology of freshwater tidal wetlands. BioSci. 33:255–259.

———, R. E. Good, R. Walker, and B. R. Frasco. 1981. Dynamics of nitrogen, phosphorous and heavy metals in Delaware River freshwater tidal wetlands. Center for Coastal and Environmental Studies. Rutgers University, New Brunswick, N.J.

Sincock, J. L. 1968. Common faults of management. Pages 222-226 *in* J. D. Newsom, ed. Proc. Marsh Estuary Management Symp., Louisiana State Univ., Baton Rouge. 250pp.

Smith, L. M., and J. A. Kadlec. 1985. Fire and herbivory in a Great Salt Lake marsh. Ecol. 66:259–265.

Smith, T. J., III, and W. E. Odum. 1981. The effects of grazing by snow geese on coastal salt marshes. Ecol. 62:98–106.

Spencer, W., and G. Bowes. 1985. Limnophila and Hygrophila: a review and physiological assessment of their weed potential in Florida. J. Aquat. Plant Manage. 23:7–16.

Suring, L. H., and M. D. Knighton. 1985. History of water impoundments in wildlife management. Pages 15-22 *in* M. D. Knighton, ed. Water impoundments for wildlife: a habitat management workshop. U.S. For. Serv. Gen. Tech. Rep. NC-100, St. Paul, Minn. 136pp.

Tiner, R. W., Jr. 1984. Wetlands of the United States: current status and recent trends. National Wetland Inventory, U.S. Fish Wildl. Serv., Washington, D.C. 59pp.

van der Valk, A. G. 1981. Succession in wetlands: a Gleasonian approach. Ecol. 62:688–696.

———. 1982. Succession in temperate North American wetlands. Pages 169-179 *in* B. Gopal, R. E. Turner, R. G. Wetzel, and D. F. Whigham, eds. Wetlands: ecology and management. National Institute of Ecology and International Scientific Publ., Jaipur, India.

———, and C. B. Davis. 1978. The role of seed banks in the vegetation dynamics of prairie glacial marshes. Ecol. 59:322–355.

Verry, E. S. 1985. Water quality and nutrient dynamics in shallow water impoundments. Pages 61-71 *in* M. D. Knighton, ed. Water impoundments for wildlife: a habitat management workshop. U.S. For. Serv. Gen. Tech. Rep. NC-100, St. Paul. Minn. 136pp.

Weller, M. W. 1978. Management of freshwater marshes for wildlife. Pages 267-284 *in* R. E. Good, D. F. Whigham, and R. L. Simpson, eds. Freshwater wetlands: ecological processes and management potential. Academic Press, New York. 377pp.

———. 1982. Workshop summary. Pages 42-44 *in* Delta Waterfowl Research Station. Workshop on the ecology of wintering waterfowl, 14-16 April, Puxico, Mo. Delta Waterfowl and Wetlands Research Station, Portage la Prairie, Manitoba. 51pp.

————, and L. H. Fredrickson. 1974. Avian ecology of a managed glacial marsh. Living Bird 12:269-291.

————, and C. E. Spatcher. 1965. Role of habitat in the distribution and abundance of marsh birds. Iowa Agric. Home Econ. Exp. Stn. Spec. Rep. 43. 31pp.

Wharton, C. H., W. M. Kitchens, and T. W. Sipe. 1982. The ecology of bottomland hardwood swamps of the Southeast: a community profile. FWS/OBS-81/37, U.S. Fish Wildl. Serv., Off. Biol. Serv., Washington, D.C. 133pp.

White, D. C. Lowland hardwood wetland invertebrate community and production in Missouri. Archiv. Hydrobiol. In press.

Wiggins, D. B., R. J. Mackay, and I. M. Smith. 1980. Evolutionary strategies of animals in annual temporary pools. Archiv. Hydrobiol. Suppl. 58:97-206.

VIII.
Harvest, Distribution, and
Population Status

35

Recoveries of North American Waterfowl in the Neotropics

Jorge E. Botero and Donald H. Rusch

Abstract: The numbers and distribution of recoveries of North American waterfowl in the Neotropics through 1980 were analyzed and summarized. A total of
18,885 bands from 30 waterfowl species was reported from Mexico, Central
America, South America, and the Caribbean islands. Blue-winged teal (*Anas
discors*) and northern pintail (*A. acuta*) were about 70% of the total Neotropical
recoveries. Mexico was an important recovery area for white-fronted geese
(*Anser albifrons*) and black brant (*Branta bernicla*). Less than 2% of the total
recoveries of diving ducks were in the Neotropics; those taken were mainly from
Mexico. About 20-25% of the total recoveries of cinnamon teal (*Anas cyanoptera*) and blue-winged teal were in the Neotropics; those taken were mainly from
Mexico and South America, respectively. Blue-winged teal recovered in Mexico
were more likely to have originated in the western United States or Canada; those
recovered in the Caribbean were most likely to have originated in the eastern
United States or Canada. Neotropics are important wintering areas for blue-
winged teal, but low band-reporting rates underemphasize the magnitude and
harvest of teal in the Neotropics.

More than 30 species of North American waterfowl winter in the Neotropics,
with distributions that extend south of the United States into Mexico, Central
America, South America, or the Caribbean islands. Leopold (1959) suggested that
9-17% of the total North American waterfowl population crosses the U.S.-Mexico
border during migration. Saunders and Saunders (1981) reported sizable numbers
of northern shoveler (*Anas clypeata*), gadwall (*A. strepera*), northern pintail (*A.

Waterfowl in Winter.© 1988 University of Minnesota. Edited by Milton W. Weller and published by
the University of Minnesota Press, Minneapolis.

acuta), green-winged teal (*A. crecca*), and redheads (*Aythya americana*) wintering in Mexico. Bellrose (1980) suggested that the majority of black brant (*Branta bernicla*), blue-winted teal (*Anas discors*), and cinnamon teal (*A. cyanoptera*) winter south of the United States.

Periodic waterfowl censuses have been conducted in Mexico since 1937 (Saunders and Saunders 1981), but only a few have been flown in Central or South America (Glover and Chamberlain (1960). The winter ecology of immigrant waterfowl in the Neotropics is essentially unknown; there is still a critical lack of information about their migratory chronology and behavior and even, in some cases, about their winter distribution in the region.

This paper summarizes data on numbers and distribution from waterfowl band recoveries in Mexico, Central America, South America, and the Caribbean islands. We discuss in more detail the implications of distribution and magnitude of blue-winged teal band recoveries in the Neotropics to migration, winter distribution, population dynamics, and management of the species.

We are grateful to R. Blohm and the Bird Banding Laboratory for making banding and recovery information available to us, to J. R. Cary for his help with the computer analysis, and to waterfowl banders throughout North America for their contributions toward understanding waterfowl ecology.

The analysis was funded through the Wisconsin Cooperative Wildlife Research Unit in cooperation with the U.S. Fish and Wildlife Service (USFWS), the University of Wisconsin, the Wisconsin Department of Natural Resources, and the Wildlife Management Institute.

Methods

The Bird Banding Laboratory provided us with tapes containing all the waterfowl band recoveries from the Neotropical region (south of the U.S.-Mexico border) that were reported through 31 August 1980. The tape included data on species, age, sex, status, date and location of banding and recovery, how obtained, why and who reported, and bird and band condition. We excerpted information on species, location of banding, and location of recovery for all types of Neotropical recoveries. Of the total of 18,885 Neotropical recoveries, 91% were from shot birds; an additional 4% of the records had no information on how the bands were recovered.

Data on numbers of birds banded and recovered worldwide through 1980 were provided by the USFWS Bird Banding Laboratory and Office of Migratory Bird Management (R. Blohm, pers. commun.). The number of waterfowl bands recovered in each Neotropical region is a function of distribution, harvest rate, reporting rate, and also partly the proportion of populations banded in respective regions of origin.

Waterfowl Band Recoveries in the Neotropics

A total of 18,885 USFWS and Canadian Wildlife Service bands from 30 waterfowl species was recovered in Mexico, Central America, South America, and the Caribbean islands and reported to the Bird Banding Laboratory. Of these, 9,468 (50%) bands were from blue-winged teal and 4,097 (22%) were from northern pintail. Eleven other species made up another 27%. White-fronted goose (*Anser albifrons*), black brant, redhead, snow goose (*Chen caerulescens*), lesser scaup (*Aythya affinis*), and American wigeon (*Anas americana*) had more than 400 recoveries each. Species with fewer than 50 bands recovered and reported were common merganser (*Mergus merganser*), American black duck (*Anas rubripes*), Mexican duck (*A. platyrhynchos diazi*), mottled duck (*A. fulvigula*), wood duck (*Aix sponsa*), greater scaup (*Aythya marila*), common goldeneye (*Bucephala clangula*), Barrow's goldeneye (*B. islandica*), bufflehead (*B. albeola*), ruddy duck (*Oxyura jamaicensis*), Ross's goose (*Chen rossii*), fulvous whistling duck (*Dendrocygna bicolor*), and tundra swan (*Cygnus columbianus*).

Goose Recoveries

Among geese, snow, white-fronted, brant, and Canada geese (*Branta canadensis*) were most often recovered south of the United States. Of 2,284 bands, white-

Table 35.1. Summary of number of bandings and recoveries of selected waterfowl species through 1980

Species	Total banded	Total recoveries	Percentage recovered	Percentage Neotropical recoveries
Snow goose	400,400	62,510	15.6	0.7
White-fronted goose	56,551	11,132	19.7	6.9
Canada goose	980,787	230,662	23.5	0.2
Black brant	42,930	5,789	13.5	11.7
Redhead	188,620	44,044	23.4	1.2
Canvasback	112,886	17,463	15.5	0.4
Lesser scaup	282,109	24,597	8.7	1.9
Ring-neck	99,636	14,988	15.0	0.4
Mallard	3,313,583	503,499	15.2	0.03
Gadwall	48,689	6,791	13.9	3.8
American wigeon	177,711	22,705	12.8	1.8
Green-winged teal	293,946	20,646	7.0	1.6
Blue-winged teal	854,675	44,186	5.2	21.4
Cinnamon teal	23,678	1,432	6.0	24.2
Shoveler	41,415	4,035	9.7	6.0
Pintail	1,047,806	122,963	11.7	3.3

fronted geese constituted 33.4% and brant 29.8%. All Neotropical recoveries of goose bands, except one from a white-fronted goose, were in Mexico.

Band recoveries from Mexico accounted for 6.9% and 11.7% of the total recoveries of white-fronted geese and black brant, respectively; Mexico is an important harvest area for these geese (table 35.1.).

Diving Duck Recoveries

Among 1,088 Neotropical band recoveries of diving ducks, 47.1% were from redheads and 41.9% from lesser scaup (table 35.2). Canvasback (*Aythya valisineria*) and ring-necked ducks (*A. collaris*) contributed only 6% and 5%, respectively.

Table 35.2. Number of Neotropical recoveries of diving ducks banded in North America through 1980

Species	Mexico	Central America	South America	Caribbean	Total
Redhead	511	1	0	1	513
Canvasback	64	0	0	1	65
Lesser scaup	384	35	1	36	456
Ring-neck	25	2	0	27	54
Total	984	38	1	65	1,088

Most of these bands (90.4%) were recovered in Mexico; some were recovered in the Caribbean (6.0%) and Central America (3.5%). Neotropical band recoveries of diving ducks outside of Mexico were primarily from lesser scaup and ring-necked ducks.

Neotropical recoveries accounted for less than 2% of the total recoveries for diving ducks (table 35.1), suggesting that most diving ducks wintered north of Mexico.

Dabbling Duck Recoveries

Recoveries of 15,298 bands from eight species of dabbling ducks were recorded in the Neotropical region (table 35.3). Blue-winged teal and northern pintail accounted for 88.7% of these; each of the other six species constituted less than 3%. In contrast to geese and diving ducks, only 53.3% of all Neotropical recoveries of dabbling duck bands were from Mexico, with 7.0% from Central America, 23.4% from South America, and 16.2% from the Caribbean islands. The majority of Neotropical recoveries of mallard, gadwall, green-winged teal, cinnamon teal, shoveler, and pintail were from Mexico. Only the American wigeon and the blue-winged teal bands were recovered in significant numbers in other Neotropical areas: 22.2% of all Neotropical recoveries of wigeon were from the Caribbean

Table 35.3. Number of Neotropical recoveries of dabbling ducks banded in North America through 1980

Species	Mexico	Central America	South America	Caribbean	Total
Mallard	138	0	0	3	141
Gadwall	260	0	0	1	261
American wigeon	304	12	9	93	418
Green-winged teal	315	3	2	2	322
Blue-winged teal	2,656	953	3,541	2,318	9,468
Cinnamon teal	329	5	11	2	347
Shoveler	227	8	1	8	244
Pintail	3,926	92	22	57	4,097
Total	8,155	1,073	3,586	2,484	15,298

islands, and South America provided 37.4% of all Neotropical recoveries of blue-winged teal.

Totals of 21.4% and 24.2% of all recoveries of blue-winged teal and cinnamon teal, respectively, were from Neotropical regions (table 35.1). About 95% of Neotropical recoveries of cinnamon teal were reported from Mexico.

Distribution of Blue-Winged Teal Recoveries

The distribution of blue-winged teal recoveries extends farther south and is much more widespread than that of any other species of North American migratory waterfowl. Of all blue-winged teal bands reported in the Neotropics, 37.4% were from South America, 10.1% from Central America, 24.5% from the Caribbean, and only 28.0% from Mexico. Most bands recovered in South America were from Colombia and Venezuela, and most recoveries in the Caribbean were from Cuba, Haiti, and the Dominican Republic (table 35.4).

The distribution of blue-winged teal bands recovered in South America includes the northeastern half of Colombia and northern Venezuela (fig. 35.1). This area includes the inter-Andean river valleys of Colombia, the seasonally flooded savannas between Colombia and Venezuela, and the Andean wetlands of Colombia and Ecuador. Large numbers of bands were recovered from the Caribbean lowlands, especially from the Magdalena River delta in Colombia and from Lake Maracaibo in Venezuela.

Bands were also recovered near the Atlantic coasts of Guyana, Suriname, French Guiana, and in the northeastern corner of Brazil, east of the Amazon River delta (fig. 35.2). Blue-winged teal bands also were recovered in Ecuador and Peru, mostly from the wetlands on the western side of the Andes, along the Pacific coast as far south as Lima (fig. 35.3).

Table 35.4. Geographical distribution of blue-winged teal and band recoveries south of the United States

Country of recovery	Number of bands	Percentage
Mexico	2,656	28.05
Belize	61	0.64
Costa Rica	100	1.06
Guatemala	172	1.82
Honduras	165	1.74
Nicaragua	116	1.23
Panama	273	2.88
El Salvador	66	0.69
Total, Central America	953	10.14
Argentina	1	. . .
Brazil	102	1.08
Colombia	1,857	19.61
Ecuador	90	0.95
French Guiana	342	3.62
Peru	59	0.62
Venezuela	1,091	11.52
Total, South America	3,542	37.41
Bahamas	164	1.73
Cuba	875	9.24
Dominican Republic and Haiti	506	5.34
Jamaica	205	2.16
Puerto Rico	144	1.52
Other Islands	424	4.48
Total, Caribbean	2,318	24.48

Most bands from the Central American isthmus were recovered in the wetlands along the Pacific coast, such as those around the Gulf of Fonseca in Honduras, the Gulf of Nicoya in Costa Rica, and the Gulf of Panama (fig. 35.4). Some bands were recovered in the Guatemalan highlands, in lakes Managua and Nicaragua, and along the Caribbean coasts of Honduras and Belize.

The distribution of blue-winged teal band recoveries in Central America covers an extensive area that includes a wide diversity of wetlands. Bands were recovered in coastal brackish wetlands and mangrove swamps, in permanent and seasonal freshwater wetlands, in tropical dry or humid lowlands, and in the high-altitude wetlands of the Andes.

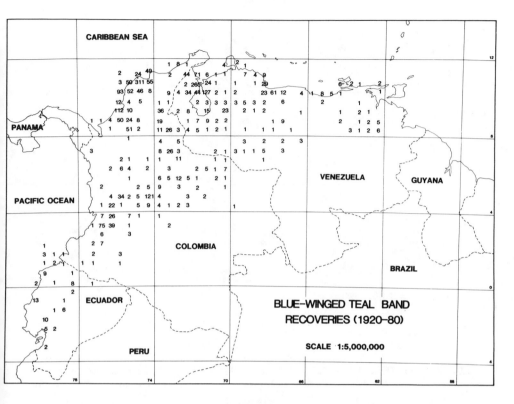

Fig. 35.1. Distribution of blue-winged teal band recoveries in northwestern South America. Numbers indicate total bands recovered in 30-minute block.

Origin of Blue-Winged Teal Recovered in the Neotropics

Blue-winged teal bands recovered south of the Rio Grande originated from an extensive area in North America that included all of the Canadian provinces and states in every flyway from the Pacific to the Atlantic. The highest numbers came from the prairie provinces of Canada (Alberta, 7.9%; Saskatchewan, 17.0%; and Manitoba, 13.2%) and from states in the Central (23.4%) and Mississippi (21.7%) flyways. Smaller numbers of bands came from Ontario (5.7%), the eastern Canadian provinces combined (4.0%), and states in the Atlantic (4.0%) and Pacific (1.1%) flyways. Only one band came from Alaska. Only 33 originated in British Columbia, where blue-winged teal populations are low and are mostly replaced by cinnamon teal (Bellrose 1980).

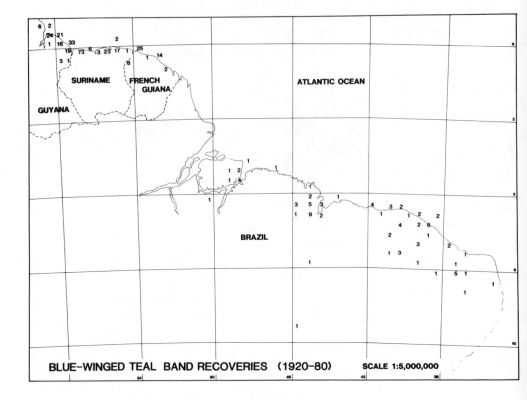

Fig. 35.2. Distribution of blue-winged teal band recoveries in northeastern South America. Numbers indicate total number of bands recovered in 30-minute block.

Teal bands from western Canadian provinces were recovered in Mexico in greater proportions than bands from the east (fig. 35.5). Conversely, teal bands from eastern provinces were recovered in the Caribbean in greater proportions than bands from the west. Substantial proportions of bands from all provinces were recoverd in South America.

A similar trend is observed in the Mexican proportions of all Neotropical recoveries of blue-winged teal bands that came from each of the flyway groups of states: teal bands from eastern states provided greater proportions recovered in the Caribbean than did teal bands from the west (fig. 35.6). Substantial proportions of bands from states in the Central, Mississippi, and Atlantic flyways were recovered in South America.

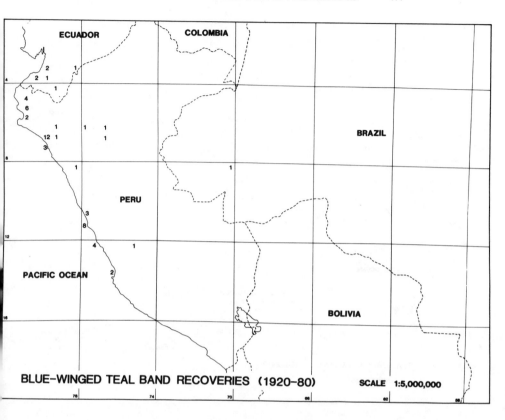

Fig. 35.3. Distribution of blue-winged teal band recovery in Peru. Numbers indicate total number of bands recovered in 30-minute block.

An estimate of derivation of the harvest for a particular recovery area requires the calculation of the size and proportion of each population banded in order to adjust or weight the number of direct recoveries (Geis 1972). The numbers of direct recoveries of blue-winged teal banded from May to August and reported to the Bird Banding Laboratory through 1980 are listed in tables 35.5 and 35.6. Large numbers of bands originated in the prairies, where teal breeding populations and the banding effort were high. There were 600 direct recoveries from Saskatchewan, 286 from Alberta, 254 from North Dakota, and 249 from South Dakota. Substantial numbers of bands also originated from several other states and provinces where populations were less well known and the banding effort was lower. For

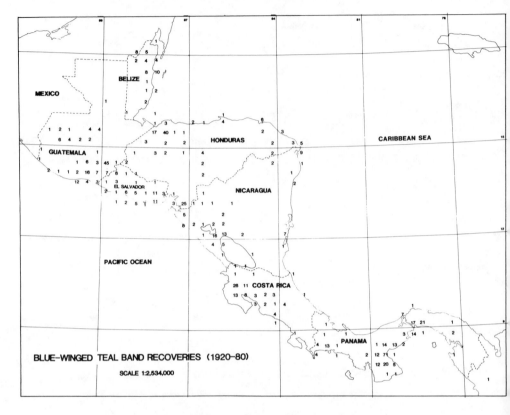

Fig. 35.4. Distribution of blue-winged teal band recoveries in Central America. Numbers indicate total number of bands recovered in 20-minute block.

example, in the four flyways, 64 bands came from New York State, 170 from Minnesota, 102 from Iowa, and 24 from Washington. Because we lack teal population estimates from some of these states, we are unable to assess the derivation of the blue-winged teal harvest in the Neotropics at this time.

Discussion

The Neotropical region is especially important to North American migratory waterfowl such as redheads, pintails, shovelers, gadwall, blue-winged teal, cinnamon teal, and black brant. Cinnamon teal, blue-winged teal, black brant, and

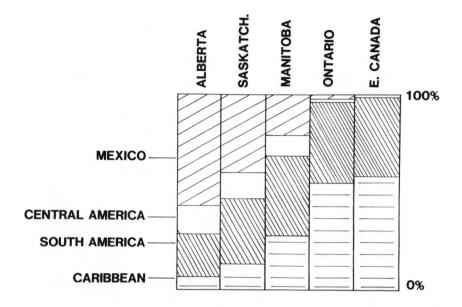

Fig. 35.5. Neotropical distribution of recoveries of blue-winged teal banded in various Canadian provinces. Total numbers of Neotropical teal recoveries were 745 from Alberta, 1,606 from Saskatchewan, 1,251 from Manitoba, 537 from Ontario, and 376 from eastern Canada.

white-fronted geese are probably harvested there at a high rate.

The distribution of reported bands in the Neotropics probably does not reflect the true winter distribution of blue-winged teal. The intensity of sport hunting is probably higher in wetlands closer or accessible to urban centers and very low in some remote areas where subsistence hunting may still occur (Leopold 1959). For example, there were relatively many bands reported from the high-altitude wetlands around Bogota, Colombia, but few from the sparsely populated plains between Colombia and Venezuela, even though the latter areas probably winter many more waterfowl (Botero 1982).

Band recoveries probably also misrepresent teal distribution in the Neotropics because reporting rates may vary from region to region. Reporting rates may be higher in areas closer to urban centers where hunters have a higher level of education and have been exposed to bird banding as a technique for the study of migration. In more remote areas, bands often are kept as souvenirs and never reported. While conducting a study on the waterfowl use of the Cienaga Grande region on the Caribbean coast of Colombia, we collected 103 blue-winged teal bands from a few small villages (Botero 1982); this small sample constituted

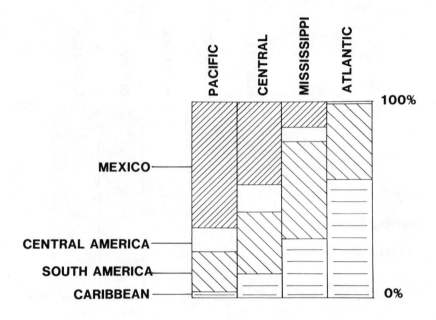

Fig. 35.6. Neotropical distribution of recoveries of blue-winged teal banded in four flyways in United States. Total numbers of Neotropical teal recoveries were 101 from Pacific Flyway, 2,218 from Central Flyway, 2,051 from Mississippi Flyway, and 538 from Atlantic Flyway.

Table 35.5. Neotropical distribution of number of direct recoveries of blue-winged teal banded in Canada from May to August through 1980

Region of banding	Region of recovery				
	Mexico	Central America	South America	Caribbean	Total
British Columbia and					
Northwest Territories	11	2	0	2	15
Alberta	166	53	54	13	286
Saskatchewan	239	89	211	61	600
Manitoba	103	57	155	83	398
Ontario	1	1	64	74	140
Eastern Canada	0	0	52	89	141

almost 6% of the total number of Colombian recoveries, or 3% of the total for South America.

Band recovery rates for blue-winged teal tend to be lower than for other waterfowl species, with the difference often attributed to lower harvest rates

Table 35.6. Neotropical distribution of number of direct recoveries of blue-winged teal banded in the United States from May to August through 1980

Region of banding	Region of recovery				
	Mexico	Central America	South America	Caribbean	Total
Pacific Flyway	21	8	4	0	33
Central Flyway	320	103	243	84	750
Mississippi Flyway	47	29	213	102	391
Atlantic Flyway	0	1	47	62	110

(Stoudt 1949, Leopold 1959). Band recovery rates, either annual or cumulative (table 35.1), are a function of survival rates, harvest rates, and band reporting rates. Relatively low survival of blue-winged teal probably contributes to the low band-recovery rates, but we believe that low band-reporting rates for teal in the Neotropics may be a major depressant of band recovery rates. We suggest that harvest rates of blue-winged teal may be considerably higher than indicated by simple comparisons of recovery rates among species.

In a review of eastward migration of blue-winged teal, Sharp (1972) concluded that blue-winged teal have a much greater tendency than other ducks to move eastward before moving south. Nevertheless, Lensink (1964) documented the tendency for blue-winged teal from Alberta to migrate down the Central and Pacific flyways to a greater extent than teal from Manitoba and Saskatchewan. We detected tendencies for both longitudinal and latitudinal migration in this analysis, but there is considerable variance and overlap in migratory routes among teal from individual breeding areas. Further description and classification of migration patterns (Salomonsen 1955) for blue-winged teal will require further study of the relationships between distribution of band recoveries and reporting rates, hunter activity, and banding effort.

The migratory waterfowl resource is shared by several countries, and it is important that international cooperation in the implementation of management programs be continued and intensified. In the case of blue-winged teal, countries in Central America, the Caribbean, and especially in northern South America should be involved with the United States and Canada in joint planning and management (Weller 1975).

Recent unexplained declines in teal numbers, continued losses of Neotropical wetlands, and intensifying human use of waterfowl in the Neotropics all emphasize the need for data on the behavior, distribution, and population ecology of blue-winged teal in the Neotropics.

LITERATURE CITED

Bellrose, F. C. 1980. Ducks, geese, and swans of North America. Stackpole Books, Harrisburg, Pa. 540pp.

Botero, J. E. 1982. Waterfowl use of the Cienaga Grande Region, Colombia. M.S. Thesis, Univ. Wisconsin, Madison. 58pp.

Geis, A. D. 1972. Use of banding data in migratory game bird research and management. U.S. Fish Wildl. Serv. Spec. Sci. Rep. Wildl. 154. 47pp.

Glover, F. A., and E. B. Chamberlain. 1960. Winter waterfowl survey: Central and South America (exploratory) January 1960. Pages 35-43 in 1960 Winter waterfowl survey, Mexico, Central and South America. U.S. Bur. Sport Fish Wildl., Washington, D.C. 43pp.

Lensink, C. J. 1964. Distribution of recoveries from bandings of ducklings. U.S. Fish Wildl. Serv. Spec. Sci. Rep. Wildl. 89. 146pp.

Leopold, A. S. 1959. Wildlife of Mexico: the game birds and mammals. Univ. California Press, Berkeley. 568pp.

Salomonsen, F. 1955. The evolutionary significance of bird-migration. Dan. Biol. Medd. 22(6):1-64.

Saunders, G. B, and D. C. Saunders. 1981. Waterfowl and their wintering grounds in Mexico, 1937-64. U.S. Fish Wildl. Serv. Resour. Publ. 138. Washington, D.C. 151pp.

Sharp, B. 1972. Eastward migration of blue-winged teal. J. Wildl. Manage. 36:1273-1277.

Stoudt, J. H. 1949. Migration of the blue-winged teal. Pages 19-20 in J. W. Aldrich et al. Migration of some North American waterfowl. U.S. Fish Wildl. Serv. Spec. Sci. Rep. Wildl. 1. 48pp. + maps.

Weller M. W. 1975. Migratory waterfowl: a hemispheric perspective. In Symposium on wildlife and its environment in the Americas. Publicaciones Biologicas Inst. Invest. Cient., Universitad Autonoma de Nuevo Leon, Mexico. 1(7):89-130.

36

Mobility and Site Fidelity of Green-Winged Teal Wintering on the Southern High Plains of Texas

Guy A. Baldassarre, Eileen E. Quinlan, and Eric G. Bolen

Abstract: Mobility and site fidelity of green-winged teal (*Anas crecca carolinensis*) wintering on the Southern High Plains of Texas (SHP) were studied on a 50-km² study area from October to March, 1980-82. Nearly all resightings of teal marked with patagial tags occurred within the study area, probably because hunting disturbance was minimal and food and water abundant in an otherwise semiarid environment. However, many teal had moved off the SHP, as reflected in resightings that averaged only 12% for both males and females from November to March, 1981-82. Resightings were highest for teal marked in December and resighted from late December to mid-February (24% for males and 31% for females). A distinct passage of females through the SHP occurred before December, but mobility of males and females after December did not appear differentially affected by cold temperatures. Direct recoveries indicated movement to coastal Texas and Louisiana. Adults were most likely to be recaptured at the banding site in subsequent years. Indirect recoveries of juvenile males were 4.2 and 1.7 times more likely to occur at different sites in subsequent winters than were those of adult males and juvenile females, respectively, whereas juveniles overall were 4.6 times more likely than adults to exhibit this behavior.

The approximately 20,000 playa lakes on the High Plains of the Texas Panhandle (Guthery and Bryant 1982) constitute major wintering habitat for green-winged teal (*Anas crecca carolinensis*) in the Central Flyway (Bellrose 1980). Green-winged teal rank second only to mallards (*A. platyrhynchos*) in numbers

Waterfowl in Winter. © 1988 University of Minnesota. Edited by Milton W. Weller and published by the University of Minnesota Press, Minneapolis.

harvested during recent years (Carney et al. 1983), yet little information exists regarding their ecology during the nonbreeding season.

However, research interest in nonbreeding waterfowl recently has accelerated (see Anderson and Batt 1983), in part because conditions during winter may control populations of some avian species (Fretwell 1972) and because reproductive performance of some waterfowl is influenced by reserves and nutrients obtained away from breeding sites (Ankney and MacInnes 1978, Raveling 1979, Krapu 1981). Selective strategies on wintering areas should therefore be important in the annual cycle of waterfowl. For example, Nichols et al. (1983) demonstrated that mallards choose different wintering sites in response to changes in habitat suitability and proposed that such flexibility can influence reproductive fitness and survival. This variability in response to habitat conditions during winter necessitates understanding annual return rates (fidelity) to wintering sites, mobility on those sites, and factors influencing mobility on wintering areas. These data can provide insights into a species' wintering strategy and can assist in identifying migration corridors as well as associated major wintering habitats, stopover areas, and staging sites.

The Southern High Plains of Texas (SHP) is an excellent area to investigate these aspects of the winter ecology of green-winged teal because it is a major wintering area for this species, with open playa lakes that maximize visibility of marked birds and very low hunter density (Funk et al. 1971). The objectives of this study were to quantify the mobility of green-winged teal banded and marked while wintering on the SHP, to test the hypothesis that severe winter weather differentially affects mobility of males vs. females, and to determine annual site fidelity to the SHP.

Segments of this study were funded by the Caesar Kleberg Foundation for Wildlife Conservation, USDA Forest Service (Great Plains Wildlife Research Laboratory), and by Organized Research from the College of Agricultural Sciences, Texas Tech University. We thank T. J. and W. J. Hill and the Hill Cattle Co. of Hart, Tex. for access to their land. R. J. Whyte assisted in all phases of the field work. R. E. Turnbull developed computer programs to plot band recovery data and prepared figures for the manuscript. This is contribution T-9-419, College of Agricultural Sciences, Texas Tech University.

Study Area and Methods

We captured green-winged teal from October to March, 1980-82, using funnel traps and a rocket net baited with corn. Birds were trapped at two playa lakes near Hart, Castro County, Texas, which is located centrally on the SHP. Bolen and Guthery (1982) discussed the SHP and associated populations of wintering waterfowl, and Baldassarre and Bolen (1984) provided a description of the specific 50-km² study area.

Each teal was banded with a U.S. Fish and Wildlife Service leg band, and a proportion of the population was also marked using colored patagial tags coded with a unique symbol (Baldassarre et al. 1980). The symbol and/or tag color were changed at about one-week intervals, thus creating a temporally marked cohort. The number of marked teal resighted in each group was recorded by surveying four playa lakes (range of 10-15 ha in size) that constituted the only permanent water sources throughout winter within the study area. Three large and permanent water playas 8-20 km outside the study area also were surveyed periodically to expand the search for marked birds. Surveys, which were conducted at about one-week intervals from 9 November 1981 to 14 March 1982, were initiated two to three hours after sunrise. Irrigation pits, stock ponds, and several small playas were not censused because only small numbers of green-winged teal used them. Also, farming activities that began shortly after sunrise disturbed many of these areas and caused teal to move to the larger playas. The percentage of males and females resighted from each marked group was recorded for each resighting period and used to describe changes through winter in the mobility of green-winged teal while on the SHP.

Most statistical comparisons of resighting data were made using t-tests. However, to examine the possibility of differential mobility of the sexes in response to winter weather we used a paired t-test (Steel and Torrie 1980) to compare the average difference between males and females in the percentage change in resightings between consecutive observation periods. Simple correlation coefficients depicted relationships between average temperature and wind speed and the percentages of males and females resighted.

Green-winged teal recovered anytime during the season banded were recorded as direct recoveries. Direct recoveries within the study area were not included in the analysis; all other band reports (through 1984) were classified as indirect recoveries. Differences among age and sex classes in recovery distribution and fidelity to the SHP were tested using chi-square analysis (Steel and Torrie 1980). Weather data were obtained from Dimmitt, Tex., which was 24 km from the study site (National Oceanic and Atmospheric Administration 1983).

Results

Resightings of Marked Birds

Totals of 1,343 (1,012 males, 331 females) and 1,067 (710 males, 357 females) of the green-winged teal captured and banded also were marked with patagial tags during the 1980-81 and 1981-82 wintering periods, respectively (table 36.1). Data from resightings during 1980-81 were not gathered consistently and thus are not presented. Resighting data also does not include the small sample of birds (17) marked before 25 October 1981.

Table 36.1. Number of green-winged teal banded on Southern High Plains of Texas from October to March, 1980-81 and 1981-82

Year	Male		Female		Total
	Adult	Juvenile	Adult	Juvenile	
1980-81	752	770	156	364	2,042
1981-82	798	711	150	499	2,158
Total	1,550	1,481	306	863	4,200

Similar numbers of male and female green-winged teal remained on the SHP from November to March ($P > 0.05$), with resightings averaging 12% for both sexes (table 36.2). However, percentages resighted were greater ($P < 0.05$) before than after 14 February, averaging 17% vs. 4% for males and 15% vs. 5% for females. These differences reflected initiation of spring migration and movement of green-

Table 36.2. Percentage of marked male and female green-winged teal resighted during winter on Southern High Plains of Texas, October-February 1981-82

Banding period	Resighting sample period (percentage resighted)											
	9 Nov	16 Nov	27 Nov	7 Dec	21 Dec	5 Jan	25 Jan	1 Feb	14 Feb	22 Feb	7 Mar	14 Mar
25 Oct-1 Nov												
33 M[a]	6	12	27	18	15	15	15	24	18	6	6	3
32 F	13	13	28	6	13	22	9	13	16	6	9	9
6-8 Nov												
34 M	7	15	0	38	7	15	32	15	8	8	8	0
13 F	0	8	8	4	8	0	0	8	0	8	0	8
20-28 Nov												
205 M				13	8	10	12	14	7	5	2	1
107 F			11	7	10	10	11	8	5	6	4	
3-11 Dec												
62 M					35	44	23	13	8	8	3	2
30 F					40	40	17	27	23	7	3	10
17-29 Dec												
107 M						47	16	18	13	4	2	1
47 F						45	38	34	17	4	2	2
3-17 Jan												
159 M							13	16	8	4	4	2
81 F							15	20	10	5	7	2
28 Jan-6 Feb												
106 M									11	3	3	5
34 F									18	0	12	3

[a]Numbers of males (M) and females (F) marked with patagial tags.

winged teal off the SHP, as also noted by Obenberger (1982). Thus, resighting data obtained after 14 February were not included in further analyses.

The highest percentage ($P < 0.05$) of resightings occurred for teal marked in December and resighted from late December to mid-February (24% vs. 14% for males and 31% vs. 10% for females). The percentage of females resighted through 14 February was different between those banded before and after 1 December (10% vs. 27%; $P < 0.001$); the difference was not significant for males (15% vs. 20%; $P = 0.11$).

The mean difference between the sexes in the percentage resighted during each census period (9 November-14 February) was not different from zero ($P = 0.52$; paired t-test). There were no significant correlations ($P > 0.05$) between average temperatures ($r = -0.11$ for males, -0.10 for females) or average wind speed ($r = 0.14$ for males, 0.13 for females) between resighting periods and the percentage of males and females resighted.

Site Fidelity and Distribution of Band Recoveries

There were 24 direct recoveries (19 males, 5 females) of green-winged teal banded during the study (fig. 36.1). Direct recoveries not shown on figure 36.1 include two from California (adult and juvenile males), one from Georgia (adult male), and

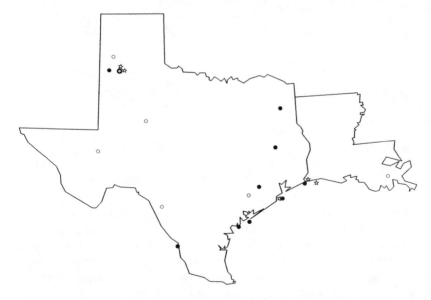

Fig. 36.1. Direct recoveries of green-winged teal from Texas and Louisiana. Closed and open circles denote adult and juvenile males, respectively, whereas closed and open stars denote adult and juvenile females, respectively. Star with solid circle marks banding site. There were four recoveries elsewhere.

one from New Mexico (adult male). There were 104 indirect recoveries (fig. 36.2) (82 males, 22 females), including 18 recaptures at the banding site (10 adult males, 3 juvenile males, 1 adult female, 4 juvenile females). Not shown on figure 36.2 are four recoveries from Mexico (three adult and one juvenile male), three from Saskatchewan (adult males), one from Alberta (juvenile female), and one from Virginia (juvenile female).

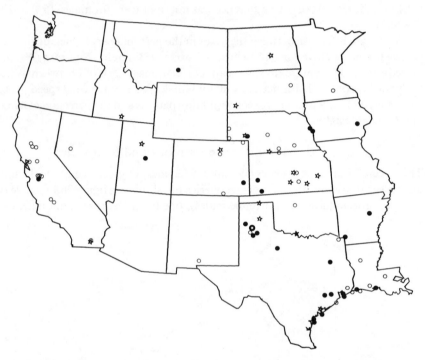

Fig. 36.2. Indirect recoveries of green-winged teal west of Mississippi River. Closed and open circles denote adult and juvenile males, respectively, whereas closed and open stars denote adult and juvenile females, respectively. Star with solid circle marks banding site. There were nine recoveries elsewhere.

Indirect recoveries indicated that juveniles, especially juvenile males, were more likely than adults to occur away from the SHP in winters following banding. For example, recaptures at the banding site totaled 11 (61%) for adults and 7 (39%) for juveniles, but chi-square tests were not signficiant ($P > 0.05$). Omitting recaptures at the banding site, 12 (32.4%) of the indirect recoveries for juvenile males occurred west of New Mexico, Colorado, Wyoming, and Montana (approximately 110° longitude), compared with only 2 (6.3%) for adult males, 3 (18.8%) for juvenile females, and 0 for adult females; there was only 1 indirect recovery of an adult female and only 1 indirect recovery east of the Mississippi River (a juvenile female).

These figures were adjusted because juvenile green-winged teal are 1.23 times more vulnerable to hunting than adults (Moisan et al. 1967), which reduced the values for juvenile males to 26.3% or 4.2 times adult males (chi-square = 7.0, $P < 0.05$). Excluding the recovery in Virginia, juvenile males were 1.7 times more likely than juvenile females to be recovered west of 110° longitude, but results were not significant (chi-square = 1.03, $P > 0.25$). Overall, indirect recoveries of juvenile green-winged teal were 4.6 times more likely than those of adults to occur west of 110° longitude (chi-square = 6.1, $P < 0.05$).

Discussion

Mobility of Green-Winged Teal

Nearly all resightings of marked green-winged teal occurred on the four playa lakes within the study area. There were less than three resightings during any survey outside the study area, indicating that within-season movements probably were off the SHP. Movements outside the study area, but still on the SHP, may not have been extensive for several reasons: (1) study area playas were among the most permanent water areas on the SHP throughout winter (Baldassarre and Bolen 1984); (2) hunting pressure was very low on the study area playas ; (3) food was not limited, with teal readily field-feeding on waste corn and foraging in playa lakes along with other waterfowl (Baldassarre and Bolen 1984, Quinlan and Baldassarre 1984); and (4) one of the study playas was associated with a cattle feedlot, where hunting was prohibited. Most feedlots in the central SHP are in close association with a large playa, and these "feedlot lakes" often act as refuges during the hunting season. This minimal human disturbance and adequate food and water in an otherwise semiarid environment could explain the lack of extensive local movements. Direct recoveries indicate that teal leaving the SHP move southeast toward coastal Texas and Louisiana, although Bellrose (1980) shows a green-winged teal migration corridor through the SHP into central Mexico.

Green-winged teal were mobile while wintering on the SHP, with resightings of either sex being usually less than 25% and averaging 12%. Female green-winged teal showed a distinct passage through the SHP before December because sightings of females banded before then averaged only 10%, compared with 27% for females banded later. Also, only 6.2% of the females banded in November were resighted, compared with 13.4% for males ($P < 0.01$). This movement of females occurred when temperatures were still comparatively warm in November, showing a 40-year average of 9.2C vs. 5.3C in December and 3.7C in January (National Oceanic and Atmospheric Administration 1983). Sex ratios of trapped birds also indicated an early passage of females, with males averaging only 45-60% in October and early November but usually over 70% thereafter (table 36.3). Similar results were noted by Obenberger (1982) from visual estimates of green-winged teal

Table 36.3. Sex ratio of green-winged teal banded on Southern High Plains of Texas from October-March, 1980-81 and 1981-82

| | Number banded | | Percentage male |
Date	Male	Female	
15-31 Oct	. . . (35)[a]	. . . (45)	. . . (44)
1-15 Nov	156 (15)	106 (36)	60 (29)
16-31 Nov	938 (215)	290 (107)	76 (67)
1-15 Dec	39 (109)	15 (56)	72 (66)
16-31 Dec	210 (227)	55 (96)	79 (70)
1-15 Jan	119 (268)	37 (155)	76 (63)
16-31 Jan	28 (119)	8 (31)	78 (79)
1-14 Feb	17 (394)	7 (114)	71 (78)
15-28 Feb	12 (65)	1 (19)	92 (77)
1-15 Mar	. . . (41)	. . . (53)	. . . (44)

[a]Figures for 1981-82 are in parentheses.

sex ratios on the SHP during 1981-82. Moisan et al. (1967) suggested a passage of adult female green-winged teal through California in late October and November, presumably toward wintering grounds in Mexico.

Green-winged teal remaining on the SHP did not exhibit differential mobility between the sexes as a response to colder winter weather, as shown by the lack of correlation between temperature and wind speed and resightings. Also, the average difference between the percentage of males and females recorded during resighting periods was not different from zero from November to mid-February. Even during periods of abnormal cold, such as 7-17 January 1982, when temperatures averaged 13C below a 40-year mean, there was no differential movement of the sexes away from the SHP. For example, the average difference between the 5 and 25 January resighting periods was −7% for males and −9% for females ($P >$ 0.05). These results conflict with Bennett and Bolen (1978), who proposed that female green-winged teal on the SHP migrate in response to severe weather, but their study did not use marked individuals. Conversely, we noted the highest percentage of resightings for both sexes during midwinter, a period when there were no sex or age differences in the lipid reserves of green-winged teal collected on the SHP (G. Baldassarre, unpubl. data). This finding suggests that individuals accumulating adequate reserves by midwinter may stay on the SHP while others migrate farther south. However, until body composition and within-season mobility of green-winged teal are compared from several geographic areas, the influence of winter lipid reserves on mobility and observed sex ratios cannot be determined.

Lebret (1950) noted differential distribution of green-winged teal (*A. crecca crecca*) in Europe and suggested that location of females farther south protected them from severe weather. However, Moisan et al. (1967, 40) questioned whether this would apply to green-winged teal in North America because populations with even sex ratios winter far north in coastal Oregon, Washington, and British Columbia. Also, sex ratios of green-winged teal wintering in North America are predominantly male, even at their major wintering sites along the Texas and Louisiana coasts, where weather conditions are relatively mild (Moisan et al. 1967). The mobility response of green-winged teal to winter weather on the SHP indicates that differential distribution of the sexes may not be caused by severe weather.

Site Fidelity and Distribution of Band Recoveries

Many indirect recoveries occurred east of the migration corridor depicted by Bellrose (1980) and toward coastal Texas and Louisiana. However, these birds could have stopped on, or passed through, the SHP: direct recoveries indicate that birds banded on the SHP move toward coastal Texas and Louisiana, and 22 indirect recoveries occurred in that direction or area; there also were 18 recaptures at the banding site. Thus, playa lakes on the SHP provide an important stopover point for green-winged teal as well as wintering habitat.

Indirect recoveries from California indicate that green-winged teal did not pass through the SHP but used a different wintering area in a subsequent year. Those recoveries toward the Mississippi River presumably were birds that had previously wintered in coastal Texas or Louisiana and were banded while passing through the SHP. Nichols et al. (1983) demonstrated the flexibility of mallards in winter distribution and suggested that juveniles were less likely to return to the same specific wintering area than adults. Dark-eyed juncos (*Junco hyemalis*) also can select different winter sites in successive years (Ketterson and Nolan 1982). However, neither study offered explanations for these movements.

Juvenile males exhibited the least site fidelity to the SHP, which may suggest a social influence on the breeding grounds that predisposes such movements in migration. For example, the first-year component of excess males in a dabbling duck population may be the least probable to acquire mates, as suggested for mallards (Ohde et al. 1983). Perhaps this group is most likely to wander from breeding sites to areas from which westward migration would be more possible. There may be no decreased fitness associated with moving to an unfamiliar wintering area because dabbling ducks are probably constantly sampling for food resources in unpredictable wetland habitats (Kaminski and Prince 1981), and the flocking behavior characteristic of wintering ducks may facilitate food finding because flocks of birds can act as information centers (Ward and Zahavi 1973). Further, because most green-winged teal pair during winter (Hepp and Hair 1983), and assuming that juvenile males recovered in California were unsuccessful in acquiring females while wintering on the SHP, it may be profitable for them to choose a different wintering site in a subsequent year and then pair successfully.

More research will be needed to elucidate patterns in mobility and fidelity of wintering green-winged teal in relationship to their overall wintering ecology. This will be necessary to understand further the response to wintering habitat conditions and the cross-seasonal effects of winter on the annual cycle of green-winged teal. We suggest that future research be conducted at multiple geographic sites and integrate concurrent studies of variations in sex ratios, aggression, pairing chronology, activity budgets, and carcass composition.

LITERATURE CITED

Anderson, M. G., and B. D. J. Batt. 1983. Workshop on the ecology of wintering waterfowl. Wildl. Soc. Bull. 11:22–24.

Ankney, C. D., and C. D. MacInnes. 1978. Nutrient reserves and reproductive performance of female lesser snow geese. Auk 95: 459–471.

Baldassarre, G. A., and E. G. Bolen. 1984. Field-feeding ecology of waterfowl wintering on the Southern High Plains of Texas. J. Wildl. Manage. 48:63–71.

———, R. J. Whyte, and E. G. Bolen. 1980. Patagial tags for pintails wintering on the Southern High Plains of Texas. Inl. Bird Banding 52:13–19.

Bellrose, F. C. 1980. Ducks, geese and swans of North America. Stackpole Books, Harrisburg, Pa. 540pp.

Bennett, J. W., and E. G. Bolen. 1978. Stress response in wintering green-winged teal. J. Wildl. Manage. 42:81–86.

Bolen, E. G., and F. S. Guthery. 1982. Playas, irrigation, and wildlife in west Texas. Trans. N. Am. Wildl. Nat. Resour. Conf. 47:528–541.

Carney, S. M., M. F. Sorensen, and E. M. Martin. 1983. Distribution of waterfowl species harvested in states and counties during 1971-80 hunting seasons. U.S. Fish Wildl. Serv. Spec. Sci. Rep. Wildl. 254. 114pp.

Fretwell, S. D. 1972. Populations in a seasonal environment. Monogr. Popul. Biol. 5. Princeton Univ. Press, Princeton, N.J. 217pp.

Funk, H. D., J. R. Grieb, D. Witt, G. F. Wrakestraw, G. W. Merrill, T. Kuck, D. Timm, T. Logan, and C. D. Stutzenbaker. 1971. Justification of the Central Flyway high plains mallard management unit. Central Flyway Technical Committee Rep. 48pp.

Guthery, F. S., and F. C. Bryant. 1982. Status of playas in the southern Great Plains. Wildl. Soc. Bull. 10:309–317.

Hepp, G. R., and J. D. Hair. 1983. Reproductive behavior and pairing chronology in wintering dabbling ducks. Wilson Bull. 95:675–682.

Kaminski, R. M., and H. H. Prince. 1981. Dabbling duck activity and foraging responses to aquatic macroinvertebrates. Auk 98:115–126.

Ketterson, E. D., and V. Nolan, Jr. 1982. The role of migration and winter mortality in the life history of a temperate-zone migrant, the dark-eyed junco, as determined from demographic analyses of winter populations. Auk 99:243–259.

Krapu, G. L. 1981. The role of nutrient reserves in mallard reproduction. Auk 98:29–38.

Lebret, T. 1950. The sex ratios and the proportion of adult drakes of teal, pintail, shoveler, and widgeon in the Netherlands, based on field counts made during autumn, winter and spring, Ardea 38:1–18.

Moisan, G., R. I. Smith, and R. K. Martinson. 1967. The green-winged teal: its distribution, migration, and population dynamics. U.S. Fish Wildl. Serv. Spec. Sci. Rep. Wildl. 100. 248pp.

National Oceanic and Atmospheric Administration. 1983. Climatological Data, Texas, May 1983. Vol. 88, No. 5. Asheville, N.C.

Nichols, J. D., K. J. Reinecke, and J. E. Hines. 1983. Factors affecting the distribution of mallards wintering in the Mississippi alluvial valley. Auk 100:932–946.

Obenberger, S. M. 1982. Numerical response of wintering waterfowl to macrohabitat in the Southern High Plains of Texas. M.S. Thesis, Texas Tech Univ., Lubbock.

Ohde, B. R., R. A. Bishop, and J. J. Dinsmore. 1983. Mallard reproduction in relation to sex ratios. J. Wildl. Manage. 47:118–126.

Quinlan, E. E., and G. A. Baldassarre. 1984. Activity budgets of nonbreeding green-winged teal on playa lakes in Texas. J. Wildl. Manage. 48:838–845.

Raveling, D. G. 1979. The annual cycle of body composition of Canada geese with special reference to control of reproduction. Auk 96:234–252.

Steel, R. G. D., and J. H. Torrie. 1980. Principles and procedures of statistics. 2d ed. McGraw-Hill, New York. 633pp.

Ward, P., and A. Zahavi. 1973. The importance of certain assemblages of birds as "information-centres" for food-finding. Ibis 115:517–534.

37

History and Status of Midcontinent Snow Geese on Their Gulf Coast Winter Range

Hugh A. Bateman, Ted Joanen, and Charles D. Stutzenbaker

Abstract: The fall migration of midcontinent snow geese (*Chen c. caerulescens*) was once a spectacular, rapid flight from the Arctic to the Gulf Coast of North America. According to historical records, most geese arrived on the Gulf Coast by mid-November. Significant changes in migration chronology have occurred. In recent years, about half of the midcontinent population of snow geese is found in the midwestern United States during mid to late November, and large numbers overwinter in the Midwest along the Missouri River. Originally, snow geese wintered mostly in the brackish marshes adjacent to the Gulf shoreline, but they sometimes ventured short distances into the adjacent wet prairie, particularly after fires removed heavy cover. The coastal tall-grass prairie now has been replaced by an extensive agricultural area dominated by rice culture, and snow geese have extended their winter range to include all of these coastal rice production areas. More goose habitat now exists along the Texas-Louisiana coast than did during historical times. Geese are able to move freely from agricultural areas to coastal marshes, the marsh thus remains an important component in the winter welfare of snow geese. During 1974-83, average annual harvest of snow geese was 119,400 in Texas and 70,100 in Louisiana. The harvest in Texas was about 45% of the total Central Flyway harvest and that in Louisiana about 48% of the total Mississippi Flyway harvest of snow geese. The foods of snow geese on the winter range vary from waste rice and soybeans to roots, tubers, and leafy portions of marsh and upland pasture vegetation. Rice is important early in fall, but green annuals become the major source of food by December. Burned, brackish marshes are particularly attractive to snow geese during late winter. Crop depredations are

Waterfowl in Winter. © 1988 University of Minnesota. Edited by Milton W. Weller and published by the University of Minnesota Press, Minneapolis.

highly variable along the Gulf Coast, but most complaints come after the goose season ends in late January or February. Because snow geese have become heavily dependent on forage associated with rice culture, large-scale reduction in the production of rice may have serious impacts on wintering geese.

The extensive coastal marshes and agricultural lands that border the northern Gulf of Mexico in Louisiana and Texas are well recognized for their importance to wintering waterfowl. Lesser snow geese (*Chen c. caerulescens*) historically have been a colorful and important part of waterfowl traditions in this region (Lynch 1967, 1975). Until the mid-1960s, populations of these arctic-nesting geese wintered exclusively along the Gulf Coast. However, substantial numbers now remain as far north as Iowa in December, and some overwinter in midwestern states. Snow geese provide important recreational and economic opportunities to thousands of waterfowl enthusiasts in Canada and in states of the Central and Mississippi flyways.

This report reviews the fall migration, winter distribution, habitat conditions, and management of midcontinent snow geese. Separate treatment is not provided for the two color phases, and the birds are referred to as midcontinent snow geese (U.S. Fish and Wildlife Service 1982). These birds may be defined as that portion of the lesser snow goose population that nests in the eastern arctic, migrates through the Central and Mississippi flyways, and winters along the northern Gulf Coast, primarily in Louisiana and Texas (fig. 37.1).

We thank G. Cooch, S. Paulus, and M. Weller for their suggestions and critical review of the manuscript.

Gulf Coast Habitat

The coastal snow goose range is divided into three major habitat zones (fig. 37.2). The first zone includes the extensive marsh belt from the Louisiana-Mississippi border to Port Lavaca, Tex. The second includes the rice production and cattle pasture region inland and adjacent to the marsh, extending from Lafayette, La., west to Port O'Connor, Tex. The third habitat zone is the brushy cattle pasture, shallow bay, and citrus and truck farm region of the lower Texas coast.

Coastal Marsh Region

Coastal marshes that border the Gulf of Mexico in Texas and Louisiana constitute some of the most valuable and productive wildlife areas in North America (Lynch 1967). These coastal wetlands extend over 800 km in a continuous band from Port Lavaca, Tex. to the Pearl River in Louisiana.

Elevation ranges from 0.6 m below and above sea level. Annual rainfall varies from 100 to 150 cm. Temperatures range from −7 to 39C ($\bar{x}$ = 20C). Normal tide

Fig. 37.1. Major breeding colonies, fall migration routes, and winter range of midcontinent snow geese.

from mean low to mean high is approximately 45 cm along the Gulf Coast, and tides are strongly influenced by winds. Salinities vary from fresh to 90% seawater, and soils range from solid clays to 80% organic matter. Average growing season for vegetation is about 300 days, and this entire coastal region is near subtropical in climatic character (O'Neil 1949).

The marsh zone can be subdivided by salinity levels into four major marsh types: saline, brackish, intermediate, and fresh (Chabreck 1970). Saline marsh is

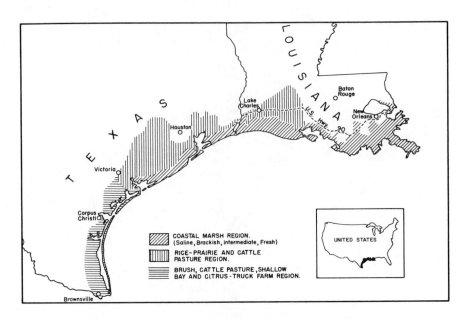

Fig. 37.2. Louisiana and Texas coastal snow goose winter habitat regions.

characterized by a plant association composed of smooth cord grass (*Spartina alterniflora*), black rush (*Juncus roemerianus*), and saltgrass (*Distichlis spicata*). The bulk of the saline marsh is found in southeast Louisiana, but small acreages are located in southwest Louisiana and in narrow strips along the immediate Texas coastline. These marshes are affected by daily tidal action.

Brackish marshes occupy that zone receiving sufficient fresh water to offset saline tidal action to a point where moderate salinity levels occur. Brackish marshes produce a plant association composed of marshhay cordgrass (*Spartina patens*), olney bulrush (*Scirpus olneyi*), saltmarsh bulrush (*Scirpus robustus*), and widgeon grass (*Ruppia maritima*).

Intermediate marshes generally lie between fresh and brackish marshes and have low salinities. These marshes produce marshhay cordgrass, bulltongue or arrowhead (*Sagittaria* sp.), coast barnyardgrass (*Echinochloa walteri*), and bullwhip bulrush (*Scirpus californicus*).

Freshwater marshes are influenced by rainfall and freshwater runoff from adjacent areas, receiving salt only during occasional storm tide surges from the gulf. Plant species include water hyacinth (*Eichornia crassipes*), pickerel weed (*Pondeteria cordata*), maidencane (*Panicum hemitomon*), and alligator weed (*Alternanthera philoxeroides*).

Distribution of shallow, open water is widespread throughout the four marsh types. Fresh and brackish marshes are punctuated with muskrat and goose "eat-outs" and by alligator holes that have been enlarged by erosion. These semipermanent water areas produce prolific stands of submerged vegetation such as widgeon grass, fennelleaf pondweed (*Potamogeton pectinatus*), hornwort (*Ceratophyllum demersum*), and southern naiad (*Najas guadalupensis*).

Rice Production and Cattle Pasture Region

This habitat zone falls into the 90- to 140-cm rainfall belt and, because of its large acreage, winters the largest component of the Texas snow goose flock. The region features rice production, cattle grazing, and, to a lesser extent, cotton, soybean, and maize farming. In Louisiana and Texas, annual rice production totals some 526,500 ha. The land is flat but with gently undulating topography along the northern limits of the coastal prairie, especially in Texas west of Houston. Soils range from deep sands to heavy clays. Five major rivers and a number of smaller streams cross in a south to southeasterly direction and empty into the Gulf of Mexico. Narrow bands of timber that follow the drainages break the continuity of the prairie environment. Original vegetation was an association of tall prairie grasses, primarily bluestem (*Andropogon* spp.). Widespread cultivation, excessive grazing, and exclusion of fire have eliminated most prairie grasses and allowed the invasions of woody species.

Extensive grasslands in the form of managed cattle pastures predominate where soils or landowner interest limits rice production. Thousands of cattle tanks and larger ponds have been constructed. The area has thousands of miles of drainage and irrigation ditches and canals that generally remain choked with water-tolerant vegetation. Characteristic of this prairie habitat are numerous small and seasonally wet ponds that hold water during most of the year, providing important water areas for wintering snow geese, particularly as roost habitat.

Brushy Cattle Pasture, Shallow Bay, and Citrus and Truck Farm Region

This highly variable habitat lies along the lower Texas coast from Port O'Connor south to the Rio Grande and extends inland approximately 40 km from the west shore of the Laguna Madre. Two major land uses dominate this area. Brushy cattle pastures prevail over the northern two-thirds, although an extensive cotton- and maize-farming community exists directly south of Corpus Christi. Remaining lower coastal habitat is dominated by agriculture. Citrus is an important crop along with cotton, maize, and irrigated and dryland vegetable crops. The coastal area directly adjacent to the Laguna Madre and the area near the mouth of the Rio Grande supports cordgrasses.

Habitat Conditions on the Gulf Coast

Industrialization, drainage, and habitat alterations along the Gulf Coast have not made overwhelming inroads into snow goose habitat. However, some important historical goose habitat along the mouths of major drainage systems has been totally eliminated, most notably the marshes along the west shore of Sabine Lake and near the mouth of the Brazos River in Texas. Both areas presently support a large petrochemical complex and associated urban developments.

Geese continue to prosper in the remaining broad expanse of marsh directly adjacent to developed areas. With the advent of rice culture and the destruction of the tall grass prairie, there presently exists more goose habitat than before early settlement.

Changes are occurring in all habitat types, but the overall trend is a continuation of land use practices that have been conducive to excellent winter conditions for geese. Cattle operators continue to manage their coastal marsh pastures in traditional ways with water management and controlled fires. Today, fur trappers burn marsh later in the winter, resulting in later goose usage than when burning occurred earlier in the fall for muskrat trapping.

Rice culture is a major agricultural activity, but it is not as profitable as during earlier decades. Consequently, rice acreage is declining in Texas but is expected to continue to provide adequate winter forage for snow geese. Reduced rice acreage could result in changing goose distribution patterns, both geographically and chronologically.

Geese have adapted well to changing conditions. Increased demand for hunting recreation should promote interest in intensive management of existing habitat for waterfowl usage at specific locations, making the future of snow geese secure along the Gulf Coast.

Historical Fall Migration and Arrival Dates

Based on historical accounts, annual fall migration of snow geese from nesting grounds to winter areas along the Texas and Louisiana coasts was a spectacular flight with only occasional short stopovers (Cooch 1958). Large concentrations of geese did not generally remain north of the Gulf Coast during fall and winter.

McIlhenny (1932) reported that the first flights of snow geese arrived on the Gulf Coast of Louisiana in early October of most years. He listed the peak migration period as 10 October to late October, with the migration completed by early November. Glazener (1946) found that the first autumn flights of geese arrived on the Texas coast during the last two weeks of September, with the heaviest movement usually during the last two weeks of October.

Surveillance of snow goose populations was maintained by biologists of the Louisiana Wildlife and Fisheries Department and the Texas Parks and Wildlife Department through the 1950s. Smith (1961) reported that the fall migration of snow geese into Louisiana was the "most regular and spectacular of any waterfowl wintering in Louisiana." In every year of observation (1952-59), he reported that the major flight arrived on the Gulf Coast during the last 10-14 days of October (table 37.1).

Table 37.1. Bimonthly mean snow geese population estimates in Louisiana, 1952-59[a]

Year	1 Oct[b]	15 Oct	1 Nov	15 Nov	1 Dec	15 Dec
1952	0	50,000	350,000	400,000	400,000	407,000
1953	50	13,000	200,000	510,000	510,000	500,000
1954	5	19,000	291,000	350,000	350,000	350,000
1955	0	28,000	329,000	421,000	410,000	410,000
1956	0	17,000	368,000	400,000	400,000	
1957	2,000	8,000	350,000	400,000	400,000	400,000
1958	0	110,000	375,000		375,000	
1959	0	7,000	350,000	375,000	375,000	472,000
1960	0		327,000	450,000	440,000	400,000

[a] Data from Smith (1961).
[b] Dates approximate.

Records from the 1967 Progress Report on Goose Management at the Squaw Creek National Wildlife Refuge in Missouri indicated virtually no snow goose usage in the 1940s. The main migrational thrust of snow geese overflew or stopped very briefly in the Midwest.

Changes in Fall Migration and Present Pattern

During the past 25 years, migrational habits of midcontinent snow geese have undergone a dramatic change. Instead of a spectacular push of birds arriving within a very short time, geese now arrive over a wider and later time period, with significant numbers overwintering in the Midwest (tables 37.2 and 37.3).

Discernible changes in migration chronology first began in the 1960s, but the phenomenon magnified in the early 1970s and a great deal of publicity developed with the "short-stopping" of geese north of their historical wintering areas (Stutzenbaker 1970, Bateman 1971). When the change in migration pattern was first recognized, the major impact areas were three national wildlife refuges: Sand Lake in South Dakota, DeSoto Bend in Iowa, and Squaw Creek in Missouri. In the early 1970s, it was common for each refuge to hold more than 200,000 snow geese during the fall migration period. Intensive crop and water management was successful in slowing and, in some cases, stopping migration. The U.S. Fish and Wildlife Service later altered refuge management policy to discourage large concentrations and overwintering of snow geese.

Migrational shifts have continued, and midcontinent snow geese now stop during fall migration in southern Canada and North Dakota. The migration

Table 37.2. Comparison of mean snow goose population size in Louisiana and Texas and in states to the north from the November coordinated snow goose survey[a]

Year	Louisiana and Texas totals	Percentage	North of Gulf Coast	Percentage	Total geese counted
1975	665,700	47	737,200	53	1,402,900
1976	790,400	65	422,600	35	1,213,000
1977	670,200	44	867,100	56	1,537,300
1978	528,400	40	806,900	60	1,335,300
1979	778,700	50	768,500	50	1,547,200
1980	681,800	47	764,600	53	1,446,400
1981[b]	835,200	43	1,117,000	57	1,952,200

[a] Data from U.S. Fish and Wildlife Service (1975-81).
[b] Last year the coordinated November survey was flown in all states. Surveys were scheduled on or about November 15 of each year.

corridor has widened throughout North Dakota, with birds using agricultural land during the fall stopover. The fall migration of snow geese from arctic nesting grounds to winter areas along the Louisiana and Texas coastal zone is no longer a spectacular, direct flight punctuated with occasional, short-term stopovers. At present, fall migrations are spread over longer period and the birds arrive much later. November snow goose survey records for the period 1975 through 1981 clearly showed that during mid-November of most years, more than half of the population observed was located north of the Gulf Coast (table 37.2).

The major change in migration to the Gulf Coast occurs before 1 January; after that date, the pattern of activity has not differed significantly (table 37.3). It can be concluded that the historical fall migration and winter distribution patterns of many midcontinent snow geese have been altered permanently. These changes are clearly related to altered land use and water availability north of the traditional Gulf Coast winter range.

Coastal Distribution and Population Status

Historical

The historical range of snow geese extended along the northern Gulf of Mexico from northeast Mexico north and east to the Mississippi River Delta, a distance of about 1,200 km. According to Bent (1925) and McIlhenny (1932), snow geese spent the entire winter period within a narrow band of brackish marsh along the Louisiana and Texas coasts. Birds seldom ventured inland more than a few miles and were not consistently associated with the bluestem prairies that lay directly north of the marshes. However, fires and floods probably created temporary suitable habitat that was used to some extent. This pattern of distribution remained unchanged until the 1920s in Texas and the 1940s in Louisiana (Lynch 1975).

Table 37.3. Present snow goose migration chronology and distribution for Louisiana and Texas.

Period	Distribution
1-15 Sept	Early pioneering flights; fewer than 2,000 birds scattered along Gulf Coast. Nearly all birds utilizing rice habitat.
15-30 Sept	Slow buildup; perhaps 10,000 geese along Gulf Coast. Most are in rice habitat.
1-15 Oct	Steady, slow buildup; geese beginning to show up at most traditional locations in small numbers. Heaviest buildup on rice prairies west of Houston and around Lacassine National Refuge in Louisiana. Perhaps 40,000-50,000 birds present.
16-31 Oct	Buildup continues but with generally fewer than 200,000 birds present along entire coast. About 90% of birds are in rice belts of Louisiana and Texas.
1-15 Nov	Major arrival flights often coincide with approaching cold fronts. Many birds arrive after front moves through, with birds arriving during both daylight and darkness.
16-30 Nov	Continued flights. During this period, about half-million-plus snow geese are present along coast zone and about 80% are found in rice habitat.
1-15 Dec	Flights arriving sporadically, coinciding with severe weather in Midwest. Some birds begin to forage in marshes and traditional use areas. About 75% remain in rice acreage. A few thousand geese (10,000+) appear in northeast Louisiana.
16-31 Dec	Same as first half of December. Increased numbers of geese moving into coastal marsh habitat. Burned marsh receiving heavy snow goose usage. One million geese may be on coastal range.
1-15 Jan	Same as December, but arrival flights strongly correlated with very severe weather in the Midwest. Up to 50% of snow geese may be utilizing marsh habitat. Increased numbers of birds are appearing in agricultural habitat in northeast Louisiana.
16-31 Jan; 1-28 Feb	During some years, a few geese migrate north, but spring migration should be considered minor during this period. In Louisiana, significant numbers of (20,000+) may occur in central and northeastern parts of state.
1-31 March	Spring migration occurs; by end of March, about 75% of snow geese have left coastal marshes of Louisiana and Texas.
1-30 April	Only a few thousand scattered birds remain, many of them gunshot cripples and lead-poisoned birds. During some years, a few thousand (<5,000) birds remain until early May. By midsummer, only a few hundred have escaped predation and remain scattered throughout coastal range from Mississippi River Delta to Rio Grande.

Expanding Use of Agricultural Areas

Geese first began using rice fields south of Beaumont, Tex., about 1920, but they did not use rice fields in Louisiana until the early 1940s. In Texas, rice fields were much closer to brackish marshes and birds had to move only a very short distance into the fields. However, in Louisiana, a band of intermediate and fresh marshes about 32 km wide separated geese from their traditional brackish marsh range and the new rice fields to the north.

The first rice fields were small and were located near country homes where disturbance factors made most of them unattractive to snow geese. As rice culture expanded, fields became larger and were developed farther from human influence and closer to the brackish marsh where they were more attractive to geese.

By the late 1940s, rice culture had expanded and dominated the original bluestem prairies of Texas and Louisiana. This encompassed the area north of the marsh zone from Lafayette, La., west to Port Lavaca, Tex., and extended inland as much as 160 km at some points. Several million hectares were diverted to rice and were widely used by wintering ducks and limited numbers of Canada (*Branta canadensis*) and white-fronted (*Anser albifrons*) geese. However, snow geese remained in their traditional brackish marsh range, making only limited excursions into rice fields that were directly adjacent to the marsh. The vast rice-producing areas located many kilometers inland from the marsh were generally devoid of snow geese.

Lynch (1975) noted that during the late 1940s snow geese began making sporadic flights from coastal marsh into the Louisiana rice production zone where they remained for a few hours to a few days. In the early 1950s, Bob Singleton (Texas Game and Fish Commission biologist) noted daily feeding flights of snow geese moving inland from the brackish marshes of the middle Texas coast, but the geese returned each evening to roost in the marsh.

During this period, interested landowners began pumping water into natural prairie ponds and rice fields and restricted hunting in and around the water areas. Snow geese began using the new water areas, and eventually daily flights back to the marsh were discontinued by the majority of the geese. Secure roost sanctuary apparently was the key to the establishment of snow geese on the inland rice prairies.

Because rice culture added over 400,000 ha of new habitat, snow geese enjoy a much wider distribution along the Gulf Coast today. Although distributional changes seem to have stabilized in Texas, the snow goose winter range in Louisiana continues to expand northward (figs. 37.3 and 37.4; Lynch 1952). Since the late 1960s, increasing numbers of snow and white-fronted geese have appeared in central and northeastern Louisiana (fig. 37.4). These birds have become associated with recently cleared bottomland hardwood forest areas where soybeans and rice are grown.

Present Snow Goose Distribution

At present, distribution of snow geese in Texas and Louisiana in late October and November is largely restricted to vast agricultural areas immediately north of the coastal marshes. Large concentrations (>10,000) are uncommon in brackish coastal marshes until December and January. In December, availability of rice and soybeans in harvested fields declines and burned marshes become attractive. By mid to late December and January, large numbers of geese move to their historical winter range to forage on native vegetation in the brackish marshes.

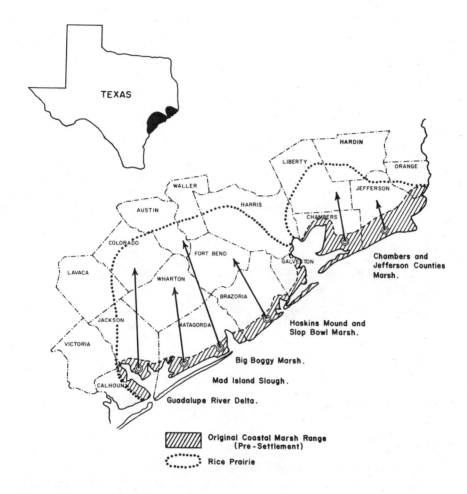

Fig. 37.3. Snow goose range extensions from coastal marsh into rice prairie, with major historical marsh use areas listed.

Texas. The coastal goose range in Texas has been divided into four population survey zones (fig. 37.5). During the 11-year period (1973-83), the mid-December aerial survey of geese indicated a snow goose population that ranged from 457,700 to 1,128,700 ($\bar{x}$ = 84,000) snow geese in the Texas Gulf Coast region.

The most important winter use area in zone 1 is the continuous expanse of brackish marsh that lies north and south of the Intracoastal Canal from Port Arthur to the west end of Bolivar Peninsula near Galveston. In this area, over 40,000 ha of marsh are contained in dedicated wildlife areas including the Murphree Wildlife Management Area, Sea Rim State Park, and the Texas Point,

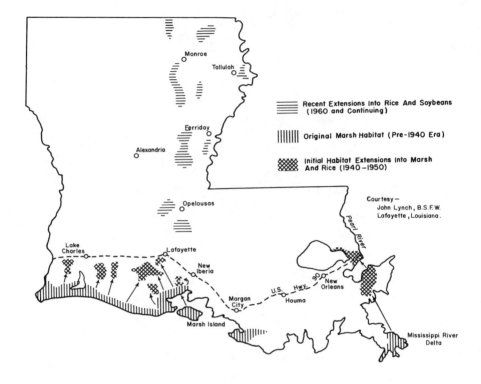

Fig. 37.4. Louisiana snow goose range extensions within coastal marsh and from marsh to agricultural lands.

McFaddin, and Anahuac national wildlife refuges. Goose usage is high on all government properties, and birds routinely move throughout this large marsh area using extensive privately owned property. During 1973-83, goose surveys in December showed that the area east of Houston accounted for 14% ($\bar{x}$ = 103,900) of all the birds located during the survey.

Heaviest goose usage along the Texas coast occurs west of Houston (zone 2) in a rice production area known collectively as the Katy, Lissie, and Garwood prairies. This was originally a bluestem prairie that did not winter geese until the 1950s. Recent inventory records show that this zone holds an average of slightly over half (52%) of the geese surveyed in Texas in mid-November (table 37.4). Birds subsist almost entirely on rice, soybeans, and native vegetation found in rice stubble and pasture land. Temporary artificial ponds are filled annually by landowners and commercial hunting interests to provide water and roost sites for geese using this water-deficient prairie environment.

Goose populations continue to build through November and December as a result of migration from the Midwest. However, by the time of the mid-December

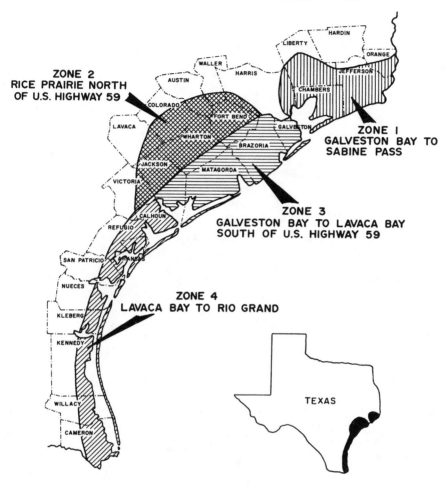

ZONE 2
RICE PRAIRIE NORTH
OF U.S. HIGHWAY 59

ZONE I
GALVESTON BAY TO
SABINE PASS

ZONE 3
GALVESTON BAY TO LAVACA BAY
SOUTH OF U.S. HIGHWAY 59

ZONE 4
LAVACA BAY TO RIO GRAND

TEXAS

Fig. 37.5. Major snow goose inventory zones along Texas Gulf Coast. Data from Texas Parks and Wildlife Department (1973-83).

goose survey, the mean percentage of birds located in this prairie zone declines from 52% to 43% as many birds leave or new migrants overfly the former prairies to spend the remainder of the winter in and near the brackish marshes of zone 3. The recent (1973-83) average November goose population for this zone is 233,000, and the December average is 317,000 (table 37.5).

Zone 3 encompasses brackish marshes in Cameron, Brazoria, Matagorda, and Jackson counties, along with extensive pasture and rice acreage south of Highway 59. Important marsh acreage is contained in the San Bernard and Brazoria national wildlife refuges and privately owned brackish marshes between Port

Table 37.4. Total number of snow geese observed in four major survey zones during mid-November aerial goose surveys for Texas Gulf Coast, 1973-81[a]

Year	Zone 1	Zone 2	Zone 3	Zone 4	Total
1973	38,500	53,200	223,700	10,600	326,000
1974	33,400	155,500	95,900	28,300	313,100
1975	76,200	216,000	57,400	40,000	389,600
1976		308,400[b]	144,400	43,400	495,800
1977	70,000	269,800	74,800	30,000	444,600
1978	70,000	174,300	58,700	18,500	321,500
1979	107,300	313,500	146,700	47,500	615,000
1980	42,000	355,000	94,200	13,900	505,100
1981	87,700	326,600	193,000	38,200	645,500
$\bar{x}$	65,600[c]	233,000[c]	118,000[c]	28,400[c]	395,600
Percentage	15	52	27	6	100

[a] Data from Texas Parks and Wildlife Department (1973-83).
[b] Zones 1 and 2 combined.
[c] Excludes 1976 data.

Table 37.5. Total number of snow geese in four major survey zones during mid-December aerial goose surveys for Texas Gulf Coast, 1973-83[a]

Year	Zone 1	Zone 2	Zone 3	Zone 4	Total
1973	76,700	114,400	227,800	38,800	457,700
1974	83,200	204,700	240,600	39,400	567,900
1975	103,800	263,000	333,900	109,500	810,200
1976	84,400	223,200	194,300	44,500	546,400
1977	150,300	516,600	412,500	49,300	1,128,700
1978	81,300	274,700	163,000	58,300	577,300
1979	122,000	410,300	169,500	45,600	747,400
1980	109,600	435,100	258,400	34,300	837,400
1981	82,600	362,600	389,500	36,600	871,300
1982	133,500	365,900	266,400	41,800	807,600
1983	115,700	316,600	346,100	42,600	821,000
$\bar{x}$	103,900	317,000	273,000	49,700	743,900
Percentage	14	43	37	6	100

[a] Data from Texas Parks and Wildlife Department (1973-83).

Lavaca and Galveston. In November (1973-81), this area supported 27% of the coastal goose flock, with an average population of 119,000 birds. Most goose usage is restricted to pasture, rice, and soybean acreage during November. In December (1973-83), average population size increased to 273,000, or 37% of the total Texas winter population. These birds take advantage of succulent green vegetation that develops in the brackish marshes after fires remove the rough growth. The San Bernard National Wildlife Refuge marsh and adjacent private marshes are important wintering sites for snow geese in December and January.

The lower Texas coast (zone 4) winters the smallest portion of snow geese in Texas. In November and December, this zone accounts for only 6% of all the geese observed during aerial surveys and averages 49,700 snow geese during the mid-December survey (1973-83). These geese are associated primarily with pasture land on the King Ranch, the Laguna Atoscosa National Wildlife Refuge in Cameron County, and an agricultural area immediately south of Corpus Christi.

Louisiana. For population survey purposes, the coastal snow goose range in Louisiana is divided into southeastern and southwestern zones (fig. 37.6). All birds found east of Marsh Island belong to the southeastern component. During the

Fig. 37.6. Major snow goose inventory zones in Louisiana.

most recent 10-year survey period (1974-83), the mid-December goose survey indicated a Louisiana coastal snow goose population ranging from a low of 188,000 to a high of 466,000 ($\bar{x}$ = 323,000) (table 37.6).

Table 37.6. Total number of snow geese observed in Louisiana during mid-December goose survey, 1974-83[a]

Year	Southeast zone	Southwest zone	Coastal zone totals	Central and northeast zone	State totals
1974	49,000	170,000[b]	219,000[b]	2,000	221,000[b]
1975	33,000	433,000	466,000	. . .	466,000
1976	36,000	394,000	430,000	5,000[c]	435,000
1977	28,000	381,000	409,000	3,000[c]	412,000
1978	80,000	268,000	348,000	2,000[c]	350,000
1979	41,000	315,000	356,000	18,000[c]	374,000
1980	20,000	284,000	304,000	2,000[c]	306,000
1981	8,000[b]	180,000[b]	188,000[b]	3,000[c]	191,000[b]
1982	41,000	219,000[b]	260,000[b]	14,000[c]	274,000[b]
1983	4,000[b]	249,000	253,000[b]	1,000[b]	254,000[b]
$\bar{x}$	34,000	289,000	323,000		
Percentage	11	89	100		

[a] Data from U.S. Fish and Wildlife Service (1974-83).
[b] Incomplete data.
[c] January survey.

Snow geese have recently expanded their winter range some 240 km north of the immediate coastline to take advantage of soybean and rice fields in central and northeast Louisiana. Since 1973, this population has ranged from a low of 2,000 birds to a high of 18,000.

Southeastern Louisiana snow goose populations are concentrated at four locations: the Mississippi River Delta, Bayou Biloxi marshes, Pearl River Delta, and west Terrebonne Parish marshes. Numbers of geese at these locations have varied during recent years, but the Mississippi River Delta has consistently wintered the majority (75%) of birds surveyed in the southeast zone. These flocks constituted about 11% ($\bar{x}$ = 34,300) of the total coastal Louisiana snow goose population as reflected by the mid-December goose survey (1974-83) (table 37.6).

Marshes and rice fields of southwest Louisiana attract most of the snow geese wintering in Louisiana. This area has accounted for about 89% of all snow geese located along the coast during the most recent 11-year period (1973-83). Snow goose usage for the southwest survey zone, as measured by the mid-December goose survey (1973-83), has averaged 289,000 birds (table 37.6).

Marsh areas of major importance are the Marsh Island-State Wildlife Refuge complex, Chenier Au Tigre, Mulberry Ridge, Rockefeller Refuge, Oyster Bayou at Cameron, Creole, Johnson Bayou, and the Sabine National Wildlife Refuge. Important rice field areas are located at Gum Cove near the Lacassine National Wildlife Refuge and at Holmwood, Sweet Lake, Klondike, Gueydan, Crowley, Jennings, Esther, and Forked Island.

Crop Depredation

During the 1950s, movement of snow geese into agricultural fields of southwest Louisiana and Texas resulted in a growing concern about crop depredations. Although this problem was new to rice farmers and inland cattle operators, people involved with cattle and fur management in the marsh had been aware of goose damage to vegetation for many years (O'Neil 1949).

In Texas and Louisiana, the muskrat (*Ondatra zibethicus*), industry has been largely replaced by nutria (*Myocastor coypus*) trapping, and only a few marshes are still intensively managed for muskrat production. As a result of waning trapping interest and shifts of wintering snow goose populations away from marshes, few complaints now come from fur trappers.

Goose damage to coastal marsh vegetation can be greatly accelerated by livestock overgrazing and overpopulations of muskrat. Marsh managers can reduce the damage to their properties by using a careful burning program designed to provide "new burns" at regular intervals throughout the winter. A staggerd marsh-burning program will attract geese from one burn to another and reduce excessive feeding in a particular area. If immediate attention is not given and large numbers of geese are allowed to remain on an area for a long time, the potential for damage increases.

During the 1960s and 1970s, cattle operators often complained when geese invaded ryegrass pastures. Most complaints were made in late winter from January to mid-February, usually after the goose hunting seasons had closed. The amount of ryegrass pasture damage in Texas and Louisiana also appears to be directly related to the severity of cold weather and the proximity of fields to goose concentration areas (Stutzenbaker and Buller 1974). Depredations of ryegrass were most severe during years when cold, dry conditions prevented emergence of green annuals. Conversely, during wet, mild winters, when native annuals were abundant, depredations on ryegrass were less severe.

To alleviate depredations in mid to late winter, Louisiana was granted an extension of the goose hunting season into late January and early February to allow disturbances associated with hunting to reduce damage to improve pastures. Normally, by the close of the late season, a general green-up of native vegetation had progressed so that most fields were free from excessive goose-feeding pressure.

Ryegrass depredation complaints have declined in recent years in Texas and Louisiana. A decline in the number of cattle, along with a corresponding decline in acres of planted ryegrass, has influenced this change. Also, many farmers now routinely initiate hazing practices to reduce goose damages in sensitive areas.

Snow Goose Hunting and Harvest on the Gulf Coast

Snow goose hunting on the Gulf Coast is an important recreational activity that dates to the 1800s (McIlhenney 1932). High-density hunting pressure around refuges, zone quotas, and "firing-line" type shooting do not occur on the Gulf Coast. Extensive goose use of privately owned habitat and the wide-ranging, frequent, and unpredictable shifts of flocks within their extensive wintering range have prevented these undesirable hunting conditions.

Increased popularity of commercial hunting clubs in Texas and, to a lesser degree, in Louisiana has made quality goose hunting available to many hunters who otherwise might not have the opportunity to hunt geese. Acreage controlled by commercial hunting operations is quite small compared with the total winter habitat available to snow geese on the Gulf Coast, but harvest levels are considerably higher in commercially hunted areas.

Commerical goose hunting has reduced law violations and crippling losses because commercial guides exert control over their hunters. Many large operators purchase water and flood-harvested or fallow rice fields to create "rest ponds." These flooded areas are not hunted, providing ideal roost sites and refuges scattered across the rice prairies.

From 1971 to 1980, approximately 96% of the harvest of snow geese in Texas occurred in 11 counties of the middle and upper coast (table 37.7). In Louisiana, a major portion of the goose kill is attributed to hunters who take geese incidental to duck hunting. However, during the past 10 years, there has been an increasing interest in commercial goose hunting on large private land holdings similar to that practiced on the rice prairies in Texas.

Table 37.7. Mean snow goose harvest by Texas counties and Louisiana parishes during 1971-80[a]

Texas county	Harvest	Percentage	Louisiana parish	Harvest	Percentage
Chambers	20,500	19.7	Calcasieu	4,000	7.3
Jefferson	7,500	7.2	Cameron	11,500	19.7
Liberty	2,500	2.4	Jefferson Davis	10,400	18.7
Jackson	4,000	3.8	Acadia	1,000	1.7
Ft. Bend	4,500	4.3	Vermilion	18,500	31.8
Matagorda	5,000	4.8	St. Tammany	1,400	2.4
Brazoria	6,000	5.8	St. Bernard	5,900	10.2
Waller	9,000	8.6			
Harris	12,000	11.5			
Wharton	14,000	13.5			
Colorado	14,900	14.3			
Total	99,900	95.5		52,700	91.8

[a] Data from Carney et al. (1983).

Some harvest of snow geese now occurs in central and northeastern portions of Louisiana, but nearly 80% occurs in the five southwest coastal parishes of Cameron, Calcasieu, Vermilion, Acadia, and Jefferson Davis (table 37.7). About 92% of the total harvest in Louisiana occurs along the Gulf Coast. During 1974-83,

Table 37.8. Mean snow goose harvest in Central and Mississippi flyways during 1974-83[a]

Year	Central Flyway	Texas	Mississippi Flyway	Louisiana
1974	247,300	79,600	171,100	41,400
1975	355,800	145,000	170,400	66,000
1976	250,100	132,700	102,100	58,100
1977	295,000	132,600	126,600	61,400
1978	191,000	69,300	136,400	84,100
1979	336,600	134,600	166,400	47,800
1980	252,000	147,300	146,700	71,200
1981	235,000	120,900	113,300	46,200
1982	239,600	133,700	122,300	83,500
1983	251,600	98,700	193,100	141,400
$\bar{x}$	265,400	119,400	144,800	70,100
Percentage	65	63	35	37

[a] Data from Carney et al. (1974-83).

estimated harvest of snow geese in the Mississippi and Central flyways averaged 144,800 and 265,400 geese, respectively (table 37.8). Louisiana (Mississippi Flyway) and Texas (Central Flyway) contributed about 48% and 45% of the average harvest in their respective flyways, and average annual snow goose harvest for Louisiana was 70,100 and for Texas was 119,400 (table 37.8).

Management Recommendations

Although the future seems clouded for prairie-oriented waterfowl, particularly puddle ducks (*Anas*), it seems much brighter for Arctic-nesting midcontinent snow geese. These geese nest in remote Arctic regions and have escaped the severe competition with agriculture and other land use activities that prairie ducks face.

Proper management of migratory game bird populations involves maintenance of breeding, migration, and winter habitats. Management recommendations for the midcontinent snow goose population wintering along the Gulf Coast are as follows:

(1) *Habitat*

a. Pursue state and federal land acquisition goals. The purchase of extensive brackish marsh acreage, especially in Texas, to ensure adequate wintering habitat if rice production declines further, should be the highest priority.

b. Manage existing state and federal waterfowl areas for more efficient control of fresh and brackish water.

c. Promote controlled burning of wildlife areas with emphasis on better timing and distribution of fire.

d. Promote managed livestock grazing on brackish marsh ranges where grazing can be an effective habitat-management tool for waterfowl.

(2) *Research*

a. Determine the effect of lead ingestion on wintering snow geese.

b. Cooperate with and support ongoing and proposed disease studies, particularly those on avian cholera.

c. Intensify aerial survey investigations in central and northeastern Louisiana to monitor changing distributional trends.

d. Initiate an intensive rice-prairie study of goose habitat to determine habitat limitations in rice-prairie habitats.

e. Continue coastal aerial goose surveys with the objective of determining population numbers by habitat types.

f. Initiate investigations into marsh burning and its long-term effects on the production of Olney bulrush and other favored snow goose forage.

g. Encourage the Fish and Wildlife Service to intensify data collection procedures to provide more accurate harvest information for snow geese.

(3) *Regulations*

a. Continue to evaluate the impact of hunting on winter populations.

b. Continue to cooperate with the flyway councils in the process of deriving annual hunting regulations.

c. Provide goose hunting opportunities on state and federal refuges and management areas where hunting recreation is feasible.

LITERATURE CITED

Bateman, H. A. 1971. Blue and snow goose shortstopping. La. Conserv. 23 (1 and 2): 4–9.

Bent, A. C. 1925. Life history of North American wild fowl. Order Anseres (part 1). U.S. Nat. Mus. Bull. 126. Washington, D.C. 244pp.

Carney, S. M., M. F. Sorensen, and E. F. Martin. 1974-83. Waterfowl harvest and hunter activity in the United States. U.S. Fish Wildl. Serv. Adm. Rep., Washington, D.C.

———, ———, and ———. 1983. Distribution of waterfowl species harvested in states and counties during 1971-80 hunting seasons. Spec. Sci. Rep. Wildl. 254. U.S. Fish Wildl. Serv., Washington, D.C. 144pp.

Chabreck, R. H. 1970. Marsh zones and vegetative types in the Louisiana coastal marshes. Ph.D. Diss., Louisiana State Univ., Baton Rouge. 113pp.

Cooch, F. G. 1958. The breeding biology and management of the blue goose (*Chen caerulescens*). Ph.D. Thesis. Cornell Univ., Ithaca, N.Y. 235pp.

Glazener, N. C. 1946. Food habits of wild geese on the Gulf Coast of Texas. J. Wildl. Manage. 10:322-329.

Lynch, J. J. 1952. Blue and snow geese on the Gulf Coast. Res. Progr. Rep. U.S. Fish Wildl. Serv., Abbeville, La. 12pp.

———. 1967. Values of the south Atlantic and Gulf Coast marshes and estuaries to waterfowl. Marsh Estuary Mgmt. Symp., Louisiana State Univ., Baton Rouge, 1:51–63.

———. 1975. Winter ecology of snow geese on the Gulf Coast. Snow Goose Symp. Midwest Fish Wildl. Conf. Toronto, Ontario, 37:45.

McIlhenny, E. A. 1932. The blue goose in its winter home. Auk 49:27.

O'Neil, T. 1949. The muskrat in the Louisiana coastal marshes. Fed. Aid Section, Fish Game Div., La. Wildl. Fish. Comm. 140pp.

Smith, M. M. 1961. Louisiana waterfowl population survey, June 1949-June 1961. La. Wildl. Fish. Comm., New Orleans. 49pp.

Stutzenbaker, C. D. 1970. Distribution dilemma. Texas Parks Wildl. 28:12-14.

———, and R. J. Buller. 1974. Goose depredation on ryegrass pastures along the Texas coast. Spec. Rep. Tex. Parks Wildl. 13pp.

Texas Parks and Wildlife Department. 1973-83. Job. Progr. Rep., Job 1, W-106-R. Austin.

U.S. Fish and Wildlife Service. 1974-83. Coordinated mid-December goose survey reports, Mississippi and Centeral Flyways. Washington, D.C.

———. 1975-81. Coordinated mid-November goose survey reports, Missisippi and Central Flyways. Washington, D.C.

———. 1982. Management plan for mid-continent snow geese. Washington, D.C. 18pp.

38

Recent Changes in Wintering Populations of Canada Geese in Western Oregon and Southwestern Washington

Robert L. Jarvis and John E. Cornely

Abstract: Despite management priority, numbers of dusky Canada geese (*Branta canadensis occidentalis*) declined from 20,000-25,000 in the 1970s to 10,000 in 1984. Beginning in the early 1970s, Taverner's Canada geese (*B. c. taverneri*) increased from a few thousand to 55,000-60,000 in the mid-1980s and now compose 85% of the combined wintering flock of about 70,000 geese. Recruitment of dusky geese declined from an average of 28% juveniles in the fall population before 1979 to about 19% since 1979. Recruitment of Taverner's geese is unknown, but juveniles constituted a larger proportion of the harvest of Taverner's geese than they did of dusky geese. Most of the mortality during winter probably was due to hunting, and dusky geese were two to three times more likely to be harvested than were Taverner's geese. Managers face a difficult task restoring the number of dusky geese to former levels because of low recruitment and high vulnerability to hunting. The large, thriving population of Taverners geese compounds the difficulties of protecting the small, unprosperous population of dusky geese.

The dusky Canada goose (*Branta canadensis occidentalis*) has been a major management priority in the Pacific Flyway for two decades because of its restricted distribution and small population (Timm et al. 1979). Management efforts included establishment of four national wildlife refuges (NWR) in western Oregon and southwestern Washington and extensive monitoring of the population on both the breeding and wintering grounds. Research has been continually supported as part of the overall management scheme (Chapman et al. 1969; Bromley 1976, 1984; Clark and Jarvis 1978; Simpson and Jarvis 1979; Cornely et

Waterfowl in Winter. © 1988 University of Minnesota. Edited by Milton W. Weller and published by the University of Minnesota Press, Minneapolis.

al. 1985; Havel and Jarvis 1987). As a result of these efforts, the population has been, until recently, maintained at levels stated in the management plan adopted in 1973 (Timm et al. 1979), despite heavy hunting pressure on the population (Hansen 1968, Chapman et al. 1969). However several recent events have resulted in the decline in the number of dusky geese while, paradoxically, there are more Canada geese in the wintering area than ever previously recorded. In this paper we review the events that led up to the current state.

Dusky geese breed almost exclusively on the Copper River Delta in southcentral Alaska and winter in the Willamette Valley of Oregon and the confluence of the Willamette and Columbia rivers on the Oregon-Washington border (fig. 38.1; Hansen 1968). Grass seed crops, which remain green and grow throughout the winter, provide abundant food for geese. Five refuges (three units of the Willamette Valley NWR, Ridgefield NWR, and Sauvie Island Wildlife Management Area) provide sanctuary for wintering geese.

Although the wintering area is managed for dusky geese, it is inhabited by five other races of Canada geese. Of these only Taverner's Canada geese (*B. c. taverneri*) occur in substantial numbers and they have increased dramatically since the early 1970s (Simpson and Jarvis 1979, Timm et al. 1979). Taverner's geese breed throughout tundra Alaska and western Canada and winter at several localities in the western United States (Bellrose 1980). The breeding grounds of Taverner's geese wintering in western Oregon and southwestern Washington have not been firmly established. We examined the change in racial composition of dusky and Taverner's geese wintering in western Oregon and southwestern Washington by analyzing population information collected for management purposes over the past two decades.

We gratefully acknowledge the contributions of the following people who provided support and information for this paper: B. H. Campbell, T. Rothe, and D. E. Timm (Alaska Department of Fish and Game); J. C. Bartonek, R.S. Rodgers, P. C. Sekora, and R. B. Wiseman (U.S. Fish and Wildlife Service); and R. L. Johnson and R. R. Denny (Oregon Department of Fish and Wildlife). Helpful comments on an early draft were provided by D. L. Boone, D. G. Raveling, D. E. Timm, and an anonymous reviewer.

Methods

Data were obtained from censuses of all geese in the wintering area and samples of subspecies composition, from brood surveys in Alaska just prior to fledging, and from subspecies composition of the harvest on refuges. Aerial censuses of the entire population were made one to four times per winter. The highest annual counts usually occurred in December or January, and we used those counts as most representative of the wintering populations. Before 1975, winter population estimates represented the number of Canada geese counted on the annual midwin-

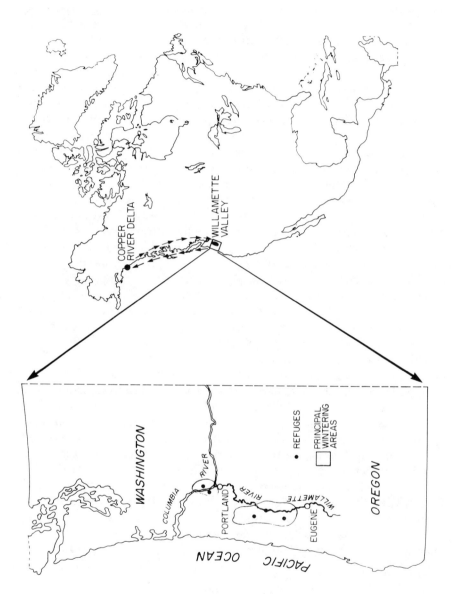

Fig. 38.1. Breeding and wintering range of dusky Canada geese.

ter survey. Usually all Canada geese counted were reported as dusky geese, but in some years "other" Canada geese were also recorded. From 1975 to 1978, subspecies composition was assessed from ground surveys conducted continually from November through February. Annual sample sizes varied from 120 to 548 flocks containing 53,000 to 230,000 geese. Surveys were conducted throughout the wintering area, which should have minimized bias from duplicate counts. From 1979 to 1984, subspecies composition was assessed from aerial photographs. From 10,000 to 15,000 geese were classified on each census, which spanned the entire wintering unit on each flight. Repeat counts of photographs revealed a misclassification rate of 10-15%, but this resulted in only a 2-5% error in overall subspecies composition because many classification errors were compensatory. In both procedures, the numbers of dusky and Taverner's geese were calculated independently in each of four to nine subunits of the wintering ground and were then aggregated to arrive at total numbers of each subspecies. Calculations were based on the number of geese counted in each subunit during aerial censuses. Partitioning of the wintering area was necessary because of differential distribution of the two subspecies (Simpson and Jarvis 1979). Counts of geese and aerial photographs generally were obtained within one week of each other. The first author was involved in all classification attempts since 1975 and classified all images on photographs. Thus, trend analysis should be appropriate, even if bias in classification was present.

Aerial brood surveys were conducted annually by the Alaska Department of Fish and Game to estimate recruitment (percentage of young) and calculate size of the fall (premigration) population of dusky geese. Timm et al. (1979) concluded that the brood surveys reliably estimated the proportion of young in the fall population. No brood surveys of Taverner's geese were conducted. Subspecies composition and age ratios of harvested geese were derived from examination of all birds bagged on the four hunting units of the Willamette Valley NWRs.

The winter population estimate, which was derived directly from total counts and subspecies composition counts, represented the size of the population at the conclusion of the hunting season. The spring population of dusky geese was calculated as the winter population less assumed natural mortaility of 0.0375 (Chapman et al. 1969) between the end of the hunting season and arrival of geese on the Copper River Delta (Timm et al. 1979). The fall population was calculated as the spring population plus recruitment of juveniles. Winter mortality was the difference between the fall population (year t) and winter population (year $t + 1$). An index to the rate of winter mortality for dusky geese was calculated as follows:

WMR = WM/ FP, where
WMR = index to rate of winter mortality
WM = winter mortality, and
FP = size of population in fall.

The information from surveys was scrutinized by the Dusky Canada Goose subcommittee of the Technical Committee of the Pacific Flyway Council and incorporated into annual reports. Because of the survey nature of the data and the potential for compounding of errors in calculated statistics, we examined the results only for broad patterns and marked changes in patterns for dusky and Taverner's geese. Similarly, we did not subject the results to statistical analysis because we believed it would imply a level of precision not warranted.

Results

Population trends of Canada geese in western Oregon and southwestern Washington, as measured by winter surveys of all subspecies combined, have generally been upward since the early 1950s (fig. 38.2). Before 1970, the increase was modest;

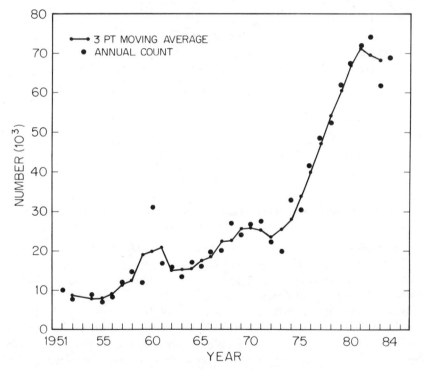

Fig. 38.2. Number of Canada geese counted in Willamette Valley, Oregon, and along lower Columbia River during midwinter census.

presumably, most of the wintering geese were duskys. Beginning in the 1970s, the wintering population increased dramatically, but dusky geese became an increasingly smaller proportion of the wintering flock (fig. 38.3). Dusky geese displayed a downward trend in the late 1970s and 1980s. Conversely, Taverner's geese have had

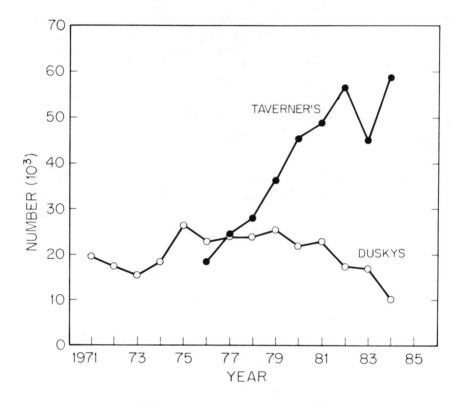

Fig. 38.3. Population trends of dusky and Taverner's Canada geese during late winter, western Oregon and southwestern Washington.

a spectacular increase in numbers and now compose 80-85% of a wintering flock of 70,000 geese. The rate of increase of Taverner's geese has averaged 20% per year since 1975. Duskys declined at an average annual rate of 8.3% during that same period, but most of that decline occurred since 1979.

Winter mortality of dusky geese, as measured by the difference between the calculated fall population and the estimated winter population, varied from 3,400 to 17,600 geese since 1971 (table 38.1). Winter mortality was variable, ranging from 16.9 to 47.7% of the fall population. Because these estimates of winter mortality were based on population-wide counts and calculations, they are probably only crude estimates of actual mortality. In addition, they are only representative of the portion of the winter from premigration (September) to posthunting season (January). Nonetheless, they were consistently derived and are suitable for investigations of trends. From 1971 to 1978, the rate of winter mortality averaged 24.0%; from 1979 to 1984, it averaged 29.6%. We judged that difference not to be real and concluded that the rate of winter mortality of dusky geese has not changed during

Table 38.1. Population levels of dusky and Taverner's Canada geese and index of winter mortality of dusky geese in western Oregon and southwestern Washington

| | Dusky | | | | Taverner's winter population |
| Year | Fall population | Winter population | Winter mortality | | |
			Number	Percentage	
1971-72	22,800	17,900	4,900	21.5	
1972-73	19,200	15,800	3,400	17.7	
1973-74	23,800	18,600	5,200	21.8	
1974-75	36,800	26,500	10,300	28.0	
1975-76	31,100	23,000	8,100	26.0	18,600
1976-77	29,200	24,100	5,100	17.5	24,300
1977-78	41,600	24,000	17,600	42.3	28,200
1978-79	30,700	25,500	5,200	16.9	36,400
1979-80	29,200	22,000	7,200	24.7	45,500
1980-81	27,800	23,000	4,800	17.3	49,000
1981-82	27,000	17,700	9,300	34.4	56,700
1982-83	22,300	17,000	5,300	23.8	45,000
1983-84	19,300	10,100	9,200	47.7	58,900

the 13-year period, although it has been quite variable.

Dusky geese made up a steadily decreasing proportion of the harvest and Taverner's geese made up an increasing proportion (table 38.2). In the mid-1970s, dusky geese were more than 75% of the geese harvested, but by the early 1980s, they were less than half. The same trend was apparent in the population (table 38.1), but dusky geese always made up a smaller proportion of the population than they did of the harvest. In the mid-1970s, more than 300 dusky geese were harvested for every 100 Taverner's geese harvested, while the population contained

Table 38.2. Proportion of dusky and Taverner's Canada geese harvested on Willamette Valley National Wildlife Refuges, Oregon

Year	N	Percentage dusky	Percentage Taverner's
1975-76	1,138	76.3	23.7
1976-77	1,132	76.2	23.8
1977-78	902	79.4	20.6
1978-79	714	60.8	39.2
1979-80	916	62.1	37.9
1980-81	1,451	51.1	48.9
1981-82	1,348	49.5	50.5
1982-83	727	46.6	53.4
1983-84	1,087	41.9	58.1

Table 38.3. Ratio of dusky Canada geese per 100 Taverner's Canada geese harvested by hunters and ratio in population, western Oregon and southwestern Washington

| Year | Harvest | | Population | | Ratio harvest/ratio population |
	N	Dusky/100 Taverner's	Number	Dusky/100 Taverner's	
1975-76	1,138	322	41,600	124	2.60
1976-77	1,132	321	48,400	99	3.23
1977-78	902	385	52,200	85	4.52
1978-79	714	155	61,900	70	2.21
1979-80	916	164	67,500	48	3.39
1980-81	1,451	105	72,000	47	2.23
1981-82	1,348	98	74,450	31	3.13
1982-83	727	87	62,000	38	2.31
1983-84	1,087	72	69,000	17	4.21
Mean	1,046	190	61,000	62	3.09

about 100 dusky/100 Taverner's geese (table 38.3). By the early 1980s, about 80 dusky/100 Taverner's geese were being harvested, but the population contained only about 30 dusky/100 Taverner's geese. The difference in these ratios of dusky/Taverner's geese being harvested and in the population indicated that dusky geese were about three times as likely to be shot, relative to their availability, as were Taverner's geese.

This estimate of the relative vulnerability to hunting of dusky geese may be slightly inflated. The data on harvest pertains to the Willamette Valley NWRs, all of which were in the southern half of the wintering area; data for the ratios in the population were gathered throughout the wintering area. Taverner's geese were more heavily represented in the northern than in the southern half of the wintering area, although differences in subspecies composition between the northern and southern halves were not large (Simpson and Jarvis 1979). Simpson and Jarvis (1979) measured subspecies composition of the harvest and of the population on each hunting unit of the Willamette Valley NWRs and estimated that dusky geese were 1.4-2.8 times more vulnerable to hunting than Taverner's geese.

Dusky geese had modest rates of recruitment during the 1970s and 1980s (table 38.4). Before 1979, reruitment averaged nearly 30%, with occasional years of high recruitment (35-50%) and occasional ones of low recruitment (10-20%). From 1979 to 1984, recruitment averaged 19% and was relatively constant, ranging from 15 to 24%. Information on recruitment of Taverner's was not available, but we did have age ratios of geese bagged on the Willamette Valley NWRs. From 1975-76 to 1983-84, a smaller proportion of the dusky geese bagged by hunters were juveniles than were the Taverner's geese bagged by hunters (table 38.5). Because of apparent differential vulnerability, we are uncertain whether Taverner's geese actually had

Table 38.4. Recruitment of dusky Canada geese as measured by percentage of young at mid to late gosling stage, Copper River Delta, Alaska[a]

Year	Percentage juveniles	Year	Percentage juveniles
1971	16.2	1979	16.0
1972	10.6	1980	23.7
1973	36.0	1981	17.9
1974	51.4	1982	23.7
1975	17.9	1983	15.0
1976	24.2	1984	18.3
1977	44.3		
1978	24.8		
Mean	28.2		19.1

[a]Data from Alaska Department of Fish and Game.

higher rates of recruitment than dusky geese. However, the age ratios of harvested Taverner's geese fluctuated annually from more than 70% to less than 40% juveniles; for dusky geese, the range was 36-53%. The large range in the proportion of juvenile Taverner's geese harvested indicated to us wide fluctuations in the annual rate of recruitment, whereas dusky geese appeared to have less variable but lower rates of recruitment.

Table 38.5. Percentage of juvenile dusky and Taverner's Canada geese bagged by hunters on Willamette Valley National Wildlife Refuges, Oregon

Year	Taverner's		Dusky	
	N	Percentage	N	Percentage
1975-76	270	51.5	868	45.4
1976-77	269	48.2	863	48.2
1977-78	186	43.5	716	53.3
1978-79	280	55.0	434	44.4
1979-80	347	51.9	569	35.9
1980-81	709	61.4	742	47.6
1981-82	681	66.8	667	39.6
1982-83	388	39.9	339	44.0
1983-84	632	71.2	455	39.3
Mean		54.4		44.2

Discussion

Our data were gathered to meet broad management goals rather than specific research objectives. Nonetheless, the trends are obvious and we think the reasons for those trends are apparent.

Depressed recruitment after 1979, combined with sustained rates of mortality during winter, resulted in decreasing numbers of dusky geese. Before 1979, recruitment was affected most strongly by timing of spring thaw and storms during nesting (Bromley 1976). Since 1979, recruitment of dusky geese appeared to have been little affected by weather, at least weather conducive to high levels of recruitment. In at least three of the years since 1979, weather was favorable for high recruitment and was favorable for average or better recruitment in the other three years (B. H. Campbell, pers. commun.). But in all six years, recruitment was below the long-term average (24%; table 38.4). Depressed recruitment in recent years appears to be a result of the interrelationship of changing habitat and predators on the Copper River Delta (Cornely et al. 1985). The lack of a strong year class since 1979 makes us believe that the downward trend of dusky geese will not be easily reversed.

Dusky geese suffered high mortality during winter (Hansen 1962, 1968; Chapman et al. 1969; Simpson and Jarvis 1979). Our analysis indicated that mortality during winter remained unchanged from 1971 to 1984. Assuming that our measure of winter mortality was reasonably reliable, then winter mortality (24%) was about equal to recruitment (28%) from 1971 to 1978. However, since 1979, winter mortality (30%) exceeded recruitment (19%). Even if our estimates are only indices to population parameters, the decline in the dusky goose population is explicable in terms of a one-third reduction in recruitment and unchanging mortality.

We believe that most mortality during winter can be attributed to hunting. Hansen (1962, 1968) and Chapman et al. (1969) reasoned that high mortality from hunting restricted the size of the dusky goose population. According to Henny (1967), 94.4% of the annual mortality of dusky geese was hunting mortality. Simpson and Jarvis (1979) estimated a 38% kill rate (harvest and crippling loss) for dusky geese in 1977-78.

We speculate that the dramatic increase in Taverner's geese resulted from a high rate of survival during winter and at least average recruitment. Taverner's geese were two to three times less vulnerable to hunting than were dusky geese. Simpson and Jarvis (1979) estimated a kill rate of 20% for Taverner's geese during 1977-78, about half the kill rate estimated for dusky geese. The low vulnerability of Taverner's geese apparently stems from their inherent behavior and activity patterns (Havel and Jarvis 1987). We had no direct measure of recruitment of Taverner's geese, but the large annual variation in age ratio of harvested Taverner's geese (40-70% juveniles) indicated that they had variable reproductive success typical of northern nesting geese. Hence, our suggestion that recruitment was at least average.

Management of geese in western Oregon and southwestern Washington has been directed at dusky geese; given their declining status, dusky geese will continue to receive special attention by managing agencies. Managers face a difficult task in stopping the decline in numbers of dusky geese and then in rebuilding the population to the management goal of 20,000-25,000 geese. Restrictions on hunting should be effective in balancing winter mortality against annual recruitment because hunting appears to be the major source of winter mortality. However, because of low recruitment and the absence of strong year classes, a cessation of hunting probably will be required to allow the population to increase. Habitat management, especially on the breeding grounds, may yield some long-term benefits, assuming that changes in habitat are responsible for the low recruitment in recent years. Additional habitat mangement on the wintering grounds may not yield dramatic results because existing refuge management is already of major benefit to dusky geese. Thus, in our view the only immediate alternative is a moratorium on hunting of Canada geese.

A moratorium on goose hunting will not be easy to sell to the goose-hunting public because of the large number of Taverner's geese. The management goal of 20,000-25,000 geese was established when only dusky geese were present in the wintering area. To cease hunting when there are 70,000 geese in the unit will require an extensive and creative public relations effort.

Assuming that managers are successful in increasing the number of dusky geese to the desired levels, and that Taverner's geese remain as abundant as at present, the challenge to managers will be to devise a scheme that will crop both populations at appropriate levels. Work should begin now on developing such a harvest system. A little forethought and aggressive action might have prevented the current crisis, one that leaves a moratorium on goose hunting as the only immediately available option.

LITERATURE CITED

Bellrose, F. C. 1980. Ducks, geese and swans of North America. 3rd ed. Stackpole Books, Harrisburg, Pa. 540pp.

Bromley, R. G. 1976. Nesting and habitat studies of the dusky Canada goose (*Branta canadensis occidentalis*) on the Copper River Delta, Alaska. M.S. Thesis, Univ. Alaska, Fairbanks. 81pp.

——. 1984. The energetics of migration and reproduction of dusky geese (*Branta canadensis occidentalis*). Ph.D. Diss., Oregon State Univ., Corvalis. 116pp.

Chapman, J. A., C. J. Henny, and H. M. Wight. 1969. The status, population dynamics and harvest of the dusky Canada goose. Wildl. Monogr. 18. 48pp.

Clark, S. L., and R. L. Jarvis. 1978. Effects of winter grazing by geese on yield of ryegrass seed. Wildl. Soc. Bull. 6:84–87.

Cornely, J. E., B. H. Campbell, and R. L. Jarvis. 1985. Productivity, mortality and population status of dusky Canada geese. Trans. N. Am. Wildl. Nat. Resour. Conf. 50:540–548.

Hansen, H. A. 1962. Canada geese of coastal Alaska. Trans. N. Am. Wildl. Nat. Resour. Conf. 27:301–320.

——. 1968. Pacific Flyway Canada goose management—Federal and state cooperation. Pages 43-49 *in* R. L. Hine and C. Schoenfeld, eds. Canada goose management: current continental problems and programs. Dembar Educ. Res. Serv., Madison, Wis.

Havel, L. H., and R. L. Jarvis. 1988. Formation of feeding flocks during winter by dusky and Taverner's Canada geese in Oregon. Pages 91-102 *in* M. W. Weller, ed. Waterfowl in winter. Univ. Minnesota Press, Minneapolis

Henny, C. J. 1967. Estimating band-reporting rates from banding and crippling loss data. J. Wildl. Manage. 31:533–538.

Simpson, S. G., and R. L. Jarvis. 1979. Comparative ecology of several subspecies of Canada geese during winter in western Oregon. Pages 223-241 *in* R. L. Jarvis and J. C. Bartonek, eds. Management and biology of Pacific Flyway geese. Oregon State Univ. Book Stores, Corvallis.

Timm, D. E., R. G. Bromley, D. McKnight, and R. S. Rodgers. 1979. Management evolution of dusky Canada geese. Pages 322-330 *in* R. L. Jarvis and J. C. Bartonek, eds. Management and biology of Pacific Flyway geese. Oregon State Univ. Book Stores, Corvallis.

39

Use of the Missouri River in South Dakota by Canada Geese in Fall and Winter, 1953-1984

S. G. Simpson

Abstract: Use of the Missouri River by Canada geese (*Branta canadensis*) in fall and winter was monitored by aerial surveys from 1953 to the present to determine impacts on migratory waterfowl of dams and reservoirs constructed under the Pick-Sloan plan. Numbers of Canada geese increased during fall migration, and more geese remained later into winter. Band recoveries, measurements of harvested geese, and surveys all indicated that Tall Grass Prairie Canada geese (*Branta canadensis hutchinsii*) shifted their migration from eastern South Dakota to the Missouri River. A northward shift occurred in concentrations of geese along the river. Observed changes were correlated with gross habitat alteration resulting from reservoir construction, including increased surface area of water, increased amount of shoreline, and a fivefold increase in area of irrigated corn bordering the river.

As early as 1804, Lewis and Clark reported use of the Missouri River in South Dakota by geese during fall (Thwaites 1969). They characterized the river as composed of braided channels with numerous sandbars and wooded islands. Canada goose hunting was well established along the southern reaches of the Missouri River by 1940 (Parker 1960).

Construction began on Fort Randall Dam, the first of four mainstem dams on the river, in 1946 (U.S. Army Corps of Engineers 1979a). Fort Randall Dam was closed in 1952 and was followed by Gavin's Point (1955), Oahe (1958), and Big Bend (1963) dams (fig. 39.1). The dams created 229,000 ha (566,000 acres) of water and over 4,800 km (3,000 miles) of shoreline by the time the reservoirs filled (U.S. Army Corps of Engineers 1979 a-d).

Waterfowl in Winter. © 1988 University of Minnesota. Edited by Milton W. Weller and published by the University of Minnesota Press, Minneapolis.

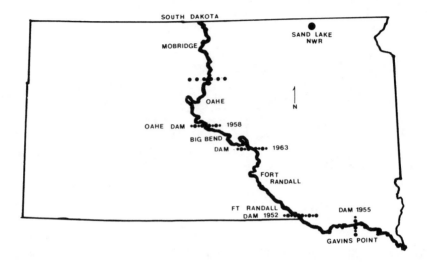

Fig. 39.1. Location of aerial survey segments, location and closure dates of dams on Missouri River in South Dakota, and location of Sand Lake National Wildlife Refuge.

Three populations of Canada geese occur on the Missouri River in South Dakota: Tall Grass Prairie (TGP) (*Branta canadensis hutchinsii* and *B c parvipes*), Western Prairie (WP) (*B c interior* and some *B c maxima*), and Great Plains (GP) (*B c maxima*). Taxonomy and delineation of populations for these geese are not agreed upon by all authorities. I follow here the usage of Vaught and Kirsch (1966); for discussion, see Nieman and Miller (1978). This paper documents changes in use of the river by Canada geese from 1953 to the present. Data were collected under the Pittman-Robertson program to determine the impact of Pick-Sloan development on migratory waterfowl. I thank K. L. Cool and J. Salyer for suggesting this summary and for editorial assistance. I also am grateful to all South Dakota Department of Game, Fish and Parks (SDGFP) and U.S. Fish and Wildlife Service (USFWS) personnel who flew aerial surveys to collect the data.

Methods

Numbers of geese on the river were estimated during aerial surveys flown weekly (biweekly in 1965) for eight weeks beginning in October in each year. The river was divided into five segments for surveys (fig. 39.1), each with a different observer. Experience of observers ranged from a single to 80 flights. The same segments, procedures, and personnel were used in special mid-December surveys. Least-squares regression lines were used to depict trends in use of particular segments of the river over time. Proportions of "small" (TGP) Canada geese in the harvest along the river were determined by measurements (culmen, tarsus, and weight in relation to age and sex) of over 5,000 hunter-killed geese from 1970 to 1974. Criteria used to classify geese as "small" (TGP) or "large" (WP, GP) were reported by Fowler (1975).

Relative abundance of small and large geese in Canada goose flocks during mid-December surveys was determined by observation from the ground at primary concentration areas along the river. Results of those ground observations were applied to aerial counts from each locale to obtain an estimate of size composition for the total.

Results

Since 1970, numbers of Canada geese on the Missouri River in South Dakota during fall have increased. Mean peak count from 1953 through 1965 was 32,300; from 1966 through 1975, 52,500; and from 1976 through 1984, over 177,000 (table 39.1). Mean weekly counts and peak counts both indicated this increasing trend (fig. 39.2).

Table 39.1. Peak numbers of Canada geese counted on weekly aerial surveys on Missouri River in South Dakota during fall, 1953-84

Year	Peak count	Year	Peak count	Year	Peak count
1953	47,800	1966	28,100	1976	91,600
1954	36,000	1967	39,200	1977	93,400
1955	45,000	1968	38,500	1978	106,500
1956	24,200	1969	44,900	1979	202,700
1957	23,500	1970	35,300	1980	259,300
1958	34,200	1971	73,200	1981	211,300
1959	29,100	1972	59,600	1982	197,500
1960	35,600	1973	97,300	1983	185,300
1961	31,300	1974	50,300	1984	247,300
1962	25,000	1975	55,500		
1963	26,400			$\bar{x} = 177,200 \pm 64,511$	
1964	36,400			$(n = 9)$	
1965	25,500	$\bar{x} = 52,200 \pm 20,604$			
		$(n = 10)$			
$\bar{x} = 32,300 \pm 7,827$					
$(n = 13)$					

More geese remained in South Dakota later into fall and winter. Mid-December surveys indicated increasing numbers of Canada geese throughout the Central Flyway (USFWS Region 6, Denver, unpubl. reports) and in South Dakota (fig. 39.2).

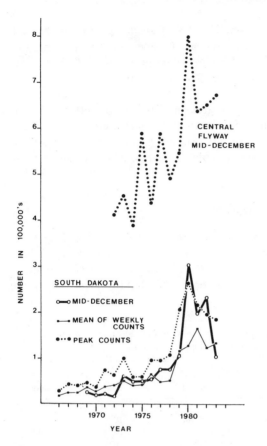

Fig. 39.2. Average of weekly counts, peak of weekly counts, and mid-December counts of Canada geese on Missouri River in South Dakota, 1966-83, and Canada geese counted on mid-December surveys in Central Flyway, 1972-83.

However, the proportion of the flyway total found in South Dakota increased from 5% in 1972 to 38% in 1980 and 1982. Comparisons of five-year means of weekly counts showed peak counts the second week in November except in the 1976-80 period, when the peak occurred the third week in November (fig. 39.3). In addition, for the 1976-80 period, the mean of mid-December counts equaled the mean of peaks (fig. 39.3).

The number of TGP Canada geese on the Missouri River increased over time. During the late 1960s, increasing numbers of TGP bands were recovered on the Missouri River (SDGFP, unpubl. data). Measurements of over 5,000 Canada geese harvested along the river from 1970 to 1974 indicated that 23.4% were small Canadas (TGP) (Fowler 1975). Mid-December surveys indicated under 20,000 TGP geese before 1980, but over 20,000 from 1980 through 1984 (fig. 39.4). Moreover, the proportion of South Dakota's TGP harvest that occurred in

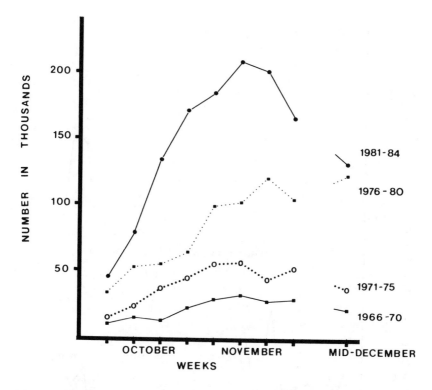

Fig. 39.3. Weekly and mid-December counts of Canada geese on Missouri River in South
Dakota, averaged over five-year periods from 1966-70 to 1981-84.

counties bordering the river increased from 60% in 1972 to over 90% in 1983
(SDGFP, unpubl. data.).

Distribution of Canada geese on the Missouri River in South Dakota changed
over time. From 1953 to 1973, the highest mean of weekly counts occurred on the
Fort Randall segment, whereas from 1974 to the present, means were highest on
the Big Bend and Oahe segments (table 39.2). The proportion of geese located on
the Fort Randall segment during peak counts decreased from 80% in 1953 to less
than 5% by 1983, whereas complementary increases occurred on Big Bend and
Oahe (fig. 39.5). This northward trend in location of concentrations of Canada
geese on the river was also suggested by harvest data. Counties bordering the Oahe
segment accounted for half the Missouri River Canada goose harvest in 1972 and
nearly 80% in 1978 (SDFGP, unpubl. data).

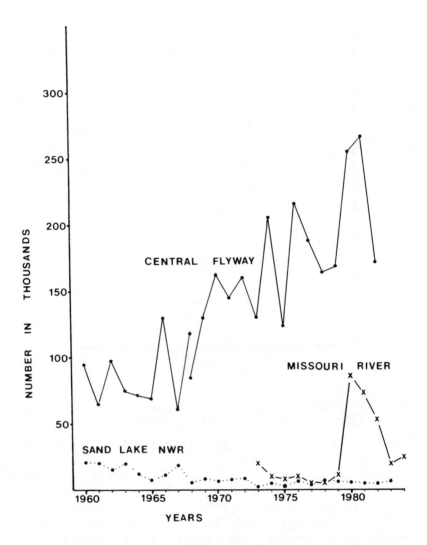

Fig. 39.4. Mid-December counts of tall grass prairie Canada geese in Central Flyway (1960-82) and on Missouri River in South Dakota (1973-84) and peak counts at Sand Lake National Wildlife Refuge (1960-83).

Discussion

Apparent increases in numbers of Canada geese on the Missouri River in South Dakota were not attributable to major changes in survey techniques, since none occurred. However, in 1978 a photographic survey was conducted the day follow-

Table 39.2. Means of weekly counts of Canada geese on three segments of Missouri River in South Dakota, 1953-84

| Year | Mean number of geese counted on | | | Number of flights |
	Ft. Randall	Big Bend	Oahe	
1953	14,030	2,902	3,268	7
1954	14,496	3,195	2,316	7
1955	22,436	1,199	1,124	8
1956	8,152	1,562	1,944	8
1947	10,601	2,996	2,244	8
1958	12,547	3,296	1,450	8
1959	13,913	2,755	2,224	8
1960	11,831	3,959	3,046	8
1961	12,099	3,894	5,160	8
1962	6,861	2,806	1,505	8
1963	9,516	1,965	2,489	8
1964	11,851	5,979	1,436	8
1965	10,386	6,759	. . .	8
1966	11,256	4,946	1,865	4
1967	12,544	5,357	2,146	3
1968	12,523	6,141	4,671	8
1969	16,330	8,851	7,955	8
1970	11,634	7,575	5,658	8
1971	20,020	11,037	7,721	7
1972	13,658	11,832	11,102	8
1973	20,758	18,841	13,559	8
1974	9,759	20,543	8,899	8
1975	12,271	10,277	16,283	
1976	12,677	23,471	24,222	8
1977	11,515	14,750	29,297	8
1978	15,363	24,292	23,748	8
1979	10,547	48,223	57,026	8
1980	4,218	59,991	63,221	8
1981	7,892	65,636	70,647	8
1982	3,371	39,230	68,706	8
1983	2,244	41,640	59,818	6
1984	4,235	63,695	100,193	8

ing the mid-December count on portions of the Oahe and Big Bend segments, and results indicated that observers underestimated the number of geese by as much as 60% (SDGFP, unpubl. data). Since that time, observers' estimates and counts from photographic surveys have converged. Weather and equipment problems preclude full use of photography to census geese on the river, but photographic surveys of Oahe and Big Bend segments are attempted annually and, if successful, are used as checks on observers' estimates. Changes in observers could not have contributed

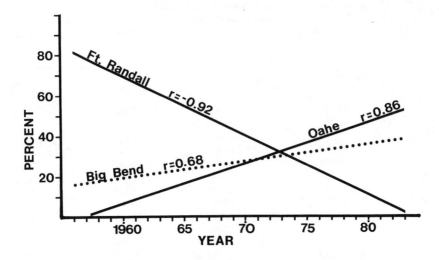

Fig. 39.5. Linear regression of percentage of peak counts of Canada geese occurring on three segments of Missouri River in South Dakota over time.

to the noted increases, since observers remained the same on the two survey segments where and when increases were greatest.

Increases could be attributed to population growth. Breeding-pair surveys in east-central Saskatchewan and Manitoba (Canadian Wildlife Service, unpubl. data), in North Dakota (North Dakota Game and Fish Department, unpubl. data), and in northeastern South Dakota (SDGFP, unpubl. data) indicated increases during the 1970s. Coordinated mid-December goose surveys also reflected increases for TGP and large Canada geese (WP and GP combined) during that period (USFWS Region 6, Denver, unpubl. reports).

Harvest management may have been partly responsible for the observed population buildups. Restrictive Canada goose bag limits were imposed in the Central Flyway in 1967 to protect TGP geese (Central Flyway Council Minutes, August 1967). In 1973, closure dates were adopted by several Central Flyway states to protect geese during restoration efforts in the Dakotas and prairie Canada (Central Flyway Committee Minutes, 1973). South Dakota retained these restrictive regulations (58 days compared with 72 days previously, one-goose daily bag) until 1979. Currently, Canada goose seasons along the Missouri River in South Dakota run 79 days with a one-goose daily bag limit until the Saturday nearest November 15, when the daily bag limit increases to two.

Gross changes in habitat along the river also were of importance in the observed increase in South Dakota. In addition to increased shoreline and area of water, the dams enabled major changes in agriculture. During the mid-1960s, center-pivot irrigation and newly developed hybrid corn combined to dominate the agricultural

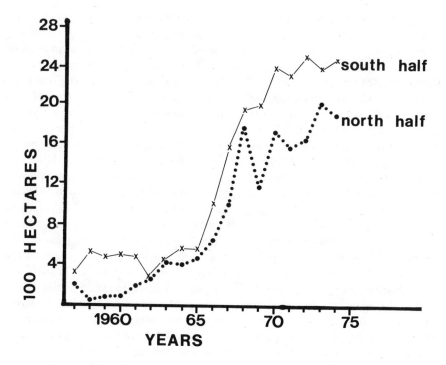

Fig. 39.6. Hectares of irrigated corn harvested in counties bordering Missouri River in South Dakota, 1957-74. Split between north and south halves lies midway between Oahe and Big Bend dams (see fig. 39.1).

landscape of central South Dakota. From 1965 to 1975, the number of hectares of irrigated corn harvested in counties bordering the river increased fivefold (fig. 39.6; South Dakota Crop and Livestock Reporting Service, 1973, 1974, 1975, 1976). This dramatic increase in available food and adjacent water provided the basis for increased use of the Missouri River by Canada geese. A similar phenomenon occurred with creation of a large lake and availability of abundant corn at Horicon Marsh (Reeves et al. 1968). Increased use by Canada geese of impoundments created for irrigation and power also were noted by W. H. Elder (in Palmer 1976, 232-233).

A primary factor determining how late geese remained was weather, including temperature and snow depth. The large, deep reservoirs remained open well into December, providing roost sites and enabling geese to remain later in South Dakota. Markgren (1963) noted southerly movements of European bean geese (*Anser fabalis*) in long periods of deep snow, but Owen (1980) pointed out that availability and high-energy content of corn afford geese some freedom from the impact of snow cover on foraging. In December 1982, when over 233,000 Canada geese were estimated on the river (fig. 39.2), the mean minimum temperature was −9.6C and snow was absent, compared with −21.9C and more than 10 cm of snow in December 1983, when less than half that number of geese were counted (U.S. Department of Commerce 1982, 1983). Concern about "short-stopping" led to an aerial reconnaissance by Central Flyway representatives in 1982. Confronted with the thousands of acres of food and water available to geese, those biologists admitted that nothing short of severe winter weather could drive the geese south (Central Flyway Technical Committee correspondence; K. Cool, pers. commun.).

Although peak counts of TGP geese at Sand Lake National Wildlife Refuge decreased from 1960 to 1975, mid-December counts for the entire Central Flyway indicated a population increase during the same period (fig. 39.4). Within South Dakota, the number of TGP geese on the river in December is difficult to determine, since observers cannot differentiate and count small and large geese from aircraft. The current methodology involving observers at key locations on the ground is subject to sampling errors. It appears likely, however, that the increase in TGP geese on the river was the result of population growth and redistribution during migration. It seems probable that increased avaiability of food and habitat was a contributing factor in the migrational shift. A second possibility is that the Missouri River TGP geese constituted a population segment with higher survival rates than the segment using Sand Lake, a concept suggested by Raveling and Dixon (1981) in a discussion of WP geese.

The buildups of Canada geese on Oahe and Big Bend began in the mid 1970s. Owen (1980) noted that provision of refuges often increased overall population levels of geese. Refuges had already been in place on Oahe and Big Bend segments since the mid-1960s, but they were not effective in concentrating geese until adequate food was available in that area. Likewise, Fort Randall Reservoir (which was designated a statutory waterfowl refuge by the state legislature in 1961) did not draw geese south beyond where their biological needs were met. Thus, refuges along the river did not result in major changes in distribution of geese, although currently they may affect local distribution within segments.

Increased numbers of Canada geese have created a situation that poses several challenges to managers. First, the economic implications of increased harvest opportunity have led to continued pressure for creation of refuges on the river including public (U.S. Army Corps of Engineers) land adjacent to private land where hunting is commercialized. This political pressure has resulted in a system of refuges that eliminates much public hunting opportunity and is cause for increasing controversy among landowners, hunters, county boards, enforcement personnel, and wildlife biologists and managers.

Second, Raveling (1978) and Raveling and Dixon (1981) pointed out that, where different subspecies or populations of Canada geese co-occur, management practices aimed at one population may affect others, possibly in unforeseen or undesired ways. The co-occurrence of three populations (TGP, WP, and GP) on the Missouri River confounds independent management based on fall flights, mid-December counts, or harvest of those populations. Since WP and GP geese cannot be separated on surveys (and distinguishing TGP geese is difficult at best), midwinter population estimates can no longer be used to monitor the WP population. As increasing proportions of the TGP population remain later in South Dakota, the importance of more accurate estimates of their numbers increases. Continued aerial surveys, improved methods of estimating numbers of TGP geese, and continued efforts to improve harvest estimates and differentiate between WP and GP geese in the harvest are necessary to successfully and responsibly manage these three populations.

LITERATURE CITED

Fowler, R. M. 1975. Investigation of Canada geese using Missouri River impoundments in South Dakota, 1974-75. P.R. Project W-75-R-17, Progr. Rep. South Dakota Dep. Game Fish Parks, Pierre. 13pp.

Markgren, G. 1963. Studies on wild geese in southernmost Sweden. Acta Vertebr. 2:229-418.

Nieman, D., and H. W. Miller. 1978. Management plan for the western prairie population Canada geese. Draft. U.S. Fish Wildl. Serv., Denver, Colo. 44pp.

Owen, M. 1980. Wild geese of the world: their life history and ecology. B. T. Batsford, London. 236pp.

Palmer, R. S. 1976. Handbook of North American birds. Vol. 2. Waterfowl (part I). Yale Univ. Press, New Haven.

Parker, D. D. 1960. History of our county and state: Charles Mix County. History Dept., South Dakota State College, Brookings.

Raveling, D. G. 1978. Dynamics of distribution of Canada geese in winter. Trans. N. Am. Wildl. Nat. Resour. Conf. 43:206-225.

———, and C. C. Dixon. 1981. Distribution and harvest of Canada geese (*Branta canadensis*) in southern Manitoba prior to development of Oak Hammock Marsh. Can. Fld. Nat. 95:276-280.

Reeves, H. M., and H. H. Dill, and A. S. Hawkins. 1968. A case study in Canada goose management: the Mississippi Valley population. Pages 150-165 *in* R. L. Hine and C. Schoenfeld, eds. Canada goose management: current continental problems and programs. Dembar Educ. Res. Serv., Madison, Wis. 195pp.

South Dakota Crop and Livestock Reporting Service. 1973. South Dakota agriculture: historic estimates 1965-1970. Sioux Falls. 106pp.

———. 1974. South Dakota agriculture 1973. Sioux Falls. 66pp.

———. 1975. South Dakota agriculture 1974. Sioux Falls. 68pp.

———. 1976. South Dakota agriculture 1975. Sioux Falls. 94pp.

Thwaites, R. G., ed. 1969. Original journals of the Lewis and Clark expedition, 1804-1806. Vol. 1. Arms Press, New York. 374pp.

U.S. Army Corps of Engineers. 1979a. Lake Francis Case, South Dakota. U.S. Gov. Print. Off., Washington, D.D. 1979-688-154.

———. 1979b. Lake Oahe, South Dakota-North Dakota. U.S. Gov. Print. Off., Washington, D.C. 1979-668-147.

———. 1979c. Lake Sharpe, South Dakota. U.S. Gov. Print. Off., Washington, D.C. 1979-768-455.

———. 1979d. Lewis and Clark Lake, Nebraska-South Dakota. U.S. Gov. Print. Off., Washington, D.C. 1979-668-146.

U.S. Department of Commerce. 1982. Climatological data: South Dakota. National Climatic Center, Asheville, N.C.

———. 1983. Climatological data: South Dakota. National Climatic Center, Asheville, N.C.

Vaught, R. W., and L. M. Kirsh. 1966. Canada geese of the eastern prairie population with special reference to the Swan Lake flock. Mo. Dep. Conserv. Tech. Bull. 3, Columbia. 91 pp.

40

Estimating Populations of Ducks Wintering in Southeast Alaska

Bruce Conant, James G. King, John L. Trapp, and John I. Hodges

Abstract: Southeast Alaska provides important coastal winter waterfowl habitat, but assessment of populations has been hampered by geographic complexity, severe winter weather, and the logistical difficulties of this remote region. An aerial survey method using random stratified plots coupled with air-to-boat correction factors offers a practical, systematic means to measure this resource. A small sample aerial plot survey in 1981 indicated a population of 151,601 ± 45% total ducks for northern southeast Alaska. Three years of replicate boat surveys showed that aerial observers recorded about 50% of the total ducks observed from small boats. The wintering duck species composition was mallard (*Anas platyrhynchos*), 16-26%; goldeneye (*Bucephala* spp.), 18-23%; scoter (*Melanitta* spp.), 33-38%; other, 14-26%. An annual wintering duck population of one million is suggested for southeast Alaska. Recommendations are given for applying the technique to a larger geographic area.

Waterfowl are common in marine habitats along the Pacific coast of Alaska in winter, but there are no reliable population figures. No standard method has been available for measuring this resource in this geographically complex area influenced by variable coastal weather systems. Sporadically over the past 30 years, biologists in the U.S. Fish and Wildlife Service (USFWS, Alaska) have been trying to develop a suitable technique to address this knowledge gap. Our objective is to develop a replicable survey method for wintering waterfowl that would yield valid population estimates with good confidence limits.

Waterfowl in Winter. © 1988 University of Minnesota. Edited by Milton W. Weller and published by the University of Minnesota Press, Minneapolis.

An aerial survey of a sample of stratified random plots conducted in late winter 1981 for northern southeast Alaska is described. Comparative aerial and boat surveys were conducted in Port Frederick during the late-winter periods of 1982-84 to establish correction factors for observations made from an airplane. Bruce Conant was pilot and observer on all air surveys. The primary air observers were James G. King on the 1981 plot survey and Rodney J. King on the comparative surveys. John L. Trapp and James G. King supervised the boat surveys. John I. Hodges provided statistical advice and helped on the boat surveys. We are grateful to the Raptor Project leader (USFWS, Alaska), Philip F. Schempf, for the use of the M/V Surfbird. Andrew Anderson maneuvered the vessel skillfully in the often treacherous waters of southeast Alaska. Additional help on the boat surveys was given by James L. Baker, Karen S. Bollinger, Robin E. Hunter, Patrick J. Gould, and Philip F. Schempf. We are grateful for the support and encouragement of Dirk V. Derksen, Migratory Bird specialist (USFWS, Alaska), and James L. Baker, chief of Wildlife Assistance (USFWS, Alaska).

Study Area

Southeast Alaska is characterized by an intricate system of fjords and mountainous islands, a product of glaciation during the Pleistocene. The climate is maritime; normal winter temperatures range from −9C to +7C (15F to 45F). Storms and moderate to heavy precipitation occur throughout the year, with associated moderate to strong surface winds (USDA 1978). This area has 23,876 km (14,836 miles) of marine coastline; 1,717 km² (663 square miles) of intertidal lands; and 5,768 km² (2,227 square miles) of marine water 18.3 m (60 ft) or less in depth (USFWS, Alaska: file data). Tidal fluctuation ranges to 7.6 m (25 ft). Saltwater bays and water passages tend to be precipitous and deep so that bottom-feeding diving ducks are confined to nearshore areas and outwash plains. Alcids and other diving birds often seek shelter near shore or in bays.

The 1981 aerial plot survey estimated birds within the perimeter (fig. 40.1) of northern southeast Alaska as dictated by U.S. Geological Survey (USGS) quadrangle map boundaries. The comparative aerial and boat survey work was accomplished in Port Frederick, a sheltered saltwater inlet within the larger study area (fig. 40.1). Port Frederick also contains a typical plot of the 1981 aerial survey (fig. 40.2).

Methods

Plot Survey

The 1981 aerial plot survey was similar to the method used to estimate bald eagle (*Haliaeetus leucocephalus*) breeding populations (King et al. 1972, Hodges and

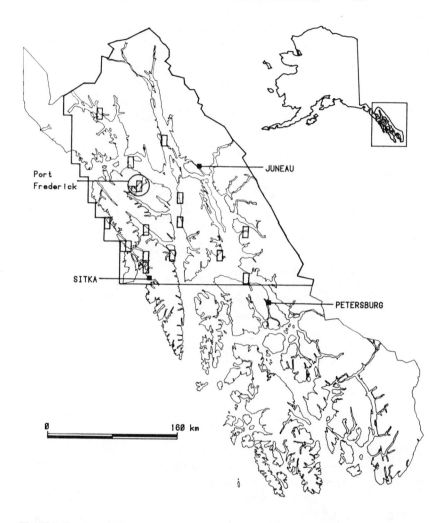

Fig. 40.1. Southeast Alaska study area boundaries, showing general location of 16 random plots flown in 1981 and Port Frederick, site of comparative aerial and boat surveys.

King 1982). For waterfowl surveys, northern southeast Alaska was subdivided by quarter sections of USGS quadrangle (1:63,360) maps. Sections containing entirely upland habitat were deleted, leaving a total of 269 plots with marine habitat. These plots were stratified into low, medium, and high categories based on expected numbers of wintering ducks (table 40.1). Stratification was based on the approximate amount of shoreline and intertidal area or previous knowledge of general densities of wintering ducks. A random set of plots (table 40.1) was selected utilizing maximum allocation of effort based on expected variability and survey

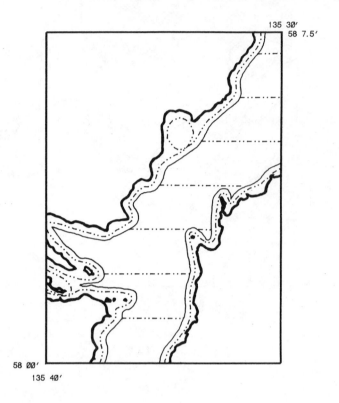

Fig. 40.2. Location of shoreline zone and transects and of open water zone and transects within typical plot.

costs (Snedecor and Cochran 1967). Percentage of coverage in a stratum was proportional to stratum size and expected standard deviation and was inversely proportional to expected cost per plot. Confidence limits are presented as proportions of the estimate, similar in concept to the coefficient of variation. All confidence limits are presented in this format.

All flights were made with a USFWS turbine Beaver aircraft specially modified for maximum observer visibility. The pilot used quarter sections of quadrangle maps for precise plot navigation. Observations were made by both pilot and observer from an altitude of 30 m (100 ft) and at a survey speed of 160 km/hr (100 mph). Data were recorded using small tape recorders and later transcribed directly into a desktop computer. Surveys were conducted 23 February 1981 to 16 March 1981 during good daylight conditions. Poor weather and short daylight hours precluded flying surveys in January.

Two techniques were used to measure the number of birds within each plot. Because the majority of ducks occurred close to shore, the airplane was flown

Table 40.1. Stratified random sample with optimum allocation of effort—aerial winter waterfowl plot survey, northern southeast Alaska, 1981

Sampling design	Plot location	
	Quarter section	Quadrangle map
Low stratum		
Sample size = 4 plots	SE[a]	Mt. Fairweather D-2
Statum size = 135 plots	NE	Sitka D-3
Percentage coverage = 3	NE	Sitka C-3
	SE	Sumdum A-5
Medium stratum		
Sample size = 7 plots	SE	Juneau C-4
Stratum size = 107 plots	SE	Juneau B-6
Percentage coverage = 7	SE	Sitka C-5
	NW	Sitka B-6
	NE	Sitka B-6
	SE	Sitka B-5
	SW	Sumdum B-6
High stratum		
Sample size = 5 plots	SW	Juneau A-5
Stratum size = 27 plots	NW	Sitka C-7
Percentage coverage = 19	SE	Sumdum C-5
	SW	Sitka B-3
	NE	Sitka A-5
Total		
Sample size = 16 plots		
Stratum size = 269 plots		
Percentage coverage = 6		

[a]Quarter sections of standard U.S. Geological Survey quadrangle maps are approximately 140 km^2 (54 square statute miles).

following a track about 0.2 km (1/8 statute mile) from the existing waterline at the time of the survey. Extensive intertidal areas were surveyed in their entirety, often necessitating a circuit of the area for adequate coverage (fig. 40.2). Birds were counted from both sides of the aircraft, resulting in transect coverage of about 0.4 km (1/4 statute mile) along the shoreline of each plot.

Beyond the shoreline zone, bird estimates were derived from either complete counting where open water areas were small or transect sampling where they were large. An area expansion factor of 4.935 was applied to observations from standard straight-line transects (0.4 km or 1/4 statute mile wide) centered on each minute of latitude (fig. 40.2). Combining the shoreline and open-water zone estimates gave a duck population figure for each plot. Mean plot values were expanded by stratum and then combined to give totals for northern southeast Alaska.

Comparative Aerial and Boat Surveys

The same techniques were used in the comparative aerial and boat surveys for the whole Port Frederick inlet. The turbine Beaver again was used for all aerial surveys. Two small skiffs duplicated the aircraft track in the shoreline zone but at about 16 km/hr (10 mph), with stops to count concentrations. Counts were made by two observers using binoculars. Open-water zone counts were done from a 20-m USFWS vessel at 18 km/hr (10 knots) or from skiffs following the straight-line transects or cruising for complete coverage. Data were recorded on forms in the field and later entered into the computer. All surveys were conducted during daylight when sufficient light was available for species identification. Survey dates were 19 February through 3 March 1982, 24 February through 2 March 1983, and 17 February through 24 February 1984.

Both aerial and boat surveys were designed for ducks. Geese and seabirds were recorded incidentally, and data for them are not presented. Duck data are presented in the survey order and groupings used in USFWS flyway reports (dabblers, divers, miscellaneous).

Results

The results of air work from the 1981 plot survey and both the air and boat surveys in Port Frederick showed that over 90% of wintering ducks occurred within the shoreline zone. The wintering duck species composition from both studies was mallard (*Anas platyrhynchos*), 16-26%; goldeneye (*Bucephala* spp.), 18-23%; scoters (*Melanitta* spp.), 33-38% and others, 14-26%.

Table 40.2 presents duck population figures from the 1981 aerial plot survey by species and zone, unadjusted for visibility. Species composition and confidence limits also are shown. Shoreline counts contained 93% of the total ducks estimated to be present in the survey area. Table 40.3 shows ducks counted by species in the shoreline zone for the three years of comparative surveys. A total of 13 replicate air and 6 replicate boat surveys was completed in three years. The number of ducks recorded in the shoreline vs. the open water zone averaged 92% for both air and boat surveys.

The percentage of ducks recorded from the air compared with that recorded from boats varied by species, averaging 50% for the species found in Port Frederick (table 40.3). The species and group composition was similar for both air and boat surveys (table 40.3). Replicate surveys found that total ducks recorded from air surveys were .47, .45, and .57 for respective years and averaged .50 ± 16% of boat survey totals (table 40.3).

Three marine habitat parameters of significance to wintering waterfowl were measured for southeast Alaska (table 40.4). About one third of each of the values is present in the northern study area. The 1981 aerial plots contained less than 10% of

Table 40.2. Population estimates of ducks for northern southeast Alaska from expansion of mean values by stratum for 1981 aerial plot survey

Species	Shoreline zone		Open water zone		Total number	95% confidence limits[a]
	Number	%	Number	%		
Mallard	23,860	17.8	0	0.0	23,860	± 76%
American wigeon	0	0.0	0	0.0	0	
Green-winged teal	0	0.0	0	0.0	0	
Northern pintail	0	0.0	0	0.0	0	
Goldeneyes	31,724	23.6	248	2.4	31,972	± 45%
Bufflehead	7,722	5.8	76	0.7	7,798	± 74%
Scaup	283	0.2	0	0.0	283	± 156%
Scoters	43,632	32.5	7,624	73.0	51,256	± 69%
Mergansers	9,889	7.4	430	4.1	10,319	± 31%
Harlequin duck	12,859	9.6	0	0.0	12,859	± 57%
Oldsquaw	4,282	3.2	2,063	19.8	6,345	± 121%
Total identified	134,251	100.0	10,441	100.0	144,692	
Unidentified	6,672		237		6,909	
Total ducks	140,923		10,678		151,601	± 45%
Shoreline/open water (%)	93		7		100	

[a]Given as proportion of total.

that third, with intertidal area being slightly underrepresented in the random sample. A significant correlation ($r^2 = .77$) was found between total ducks and the square kilometers of intertidal area.

Populations of total ducks as derived from three aerial surveys—from the 1981 plot survey, expanded by both intertidal area and by plots; from an independent 1980 plot survey only along shorelines; and from a 1975 limited shoreline-only sample—compare favorably (table 40.5). Application of the visibility-expansion factor derived from the Port Frederick work indicates an estimated population of about one-third million ducks for the northern half of southeast Alaska. If the relationship continues for the southern half, a total wintering duck population of about one million is suggested for all of southeast Alaska.

Discussion

The aerial plot survey system described provides a practical way to complete a winter waterfowl survey in southeast Alaska. A survey accomplished prior to early March measures essentially a wintering population in these latitudes. It yields duck population estimates with confidence limits that can be further narrowed. A fourfold increase in sample size should reduce the confidence limits by one half. Adjusting expanded air-survey results with reliable air-to-boat visibility-correction

Table 40.3. Comparison of air and boat surveys of winter waterfowl in Port Frederick, 1982-84

Species	1982 survey[a]		1983 survey[b]		1984 survey[c]		$\bar{x}$		Count by air/boat (%)	Percentage of total count	
	Air	Boat	Air	Boat	Air	Boat	Air	Boat		Air	Boat
Dabblers											
Mallard	1,089	2,925	1,395	2,866	2,094	3,799	1,526	3,197	48	25	26
Am. wigeon	1	0	0	0	1	0	2	0	. . .	. . .	. . .
G. W. Teal	7	12	5	9	0	40	4	20	. . .	. . .	. . .
No. pintail	36	221	11	44	79	100	42	122	35	1	1
Unidentified	77	209	13	0	0	0	26	70	37	. . .	. . .
Total	1,210	3,367	1,424	2,919	2,174	3,939	1,598	3,408	47	26	28
Divers											
Goldeneyes	1,435	1,977	1,483	2,563	1,182	2,176	1,367	2,239	61	23	18
Bufflehead	188	640	243	838	239	892	223	790	28	4	6
Scaup	42	373	84	420	326	590	151	461	33	2	4
Unidentified	7	14	21	0	2	0	3	5	. . .	. . .	. . .
Total	1,672	3,004	1,831	3,821	1,749	3,658	1,744	3,494	50	29	29
Scoters	1,902	3,973	2,741	5,466	2,203	2,904	2,282	4,035	57	38	33
Mergansers	117	165	76	173	130	247	108	198	54	2	2
Harlequin duck	125	660	268	641	221	597	205	613	33	3	5
Oldsquaw	239	112	68	1,133	59	154	122	463	26	2	4
Unidentified	0	0	0	0	0	0	0	0	. . .	. . .	. . .
Total	2,383	4,910	3,153	7,413	2,613	3,902	2,716	5,309	51	45	43
Total ducks	5,267	11,281	6,408	14,153	6,536	11,499	6,058	12,212	50	100	100
Air/boat	.47		.45		.57		$.50 \pm 16\%$[d]		. . .	. . .	. . .

[a]For air surveys, data represent mean values. Three air surveys were conducted, with 93% of the ducks being counted in the shoreline zone and the rest in open water; one boat survey was conducted, with 98% of the ducks being counted in the shoreline area.

[b]Data represent mean values. Four air surveys were conducted, with 88% of the ducks being counted in the shoreline zone and the rest in open water; two boat surveys were conducted, with 84% of the ducks being counted in the shoreline zone.

[c]Data represent mean values. Six air surveys were conducted, with 95% of the ducks being counted in the shoreline zone and the rest in open water; three boat surveys were conducted, with 94% of the ducks being counted in the shoreline zone.

[d]95% confidence limits computed from the three annual ratios.

factors should provide reasonable estimates of total wintering ducks. The method is repeatable and needs to be applied broadly over several years to establish a sound baseline.

The credibility of the comparative air and boat survey results was enhanced by replicate counts within each year. Replicate counts helped to reduce the components of variance caused by the various environmental factors that fluctuated between surveys. Repetitive surveys are not a luxury and should be considered by anyone developing new population-estimating methods.

Table 40.4. Significant marine habitat relationships from southeast Alaska[a]

Area	Kilometers of shoreline	Square kilometers of intertidal	Square kilometers water < 18.3 m
Total SE Alaska	23,876	1,717	5,768
Northern SE Alaska[b]	8,487 (36%)	585 (34%)	2,183 (38%)
1981 plots[c]	703 (8.3%)	39 (6.7%)	155 (7.1%)
Correlations of total ducks to habitat (r^2)[d]	.07	.77	.10
1975 survey[e]	853 (3.6%)		

[a] Unpublished data (U.S. Fish and Wildlife Service, Juneau, Ala.).
[b] Study area: figure 40.1 (% of total southeast Alaska).
[c] Plots: figure 40.1 (% of northern southeast Alaska).
[d] Data from the 1981 aerial plot survey, $n = 16$.
[e] Data from Conant (1975) (% of total Southeast Alaska).

Table 40.5. Expanded estimates of total ducks counted in three aerial surveys in southeast Alaska (in thousands)[a]

Area	1981 Plot survey[b]		1980 Plot survey Expanded by plots[c]	1975 Shoreline survey Expanded by miles of shoreline[d]
	Expanded by intertidal area	Expanded by plots		
Northern SE Alaska	213.0	151.6 ± 45%	141.4 ± 24%	156.2
Total SE Alaska	530.8			439.4

[a] Not expanded with air-to-boat visibility factor. Confidence limits at 95%.
[b] From tables 40.4 and 40.2.
[c] From a 0.4-km (1/4-mile) aerial shoreline-only plot sample in the central part of northern southeast Alaska (Conant et al. 1980).
[d] From table 40.4 and a 0.2-km (1/8-mile) aerial shoreline-only sample throughout southeast Alaska (Conant 1975).

The limited data collected during comparative surveys in the open water zone are not presented (table 40.3). Scoters and oldsquaw (*Clangula hyemalis*) were the primary species found in this zone. Although more comparative data here would be valuable in establishing species visibility-correction factors, the lack of it does not much affect the total population estimates presented since this zone contained less than 10% of the total ducks.

The marine habitat measurements (table 40.4) were not available for use in stratification of samples for the 1981 aerial plot survey. An increase in the precision of stratification of wintering habitat may be possible where such habitat parameters are available by plot. The strong correlation between amounts of intertidal area and total ducks (table 40.4) suggests that this factor may be the most important consideration. A stratification approach such as this may be especially useful in regions where little is known about waterfowl distribution.

Because of the strong intertidal correlation, the 1981 plot data also were expanded by the measured amounts of intertidal area for northern and total southeast Alaska (table 40.5). Although the results of the 1980 and 1975 surveys are not strictly comparable (table 40.5), they provide independent assessments of the magnitude of wintering duck populations. The 1980 estimate is low because it contains only shoreline counts and was expanded for a slightly smaller area. The 1975 estimates likewise are slightly deficient since they were derived from a widely distributed random sample of shoreline counts that did not include observations from the pilot side of the aircraft. Both estimates demonstrate phases in the development of the 1981 aerial survey scheme.

Bias is present with any aerial survey. Observers vary in their ability to identify and enumerate waterfowl species from aircraft. Some birds dive; some blend into the background; some fly ahead, and could be counted twice. Waterfowl distribution is influenced by wind, temperature, tide, food availability, and other factors. Air survey variability was kept to a minimum by following a standardized survey design and by using only experienced observers seated in the front of an airplane with good visibility.

Boat surveys are confronted with most of the same biases, but they were minimized by again following a standardized survey design and by using experienced boat observers familiar with southeast Alaska waterfowl and their habitats. The results of our comparative air and boat surveys are similar to those found from ground truth work along New Hampshire and Massachusetts shorelines (Stott and Olson 1972) and in British Columbia (Savard 1982). Although their air survey methods differ from ours, they also found that about half as many ducks were recorded from the air as from the ground.

We conclude that the numbers of ducks recorded on boat surveys are much closer to actual numbers present than those recorded from the air. More air-to-boat or ground truth-comparison work may increase confidence in visibility-correction factors by species. Application of good species-correction factors could increase the precision of estimates of individual species and total population.

An expanded plot survey for wintering ducks for all of southeast Alaska is planned. Additional comparative survey work in the southern half would be useful. The plot method appears to hold promise for other north Pacific coastal marine habitats such as Prince William Sound, Kodiak Island, and British Columbia. Concurrent comparative survey studies in these areas could increase the precision of those population estimates. The method probably can be used successfully in other similar waterfowl habitats of the world.

LITERATURE CITED

Conant, B. 1975. Southeast Alaska coastal foundation studies, aerial waterfowl survey addendum 1973-1975. U.S. Fish Wildl. Serv. Rep. Juneau, Ala. 129pp.

———, R. J. King, J. I. Hodges, and J. G. King. 1980. A winter waterfowl survey in southeastern Alaska. U.S. Fish Wildl. Serv. Rep. Juneau, Ala. 7pp.

Hodges, J. I., and J. G. King. 1982. Bald eagle (Alaska). Pages 50-51 *in* D. E. Davis, ed. CRC handbook of census methods for terrestrial vertebrates. CRC Press, Boca Raton, Fla.

King, J. G., F. C. Robards, and C. J. Lensink. 1972. Census of the bald eagle breeding population in southeast Alaska. J. Wildl. Manage. 36:1292–1295.

Savard, J.-P. L. 1982. Variability of waterfowl aerial surveys: observer and air-ground comparisons. A preliminary report. Progr. Notes 127. Canadian Wildl. Serv., Ottawa.

Snedecor, G. W., and W. G. Cochran. 1967. Statistical methods. 6th ed. Iowa State Univ. Press, Ames. 593pp.

Stott, R. S., and D. P. Olson. 1972. An evaluation of waterfowl surveys on the New Hampshire coastline. J. Wildl. Manage. 36:468–477.

U. S. Department of Agriculture. Forest Service, Alaska Region. 1978. Tongass land management plan—draft environmental statement. June. Series R 10-29:11.

41

Dabbling Duck Harvest Dynamics in the Central Valley of California— Implications for Recruitment

Michael R. Miller, John Beam, and Daniel P. Connelly

Abstract: Age and sex ratios and body weights were obtained for northern pintails (*Anas acuta*), mallards (*A. platyrhynchos*), American wigeon (*A. americana*), green-winged teal (*A. crecca*), and northern shovelers (*A. clypeata*) shot at Mendota State Wildlife Area in the San Joaquin Valley (SANJV) and at Sacramento National Wildlife Refuge in the Sacramento Valley (SACV) during 1982-83 and 1983-84. Age ratios were determined for pintails at four locations during 1980-83. Cooperative Waterfowl Parts Collection Survey (1982-84; U.S. Fish and Wildlife Service) and California preseason-banding data (1973-77, for mallards and pintails) also were used to measure age ratios of the California harvest. Harvest rate (ducks shot per day) was obtained and summed from all SACV and SANJV public hunting areas in 1982-84. All species except female wigeon and adult female mallards lost weight between October and January. Except for wigeon, harvest rate was high in October when hunting began. Harvest rates were low in November and December but rose markedly in January in the SACV for all species and for all except pintails in the SANJV. Proportion of adults in the bag as measured by all methods increased progressively through the hunting season. Proportion of adults in the harvest was higher in 1982-83 than in 1983-84 and was greater in the SACV than the SANJV both years for most species. Adult females formed a small component of total kill but 50% or more of female kill. The harvest of pintails at a SACV and a SANJV location consistently contained about half as many immatures per adult as that at two other California locations for 1980-83. The substantial harvest of adults in January eliminates the most productive breeders from the

Waterfowl in Winter.© 1988 University of Minnesota. Edited by Milton W. Weller and published by the University of Minnesota Press, Minneapolis.

population. Thus, winter hunting mortality may influence age composition of the spring flight and, hence, recruitment potential of the breeding population.

Recent proposals to extend California duck hunting seasons into February (Bartonek 1983) and implementation of stabilized duck-hunting regulations by the U.S. Fish and Wildlife Service (USFWS) nationwide have led to a need for age, sex, and body weight data of harvested ducks to evaluate the potential impact of regulation changes on population status and recruitment potentials. Present estimates of age and sex ratios of harvested ducks are based on national wing collections from the USFWS's Cooperative Waterfowl Parts Collection Survey (Martin and Carney 1977, Carney et al. 1982) and are issued as annual state summaries. More detailed temporal (five-day period) and geographic (county) compilations are available upon request, but wing samples are small. Wing collections may be biased to early-season samples (Martin and Carney 1977), and detailed, comprehensive analyses have been published only for mallards (Martin and Carney 1977). Body weight, often adjusted for structural size, may measure condition (Hanson 1962, Owen and Cook 1977, Wishart 1979, Bailey 1979, Chappel and Titman 1983) or stress (Harris 1970, Bennett and Bolen 1978) and thus be sensitive to harvest regulations. Virtually no information is available on seasonal changes in age and sex composition of the duck harvest or body weights of ducks in California at specific state wildlife area (SWA) and national wildlife refuge (NWR) hunting areas.

Our purpose is to report results of a multiyear effort to obtain baseline information on age and sex composition of the harvest and on body weights of five dabbling duck species shot at public hunting areas in California. We offer possible explanations for the patterns detected and assess the potential impact of extended hunting seasons on recruitment.

We thank R. K. Anstead, J. A. Bauer, J. M. Bigham, H. A. George, and numerous seasonal aides of the California Department of Fish and Game (CDFG) and T. J. Charmley, L. N. Dean, J. M. Hicks, and G. Kramer of the USFWS for cooperation and assistance at check stations. We are grateful to J. Y. Pirot, W. C. Reinecker, and R. D. Titman for permission to use unpublished data. S. M. Carney kindly provided printed summaries of age-ratio data from the Parts Collection Survey. We thank California hunters who patiently and willingly allowed us to examine their ducks. D. S. Gilmer provided administrative support and encouragement for the study and provided helpful suggestions to improve the manuscript. L. J. Adams compiled harvest data and J. M. Hicks typed the manuscript. We thank J. C. Bartonek, L. M. Cowardin, D. S. Gilmer, P. A. Opler, and A. B. Sargeant for careful review and helpful comments on earlier drafts of the manuscript. D. H. Johnson and D. W. Sparling conducted statistical analyses and reviewed the manuscript.

Methods

During the 1982-83 and 1983-84 waterfowl seasons, sex, age, and weight were determined for samples of northern pintails (*Anas acuta*), mallards (*A. platyrhynchos*), American wigeon (*A. americana*), green-winged teal (*A. crecca*), and northern shovelers (*A. clypeata*) shot by hunters at Mendota SWA and Sacramento NWR in the San Joaquin (SANJV) and Sacramento (SACV) valleys, respectively (together making up the Central Valley; fig. 41.1). These five species were chosen because they collectively form more than 80% of the duck harvest on public areas in California. Harvest on these areas forms about 10% of the statewide total (CDFG, unpubl. data). Sex was determined from external morphological charac-

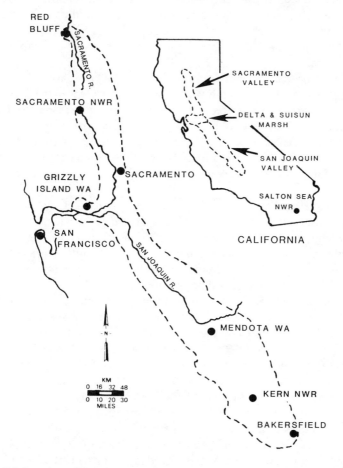

Fig. 41.1. Locations of Sacramento, Kern, and Salton Sea national wildlife refuges (NWR) and of Mendota and Grizzly Island state wildlife areas (SWA) in California.

teristics and age was determined from wing plumage characters (Carney 1964). Weights were obtained to the nearest 5 g using Pesola spring scales (mention of specific product name does not constitute endorsement by USFWS).

Samples were obtained at each area on two to five Wednesdays and Saturdays per month during October, November, December, and January each year (legal shoot days were weekends and Wednesdays). October samples included opening day of the season (Saturday) and the following Wednesday; January samples included the last Wednesday and Saturday of the season. November and December were each sampled during the second and third weeks. On each sampling day, all ducks from as many hunters as possible were examined (about 75-95% of all ducks checked out at Sacramento NWR and about 33-50% at Mendota SWA). Additionally, pintail wings were collected from hunters at Kern NWR, Salton Sea NWR, Sacramento NWR, and Grizzly Island SWA (fig. 41.1) during the 1980-81, 1981-82, and 1982-83 hunting seasons to measure geographic variation in age ratios.

Harvest rate (mean number of ducks per day) was obtained from daily hunter success reports from all SWA and NWR public hunting areas in the SACV (five areas) and SANJV (six areas). Recoveries of California preseason-banded pintails and mallards (1973-77) were used to compare recovery rates of adults and immatures (W. R. Reinecker, unpubl. data). Cooperative Waterfowl Parts Collection Survey data for 1982-83 and 1983-84 were used to determine age composition of the total California harvest of the five species to compare with check station results.

We measured selected factors possibly associated with harvest rate. We obtained the numbers of hunters per week and of ducks bagged per day from Sacramento NWR and Mendota SWA. Population size is of interest, but meaningful correlation analysis was not possible between monthly means of population size and harvest rate because only three months' data were available. Therefore, we ocularly compared trends of harvest rate and population size (aerial and ground counts of NWRS, SWAs, and private lands) for November through January. Total kilometers of wind per month, a measure of storm activity, and temperature were obtained for the SACV from Climatological Data reports (National Oceanic and Atmospheric Administration 1982-84). The number of hunting days with fog and other weather types and bag per hunter were determined from records kept at the hunter check station at Sacramento NWR.

We analyzed harvest rates (ducks per day) with a two-way analysis of variance (ANOVA) using location (SACV or SANJV), month, and their interaction as explanatory variables to test the hypothesis that there was no difference among months or between locations in the rate of duck harvest. To test a posteriori monthly contrasts, we used Tukey's studentized range test (Steel and Torrie 1980). We tested the hypothesis that body weights did not vary among locations, years, or months with a three-way ANOVA. Only months displayed consistent differences in preliminary tests, so we further tested these with Tukey's test. We used the Functional Categorical Technique (PROC FUNCAT; Statistical Analysis System 1982) to analyze age and sex-ratio variation among years, months, and locations (Sacramento NWR or Mendota SWA) for each species. This method is analogous to an ANOVA for categorical data. PROC FUNCAT was also applied to the Parts Collection Survey data. We transformed age ratios of pintail wings collected from 1980 to 1983 at Sacramento, Salton Sea, and Kern NWRs, and at Grizzly Island SWA with the arcsine transformation and tested the hypothesis of no difference among location or years with a two-way ANOVA followed by Tukey's test.

Results

Harvest Rate

Significant differences were found in harvest rate among months for each species and area ($P < 0.004$). Tukey's tests showed that the harvest rate was higher in October than in midwinter (November and December; $P < 0.05$) except for shovelers and wigeon in the SANJV ($P > 0.05$; fig. 41.2). Harvest rate increased markedly in January for all species in the SACV ($P < 0.05$). In the SANJV,

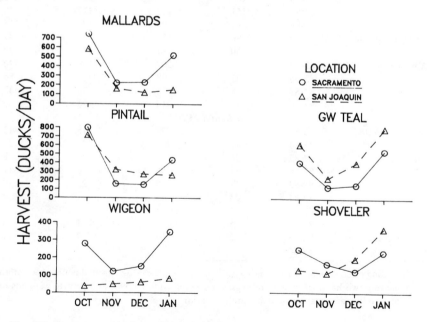

Fig. 41.2. Harvest rate (ducks per day) of dabbling ducks shot during October, November, December, and January (all legal shoot days per month) at all Sacramento (five areas) and San Joaquin (six areas) Valley public hunting areas, 1982-83 and 1983-84.

January harvest rates exceeded those at midwinter or October ($P < 0.05$) except for pintails ($P < 0.05$).

Ocular examination of trends in duck numbers (table 41.1) vs. harvest rate (see fig. 41.2) in individual years showed increasing harvest rates with declining populations in 9 of a possible 20 (five species, two years, two valleys) comparisons. Marked increases in harvest rate in January occurred in another nine comparisons, whereas little or no change occurred in duck abundance. A potential positive relation was found in the other two comparisons (shovelers and wigeon in the SANJV).

Table 41.1. Numbers (thousands) of dabbling ducks recorded each month on Sacramento[a] and San Joaquin[b] Valley wetlands during 1982-83 and 1983-84

Species	Year	Month			
		October	November	December	January
Sacramento Valley					
Northern pintail	82-83	480	340	357	225
	83-84	188	175	398	280
Mallard	82-83	151	137	177	178
	83-84	82	96	128	125
Green-winged teal	82-83	80	128	148	107
	83-84	60	81	90	78
American wigeon	82-83	88	207	149	120
	83-84	33	78	106	85
Shoveler	82-83	18	71	76	43
	83-84	12	18	76	60
San Joaquin Valley					
Northern pintail	82-83	28	28	18	13
	83-84	73	58	42	33
Mallard	82-83	26	30	25	8
	83-84	38	53	38	17
Green-winged teal	82-83	12	20	29	20
	83-84	24	19	61	38
American wigeon	82-83	0.1	1	1	2
	83-84	0.5	1	1	4
Northern shoveler	82-83	2	3	7	11
	83-84	7	5	9	21

[a] Including three national wildlife refuges. Values are means of two ground counts per month.
[b] Including two national wildlife refuges, three state wildlife areas, and private wetlands and reservoirs. Values are from one aerial count per month.

In 1982-83, the number of hunters per week increased 20% (396 to 472) at Sacramento NWR and 50% (581 to 879) at Mendota SWA from December to January. Furthermore, ducks bagged per hunter increased 75% (1.04 to 1.82) and

33% (1.94 to 2.59) over the same period on the two areas, respectively. Similar trends were found in 1983-84.

Harvest Age and Sex Ratios

Sex and age were determined for 9,457 ducks sampled at Sacramento NWR and Mendota SWA. Females formed a smaller proportion of sampled adults than of immatures for pintails, wigeon, and shovelers ($P < 0.001$; fig. 41.3). There were no

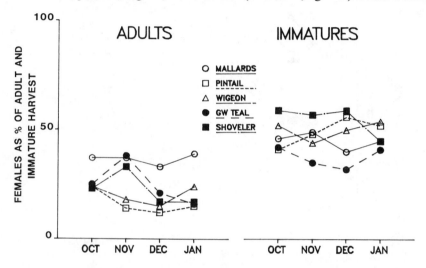

Fig. 41.3. Females as percentage of mallard, northern pintail, American wigeon, green-winged teal, and northern shoveler harvest sampled at check stations (Sacramento National Wildlife Refuge and Mendota State Wildlife Area, 1982-83 and 1983-84 data combined).

differences ($P = 0.252$) in green-winged teal because of a large proportion of females in the kill of adults in November. In mallards, females made up a similar proportion of the kill of adults and immatures ($P = 0.652$). There were no location or year differences in sex ratio of immatures for any species or for adult mallards ($P > 0.05$). There were more females in the harvest of adult teal and pintails in 1982-83 than in 1983-84 ($P < 0.001$) and at Sacramento than at Mendota ($P < 0.001$). The proportion of females among sampled adults declined through the season ($P < 0.001$) except for no change in mallards ($P = 0.656$) and an increase in January for wigeon ($P < 0.001$; fig. 41.3); there were no monthly changes for immatures consistent among species.

The proportion of adult males in the sampled harvest at check stations ($P < 0.001$) and as measured by the Cooperative Waterfowl Parts Collection Survey ($P < 0.001$; fig. 41.4) increased for all five species as the season progressed. Adult females made up a small but increasing (except green-winged teal; $P > 0.05$)

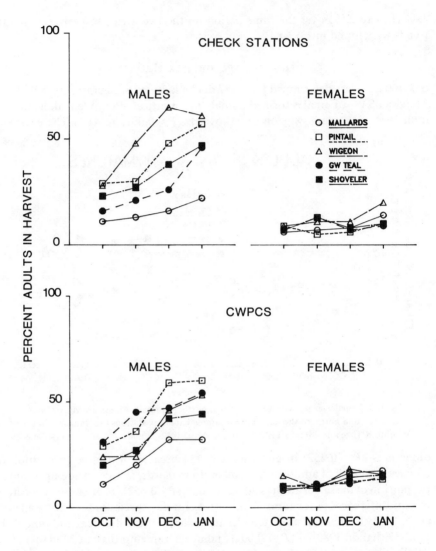

Fig. 41.4. Adults as percentage of harvest of mallards, northern pintails, American wigeon, green-winged teal, and northern shovelers sampled at check stations. Top: Sacramento National Wildlife Refuge and Mendota State Wildlife Area, 1982-83 and 1983-84 data combined; bottom: as determined from 1982-84 Cooperative Waterfowl Parts Collection surveys (CWPCS) for California.

component of the sampled harvest ($P < 0.001$) through the season. At check stations, adult males as a percentage of male harvest, and adult females as a percentage of female harvest, increased markedly to January each year for all

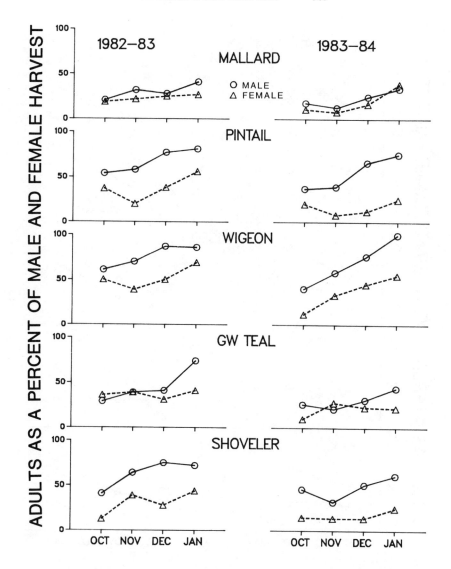

Fig. 41.5. Adult males as percentage of male harvest and adult females as percentage of female harvest of mallards, northern pintails, American wigeon, green-winged teal, and northern shovelers sampled at check stations (Sacramento National Wildlife Refuge and Mendota State Wildlife Area data combined) in 1982-83 and 1983-84.

species ($P < 0.001$) except female green-winged teal ($P > 0.05$; fig. 41.5). In 1982-83, there was a greater proportion of adults in the bag than in 1983-84 for all species ($P < 0.008$) except mallards ($P > 0.05$; fig. 41.5).

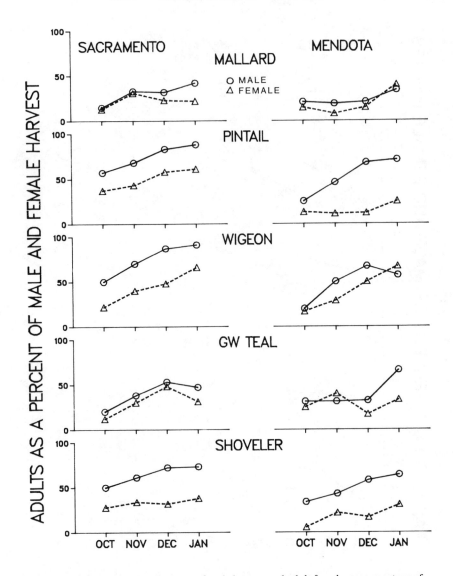

Fig. 41.6. Adult males as percentage of male harvest and adult females as percentage of female harvest of mallards, northern pintails, American wigeon, green-winged teal, and northern shovelers (1982-83 and 1983-84 combined) sampled at Sacramento National Wildlife Refuge and Mendota State Wildlife Area.

Geographic differences existed in the proportion of adult males and females in the harvest ($P < 0.001$; fig. 41.6). Greater proportions of adult male and female pintails and shovelers were taken on Sacramento NWR than on Mendota SWA ($P < 0.007$). Too few wigeon were sampled at Mendota for valid comparisons (0-23 per month), and no differences were detected between areas for mallards and green-winged teal ($P > 0.05$). Geographic differences may be consistent among years: examination of 6,016 wings showed that the harvest of pintails at Sacramento and Kern NWRs consistently contained about half as many immatures per adult as those at Grizzly Island SWA and Salton Sea NWR from 1980 to 1983 ($P < 0.001$; table 41.2).

Table 41.2. Immature ducks per adult duck in pintail harvest at specific geographic areas in California, 1980-83 ($N = 6,016$)

Area	1980-81	1981-82	1982-83
Sacramento National Wildlife Refuge	0.46	0.45	0.43
Kern National Wildlife Refuge	0.43	0.38	0.57
Grizzly Island State Wildlife Area	1.03	0.85	1.18
Salton Sea National Wildlife Refuge	0.97	0.70	. . .[a]

[a]No wings collected.

Band returns of California preseason-banded pintails and mallards showed that the harvest of immatures was concentrated in the first third and of adults in the last third of the season. For example, weekly percentages of total season recoveries increased from 4-6% the first week to 13-14% the last week for adults, but they declined from 15-18% to 4-5% during this period for immatures (93-day season beginning mid-October). Over half (50-53%) of recoveries occurred during the last third of the season for adults, compared with 21-26% for immatures.

Body Weights

Body weights were obtained from 4,172 ducks. Except for adult female mallards and immature male and adult and immature female wigeon ($P < 0.05$), each age-sex class of all species lost weight between October and January ($P < 0.03$; fig. 41.7). There were no consistent differences in these patterns between years or areas. Females weighed less than males, and immatures weighed less than adults ($P < 0.05$).

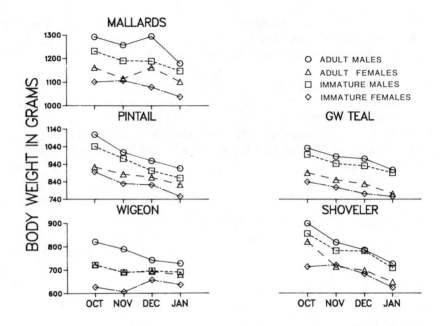

Fig. 41.7. Monthly mean body weight (grams) of mallards, northern pintails, American wigeon, green-winged teal, and northern shovelers (Sacramento National Wildlife Refuge and Mendota State Wildlife Area, 1982-83 and 1983-84 data combined).

Discussion

Harvest Rate

Naiveté of ducks to hunting and large proportions of juveniles in local populations during opening weekend caused high harvest rates in October (Bellrose et al. 1961, Martin and Carney 1977, Hochbaum and Walters 1984). Presumably, experienced ducks were less available to shooting in November and December when harvest rate was low, but seemingly not in January when harvest rate increased. January harvest rate may have reflected any or a combination of (1) increased populations in the area of harvest, (2) migration and distributional changes of subpopulations, (3) increased hunter participation and success, (4) low body weight and behavioral changes in January, and (5) adverse meteorological conditions conducive to harvest, e.g., wind and fog.

The absence of a consistent positive relationship between population size and harvest rate suggests that duck abundance on NWR and SWA sanctuaries does not necessarily govern daily harvest rate. However, this result is tentative in the absence of rigorous correlation analyses. In Manitoba, the number of ducks passing within 35 m of a hunting site and retrieved kill per hour were independent of local population size (Hochbaum and Walters 1984).

Major shifts in population among areas within the Central Valley occur during winter (W. C. Reinecker, unpubl. data) and could increase vulnerability until ducks became familiar with the new area. Migration and local movements could become more common in late winter because of poor weather and the expansion of habitat by flooding.

Increased hunter participation was a factor in the high January harvest rate, but kill in January was associated also with increased bag per hunter. Thus, more hunters took more ducks per hunter, suggesting that ducks were more available for harvest late in the year. This is contrary to results in Manitoba during October, where vulnerability of ducks was inversely proportional to hunter numbers (Hochbaum and Walters 1984).

All species except female wigeon weighed least in January when harvest rate was high. Weight losses in dabbling ducks are common during winter (Folk et al. 1966, Douthwaite 1976, Owen and Cook 1977, Paulus 1980), perhaps resulting in increased probability of hunting mortality if thin ducks forage more in areas subject to hunting. Courtship activity in midwinter (Hepp and Hair 1983) also may affect availability of ducks to hunting.

High duck harvests are traditionally, though not consistently (see Hochbaum and Walters 1984), associated with poor weather conditions. Stormy and cold weather is most common in the Central Valley in December and January (National Oceanic and Atmospheric Administration 1982-84), so harvest could be expected to increase then. However, total kilometers of wind per month was less during January (1983: 4,026 km; 1984: 4,229 km) than December (1982: 5,768 km; 1983: 5,253 km), and wind was recorded at Sacramento's check station on only four shoot days over two years. Wind increased the hunting vulnerability of mallards, but not of canvasbacks (*Aythya valisineria*) or lesser scaup (*A. affinis*), in Manitoba (Hochbaum and Walters 1984). Average daily temperature in the Central Valley was nearly the same in December (9.1-10.4C) and January (8.7-9.4C) both years, so it probably contributed little to the increased harvest rate in January. Foggy days produced larger average bags per hunter than other weather types in January ($P <$ 0.05; t-test), but not in other months. Thus, fog could have contributed to the increased January harvest rates.

Harvest Age and Sex Ratios

The seasonal increase in proportionate harvest of adults that we recorded for all species is supported by data of Munro and Kimball (1982), who found that mean band-recovery dates for mallards across the continent were later for adults than for immatures, and Martin and Carney (1977), who used wing ratios, to show that adults formed an increasing proportion of mallard harvest as the season advanced.

As the season advances, young birds should become as wary as adults, and the harvest age-ratio should thereafter remain the same (Martin and Carney 1977). Where such stability in age ratios was not detected, any or a combination of the following could have occurred: (1) relative vulnerability between adults (low) and immatures (high) did not change during the winter, (2) immatures became less vulnerable relative to adults at a constant or variable rate, or (3) differential age-related migration occurred (Bellrose et al. 1961, Martin and Carney 1977). The last two alternatives have obvious consequences for harvest age-ratios, and the first, though unlikely (see Bellrose et al. 1961), results in a straight-line increase in the proportion of adults harvested as the number of immatures in the population declines. For example, based on the slope of lines in check station data (fig. 41.4), harvest age-ratios may have stabilized in male wigeon; immatures may have become less vulnerable relative to adults, or differential migration may have occurred, in male green-winged teal; and adults and immatures may have maintained their relative vulnerability through the season in male shovelers and pintails.

The breeding season of 1983 was projected to be a better production year than 1982 for the Pacific Flyway (USFWS and Canadian Wildlife Service 1983). This was confirmed by the Cooperative Waterfowl Parts Collection Survey (Sorensen et al. 1984). Check station data for local harvest in 1983-84 reflected this increased availability of immatures. Similarly, assuming immatures were equally vulnerable to shooting relative to adults throughout the Central Valley, proportionately more immatures were available for harvest in the SANJV than the SACV.

In California, 90% of female mallards, pintails, and shovelers and 80% of green-winged teal have mates by January (R. D. Titman and J. Y. Pirot, unpubl. data). Early pairing in American wigeon (Wishart 1983) and gadwalls (*Anas strepera*) (Paulus 1983) is by adults. Pairs formed early are dominant and establish priority to feeding areas (Paulus 1983, Hepp and Hair 1984), are less vulnerable to predation (Wishart 1983), and may be more productive during nesting (Spurr and Milne 1976a, b) than pairs formed later. Thus, continual pair breakup caused by high harvest of paired adults in late season may affect productivity. Increased harvest of adult ducks is important to recruitment because adult female mallards older than one year are nearly twice as effective at hatching nests as first-year nesters (Cowardin et al. 1985). Thus, as hunting continues later into winter, increasing harvest removes from the population an increasing proportion of the most productive breeders.

Few adult females are harvested because hunters select males (Bellrose et al. 1961, Bellrose 1980) and because a large number of adult females have been eliminated by predation; paired and unpaired and adult and immature ducks also select habitat differentially. Males predominated in harvests of adults in the Central Valley, but the sex ratios of harvested immatures were more nearly equal (fig. 41.3), indicating that immature females were more available to hunters than were adult females. Johnson and Sargeant (1977) showed that disparate sex ratios in mallards in North Dakota could be explained by red fox (*Vulpes vulpes*) predation on females during the nesting season. Adult females are more likely to nest than are young birds (Cowardin et al. 1985), so they could suffer higher predation losses. Paulus (1983), for gadwalls in Louisiana, and Hepp and Hair (1984), for several dabblers in North Carolina, found that unpaired females (most likely to be immatures) are displaced from prime winter habitat by adults and pairs. Low body weights and high availability of immatures and low representation of adult females in the California harvest may result if pair habitat is less subject to shooting pressure (e.g., refuge closed zones). Young female mallards survive at rates lower than other sex-age classes (Anderson 1975), and this probably is true for other species.

Management Implications

Low body weights, high pair-formation and harvest rates, and a large proportion of adults in the harvest suggest that January is particularly critical to dabbling duck population dynamics and, thus, management. Geographic and temporal characteristics associated with winter waterfowl harvest may influence survival rates, population levels, age structure of the spring flight, and ultimately recruitment rates. Tacha and Vohs (1984) showed that adults increased proportionately in the harvest of lesser sandhill cranes (*Grus canadensis*) as the hunting season progressed and suggested that shortened seasons may protect adults, the most productive component of the population.

Harvest of male mallards seems to be fully compensated for by reduced natural mortality (Anderson and Burnham 1976, Rogers et al. 1979, Nichols and Hines 1983, Burnham et al. 1984, Burnham and Anderson 1984, Nichols et al. 1984). Analyses, however, were inconclusive for adult (Burnham et al. 1984, Burnham and Anderson 1984) and immature females (Nichols and Hines 1983), and data from other species generally are not of sufficient quality or quantity to differentiate between compensatory or additive mortality processes (Nichols et al. 1984). Anderson and Burnham (1976) suggested a threshold point above which hunting mortality becomes additive. This point may be exceeded when, and in areas where, ducks are numerous and particularly vulnerable. Hunting mortality may not be compensatory for adult females in years of poor production (e.g., 1982) when adults formed a relatively large proportion of the harvest.

Our data suggest that modification of timing and geography of harvest, especially in years of poor production, may improve recruitment by increasing survival of the most productive components of the population. However, the trends we have identified need to be verified by expanded studies to obtain information on the much larger (90%) harvest on private lands. Finally, application of our results to harvest management awaits final resolution of the debate concerning the compensatory or additive nature of hunting mortality.

LITERATURE CITED

Anderson, D. R. 1975. Population ecology of the mallard: V. Temporal and geographic estimates of survival, recovery, and harvest rates. U.S. Fish Wildl. Serv. Resour. Publ. 125. 110pp.

———, and K. P. Burnham. 1976. Population ecology of the mallard: VI. The effect of exploitation on survival. U.S. Fish Wildl. Serv. Resour. Publ. 128. 66pp.

Bailey, R. O. 1979. Methods of estimating total lipid content in the redhead duck (*Aythya americana*) and an evaluation of condition indices. Can. J. Zool. 57:1830–1833.

Bartonek, J. C. 1983. Pacific Flyway study committee minutes. Pac. Fly. Waterfowl Rep. 90:1–12.

Bellrose, F. C. 1980. Ducks, geese and swans of North America. Stackpole Books, Harrisburg, Pa. 540pp.

———, T. G. Scott, A. S. Hawkins, and J. B. Low. 1961. Sex ratios and age ratios in North American ducks. Ill. Nat. Hist. Surv. Bull. 27:391–474.

Bennett, J. W., and E. G. Bolen. 1978. Stress response in wintering green-winged teal. J. Wild. Manage. 42:81–86.

Burnham, K. P., and D. R. Anderson. 1984. Tests of compensatory vs. additive hypotheses of mortality in mallards. Ecol. 64:105–112.

———, G. C. White, and D. R. Anderson. 1984. Estimating the effect of hunting on annual survival rates of adult mallards. J. Wildl. Manage. 48:350–361.

Carney, S. M. 1964. Preliminary keys to waterfowl age and sex identification by means of wing plumage. U.S. Fish Wildl. Serv. Spec. Sci. Rep. Wildl. 82. 47pp.

———, M. F. Sorensen, and E. M. Martin. 1982. Waterfowl harvest surveys. Pages 15-17 *in* J. F. Voelzer, E. Q. Lauxen, S. L. Rhoades, and K. D. Norman, eds. Waterfowl status report 1979. U.S. Fish Wildl. Serv. Spec. Sci. Rep. Wildl. 246.

Chappell, W. A., and R. D. Titman. 1983. Estimating reserve lipids in greater scaup (*Aythya marila*) and lesser scaup (*A. affinis*). Can. J. Zool. 61:35–38.

Cowardin, L. M., D. S. Gilmer, and D. W. Shaiffer. 1985. Mallard recruitment in the agricultural environment of North Dakota. Wildl. Monog. 92. 37pp.

Douthwaite, R. J. 1976. Weight changes and wing moult in the red-billed teal. Wildfowl 27:123–127.

Folk, C., K. Hudec, and J. Toufar. 1966. The weight of the mallard, *Anas platyrhynchos* and its changes in the course of the year. Zool. Listy 15:249–260.

Hanson, H. C. 1962. The dynamics of condition factors in Canada geese and their relation to seasonal stresses. Arct. Inst. N. Am. Tech. Pap. 12:1–68.

Harris, H. J., Jr. 1970. Evidence of stress response in breeding blue-winged teal. J. Wildl. Manage. 34:747–755.

Hepp, G. R., and J. D. Hair. 1983. Reproductive behavior and pair chronology in wintering dabbling ducks. Wilson Bull. 95:675–682.

———, and ———. 1984. Dominance in wintering waterfowl (Anatini): effects on distribution of sexes. Condor 86:251–257.

Hochbaum, G. S., and C. J. Walters. 1984. Components of hunting mortality in ducks: a management analysis. Can. Wildl. Serv. Occas. Pap. 52. 29pp.

Johnson, D. H., and A. B. Sargeant. 1977. Impact of red fox predation on the sex ratio of prairie mallards. U.S. Fish Wildl. Serv. Resour. Rep. 6. 56pp.

Martin, E. M., and S. M. Carney. 1977. Population ecology of the mallard: IV. A review of duck hunting regulations, activity, and success with special reference to the mallard. U.S. Fish Wildl. Serv. Resour. Publ. 130. 137pp.

Munro, R. E., and C. F. Kimball. 1982. Population ecology of the mallard: VII. Distribution and derivation of the harvest. U.S. Fish Wildl. Serv. Resour. Publ. 147. 127pp.

National Oceanic and Atmospheric Administration. 1982-84. Climatological data, California. 86:10–12; 87:1, 10–12; 88:1.

Nichols, J. D., M. J. Conroy, D. R. Anderson, and K, P. Burnham. 1984. Compensatory mortality in waterfowl populations: a review of the evidence and implications for research and management. Trans. N. Am. Wildl. Nat. Resour. Conf. 49:535–554.

———, and J. E. Hines. 1983. The relationship between harvest and survival rates of mallards: a straightforward approach with partitioned data sets. J. Wildl. Manage. 47:334–348.

Owen, M., and W. A. Cook. 1977. Variations in body weight, wing length, and condition of mallard *Anas platyrhynchos platyrhynchos* and their relationship to environmental changes. J. Zool. Lond. 183:377–395.

Paulus, S. L. 1980. The winter ecology of the gadwall in Louisiana. M.S. Thesis, Univ. North Dakota, Grand Forks. 357pp.

———. 1983. Dominance relations, resource use, and pairing chronology of gadwalls in winter. Auk 100:947–952.

Rogers, J. P., J. D. Nichols, F. W. Martin, C. F. Kimball, and R. S. Pospahala. 1979. An examination of harvest and survival rates of ducks in relation to hunting. Trans. N. Am. Wildl. Nat. Resour. Conf. 44:114–126.

Sorensen, M. F., S. M. Carney, and E. M. Martin. 1984. Age and sex composition of ducks and geese harvested in the 1983 hunting season in comparison with prior years. U.S. Fish Wildl. Serv., Off. Mig. Bird Manage., Admin. Rep. 28 June.

Spurr, E. B., and H. Milne. 1976a. Adaptive significance of autumn pair formation in the common eider *Somateria mollissima*. Ornis Scand. 7:85–89.

———, and ———. 1976b. Factors affecting laying data in the common eider. Wildfowl 27:107–109.

Statistical Analysis System. 1982. User guide: statistics. SAS Institute, Cary, N.C. 584pp.

Steel, R. G. D., and J. H. Torrie. 1980. Principles and procedures of statistics. McGraw-Hill, New York. 633pp.

Tacha, T. C., and P. A. Vohs. 1984. Some population parameters of sandhill cranes from mid-continental North America. J. Wildl. Manage. 48:89–98.

U.S. Fish and Wildlife Service and Canadian Wildlife Service. 1983. Status of waterfowl and fall flight forecast. U.S. Fish Wildl. Serv., Off. Mig. Bird Manage. 26pp.

Wishart, R. A. 1979. Indices of structural size and condition of American wigeon (*Anas americana*). Can. J. Zool. 57:2369–2374.

———. 1983. Pairing chronology and mate selection in the American wigeon (*Anas americana*). Can. J. Zool. 61:1733–1743.

42

Workshop Summary: Species and Population Status and Distribution

James D. Nichols, Dirk V. Derksen, Robert L. Jarvis, and John T. Ratti

Population Estimation and Assessment

Estimation of the size of a free-ranging avian population is a difficult task, and a great deal of effort has been devoted to the development of methodologies to be used for this purpose (e.g., see Ralph and Scott 1981, Seber 1982). Historically, there have been numerous efforts to estimate the size of various wintering waterfowl populations. The success of these efforts has varied substantially, depending on such factors as methods used, geographic range of the population of interest, habitat characteristics of surveyed areas, and behavioral characteristics of the species. It probably is unrealistic to try to develop a general winter waterfowl survey that provides precise, reliable estimates of population size for all species wintering in North America. Instead, it is perhaps more reasonable to monitor the more abundant, prairie-nesting species using estimates from the May breeding-ground survey (Martin et al. 1979). For species not covered well by this survey, but for which information on population size is critical, special winter surveys can be designed, as has been done experimentally for the American black duck (*Anas rubripes*) (M. J. Conroy, pers. commun.), canvasback (*Aythya valisineria*) (Haramis et al. 1985), and many specific populations of geese. Conant, et al. (1987) demonstrated that it is possible to obtain reliable estimates of the size of wintering waterfowl populations even under adverse conditions, provided that sufficient effort is directed at the estimation problem. The survey effort reported by Conant et al. differed from many other winter waterfowl surveys in three critical respects: it was established using a formal sampling design, it included replicate counts, and it included a ground-truth effort to estimate the proportion of birds not seen from the air.

The allocation of funds and effort to surveys designed to estimate population size is a decision that requires careful consideration. Wildlife biologists sometimes place too much emphasis on the need for accurate estimates of such quantities as population size. Even if we knew the exact number of birds in a population for each of a number of years, this information alone would not be adequate for informed population management. For this, we would require some knowledge of the functional relationships between reproductive and survival rates (the two variables that effect change in population size) and such things as management actions and various environmental variables. Certainly, good estimates by themselves will not necessarily result in good management.

Population Status

Population status is neither easily defined nor assessed. Possible metrics reflecting status include the rate of population increase or the probability of a population declining by a specified amount. Management plans for many North American waterfowl species include *population objectives*, which are simply population sizes judged desirable by managers. When population size is estimated to be below such a numerical objective, efforts are made to bring about increases through available management options (including harvest regulations). Some biologists believe that it is inappropriate to set specific numerical objectives in the face of ever-changing habitat conditions and environmental fluctuations. However, other biologists believe that, in the absence of any other method of specifying management objectives, some sort of population goal is needed. A major challenge to waterfowl managers will be to develop at least semiobjective decision criteria and associated management strategies for use in times of decreasing habitat bases.

A Case History: Alaskan Geese

Three species of geese that nest primarily on the Yukon-Kuskokwim Delta in western Alaska have been significantly reduced in their populations in the past 20 years. Cackling Canada geese (*Branta canadensis minima*) have declined over 90%, from the 1965 estimate of 350,000 to 26,200 in 1983 and 21,800 in 1984. Pacific white-fronted geese (*Anser albifrons frontalis*) have declined by 78%, from 450,000 counted in the fall of 1967 to 112,900 in 1983 and 100,200 in 1984. Emperor geese (*Chen canagica*) have declined 49% in twenty years; 139,000 were counted in 1964, whereas only 71,000 were found in a spring survey conducted in 1984. Additionally, estimated numbers of black brant (*Branta bernicla nigricans*) nesting on the Yukon-Kuskokwim Delta have declined by about 50% from 1981 to 1984.

The factors responsible for these dramatic declines of goose populations may include alteration or loss of wintering habitat, disease and contaminants, and overharvest. Spring and summer hunting on the Delta includes harvest of prenesting birds, nesting birds and their eggs, molting birds, and adults with goslings. Relatively few reliable quantitative data on the magnitude and composition of the spring and summer harvest are available. Monitoring of the harvest is impeded by the remoteness of the area where hunting occurs, the inability of resource agencies to overcome political considerations, and cultural and language differences between Yupik Eskimos and management personnel. The situation is further complicated by a suit brought against the Department of Interior and the Alaska Department of Fish and Game by a private sportsmen's group in late May 1984. That suit charges the defendants with violation of the Migratory Bird Treaty Act (MBTA) of 1918 and four treaties with foreign countries (Canada, Mexico, Japan, and the Soviet Union). Furthermore, a statewide native organization filed a cross-claim against the U.S. Fish and Wildlife Service charging that the Alaska Game Act of 1925 amended the MBTA to permit Alaska natives to harvest migratory waterfowl for subsistence uses without regard to regulations adopted pursuant to the MBTA. The 1916 Migratory Bird Treaty between the United States and Canada (as implemented by the MBTA of 1918) prohibits virtually all hunting of waterfowl between 10 March and 1 September. However, spring and summer hunting of waterfowl has been a customary and traditional subsistence activity that continues to be practiced today in some rural Alaska communities. The United States and Canada have been negotiating a protocol amendment to the treaty that would allow a managed subsistence harvest of waterfowl, but the matter has not yet been resolved.

In the meantime, the Association of Village Council Presidents, which represents natives in western Alaska; the U.S. Fish and Wildlife Service; Alaska Department of Fish and Game; and agencies in other Pacific Flyway states have developed written agreements in 1984 and 1985 to reduce the harvest of geese throughout the flyway, to set population goals for these species, and to conduct additional research on population dynamics and ecology of arctic nesting geese in Alaska and wintering areas.

Recovery of these populations to historical levels may take decades, requiring the cooperation of resource agency personnel, sport and subsistence hunters, and the general public. Clearly, this is one of the most challenging resource issues of the 1980s.

Concluding Comments

Obtaining some knowledge of population status and then acting on that knowledge to try to bring about desired changes in population size are central to the management of natural animal populations. When viewed from one perspective, all of the contributions to this volume can be thought of as efforts to understand the factors associated with changes in waterfowl population status. The logistical constraints imposed by the great mobility and widespread distribution of North American waterfowl combine with tight social and political constraints to make population-level experimentation virtually impossible. The central challenge to waterfowl managers and biologists is to learn enough about the workings of waterfowl populations, in spite of these formidable constaints, to do a reasonable job of population management.

LITERATURE CITED

Conant, B., J. G. King, J. L. Trapp, and J. I. Hodges. 1988. Estimating populations of ducks wintering in southeast Alaska. Pages 541-551 *in* M. W. Weller, ed. Waterfowl in winter. Univ. Minnesota Press, Minneapolis.

Haramis, G. M., J. R. Goldsberry, D. G. McAuley, and E. L. Derleth. 1985. An aerial photographic census of Chesapeake Bay and North Carolina canvasbacks. J. Wildl. Manage. 49:449-454.

Martin, F. W., R. S. Pospahala, and J. D. Nichols. 1979. Assessment and population management of North American migratory birds. Pages 187-239 *in* J. Cairns, G. P. Patil, and W. E. Waters, eds. Environmental biomonitoring, assessment, prediction, and management—certain case studies and related quantitative issues. Stat. Ecol. 11. Int. Coop. Publ. House, Fairland, Md.

Ralph, C. J., and J. M. Scott, eds. 1981. Estimating numbers of terrestrial birds. Stud. Avian Biol. 6. 630pp.

Seber, G. A. F. 1982. The estimation of animal abundance and related parameters. Macmillan, New York. 672pp.

43

Workshop Summary: Hunting Vulnerability and Mortality

Frank Montalbano III, Douglas H. Johnson, Michael R. Miller, and Donald H. Rusch

During the past decade, Anderson and Burnham (1976) challenged traditional theory regarding the relationships between hunting mortality and annual survival rates for North American mallards (*Anas platyrhynchos*). They argued that the considerable evidence suggesting relationships between harvest rates and annual mortality rates for a number of waterfowl species was based on inappropriate correlations of statistically dependent data. Anderson and Burnham (1976) defined and tested two distinct hypotheses and reexamined the effect of harvest on survival rate using independent measurements. They subsequently rejected the hypothesis that hunting is a completely additive form of mortality in the populations studied and concluded that the relationship between natural and hunting mortality was a largely compensatory process below a threshold mortality rate. They also reasoned that once this threshold rate was exceeded, hunting mortality became additive.

Subsequent work (Rogers et al. 1979. Anderson et al. 1982, Nichols and Hines 1983, Burnham and Anderson 1984, Burnham et al. 1984, Nichols et al. 1984) has generally supported and expanded upon the findings of Anderson and Burnham (1976) for mallard populations banded before the hunting season. Rakestraw (1981) provided evidence consistent with the compensatory mortality hypothesis for a sample of postseason-banded mallards. The relationship between hunting mortality and annual survival rates also has been investigated for canvasbacks (*Aythya valisineria*) (Nichols and Haramis 1980) and ring-necked ducks (*Aythya collaris*) (Conroy and Eberhardt 1983), but results were inconclusive with respect to competing hypotheses of additive and compensatory mortality.

Waterfowl in Winter.© 1988 University of Minnesota. Edited by Milton W. Weller and published by the University of Minnesota Press, Minneapolis.

Compensatory mortality theory has become a philosophical cornerstone of regulatory programs for waterfowl since publication of Anderson and Burnham's (1976) findings (Burnham et al. 1984, 351). However, several authors (Pollock and Raveling 1982, Bartonek et al. 1984, Johnson et al. 1987) have raised questions regarding the appropriate interpretation and application of current theory in the regulatory process. Pollock and Raveling (1982) and Johnson et al. (1987) suggested that heterogeneous survival or recovery rates in banded samples may contribute to spurious conclusions regarding population status. Of particular concern is the suggestion that heterogeneity can foster an illusion of compensation in band-recovery analyses (Johnson et al. 1987). Heterogeneity within sex and age groups is documented in certain populations of Canada geese (*Branta canadensis*) (Pollock and Raveling 1982) and mallards (Anderson 1975, 18; Johnson and Sargeant 1977; G. Hepp, pers. commun.). Nichols et al. (1982) acknowledged and further discussed the problems resulting from heterogeneity in banding data, but they concluded that the level of heterogeneity normally encountered in real data sets produces relatively small biases in average survival rates. Nevertheless, heterogeneity as a false indicator of compensation (Johnson et al. 1987) remains a problem in band-recovery analyses.

Johnson et al. (1984) and Bartonek et al. (1984), respectively, expressed concern that the threshold beyond which hunting mortality becomes additive may be frequently exceeded in some mottled duck (*Anas fulvigula*) and mallard populations. Anderson and Burnham (1976) indeed acknowledged that the threshold may easily be exceeded on a local basis.

Although compensatory mortality is well documented for male mallards, studies have been less conclusive for females (Nichols and Hines 1983, Burnham et al. 1984, Burnham and Anderson 1984, Nichols et al. 1984). This population segment would seem especially critical to maintenance of overall population stationarity.

Thus, the conclusion that hunting mortality is largely compensatory in the North American mallard population during the periods examined may provide a false sense of security regarding the effects of harvest on populations of other species of waterfowl, on certain geographic populations of mallards, and on North American mallard populations in the very recent past. For these reasons, the group participants believed that a discussion of the competing hypotheses of additive and compensatory mortality was timely and appropriate.

Discussion

Authority and responsibility for formulation of annual waterfowl harvest regulations in the United States were traced from several treaties involving the United States, Great Britain, Canada, the United Mexican States, and Japan, through the Migratory Bird Treaty Act (as amended), to the secretary of the interior. The secretary solicits and considers the suggestions and comments of representatives of the several states, Canadian provinces, and the Canadian federal government through the regional waterfowl flyway councils. A significant amount of information on the status of continental waterfowl populations is collected annually and provided as reports and recommendations by the flyway council technical sections and the U.S. Fish and Wildlife Service's Office of Migratory Bird Management. Despite the quality of the data base that supports the process, sociopolitical considerations often outweigh biological influences.

Recently, stabilized harvest regulation studies have been implemented in the United States and Canada. The belief is widespread among resource managers that these studies focus on compensatory mortality questions. Although the topic is highly debatable, most population biologists seem to agree that (1) stabilized regulations were implemented in an effort to assess the effect of nonregulatory factors on waterfowl harvest, (2) expanded inferences on compensatory mortality were not objectives of the study, and (3) few insights on compensatory/additive mortality hypotheses were expected.

The compensatory mortality theory has become a foundation of the regulatory process. Until the mid 1970s, harvest regulations, and ultimately the magnitude of the annual continental waterfowl harvest, were perceived as important determinants of the size of the subsequent year's breeding population for a number of species. As a result, harvest regulations reflected dramatic shifts in the magnitude of projected fall flights in an effort to stockpile breeding birds during periods of depressed production or survival. The findings of Anderson and Burnham (1976) implied that breeding mallards could not be stockpiled because of the influence of density-dependent factors on population mortality.

Much of the corroborating evidence published subsequent to Anderson and Burnham's (1976) work represents a reexamination of the same or overlapping data sets using different approaches and techniques. Thus, there is some question as to whether such alternative methodologies could be accurately termed *corroboration*. In all probability, the existing North American mallard data sets have been exhausted with regard to their potential to shed light on the question of compensatory mortality.

Information Needs and New Approachs

Most rigorously controlled population studies of lower life forms suggest compensation in survival processes (Anderson and Burnham 1976, 7; Burnham et al. 1984, 358). Several studies supporting the compensatory mortality hypothesis have produced less than conclusive results for certain segments of mallard populations, notably adult females (Anderson and Burnham 1976, Burnham and Anderson 1984, Burnham et al. 1984, Nichols et al. 1984). Although Burnham et al. (1984) could not reject either of the competing hypotheses for the female segment of the population they examined, they concluded that females probably also exhibited highly compensatory nonhunting mortality (Burnham et al. 1984, 358). It was suggested that stronger inferences regarding compensation in male mallards were a function of banded sample sizes (D. R. Anderson, pers. commun.). Burnham et al. (1984, 358) even indicated that the capacity for compensatory mortality was greater in the female segment of the mallard population examined. Nevertheless, a more conclusive assessment of the competing hypotheses with respect to female mallards would contribute greatly to competent management of this species.

More definitive studies of survival processes might best be conducted on geographically isolated populations. Repeated observation of individually marked birds may provide improved estimates of survival in such studies (Pollock and Raveling 1982). The opportunity for repeat observations of each marked bird confers an obvious advantage over conventional banding approaches that generated cumulative recovery rates of only about 15% and 23% for mallards and Canada geese, respectively (file data, U.S. Fish and Wildlife Service, Bird Banding Laboratory).

Low band-reporting rates reduce the precision of survival estimates generated by banding studies. The U.S. Fish and Wildlife Service has traditionally resisted operational reward banding programs because of perceived difficulties that might result from artificially stimulated geographic and temporal variability in reporting rates. However, modern approaches to banding data analysis are not influenced by variability in reporting rates (Anderson 1975, 7). Band solicitation efforts can markedly improve the cost-effectiveness of banding operations, and little justification remains for U.S. Fish and Wildlife Service reluctance in this area.

Past studies attempted to demonstrate correlations between survival and harvest rate estimates from existing data sets (Anderson and Burnham 1976, Rogers et al. 1979, Nichols and Haramis 1980, Anderson et al. 1982, Nichols and Hines 1983, Conroy and Eberhardt 1983, Burnham and Anderson 1984, Burnham et al. 1984). An experimental approach to testing competing mortality hypotheses might provide additional insights. This approach differs from previous studies in that it would seek to vary the survival rate experimentally in a marked population by implementing alternately very liberal and very restrictive harvest regulations over two or more multiyear periods. Black ducks (*Anas rubripes*), Canada geese, and mallards were mentioned as candidate species for this approach. These studies would be labor intensive and involve a multitude of potential problems with public opinion. Nevertheless, such an approach may provide our best hope for additional insights on compensatory/additive mortality hypotheses in wild waterfowl populations.

We are indebted to D. H. Brakhage and F. A. Johnson for their comments on an earlier draft of the manuscript.

LITERATURE CITED

Anderson, D. R. 1975. Population ecology of the mallard: V. Temporal and geographic estimates of survival, recovery and harvest rates. U.S. Fish Wildl. Serv. Resour. Publ. 125. 110pp.

———, and K. P. Burnham. 1976. Population ecology of the mallard: VI. The effect of exploitation on survival. U.S. Fish Wildl. Serv. Resour. Publ. 128. 66pp.

———, ———, and G. C. White. 1982. The effect of exploitation on annual survival of mallard ducks: an ultrastructural model. Int. Biometric Conf. 11:33–39.

Bartonek, J. C., R. J. Blohm, R. K. Brace, F. D. Caswell, K. E. Gamble, H. W. Miller, R. S. Pospahala, and M. M. Smith. 1984. Status and needs of the mallard. Trans. N. Am. Wildl. Nat. Resour. Conf. 49:501–518.

Burnham, K. P., and D. R. Anderson. 1984. Tests of compensatory vs. additive hypotheses of mortality in mallards. Ecol. 65:105–112.

———, G. C. White, and D. R. Anderson. 1984. Estimating the effect of hunting on annual survival rates of adult mallards. J. Wildl. Manage. 48:350–361.

Conroy, M. J., and R. T. Eberhardt. 1983. Variation in survival and recovery rates of ring-necked ducks. J. Wildl. Manage. 47:127–137.

Johnson, D. H., J. D. Nichols, M. J. Conroy, and L. M. Cowardin. 1988. Some considerations in modeling the mallard life cycle. Pages 9-20 in M. W. Weller, ed. Waterfowl in winter. Univ. Minnesota Press, Minneapolis.

———, and A. B. Sargeant. 1977. Impact of red fox predation on the sex ratio of prairie mallards. U.S. Fish Wildl. Serv. Wildl. Res. Rep. 6. 56pp.

Johnson, F. A., F. Montalbano III, and T. C. Hines. 1984. Population dynamics and status of the mottled duck in Florida. J. Wildl. Manage. 48:1137–1184.

Nichols, J. D., M. J. Conroy, D. R. Anderson, and K. P. Burnham. 1984. Compensatory mortality in waterfowl populations: a review of the evidence and implications for research and management. Trans. N. Am. Wildl. Nat. Resour. Conf. 49:535–554.

———, and G. M. Haramis. 1980. Inferences regarding survival and recovery rates of winter-banded canvasbacks. J. Wildl. Manage. 44:164–173.

———, and J. E. Hines. 1983. The relationship between harvest and survival rates of mallards: a straightforward approach with partitioned data sets. J. Wildl. Manage. 47:334–348.

———, S. L. Stokes, J. E. Hines, and M. J. Conroy. 1982. Additional comments on the assumption of homogeneous survival rates in modern bird banding models. J. Wildl. Manage. 46:953–962.

Pollock, K. H., and D. G. Raveling. 1982. Assumptions of modern band-recovery models, with emphasis on heterogeneous survival rates. J. Wildl. Manage. 46:88–98.

Rakestraw, J. L. 1981. Survival and recovery rates of mallards banded postseason in South Carolina. J. Wildl. Manage. 45:1032–1036.

Rogers, J. P., J. D. Nichols, F. W. Martin, C. F. Kimball, and R. S. Pospahala. 1979. An examination of harvest and survival rates of ducks in relation to hunting. Trans. N. Am. Wildl. Nat. Resour. Conf. 44:114–126.

IX.
Decimating Influences: Habitat Loss, Toxins, and Disease

44

Wintering Waterfowl Habitat in Texas: Shrinking and Contaminated

Brian W. Cain

Abstract: Bays and marshes along the Texas coast are wintering habitat for millions of migratory waterfowl. Encroachment into these areas by agriculture, industry, and urbanization accelerated during the 1960s and led to environmental contamination by pesticides, herbicides, petroleum hydrocarbons, heavy metals, and other industrial pollutants. Hazardous waste storage and disposal in coastal lowlands further contaminated wintering waterfowl habitat. Data collected from sediment, water, and fish and wildlife species indicate that these contaminants may pose a chronic and sublethal hazard to wintering waterfowl along the Texas coast. Contamination of the remaining winter habitat may eliminate management options to provide quality habitat that produce food resources essential to wintering waterfowl.

The bays and marshes along the Texas coast provide wintering habitat for millions of migratory waterfowl (table 44.1). During the 1960s, these areas suffered increasing encroachment from agriculture, industry, and urbanization. The result of this encroachment has been loss of habitat through draining or filling and contamination by pesticides, petroleum hydrocarbons, heavy metals, and other industrial pollutants. Data have been collected by various agencies from sediment, water, and birds to determine whether these contaminants may pose a chronic and sublethal hazard to wintering waterfowl along the Texas coast. The purpose of this review is to identify the nature of habitat losses, to summarize data on contaminants in wintering habitat in Texas, and to indicate possible consequences of continuing contamination on waterfowl and other waterbirds.

Waterfowl in Winter.© 1988 University of Minnesota. Edited by Milton W. Weller and published by the University of Minnesota Press, Minneapolis.

Table 44.1. Winter waterfowl survey data for Texas and the Texas coast, 1980-81[a]

Species	Texas	Texas coast	Percentage of coast population to central Flyway population[b]	
Mallard	379,000	63,700	3	(05)
Mottled duck	37,400	37,400	100	(99)
Gadwall	137,800	95,400	65	(72)
Widgeon	82,200	34,200	32	(49)
Green-winged teal	385,400	366,400	92	(91)
Blue-winged teal	1,700	1,300	75	(100)
Northern shoveler	30,500	30,400	92	(86)
Northern pintail	326,700	221,100	63	(64)
Total dabblers	1,381,000	849,900	26	(46)
Redhead	209,300	208,100	96	(99)
Canvasback	40,000	37,100	87	(88)
Scaup	59,400	55,100	88	(97)
Ring-necked duck	4,500	4,100	65	(38)
Common goldeneye	1,600	100	T[c]	(01)
Bufflehead	5,500	5,300	47	(92)
Ruddy duck	4,900	4,800	58	(91)
Total divers	325,300	314,600	86	(97)
Total ducks[d]	1,745,200	1,202,100	31	(52)
Snow goose	838,700	837,400	89	(87)
White-fronted goose	108,900	108,900	99	(83)
Canada goose	191,300	95,500	12	(15)
Total geese	1,138,900	1,041,800	58	(61)
American coot	309,700	181,300	57	(69)
Total waterfowl	3,193,800	2,425,200	39	(54)

[a] Data from U.S. Fish and Wildlife Service (1981).
[b] Mean percentages for 1974-75 and 1975-76 are given in parentheses.
[c] T = trace.
[d] Includes mergansers and unidentified ducks.

National Losses of Wintering Waterfowl Habitat

During the 1950s, the U.S. Fish and Wildlife Service conducted a national inventory of wetlands (Shaw and Fredine 1956) as an aid to waterfowl management planning. Since 1974, the National Wetlands Inventory has been preparing detailed maps showing the location and category of wetlands in the United States. Roe and Ayres (1954) estimated the original wetland acreage of the lower 48 states to be 87 million hectares (roughly the size of Texas), of which only 40 million (less than half) remained by the mid 1970s (Frayer et al.

The inventory of wetland changes in the Atlantic and Gulf coasts, where 30% of the nation's wetlands occur, indicates that estuarine intertidal emergent habitat has declined 8.3% (57,800 ha) and that palustrine emergent habitat has declined 17.8% (232,000 ha) during the period 1954-76. Nationwide during this period, the average loss of all wetlands was 185,000 ha per year (4.4 million total ha), whereas 808,000 ha of new wetlands was created, for a net loss of 3.6 million ha—an area twice the size of New Jersey (Tiner 1984). The current rate of marsh loss in Louisiana is 12,900 ha (46 square miles) per year as a result of erosion of shorelines, inundation, and saltwater intrusion. Saint Bernard Parish changed from 78% water in 1955 to more than 81% water in 1978 (Frayer et al. 1983). Greatest losses of forested wetlands occurred in the lower Mississippi Valley with the conversion of bottomland hardwood forests to farmland. Agricultural development was responsible for 87% of recent national wetland losses, urban development caused 8%, and other development caused 5% of the losses (Tiner 1984).

Wintering Waterfowl Habitat in Texas

The U.S. Fish and Wildlife Service ranked the Texas Gulf Coast eighth out of 33 categories on a national priority scale based on its importance to the nation's waterfowl resource (U.S. Fish and Wildlife Service 1981). The area contains about 64,750 km² of high-quality natural breeding and wintering habitat. The important waterfowl habitat is a narrow band approximately 233 km long that consists of bays, tidal marshes, estuaries, and agricultural lands that support over three million wintering waterfowl (table 44.1).

A second area that supports a large concentration of wintering waterfowl is the playa lake district on the southern High Plains. During years of adequate moisture, this region may support a million ducks, mostly mallards (*Anas platyrhynchos*) (Simpson et al. 1981), on about 25,000 playas. The principal functions served by wintering waterfowl habitat are to furnish sufficient food to carry waterfowl through the energy-demanding time of winter, to keep natural mortality to a minimum, and to provide proper food for spring migration and onset of egg production. These functions of wintering habitat are being reduced both by the size of the area left and by its inability to provide enough food for the various feeding guilds (diving, dabbling, grazing) because of the pollution impacts on primary production. The pollutants from agriculture, urbanization, industrialization, and fossil-fuel handling that are chronically discharged into this wintering waterfowl habitat are toxic to plants and aquatic invertebrates.

Agricultural Contamination

Historically, waterfowl wintered in remote coastal marshes, but in the 1940s they began expanding into rice-farming lands that bordered the Texas and Louisiana marshes (West and Newsom 1977). Rice is planted between late February and May in a 100-km-wide belt from Victoria County in south Texas to near the Atchafalaya Basin in Louisiana. Between 1960 and 1974, rice seeds were treated with aldrin to protect against larvae of the rice water weevil (*Lissorhoptrus oryzophilus*) and with granosan, a mercurial fungicide, to control rice seedling blight (Flickinger and King 1972, Flickinger 1979). Rice fields are sprayed with propanil, a herbicide used to control grasses and weeds, two to four weeks after planting and while the rice is flooded. A variety of organophosphates also are applied to prevent insect damage as rice heads form. All of the pesticides are applied to rice while the fields are flooded; after each rainfall, these fields drain into coastal bayous, rivers, and adjacent wetlands.

South of the rice belt in Texas, the coastal marshes are bordered by agricultural lands that produce cotton and soybeans; in the lower Rio Grande Valley, citrus, sugarcane, and winter vegetables are additional crops. Pesticides are applied in the southern tip of Texas every month, with major drainage into the lower Laguna Madre, which winters nearly 80% of the U.S. redhead (*Aythya americana*) population (Weller 1964).

Sediment Samples. A total of 433 silt samples from 50 stations on eight major Texas rivers were collected over a 23-month period between 1970 and 1972 by the Texas Department of Agriculture (Tidswell and McCasland 1972) and analyzed for organochlorine pesticide residues. The highest frequencies of occurrence were found in the Brazos River, the San Antonio River, two small watersheds of the Tres Palacio Creek, and the Arroyo Colorado River in the lower Rio Grande Valley (Tidswell and McCasland 1972). These authors concluded that agricultural lands account for a constant burden of pesticides in these streams.

The Texas Department of Water Resources and the U.S. Geological Survey made 2,000 analytical determinations for pesticides in water and sediment from 220 sites between 1973 and 1977 (Dick 1982). Percentages of positive determinations for 19 pesticides are presented in table 44.2. Sediment samples taken in 1980 from Taylor's Bayou near Beaumont, Tex., had an average of 22.5 ppm heptachlor, 3.1 ppm dieldrin, and 39.6 ppm total DDT isomers (U.S. Army Corps of Engineers, Galveston, unpubl. data). A comparison of the water quality criteria set by the U.S. Environmental Protection Agency (EPA) to protect aquatic life with the percentage of positive determinations for 10 pesticides (table 44.3) indicates that residue concentrations in many Texas sites exceed the criteria.

In June 1977, the U.S. Army Corps of Engineers analyzed sediment and soil samples from 34 agricultural drainage outfalls in the lower Rio Grande Valley and in the Laguna Madre. Detectable amounts of 20 pesticides were present, with

Table 44.2. Pesticide residue data in samples collected by U.S. Geological Survey from October 1973 to December 1977[a]

	Determinations (No.)		Positive determinations (%)	
Pesticide	Fresh water	Sediment	Fresh water	Sediment
Chlorophenoxy herbicides				
2,4-D	555	...	27	—
2,4,5-T	551	—	26	—
Silvex	555	—	9	—
Chlorinated hydrocarbons				
Aldrin	563	346	2	2
Chlordane	563	344	9	38
DDD	567	351	4	45
DDE	567	351	5	53
DDT	567	350	6	33
Dieldrin	567	350	16	39
Endrin	566	351	0.2	0
Heptachlor	567	351	0.5	2
Heptachlor epoxide	568	351	2	6
Lindane	566	351	9	2
Methoxychlor	53	17	0	0
Toxaphene	271	159	0	2
Organophosphates				
Diazinon	567	16	35	0
Malathion	561	14	7	0
Methylparathion	567	13	0.7	0
Parathion	565	13	0.5	0

[a]Data modified from Dick (1982). Use of trade names here and throughout the paper does not represent endorsement by the U.S. Fish and Wildlife Service.

carbophenothion and phorate having the highest concentrations (U.S. Army Corps of Engineers 1982). At the mouth of the Raymondville Drain into the Laguna Madre, phorate concentrations were 9.9 and 8.3 ppb, respectively. Carbophenothion in sediments of La Sal Vieja reached 24.5 ppb; the Raymondville Drain, 15.5 ppb; and at the mouth, 17.6 ppb. Concentrations of DDT, dieldrin, endosulfan, endrin, guthion, and PCBs exceeded EPA criteria for propagation of fish and wildlife (U.S. Army Corps of Engineers 1982).

Wintering Waterbirds. DDE residues increased significantly in bodies of shorebirds between October and December after they arrived at mud flats that had developed at agricultural drains in South Texas (White et al. 1983). Levels of DDE reached 12-68 ppm in 40% of the long-billed dowitchers (*Limnodromus scolopaceus*). At Corpus Christi, DDE residues were 9 ppm in sanderlings (*Calidris alba*), dunlins (*Calidris alpina*), and lesser yellowlegs (*Tringa flavipes*) (White et al. 1980). These data indicate that the lower Texas coast has considerable organochlorine

Table 44.3. U.S. Environmental Protection Agency 1980 revisions of water quality criteria to protect aquatic life compared with levels detected in Texas waters[a]

| Pesticide | Levels of protection (μg/l) | | Detection level (μg/l) | Percentage of determinations at or above detection level |
	Concentration not to be exceeded at any time	Concentration not to be exceeded on 24-hour average		
Aldrin	3.00	. . .	.01	2.0
Chlordane	2.40	.0043	.10	9.0
DDD	1.10	.0010	.01	4.0
DDE	1.10	.0010	.01	5.0
DDT	1.10	.0010	.01	16.0
Dieldrin	2.50	.0019	.01	0.2
Endrin	0.18	.0023	.01	0.5
Heptachlor	0.52	.0038	.01	0.5
Lindane	2.00	.0800	.01	9.0
Toxaphene	1.60	.0130	.01	0.0

[a]Data from Dick (1982).

contamination that is being assimilated into migrant waterbirds and that may contaminate wintering waterfowl. Analysis of residue data from eggs collected in 1979 near Port Mansfield indicates that laughing gull (*Larus atricilla*) eggs had a median of 4.0 ppm DDE and that black skimmer (*Rynchops niger*) eggs had a 9.3 ppm median DDE level (White et al. 1980).

Dieldrin-induced mortality of snow geese (*Chen caerulescens*) and other migratory birds occurred in 1972 and 1974 after heavy rains flooded rice fields in early March (Flickinger 1979). Dieldrin is a metabolite of aldrin that, until 1974, was a legal pesticide applied to rice seedlings at planting. During 1984, two hundred 55-gallon drums of illegal, technical-grade aldrin were seized in the rice-growing areas of Texas and Louisiana (USFWS, Enforcement Division, unpubl. information). According to area farmers and aerial applicators, it is not uncommon in the rice belt for persons to soak rice seeds with aldrin, bidrin, or parathion and to distribute those seeds over a field previously planted to kill birds and reduce seedling damage. Rice seeds soaked with azodrin caused the death of ducks and geese in rice fields of Louisiana in 1981 (White et al. 1983). These authors stated that the azodrin-soaked seeds were aerially broadcast with the sole intention of poisoning depredating waterfowl and blackbirds. They were informed that this illegal practice had been going on for years.

Fulvous whistling ducks (*Dendrocygna bicolor*) were numerous during the 1950s along the Texas coast. Singleton (1953) reported over 4,000 fulvous whistling ducks in Brazoria County, but in 1969 only 50 were reported by Flickinger and King (1972). Rice fields are a favorite nesting area for this species. I found only six pairs of fulvous whistling ducks during the summer of 1984 in the rice fields of Brazoria County.

Industrial Contaminants

Large complexes of petroleum-refining, petrochemical-manufacturing, and pesticide-formulating industries have developed around every major coastal bay system from New Orleans, La., to Corpus Christi, Tex. Waste disposal of these industries has created numerous hazardous waste sites and contaminated wetlands along the Texas coast (U.S. Environmental Protection Agency 1984). Heavy rains and storm surges associated with hurricanes have flushed these materials (table 44.4) into Galveston Bay and surrounding wetlands.

Table 44.4. Organic priority pollutants and metals identified in waste pit samples[a]

Compound	Range of concentration (ppm)[b]
Volatile Organics	
Benzene	ND - 2,800
Chlorobenzene	ND - 400
Ethylbenzene	ND - 5,100
Chloroform	ND - 700
1,1-Dichloroethane	ND - 800
1,2-Dichloroethane	38 - 20,000
1,1,2-Trichloroethane	ND - 15,000
1,1,1-Trichloroethane	ND - T (1.0)
1,1,2,2,-Tetrachloroethane	ND - 3,200
1,1-Dichloroethylene	ND - 5,100
1,2-*trans*-Dichloroethylene	ND - 5,200
Trichloroethylene	ND - 400
Methylene chloride	ND - 11
Toluene	ND - 2,500
Vinyl chloride	ND - 6,600
1,2-Dichloropropane	ND - 200
1,2-Dichloropropylene	ND - 200
Tetrachloroethylene	ND - 600
Pesticides/PCBs	
PCBs (total)	ND - 30.2
Dieldrin	ND - 17.0
Acid-fraction organics	
Pentachlorophenol	ND - 34.0
Base/neutral organics	
Acenaphthene	ND - 1,300
Acenapthylene	ND - 5,400

continued on next page

Table 44.4. *Continued*

Compound	Range of concentration (ppm)[b]
Antracene/phenanthrene	ND - 10,000
Benzo(a)antracene/chrysene	ND - 490
Fluoranthene	ND - 1,100
3,4-Benzofluoranthene/benzo(k)fluoranthene	ND - 34
Fluorene	ND - 4,200
Napthalene	ND - 36,000
Benzo(g,h,i)perpylene	ND - T (25)
Pyrene	11 - 2,300
Benzo (a) pryene	ND - 140
n-Nitrosodiphenylamine	ND - 4,700
Metals	
Aluminum	32 - 4,500
Boron	ND - I
Barium	ND - 95
Chromium	2 - 75
Cobalt	ND - 10
Copper	ND - 890
Iron	14 - 1,400
Manganese	ND - 14
Nickel	ND - 9
Zinc	ND - 210
Arsenic	ND - 3
Cadmium	ND - 3
Mercury	ND - 5
Lead	7 - 660
Antimony	ND - 3
Calcium	22 - 810
Magnesium	ND - 220
Sodium	160 - 1,350

[a] Data from Anonymous (1980).

[b] ND = not detected; T = trace quantity detected but concentration was less than quantitation limit given in parentheses; and I = sample interference precluded analysis.

Many industries have their own waste-treatment ponds where aeration and evaporation reduce the chemical oxygen demand of the wastewater before it is discharged into surface streams. There are currently more than 2,000 industrial point-source discharges permitted into the Galveston Bay system, which carries a variety of hazardous chemicals (table 44.5) to this habitat. Waste-treatment ponds attract ducks, American coots (*Fulica americana*), and other waterbirds as loafing or roosting areas. One plant security guard reported that ducks fly into an acid-waste

Table 44.5. Hazardous chemicals potentially present in waste streams from refineries and other basic chemical industries located in Galveston Bay watershed[a]

Acetaldehyde	Cresols	Nickel
Acetic acid	Cresylic acid	Nickel carbonyl
Aldehydes	Cyanides	Nitrogen oxides
Alkenes	1,2-Cyclohexanediamine	C[4] Olefins and diolefins
Alkyl sulfide	Dibenzothiophene	Phenanthrene
Ammonia	1,3-Dichloroacetone	Phenol
Antracenes	Dichlorobenzene	Propylene
Aromatic Amines	Diethylamine	Pyrene
Barium	Dimethylphenol	Pyridines
Benidine	Ethylene	Pyrroles
Benzene	*bis*(2-Ethylhexylphthalate)	Quinolines
Benzoic acid	Fluoranthrene	Spent caustic soda brine
Benzo(g,h,i)perylene	Formaldehyde	Strontium
Benzo(a)pyrene	Formic acid	Succinc acid
Benzo(e)pyrene	Furans	Sulfates
Carbon disulfide	Halogenated alkenes	Sulfides
Carbon monoxide	Hydrogen sulfide	Sulfonates
Carbonyl sulfide	Hypochlorite	Suflones
Carbozoles	Indoles	Sulfur oxides
Catalyst fines	Ketones	Sulfur particulates
Chlorides	Lead	Sufluric acid
Chlorine	Maleic acid	Tetraethyl lead
Chlorine dioxide	Mercaptans	Thiopenes
2-Chloropropenal	Metaloporphines	Thiopenols
Chromates	Methanol	Thiosulfide
Cobalt	Methylethylamine	Toluene
Cobalt carbonyl	Methylmercaptan	Vanadium
Coke fines	Mixed cresols	Xylenes
Copper	Molybdenum	Xylenols
Coronene	2-Naphthylamine	Zinc

[a]Data from Andreasen (in press).

pit but that they "never leave." Effects of waste-treatment ponds on migratory waterfowl are not known, nor are they being evaluated at the present time.

Oil and gas production along the coasts of Texas and Louisiana is associated with enormous amounts of wastewater (brine), which is separated from the oil or gas and then injected into disposal wells or discharged into evaporation ponds or surface water. Evaporation ponds may develop a layer of oil on the surface and become a trap for any waterbird that lands in the water. More than 2,000 permits issued by the Texas Railroad Commission allow direct discharge into surface waters of Texas. Galveston Bay receives three million gallons of brine effluent per day (Andreasen and Spears 1983).

Sediment Samples. Analysis of sediment for industrial contamination along the Texas coast has been performed in connection with the maintenance dredging of the Gulf Intracoastal Waterway (GIWW) and numerous side channels by the U.S. Army Corps of Engineers. Regulation of disposal of this dredge material into open bay water or confined areas is determined by the amount and kinds of contaminants present in the material. Sediment samples collected and analyzed by the corps before dredging indicate that oil and grease are major contaminants in certain areas. Oil and grease residues as high as 9,000 mg/kg (ppm) have been found since 1980 in the Houston Ship Channel, the Texas City Ship Channel, and the GIWW along the Aransas National Wildlife Refuge. Sediment samples collected from one management cell on the J. D. Murphree Wildlife Management Area near Port Arthur, Tex., had oil and grease residues of 104,000 ppm.

The toxic components of oil and grease are the polycyclic aromatic hydrocarbons (PAHs) that adsorb to and accumulate in sediments. Samples collected and analyzed by the USFWS from Swan Lake at Texas City, Tex., contained pyrene (120 ppb), chrysene (290 ppb), benzo(a)anthracene (84ppb), benzo(a)pyrene (110 ppb), fluoranthene (180 ppb), and phenanthene (100 ppb). Naphthalene and methylated naphthalenes accumulated in the sediments near the oil-field brine discharge in Trinity Bay (Armstrong et al. 1979) to parts per million levels. All these PAHs are known carcinogens to mammal and fish liver tissue (Heseltine 1983).

Other industrial contaminants such as PCBs and di(2-ethylhexyl)phthalate were found in Galveston Bay sediments (Murray et al. 1981). Detectable levels of octachlorinated styrene, hexachlorobenzene, and pentachlorophenol have also been detected in sediment samples analyzed from near industrial outfalls. Heavy metals such as arsenic, cadmium, lead, mercury, selenium, and zinc were detected in sediment samples from Lavaca Bay at levels that exceed EPA criteria for open-water disposal (Texas Department of Water Resources, unpubl. data).

Wintering Waterbirds. Waterfowl tissues from the southern coastal areas have not been analyzed for the presence of residues of most industrial contaminants. Lethal levels of mercury and selenium were discovered in tissues from common loons (*Gavia immer*) collected during a die-off of 2,500 loons along the coasts of Georgia, Alabama, and Mississippi from January to April 1983 (National Wildlife Health Laboratory, unpubl. information).

Researchers at the Gulf Coast Field Station of the Patuxent Wildlife Research Center collected 10 olivaceous cormorants (*Phalacrocorax olivaceus*) for chemical analysis in 1980 and found an average of 0.23 ppm chlorinated styrenes in 7 of the 10 carcasses, and PCB residues ranged up to 24 ppm in these fish-eating waterbirds (K. King, pers. commun.). In November 1982 and February 1983, these researchers collected 10 double-crested cormorants (*Phalacrocorax auritus*) from the Houston Ship Channel in an area below its confluence with the San Jacinto River to Morgan's Point. All 20 cormorants were analyzed for petroleum hydrocarbons, and significant increases in the residue levels of C_{12}-C_{20} alkanes and some PAHs were found between the November and February collections (K. King, pers. commun.). It is assumed that these fish-eating birds are accumulating the petroleum compounds from their wintering habitat along the Houston Ship Channel.

Impact of Contamination in Wintering Waterfowl Habitat

The coastal bays and marshes that provide a large percentage of habitat to wintering waterbirds also are sediment traps for all contaminants associated with agricultural drainage, urban stormwater runoff, treated domestic sewage, industrial discharge, and effluents from energy production and exploration facilities. These contaminant sources release toxic chemicals into waterfowl habitat at parts per million levels daily. Impacts of several agricultural chemicals on waterfowl reproduction and survival were addressed by White and Stickel (1975), but nothing is reported about the impacts of these other contaminants on waterfowl health.

The lower Laguna Madre, which borders the rich agricultural lower Rio Grande Valley, receives runoff from two major drains, the Arroyo Colorado and the Raymondville. In 1973, this area received 26.6 kg of insecticides per hectare of cotton as well as 0.8 kg/ha of herbicides and 4.2 kg/ha of defoliants (Cornelius 1975).

During the 20-year period between 1956 and 1975, the distribution of wintering redhead ducks in the lower Laguna Madre dropped from 84% of the wintering population to 24% (Cornelius 1975). These ducks consume large amounts of American shoalgrass (*Halodule wrightii*) during their winter visit to the Texas coast (Koenig 1969, Cornelius 1977, Marsh 1979). Vegetative sampling since 1960 indicates that shoalgrass beds have declined over 50% and that slender syringodium (*Syringodium filiforme*) has expanded throughout the Laguna Madre (Cornelius 1975, Marsh 1979). Syringodium is not used by redhead ducks in Texas as a food source (Koenig 1969).

Although the direct cause of the decline of shoalgrass has not been identified, major contaminants to the Laguna Madre that may affect vegetation are cotton defoliants, herbicides, and oil- or gas-well brine discharge. The organophosphorus defoliant S,S,S-tributyl phosphorotrithioate (DEF) is applied to cotton throughout the South. In soil, DEF persists for up to two weeks and in brackish water for up to eight days. DEF in fresh water reduced survival and growth of catfish and trout at levels of less than 20 ppb (Cleveland and Hamilton 1983) and also caused spinal deformities. In the agricultural runoff to the lower Laguna Madre, enough herbicides may be present during the summer to stress aquatic vegetation and thus lower its vitality.

Preemergence herbicides such as alachlor and dinoseb are widely used for weed control in corn, soybean, peanuts, and other legume crops. These herbicides are leached from soil if rainfall occurs soon after application and can be transported to bays and marshes. The impact of these herbicides as well as of postemergents and defoliants, on the stand quality of shoalgrass in the Laguna Madre needs evaluation. A similar situation of submerged aquatic vegetation decline and reduced wintering-waterfowl populations between 1955 and 1979 was reported by Perry et al. (1981) for the Chesapeake Bay. Toxic substances in the Chesapeake Bay are currently being addressed in the EPA's Chesapeake Bay Program (Bricker 1981).

Agricultural pesticides such as organophosphates and carbamates usually are toxic to waterfowl in small amounts if ingested. Misuse of monocrotophos and dicrotophos killed about 1,100 birds of 12 species on the Texas coast in March and May of 1982 (Flickinger et al. 1984). Many birds that are not killed but that suffer from organophosphate poisoning simply stop feeding for a period of time, which may retard their fat buildup before migration. Thus, waterfowl may leave their wintering habitat without enough energy to begin nesting as they arrive at their breeding area. Acetylcholinesterase inhibition as a result of organophosphate ingestion changes waterfowl behaviors so that feeding, courtship, escape, and migration are not performed. The impact on reproduction is not known. Hunter et al. (1984) showed that aerially applied carbaryl reduced the biomass and number of macroinvertebrates in ponds and led to decreased growth rates of American black duck (*Anas rubripes*) and mallard young.

Wintering waterfowl habitat along the Texas coast has been contaminated and altered most by discharge of petroleum compounds in effluents from production sites (wells), refineries, and runoff from petroleum-sludge land farms or storage pits. Brine discharge from production sites contains from 15 to 60 ppm water-soluble fractions of oil, many of which are PAHs that are extremely toxic to aquatic flora and fauna. One brine-discharge point in Trinity Bay caused reduced populations of benthic invertebrates in a 7-ha area, with sediment accumulation of 60 ppm toxic aromatic hydrocarbons (Armstrong et al. 1979). Research summarized by Andreasen and Spears (1983) indicated that a 40% dilution of petroleum brine was toxic to larval shrimp and crabs and that exposed sheepshead minnows (*Cyprinodon variegatus*) also lost their salinity tolerance in a laboratory study.

More than 2,000 brine-discharge points are permitted into surface waters of Texas. Vegetation is killed at each point and benthic organisms are reduced. These discharge points are a continual source of toxic compounds for as long as the oil field is producing, which in some cases exceed 30 years. In areas along the coast and inland where discharge to surface waters has not been permitted, evaporation pits receive the discharge. Evaporation pits may cover several hectares and may contain a film of oil on the surface. All these pits lack vegetation and contain water-soluble fractions of oil that are toxic compounds. The pits attract waterfowl as loafing sites and become death traps for them, as well as for a variety of other migratory birds (Flickinger 1981). Chronic effects of aromatic hydrocarbons that are present in brine discharge caused an increase in liver weight of mallards (Patton and Dieter 1980) similar to liver hypertrophy induced by other xenobiotics.

Research efforts to slow the decline in wintering waterfowl habitat should focus not on what ducks are eating but on what is becoming of their food sources. All waterfowl cannot move into rice fields, which themselves are dwindling, for their winter habitat along the Texas and Louisiana coasts. Texas has grown from 5.8 million people in 1930 to more than 15 million in 1983. This population growth will continue and will bring more development and more discharge points to coastal areas. Answers are needed now on the effects of contaminants on the habitat quality of wintering waterfowl, or the 20 million Texans projected for the year 2020 may find that they have few waterfowl with which to concern themselves.

LITERATURE CITED

Andreasen, J. K. The potential impact of contaminants on resources of Galveston Bay: a map and planning guide. U.S. Fish Wildl. Serv., Washington, D.C. In press.

————, and R. W. Spears. 1983. Toxicity of Texan petroleum brine to the sheepshead minnow (*Cyprinodon variegatus*), a common estuarine fish. Bull. Environ. Contam. Toxicol. 30:277–283.

Anonymous. 1980. Remedial Action Master Plan Motco Hazardous Waste Site La Marque, Texas. EPA Contract 68-01-6692. Available from U.S. Environ. Protection Agency, Region VI, Dallas, Tex.

Armstrong, H. W., K. Fucik, J. W. Anderson, and J. M. Neff. 1979. Effects of oilfield brine effluent on sediment and benthic organisms in Trinity Bay, Texas. Mar. Environ. Res. 2:55–69.

Bricker, O. P. 1981. Toxic substances in the Chesapeake Bay estuary. Trans. N. Am. Wildl. Nat. Resour. Conf. 46:250–258.

Cleveland, L., and S. J. Hamilton. 1983. Toxicity of the organophosphorus defoliant DEF to rainbow trout (*Salmo gairdneri*) and channel catfish (*Ictalurus punctatus*). Aquat. Toxicol. 4:341–355.

Cornelius, S. E. 1975. Human activity as a factor influencing distribution and wintering habitat of redhead ducks in lower Laguna Madre, Texas. Redhead Res. Rep. Dep. Wildl. Fish. Sci., Texas A&M Univ., College Station. 60pp.

————. 1977. Food resource utilization by wintering redheads on lower Laguna Madre. J. Wildl. Manage. 41:374–385.

Dick, M. 1982. Pesticide and PCB concentrations in Texas—water, sediment and fish tissue. Rep. 264, Texas Dep. Water Res., Austin. 77pp.

Flickinger, E. L. 1979. Effects of aldrin exposure on snow geese in Texas rice fields. J. Wildl. Manage. 43:94–101.

————. 1981. Wildlife mortality at petroleum pits in Texas. J. Wildl. Manage. 45:560–564.

————, and K. A. King. 1972. Some effects of aldrin-treated rice on Gulf Coast wildlife. J. Wildl. Manage. 36:706–727.

————, D. H. White, C. A. Mitchell, and T. G. Lamont. 1984. Monocrotophos and dicrotophos residues in birds as a result of misuse of organophosphates in Matagorda County, Texas. J. Assoc. Off. Anal. Chem. 67:827–828.

Frayer, W. E., T. J. Monahan, D. L. Bowden, and F. A. Graybill. 1983. Status and trends of wetlands and deepwater habitats in the conterminous United States, 1950's to 1970's. U.S. Fish Wildl. Serv., Washington, D.C. 31pp.

Heseltine, E., ed. 1983. IARC monographs on the evaluation of the carcinogenic risk of chemicals to humans. Polynuclear aromatic compounds, part 1. Agency Res. Cancer, World Health Organization. Vol. 32. Lyon, France. 477pp.

Hunter, M. L., J. W. Witham, and H. Dow. 1984. Effects of a carbaryl-induced depression in invertebrate abundance on the growth and behavior of American black duck and mallard ducklings. Can. J. Zool. 62:452–456.

Koenig, R. L. 1969. A comparison of the winter food habits of three species of waterfowl from the upper Laguna Madre of Texas. M.S. Thesis, Texas A&I Univ., Kingsville. 59pp.

Marsh, S. L. 1979. Factors affecting the distribution, food habits and lead toxicosis of redhead ducks in the Laguna Madre, Texas. M.S. Thesis, Texas A&M Univ., College Station. 47pp.

Murray, H. E., L. E. Ray, and C. S. Giam. 1981. Phthalic acid esters, total DDT's and polychlorinated biphenyls in marine samples from Galveston Bay, Texas. Bull. Environ. Contam. Toxicol. 26:769-774.

Patton, J. F., and M. P. Dieter. 1980. Effects of petroleum hydrocarbons on hepatic functions in the duck. Comp. Biochem. Physiol. (c) 65:33-36.

Perry, M. C., R. E. Munroe, and G. M. Haramis. 1981. Twenty-five year trends in duck diving populations in Chesapeake Bay. Trans. N. Am. Wildl. Nat. Resour. Conf. 46:299-310.

Roe, H. B., and Q. L. Ayres. 1954. Engineering for agricultural drainage. McGraw-Hill, New York. 501pp.

Shaw, S. P., and C. G. Fredine. 1956. Wetlands of the United States. Circular 39. U.S. Fish Wildl. Serv., Washington, D.C. 67pp.

Simpson, C. D., E. G. Bolen, R. L. Moore, and F. A. Stormer, 1981. Signifiance of playas to migratory wildlife. Pages 35-45 in Playa lakes symposium proceedings, FWS/OBS-81-07. U.S. Gov. Print. Off., Washington, D.C.

Singleton, J. R. 1953. Texas coastal waterfowl survey. Tex. Game Fish Comm. Ser. 11, P-R Rep. 128pp.

Tidswell, B., III, and W. E. McCasland. 1972. An evaluation of pesticide residues on silt and sediment in Texas waterways. Tex. Dep. Agric., Austin. 45pp.

Tiner, R. W., Jr. 1984. Wetlands of the United States: current status and recent trends. U.S. Fish Wildl. Serv., Washington, D.C. 59pp.

U.S. Army Corps of Engineers. 1982. Lower Rio Grande Basin, Texas, Flood Control and Major Drainage Project. Phase 1, appendix VI. Environmental resources. 326pp.

U.S. Environmental Protection Agency. 1984. National priorities list. HW-7.2. 1st ed. U.S. Environ. Protection Agency, Washington, D.C. 75pp.

U.S. Fish and Wildlife Service. 1981. Category 8, Texas Gulf Coast. Wetland Preservation Program report. U.S. Fish Wildl. Serv., Region 2, Albuquerque, N.M. 145pp.

Weller, M. W. 1964. Distribution and migration of the redhead. J. Wildl. Manage. 28:64-103.

West, L. D., and J. D. Newsom. 1977. Lead and mercury in lesser snow geese wintering in Louisiana. Proc. Southeast. Assoc. Game Fish Comm. 31:180-187.

White, D. H., K. A. King, and R. M. Prouty. 1980. Significance of organocholorine and heavy metal residues in wintering shorebirds at Corpus Christi, Texas, 1976-77. Pestic. Monit. J. 14:58.

————, C. A. Mitchell, and T. E. Kaiser. 1983. Temporal accumulation of organochlorine pesticides in shorebirds wintering on the south Texas coast, 1979-80. Arch. Environ. Contam. Toxicol. 12:241-245.

————, and L. F. Stickel. 1975. Impacts of chemicals on waterfowl reproduction and survival. Int. Waterfowl Symp. 1:132-142.

45

Ingestion of Shotshell Pellets by Waterfowl Wintering in Texas

Daniel W. Moulton, Carl D. Frentress,
Charles D. Stutzenbaker, David S. Lobpries,
and William C. Brownlee

Abstract: Data are given on the incidence of ingested shot in the gizzards of waterfowl collected from 1973 through 1984 in Texas. The progressive implementation of steel-shot zones on the Texas Gulf Coast, initiated in 1978-79, is reviewed. Ingestion data from before the steel-shot period are compared with those from the steel-shot period in an effort to assess the effects of steel-shot zone implementation. Mottled ducks (*Anas fulvigula*) had the highest incidence of ingested shot of any species sampled. Gizzards of this species from the public hunting areas of Jefferson and Chambers counties consistently showed proportions between 30% and 50% with ingested shot. Since 1978-79, the proportions of waterfowl gizzards containing only steel shot have increased in steel-shot zones. The estimated proportions of gizzards containing lead shot have been about halved for some species. A comparison between visual examination and X-ray radiography for the 1983-84 gizzard sample showed that visual ingestion rates required an upward adjustment of 42.7% (average for all species) to approximate actual shot-ingestion rates.

In 1972, the U.S. Fish and Wildlife Service (USFWS) began a study to determine lead concentrations in the wing bones of waterfowl throughout the United States (U.S. Fish and Wildlife Service 1976). The highest lead levels observed during the study were in mottled ducks (*Anas fulvigula*) from Texas, Louisiana, and Florida. An earlier study by Bellrose (1959) indicated that ducks from Texas had the highest incidence of ingested lead shot among those gizzards collected in the Central Flyway.

Waterfowl in Winter.© 1988 University of Minnesota. Edited by Milton W. Weller and published by the University of Minnesota Press, Minneapolis.

Results from these studies were not surprising because the two elements that result in the ingestion of shot by waterfowl—large numbers of waterfowl and of waterfowl hunters—are concentrated on limited areas of habitat in Texas, which is a major waterfowl-wintering area and a major waterfowl-harvest area. Texas annually winters 3 million to 5 million waterfowl, about 50% of the total surveyed in the Central Flyway during the midwinter waterfowl surveys throughout the flyway (Texas Parks and Wildlife Department 1983a). About 90% of the geese and 50% of the ducks surveyed in Texas are found on the Gulf Coast. During the 1979-80 hunting season, Texas accounted for 33% of the federal duck stamps sold and 43% of the waterfowl harvested in the Central Flyway (Texas Parks and Wildlife Department 1983a).

In 1973, the Texas Parks and Wildlife Department (TPWD) began a long-term study to examine the problem of shot ingestion by waterfowl wintering in Texas. The objectives of the study were to determine the extent of the shot-ingestion problem among waterfowl wintering in Texas and to assess the effects of the progressive implementation of steel-shot use upon observed incidence of ingested shot.

We gratefully acknowledge the efforts of all TPWD and USFWS biologists involved in collecting and analyzing waterfowl gizzards over the past decade. We thank J. G. Barron (TPWD) for computer assistance, F. M. Fisher (Rice University) for X-ray radiography studies of waterfowl gizzard contents, and S. L. Stokes (University of Texas) for statistical advice. This study was partially funded under Pittman-Robertson Project W-106-R.

Study Area

Texas can be divided into six waterfowl habitat regions (fig. 45.1) on the basis of similarity of waterfowl habitat features and wintering waterfowl concentrations (Texas Parks and Wildlife Department 1982): region 1 (Panhandle) is typified by playas and extensive grain fields; region 2 (north central Texas) by hardwood bottoms, large water-project reservoirs, and numerous farm ponds and tanks; region 3 (Piney Woods) by hardwood bottoms, swamps, sloughs, and large reservoirs; region 4 (upper Gulf Coast) by deep coastal marshes and adjacent rice prairies; region 5 (lower Gulf Coast) by large, shallow, saline bays and salt marshes; and region 6 (south and west Texas) by widely scattered rivers, streams, ponds, and tanks.

During the 1982-83 hunting season in Texas, 120,000-130,000 hunters harvested about 1.1 million to 1.2 million birds. The estimated proportions of total hunters and total harvest for the various regions were, for region 1, 6% of hunters and 6% of harvest; for region 2, 21% of hunters and 15% of harvest; for region 3, 10% of hunters and 7% of harvest; for region 4, 52% of hunters and 56% of harvest; for region 5, 8% of huntes and 12% of harvest; and for region 6, 3% of hunters and 4% of harvest (Texas Parks and Wildlife Department 1983b).

Fig. 45.1. Texas waterfowl habitat regions delineated on basis of similarity of habitat features and wintering waterfowl concentrations. J/C = Jefferson and Chambers counties.

Methods

Waterfowl gizzards examined during this study were solicited from hunters at areas where hunters concentrated. It was not practical to attempt random sampling over entire regions or counties. Each year, gizzards were collected throughout the entire hunting season and frozen for analysis after its close. For analysis, gizzards were opened and washed to collect the contents. Pellets were examined by dissecting scope to identify shot-in pellets because only pellets that showed erosion were considered ingested. Magnets were used to aid observers in detecting steel shot. The washed contents (and washing fluid) of gizzards collected in 1983-84 were examined by X-ray radiography following visual examination, and the results of these examinations were compared.

Incidences of lead-shot ingestion before and after the implementation of steel-shot regulations were compared using a binomial test for the difference in proportions.

Results

Period before Steel Shot, 1973-75

Data from the 1973-74 and 1974-75 hunting seasons represent baseline data for lead-shot ingestion preceding the implementation of any steel-shot zones in Texas (table 45.1). Gizzards were collected from 82 of 254 counties during the two-year

Table 45.1. Incidence of ingested shot in waterfowl gizzards collected in Texas, 1973-75 and 1980-84

Species	Locale[a]	1973-74 N	With lead (%)	1974-75 N	With lead (%)	1980-81[b] N	With lead (%)	With shot (%)	1981-82[c] N	With lead (%)	With shot (%)	1982-83[d] N	With lead (%)	With shot (%)	1983-84[e] N	With lead (%)	With shot (%)
Mallard	1+2+																
	3+6	452	2.2	295	2.7	...	...		...	...	...	634	1.9	2.1	577	2.8	3.1
	4+5	23	0.0	107	2.8	201	7.0	7.0	194	5.2	6.2	75	1.3	1.3	169	3.0	4.1
	J/C	31	29.0	129	36.4	15	6.7	13.3	214	25.2	39.3	288	12.2	20.5	202	14.4	26.2
Mottled	4	17	0.0	57	5.3	253	4.7	5.1	192	11.5	12.5	107	11.2	15.0	234	4.3	8.1
duck	J/C	195	43.6	192	31.3	369	27.9	38.8	372	17.5	33.1	555	26.7	39.1	291	21.0	54.3
	5	3	33.3	12	25.0	12	33.3	33.3	88	12.5	17.0	33	3.0	6.1	32	0.0	0.0
Northern	1+2																
pintail	3+6	79	0.0	39	2.6	...	...		...	...	...	106	3.8	3.8	73	0.0	0.0
	4	63	0.0	130	3.8	400	6.5	8.8	422	7.6	7.8	216	2.8	2.8	345	1.2	2.3
	J/C	82	34.1	311	28.0	...	...		...	464	29.5	46.1	326	12.9	17.8	399	13.8	25.3
	5	91	5.5	95	8.4	316	7.9	7.9	933	5.7	5.8	166	1.8	4.2	162	0.0	2.5
Gadwall	1+2+																
	3+6	109	0.0	27	0.0	...	...		...	...	...	98	2.0	2.0	37	13.5	13.5
	J/C+																
	4+5	28	0.0	49	0.0	76	2.6	2.6	332	0.0	0.3	139	0.0	0.7	50	0.0	4.0
Wood	2+3+																
duck	4+5	56	0.0	22	0.0	16	0.0	0.0	17	5.9	5.9	56	1.8	1.8	89	1.1	1.1
Ring-	1+2+																
necked	3+6	27	0.0	14	14.3	...	...		...	...	...	149	2.0	2.0	184	10.3	10.3
duck	4+5	...	...	3	33.3	10	0.0	0.0	23	17.4	17.4	6	0.0	0.0	6	0.0	0.0
	J/C	4	0.0	23	30.4	...	...		...	113	16.8	32.7	113	34.5	49.6	121	15.7	30.6
Lesser	1+2+																
scaup	3+6	85	10.6	37	8.1	...	...		...	...	...	16	12.5	12.5	24	12.5	12.5
	4+5	10	20.0	11	18.2	40	7.5	7.5	494	12.8	14.4	46	13.0	13.0	44	9.1	11.4
	J/C	50	20.0	155	35.5	...	...		...	169	37.3	48.5	95	23.2	32.6	124	17.7	29.8
Redhead	1+2+																
	3+6	1	0.0	19	15.8	...	...		...	...	...	9	0.0	0.0	9	0.0	11.1
	J/C+																
	4+5	...	...	5	0.0	32	25.0	28.1	224	26.8	27.2	66	7.6	9.1	85	17.6	28.2

Continued on next page

Table 45.1. *Continued*

Species	Locale[a]	N (1973-74)	With lead (%)	N (1974-75)	With lead (%)	N (1980-81[b])	With lead (%)	With shot (%)	N (1981-82[c])	With lead (%)	With shot (%)	N (1982-83[d])	With lead (%)	With shot (%)	N (1983-84[e])	With lead (%)	With shot (%)
Canvas-back	2+3+ 4+5+ J/C	3	0.0	...	...	10	50.0	50.0	16	18.8	18.8	23	8.7	8.7	36	22.2	25.0
American wigeon	1+2+ 3+6	79	0.0	23	0.0	...	...	...	...	...	...	104	1.9	1.9	22	0.0	0.0
	4+J/C	22	4.5	23	4.3	20	0.0	0.0	75	2.7	2.7	41	0.0	0.0	10	0.0	0.0
	5	15	0.0	19	0.0	75	0.0	0.0	234	0.0	0.0	64	0.0	1.6	...	...	...
Blue-winged teal	2+3+6	23	0.0	23	0.0	...	...	...	...	...	...	...	...	...	...	...	...
	4+J/C	29	20.7	71	11.3	21	0.0	0.0	238	2.1	2.1	...	...	...	...	...	...
	5	10	0.0	5	0.0	110	1.8	1.8	72	5.6	5.6	...	...	...	...	...	...
Green-winged teal	1+2+ 3+6	121	0.8	29	0.0	...	...	...	...	...	...	69	0.0	0.0	11	9.1	9.1
	4+J/C	45	0.0	179	2.2	284	0.4	0.7	474	0.6	1.1	21	0.0	0.0	...	...	...
	5	10	0.0	8	0.0	276	1.4	1.4	248	1.2	1.2	46	0.0	0.0	...	...	...
Northern shoveler	1+2+ 3+6	22	0.0	14	0.0	...	...	...	...	...	...	8	0.0	0.0	...	...	...
	4+J/C	12	0.0	158	4.4	21	9.5	9.5	35	0.0	0.0	11	0.0	0.0	...	...	...
	5	10	0.0	12	0.0	55	1.8	1.8	116	4.3	5.2	28	7.1	10.7	...	...	...
Snow goose	2+5	...	...	...	...	...	...	...	17	11.8	11.8	162	1.2	1.9	33	0.0	3.0
	4	...	...	...	...	3	0.0	0.0	785	2.2	3.6	155	5.8	6.5	628	1.3	5.1
	J/C	...	...	...	...	...	...	...	71	0.0	11.3	62	8.1	11.3	286	3.1	11.2
White-fronted goose	2+5	...	...	...	...	...	...	...	15	6.7	6.7	80	2.5	5.0	26	0.0	0.0
	4+J/C	...	...	...	...	...	...	...	167	4.2	4.2	232	3.9	3.9	224	1.3	4.9
Canada goose	1+2+5	...	...	...	...	...	...	...	17	0.0	0.0	8	0.0	0.0	15	0.0	6.7
	4	...	...	...	...	5	0.0	0.0	82	1.2	1.2	191	2.6	3.1	157	0.0	1.9

[a]Numbers represent waterfowl habitat regions: 1 = Panhandle, 2 = north-central Texas, 3 = Piney Woods, 4 (excluding Jefferson and Chambers counties) = upper Gulf Coast and rice prairies, 5 = lower Gulf Coast, and 6 = south and west Texas. J/C = public hunting areas of Jefferson and Chambers counties.

[b]Steel shot required in all gauges on all public hunting areas in Jefferson County.

[c]Steel shot required in all gauges in most of region 4.

[d]Steel shot required in all gauges in most of region 4 and the northern half of region 5.

[e]Steel shot required in all gauges in all of regions 4 and 5—i.e., the entire Gulf Coast and the rice prairies.

study. High incidence of ingested lead shot was documented for the following species of ducks taken from the public hunting areas of Jefferson and Chambers counties (J/C): mottled duck, 38%; mallard (*Anas platyrhynchos*), 35%; lesser scaup (*Aythya affinis*), 32%; northern pintail (*Anas acuta*), 29%; ring-necked duck

(*Aythya collaris*), 26%; and blue-winged teal (*Anas discors*), 16%. Lower incidences of ingested lead shot occurred for northern shovelers (*Anas clypeata*), 5%; green-winged teal (*Anas crecca*), 2%; gadwall (*Anas strepera*), 0%; wood duck (*Aix sponsa*), 0%; and American wigeon (*Anas americana*), 0%.

The remaining gizzards sampled from region 4 (excluding the J/C samples) were lower in proportions that contained ingested lead shot: mallards, 2%; mottled ducks, 4%; northern pintails, 3%; gadwalls, 0%; wigeon, 4%; blue-winged teal, 11%; green-winged teal, 2%; and northern shovelers, 4%.

Ingestion rates of 5% or greater were found for the following samples from other habitat regions: mallards from region 6 (6%); mottled ducks from region 5 (27%); northern pintails from regions 5 (7%) and 6 (5%); ring-necked ducks from region 2 (9%); and lesser scaup from regions 1 (7%), 2 (9%), 3 (10%), 5 (19%), and 6 (12%).

Implementation Period for Steel-Shot Zones

Progressive implementation of steel-shot zones on the Texas coast began in 1978. For the 1978-79 and 1979-80 hunting seasons, steel shot was required in only 12-gauge guns used on state-owned hunting areas in Jefferson County. In 1980-81, steel shot was required in all gauges on all federal and state public hunting areas in Jefferson County. In 1981-82, the steel-shot zone was expanded to include most counties along the upper Gulf Coast. In 1982-83, the zone was again expanded to include the northern half of the lower Gulf Coast (region 5). In 1983-84, the zone was expanded to include all of regions 4 and 5—the entire Gulf Coast and adjacent rice prairies.

By 1983-84, J/C samples indicated that nearly half of the pellets ingested by mallards, mottled ducks, northern pintails, ring-necked ducks, lesser scaup, snow geese (*Chen caerulescens*), white-fronted geese (*Anser albifrons frontalis*), and Canada geese (*Branta canadensis*) were steel.

Steel shot was not required outside Jefferson County until the 1981-82 hunting season. Gizzards collected in 1983-84 from region 4 (excluding J/C) indicated lower ingestion incidence than in J/C samples. However, ingestion rates were high for mottled ducks (8%) and lesser scaup (12%).

We found high ingestion rates in region 5 for some species in some years. Examples are mottled ducks (17% in 1981-82), northern pintails (8% in 1980-81, 6% in 1981-82), ring-necked ducks (15% in 1981-82), lesser scaup (13% in 1981-82), snow geese (12% in 1981-82), and white-fronted geese (7% in 1981-82).

There are no steel-shot zones in Texas other than regions 4 and 5. Therefore, we found very little ingested steel shot outside those regions. In general, ingestion rates observed outside regions 4 and 5 were not nearly as high as those that were observed within. However, high ingestion rates were observed for ring-necked ducks ($N = 129$) in region 2 (12% in 1983-84) and snow geese ($N = 69$) in region 2 (4% in 1982-83).

J. D. Murphree Area—A Case Study

The J. D. Murphree Wildlife Management Area (Big Hill Bayou Unit), which is located near Port Arthur in Jefferson County, contains 3,400 ha. The TPWD acquired the area in 1958 and has operated public hunts on half of it since that time. Before 1958, the area was a private duck-hunting club. In 1978-79 and 1979-80, steel shot was required only for 12-gauge shotguns on the Murphree Area. As a result, the proportion of hunters using 12-gauge shotguns dropped from 76% to 50% because many switched to other gauges to avoid using steel shot. In 1980-81, steel shot was required in all gauges and the proportion of hunters using 12-gauge shotguns increased to 97%. The 1980-81 steel-shot zone included all public hunting areas in Jefferson County. After 1980-81, the steel-shot zone was expanded to include most counties along the upper Gulf Coast.

Table 45.2 summarizes gizzard data from the Murphree Area, 1973-75 to 1983-84. In 1973-75, gizzards from most species sampled had large proportions with ingested lead shot. Proportions of gizzards with ingested lead (two-year averages) ranged from 38% in mottled ducks to 0% for small samples of gadwall and wigeon. Mottled duck samples have consistently indicated ingestion rates between 30% and 50% (total shot). By 1983-84, gizzards from mottled ducks, mallards, northern pintails, and lesser scaup all indicated much lower rates of lead-shot ingestion.

Eleven years of ingestion data for mottled ducks from the Murphree Area reflect the changing proportions of gizzards containing lead and steel shot (fig. 45.2). A comparison of the proportion of mottled duck gizzards with ingested lead (37%, N = 926) before any steel-shot regulations (i.e., before 1978-79), with the proportion with lead (24.5%, N = 550) for the last two years (1982-84) showed a significant difference (z = 4.96, $P < .001$). The objective of implementing steel-shot zones was to reduce ingestion of toxic lead shot by waterfowl (and other birds). The data in table 45.3 indicate that this objective was met on the public hunting areas of Jefferson and Chambers counties.

X-Ray Radiography

The contents of more than 4,000 gizzards from 15 species collected in Texas during 1983-84 were examined by X-ray radiography after visual examination (Fisher et al. 1986). It is assumed that all shot was detected with X-ray radiography. The comparison showed that visual examination considerably underestimated the proportions of gizzards that contained shot. Therefore, the data on proportions of gizzards with shot given in this paper are conservative. For the entire sample (all species), the average proportion by which visual totals would need to be increased is 42.7%. Similar comparisons have shown a need to correct visually determined estimates by 30% (Anderson and Brewer 1980) and 32% (Montalbano and Hines 1978).

Table 45.2. Incidence of ingested shot in waterfowl gizzards collected on J. D. Murphree Wildlife Management Area, Jefferson County, Texas, 1973-84

Species	1973-75 N	With lead (%)	1975-76 N	With lead (%)	1976-77 N	With lead (%)	1977-78 N	With lead (%)	1978-79[a] N	With lead (%)	With shot (%)	1979-80[a] N	With lead (%)	With shot (%)	1980-81[b] N	With lead (%)	With shot (%)	1981-82[c] N	With lead (%)	With shot (%)	1982-83[d] N	With lead (%)	With shot (%)	1983-84[e] N	With lead (%)	With shot (%)
Lesser scaup	187	33.7	…	…	…	…	…	…	…	…	…	…	…	…	…	…	…	152	40.1	52.0	72	20.8	31.9	75	18.7	34.7
Mallard	129	37.2	7	42.9	…	…	…	…	…	…	…	…	…	…	…	…	…	207	24.6	39.1	140	12.1	23.6	164	15.2	28.0
Mottled duck	340	38.2	180	38.9	202	37.6	204	33.8	248	41.9	49.6	132	40.9	50.0	369	27.9	38.8	355	16.9	33.2	347	25.6	38.6	203	22.7	63.5
Northern pintail	362	31.2	8	0.0	…	…	…	…	…	…	…	…	…	…	…	…	…	361	30.5	49.9	119	16.8	24.4	229	13.5	27.1
Ring-necked duck	26	23.1	…	…	…	…	…	…	…	…	…	…	…	…	…	…	…	113	16.8	32.7	111	34.2	49.5	97	17.5	35.1

[a]Steel shot required on state-owned, public hunting areas in Jefferson County in 12-gauge only.
[b]Steel shot required in all gauges on all public hunting areas in Jefferson County.
[c]Steel shot required in all gauges in most of region 4.
[d]Steel shot required in all gauges in most counties of region 4 and the northern half of region 5.
[e]Steel shot required in all gauges in all of regions 4 and 5—i.e., the entire Gulf Coast and the rice prairies.

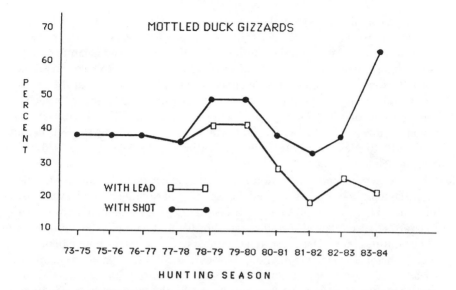

Fig. 45.2. Proportions of mottled duck gizzards containing shot (lead only, steel only, and both lead and steel) and lead shot (lead only and both lead and steel) from J. D. Murphree Area in Jefferson County, Texas. Difference between proportions for total shot and lead shot for any year is proportion of gizzards that contained only steel shot. Implementation of steel-shot zones began in 1978-79. Sample sizes ranged from 132 (1979-80) to 369 (1980-81).

Table 45.3. Incidence of ingested lead shot in waterfowl gizzards collected on public hunting areas of Jefferson and Chambers counties before (1973-75) and after (1982-84) implementation of steel-shot regulations

Species	Baseline, 1973-75		Steel shot, 1982-84		Significance of Difference	
	N	With lead (%)	N	With lead (%)	z	P
Lesser scaup	205	31.7	219	20.1	2.73	<.001
Mallard	160	35.0	490	13.1	6.19	<.001
Mottled duck	387	37.5	846	24.7	4.59	<.001
Northern pintail	393	29.3	725	13.4	6.47	<.001

Discussion

Throughout the period of study, high incidence of ingested shot was found in mottled duck gizzards collected on the upper Gulf Coast (region 4) of Texas.

Results were similar to those of Bateman (n.d.) for Louisiana mottled ducks. High incidence of ingested shot was also found in the gizzards of most other species of waterfowl taken from the public hunting areas of Jefferson and Chambers counties in region 4. Incidence of ingested shot in waterfowl taken from counties other than Jefferson and Chambers on the upper Gulf Coast was lower but still of concern. Results were comparable to other heavily hunted areas in states such as Illinois (Anderson 1982), Ohio (Bednarik and Shieldcastle 1980), Missouri (Humburg and Babcock 1982), Maine (Longcore et al. 1982), Michigan (Nelson and Johnson 1980), New York (Moser 1983), California (Moore and King 1980), and Arkansas (Sullivan 1980).

The progressive implementation of steel-shot zones on the Texas coast, which was initiated in 1978-79, has reduced the ingestion of toxic lead shot by waterfowl wintering on the upper Gulf Coast of Texas. In 1983-84, the observed proportions of gizzards that contained ingested lead shot for several species taken from the public hunting areas of Jefferson and Chambers counties were about half of those observed before steel-shot regulations. However, there is an apparent residual level of lead shot present on the upper Gulf Coast, even though steel shot is now required along the entire coast. For mottled ducks, this level results in lead in 20% of the gizzards examined, at least during the hunting season. There are three possible sources of this residual lead: old lead shot deposited in previous years; illegal use of lead shot, as discussed by Young and Ferrigno (1980); and lead shot ingested outside the steel-shot zone.

LITERATURE CITED

Anderson, W. L. 1982. Lead poisoning in Illinois waterfowl 1979 through January 1982: ingested shot, blood chemistry, and die-offs. Per. Rep. 35. Ill. Dep. Conserv., Div. Wildl. Resour. 13pp.

————, and P. Brewer. 1980. Incidence of ingested shotgun shell pellets in Illinois mallards as determined by radiology: 1979 season. Ill. Dep. Conserv., Div. Wildl. Resour. Invest. Surv. Sec. 14pp.

Bateman, H. n.d. A study of lead shot ingestion in Louisiana game ducks collected during the 1977-78 hunting season. La. Dep. Wildl. Fish. Pittman-Robertson Proj. W-29-25. 11pp.

Bednarik, K. E., and M. Shieldcastle. 1980. Analysis of a three-year (1977-1979) shot ingestion study in Ohio waterfowl. Ohio Dep. Nat. Resour., Div. Wildl. Inserv. Note 435. 9pp.

Bellrose, F. C. 1959. Lead poisoning as a mortality factor in waterfowl populations. Ill. Nat. Hist. Surv. Bull. 27:235–288.

Fisher, F. M., Jr., S. L. Hall, W. R. Wilder, C. D. Stutzenbaker, and D. S. Lobpries. 1986. An evaluation of spent shot ingestion in Texas wintering waterfowl by X-ray radiography. Proc. Lead Poisoning Waterfowl Workshop, Nat. Wildl. Fed., Washington, D.C.

Humburg, D. D., and L. M. Babcock. 1982. Lead poisoning and lead/steel shot: Missouri studies and a historical perspective. Mo. Dep. Conserv. Tech. Rep. Terrestrial Ser. 10. 23pp.

Longcore, J. R., P. O. Corr, and H. E. Spencer, Jr. 1982. Lead shot incidence in sediments and waterfowl gizzards from Merrymeeting Bay, Maine. Wildl. Soc. Bull. 10:3–10.

Montalbano, F., and T. C. Hines. 1978. An improved X-ray technique for investigating ingestion of lead by waterfowl. Proc. Southeast. Assoc. Game Fish Comm. 32:364–368.

Moore, K. C., and J. T. King. 1980. Investigations of lead poisoning in waterfowl in California, October 1, 1979 to March 31, 1980. Calif. Dep. Fish Game. Wildl. Invest. Lab. 9pp.

Moser, J. D. 1983. The incidence of shot ingestion in New York waterfowl. Abstr. Northeast Fish Wildl. Conf., 15-18 May, Mt. Snow. Vt.

Nelson C., and M. Johnson. 1980. Lead-steel shot report: Michigan ingestion study (1976-1979). Mich. Dep. Nat. Resour., Wildl. Div. Rep. 2852. 4pp.

Sullivan, J. D. 1980. Investigations of waterfowl lead shot ingestion in Arkansas. Ark. Game Fish Comm. Unpubl. Rep. 29pp.

Texas Parks and Wildlife Department. 1982. The future of waterfowl in Texas: an issue of habitat. Spec. Admin. Rep., Wildl. Div. PWD Rep. 7000-80. 20pp.

———. 1983a. Lead poisoning in waterfowl. A resource issue. Spec. Admin. Rep., Wildl. Div. PWD Rep. 7000-82. 13pp.

———. 1983b. Texas waterfowl harvest survey, 1982-83. Spec. Admin. Rep., Wildl. Div. Pittman-Robertson Proj. W-106-R. 45pp.

U.S. Fish and Wildlife Service. 1976. Proposed use of steel shot for hunting waterfowl in the United States. Final environmental statement. Washington, D.C. 276pp.

Young, B. D., and F. Ferrigno. 1980. Steel shot program: law compliance N.J. Div. Fish. Game Wildl. Pittman-Robertson Proj. W-58-R. 12pp.

46

Workshop Summary: Toxins, Disease, and Lead Poisoning

Brian W. Cain and J. Scott Feierabend

Because of the location of the Waterfowl in Winter Symposium and the importance of the area for waterfowl, considerable emphasis was focused on problems in the Gulf of Mexico. However, certain of the problems have nationwide or worldwide significance.

Historically, wintering waterfowl habitat along the Gulf Coast has not been plagued with die-offs such as those recorded in upland playas and western lakes. The workshop focused on contamination of wintering habitat—especially the Gulf Coast—by industrial sources, agricultural runoff, lead-shot deposition, and discharges from hazardous waste sites and petroleum production. Southern coastal marshes now receive discharges that contain phenolic compounds, halogenated organics, aromatic hydrocarbons, and other priority pollutants. These discharges are regulated by the U.S. Environmental Protection Agency through the National Pollutant Discharge Elimination System permits. Lack of adequate information concerning the effects of these pollutants on the aquatic system has resulted in their being discharged at levels that accumulate in sediments; inhibit planktonic growth; reduce larval survival for shrimp, crabs, and fish; and inhibit bay grasses.

Many industrial complexes have developed near coastal marshes in response to lower shipping costs and availability of sites and raw materials. Disposal of waste by-products from these industries in past decades created hazardous waste sites that are in tidal areas or near drainages that empty into coastal marshes. Heavy metals such as arsenic, cadmium, led, mercury, selenium, and zinc have built up to high levels in the sediments of the coastal marshes. The impact of

Waterfowl in Winter. © 1988 University of Minnesota. Edited by Milton W. Weller and published by the University of Minnesota Press, Minneapolis.

wintering waterfowl from these heavy metals is difficult to assess. Cadmium, for example, can be measured in tissues of these organisms, but what does a certain level mean to the animal? It is well known that cadmium induces production of metallothionein in animals, but is that good or bad? Another complexity to assessment of harm to waterfowl is a lack of information concerning heavy metal exposure and the physiological adjustment necessary for the organism to survive in a changing environment.

The second source of major contaminants entering coastal marshes is the water-soluble fraction (WSF) of oil and grease associated with brine disposal from oil and gas production facilities. Coastal oil wells produce up to eight barrels of brine water for each barrel of oil, and the water is tidally discharged in coastal areas. This brine water contains many aromatic hydrocarbons that are toxic to larval stages of aquatic life and are known to be carcinogenic to fish and mammals. Effects of these WSF compounds on waterfowl are not known. Sublethal effects such as enzyme induction, mixed-function oxidase reduction, or reduced spermatogenesis caused by these WSF have not been studied in waterfowl. The real challenge for future research is to determine sublethal effects of such contaminants to waterfowl populations.

A third source of contamination to wintering waterfowl habitat is agricultural runoff. Herbicides and pesticides are applied to agricultural land that borders coastal marshes as well as harbors wintering waterfowl. These chemicals are washed from fields during rainfall runoff into drainage lakes and coastal lagoons. Bay grasses and other macrophytes may suffer from these pulses of herbicides by reduced regeneration or diebacks, in turn reducing the area that aquatic invertebrates, many of which are food items for wintering waterfowl, inhabit.

The sublethal effects of organophosphates on waterfowl behavior and physiological responses to weather are not yet known. At field application levels, these chemicals alter a duck's feeding intensity for a short time, in turn perhaps affecting the bird's ability to migrate on time or to store the proper energy to produce eggs in a timely manner. Behavioral changes resulting from minor organophosphate ingestion may also affect breeding behavior, which could delay nesting.

Deposition of lead shot by waterfowl hunters and the need to explore options for nontoxic-shot zones was the fourth major contamination issue discussed. The lead-shot poisoning issue has provoked controversy and debate among administrators, biologists, and hunters for decades (Feierabend 1983, in press). The complexion and direction of this issue is changing rapidly, however, and there is now a growing consensus among conservationists that it is finally "time to get the lead out." Lead has already been eliminated from paint and plumbing; it will soon be eliminated from gasoline, and it may be only a matter of time before lead shot is completely outlawed for waterfowl hunting. Several recent developments signal that the inevitable widespread conversion to nontoxic (steel) shot for waterfowl is well under way:

(1) All four flyway technical committees have recommended to their respective flyway councils that nontoxic shot be required, throughout the flyway, for all waterfowl hunting within the next few years. Three of the four flyway councils (Atlantic, Mississippi, Central) have passed resolutions adopting these recommendations.

(2) At least two states (Nebraska, Iowa) required nontoxic shot for all waterfowl hunting beginning with the 1985-86 season. A number of other states are actively considering similar proposals.

(3) The Wildlife Society has adopted a statement calling for the nationwide elimination of lead shot for all waterfowl hunting as soon as possible, but no later than 1989-90.

(4) The numbers and types of commercially available steel-shot factory loads continue to expand. Hunters can now select from a wide variety of gauges, pellet sizes, and shotshell lengths.

(5) Safe and reliable nontoxic-shot reloading components and recipes are now available to handloaders. The availability of these components will enable handloaders to produce steel shotshells at about half the cost of factory steel loads.

(6) The U.S. Fish and Wildlife Service appears to be moving forward once again on the lead poisoning-nontoxic shot issue. Several federal regulatory and administrative initiatives designed to reduce lead poisoning in waterfowl and other wildlife are now under way. The service is developing a lead poisoning-nontoxic shot information and education program to provide hunters with objective and unbiased information. Strong federal leadership on the issue is essential to resolving the lead-poisoning problem.

(7) The U.S. Department of the Interior is working with Congress to eliminate legislation that prohibits the U.S. Fish and Wildlife Service from establishing or enforcing nontoxic-shot zones without prior consent from the state agency. Commonly referred to as the "Stevens Amendment" or the "steel-shot rider," this restrictive language has been a major stumbling block to effective federal management of migratory birds authorized by the Migratory Bird Treaty Act. If the department is successful in removing the Stevens Amendment, then Federal authority to implement and enforce nontoxic-shot zones will be restored. Restoring federal purview to the nontoxic-shot program is critical to the successful elimination of lead shot from the environment.

Contrary to the turmoil that surrounded the issue in the 1970s, conservationists today are less split on the issue. Although a few vocal opponents to steel shot remain, there are increasing numbers of hunters who support steel shot. As time, reason, and concern for the waterfowl resource prevail, this remaining handful of steel-shot opponents will become insignificant. The outlook on the lead-poisoning issue, therefore, is positive.

The conclusion of the workshop was that it is extremely difficult to evaluate the effects of contaminants on a migratory resource but that a start must be made. The result of inaction will be smaller and smaller populations of waterfowl in the future.

LITERATURE CITED

Feierabend, J. S. 1983. Steel shot and lead poisoning in waterfowl. An annotated bibliography of research, 1976-1983. Natl. Wildl. Fed. Sci. Tech. Ser. 8. 62pp.
———. Legal challenges to nontoxic (steel) shot regulations. Proc. Southeast. Assoc. Game Fish Comm. In press.

47

Workshop Summary: Habitat Loss and Its Effect on Waterfowl

Robert E. Stewart, Jr., Gary L. Krapu, Bruce Conant, H. Franklin Percival, and David L. Hall

Historically, waterfowl research has focused principally on breeding biology and habitat. In part, this emphasis stemmed from the recognized importance of recruitment and factors related to the size of the fall flight. It has long been assumed that wintering habitat does not have a long-term limiting effect on waterfowl populations. Yet the rates of wintering habitat loss and modification have been staggering in the last 25 years, and these changes certainly are affecting the distribution and abundance of wintering waterfowl. Recent evidence suggests that the general health of waterfowl and their annual survival rates are influenced by habitat conditions on the wintering grounds (Heitmeyer and Fredrickson 1981). The increasing awareness of the importance of wintering grounds has prompted growing concern over the limited information available on the wintering phase of waterfowl life cycles.

Examples of selected habitat loss rates of waterfowl wintering areas are shown on table 47.1. Along the Atlantic coast, habitat losses are most severe in the coastal marshes from Connecticut to Maryland (Tiner 1984). The southeastern United States has had very high habitat losses since settlement and an estimated 14% loss between the mid-1950s and mid-1970s (Hefner and Brown 1984). Loss rates in Florida have been especially high (table 47.1).

Louisiana once had enormous areas of forested wetlands and coastal marshes that seemed limitless. Yet more than half of these forested wetlands have disappeared since settlement, and between the 1950s and 1970s Louisiana's coastal marshes eroded to open water at a rate of almost 10,368 ha per year (National

Waterfowl in Winter. © 1988 University of Minnesota. Edited by Milton W. Weller and published by the University of Minnesota Press, Minneapolis.

Table 47.1. Selected wetland habitat changes in the United States

Region	Percentage of wetland lost		Estimated recent loss rate (ha/yr)[a]	Source
	Since settlement	Since 1950s		
United States total	54	9	185,300[b]	Frayer et al. 1983; Tiner 1984
Connecticut coastal marshes	50			Niering (in Tiner 1984)
New York estuarine marshes			300	O'Connor and Terry 1972 (in Tiner 1984)
New Jersey coastal marshes			1,250	Ferrigno et al. 1973 (in Tiner 1984)
Delaware coastal marshes			180	Hardisky and Klemas 1983 (in Tiner 1984)
Maryland coastal wetlands			405	Redelfs 1980 (in Tiner 1984)
Southeastern United States[c]		14	156,000	Hefner and Brown 1984
North Carolina pocosins	40		17,600	Richardson et al. 1981 (in Tiner 1984)
Palm Beach County, Fla.			1,240	USFWS 1982
Florida-Apalachicola to Alabama line (selected marshes)		43	150	NCET[d]
Mobile Bay, Alabama marshes		36	300	NCET
Mississippi coastal marshes		8		NCET
Mississippi Deltaic Plain, La.		20	11,300	NCET
Mississippi River Delta, La.		51	1,700	NCET
Barataria Bay, La.		25	2,500	NCET
Terrebonne Bay, La.		22	2,500	NCET
Louisiana forested wetlands			35,300	Turner and Craig 1980 (in Tiner 1984)
Galveston Bay, Tex.		17	505	NCET
Port Isabel, Tex.		4	8	NCET
San Francisco Bay	80			USFWS/Calif. Dep. Fish Game 1979
California—all wetlands	91			USFWS 1977

[a] Metric conversions have been made from original data reported in acres.

[b] Based on changes between 1950s and 1970s.

[c] Alabama, Arkansas, Florida, Georgia, Kentucky, Louisiana, Mississippi, North Carolina, South Carolina, and Tennessee.

[d] National Coastal Ecosystems Team, U.S. Fish and Wildlife Service, Slidell, La.

Coastal Ecosystems Team data). Wintering habitats in Texas also are changing rapidly (table 47.1).

The highest percentage of wetland loss nationally for wintering waterfowl has occurred along the West Coast. California has lost an estimated 90% or more of the wetlands that were present at settlement (U.S. Fish and Wildlife Service 1977; cited by Tiner 1984).

Habitat changes of these magnitudes are to be expected over a geologic time frame, but not in a span of 20-30 years. Moreover, most of the habitat losses are directly attributable to human development activities. The largest acreage of wetland loss on the wintering grounds is the result of agricultural development. In many coastal areas, however, river levee systems, canals, energy development, and urban development are an integral part of the problem.

Although changes in the status of wintering habitat have been well documented during the past 20 years, we have limited information on impacts of habitat change on wintering waterfowl populations. In short, we can do little more than make educated guesses at what will happen to waterfowl diversity, distribution, abundance, survival, and other population parameters as these habitat changes continue.

Research Needs and Strategy

The direction of wintering ground research will be affected by varying perspectives of what is needed. There tend to be notable differences in perspective between individuals in resource operations and those in research. Generally, individuals from operations need information for solving immediate problems, such as better information on waterfowl numbers, distributions, and habitat conditions. They want researchers to serve as expert witnesses to assist in resolving operational issues that affect wintering waterfowl and their habitat. Operations personnel also want researchers to disseminate the results of their research to the general public, not just to the research community.

Researchers, on the other hand, tend to be concerned with scientific methodology, accuracy, reliability, and habitat or population studies conducted over several or more seasons to measure seasonal as well as annual variation. Professional expertise and research reputations, on which operational personnel depend, require years to develop. However, researchers do note that studies lasting 10-15 years can often produce useful results after only 1-2 years.

Despite obvious differences in background, outlook, and philosophy between these groups, there is no disagreement about the need for wintering ground studies. Information required from such studies includes the following:

(1) Habitat-related waterfowl distribution data:
    a. Where are the waterfowl?
    b. When are they there?

   c. How many are there?

   d. What are they doing?

(2) Mortality factors and survival rates as influenced by habitat.

(3) Time budgets and behavior in various habitat types.

(4) Habitat-related changes in migration patterns (i.e., larger numbers migrating across the Gulf of Mexico due to changes in U.S. wintering habitat).

(5) Effects of concentrating waterfowl (on predation, disease, food shortage, etc.).

(6) Improved inventory techniques relating wintering waterfowl and habitat to increase the accuracy and reliability of broad and site-specific waterfowl surveys.

(7) Long-term effects of trading natural wintering-ground habitats for human-made habitats, particularly agricultural lands, and effects of more efficient farming practices.

(8) Effects of removing "hidden" federal subsidies for wetland destruction (e.g., tax advantages and insurance).

(9) Food availability, utilization, and nutritional needs.

A long-term, interdisciplinary research program on wintering waterfowl habitat is essential. It has been suggested that such a program might be initiated by the U.S. Fish and Wildlife Service and have the following characteristics: (1) a life span of 20 or more years; (2) involvement of varied disciplines (plant ecology, limnology, hydrology, soils, waterfowl biology, etc.); (3) a focus on defining habitat requirements and relationships of wintering waterfowl, as well as on management methodologies to sustain wintering waterfowl populations; and (4) a focus on waterfowl, migration, distributions, and abundance and how these change on the wintering ground.

Other Needs

More efforts need to go into a national public information program. Such a program might be more valuable to the conservation of wintering habitat than all the research and operational activities ongoing or planned. An emphasis on socioeconomic values is essential in such a public awareness program.

Many biologists are particularly concerned over incrementally small losses of wintering habitat that cumulatively result in enormous losses. To address these cumulative losses, the highest levels of federal and state governments must provide policy and legislative direction that is responsive, clear, and action oriented.

LITERATURE CITED

Ferrigno, F., L. Widjeskog, and S. Toth. 1973. Marsh destruction. N.J. Pittman-Robertson Rep. Proj. W-53-12-1, job I-G. 20pp.

Frayer, W. E., T. J. Monahan, D. C. Bowden, and F. A. Graybill. 1983. Status and trends of wetlands and deepwater habitats in the conterminous United States, 1950's to 1970's. U.S. Fish Wildl. Serv., Washington, D.C. 32pp.

Hardisky, M. A., and V. Klemas. 1983. Tidal wetlands—natural and human-made changes from 1973 to 1979 in Delaware: mapping techniques and results. Environ. Manage. 7(4):1–6.

Hefner, J. M., and J. D. Brown. 1984. Wetland trends in the southeastern United States. National Wetlands Inventory, St. Petersburg, Fla.

Heitmeyer, M. E., and L. H. Fredrickson. 1981. Do wetland conditions in the Mississippi Delta hardwoods influence mallard recruitment? Trans. N. Am. Wildl. Nat. Resour. Conf. 46:44–57.

O'Connor, J., and O. W. Terry. 1972. The marine wetlands of Nassau and Suffolk Counties, New York. Marine Science Research Center, State Univ. New York, Stony Brook. 99pp.

Redelfs, A. E. 1980. Wetland values and losses in the United States. M.S. Thesis, Oklahoma State Univ., Stillwater. 143pp.

Richardson, C. J., R. Evans, and D. Carr. 1981. Pocosins: an ecosystem in transition. Pages 3-19 *in* C. J. Richardson, ed. Pocosin wetlands. Hutchinson Ross, Stroudsburg, Pa.

Tiner, R. W. 1984. Wetlands of the United States: current status and recent trends. U.S. Fish Wildl. Serv., Washington, D.C. 59pp.

Turner, R. E., and N. J. Craig. 1980. Recent areal changes in Louisiana's forested wetland habitat. Proc. La. Acad. Sci. 43:61–68.

U.S. Fish and Wildlife Service. 1977. Concept plan for waterfowl wintering habitat preservation. Central Valley, California. FWS Region 1, Portland, Ore. 116pp. and appendices.

———. 1982. Agricultural resources and wetland changes 1972-1980, Palm Beach County, Florida. National Wetlands Inventory, St. Petersburg, Fla.

———, and California Department of Fish and Game. 1979. Protection and restoration of San Francisco Bay fish and wildlife habitat. U.S. Fish Wildl. Serv., Washington, D.C. 23pp. and maps.

Index

Index

Activity budget, 135-167, 169-187
Afton, A. D., 399
Agriculture, 325-336, 495-515
Alaska, 72-73, 541-550, 572-578
Anatidae, 136-149
Anderson, B. W., 191, 399
Anderson, M. G., 123
Ankney, C. D., 299
Annual cycle, 257-267, 302-321

Baldassarre, G. A., 181, 483
Band recoveries, 469-492, 575-578
Barkley, R. C., 325
Bateman, H. A., 495
Bates, G., 419
Batt, B. D. J., 3
Baxter, C. K., 325
Beam, J., 553
Behavior, agonistic, 39-61, 64-68, 103-120
Behavior, courtship, 39-68, 123-127
Behavior, diurnal, 153-167
Behavior, dominance, 59-68
Behavior, feeding/foraging, 77-79, 81-87,
    91-120, 153-167
Behavior, nocturnal, 169-177
Behavior, social, 59-68
Bellrose, F., 5
Bennett, L., 5
Bioenergetics, 257-267
Black, J. M., 23, 39
Body weight, 103-120, 257-267,
    271-296, 353-374

Bolen, E. G., 483
Botero, J. E., 469
Bottomland hardwoods, 307-321, 325-336, 413
Brant, black, 470, 472
Breeding success, 26, 29-36
Britain, 23, 25
Brownlee, W. C., 597
Bufflehead, 200-208, 224-228, 242, 416, 471, 584

Cain, B. W., 583, 609
California, 71-87, 553-567
Canvasback, 103-120, 237-247, 415-417,
    472, 565, 571, 575, 584
Captives, 103-120
Catfish ponds, 413-418
Cattle pasture, 496-500, 511
Chabreck, R. H., 339, 427, 459
Christopher, M. W., 413
Colorado, 277-284
Colorado River, 191-233
Columbia River, 153-167
Competition, 410
Conant, B., 541, 613
Condition body, 277-284, 299-302, 354-374
Condition index, 277-284
Connelly, D. P., 459
Conroy, M. J., 9, 103
Contaminants, 14, 583-595
Cooke, W. W., 4
Coot, American, 162, 415-417, 430, 433,
    449-453, 584, 590

Cornely, J. E., 517
Cover types, 391-398
Cowardin, L. M., 9
Crayfish culture, 427-438
Crop depredation, 511

Day, A., 5
Derksen, D. V., 571
Diet, 103-120, 139, 143-145, 354-374, 441-456
Disease, 14, 609-612
Displays, 39, 59
Distribution, 103-120, 405-411, 469-514
Dominance, sex-related, 103-120
Drainage, 325-336
Duck, black, 139, 354, 377-387, 391-398, 410-411, 471, 571, 578, 594
Duck, Mexican, 471
Duck, mottled, 59-68, 142-146, 471, 576, 584, 597-606
Duck, ring-necked, 142, 162, 205-208, 223, 242, 257-267, 313, 415, 432, 472, 575, 584, 601
Duck, ruddy, 201, 206, 242, 415, 453, 471, 584
Duck, tufted, 138-139, 147
Duck, wood, 315-319, 432-433, 471, 600, 602
Ducks, dabbling, 153-167, 553-567
Ducks, diving, 136-149, 153-167, 184

Ecophysiology, 301
Eider, 144, 354
Energy budgets, 177
Energy requirements, 299-302
Estel, B. L., 271

Fasting, 103-120
Feeding ecology, 237-247, 251-252
Feeding flocks, 77-87, 91-101
Feierabend, J. S., 609
Flock distribution, 377-387
Flock size, 381-387
Flood control, 419-425
Flood control, history of, 325-336
Flooding, 302-321
Floodplain management, 320-321, 325-336
Floodwater retarding structures, 419-425
Flyway biologists, 5
Foods, 82, 86, 138-140, 194-207, 215, 221-235, 271-275, 299-300, 339-355, 423-456
Forest openings, 339-349
Forested wetlands, 307-321, 339-349

Fredrickson, L. H., 307, 459
Frentress, C. D., 597

Gadwall, 137-147, 201-222, 314-315, 354, 416-417, 449-452, 469-473, 566, 584, 600-602
George, L. S., 237
Gibbs, J. P., 377
Gillham, C., 5
Goldeneye, 139, 142-144, 147, 200-208, 225-228, 471, 546-548, 584
Goldman, L. J., 5
Goose, barnacle, 23-56, 140, 144
Goose, bean, 537
Goose, cackling Canada, 71-87, 572
Goose, Canada, 24, 32, 71, 146, 153, 158-161, 271-275, 314, 416, 471, 504, 517-539, 576, 584, 601
Goose, dusky Canada, 517-527
Goose, emperor, 572
Goose, greylag, 144
Goose, Ross's, 471
Goose, snow, 24-35, 140, 334, 417, 495-514, 588, 601
Goose, Taverner's Canada, 517-527
Goose, white-fronted, 24, 140, 430, 469-471, 504, 572, 584, 601
Green, W. L., 237
Gulf coast, 353-374, 495-515, 597-606, 609-612

Habitat, coastal marsh, 495, 503
Habitat, freshwater, 353-374
Habitat, saltwater, 353-374
Habitat contamination, 583-595
Habitat evaluation, 391-398
Habitat fidelity, 357-371
Habitat loss, 583-595, 613-616
Habitat management, 459-463
Habitat selection, 399-402
Habitat suitability, 391-402
Habitat use, 307-321, 339-349, 354-374, 391-398, 413-425
Hale, P. E., 441
Hall, D., 613
Harrison, A. J., 339
Harvest, 512-514, 531, 539, 553-567
Havel, L. H., 91
Hayden, D. C., 427
Heitmeyer, M. E., 307
Hepp, G. R., 123
Heterogeneity, 16-19, 576

Heusmann, H W, 405
Hill, E. P., 413
Hodge, J. I., 541
Hohman, W. L., 257
Hunting, 147-149, 218, 232, 512-514
Hunting regulations, 575-577
Hunting vulnerability, 517-527, 564-567
Hybridization, 410
Hydroelectric impacts, 153-167
Hydrological cycle, 307-321
Hydrology, 325-336

Impoundments, 419-425, 427-438, 441-456
Iowa, 287-296

Jarvis, R. L., 91, 517, 571
Joanen, T., 495
Johnson, A. S., 441
Johnson, D. H., 9, 575
Johnson, J. C., 71
Jorde, D. G., 169, 399
Joyner, R. L., 441

Kaminski, R. M., 399
King, J. G., 541
Korschgen, C. E., 237, 251
Krapu, G. L., 299, 613

LaGrange, T. G., 287
Lead shot, 597-606, 609-612
Lewis, J. C., 391
Liber, H., 23
Lincoln, F. C., 4
Lipids, 287-296
Lobpries, D. S., 597
Longcore, J. R., 377, 399
Loon, common, 592
Louisiana, 59-68, 339-349, 495-514
Lynch, J. J., 5

Maine, 377-387
Mallard, 9, 60, 143, 161, 203, 277-300,
314-336, 354, 405-417, 432, 483,
546-606
Management, 147-149, 423-424, 513-514
Management population, 567
Mate choice, 125
McKinney, F., 123
Merganser, common, 200-208, 228-229
Merganser, hooded, 314, 416

Merganser, red-breasted, 201, 205-207,
228-229
Mergansers, 139, 142, 200, 207-208, 228-229
Mexico, 469-482
Migration, 287-296, 313, 469-482, 495-515
Miller, M. R., 553, 575
Mississippi Alluvial Valley, 271-275, 307-321,
325-336
Mississippi Delta, 413-418
Mississippi River, 237-247, 325-336
Mississippi River Delta, 325-336
Missouri, 307-321
Missouri River, 529-539
Mobility, 483-492
Moffitt, J., 5
Molt, 291-292, 316
Montalbano, F., III, 575
Mortality, 575-578
Mortality, compensatory, 12, 575-578
Mortality, hunting, 11-19
Moulton, D. W., 597
Munro, J. A., 5
Murkin, H. R., 459

Nassar, J. R., 427
Nelson, M., 391
Neotropics, 469-482
Nichols, J. D., 9, 103, 571
Nocturnal activity, 169-177, 183-184
Northeast, 405-411
Nutrient reserves, 287-296
Nutrition, 299-302

Obrecht, H. H., III, 103
Ohmart, R. D., 191
Oldsquaw, 549
Oregon, 153-167, 517-527
Owen, M., 23, 39
Owen, R. B., Jr., 169, 299

Pairing, 23-56, 59-68, 75-81, 86-87
Park habitat, 405-411
Paulus, S. L., 59, 135, 181
Pederson, R. L., 459
Percival, H. F., 613
Perry, M. C., 103
Peters, H. S., 4
Pintail, northern, 143-145, 161, 200-218, 315,
416-417, 449-452, 553-567, 584-605
Playa lakes, 483-492

Pollutants, 583-595, 609-612
Ponds, 413-418
Population model, 9-19
Population status, 405-411, 571-574
Prince, H. H., 299

Quinlan, E. E., 483

Range expansion, 405-411
Ratti, J. T., 571
Raveling, D. G., 71, 299
Recruitment, 522-527, 553, 567
Redhead, 162-163, 205, 223, 242, 373, 414,
    469, 584, 600-601
Reid, F. A., 251
Reinecke, K. J., 299, 325
Reservoir, 153-167, 191-233, 529-539
Rice culture, 496-511
Rusch, D. H., 469

Salt marsh habitat, 353-374, 441-456, 495-514
Saunders, G., 5
Scaup, 584
Scaup greater, 205-224, 471-472
Scaup lesser, 162-163, 205, 224, 373, 415, 417,
    431-433, 492, 597, 600, 606
Scoter, 546-549
Scotland, 39
Seed production, 339-349
Serie, J. R., 251
Sexual dimorphism, 103-120
Shelduck, 140, 144
Shoveler, northern, 119, 201-217, 353-374, 417,
    418, 432, 449-453, 469, 555-567, 584,
    601-602
Simpson, S. G., 529
Site fidelity, 483-492
South America, 469-482
South Carolina, 441-456
South Dakota, 529-539
Spitsbergen, 23, 25, 40
Spitzkeit, J. W., 271
Sprague, F. H., 419
Steel shot, 597-606, 609-612
Steffen, D. E., 413
Stewart, R. E., Jr., 613
Stutzenbaker, C. D., 495, 597
Survey correction factor, 541-550

Surveys, aerial, 541-550
Surveys, boat, 541-550
Swan, trumpeter, 314
Swan, tundra, 24, 471
Swiderek, P. K., 441

Tabor, J. E., 153
Tacha, T. C., 271
Tamisier, A., 181
Taylor, T. S., 257
Teal, blue-winged, 5, 431-432, 441, 449-452,
    469-482, 584, 601-602
Teal, cinnamon, 200, 217, 470-471, 473
Teal, common, 139, 143
Teal, green-winged, 139-145, 202-204, 214,
    313, 354, 414, 417, 449, 470, 483-492, 555,
    584, 601
Techniques, activity budget, 169-177, 181-187
Techniques, timing activity, 181-187, 541-550
Teer, J. G., 353
Texas, 483-492, 495-515, 583-595, 597-606
Thermoregulation, 386
Thompson, B. C., 153
Thornburg, D. D., 271
Tietje, W. D., 353
Time budget, 135-149, 153-167, 169-187
Titman, R. D., 181
Toxins, 609-612
Trapp, J. L., 541
Turner, C. L., 153

Urban populations, 405-411

Valentine, G. L., 419

Washington, state of, 153-167, 517-527
Weller, M. W., 3, 257
Whistling duck, fulvous, 471, 588
Wigeon, American, 161-162, 200-204, 208-220,
    356, 414-417, 449, 473, 555, 584, 597-601
Wigeon, European, 139, 142-144
Williams, B. K., 103
Winter habitat, 15, 277, 325, 339, 529, 539,
    541-550
Winter mortality, 517-527
Winter range, 495-514
Wintering site, 483-492